Thirteenth Edition

Principles of California Real Estate

Kathryn J. Haupt
David L. Rockwell

Rockwell Publishing Company

Table of Contents

The Nature of Real Property

▲ 🏠 ▲ 🏠 ▲ Chapter Overview

Real estate agents are concerned not just with the sale of land and houses, but with the sale of real property. Real property includes the land and improvements, and it also encompasses the rights that go along with ownership of land. The first part of this chapter explains those rights, which are known as appurtenances. It also explains natural attachments and fixtures, which are sold as part of the land, and the distinction between fixtures and personal property, which ordinarily is not transferred with the land. The second part of this chapter explains methods of legal description—the different ways in which a parcel of land may be identified in legal documents to prevent confusion about its boundaries or ownership.

What Is Real Property?

There are two types of property: real property (realty) and personal property (personalty). Real property is commonly described as land, anything affixed to the land, and anything incidental or appurtenant to the land. Sometimes it is referred to as "that which is immovable." Personal property, on the other hand, is usually movable. A car, a sofa, and a hat are simple examples of personal property.

The distinction between real and personal property is very important in real estate transactions. When a piece of land is sold, anything that is considered part of the real property is transferred to the buyers along with the land, unless otherwise agreed. But if an item is considered personal property, the sellers can take it with them when they leave.

Of course, the principal component of real property is land. But real property is more than just the surface of the earth. It also includes everything beneath the surface down to the center of the earth, and everything above the surface, to the upper reaches of the sky.

A parcel of real property can be imagined as an inverted pyramid, with its tip at the center of the globe and its base above the earth's surface. The landowner owns not only the earth's surface within the boundaries of the parcel, but also everything under or over the surface.

The rights, privileges, and interests associated with land ownership are also considered part of the real property. Think of real property as the land plus a bundle of rights. The

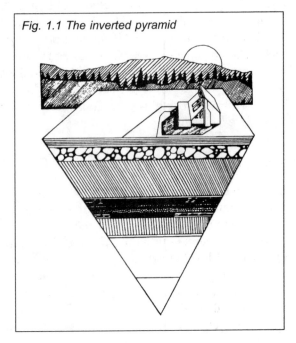

Fig. 1.1 The inverted pyramid

owner's bundle of rights includes the right to possess, use, enjoy, encumber, will, sell, or do nothing at all with the land. (Naturally, these rights are not absolute; they are subject to government regulation.)

Appurtenances

In addition to the basic bundle of ownership rights, a landowner has appurtenant rights. An appurtenance is a right or interest that goes along with or pertains to a piece of land. A landowner's property may include any or all of these appurtenances:

- air rights,
- water rights,
- solid mineral rights,
- oil and gas rights, and
- support rights.

Appurtenances are ordinarily transferred along with the land, but the landowner can sell certain appurtenant rights separately from the land. For example, the owner may keep the land but sell his or her mineral rights to a mining company.

Air Rights

In theory, a landowner's rights extend to the upper limits of the sky. In practice, however, this is no longer true. Congress gave the federal government complete control over the nation's airspace. A landowner still has the exclusive right to use the lower reaches of airspace over his or her property, but may do nothing that would interfere with normal air traffic.

On the other hand, sometimes air traffic interferes with a property owner's right to the normal use of his or her land. If aircraft overflights cause substantial harm to a landowner, he or she may sue the government for some form of reimbursement. The classic example is an airport built next door to a chicken farm. The noise and vibrations from overflights are so severe that the chickens no longer lay eggs. If the land cannot be used for any other reasonable purpose, the value of the land is significantly diminished. The landowner may be able to force the government to condemn the property and compensate him or her for its fair market value.

Water Rights

The right to use water can also be an appurtenant right. Because water is vital for agriculture, industry, and day-to-day living, water rights are an important issue in many areas.

Water is found both on the surface of the earth and beneath the surface. (The natural level at which water can be located is called the **water table**.) Surface water may be confined to a channel or basin, or it may be unconfined water, such as runoff or flood water. The water beneath the surface may also be "confined" in the sense that it runs in recognizable underground streams, or it may collect in porous ground layers called aquifers.

In regard to confined surface waters, there are two types of property rights:

1. riparian rights, and
2. appropriative rights.

Riparian Rights. Riparian rights are the water rights of a landowner with respect to water that flows through or adjacent to his or her property. Such a landowner, called a riparian landowner, has a right to make reasonable use of the stream's natural flow. A riparian landowner also has the right to use stream water for domestic uses, such as drinking, bathing, and watering a personal-use produce garden. However, upstream landowners are prevented from substantially diminishing the flow in quantity, quality, or velocity.

Whether a riparian owner also owns the land under the stream depends on whether the stream is considered navigable or not. A waterway is generally considered navigable if it is large enough to be used in commerce. If a stream is not navigable, the riparian owner owns the land under the water to the midpoint of the streambed. If a stream is navigable, the government owns the land under the water and the riparian landowner only owns the land to the mean high water mark of the streambed. The general public has the right to use navigable waterways for transportation and recreation.

Property located beside a lake, as opposed to a river or stream, is called **littoral** property. The owner of littoral property is entitled to have the lake maintained at its natural level, and to use the lake for fishing or recreation. The owner is also entitled to have the natural purity of the lake's waters maintained. If the lake is non-navigable, each littoral owner owns a portion of the lake bed adjacent to his or her property.

There is an important restriction on a riparian or littoral owner's water rights. A riparian or littoral owner is never permitted to divert water from a stream or lake for use on non-riparian land—that is, land that does not adjoin the stream or lake from which the water is taken.

> **Example:** Brown is a riparian landowner. She owns Parcel C, property that borders Swiftwater River. She also owns Parcel D, property that is about 300 feet inland. She cannot divert water from Swiftwater River to irrigate the crops on her non-riparian property.

Appropriative Rights. Riparian and littoral rights are tied to ownership of land beside a body of water. The second major type of water rights, appropriative rights, do not depend on land ownership. Instead, appropriative rights are based on a permit system called the prior appropriation system.

To establish an appropriative right, someone who wants to use water from a particular lake or stream applies to the state government for a permit. It is not necessary for the applicant to own land beside the body of water. Water taken by a permit holder does not have to be used on property adjacent to the water source.

If someone with an appropriative right fails to use the water for a certain period of time, he or she is likely to lose the appropriative right. Another person can then apply for a permit to use the water.

Water Rights in California. The appropriation system is primarily used in the western United States, where water resources are scarce and are therefore carefully controlled. This is certainly true of California. As a result of years of legislation and litigation, California has an extremely complex body of law that regulates the use of water in the state. The basis of this body of law is the system of prior appropriation, the most common method of obtaining water rights in California. California also recognizes a limited form of riparian rights.

Ground Water. Landowners have **overlying rights** in regard to the ground water in aquifers beneath their property. Overlying rights are similar to riparian rights; the landowner is allowed to make reasonable use of the ground water, but may not transport the water for use on land outside the ground water basin from which it was removed. The prior appropriation system may also be applied to ground water.

Solid Mineral Rights

A landowner owns all the solid minerals within the "inverted pyramid" under the surface of his or her property. These minerals are considered to be real property until they are extracted from the earth, at which point they become personal property.

Remember that a landowner can sell his or her mineral rights separately from the rest of the property. When rights to a particular mineral are sold, the purchaser automatically acquires an implied easement—the right to enter the land in order to extract the minerals.

Oil and Gas Rights

Ownership of oil and gas is not as straightforward as ownership of solid minerals. In their natural state, oil and gas lie trapped beneath the surface in porous layers of earth. However, once an oil or gas reservoir has been tapped, the oil and gas begin to flow toward the point where the reservoir has been pierced by the well. A well on one parcel of land can attract all the oil and gas from the surrounding properties.

Ownership of oil and gas is governed by the "rule of capture." That is, a landowner owns all of the oil and gas produced from wells on his or her property. The oil and gas become the personal property of the landowner once they are brought to the surface. The rule of capture has the effect of stimulating oil and gas production, since the only way for a landowner to protect his or her interest in the underlying gas and oil is to drill an offset well to keep the oil and gas from migrating to the neighbor's wells.

Fugitive Substances. Oil, gas, and water are sometimes referred to as "fugitive substances," because they are not stationary in their natural state. As we've discussed, appurtenant rights to extract oil and gas and to use water are classified as real property; and the substances themselves become personal property once they have been captured or contained. Until that point, however, oil, gas, and water are not considered property.

Other Appurtenant Rights

In addition to rights concerning air, water, minerals, and oil and gas, there are some other important appurtenant rights.

A piece of land is supported by the other land that surrounds it. A landowner has **support rights**—the right to the natural support provided by the land beside and beneath his or her property. **Lateral support** is support from adjacent land, which may be disturbed by construction or excavations on the adjacent property. **Subjacent support**—support from the underlying earth—may become an issue when a landowner sells his or her mineral rights.

Easements and restrictive covenants also create appurtenant rights. These are discussed in detail in Chapter 4.

Stock in a **mutual water company** is considered appurtenant to real property. A mutual water company is a company that is created to secure adequate water supplies at reasonable rates for water users in a particular area. The company's stock is issued to the water users.

Attachments

You have seen that the land and appurtenances are considered part of the real property. The third element of real property is attachments. There are two types of attachments:

1. natural, and
2. man-made.

Natural Attachments

Natural attachments are things attached to the earth by roots, such as trees, shrubs, and crops. This includes plants that grow spontaneously, without the help of humans; these are almost always classified as real property. Natural attachments also include plantings cultivated by people, which are also a part of the real property. However, crops from cultivated plantings are treated as personal property. Thus, a cultivated apple orchard would be realty, but the apples themselves would be personalty.

A special rule, called the **doctrine of emblements**, applies to crops planted by a tenant farmer. If the tenancy is for an indefinite period of time and the tenancy is terminated through no fault of the tenant before the crops are ready for harvest, he or she has the right to re-enter the land and harvest the first crop that matures after the tenancy is terminated.

Man-made Attachments: Fixtures

Articles attached to the land by people are called **fixtures**. Houses, fences, and cement patios are all examples of fixtures. Fixtures are considered part of the real property.

Fixtures always start out as personal property—for example, lumber is personal property, but it becomes a fixture when it's used to build a fence. So it is sometimes difficult to determine whether a particular item has become a fixture or is still personal property. If the item remains personal property, the owner can remove it from the property when the land is sold. But if the item is a fixture, it's transferred to the buyer along with the land unless otherwise agreed.

Distinguishing Fixtures from Personal Property

Buyers and sellers often disagree as to exactly what has been purchased and sold. For instance, is the heirloom chandelier installed by the seller real property that's transferred to the buyer, or can the seller remove it when he moves out?

The easiest way to avoid such a controversy is to put the intentions of the parties in writing. If there is a written agreement between a buyer and seller (or a landlord and tenant, or a lender and borrower) stipulating how a particular item shall be treated—as part of the real estate or as personal property—then the court will respect and enforce that agreement. The stipulation between a buyer and seller would ordinarily be found in their purchase and sale agreement. For example, if a seller plans to take certain shrubs from the property before the transaction closes, a statement to that effect ought to be included in the purchase and sale agreement, since shrubs are usually considered part of the real property.

Similarly, if the seller intends to transfer personal property, such as a couch, to the buyer, that should also be stated in the purchase agreement. In addition to the deed conveying title to the real property, a separate document called a **bill of sale** will be needed if the personal property is worth $500 or more. A bill of sale conveys title to personal property.

In the absence of a written agreement, courts apply a series of tests to classify the item in dispute. These tests include:

- the method of attachment,
- adaptation of the item to the realty,
- the intention of the annexor, and
- the relationship of the parties.

Method of Attachment. As a general rule, any item a person permanently attaches to the land becomes a part of the real estate. A permanent attachment occurs when the item is:

- annexed to the land by roots, as with trees and shrubs;
- embedded in the earth, like sewer lines or septic tanks;
- permanently resting on the land, like certain types of buildings; or
- attached by any other enduring method, such as by cement, plaster, nails, bolts, or screws.

It isn't absolutely necessary for an item to be physically attached to the real property in order to be considered a fixture. Often there is physical annexation even without actual attachment. The force of gravity alone may be sufficient, as in the case of a building with no foundation. Also, an article enclosed within a building may be considered annexed to the real property if it cannot be removed without dismantling it or tearing down part of the building.

Even easily movable articles may be considered "attached" to the real property, if they are essential parts of other fixtures. For example, the key to the front door of a house is a fixture. Also, fixtures that have been temporarily removed for servicing or repair remain legally attached to the real property. For example, a built-in dishwasher that has been sent to the repair shop is still considered to be a part of the house in which it is ordinarily installed.

Adaptation of the Item to the Realty. If an unattached article was designed or adapted specifically for use on a particular property, it is probably a fixture. Examples include the pews in a church, and storm windows made for a particular building.

Fig. 1.2 Fixture tests

- Method of attachment
- Adaptation to the realty
- Relationship of the parties
- Intention of the annexor
- Agreement in writing

The acronym MARIA is often used as a memory aid for the fixture tests.

Intention of the Annexor. Method of attachment was once regarded as the most important test in determining whether an item was a fixture, but over time courts decided that test was too rigid. It didn't allow for special situations where something permanently affixed would be more justly classified as personal property. Now the intention of the annexor is considered a more important test. Courts try to determine what the person who annexed the item to the property intended. Did he or she intend the item to become part of the realty or remain personal property? Each of the other tests is viewed as objective evidence of this intention. For instance, permanently imbedding a birdbath in concrete indicates an intention to make the item a permanent fixture, while just setting a birdbath out in the yard does not.

Relationship of the Parties. Intent is also indicated by the relationship between the parties: landlord/tenant, buyer/seller, borrower/lender. For example, it is generally held that a tenant who installs an item, such as new lighting, probably does so with the intention of removing it at the expiration of the lease. On the other hand, it's assumed that an owner making the same alteration is trying to improve the property and does not intend to remove the item. So an item that would be considered personal property if installed by a tenant might be considered a fixture if installed by an owner.

Items installed by a tenant so he or she can carry on a trade or business are called **trade fixtures**. Trade fixtures generally remain personal property and may be removed by the tenant unless there is a contrary provision in the lease, or the fixtures have become an integral part of the land or improvements. In the latter case, if the tenant still wants to remove the fixtures, it is his or her responsibility to either restore the property to its original condition, or compensate the landlord for any physical damage resulting from the removal. Trade fixtures that are not removed by the tenant become the property of the landlord.

Mobile Homes

The distinction between personal property and real property has special significance in relation to mobile homes, also called manufactured homes. A mobile home is mostly assembled in a factory, then transported to the property it will occupy. (This is in contrast to traditional houses that are built on the property they occupy, sometimes called site-built or stick-built homes.)

Mobile homes leave the factory as personal property but may become real property later on. As long as a mobile home is classified as personal property, a real estate licensee may list and sell it only if it has been registered with the Department of Housing and Community Development. (Unregistered mobile homes are considered "new" and cannot be listed or sold by a real estate licensee who doesn't also have a mobile home dealer's license.) When a registered mobile home is sold, the broker must notify the Department of Housing and Community Development in writing within ten calendar days.

To become real property, a mobile home must be permanently affixed to land. It must be installed on a foundation, the installation must be inspected and approved, a certificate of occupancy must be issued, and the vehicle registration must be canceled. The final step in the process is recording a document that identifies the property and the property owner and states that the mobile home has been affixed to the real property on a foundation system.

A mobile home can be installed on a foundation without becoming real property. It becomes real property only if all of the steps listed above are taken.

Once a mobile home has become real property, it's treated just like a site-built home. So an agent who lists or sells a mobile home and the land it's attached to must have a real estate license.

When a house attached to real property is purchased separately from the land so that it can be moved to another site, it's severed from the real property and becomes personal property. This is true whether it was originally a mobile home or site-built. Since the house is personal property, the sale is subject to sales tax. The house will become real property again when installed on its new site.

Methods of Legal Description

When real property is transferred from one party to another, an accurate description of the land being conveyed is essential. An ambiguous or uncertain land description could make a contract or a deed invalid, and confusion over exactly what land was transferred could cause problems not only for the parties involved in the current transaction, but also for the parties in future transactions.

There are three major methods used to describe land in legal documents:

- the metes and bounds method,
- the government survey method, and
- the recorded map method.

Metes and Bounds

The metes and bounds method describes a parcel by establishing its boundaries. The boundaries are described by reference to three things:

- monuments, which may be natural objects such as rivers or trees, or man-made objects such as roads or survey markers;
- directions or courses, in the form of compass readings; and
- distances, measured in any convenient units of length.

Point of Beginning. A metes and bounds description begins at a convenient and well-defined point along the boundary of a tract of land (called the point of beginning). It then sets out directions that would allow a surveyor to trace the boundaries of the tract all the way back to the point of beginning. The point of beginning will always be described by reference to a monument, such as "the SW corner of the intersection of Front and Cherry," or "200 feet north of the old barn." Notice that the point of beginning does not have to be a monument itself, but can be described by referring to a monument.

Tracing Boundaries by Course and Distance. The point of beginning is established, then courses and distances are given. For example, "north, 100 feet" is a course and distance. Both the course and the distance may be de-

Fig. 1.3 Metes and bounds description
"A tract of land, located in Smith County and described as follows: Beginning at the old oak tree, thence south 15° east, 200 feet, thence north 90° west, 310 feet more or less to the centerline of Smith Creek, thence northwesterly along the centerline of Smith Creek to a point directly west of the old oak tree, thence north 90° east, 430 feet more or less to the point of beginning."

scribed in terms of a monument; for example, "northerly along the eastern edge of Front Street 100 feet" or "north, 100 feet more or less, to the centerline of Smith Creek."

If there is a discrepancy between a monument and a course or distance, the monument will take precedence. In the examples above, the first boundary would be along the edge of Front Street, even if that edge does not run due north, and the second boundary would extend to the center of Smith Creek even if the actual distance to that point is not 100 feet.

A metes and bounds description continues with a series of courses and distances, until the parcel's boundaries have been described all the way around, back to the point of beginning. A metes and bounds description must end at the point of beginning, or else it will not describe a totally enclosed tract.

Metes and bounds descriptions tend to be quite lengthy, and they are often confusing. Furthermore, monuments and reference points do not always maintain their exact locations over the years. An actual survey of the property is usually necessary when dealing with a metes and bounds description.

Conflicting Directions. As noted above, discrepancies may occur between the various elements of a metes and bounds description. In resolving them, the order of priority is as follows:

1. natural monuments,
2. then man-made monuments,
3. then courses,
4. then distances,
5. then names (e.g., "Smith Farm"),
6. then areas (e.g., "40 acres").

If any two of these elements conflict, the one with higher priority will prevail.

Compass Bearings. Directions or courses in metes and bounds descriptions are given in a peculiar fashion. A direction is described by reference to its deviation from either north or south, whichever is closer. Thus, northwest is written as north 45° west, since it is a deviation of 45° to the west of north. Similarly, south-southeast is written south 22½° east, since it is a deviation of 22½° to the east of south. East and west are both written relative to north: north 90° east and north 90° west, respectively.

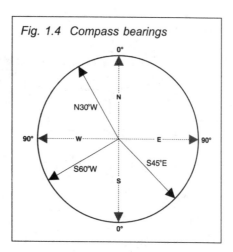

Fig. 1.4 Compass bearings

Government Survey

The government survey system, also called the rectangular survey system, describes land by reference to a series of grids. This system of land description was established after many of the northeastern states were already surveyed. Thus, it is mainly used west of the Mississippi River.

The grids and terms used in the government survey system may seem confusing at first, and we recommend that you study the accompanying diagrams closely.

The grids are composed of two sets of lines, one set running north/south, the other east/west. Each grid is identified by a **principal meridian**, which is the original north/south line established in that grid, and by a **base line**, which is the original east/west line. (See Figure 1.7.) In California, there are three principal meridians: **Humboldt**, **Mt. Diablo**, and **San Bernardino**. Each has its own base line. (See Figure 1.5.)

Grid lines run parallel to the principal meridian and the base line at intervals of six miles. The east/west lines are called **township lines**, and they divide the land into rows or tiers called **township tiers**. The north/south lines, called **range lines**, divide the land into columns called **ranges**. Every fourth range line is a **guide meridian**. (See Figure 1.7.)

A particular area of land that is located at the intersection of a range and a township tier is called a **township**, and it is identified by its position relative to the principal meridian and base line. For example, the township that is located in the fourth tier north of the base line and the third range east of the principal meridian is called "Township 4 North Range 3 East." (See Figure 1.7.) This is often abbreviated "T4N, R3E."

Grid systems are identical across the country, so it is necessary to include in the description the name of the principal meridian that is being used as a reference. (Since each principal meridian has its own base line, it is not necessary to specify the base line.) It's also a good practice to mention the county and state where the land is situated, to avoid any possible confusion. Thus, for example, a complete description of a township might be T4N, R3E of the Mt. Diablo Meridian, Sacramento County, State of California.

Each township measures 36 square miles and contains 36 sections. Each section is one square mile, or 640 acres. (See Figure 1.8.) These sections are

Fig. 1.5 Principal meridians and base lines

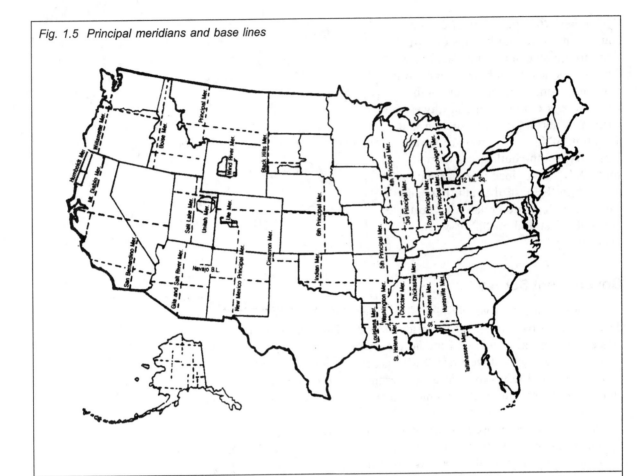

Fig. 1.6 Units of land measurement

UNITS OF MEASUREMENT FOR LAND	
UNITS OF AREA	1 Tract = 24 mi. x 24 mi. (576 sq. mi) = 16 townships 1 Township = 6 mi. x 6 mi. (36 sq. mi) = 36 sections 1 Section* = 1 mi. x 1 mi. (1 sq. mi) = 640 acres 1 Acre = 43,560 sq. ft. = 160 sq. rods 1 Square Acre = 208.71 ft. x 208.71 ft.
UNITS OF LENGTH	1 Mile = 5,280 ft. = 320 rods = 80 chains 1 Rod = 16½ ft. 1 Chain = 66 ft. = 4 rods

* Note: To determine the area of partial sections, simply multiply the fraction of the section by 640. For example,

1 half-section = ½ x 640 = 320 acres
1 quarter-section = ¼ x 640 = 160 acres
1 quarter-quarter section = ¼ x ¼ x 640 = 40 acres

Fig. 1.7 East/west lines are township lines; north/south lines are range lines.

Township 4 North, Range 3 East

Fig. 1.8
  A township contains 36 sections.

6	5 640 acres	4	3	2	1
7	8	9	10	11	12
18	17	16	15	14	13
19	20	21	22	23	24
30	29	28	27	26	25
31	32	33	34	35	36

NW   1 Mile   NE

SW   6 Miles   SE

Fig. 1.9
  A section can be divided up into smaller parcels.

Fig. 1.10 Plat map

numbered in a special way, starting with the northeast corner and moving west, then down a row and eastward, snaking back and forth and ending with the southeast corner.

Smaller parcels of land can be identified by reference to sections and partial sections, as illustrated in Figure 1.9.

Government Lots. A government lot is a section of land of irregular shape or size that is referred to by a lot number. Because of the curvature of the earth, range lines converge, so it is impossible to keep all sections exactly one mile square. As a result, the sections along the north and west boundaries of each township are irregular in size. The quarter sections along the north and west boundaries of these sections are used to take up the excess or shortage. The quarter-quarter sections, then, along the north and west boundaries of a township are given government lot numbers.

Another situation in which government lots occur is when a body of water or some other obstacle makes it impossible to survey a square-mile section. The irregularly shaped sections are assigned government lot numbers.

Recorded Map

The recorded map method of land description is sometimes referred to as the lot and block method, or the maps and plats system. When land is subdivided, lots and blocks (groups of lots surrounded by streets) are mapped out by a surveyor on a subdivision map called a **plat**. The plat is then recorded in the county where the land is located.

After the plat has been recorded, a reference to one of the lot numbers on the specified plat is a sufficient legal description of the lot. Since a detailed description of the lot is already on file in the county recorder's office, that description may be incorporated into any legal document simply by reference to the lot number and subdivision plat.

To find the precise location and dimensions of the parcel, you would look in the map book at the county recorder's office. Here is an example of a recorded map description:

Lot 2, Block 4 of Tract number 455, in the City of Fresno, County of Fresno, State of California, as per map recorded in Book 25, page 92, of maps, in the office of the recorder of said county.

Plat maps frequently contain a considerable amount of useful information beyond a detailed description of lot boundaries. For example, they may include area measurements, the locations of various easements, right-of-way dimensions, the location of survey markers, and a list of use restrictions applying to the land. (However, studying a plat map is not a substitute for a thorough title search.)

Other Methods of Land Description

There are other methods of describing land besides the three major systems discussed above. When an adequate description of property is already a matter of public record—contained in a recorded document—then a simple reference to that earlier document serves as an adequate property description in a new document. (For example, "All that land described in the grant deed recorded under recording number 92122401503 in Orange County, California.") References to records of survey or tax assessor's maps may be used, as long as those records or maps have been recorded in the county where the property is located. Also, generalized descriptions such as "all my lands" or "Smith Farm" can be adequate, as long as they make it possible to determine exactly what property is being described. But it's always best to use the least ambiguous description possible, to prevent future problems. This is especially true if the property owner has several properties in one area.

It should be noted that a property's street address is usually not an adequate legal description. It's also not a good idea to use the property description shown on a property tax bill.

Air Lots. Not every parcel of real property can be described simply in terms of its position on the face of the earth. Some forms of real property (e.g., condominiums) require description in terms of elevation above the ground as well. These descriptions are made by reference to an established plane of elevation, called a **datum**. Most large cities have their own official datum, and frequently subsidiary reference points, called bench marks, are also established. A **bench mark** is a point whose position relative to a datum has been accurately measured. Thereafter, surveyors can use the bench mark as a reference when it is more convenient than the datum.

📖 Chapter Summary

1. There are two types of property: real property and personal property. Real property is the land, anything affixed to the land, and anything appurtenant to the land. Movable items, such as furniture, are usually personal property.

2. Appurtenances to land include air rights, water rights, mineral rights, oil and gas rights, and support rights.

3. Attachments may be natural (growing plants) or man-made (fixtures). In the absence of a written agreement, the tests used to distinguish fixtures from personal property include: the method of attachment, the adaptation of the item to the realty, the intention of the annexor, and the relationship of the parties.

4. For real property to be transferred, there must be an adequate description of it. There are three major methods of legal description: metes and bounds, government survey, and recorded map.

🔑 Key Terms

Real property—Land, attachments, and appurtenances.

Personal property—Anything that is not real property. Its main characteristic is movability.

Appurtenance—A right incidental to the land that is transferred with it.

Emblements—Crops, such as wheat, produced annually through the labor of the cultivator.

Trade fixtures—Personal property attached to real property by a tenant for use in his or her trade or business. Trade fixtures are removable by the tenant.

Riparian rights—The water rights of a landowner whose land borders on a stream or other surface water. Riparian rights allow only reasonable use of the water.

Littoral land—Land bordered by a stationary body of water, such as a lake or pond.

Appropriative rights—Water rights established by obtaining a government permit, and not based on ownership of land beside a body of water.

Lateral support—The support that a piece of land receives from the surrounding land.

Subjacent support—The support that a piece of land receives from the underlying earth.

Metes and bounds—A system of land description in which the boundaries of a parcel of land are described by reference to monuments, courses, and distances.

Monument—A visible marker (natural or artificial) used in a survey or a metes and bounds description to establish the boundaries of a piece of property.

Point of beginning—The starting point in a metes and bounds description; a monument or a point described by reference to a monument.

Course—In a metes and bounds description, a direction, stated in terms of a compass bearing.

Distance—In a metes and bounds description, the length of a boundary, measured in any convenient unit of length.

Government survey—A system of land description in which the land is divided into squares called townships, and each township is, in turn, divided up into 36 sections, each one square mile.

Principal meridian—In the government survey system, the main north-south line in a particular grid, used as the starting point in numbering the ranges and township tiers. California's principal meridians are the Humboldt, Mt. Diablo, and San Bernardino meridians.

Range—In the government survey system, a strip of land six miles wide, running north and south.

Township—The intersection of a range and a township tier in the government survey system. It is a parcel of land that is six miles square and contains 36 sections.

Section—One square mile of land, containing 640 acres. There are 36 sections in a township.

Government lot—In the government survey system, a parcel of land that is not a regular section.

Recorded map—The system of description used for subdivided land. The properties within a subdivision are assigned lot numbers on a plat map, which is then recorded. The location and dimensions of a particular lot can be determined by consulting the recorded plat.

Air lot—A parcel of property above the surface of the earth, not containing any land: for example, a condominium unit on the third floor.

Chapter Quiz

1. Real property is equivalent to:

    a) land
    b) personal property
    c) land, attachments, and appurtenances
    d) land and water

2. The most important consideration in determining whether an article is a fixture is:

    a) physical attachment
    b) the annexor's intention
    c) adaptation of the article to the realty
    d) the intended use of the article

3. Articles installed in or on realty by tenants for use in a business are called:

    a) personalty
    b) trade fixtures
    c) emblements
    d) easements

4. A right that goes with or pertains to real property is called:

    a) an attachment
    b) an appurtenance
    c) personal property
    d) a fixture

5. A landowner's rights regarding water in a stream flowing through his or her land are called:

    a) riparian rights
    b) littoral rights
    c) appropriative rights
    d) easement rights

6. Minerals become personal property when they are:

    a) surveyed
    b) extracted from the land
    c) taken to a refinery
    d) claimed

7. Rights to oil and gas are determined by:

    a) the rule of capture
    b) offset wells
    c) the Bureau of Land Management
    d) the Department of the Interior

8. Whether land borders on a lake or stream is irrelevant under the system of:

    a) riparian rights
    b) capture rights
    c) littoral rights
    d) appropriative rights

9. Ted's property is damaged by sinkholes caused by old coal mining tunnels beneath his land. The rights implicated in this situation are:

    a) riparian rights
    b) subjacent support rights
    c) proximate support rights
    d) lateral support rights

10. Which of the following is most likely to be considered part of the real property?

    a) Piano
    b) Dining room table
    c) Living room drapes
    d) Kitchen sink

11. Which of the following benefits tenant farmers?

    a) Doctrine of emblements
    b) Rule of capture
    c) Overlying rights
    d) Method of attachment test

12. A section of a township contains the following number of acres:

    a) 360
    b) 580
    c) 640
    d) 560

13. A parcel that measures ¼ of a mile by ¼ of a
    mile is:

    a) ¼ of a section
    b) ⅛ of a section
    c) 1/16 of a section
    d) 1/36 of a section

14. The distance between the east and west
    boundary lines of a township is:

    a) one mile
    b) two miles
    c) six miles
    d) ten miles

15. A township contains 36 sections that are
    numbered consecutively 1 through 36. The
    last section in the township is located in the:

    a) southeast corner
    b) southwest corner
    c) northeast corner
    d) northwest corner

👉 Answer Key

1. c) Real property is made up of land, everything that is attached to the land (e.g., fixtures), and everything that is appurtenant to the land (e.g., water rights).

2. b) The intention of the party who attached the item is the primary consideration in determining whether it is a fixture. The other tests provide evidence of the party's intention.

3. b) An article installed by a tenant for use in a business is called a trade fixture, and it remains the tenant's personal property.

4. b) An appurtenance is a right or interest that goes with the property. Riparian rights are an example.

5. a) Riparian rights include the right to reasonable use of the water that flows through a property owner's land.

6. b) When minerals are extracted from the land, they become personal property.

7. a) The rule of capture determines ownership of oil and gas. This rule provides that the landowner owns all the oil and gas removed from a well on his or her property, even if the oil or gas was originally beneath someone else's property.

8. d) To obtain a water appropriation permit, it is not necessary to own riparian or littoral land.

9. b) Subjacent support rights involve support from the underlying earth.

10. d) Unlike the other items listed, the kitchen sink is a fixture, and therefore part of the real property.

11. a) The doctrine of emblements allows a tenant farmer to return and harvest crops after the lease expires.

12. c) In the government survey system of land description, one section contains 640 acres.

13. c) A section is one mile on each side, a quarter section is ½ mile on each side, and a quarter of a quarter section is ¼ mile on each side.

14. c) A township measures six miles by six miles.

15. a) Section 36 is always in the southeast corner of a township.

Chapter 2

Estates in Land and Methods of Holding Title

I. Estates
   A. Freehold estates
      1. fee simple estate
      2. fee simple defeasible estate
      3. life estate
   B. Leasehold estates
      1. term tenancy
      2. periodic tenancy
      3. tenancy at will
      4. tenancy at sufferance
II. Methods of Holding Title
   A. In severalty
   B. Concurrently
      1. tenancy in common
      2. joint tenancy
      3. community property
      4. tenancy in partnership
   C. Forms of business ownership
      1. partnerships
      2. corporations
      3. limited liability companies
      4. joint ventures
      5. real estate investment trusts
   D. Condominiums and cooperatives

Chapter Overview

Real property ownership can take many different forms. An owner typically has full title to the property and full possession of it, but that isn't necessarily the case. An owner may have a more limited interest instead of full title, or may allow someone else (a tenant) to take possession of the property without taking title. In addition, a property may be owned by more than one person at the same time, which is called concurrent ownership. The first part of this chapter explains the various types of ownership interests, and also the types of interests that tenants may have. The second part of this chapter explains concurrent ownership and the different ways co-owners may hold title.

Estates

The word "estate" refers to an interest in land that is or may become possessory. In other words, someone has now, or may have in the future, the right to possess the property—the right to exclusively occupy and use it. An estate may also be called a tenancy.

The different types of estates are distinguished by two features: the duration (how long the estate holder has the right of possession); and the time of possession (whether the estate holder has the right to possess the property right now, or not until sometime in the future).

It is important to note that while all estates are interests in land, not every interest in land is an estate. Interests that are not estates are called non-possessory interests. For example, a mortgage gives a lender a financial interest in the property (a lien), but this interest is not an estate, because it is not a possessory interest. Non-possessory interests are covered in Chapter 4.

Estates fall into two categories:

1. freehold estates, and
2. leasehold (less-than-freehold) estates.

A freehold estate is an interest in real property that has an indeterminable (not fixed or certain) duration. The holder of such an estate is usually referred to as an owner. All other possessory interests are leasehold (less-than-freehold) estates. A leasehold estate has a limited duration (a one-year lease is an example). The holder of a leasehold estate is referred to as a tenant; a tenant has possession of the property but not title.

Both types of estates can exist in the same piece of property at the same time. For instance, the owner of a freehold estate may lease the property to a tenant, who then has a leasehold estate in the same property. (When two or more parties have interests in the same property, their mutual relationship is referred to as "privity.")

Freehold Estates

The freehold estate got its name back in the Middle Ages—it originally referred to the holdings of a freeman under the English feudal system. Freehold estates can be subdivided into fee simple estates and life estates.

Fee Simple Estates. The fee simple estate (also called the "fee," the "fee simple," or the "fee simple absolute") is the greatest estate that can exist in land, the highest and most complete form of ownership. It is of potentially infinite duration and represents the whole "bundle of rights."

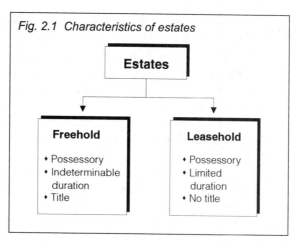

Fig. 2.1 Characteristics of estates

A fee simple estate is freely transferable and inheritable, so it is sometimes referred to as the **estate of inheritance**. A fee simple estate has no set termination point, and theoretically can be owned forever by the titleholder and his or her heirs. When a fee simple owner transfers title by deed, it is presumed that the grantee (the new owner) receives a fee simple absolute estate, unless the deed includes language that indicates an intent to confer a lesser estate (such as a life estate, described below).

Fee Simple Defeasible Estates. A fee simple estate may be qualified when it is transferred from one owner to another. For example, in a deed, the grantor may specify that the grantee's estate will continue only as long as a certain condition is met ("on the condition that the property is used as low-cost housing"), or until a certain event occurs ("until Aunt Jolene has a daughter"). If the requirement is not met, or if the event occurs, the new owner could forfeit title to the property. These types of estates are referred to as fee simple defeasible estates.

Until the 1980s, certain types of fee simple defeasible estates terminated automatically if the condition stated in the deed was not met. These types of estates were abolished by the California legislature. Now, the only type of defeasible estate recognized in California is called a **fee simple subject to a condition subsequent** (sometimes called a **conditional fee**). This estate does not end automatically when the condition is breached. Instead, the grantor must file a lawsuit to get the property back.

Life Estates. An estate for life is a freehold estate whose duration is limited to the lifetime of a specified person or persons.

> **Example:** Noel gives a parcel of property to Beatrice for her lifetime, calling for a reversion of title to Noel upon Beatrice's death. Beatrice is the life tenant (holder of the life estate), and the duration of the life estate is measured by her lifetime.

The measuring life may be that of the life tenant (as in the example above, where Beatrice's life is the measuring life) or it may be the life of another person. Suppose, for example, Catalina gives a parcel of property to Howard for the life of Charlie. Howard has a life estate which will end when Charlie dies. The fee simple estate is a perpetual estate; the life estate is a lesser estate because it is limited in duration. In granting a life estate, a fee simple owner transfers only part of what he or she owns, so there must be something left over after the life estate terminates. What remains is either an estate in reversion or an estate in remainder. These are known as future interests.

Estate in Reversion. If the grantor stipulates that the property will revert back to the grantor at the end of the measuring life, the grantor holds an estate in reversion. The grantor has a future possessory interest in the property. Upon the death of the person whose life the estate is measured by, the property will revert to the **reversioner**—the grantor or his or her heirs.

Estate in Remainder. If the grantor stipulates that the property should go to a person other than the grantor at the end of the measuring life, that other person has an estate in remainder and is called the **remainderman**. The only difference between reversion and remainder estates is that the former is held by the grantor and the latter by a third party. (If the grantor doesn't name a remainderman, an estate in reversion is created.) The interest that will pass to the designated party on the death of the life tenant is a fee simple estate.

Rights and Duties of Life Tenants. A life tenant has the same rights as a fee simple absolute owner, including the right to profits or rents, and the right to lease or mortgage the property. And a life tenant has the same duties as a fee simple owner: to pay taxes, assessments, and liens. A life tenant also has certain additional duties, because someone else has a future interest in the property:

- A life tenant must not commit **waste**, which means that the life tenant must not engage in acts that will permanently damage the property and harm the interests of the reversionary or remainder estate.
- A life tenant must also allow for the reasonable inspection of the property by the reversioner or remainderman, who is permitted to check the property for possible waste.

The life tenant may transfer or lease his or her interest in the property. But it should be noted that the life tenant can give, sell, or lease only that which he or

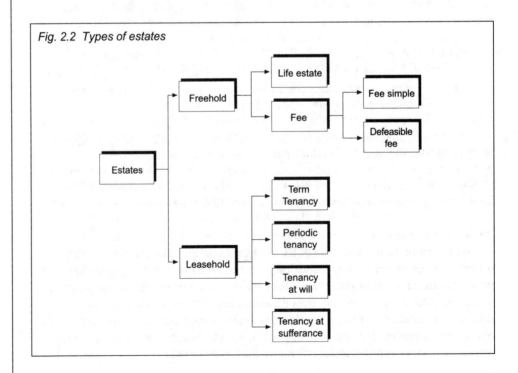

Fig. 2.2 *Types of estates*

she has. In other words, a lease given by a life tenant will terminate upon the death of the person designated as the measuring life. The lease need not be honored by a remainderman. Similarly, a mortgage on a life estate loses its status as a valid lien upon the death of the person named as the measuring life. However, if a life tenant leases or mortgages the property and later dies, but the life estate continues because the person who is the measuring life is still alive, the lease or mortgage will continue according to its terms.

Leasehold Estates

Less-than-freehold estates are more commonly called **leasehold estates**. (They may also be called "chattels real.") The holder of a leasehold estate is the tenant, who does not own the property, but rather has a right to exclusive possession of the property for a specified period.

The leasehold is created with a **lease**. The parties to a lease are the **landlord (lessor)**, who is the owner of the property, and the **tenant (lessee)**, the party with the right of possession. The lease creates the relationship of landlord and tenant. It grants the tenant the right of exclusive possession, with a reversion of the possessory rights to the landlord at the end of the rental period. The lease is a contract and its provisions are interpreted under contract law.

There are four types of leasehold estates:

1. term tenancy (estate for years),
2. periodic tenancy,
3. tenancy at will, and
4. tenancy at sufferance.

Term Tenancy. The term tenancy, or estate for years, is a tenancy for a fixed term. The name "estate for years" is misleading in the sense that the duration need not be for a year or a period of years; it must only be for some fixed term.

> **Example:** Bob rents a cabin in the mountains from Clark for a period from June 1 through September 15. Bob has a term tenancy because the rental term is fixed.

A term tenancy can be created only by express agreement. It terminates automatically when the agreed term expires; neither party has to give notice of termination. If either the landlord or the tenant wants to terminate a term tenancy before the end of the lease period, he or she may do so only if the other party consents. Termination of a lease by mutual consent is called **surrender**.

Unless the lease includes a no-assignment clause, a term tenancy is assignable—that is, the tenant can assign his or her interest to another person.

Periodic Tenancy. A periodic tenancy, sometimes called a periodic estate, has no fixed termination date. It lasts for a specific period (for example, one year, one month, or one week) and continues for successive similar periods (another year, month, or week) until either party gives the other proper notice of termination. Unlike a term tenancy, which terminates automatically, a periodic tenancy automatically renews itself at the end of each period, unless one of the parties gives notice. Failure to give proper notice of termination results in the automatic extension of the lease for an additional period.

Like a term tenancy, a periodic tenancy is assignable unless assignment is prohibited by the terms of the lease agreement.

Tenancy at Will. A tenancy at will is usually created after a periodic tenancy or term tenancy has terminated. This estate is created with the agreement of both parties and can be terminated at the will of either. A tenancy at will often arises when a lease has expired and the parties are in the process of negotiating the terms of a new lease. The term of the tenancy is indefinite; it will continue until either party gives proper notice of termination (in California, 30 days). Note, however, that unlike a term tenancy or periodic tenancy, which are not affected by the death of the landlord or tenant, a tenancy at will automatically expires upon the death of either the landlord or the tenant. Also, a tenancy at will is not assignable.

Tenancy at Sufferance. The tenancy at sufferance is the lowest type of estate; in fact, though it's sometimes called an "estate at sufferance," technically it isn't an estate at all. In a tenancy at sufferance, a tenant who came into possession of the property lawfully, under a valid lease, holds over after the lease has expired. The tenant continues in possession of the premises, but without the consent of the landlord.

> **Example:** Tenant Joe has a one-year lease with Landlord Sam. At the end of the term, Joe refuses to move out. Joe initially obtained possession of the property legally (under a valid lease), but he is remaining on the property without Sam's consent.

Tenancy at sufferance is simply a way of distinguishing between someone who entered into possession of the property legally but no longer has a right to possession, and a trespasser, who never had permission to enter the land in the first place. Because a tenant at sufferance does not hold an estate (a possessory interest in the property), the landlord is not required to give the tenant notice of termination. Even so, the tenant at sufferance cannot simply be forced off the property; the landlord is required to follow the proper legal procedures for eviction.

Methods of Holding Title

Title to real property may be held by one person, which is ownership in severalty, or it may be held by two or more persons at the same time, which is concurrent ownership.

Ownership in Severalty

When one person holds title to property individually, the property is owned in severalty. The term is derived from the word "sever," which means to keep separate or apart. A sole owner is free to dispose of the property at will. Real property may be owned in severalty by a natural person (a human being) or an artificial person (such as a corporation, a city, or a state).

Concurrent Ownership

Concurrent ownership (also called co-ownership) exists where two or more people simultaneously share title to a piece of property. There are several forms of concurrent ownership, each with distinctive legal characteristics. Under California law, four forms of concurrent ownership are recognized:

- tenancy in common,
- joint tenancy,
- community property, and
- tenancy in partnership.

Tenancy in Common. Tenancy in common is the most basic form of concurrent ownership. In a tenancy in common, two or more individuals each have an **undivided interest** in a single piece of property. This means that each tenant in common has a right to share possession of the whole property, not just a specified part of it. This is referred to as unity of possession.

Tenants in common may have equal or unequal interests. For example, if three people own property as tenants in common, they might each have a one-third interest in the property, or one of them might have a one-half interest in the property and each of the other two a one-quarter interest. But no matter how small a tenant in common's ownership interest is, he or she is still entitled to share possession of the whole property.

A tenant in common may deed his or her interest to someone else, without obtaining the consent of the other co-tenants. A tenant in common may also mortgage his or her interest without the others' consent. At death, a tenant in common's interest is transferred according to the terms of his or her will, or to the legal heirs.

Termination of Tenancy in Common. A tenancy in common may be terminated by a **partition suit**, a legal action that divides the interests in the property and destroys the unity of possession. If possible, a court will actually divide the land into separate parcels. If the property cannot be divided fairly, the court will order the property to be sold and the proceeds divided among the tenants in accordance with their fractional interests.

Joint Tenancy. The second form of concurrent ownership is joint tenancy. In a joint tenancy, two or more individuals are joint and equal owners of the property. The key feature that distinguishes joint tenancy from tenancy in common is the **right of survivorship**: on the death of one of the joint tenants, his or her interest automatically passes by operation of law to the other joint tenant(s). To create a joint tenancy, the "four unities of title" must exist. These unities are:

- unity of interest,
- unity of title,
- unity of time, and
- unity of possession.

These four unities signify that each joint tenant has an equal interest in the property (unity of interest), that each received title through the same deed or will (unity of title), which was executed and delivered at a single time (unity of time), and that each is entitled to undivided possession of the property (unity of

Fig. 2.3 Tenancy in common vs. joint tenancy: death of a co-owner

A, B, and C owned property as tenants in common. Then C died, and his heirs inherited his share of the property. Now the property is owned by A, B, and C's heirs as tenants in common.

A, B, and C owned property as joint tenants, each with a 1/3 interest. Then C died. Now, by the right of survivorship A and B own the property as joint tenants, each with a 1/2 interest.

possession). If any one of these unities does not exist when the tenancy is created, a joint tenancy is not established.

Since title passes directly to the other joint tenant(s) upon the death of one joint tenant (because of the right of survivorship), property held in joint tenancy can't be willed. The heirs of a deceased joint tenant have no interest in the joint tenancy property.

> **Example:** Jim, Sue, and Bill own property as joint tenants. Jim dies. Sue and Bill now own the entire property fifty-fifty. Jim's heirs cannot make any legal claim to the property. On his death, it ceased to be a part of his estate. Accordingly, the property is not subject to probate and could not have been willed by Jim.

Avoiding the delay and cost of probate proceedings is one of the primary advantages of joint tenancy. Also, the survivors hold the property free from the claims of the deceased tenant's creditors and from any liens against his or her interest. The main disadvantage is that a joint tenant gives up the right to dispose of his or her property by will.

Termination of Joint Tenancy. Like a tenancy in common, a joint tenancy can be terminated through a partition suit. But a joint tenancy also terminates automatically if any one of the four unities is destroyed. A joint tenant is free to convey his or her interest in the property to someone else. However, a conveyance destroys the unities of time and title. This terminates the joint tenancy with respect to the ownership of the conveying joint tenant.

Example: Aaron, Bob, and Carrie own a piece of property as joint tenants. If Aaron conveys his interest to Alice, that terminates the joint tenancy with respect to that one-third interest. Since Alice didn't receive title through the same deed or at the same time as Bob and Carrie, Alice can't be a joint tenant. Bob and Carrie are still joint tenants in relation to one another, but Alice holds title as a tenant in common.

However, if a joint tenant executes a mortgage against his or her interest, that doesn't break the unity of title. The joint tenancy remains intact and valid.

Community Property. The community property system of ownership is of Spanish origin; for historical reasons, it is used in several western states, including California. In those states, all the property owned by a married couple is classified either as the separate property of one spouse or as the community property of husband and wife.

A spouse's separate property is the property he or she owned before the marriage, and any property he or she acquires during the marriage by inheritance, will, or gift. All other property the husband or wife acquires during the marriage is community property. For example, property purchased with wages earned by either spouse during the marriage is community property. Each spouse has an undivided one-half interest in the community property.

The separate property of either spouse is free from the interests and claims of the other spouse; it may be transferred or encumbered without the approval or interference of the other spouse. Any conveyance or encumbrance of community property, however, requires the approval of both spouses.

Since 2001, California law has allowed married couples to hold property as **community property with right of survivorship**. In this form of ownership, the usual community property rules apply; however, as with joint tenancy, the right of survivorship allows title to pass directly to a surviving spouse without probate. This form of ownership offers certain tax benefits over a standard joint tenancy.

In 2005, California's community property laws were extended to apply to registered domestic partners as well as married couples. Domestic partners may now hold title to property as community property or as community property with right of survivorship.

In some states that do not have a community property system, married couples may hold title to property as tenants by the entireties. A **tenancy by the entireties** is quite similar to a joint tenancy, but there are some differences. A tenancy by the entireties can only be created by a married couple, and (unlike a joint tenant) a tenant by the entireties cannot convey his or her interest without the other tenant's consent. Tenancy by the entireties is not recognized in community property states such as California, and it has been abolished in a number of other states as well.

Tenancy in Partnership. The last form of concurrent ownership in California is tenancy in partnership. Ownership takes this form when a business organized as a partnership owns property. Partnerships are covered later in this chapter.

Forms of Business Ownership

The discussion so far has focused on real property ownership by individuals, whether in severalty or concurrently. Real property can also be owned by business entities.

A **syndicate** is a group of individuals who come together and pool their resources to carry out an enterprise. The syndicate, as such, is not a recognized legal entity. A syndicate may be a business association or a nonprofit organization, and it may be organized as a:

- partnership,
- corporation,
- limited liability company,
- joint venture, or
- trust.

The parties who create a syndicate usually decide which form of organization to use based on tax consequences and other considerations, such as the members' personal liability for the syndicate's debts. The form of organization affects how a syndicate holds title to real property.

Partnerships. A partnership is generally defined as an association of two or more persons to carry on, as co-owners, a business for profit. There are two types of partnerships: general and limited.

A **general partnership** is formed by contract. Although the agreement need not be in writing, it's wise to spell out all the terms in a written agreement. If the agreement isn't in writing, the partnership will be governed by the terms of California's Uniform Partnership Act. If the agreement is in writing, the terms of the written agreement will govern, instead of the terms of the Uniform Partnership Act.

The partners in a general partnership all share in the profits and management of the partnership. Unless otherwise agreed, each one has an equal share of the profits and losses, and each has an equal voice in management and control of the business. Each partner can be held personally liable for the debts of the partnership.

Also, each partner is both a principal for and an agent of the general partnership for business purposes. Thus, the authorized acts of one partner (including the execution of legal documents) are binding on the partnership. A partnership is a fiduciary relationship; all the partners have a duty to act with utmost good faith toward one another. (See Chapter 8 for a discussion of agency.)

In general, property acquired for the partnership's business is **partnership property**. Title to partnership property may be held in the partnership's name. Alternatively, it may be held in the name of one or more of the partners, as long as the deed makes reference to the partnership.

Unless otherwise agreed, each partner has an equal right to possess and use all partnership property for partnership purposes. However, a partner is not a co-owner of the partnership property and has no transferable interest in it. Partnership property is not subject to the claims of creditors of individual partners; it can be reached only by creditors of the partnership.

When title to partnership property is held in the partnership's name, it must also be conveyed in the partnership's name. Since each partner is an agent for the partnership, any authorized partner can sign the deed.

Many real estate syndicates in California are limited partnerships. A **limited partnership** is a partnership with one or more general partners and one or more limited partners. Limited partnerships must strictly conform to the statutory requirements of the California Uniform Limited Partnership Act, and there must be a written limited partnership agreement.

The general partners in a limited partnership have unlimited liability for the partnership's debts and obligations, and they have the exclusive right to manage the business. By contrast, the limited partners have limited liability (that is, they cannot be held personally liable for the partnership's debts and obligations), and they have no voice in management. In fact, if a limited partner took part in the day-to-day control of the business, he or she could be held liable to the same extent as a general partner.

Corporations. A corporation is owned by its shareholders, individuals who purchase shares of stock in the company as an investment. But the corporation is legally a separate entity from its shareholders. In the eyes of the law, a corporation is an "artificial person." It can enter into contracts, own property, and incur debts and liabilities, just like a natural person (a human individual).

Shares in a corporation are **securities**. A security is an ownership interest that represents only an investment in an enterprise, without managerial control over it. Securities are regulated by the federal government through the Securities and Exchange Commission.

A corporation is capable of perpetual existence; the death of a shareholder does not affect its operation. Corporate property is owned by the corporation in severalty, not by the shareholders. The shareholders own only a right to share in the profits of the business. Their liability is limited.

The main drawback to the corporate form of organization is double taxation. First the corporation must pay income taxes on any profits it generates. Then if the profits are distributed to shareholders as dividends, the same money is taxed again as the personal income of the shareholders. Business investors can avoid double taxation by choosing a different form of organization, such as a partnership or trust.

A corporation formed under the laws of California is called a **domestic corporation**. All other corporations, incorporated in other states or foreign countries, are called foreign corporations. Foreign corporations may conduct business in California, but they must obtain a certificate of qualification from the Secretary of State and abide by any conditions or limitations imposed.

Note that a corporation cannot co-own property in joint tenancy. Since a corporation has a potentially perpetual existence, the other joint tenant could not really have a right of survivorship. Thus, when a corporation co-owns real property with another entity or person, they hold title as tenants in common.

Limited Liability Companies. In the eyes of many business experts, a limited liability company (LLC) is the best of both worlds. It combines many of the advantages of a corporation with many of the advantages of a partnership.

An LLC is easily created. Any two business owners (called members) draw up an LLC operating agreement and file articles of organization with the Secretary of State. LLC agreements can be quite flexible: members can choose virtually any manner of allocating income, losses, or appreciation among themselves. Once the LLC is created, annual statements must be filed with the state and an annual fee must be paid.

LLC members have the flexibility of a general partnership when it comes to managing the business. Certain members may be appointed to manage the company, or all of the members may manage the company. All managing members can bind the LLC with their actions. However, unlike the general partnership, all managing members are not personally liable for the company's contractual liabilities. LLC members have the same type of limited liability enjoyed by corporate stockholders or limited partners. Regardless of their level of participation in the company, LLC members risk only their initial investment in the company.

As noted earlier, a major disadvantage of the corporate form of ownership is the double taxation imposed on corporations and their stockholders. Income earned by an LLC, on the other hand, is taxed at only one level—the member level. LLC income is taxed as the personal income of each member, in the same manner as partnership income.

Joint Ventures. A joint venture is similar to a partnership, except that it is created for a single business transaction or for a series of individual transactions. It is not intended to be an ongoing business of indefinite duration. Joint ventures are generally governed by the same rules as partnerships. An example of a joint venture would be a property owner, an architect, and a building contractor joining together to design and construct a particular building.

Real Estate Investment Trusts. In a trust, one or more **trustees** manage property for the benefit of others (the **beneficiaries**). A trust instrument vests title to the property in the trustees, who have only the powers expressly granted in the instrument.

A real estate investment trust is an unincorporated syndicate created by investors to finance large real estate projects. The Internal Revenue Code offers tax benefits to real estate investors who organize their syndicate as a real estate investment trust. An REIT must have at least 100 investors and must invest exclusively in real estate and real estate mortgages. Shares in an REIT are securities, subject to federal regulation.

Because an REIT is unincorporated, it avoids double taxation. As long as at least 95% of its income is distributed to the shareholders, the trust pays taxes only on the earnings it retains. Yet the investors, like corporate shareholders, are shielded from liability for the REIT's debts.

Condominiums and Cooperatives

Condominiums and cooperatives provide alternatives to ownership of a traditional single-family home. In a sense, they combine aspects of individual ownership with aspects of concurrent ownership. They are becoming increasingly popular because of their efficient use of increasingly valuable land.

Condominiums. Someone who buys a unit in a condominium owns the unit itself in severalty, but shares ownership of the common elements with other unit owners as tenants in common. **Common elements** (also called common areas) are aspects of the condominium property that all of the unit owners have the right to use, such as the driveway or the elevator.

Some features may be designated as **limited common elements**, which are reserved for the owners of certain units. For example, an assigned parking space would be a limited common element. A feature such as a balcony, which is designed for use with a particular unit but is outside of the unit itself, would also be a limited common element.

Each unit owner obtains separate financing to buy his or her unit, receives an individual property tax bill, and may acquire a title insurance policy for the unit. A lien can attach to a single unit, so that the unit can be foreclosed on separately, without affecting the other units in the condominium.

An elected governing board usually manages the condominium, and monthly assessments are made to cover maintenance costs for the common elements. The sale of a unit ordinarily doesn't require the approval of the other unit owners. The seller's interest in the common elements passes to the buyer. When selling a condominium unit, the seller is generally required to give the prospective buyer a copy of the bylaws, the latest financial statement, and the CC&Rs (covenants, conditions, and restrictions) of the condominium project.

A condominium usually involves one or more multifamily residential buildings, but commercial and industrial properties can also be developed as condominiums. To establish a condominium, the developer must record a condominium plan and declaration. Condominium projects are generally regulated as subdivisions.

Sometimes the owner of an apartment complex will find it profitable to change the complex into a condominium. This process, called **conversion**, is regulated to protect renters who will be displaced. For instance, when an apartment is converted to a condominium project, each tenant must be given 180 days' advance written notice of the conversion.

Cooperatives. In a cooperative, ownership of the property is vested in a single entity—usually a corporation. The residents of the cooperative building own shares in the corporation, rather than owning the property itself. They are tenants with long-term proprietary leases on their units; they do not hold title to their units. In other words, they have leasehold estates in the property.

To establish a cooperative, the corporation gets a mortgage loan to buy or construct the building, and other funds are raised by selling shares in the corporation to prospective tenants. The rent that each tenant pays to the corporation is a pro rata share of the mortgage, taxes, operating expenses, and other debts for the whole property. The cooperative corporation is managed by an elected board of directors.

In many cooperatives, a tenant cannot transfer stock or assign his or her proprietary lease without the consent of the governing board or a majority of the members. This approval process is used to screen out undesirable tenants; however, discrimination in violation of fair housing laws is not allowed (see Chapter 14). Like condominiums, cooperatives are generally regulated as subdivisions.

Differences Between Condominiums and Cooperatives. In a condominium, each unit is owned individually. In a cooperative, a corporation owns the whole project; the tenants own shares in the corporation and have proprietary leases on their units.

In a condominium, each unit owner secures individual financing to buy the unit. In a cooperative, the corporation takes out one blanket loan for the entire project. One advantage of condominiums over cooperatives is that a condominium owner is not responsible for any default on another unit owner's loan. In a cooperative, if one tenant defaults on his or her share of the mortgage payments, the other tenants must cure the default or risk having the mortgage on the entire project foreclosed. This is also true for tax assessments and other liens.

A condominium owner can usually sell his or her unit to anyone who can pay for it. In a cooperative, the corporation usually must approve of the proposed tenant.

📖 Chapter Summary

1. An estate is a possessory interest in real property. Someone who has a freehold estate has title to the property and is considered an owner. Someone who has a leasehold (less-than-freehold) estate has possession of the property, but does not have title.

2. Freehold estates include the fee simple absolute, the fee simple defeasible, and the life estate. A life estate lasts only as long as a specified person is alive; then the property either reverts to the grantor or else passes to the remainderman. Leasehold estates include the term tenancy, the periodic tenancy, and the tenancy at will. (The tenancy at sufferance, which arises when a tenant holds over without the landlord's permission, is not really an estate.)

3. Title to real property can be held in severalty or concurrently. In California, the methods of concurrent ownership are joint tenancy, tenancy in common, community property, and tenancy in partnership.

4. Real property can be owned by a syndicate, which may be organized as a general or limited partnership, a corporation, a limited liability company, a joint venture, or a real estate investment trust.

5. In a condominium, each unit is separately owned, and all the unit owners own the common elements as tenants in common. A cooperative is owned by a corporation; a resident owns shares in the corporation, and has a proprietary lease for a particular unit.

🔑 Key Terms

Estate—An interest in land that is or may become possessory.

Freehold estate—A possessory interest that has an indeterminable duration.

Less-than-freehold (leasehold) estate—A possessory interest that has a limited duration.

Fee simple absolute—The highest and most complete form of ownership, which is of potentially infinite duration.

Fee simple defeasible—A fee simple estate that carries a qualification, so that ownership may revert to the grantor if a specified event occurs or a condition is not met. Also called a defeasible fee.

Life estate—A freehold estate whose duration is measured by the lifetime of one or more persons.

Waste—Permanent damage to real property caused by the party in possession, harming the interests of other estate holders.

Term tenancy (estate for years)—A leasehold estate with a fixed term.

Periodic tenancy—A leasehold estate that is renewed at the end of each period unless one party gives notice of termination. Also called a periodic estate.

Tenancy at will—A leasehold estate that may arise after a periodic tenancy or a term tenancy terminates. Also called an estate at will.

Ownership in severalty—Sole ownership of property.

Tenancy in common—Joint ownership where there is no right of survivorship.

Joint tenancy—Joint ownership with right of survivorship.

Right of survivorship—The right by which the surviving joint tenant(s) acquire a joint tenant's interest in the property upon his or her death.

Community property—Property owned jointly by husband and wife (in California and other community property states).

Corporation—An artificial person; a legal entity separate from its shareholders.

Limited liability company—A form of business entity that offers limited liability and tax benefits.

Real estate investment trust—An unincorporated trust that invests exclusively in real estate and real estate mortgages.

Condominium—A property that has been developed so that individual unit owners have separate title to their own units, but share ownership of the common elements as tenants in common.

Cooperative—A property that is owned by a corporation and tenanted by shareholders in the corporation who have proprietary leases for their units.

Chapter Quiz

1. A fee simple title in real estate is of indefinite duration, and can be:

   a) freely transferred
   b) encumbered
   c) inherited
   d) All of the above

2. A conveyance of title with the condition that the land shall not be used for the sale of intoxicating beverages creates:

   a) a less-than-freehold estate
   b) a fee simple defeasible
   c) a life estate
   d) a reservation

3. Lewis was given real property for the term of his natural life. Which of the following statements is incorrect?

   a) Lewis has a freehold estate
   b) Lewis has a fee simple estate
   c) Lewis is the life tenant
   d) If Lewis leases the property to someone else, the lease will terminate if Lewis dies during its term

4. Baker sold a property to Lane, but reserved a life estate for himself and remained in possession. Later Baker sells his life estate to Clark and surrenders possession to Clark. Lane then demands immediate possession as fee owner. Which of the following is true?

   a) Lane is entitled to possession
   b) Clark should sue Baker for return of the purchase price
   c) Baker is liable for damages
   d) Clark can retain possession during Baker's lifetime

5. Cobb owns a property in fee simple; he deeds it to Smith for the life of Jones. Which of the following is true?

   a) Jones holds a life estate; Smith holds an estate in reversion
   b) Smith holds a life estate; Cobb holds an estate in remainder
   c) Smith holds a fee simple estate; Jones holds a life estate
   d) Smith holds a life estate; Cobb holds an estate in reversion

6. Johnston, a life tenant, decides to cut down all the trees on the ten-acre property and sell them for timber. Mendez, the remainderman, can stop Johnston's actions because:

   a) a life tenant is never permitted to cut down any trees on the property for any reason
   b) a life tenant cannot commit waste
   c) Mendez's interest is superior to Johnston's, since it is a possessory estate
   d) None of the above; Mendez has no legal grounds for stopping Johnston

7. Jones and Adams signed an agreement for the use and possession of real estate, for a period of 120 days. This is a:

   a) term tenancy
   b) tenancy at sufferance
   c) periodic tenancy
   d) tenancy at will

8. The four unities of title, time, interest, and possession are necessary for a:

   a) tenancy in common
   b) partnership
   c) mortgage
   d) joint tenancy

9. Which of the following is incorrect? Joint tenants always have:

   a) equal rights to possession of the property
   b) the right to will good title to heirs
   c) the right of survivorship
   d) equal interests in the property

10. A, B, and C own property as joint tenants. C dies and B sells her interest in the property to D. The property is now owned:

    a) as joint tenants by A, D, and C's widow E, his sole heir
    b) by A and D as joint tenants
    c) by A and D as tenants in common
    d) None of the above

11. Asher and Blake own real property together. Asher has a one-third interest and Blake has a two-thirds interest. How do they hold title?

    a) Community property
    b) Tenancy at will
    c) Joint tenancy
    d) Tenancy in common

12. All of the following statements about a corporation are true, except:

    a) A corporation has a potentially perpetual existence
    b) Each shareholder is individually liable for the corporation's acts
    c) Corporations are subject to double taxation
    d) A corporation can enter into contracts in essentially the same way as an individual person

13. A real estate investment trust is required to:

    a) invest exclusively in real estate and mortgages
    b) have at least 150 participating investors
    c) have investors accept liability for the trust's acts
    d) be incorporated in the state in which it does business

14. In a condominium:

    a) individual units are owned in severalty, while common elements are owned in joint tenancy
    b) individual units are owned in joint tenancy, while common elements are owned in severalty
    c) individual units are owned in severalty, while common elements are owned in tenancy in common
    d) the entire building is owned in tenancy in common, with residents owning shares

15. A unit in a cooperative is owned:

    a) in severalty by its resident
    b) by the corporation that owns the building, in which the resident owns shares
    c) in tenancy in common among all residents of the building
    d) in partnership among all residents of the building

☛ Answer Key

1. d) A fee simple owner has the full bundle of rights.

2. b) A fee simple defeasible is an estate that will fail if a certain event occurs.

3. b) Although a life estate is a freehold estate, it is not a fee simple estate.

4. d) Baker was entitled to sell his life estate to Clark. Clark can retain possession during Baker's lifetime.

5. d) Smith has possession of the property for the duration of Jones's life, so Smith has a life estate. Cobb has an estate in reversion, because the property will revert to Cobb after Jones's death.

6. b) A life tenant cannot commit waste, which means that the life tenant cannot damage the property or harm the interests of the remainderman.

7. a) A term tenancy has a set termination date.

8. d) A valid joint tenancy requires all four unities: title, time, interest, possession.

9. b) A joint tenant cannot will his or her interest in the property. The right of survivorship means the surviving joint tenants acquire the deceased tenant's title.

10. c) When C dies, his interest in the property goes to the other joint tenants, A and B. When B sells her interest to D, the joint tenancy is terminated and a tenancy in common is created between A and D.

11. d) Because their interests in the property are unequal, Asher and Blake must be tenants in common.

12. b) A corporation's shareholders have limited liability for the corporation's actions.

13. a) A real estate investment trust is restricted to investment in real estate and real estate mortgages. The minimum number of investors is 100, not 150.

14. c) In a condominium, residents own their individual units in severalty, but own the common elements as tenants in common.

15. b) A cooperative is owned by a business entity, usually a corporation. Residents purchase shares in the corporation and receive long-term leases, rather than title to their units.

Transfer of Real Property

Chapter Overview

A property owner may transfer property to someone else by choice, as when an owner deeds property to a buyer or wills it to a friend. Property may also be transferred involuntarily, as in a foreclosure sale or a condemnation. This chapter describes the various types of transfers, voluntary and involuntary. It also discusses how and why deeds and other documents are recorded, and how title insurance works.

Alienation

The process of transferring ownership of real property from one party to another is called **alienation**. Alienation may be either voluntary or involuntary. Voluntary alienation includes transferring property by patent, deed, or will. Involuntary alienation, a transfer of property without any action by the owner, can be the result of rule of law, accession, or occupancy (adverse possession).

Voluntary Alienation

Patents

Title to all real property originates with the sovereign government. The government holds absolute title to all the land within its boundaries, except what it grants to various other entities or persons. Title to land passes from the government to a private party by a document known as a **patent**. The patent is the ultimate source of title for all the land under private ownership.

Deeds

The most common form of voluntary alienation is transfer by deed. With a deed, the owner of real property, called the **grantor**, conveys all or part of his or her interest in the property to another party, called the **grantee**. The process of transferring real property by deed is known as conveyance. A grantor conveys real property to a grantee by means of a deed.

Types of Deeds. There are many different types of deeds. The ones used most often in California are the grant deed, quitclaim deed, trustee's deed, and deed executed under court order.

Grant Deed. The grant deed is the most commonly used deed in California. A grant deed uses the term "grant" in its words of conveyance and carries two warranties:

1. the grantor has not previously conveyed title to anyone else, and
2. the grantor has not caused any encumbrances to attach to the property other than those already disclosed.

These two basic warranties apply even if they are not expressly stated in the grant deed. Additional warranties and covenants (promises) may be stated in the deed if the parties so desire.

The grant deed also conveys to the grantee all **after-acquired title** of the grantor. This means that if the grantor's title was defective at the time of transfer, but the grantor later acquires a more perfect title, the additional interest passes automatically to the grantee under the original deed.

> **Example:** Warner conveyed her property to Meyers on June 1, by a grant deed. However, Warner did not have valid title to the property on June 1 because she held title under a forged deed. On August 12, Warner received good title to the property under a properly executed deed. Meyers automatically acquired good title to the property on August 12.

Quitclaim Deed. The quitclaim deed contains no warranties of any sort, and it does not convey after-acquired title. It conveys only the interest the grantor has when the deed is delivered. It conveys nothing at all if the grantor has no interest at that time. But if the grantor does have an interest in the property, the quitclaim deed will convey it just as well as any other type of deed.

One common reason for using a quitclaim deed is to cure "clouds" on the title; in such situations, a quitclaim deed may be referred to as a **reformation deed**. A cloud is a title defect, often the result of a technical flaw in an earlier conveyance. Perhaps one of the parties' names was misspelled, or the land was inaccurately described. A quitclaim deed is also used when the grantor is unsure of the validity of his or her title and wishes to avoid giving any warranties.

> **Example:** Alvarez holds title by virtue of an inheritance that is being challenged in probate court. If Alvarez wants to transfer the property, she will probably use a quitclaim deed, because she is not sure that her title is valid.

In a quitclaim deed, words such as "grant" or "convey" should be avoided. The use of these words may imply that the grantor is warranting the title. A quitclaim deed should use only terms such as "release," "remise," or "quitclaim" to describe the transfer.

Trustee's Deed. When property is foreclosed under a deed of trust, the trustee conveys the property to the buyer at the foreclosure sale with a trustee's deed. The trustee's deed states that the conveyance is in accordance with the trustee's powers and responsibilities under the deed of trust. (Deeds of trust are discussed in Chapter 9.)

Deeds Executed by Court Order. Court-ordered deeds are used after a court-ordered sale of property. A common example is the sheriff's deed used to transfer property to the highest bidder at a court-ordered foreclosure sale (see Chapter 9). Court-ordered deeds usually state the exact amount of the purchase price approved by the court, and carry no warranties of title.

Other Deeds. Two other types of deeds, the **warranty deed** and the **special warranty deed**, are rarely used in California. (This is because title insurance has largely replaced the buyer's reliance on the warranties that appear in the deed.) The warranty deed gives the greatest protection to a real estate buyer. Under a warranty deed, the grantor makes five basic promises, or covenants, to

Fig. 3.1 Grant deed

RECORDING REQUESTED BY

AND WHEN RECORDED MAIL THIS DEED AND, UNLESS
OTHERWISE SHOWN BELOW, MAIL TAX STATEMENTS TO:

NAME

STREET
ADDRESS

CITY,
STATE
ZIP

Title Order No.............. Escrow No.................

This space for Recorder's use

GRANT DEED

THE UNDERSIGNED GRANTOR(s) DECLARE(s)
DOCUMENTARY TRANSFER TAX is $_____

☐ computed on full value of property conveyed, or
☐ computed on full value less value of liens or encumbrances remaining at time of sale, and

FOR A VALUABLE CONSIDERATION, receipt of which is hereby acknowledged,

hereby GRANT(S) to

the following described real property in the
County of   , State of California:

Dated _____

_____

_____

_____

_____

STATE OF CALIFORNIA
COUNTY OF _____} SS.
On _____before me, the under-
signed, a Notary Public in and for the said State, personally appeared

known to me to be the person(s) whose name(s) is (are) subscribed
to the within instrument and acknowledged that................................
executed the same. Witness my hand and official seal.
Signature _____

(Space above for official notarial seal)

MAIL TAX STATEMENTS TO PARTY SHOWN ON FOLLOWING LINE; IF NO PARTY SHOWN, MAIL AS DIRECTED ABOVE

| Name | Street Address | City & State |

the grantee. These covenants warrant against defects in the title that arose either before or during the grantor's period of ownership (tenure).

The special warranty deed contains the same covenants found in the general warranty deed, but the scope of the covenants is limited to defects that arose during the grantor's tenure. The grantor makes no assurances regarding defects that may have existed before he or she obtained title. This type of deed may be used by entities such as corporations, which may not have the authority to make further warranties.

Requisites of a Valid Deed. A deed will transfer title only if it meets the requirements for validity. To be valid, a deed must:

- be in writing,
- identify the parties,
- be signed by a competent grantor,
- have a living grantee,
- contain words of conveyance (the granting clause), and
- include an adequate description of the property.

In Writing. The statute of frauds is a state law that requires certain contracts and other legal transactions to be in writing. With only a few minor exceptions, the statute of frauds applies to any transfer of an interest in real property. An unwritten deed cannot transfer title; it has no legal effect.

Identification of the Parties. Both the grantor and the grantee must be identified in the deed. The name of the grantee is not required, as long as an adequate description is given; for example, "John T. Smith's only sister." The grantee may also take title under a fictitious name.

When property was conveyed by or to a husband and wife, it used to be common for the deed to say (for example), "John T. Smith, et ux." "Et ux." is a Latin abbreviation that means "and wife." Now it is standard practice to give the names of both spouses in full.

Signed by a Competent Grantor. In addition to requiring a deed to be in writing, the statute of frauds also requires that the deed must be signed by the party to be bound by the transfer. Thus, the grantor must sign the deed. The deed is considered to be executed at the time of the grantor's signature. Note that if the grantor's signature is a forgery, the deed is void.

If the grantor can't sign his or her full name (due to disability or illiteracy), he or she may sign by making a mark. But a signature by mark must be accompanied by the signatures of witnesses who can attest to the grantor's execution of the deed.

A deed can also be signed by the grantor's **attorney in fact**. The attorney in fact (not necessarily a lawyer) is someone the grantor has appointed to act on his or her behalf in a document called a **power of attorney**. The power of attorney must specifically authorize the attorney in fact to convey the property, and it must be recorded in the county where the property is located.

Deeds from corporations are usually signed by an authorized officer of the corporation, and the signature must be accompanied by the corporate seal.

If there is more than one grantor, all of the grantors must sign the deed. If a prior deed named several grantees, all of them must sign as grantors of a new deed. The signatures of both the husband and the wife are required to convey community property (see Chapter 2). For this reason, it is a good idea (although not required) to state the grantor's marital status in the deed and to obtain the spouse's signature if the grantor is married, even if the property is not community property.

A grantor must be legally competent when he or she signs the deed. This means that the grantor must be an adult (at least 18 years old) and sane. If the grantor is not competent, the deed is not valid.

Living Grantee. The grantee does not have to be competent in order for the deed to be valid. It is only necessary for the grantee to be alive (or, if the grantee is a corporation, legally in existence) and identifiable when the deed is executed.

Words of Conveyance. The requirement of words of conveyance, the granting clause, is easily satisfied. The single word "grant" or a similar word is sufficient. Additional technical language usually does more harm than good, and should be avoided since it adds nothing to the validity of the deed.

Description of the Property. A valid deed must contain an adequate description of the property to be conveyed. A legal description of the property should always be included. (Land description is discussed in Chapter 1.)

Acknowledgment, Delivery, and Acceptance. To convey real property successfully, more than a valid deed is necessary; a proper conveyance also requires acknowledgment, delivery, and acceptance.

Acknowledgment occurs when the grantor swears before a notary public or other official witness that his or her signature is genuine and voluntary. The witness cannot be a person who has an interest in the transfer. For example, if Grandma deeds her property to Granddaughter, who is a notary public, Granddaughter should not be the one to notarize the deed.

Technically, a deed may be considered valid even if the grantor's signature is not acknowledged. However, an unacknowledged deed cannot be recorded.

A valid deed becomes effective, so that title is transferred, when the deed is **delivered** to the grantee. Delivery must occur while the grantor is alive.

> **Example:** When Sam Wiggins died, a deed was found in his safe deposit box. The deed transferred his property to his nephew, Frank Wiggins. The deed was void because it was not delivered during Sam's lifetime.

Delivery is more than the mere physical transfer of the document; the grantor's intent is a key element of delivery. The grantor must have the intention of immediately transferring title to the grantee. The conveyance is completed when the grantee **accepts** delivery of the deed. The grantee may accept delivery of the deed through an agent.

> **Example:** Clark deeds his property to Martinez. Clark hands the deed to Martinez's attorney, with the intention of immediately transferring ownership to Martinez. This is considered delivery to an agent of the grantee, and the title transfer is effective.

Because delivery of a deed involves some complicated legal issues, a real estate lawyer should be consulted when there is a question concerning delivery.

Nonessential Terms. There are some elements that should be included in a deed, even though they aren't required. A deed should include a **habendum clause** (also called a "to have and to hold" clause), which states the nature of the interest the grantor is conveying. Is the grantor conveying a fee simple absolute or a life estate? Unless otherwise specified, the grantor's entire interest is presumed to pass to the grantee. If there is more than one grantee, the deed should say how they will hold title: is this a tenancy in common or a joint tenancy?

Many deeds have an **exclusions and reservations clause**, which is a list of any encumbrances (easements, private restrictions, or liens) that the grantee will be taking title subject to. However, valid encumbrances usually remain in force even if they aren't listed in the deed.

A recital of the purchase price is helpful because it indicates that the transfer is a purchase instead of a gift. (If the transfer were a gift, the grantee might be vulnerable to the claims of the grantor's creditors.) The recital of consideration usually says something like, "for $1.00 and other valuable consideration."

The date of conveyance is standard, but not legally required. Other non-essential items include the grantor's seal, warranties, and technical terminology. "I hereby grant Greenacres Farm to Harry Carter. (signed) Hector Valdez" is a valid deed, assuming that Hector Valdez is legally competent. Note that the grantee does not ordinarily sign the deed.

Wills

The will (or testament) is another method of voluntary alienation. In general, a will must be:

1. in writing,
2. signed by the person making it (the testator), and
3. attested to by at least two competent witnesses.

The will must be signed by the testator in the presence of the witnesses. The witnesses must also sign an acknowledgment that the testator declared the document to be his or her will.

California also recognizes a type of unwitnessed will, called a **holographic will**. A holographic will is one that is completely handwritten, signed, and dated by the testator. Holographic wills do not need to be signed in the presence of witnesses. If a portion of a holographic will is typewritten or preprinted, those provisions will be disregarded by the probate court.

Terminology. The person who makes a will is referred to as the **testator**. A testator **bequeaths** personal property to **legatees** and **devises** real property to **devisees**. An amendment to a will is called a **codicil**. The directions contained in the will are carried out by an **executor** named in the will, under the supervision of the probate court (in California, the superior court).

Probate. Probate is the procedure by which a will is proved valid and the testator's directions

Fig. 3.2 Will terminology

Will Terminology

Testator: One who makes a will.

Bequeath: To transfer personal property by will.

Devise: To transfer real property by will.

Executor: Appointed by the testator to carry out the instructions in the will.

Administrator: Appointed by the court if no executor named.

Probate: Procedure to prove a will's validity.

are carried out. If no executor is named in the will, the court will appoint an **administrator** to manage and distribute the estate. Note that a will does not create any interest in property until the testator has died and the will has been probated.

If real property devised in a will is going to be sold by the executor or administrator on behalf of the devisees, then the conveyance may have to be approved by the probate court. (And if a real estate broker handles the sale, the listing agreement and commission rate will also be subject to court approval.) Alternatively, if the will is being administered under the Independent Administration of Estates Act, the executor or administrator may sell the real property without court approval if none of the estate beneficiaries object.

Involuntary Alienation

The patent, the deed, and the will are the three most common methods of transferring property voluntarily. We will now look at the different ways interests in real property can be conveyed without any voluntary action on the part of the owner.

Involuntary alienation of real property can be the result of rule of law, adverse possession, or accession. Alienation by rule of law includes dedication, intestate succession and escheat, condemnation, and court decisions regarding real property.

Dedication

When a private owner gives real property to the public, it is called dedication. While dedication may be voluntary, most often it is required in exchange for a benefit from a public entity.

> **Example:** The county requires a land developer to dedicate land within a new subdivision for public streets. Otherwise, the county will deny permission to subdivide.

This type of dedication is called **statutory dedication** because it involves compliance with relevant statutory procedures. In the example above, the subdivision statutes require that land for streets and utilities must be dedicated before a parcel can be subdivided.

A second type of dedication is called **common law dedication**. The usual requirement for common law dedication is the owner's acquiescence in the public's use of his or her property for a prolonged period of time. If property has been used by the public long enough, a government entity can pass an ordinance accepting a common law dedication. The dedication may be treated as a transfer of ownership, or it may establish only a public easement, depending on the circumstances. (Easements are discussed in Chapter 4.)

> **Example:** Barker owns some lakefront property. For many years, people from town have walked across a corner of his lot to gain access to the lake, and Barker has done nothing to prevent this. Barker's acquiescence to this public use would probably be considered a common law dedication.

Intestate Succession and Escheat

A person who dies without leaving a will is said to have died intestate. The law provides for the distribution of his or her property by a process called **intestate succession**. The procedure varies from state to state, but in general the property passes first to the surviving spouse, then to any surviving children, then to various other relatives. In California, a surviving spouse is entitled to all of the community property. If there is one child, the decedent's separate property is divided evenly between the surviving spouse and that child. If there is more than one child, the surviving spouse gets one-third of the separate property, and the children share equally in the remaining two-thirds.

Persons who take property by intestate succession are called **heirs**. Those who receive property by intestate succession are said to have received property by **descent**, rather than by devise or bequest. Intestate succession is supervised by the probate court. The court appoints an administrator, who is responsible for distributing the property in the manner required by statute.

If a person dies intestate (or with an invalid will) and the probate court is unable to locate any heirs, then the intestate person's property will pass back to the state according to the law of **escheat**. Since the state is the ultimate source of title to property, it is also the ultimate heir when there are no intervening interested parties. To obtain title to the property, the state Attorney General must follow the appropriate legal procedures. The state may also take ownership of abandoned property through escheat.

Condemnation

The government has the constitutional power to take private property for public use, as long as it pays just compensation to the owner of the condemned property. The government's power to condemn (take) property is called the power of **eminent domain**. Before the power of eminent domain can be exercised, the following requirements must be met:

- The use must be a **public use**—that is, it must benefit the public. Taking property for a public park would qualify as a public use. In cases of mixed public and private benefit the question is more difficult, but generally there is no authority for the government to take one person's land for the sole purpose of turning it over to another person.
- The condemning entity must pay **just compensation** to the owner. As a general rule, just compensation is the fair market value of the property.

The power of eminent domain may be exercised by any government entity, and also by some semi-public entities, such as utility companies.

Inverse Condemnation. If a property owner feels that his or her property has been taken or damaged by a public entity, the owner may file a lawsuit called an inverse condemnation action to force the government to pay the fair market value of the property.

Court Decisions

Title to property can also be conveyed by court order in accordance with state statutes and the precedents of the common law. The most common forms of court action affecting title to property are the quiet title action, the suit for partition, and foreclosure.

Quiet Title. The quiet title action is used to remove a cloud on the title when the title cannot be cleared by the more peaceful means of an agreement and a quitclaim deed. In a quiet title action, the court decides questions of property ownership. The result is a binding determination of the various parties' interests in a particular piece of real estate.

> **Example:** A seller has found a potential buyer for his property. However, a title search uncovers a gap in the title: the public record doesn't indicate who owned the property for a certain time period.
>
> The seller brings a quiet title action. The defendants in the action are all persons who have a potential interest in the seller's property. This includes whoever the mystery person was who held title during the gap, even though his or her name is unknown.
>
> The seller asks the court to declare his title valid, thereby "quieting title" to the land. If no defendants appear to challenge the seller's title, the court will grant the seller's request. The buyer can then safely rely on the court's decision and consummate the sale.

Suit for Partition. A suit for partition is a means of dividing property held by more than one person when the co-owners cannot agree on how to divide it. For example, joint tenants may wish to end their joint tenancy but be unable to decide among themselves who gets what portion of the property. The court divides the property for them, and the owners are then bound by the court's decision. In many cases, the court will order the property sold and the proceeds divided among the co-owners.

> **Example:** Green and Black are joint tenants. The joint tenancy property is a vacation home in the mountains. After a serious argument, Green and Black decide they want to terminate their joint tenancy. However, they can't agree on how to divide the property. Green wants to put the property up for sale and divide the proceeds. Black wants to buy out Green's interest and keep the vacation home for himself, but Green says Black isn't offering him enough money.
>
> Finally, Green files a suit for partition. The court orders the vacation home sold and divides the proceeds between Green and Black. Black must abide by this decision, even though he doesn't like it.

Foreclosure Actions. Persons holding liens against real property may force the sale of the property if the debts secured by their liens are not paid. Foreclosure is available for any type of lien that attaches to real property, including mortgages, deeds of trust, construction liens, and judgment liens. (See Chapter 9 for further discussion of foreclosure.)

Adverse Possession

Adverse possession, another form of involuntary alienation, is the process by which the possession and use of property can mature into title. The law of adverse possession encourages the fullest and most productive use of land. It provides that someone who actually uses property may eventually attain a greater interest in that property than the owner who does not use it. The precise requirements for obtaining title by adverse possession vary from state to state. These requirements are often highly technical, and they must be followed exactly in order to obtain title. Legal counsel should be obtained in transactions where title may be affected by adverse possession.

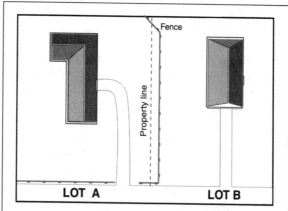

Fig. 3.3 Adverse possession
Use of property (here, the strip between Lot A's fence and the true property line) can mature into title by the process of adverse possession.

Requirements. In California, there are five basic requirements for adverse possession. Possession of the land must be:

1. actual, open, and notorious,
2. hostile to the owner's interest,
3. under claim of right or color of title,
4. continuous and uninterrupted for a specific period of time, and
5. the adverse possessor must have paid the property taxes during the required period of possession.

Actual, Open, and Notorious. Actual possession means occupation and use of the property in a manner appropriate to the type of property. It does not require residence on the property unless residence is an appropriate use. Thus, actual possession of farmland may be achieved by fencing the land and planting crops, while actual possession of urban property would require a residential or commercial use of the property.

The requirement of "open and notorious" possession means that the possession must put the true owner on notice that his or her interest in the property is being threatened. "Open and notorious" and "actual" possession overlap. Actual possession generally constitutes reasonable notice to the world that the adverse possessor is occupying the property.

Hostile. The adverse possessor must intend to claim ownership of the property and defend that claim against all parties. Hostile intent is proven by the adverse possessor's actions. If the adverse possessor uses the property in the same fashion as an owner would use it, then hostile intent exists. Note that the hostility requirement cannot be satisfied if the possession is with the permission of the actual owner.

Claim of Right or Color of Title. The "claim of right or color of title" requirement basically means that the adverse possessor must have a good faith but mistaken belief that he or she is the owner of the land. An example of an adverse possessor with color of title is one who takes possession under an invalid deed. Under those circumstances, the adverse possessor may acquire title to all the property described in the defective instrument, even if he or she occupies only part of the property.

Continuous and Uninterrupted. An adverse possessor must have continuous and uninterrupted possession of the property for the length of time prescribed by state statute. In California, the possession must be continuous and uninterrupted for five years, and the adverse possessor must pay the taxes on the property during that period.

In some cases, intermittent use of the property may be enough to fulfill the continuity requirement. This is true if the property is a type that an owner would ordinarily use only at certain times of year, such as seasonal farmland or summer resort property. However, the continuity requirement is not met if the adverse possessor fails to use the property for a significant period when it would ordinarily be used, or if the true owner interrupts the period of exclusive possession.

Successive adverse possessors can add together their periods of possession to equal the statutory time period; this is called **tacking**.

Example: Tanaka adversely possesses property for four years, and then transfers possession to White, who possesses the property for three years. White can claim title because the total period of adverse possession is more than five years.

Note that title to government property can never be acquired by adverse possession.

Perfecting Title. Since the adverse possessor's interest is not recorded, he or she must take additional steps to acquire marketable title. Unless the true owner is willing to provide a quitclaim deed, the adverse possessor has to file a quiet title action.

Accession

Accession is any addition to real property from natural or artificial causes. It can result in involuntary alienation. Accession includes:

- accretion,
- reliction, and
- avulsion.

Accretion. When riparian or littoral land is slowly enlarged by waterborne soil deposits (called alluvion or alluvium), the riparian or littoral owner acquires title to the new land. A key feature of accretion is that the buildup of soil must be so gradual that the process is virtually imperceptible.

Reliction. When riparian or littoral land is enlarged by the gradual retreat of the body of water, the landowner acquires title to the newly exposed land. Like accretion, reliction must be very gradual. Reliction is also called dereliction.

Avulsion. Accretion and reliction are both gradual processes. By contrast, avulsion occurs when land is violently torn away by flowing water or waves and deposited somewhere else, or when land is exposed by a sudden change in a watercourse. Unlike accretion and reliction, avulsion does not necessarily result in involuntary alienation of the land that has been moved or exposed. The original owner still has title to that land, if there is some way to claim it. If unclaimed, it eventually becomes part of the property it is now attached to.

Recording

Once an interest in property has been transferred (voluntarily or involuntarily), the new owner protects his or her interest by recording the document of conveyance with the county clerk. Recording is a way to provide convenient access to information regarding ownership of a property to anyone who's interested.

The Recording Process

Recording is accomplished by filing a copy of the deed or other document at the county clerk's office in the county where the property is located. The recorder catalogs, or **indexes**, the document twice, once under the grantor's last name and once under the grantee's last name. Sometimes a document will also be indexed according to tract, so that all documents affecting a particular property are listed together.

These indexes serve as the basis for **title searches**. A purchaser can search the grantor index to determine if the seller has already conveyed the interest to another party. The purchaser can also search the grantee index to discover the source of the seller's title, and trace the title back through a **chain of title** (successive grantors and grantees) that is long enough to ensure the validity of the seller's title.

Almost any document affecting title to land may be recorded: a deed, a mortgage, an abstract of judgment, a lis pendens (a notice of pending legal proceedings that may affect property), and so on. A deed or other document of conveyance must be acknowledged before it can be recorded, mainly to protect against forgeries. Also, the Federal Fair Housing Act prohibits the recording of any deed that contains a racially restrictive covenant (see Chapter 14).

The Effect of Recording

Recording has two significant consequences. Most importantly, it gives **constructive notice** of recorded interests to "the world." In other words, anyone who later acquires an interest in the property is held to know about all the other recorded interests, even if he or she does not check the record.

Example: Jones owns Haystack Farm. She sells the farm to Chin, who immediately records his deed. One week later, Jones sells Haystack Farm to Brown. Jones pretends she still owns the farm, and Brown simply takes her word for it; he doesn't do a title search. When Brown tries to record his deed, he discovers that Jones did not have title to Haystack Farm when she sold it to him.

Although Brown didn't actually know about the conveyance from Jones to Chin, he had constructive notice of that conveyance. He could have found out about it by checking the public record. As a result, he has no claim to the property. Chin owns Haystack Farm. Brown could sue Jones to get his money back, but she has probably left town by now.

Constructive notice is contrasted with actual notice. A party has **actual notice** of something if he or she actually knew about it.

A grantee who fails to record his or her deed can lose title to a subsequent good faith purchaser who did not have notice of the earlier conveyance. In a conflict between two purchasers, the one who records his or her deed first has good title to the property—even if the other purchaser's deed was executed first.

> **Example:** Jones sells Haystack Farm to Chin, but Chin does not record his deed. One week later, Jones sells the same property to Brown. No one tells Brown about the previous conveyance to Chin.
>
> Since Chin's deed isn't recorded, Brown doesn't have constructive notice of Chin's interest in the property. Even if Brown does a title search, there's nothing in the public record to indicate that Jones no longer owns the property.
>
> Brown qualifies as a subsequent good faith purchaser without notice. If he records his deed before Chin records his, Brown has good title to the property.

In addition to providing constructive notice, recording also creates a presumption that the recorded instrument is valid and effective. Recording will not serve to validate an otherwise invalid deed, nor will it protect against interests that arise by operation of law, such as adverse possession.

Wild Deeds. Because of the grantor/grantee system of indexing, it is possible for a deed to be recorded in such a way that a title search would not discover it.

> **Example:** Suppose Smith sells property to Montgomery, who fails to record her deed. Not long thereafter, Montgomery conveys the property to Klein, who promptly records his deed.
>
> If Smith then makes another conveyance of the same property to Walker, Walker will not be able to discover Klein's interest because Klein is not in Smith's chain of title. There is a break in the chain of title between Smith and Klein because the connecting deed was not recorded.

The general rule in these situations is that the subsequent purchaser (in the example above, Walker) is not charged with constructive notice of a deed that is not in the chain of title. A deed outside the chain of title is called a wild deed.

Possession and Notice. Possession of the land by someone other than the seller gives notice to the buyer that the possessor may have an interest in the property, and the buyer then has a duty to inquire into the matter further. This is sometimes called "inquiry notice" or "implied notice."

Title Insurance

Given the complexity of real property law and the high cost of real estate, it's natural that a prospective buyer will want to do everything possible to protect his or her interest. One means of accomplishing this is to obtain warranties of title from the seller, but warranties aren't very valuable if the seller is financially unable to back them up.

The buyer could also obtain a complete history of all the recorded interests in the property (called a **chain of title**) or a condensed history of those interests (called an **abstract of title**), and then have the history examined by an attorney who could render an opinion on the condition of the title. But the buyer would still have no protection against latent or undiscovered defects in the title. Therefore, most buyers will protect their interests with a title insurance policy.

In a title insurance policy, the title insurance company agrees to indemnify the policy holder against (reimburse him or her for) losses caused by defects in the title, except for any defects specifically excluded from coverage. The title company will also handle the legal defense of any claims covered by the policy.

Obtaining Title Insurance

There are two steps in getting a title insurance policy. First, the buyer (or the seller) pays a fee to the title company to cover the cost of a title search. Most title companies have their own sets of records (called title plants), so they do not have to search the files in the county recorder's or county clerk's office. (Title companies may also search the records of the Federal Land Office.)

After the title search is completed, the title company issues a **title report** describing the condition of the title. The report lists all defects and encumbrances of record; these items will be excluded from the policy coverage. If the buyer is satisfied with the report, he or she purchases an insurance policy by paying the required premium; one payment covers the entire life of the policy.

Limits on Coverage

Title insurance policies may be limited in a number of ways. As mentioned above, all defects and encumbrances of record are listed in the policy and excluded from coverage. In addition, the liability of the title company cannot

Fig. 3.4 Title insurance coverage

Standard Coverage	Extended Coverage

• Marketable title
• Latent defects in title
   forged deed
   incompetent grantor
• Right of access
	• Marketable title
	• Latent defects in title
	   forged deed
	   incompetent grantor
	• Right of access
	• Parties in possession
	   tenants
	   adverse possessors
	• Matters discovered by survey
	   boundary lines
	   encroachments
	   area
	• Unrecorded mechanic's liens
	• Tax liens

exceed the face value of the policy. The extent of protection also varies according to the nature of the policy. The two most common types of policies are the standard coverage policy and the extended coverage policy.

The **standard coverage** policy (sometimes called a CLTA policy, after the California Land Title Association) insures against defects in title, including hidden risks such as forgery. It does not insure against the interests of a person in actual possession of the property (such as an adverse possessor), against title defects known by the owner but not disclosed to the title insurer, nor against interests that would be disclosed by an inspection of the premises (such as an encroachment).

Standard coverage is most often used to protect the buyer's interest in the property; this is called an owner's policy, since the buyer is the new owner. If a buyer wants coverage for a specific item not included in the standard policy, it may be possible to purchase an endorsement to cover that item.

The **extended coverage** policy (sometimes called an ALTA policy, after the American Land Title Association) insures against all matters covered by the standard policy, plus matters not of public record, such as the rights of parties in possession of the property, unrecorded mechanic's liens, and encroachments. Extended coverage is most often purchased by the buyer to insure his or her lender; this is known as a mortgagee's policy.

Title insurance never protects a landowner from losses due to governmental action such as condemnation or zoning changes.

Title insurance coverage is also limited to losses resulting from defects in the particular interest covered. Thus, an owner's policy covers only defects in title; a mortgagee's policy insures only the lender's lien priority. There is also a type of policy called a leaseholder's policy, which insures only the validity of a lease.

Chapter Summary

1. A transfer of ownership of property from one person to another is called alienation. Alienation may be either voluntary or involuntary.

2. Property may be transferred voluntarily by patent, deed, or will. The deed is the most common way of voluntarily transferring property. To be valid, a deed must be in writing, identify the parties, be signed by a competent grantor, have a living grantee, contain words of conveyance, and include an adequate description of the property. For property to be successfully conveyed, there must be delivery and acceptance as well as a valid deed. Once the deed is delivered and accepted, it should be recorded to protect the new owner's interest.

3. When a person dies, his or her real property is transferred to devisees under a will, or to heirs by the rules of intestate succession. A person who dies without a will is said to have died intestate. Property from an estate is distributed under the jurisdiction of the probate court. If a person dies without a valid will and without heirs, the property escheats to the state.

4. In addition to intestate succession and escheat, there are several other methods of involuntary alienation, including dedication, condemnation, court decisions, and adverse possession. When someone uses property openly and continuously without the owner's permission for five years, he or she may acquire title by adverse possession.

5. Ownership of property may be transferred by accession. Accession refers to an addition to real property by various natural means, including accretion, reliction, and avulsion.

6. Documents affecting real property are recorded to provide constructive notice of their contents to anyone interested in the property. Recording also creates a presumption that a document is valid.

7. To protect a newly acquired interest in real property, the owner usually obtains a title insurance policy. The title insurance company will reimburse the owner for losses caused by defects in title, and will defend the title against the legal claims of others.

O—🔑 Key Terms

Alienation—The transfer of title, ownership, or an interest in property from one person to another. Alienation may be voluntary or involuntary.

Deed—A written instrument that, when properly executed, delivered, and accepted, conveys title or ownership of real property from the grantor to the grantee.

Grant deed—The deed most commonly used in California. It carries two warranties: the covenant of the right to convey, and the covenant against encumbrances caused by the grantor.

Quitclaim deed—A deed that conveys and releases any interest in a piece of real property that the grantor may have. It contains no warranties of any kind, but does transfer any right, title, or interest the grantor has at the time the deed is executed.

Acknowledgment—A formal declaration made before an authorized official, such as a notary public or county clerk, by a person who has signed a document; he or she states that the signature is genuine and voluntary.

Will—The written declaration of an individual that designates how his or her estate will be disposed of after death.

Intestate—When a person dies without leaving a valid will, he or she dies intestate.

Escheat—The reversion of property to the state when a person dies without leaving a valid will and without heirs entitled to the property.

Adverse possession—A means by which a person may acquire title to property by using it openly and continuously without the owner's permission for the required statutory period.

Dedication—When a private owner voluntarily or involuntarily gives real property to the public.

Eminent domain—The power of the government to take (condemn) private property for public use, upon payment of just compensation to the owner.

Condemnation—The act of taking private property for public use under the power of eminent domain.

Accession—Any addition to real property from natural or artificial causes.

Constructive notice—Notice of a fact that a person is held by law to have (as opposed to actual notice). He or she had the opportunity to discover the fact in question by searching the public record.

Title search—An inspection of the public record to determine all rights to a piece of property.

Chain of title—A complete history of all of the recorded interests in a piece of real property.

Abstract of title—A condensed history of the recorded interests in a piece of real property.

Title report—A report issued after a title search by a title insurance company, listing all defects and encumbrances of record.

Wild deed—A recorded deed that cannot be located under the grantor-grantee system of indexing.

⦿⦿ Chapter Quiz

1. The process of transferring real property is called:

   a) avulsion
   b) quitclaim
   c) alienation
   d) dereliction

2. The government transfers title to private parties by means of a:

   a) patent
   b) deed
   c) quitclaim
   d) escheat

3. A grant deed warrants that:

   a) no one has adversely possessed the property
   b) the grantor has not previously conveyed title to anyone else
   c) the purchase price was fair and equitable
   d) title has been duly recorded

4. Clouds on title are usually cleared by:

   a) a suit for partition
   b) title insurance
   c) adverse possession
   d) a quitclaim deed

5. A valid deed must refer to a grantee who is:

   a) competent
   b) over 21 years old
   c) identifiable
   d) intestate

6. Conveyance requires a valid deed, plus:

   a) recording
   b) delivery
   c) acceptance
   d) Both b) and c)

7. A person who makes a will is called a/an:

   a) grantor
   b) executor
   c) testator
   d) escheat

8. An unwitnessed, handwritten will is called a:

   a) witnessed will
   b) holographic will
   c) nuncupative will
   d) None of the above

9. The process by which possession of property can result in ownership of the property is called:

   a) fee simple
   b) succession
   c) adverse possession
   d) reliction

10. A quitclaim deed conveys:

    a) whatever interest the grantor has
    b) only a portion of the interest held by the grantor
    c) only property acquired by adverse possession
    d) None of the above

11. The main reason why a grantee should make sure the deed gets recorded is to:

    a) give constructive notice of his or her interest in the property
    b) show acceptance of the conveyance
    c) make the transfer of title effective
    d) prevent adverse possession

12. To be valid, a deed must:

    a) include a recital of consideration
    b) be in writing
    c) have a habendum clause
    d) transfer after-acquired title

13. When a cloud on the title cannot be cleared
    with a quitclaim deed, this judicial proceeding
    decides ownership:

    a) quiet title action
    b) suit for partition
    c) interpleader action
    d) reformation action

14. All of the following are requirements for
    adverse possession, except:

    a) actual, open, and notorious possession
    b) continuous and uninterrupted possession
    c) hostile possession
    d) tacking

15. A standard title insurance policy would protect
    against:

    a) adverse possession
    b) encroachments
    c) a forged deed
    d) condemnation

Answer Key

1. c) The general term for a transfer of ownership of real property from one party to
another is alienation.

2. a) The government transfers title to property
with a patent.

3. b) A grant deed warrants that the grantor has
not conveyed title to anyone else.

4. d) A quitclaim deed is commonly used to
clear clouds on title.

5. c) The grantee is only required to be identifiable. He or she need not be competent.

6. d) To convey title successfully, the deed must
be delivered and accepted.

7. c) A testator is the person who makes a will.

8. b) A holographic will is one that is handwritten by the testator and not witnessed.

9. c) Adverse possession encourages the full use
of land by providing a means by which a
user may acquire ownership rights.

10. a) A quitclaim deed transfers whatever
interest the grantor has. If the grantor has
good title, it conveys good title. If the
grantor has no interest in the property, it
conveys nothing at all.

11. a) Recording a deed gives constructive notice
of the grantee's interest.

12. b) Under the statute of frauds, a deed must be
in writing to be valid.

13. a) A quiet title action provides a binding
determination of the parties' interests in a
piece of real estate.

14. d) All of these are among the requirements for
adverse possession, except tacking.
Although an adverse possessor may use
tacking to fulfill the statutory time requirement, tacking is not itself a requirement.

15. c) Standard title insurance coverage insures
only against title defects (such as a forged
deed), not against matters that are not part
of the public record.

Chapter 4

Encumbrances

I. Financial Encumbrances (Liens)
   A. Types of liens
      1. mortgages
      2. deeds of trust
      3. mechanic's liens
      4. judgment liens
      5. attachment liens
      6. property tax liens
      7. special assessments
      8. other tax liens
   B. Lien priority
   C. Homestead law
II. Nonfinancial Encumbrances
   A. Easements
      1. types of easements
      2. creating an easement
      3. terminating an easement
   B. Profits
   C. Related concepts
      1. licenses
      2. encroachments
      3. nuisances
   D. Private restrictions

Chapter Overview

An interest in real property may be held by someone other than the property owner or a tenant; such an interest is called an encumbrance. Nearly every property has encumbrances against it. Some encumbrances represent another person's financial interest in the property. Other encumbrances involve another person's right to make use of the property or to restrict how the owner uses it.

The first part of this chapter explains financial encumbrances, including mortgages and other types of liens. The second part of this chapter covers the nonfinancial encumbrances, including easements and private restrictions, and some related concepts.

Encumbrances

An encumbrance is a nonpossessory right or interest in real property held by someone other than the property owner. The interest can be financial or non-financial in nature. A financial encumbrance affects title only; a nonfinancial encumbrance also affects the use or physical condition of the property.

Financial Encumbrances (Liens)

Financial encumbrances are more commonly called **liens**. A lien is a security interest in property; it is held by a creditor of the property owner. If the owner doesn't pay off the debt owed to the creditor, the security interest allows the creditor to force the property to be sold, so that the creditor can collect the debt out of the sale proceeds. This is called **foreclosure**. The most familiar example of a lien is a mortgage.

A lien may also be defined as a charge imposed on real property as security for a specific act.

A creditor who has a lien against (a security interest in) the debtor's property is called a **secured creditor**. The lien does not prevent the debtor from trans-ferring the property, but the new owner takes title subject to the lien. The creditor can still foreclose if the debt is not repaid.

Liens may be voluntary or involuntary. A **voluntary lien** is one the debtor voluntarily gives to the creditor, usually as security for a loan. The two types of voluntary liens are mortgages and deeds of trust. **Involuntary liens** (some-times called statutory liens) are given to creditors without the property owner's consent, by operation of law. Examples of involuntary liens are property tax liens and judgment liens.

Example: Dunn sues Bronson for injuries sustained in a car crash and wins a $125,000 judgment. The judgment can become a lien against Bronson's property.

Liens may also be general or specific. A **general lien** attaches to all of the debtor's property. For instance, the judgment lien in the example is a general lien. Any property owned by Bronson could be encumbered by the judgment lien. On the other hand, a **specific lien** attaches only to a particular piece of property. A mortgage is an example of a specific lien. It is a lien against only the particular piece of property offered as security for the loan.

Types of Liens

The most common types of liens against real property include mortgages, deeds of trust, mechanic's liens, judgment liens, attachment liens, and tax and assessment liens.

Mortgages. A mortgage is a specific, voluntary lien created by a contract between the property owner (the **mortgagor**) and the creditor (the **mortgagee**). The mortgagee is usually a lender, who will not loan money unless the borrower gives a lien as security for repayment.

Deeds of Trust. A deed of trust (also called a trust deed) is used for the same purpose as a mortgage. However, there are three parties to a trust deed rather than the two found in a mortgage transaction. The borrower is called the **trustor**; the lender or creditor is called the **beneficiary**; and there is an independent third party (often an attorney or title insurance company) called the **trustee**. The most significant difference between mortgages and deeds of trust is in the foreclosure process. Mortgages and deeds of trust are discussed in more detail in Chapter 9.

Mechanic's liens. A person who provides labor, materials, or professional services for the improvement of real property may be entitled to claim a mechanic's lien against the property. For example, if a plumber who is involved in remodeling a bathroom isn't paid, he or she can claim a lien against the property for the amount owed. Eventually, if necessary, the plumber could foreclose on the lien, forcing the property to be sold to pay the debt.

A mechanic's lien is a specific, involuntary lien, attaching only to the property where work was performed or materials were supplied. Mechanic's liens are sometimes called **construction liens**; a lien claimed by someone who provides materials (as opposed to labor) is sometimes called a **materialman's lien**.

Many improvement projects involve a complex hierarchy of contractors, subcontractors, laborers, and materials suppliers, all of whom may be entitled to claim liens. However, before a mechanic's lien can be successfully created, the lien claimant must comply with numerous statutory requirements.

Preliminary Notice. California law requires a mechanic's lien claimant to give the property owner a preliminary notice of his or her right to claim a lien within 20 days after he or she begins providing services or materials. However, this notice is not necessary if the claimant has a contract directly with the owner. (The general contractor probably

Fig. 4.1 Lien classifications		
	Voluntary	**Involuntary**
Specific	Mortgages Deeds of trust	Property taxes Special assessments Mechanic's liens
General		Judgment liens IRS liens

has a contract directly with the owner; the electrician, for example, probably does not.)

Claim of Lien. The period of time during which a claim of lien can be filed and recorded varies, depending on whether a notice of completion or notice of cessation has been filed by the property owner.

When a project has been completed, the property owner has ten days in which to file a **notice of completion** at the recorder's office. A project is considered completed:

- if the project is subject to acceptance by any public entity, on the date of that acceptance; or
- 30 days after all labor on the project has ceased.

A property owner is allowed to file a **notice of cessation** after all work on the project has been stopped for a continuous period of 30 days, regardless of whether the project is actually completed.

When the property owner files a notice of completion or notice of cessation, all mechanic's liens must be filed and recorded within 30 days. The only exception to this rule is that the original or general contractor may file and record a lien within 60 days after the notice is filed. If the property owner fails to file a notice of completion or a notice of cessation, all mechanic's liens may be filed and recorded up to 90 days after the work on the project has ceased.

Foreclosure. To foreclose a mechanic's lien, the lienholder must file a court action within 90 days after the lien was filed and recorded. Otherwise, the lien automatically becomes null and void, and has no further force or effect.

Notice of Nonresponsibility. Occasionally, construction workers begin a project that has not been approved by the property owner. For instance, a tenant may order work done on the leased property without the landlord's knowledge or consent. If the tenant fails to pay for the work, the construction workers and suppliers could file mechanic's liens against the property, and the owner would be held responsible for the cost of the project.

There is a way for owners to protect themselves against mechanic's liens. Within ten days of becoming aware of the construction project, a property owner can give notice that he or she will not be responsible for the work. This is done by posting a **notice of nonresponsibility** in a conspicuous place on the property, and then recording that notice. The notice must contain a description of the property, the name of the person giving the notice and his or her interest in the property, the name of any lessee or purchaser of the property, and a statement that the person giving the notice will not be responsible for any claims arising from the work done.

Judgment Liens. Judgment liens are involuntary, general liens. If a lawsuit results in a money judgment against the loser, the winner (the judgment creditor) may obtain a lien against the loser's (the judgment debtor's) property. The lien attaches to all the property owned by the debtor in the county where the judgment was entered, and also attaches to any property acquired by the debtor during the lien period (the length of time the judgment creditor has to take action on the lien). The judgment lien may also be recorded in other counties in the state, if the debtor owns property in other counties.

Once a judgment lien has attached, the debtor must pay the judgment to free the property from the lien. If it's not paid, the property can be sold by a designated official to satisfy the judgment. To order this done, the court issues a **writ of execution**.

Attachment Liens. When someone files a lawsuit, there is a danger that by the time a judgment is entered, the **defendant** (the party sued) will have sold his or her property and disappeared, leaving the other party with little more than a piece of paper. To prevent this, the **plaintiff** (the person who started the lawsuit) can ask the court to issue a writ of attachment. A **writ of attachment** directs the sheriff to seize enough of the defendant's property to satisfy the judgment the plaintiff is seeking. The writ of attachment is recorded and creates a lien on the defendant's real property. An attachment lien is valid for three years and is renewable.

Also, when a lawsuit that may affect title to real property is pending, the plaintiff may record a document called a **lis pendens**, which is Latin for "action pending." While a lis pendens is not a lien, anyone who purchases the property identified in the lis pendens has constructive notice of the pending lawsuit and therefore is bound by any judgment that results from the suit, even though that person is not a party to the lawsuit. If the need for the lis pendens disappears before the lawsuit is concluded, the lis pendens may be removed by the person who originally recorded it.

Property Tax Liens. Property is assessed (appraised for tax purposes) and taxed according to its value. When property taxes are levied, a lien attaches to the property until they are paid. Property tax liens are involuntary, specific liens. (Property taxation is discussed in more detail in Chapter 5.)

Special Assessments. Special assessments result from local improvements, such as road paving or sewer lines, that benefit some, but not all, property owners within the county. The properties that have benefited from the improvement are assessed for their share of the cost of the improvement. The assessment creates an involuntary, specific lien against the property. (Special assessments are also discussed in Chapter 5.)

Other Tax Liens. Many other taxes, such as federal income taxes, estate or inheritance taxes, and gift taxes, can result in liens against property.

Lien Priority

It is not at all unusual for a piece of property to have more than one lien against it. In fact, the dollar amount of all the liens may add up to more than the property will sell for at a foreclosure sale. When this happens, the sale proceeds are not allocated among all the lienholders in a pro rata fashion (proportionate distribution). Instead, the liens are paid according to their priority. This means that the lien with the highest priority is paid first. If any money is left over, the lien with the second highest priority is paid, and so forth.

As a general rule, lien priority is determined by the date a lien was recorded. The lien that was recorded first will be paid first, even though another lien may have been created first.

Example: Suppose Baker borrows money from two banks—$5,000 from National Bank on March 17, and $5,000 from State Bank on May 5 of the same year. Baker gives mortgages to both banks when the loan funds are received. If National Bank does not record its mortgage until July 14, but State Bank records its mortgage promptly on May 5, State Bank's lien will be paid before National Bank's in the event of foreclosure.

While "first in time (to record), first in right" is the general rule, there are some exceptions; some types of liens are given special priority. In California, special priority is given to property tax and special assessment liens; they have priority over all other liens. Mechanic's liens are another exception. Their priority is determined by the date that work on the project began, even though the claim of lien was recorded later on.

The Homestead Law

Homestead laws are state laws that give homeowners limited protection against lien foreclosure. In California, the homestead law offers protection only against judgment liens. It does not apply to mortgages, deeds of trust, mechanic's liens, or liens for child support or spousal maintenance.

A **homestead** is an owner-occupied dwelling, together with any appurtenant buildings and land. Homestead protection may be claimed by filing a **declaration of homestead** at the county recorder's office, or by claiming the exemption after the property has become subject to a judgment lien foreclosure proceeding. A declaration of homestead may be filed by the owner, by the owner's spouse, or by a guardian, attorney in fact, or other person authorized to act on behalf of the owner.

Exemption. After a homestead declaration has been filed, the homestead property is exempt from judgment liens to the extent of the homestead exemption. Currently, the standard exemption is $50,000. The exemption for a member of a family unit is $75,000. The exemption is $150,000 if the debtor or the debtor's spouse is over 65 or unable to work because of a disability. It's also $150,000 if the debtor or spouse is over 55 and low income and the sale is involuntary.

A judgment creditor cannot foreclose on a homestead unless the net value of the property is greater than the amount of the exemption.

When a judgment lien is foreclosed on and homestead property is sold, the sale proceeds are applied in the following manner:

1. to pay all liens and encumbrances not subject to the homestead exemption (a deed of trust, for example);
2. to the homestead claimant in the amount of the exemption ($50,000, $75,000, or $150,000);
3. to pay the costs of sale;
4. to the judgment creditor to satisfy the debt; and
5. any surplus to the homestead claimant.

Money paid to the former owner as a result of the homestead exemption is protected from judgment creditors after the foreclosure sale for up to six months, during which time the funds may be reinvested in another homestead property.

Termination. Homestead protection is terminated when the property is sold, when the homesteader files a declaration of abandonment, or when the homesteader files a declaration of homestead on another property. Funds from the voluntary sale of the homestead property (up to the amount of the homestead exemption) are protected from judgment creditors just as the proceeds of a forced sale are protected—for up to six months, to allow the homesteader to purchase another home.

Homestead protection does not terminate auto-

Fig. 4.2 Types of encumbrances

Financial Encumbrances	Nonfinancial Encumbrances
• Mortgages • Deeds of trust • Mechanic's liens • Judgment liens • Attachment liens • Property tax liens • Other tax liens	• Easements • Profits • Private restrictions

matically on the death of the homesteader. It continues for the benefit of the spouse, children, or other family members living on the property.

Nonfinancial Encumbrances

While financial encumbrances affect only title to property, nonfinancial encumbrances affect the physical use or condition of the property itself. Thus, a property owner can find the use of his or her land limited by a right or interest held by someone else. Nonfinancial encumbrances include easements, profits, and private restrictions. We'll also cover licenses, encroachments, and nuisances in this section; they too involve someone using another's property or affecting the owner's use of it, although they aren't actually interests in real property.

Easements

An easement is a right to use another person's land for a particular purpose. It is a nonpossessory interest in land; the easement holder has a right to use the land, but has no title or right of possession. An easement is not an estate.

Example: A landowner has an easement across her neighbor's lot for access to the public road. She has a right to make reasonable use of that easement to get to and from her property. However, she does not have the right to build a shed on the easement, or to use the easement in any way other than as a driveway.

Types of Easements. There are two main types of easements: easements appurtenant and easements in gross.

Easements Appurtenant. An easement appurtenant burdens one parcel of land for the benefit of another parcel of land. The parcel with the benefit is called the **dominant tenement**; the one with the burden is called the **servient tenement**. The owner of the dominant tenement is called the **dominant tenant**; the owner of the servient tenement is the **servient tenant**. Do not confuse the term "tenement," which is the land, with "tenant," which is the landowner.

Probably the most common example of an easement appurtenant is a driveway easement providing access across one parcel of land to another. (A driveway easement is often called an easement for **ingress and egress**, which means entering and exiting.) In Figure 4.3, Lot B has an easement appurtenant across Lot A. The easement provides access to a public road. Lot B is the dominant tenement. Lot A is the servient tenement.

Fig. 4.3 Easement appurtenant

An easement appurtenant passes with or "runs" with the land. This means that if either the dominant or servient tenement is transferred to a new owner, the new owner also acquires the benefit or the burden of the easement. Refer to Figure 4.3 again. If Lot B were sold, the new owner would still have an easement across Lot A. If Lot A were sold, the new owner would still bear the burden of allowing the owner of Lot B to use the easement.

An easement that benefits a parcel of land is called an easement appurtenant because it goes along with ownership of the land like other appurtenances (air rights, for example). The easement is appurtenant to the dominant tenement.

Easements in Gross. An easement in gross benefits a person (a dominant tenant) rather than a parcel of land. When someone has an easement in gross, there is no dominant tenement, only a servient tenement.

> **Example:** Wilson has the right to enter Able's land and fish in Able's stream. Wilson is a dominant tenant with an easement in gross over Able's land (the servient tenement). The easement serves Wilson, not a parcel of land.

Since an easement in gross belongs to an individual, and not a parcel of land, it is a personal right that is extinguished on the death of the dominant tenant. In the example above, when Wilson dies, the easement will disappear. A personal easement in gross may not be assigned by its owner to a third party.

Most easements in gross are commercial easements. The most common example is the easement held by a utility company, which allows company employees to enter property to install and service the utility lines. Because commercial easements in gross are considered more substantial interests than personal easements, they can be assigned from one utility company to another.

Creating an Easement. Easements (whether appurtenant or in gross) can be created in any of the following ways:

- express grant,
- express reservation,
- implication,
- prescription,
- reference to a recorded plat,
- dedication, or
- condemnation.

Express Grant. An easement is created by express grant when a property owner grants someone else the right to use the property. The grant must be put into writing and comply with all the other requirements for conveyance of an interest in land (see Chapter 3).

When granting an easement, the grantor does not have to specify the location of the easement. For example, a grant of an easement "across Lot A for purposes of ingress and egress" would be valid (assuming that all the other requirements for a proper conveyance are met).

A person can grant an easement only in the interest that he or she holds. For instance, if a tenant grants an easement in the leased property, the easement will exist only for the term of the lease.

A fee simple owner may grant an easement that will last in perpetuity (indefinitely), or for the life of the grantor, or only for a specified term.

Express Reservation. A landowner who is conveying a portion of his or her property may reserve an easement in that parcel to benefit the parcel of land that is retained. Like an express grant, an express reservation must be put into writing.

> **Example:** Carmichael owns 100 acres beside a state highway. She sells 40 acres, including all the highway frontage. In the deed, she reserves to herself an easement across the conveyed land so that she will have access to her remaining 60 acres.

Implication. An easement by implication (sometimes called an easement by necessity) can be either an implied grant or an implied reservation. This type of easement can arise only when a property is divided into more than one lot, and the grantor neglects to grant or reserve an easement on one lot for the benefit of the other. There are two requirements for an easement to be created by implication:

1. it must be reasonably necessary for the enjoyment of the property, and
2. there must have been apparent prior use.

The second requirement is fulfilled if the use was established before the property was divided, and would have been apparent from an inspection of the property.

Prescription. An easement by prescription is created through long-term use of land without the permission of the landowner. Acquiring an easement by prescription is similar to acquiring ownership through adverse possession. Here are the requirements for an easement by prescription:

- the use is **open and notorious** (apparent to the landowner);
- the use is **hostile** (without the permission of the landowner);
- the use is **reasonably continuous** for five years;
- the use is under some **claim of right**; and
- if **property taxes** are assessed separately against the easement, they are paid by the easement claimant for the five-year period.

Reference to a Recorded Plat. When a landowner subdivides and sells his or her land under a recorded plat, the lot purchasers acquire easements to use the roads and alleys shown on the plat.

Dedication. A private landowner may grant an easement to the public to use some portion of his or her property for a public purpose, such as a sidewalk. The dedication may be expressly stated, or it may be implied.

Condemnation. The government may exercise its power of eminent domain and condemn private property to gain an easement for a public purpose, such as a road. This power may also be exercised by private companies that serve the public, such as railroad and power companies.

Terminating an Easement. An easement can be terminated in any of the following ways:

- release,
- merger,
- failure of purpose,
- abandonment, or
- prescription.

Release. The holder of an easement may release his or her rights in the servient tenement. This would be accomplished with a written document, usually a quitclaim deed from the easement holder to the owner of the servient tenement.

Merger. Since an easement is, by definition, the right to make some use of another person's land, if the dominant and servient tenements come to be owned by the same person, the easement is no longer necessary and therefore is terminated. This is called merger; ownership of the dominant and servient tenements has merged.

Failure of Purpose. If the purpose for which an easement was created ceases, then the easement terminates. For example, if an easement was created for a railroad and the railroad company later removes the rails and discontinues its use, the easement would be terminated through failure of purpose.

Abandonment. An easement is also terminated if the easement holder abandons it. This requires acts by the holder indicating an intent to abandon the easement. Mere non-use is not abandonment.

> **Example:** The dominant tenant builds a fence that blocks any further use of an easement that had been used for ingress and egress. Under the circumstances, it would be reasonable for the servient tenant to conclude that the easement has been abandoned.

Note that a servient tenant can bring a suit to have a prescriptive easement terminated after five years of non-use. If the court finds non-use, the easement will be terminated.

Prescription. An easement is extinguished by prescription if the servient tenant prevents the dominant tenant from using the easement for the statutory period (five years).

> **Example:** The servient tenant builds a brick wall around his property. The dominant tenant can no longer use her easement for ingress and egress. If the wall remains undisturbed for five years, then the easement will be terminated by prescription.

Profits

A profit is the right to take something away from land that belongs to someone else. For example, it might be the right to take timber, peat, or gravel from someone else's land. The difference between a profit and an easement is that the easement is just a right to use another's land, but a profit allows the removal of something from the land. A profit must be created in writing or by prescription.

Fig. 4.4 Encroachments

Licenses

Like an easement, a license gives someone the right to make some use of another person's land. However, easements and licenses are different in many ways. An easement is created in writing or through action of law. Ordinarily, a license is just spoken permission to cross, hunt, fish on, or make some other use of a landowner's property. An easement is irrevocable, but a license can be revoked at the will of the landowner. In general, easements are permanent and licenses are temporary. A license is a personal right that does not run with or pass with the land. It cannot be assigned. Since the license is revocable at the will of the landowner, it is not actually considered an encumbrance or an interest in the property.

Encroachments

An encroachment is a physical object that is wholly or partially on someone else's property, such as a fence or garage built partially over the property line onto the neighbor's land (see Figure 4.4). Most encroachments are unintentional, resulting from a mistake concerning the exact location of the property line.

An encroachment may be a **trespass** if it violates the neighboring owner's right to possession. A court can order an encroachment to be removed through a judicial action called an **ejectment**, or if the cost of the removal would be too high, order the encroacher to pay damages to the neighbor. There is a three-year statute of limitations on court actions for trespass on real property. That means that a property owner must file suit within three years of the time he or she discovered (or should have discovered) an encroachment, or the right to sue for damages or the removal of the encroachment will be lost.

Nuisances

A nuisance is an activity or a condition on neighboring property that interferes with a property owner's reasonable use or enjoyment of his or her own property. Common examples include odors, noises, and interference with communication signals. Like an encroachment, a nuisance isn't truly an encumbrance, but rather a violation of an owner's possessory rights.

A private nuisance affects only a few surrounding people. For example, rotting garbage in a neighbor's backyard would be a private nuisance. A public nuisance affects a larger community's health or welfare; jet noise and industrial emissions are examples. A property owner may ask a court for an injunction against a private or public nuisance, or may sue for damages.

A related concept is the **attractive nuisance** doctrine. The owner of a property with a feature that is dangerous and attractive to children, such as an unfenced swimming pool or construction site, will be held liable for any harm resulting from failure to keep out trespassing children.

Private Restrictions

Private restrictions (also known as deed restrictions) are restrictions on the use of a property that were imposed by some previous owner. For example, when selling a house long ago, a previous owner might have stated in the deed that the poplar trees in the front yard must not be cut down. Like easements, private restrictions can "run with the land," binding all subsequent owners of the property.

As long as a private restriction isn't unconstitutional, in violation of a law, or contrary to a judicial determination of public policy, it can be enforced in court. (An example of an unenforceable restriction is one prohibiting the sale of property to non-white buyers; see Chapter 14.)

Most subdivision developers impose a list of restrictions on all lots within the subdivision, before they begin selling individual lots. This is called a declaration of restrictions, or **CC&Rs** (covenants, conditions, and restrictions). The CC&Rs typically include rules limiting all the lots to single-family residential use, requiring property maintenance, and preventing activities that would bother the neighbors. The rules are intended to ensure that the subdivision will remain a desirable place to live. The CC&Rs are recorded, and then referenced in the deeds used to convey the lots in the subdivision.

Note that private restrictions can also be created by written agreement.

Covenants vs. Conditions. A private restriction is either a covenant or a condition. A **covenant** is a promise to do or not do something, as in a contract. A property owner who violates a covenant may be sued, leading to an injunction (a court order directing the owner to comply with the covenant) or, less often, payment of damages for failure to comply. Violation of a **condition** can have more serious consequences. A condition in a deed makes the grantee's title conditional, so that he or she owns a defeasible fee (rather than a fee simple absolute; see Chapter 2). Breach of the condition could result in forfeiture of title.

Whether a particular restriction is a covenant or a condition depends on the wording in the deed. Courts try to avoid forfeitures, so they will usually interpret a restriction as a covenant rather than a condition, if there is any ambiguity. (CC&Rs are virtually always covenants, even though the term includes the word "conditions.")

Termination of Restrictions. It is up to the property owners within a subdivision to enforce the CC&Rs. If the residents have failed to enforce a particular restriction in the past, they may no longer be able to enforce it.

> **Example:** The subdivision's CC&Rs state that recreational vehicles may not be parked within view of the street. Over the years, however, many homeowners have broken this rule and their neighbors haven't complained. If someone tries to start enforcing the parking restriction now, a court might rule that it has been abandoned and is no longer enforceable.

A private restriction will also terminate if its purpose can no longer be achieved. For example, this might occur because zoning changes and other factors have dramatically altered the character of the neighborhood. If there is a private restriction limiting a property to single-family residential use, but most of the surrounding properties are now used for light industry, the restriction is probably no longer enforceable.

Chapter Summary

1. An encumbrance is a nonpossessory right or interest in real property held by someone other than the property owner. Encumbrances may be financial or nonfinancial.

2. A financial encumbrance (a lien) affects title to property. It gives a creditor the right to foreclose and use the sale proceeds to pay off the debt. A lien is either voluntary or involuntary, and either general or specific. The most common types of liens include mortgages, deeds of trust, mechanic's liens, tax liens, judgment liens, and attachment liens.

3. A nonfinancial encumbrance affects the use or condition of the property. Nonfinancial encumbrances include easements, profits, and private restrictions.

4. An easement gives the easement holder the right to use a portion of someone else's property for a specified purpose. An easement runs with the land, affecting the title of subsequent owners of the property or properties in question.

5. An easement appurtenant burdens one parcel of land (the servient tenement) for the benefit of another parcel (the dominant tenement). An easement in gross burdens a parcel of land for the benefit of a person, not another parcel of land.

6. Licenses, encroachments, and nuisances may also affect the use or condition of property. They are not classified as encumbrances, however, because they are not interests in real property.

7. Private restrictions affect how an owner may use his or her own property. Like easements, private restrictions run with the land. A declaration of CC&Rs recorded by a subdivision developer is binding on the future owners of the subdivision lots.

🔑 Key Terms

Encumbrance—An interest in real property held by someone other than the property owner.

Voluntary lien—A security interest given to a creditor voluntarily.

Involuntary lien—A security interest given to a creditor by operation of law.

General lien—A lien that attaches to all of a debtor's property.

Specific lien—A lien that attaches only to one particular piece of property.

Mechanic's lien—A lien on property in favor of someone who provided labor or materials to improve it. Also called a construction lien or materialman's lien.

Judgment lien—A lien held by someone who has won a judgment in a lawsuit, attaching to property owned by the person who lost the lawsuit.

Easement—The right to use another's land for a particular purpose.

Easement appurtenant—An easement that burdens one parcel of land (the servient tenement) for the benefit of another parcel (the dominant tenement).

Easement in gross—An easement that benefits a person rather than a parcel of land.

Easement by implication—An easement created automatically because it is necessary for the enjoyment of the benefited land.

Prescriptive easement—An easement created by continuous use for the statutory period, without the landowner's permission.

Merger—When both the dominant and servient tenements are acquired by one owner, resulting in termination of the easement.

Abandonment—A way in which an easement may terminate. It requires action by the easement holder, not simply non-use.

Profit—The right to take something (such as timber) from another's land.

License—Revocable permission to enter another's land, which does not create an interest in the property.

Encroachment—A physical object that intrudes onto another's property, such as a tree branch or a fence.

Nuisance—An activity or condition on nearby property that interferes with a property owner's reasonable use and enjoyment of his or her property.

CC&Rs—Covenants, conditions, and restrictions; private restrictions imposed by a subdivision developer.

Condition—A restriction on the use of land, the violation of which may result in forfeiture of title.

Covenant—A promise by a landowner to refrain from using his or her land in a particular manner.

Chapter Quiz

1. Real estate property tax liens are:

   a) general, involuntary liens
   b) general, voluntary liens
   c) specific, voluntary liens
   d) specific, involuntary liens

2. A lawsuit against Thatcher is pending. The court rules that a lien should be placed on his farm, holding it as security in case of a negative judgment. This is:

   a) adverse possession
   b) prescription
   c) an attachment
   d) an easement

3. A recorded document that informs potential buyers that the property may become subject to a judgment in a lawsuit is a:

   a) lis pendens
   b) writ of execution
   c) writ of attachment
   d) habendum clause

4. Which of the following has priority over a mortgage that has already been recorded?

   a) A deed of trust
   b) A judgment lien
   c) A property tax lien
   d) None of the above

5. If there were two deeds of trust against the same property and you needed to know which one had higher priority, you could find this information at the county recorder's office. The priority is usually established by:

   a) the printed trust deed forms, which have the words "first deed of trust" and "second deed of trust" on their face
   b) the date and time of recording
   c) the county auditor's stamp, which says "first trust deed" or "second trust deed"
   d) the execution date of each document

6. When there's an easement appurtenant, the dominant tenement:

   a) can be used only for purposes of ingress and egress
   b) is burdened by the easement
   c) receives the benefit of the easement
   d) cannot be sold

7. You have the right to cross another's land to get to your house. You probably own a:

   a) dominant tenement
   b) servient tenement
   c) Both of the above
   d) Neither of the above

8. An easement in gross benefits a:

   a) dominant tenement
   b) servient tenement
   c) Both of the above
   d) Neither of the above

9. Unlike a personal easement in gross, a commercial easement in gross:

   a) is not an encumbrance
   b) is considered a possessory interest in real property
   c) can be assigned to another party
   d) can be revoked by the owner of the servient tenement

10. Which of the following is not a method of creating an easement?

    a) Implication
    b) Express grant in a deed
    c) Dedication
    d) Spoken grant

11. The creation of an easement by prescription is similar to acquiring ownership of property by:

    a) adverse possession
    b) escheat
    c) alluvium
    d) intestate succession

12. A has an easement over B's property. If A buys B's property, the easement is:

    a) abandoned
    b) terminated by merger
    c) unaffected
    d) None of the above

13. A porch or balcony that hangs over the established boundary line of a parcel of land is called:

    a) an easement in gross
    b) an encroachment
    c) an easement appurtenant
    d) a license

14. All of the following would be considered nuisances, except:

    a) fumes from a paper mill
    b) a house with regular drug-dealing activity
    c) radiation from a microwave tower
    d) a garage built on top of the property line

15. The private restrictions in a subdivision's CC&Rs:

    a) do not run with the land
    b) were imposed by the developer
    c) can terminate only with the approval of a majority of the lot owners
    d) create a lien against the property

☞ Answer Key

1. d) Property tax liens are specific (they attach only to the taxed property) and involuntary.

2. c) In an attachment, a lien is created against the defendant's property, pending the outcome of the lawsuit.

3. a) A lis pendens provides constructive notice of a pending lawsuit that may affect the property described in the document.

4. c) Property tax liens always have priority over other liens.

5. b) The date of recording governs lien priority, rather than the date of execution of the documents.

6. c) The dominant tenement is benefited by the easement; the servient tenement is burdened by the easement. An easement appurtenant is not necessarily an easement for ingress and egress.

7. a) Since you have the right to use another's property to reach your own, you probably own a dominant tenement.

8. d) An easement in gross benefits an individual (the dominant tenant) rather than any parcel of land.

9. c) A commercial easement in gross can be assigned to another party, but a personal easement in gross cannot be.

10. d) Like any other interest in land, an easement must be granted in writing, unless it is created by operation of law.

11. a) An easement by prescription is obtained in much the same way as ownership by adverse possession: the use must be open and notorious, hostile, and continuous for five years.

12. b) Merger occurs when one person acquires ownership of both the dominant tenement and the servient tenement. Merger terminates the easement.

13. b) An overhanging porch or balcony is an encroachment.

14. d) A structure built on the property line is an encroachment, not a nuisance. A nuisance is an activity or condition on neighboring property that negatively affects an owner's use and enjoyment of his or her property.

15. b) CC&Rs are usually imposed by the developer. They run with the land, which means that subsequent owners of the subdivision lots must abide by them.

Public Restrictions on Land

▲▪▲▪ Chapter Overview

Although a property owner has many rights in regard to his or her property, those rights are limited by certain powers of the federal, state, and local governments. This chapter examines the ways in which governmental powers affect property ownership most directly. The first part of the chapter explains planning, zoning, and other public restrictions on land use. The second part discusses the government's power to tax property.

Land Use Controls

In the United States, the powers of government are determined by the federal and state constitutions. Thus, efforts by the federal, state, and local governments to control the use of private property raise constitutional issues. When a property owner objects to a land use law, the central question is often whether the law is constitutional—whether the Constitution gives the government the power to interfere with private property rights in this way.

The constitutional basis for land use control laws is the **police power**. This is the power vested in a state to adopt and enforce laws and regulations necessary for the protection of the public's health, safety, morals, and general welfare. A state may delegate its police power to local governmental bodies.

It is the police power that allows state and local governments to regulate the use of private property. The Constitution does not give the federal government a general power to regulate for the public health, safety, morals, and welfare. But the federal government does have authority to use its other powers (such as the power to regulate interstate commerce) to advance police power objectives.

Exercises of the police power must meet constitutional limitations. As a general rule, a land use law or regulation will be considered constitutional if it meets these four criteria:

1. It is reasonably related to the protection of the public health, safety, morals, or general welfare.
2. It applies in the same manner to all property owners who are similarly situated (it is not discriminatory).
3. It does not reduce a property's value so much that the regulation amounts to a confiscation.
4. It benefits the public by preventing harm that would be caused by the prohibited use of the property.

Government land use controls take a variety of forms: comprehensive plans, zoning ordinances, building codes, subdivision regulations, and environmental laws. All of these are intended to protect the public from problems that unrestricted use of private property can cause.

If two different governmental entities have passed conflicting laws or ordinances based on the police power, the one with the higher standards of health and safety will apply.

Comprehensive Planning

To alleviate problems caused by haphazard, unplanned growth, California requires cities and counties to have a planning agency, usually called a planning commission.

The planning commission is responsible for designing and adopting a comprehensive, long-term plan for all the development within the city or county. This is often called the "master plan" or "general plan." The purpose of the general plan is to outline the community's development goals and design an overall physical layout to achieve those goals. Once the general plan has been adopted, all development and all land use regulations (such as zoning laws) must conform to it.

Fig. 5.1 Setbacks and side yards

Setback 10'

Side yard 5'

Buildable Area

Side yard 5'

Setback 10'

The government uses both its police power and its power of eminent domain (discussed later) to implement the planning commission's general plan.

Zoning

Zoning ordinances divide a community into areas (or zones) that are set aside for specific types of uses, such as agricultural, residential, commercial, or industrial use. Each of these basic classifications may be further divided. For instance, an industrial district may be divided into a light industrial zone and a heavy industrial zone. A residential district may be divided into single-family zones (often designated as R-1 zones) and multifamily zones (often designated as R-3 zones). Keeping various uses in separate zones helps ensure that only compatible uses are located in the same area. In addition, areas zoned for incompatible uses may be separated by undeveloped areas called **buffers**.

Zoning ordinances regulate the height, size, and shape of buildings, as well as their use. The laws also usually include setback and side-yard requirements, which prescribe the minimum distance between a building and the property lines (see Figure 5.1). These regulations control population density, provide aesthetic guidelines, and help preserve adequate open space and access to air and daylight.

To be valid, zoning ordinances cannot be applied retroactively, cannot discriminate against a particular parcel of property, and cannot create a patently unfair situation.

Zoning Exceptions and Amendments. Complications inevitably arise when zoning regulations are administered and enforced. So zoning ordinances provide for certain exceptions and changes to their rules, including:

- nonconforming uses,
- variances,
- conditional uses, and
- rezones.

A zoning exception or change can be requested by an individual property owner, a developer, or a city or county government.

Nonconforming Uses. A **nonconforming use** can arise when an area is zoned for the first time, or when a zoning ordinance is amended. Certain established uses that were previously lawful may not conform to the rules laid down in the new ordinance. These nonconforming uses will be permitted to continue.

> **Example:** Smith has been lawfully operating a bakery for seven months when his property is rezoned for single-family residential use. Smith's bakery will be allowed to continue as a nonconforming use. He is not required to apply for a permit.

Even though nonconforming uses are allowed to remain, the local government wants all uses to conform to the current zoning laws at some point. Consequently, the owners of a nonconforming use property are often prohibited from enlarging the use, rebuilding if the property is destroyed, or resuming the use after abandoning it.

> **Example:** Smith's bakery burns to the ground in a terrible fire. The zoning authority will not allow him to rebuild the bakery in this residential zone. He will have to sell the property and use the insurance proceeds to buy a suitable property located in a commercial zone.

Variances. In some cases, if a zoning law were strictly enforced, the property owner's injury would far outweigh the benefit of enforcing the zoning requirement. Under these circumstances, a **variance** may be available. A variance is authorization to build or maintain a structure or use that is prohibited by the zoning ordinance. For example, a variance might authorize construction of a house even though the topography of the lot makes it virtually impossible to comply with normal setback requirements. In most communities, the property owner applies to the local zoning authority for a variance.

A variance usually will not be granted unless the property owner faces severe practical difficulties or undue hardship (not created by the property owner him or herself) as a result of the zoning. The owner is generally required to prove that the zoning prevents any reasonable use of the land, not merely the most profitable use.

> **Example:** Martinez owns a piece of property that would make a perfect site for a fourplex. However, because of the setback and side-yard requirements, the largest structure Martinez could build is a duplex. Martinez will not be able to get a variance by claiming that she could make much more money by building a fourplex than she could by building a duplex.

Most variances authorize only minor deviations from the zoning law. A variance should not change the essential character of the neighborhood or conflict with the community's general plan.

In California, local authorities may not grant **use variances**—variances that authorize a land use not otherwise permitted in a zone. For instance, a variance allowing a commercial or retail use in a single-family residential zone cannot be granted.

> **Example:** Corelli owns a piece of property in a single-family residential zone. Unfortunately, the land does not drain properly, so he is not permitted to construct a single-family home on the lot. However, the lot would make a perfect site for storage units. Corelli requests a variance, but the request is denied. Whether or not

Corelli is suffering undue hardship because of the zoning law is immaterial; the local authority does not have the power to grant a variance that would allow a commercial use in a residential zone.

Conditional Uses. Various special uses, such as schools, hospitals, and churches, don't fit into the ordinary zoning categories. These uses are necessary to the community, yet they may have adverse effects on neighboring properties. So in most communities, the zoning authority can issue **conditional use permits** (also called special exception permits), allowing a limited number of these uses to operate in compliance with specified conditions. For example, a property owner might be given a conditional use permit to build a private school in a residential neighborhood, as long as the school meets certain requirements for parking, security, and so on.

Rezones. A property owner who believes that his or her property has been zoned improperly may petition the local appeals board for a **rezone** (sometimes called a zoning amendment). Usually, notice must be given to surrounding landowners and a hearing must be held before a decision is made on a petition.

When an area is rezoned to a more restrictive use (for example, a change from multifamily dwellings to single-family dwellings), it is referred to as **downzoning**.

Zoning vs. Private Restrictions. Sometimes private restrictions impose stricter limits on property than the local zoning ordinances. For example, suppose a property is in a zone that requires lots to be a minimum of 15,000 square feet, while a private restriction on the property prevents it from being subdivided into lots smaller than half an acre (21,780 square feet). The general rule is that the more restrictive requirement must be met. In our example, the private restriction would take precedence over the zoning ordinance, because it is the more restrictive of the two. On the other hand, in cases where the zoning is more restrictive than a private restriction, the zoning will take precedence.

Building Codes

The enactment of building codes is another exercise of the police power. Building codes protect the public from unsafe or unworkmanlike construction. They are generally divided into specialized codes, such as a fire code, an electrical code, and a plumbing code. The codes set standards for construction methods and materials. A structure that was built before a new, stricter standard is enacted may still be required to meet the new standard.

Enforcement of building codes is usually accomplished through the building permit system. A property owner must obtain a permit from the city or county before constructing a new building or repairing, improving, or altering an existing building. For example, it is usually necessary to have a building permit in order to add on to a home, to convert a carport into a garage, or even to build a fence. The permit requirement allows officials to inspect the building plans to verify that building codes and zoning ordinances have been satisfied. Once the completed construction has been inspected and found satisfactory, a **certificate of occupancy** is issued.

In California, the state Housing Law sets forth minimum construction and occupancy requirements for residential construction. These requirements are enforced by local building inspectors.

Subdivision Regulations

Another way in which state and local governments control land use is by regulating subdivisions. A **subdivision** is a division of one parcel of land into two or more parcels.

Types of Subdivisions. There are various types of subdivisions in California, including standard, common interest, and undivided interest subdivisions. Subdivisions are usually residential, but may be commercial, industrial, or recreational.

Standard Subdivisions. The typical housing development—where each individual owner owns his or her own parcel of land—is considered to be a standard subdivision. A standard subdivision is technically defined as one with no common rights of either ownership or use among the various owners of the individual parcels created by the division.

Standard subdivisions usually consist of five or more lots that have been improved with utilities. Individuals may purchase a lot on which to build their own home, or developers may purchase several or all of the lots, build houses on the lots, and then sell the homes to individual homeowners.

Common Interest Subdivisions. These are subdivisions where individual owners own or lease a separate lot or unit along with an undivided interest in the common areas of the project. Condominium and cooperative projects are examples of common interest subdivisions. For example, a condominium owner owns the residential unit in severalty, and has an undivided interest in the common areas of the condominium project, such as the lobby, elevators, parking lot, and recreational areas. (See Chapter 2.)

Planned developments are also considered common interest subdivisions. A planned development consists of lots that are separately owned, plus areas that are owned in common and reserved for the use of some or all of the individual lot owners. The common areas are generally managed and maintained by an owners' association. The association charges the lot owners fees to pay for the management and maintenance of the common areas.

A timeshare is another type of common interest subdivision. In a timesharing arrangement, buyers purchase the exclusive right to possession of the property for a specified period each year. A timeshare could be developed for any kind of housing, but it is most commonly used for resort condominiums.

Undivided Interest Subdivisions. In an undivided interest subdivision, individual owners own undivided interests in a parcel of land and have a non-exclusive right to use and occupy the property. The undivided interests are typically tenancies in common. An example of an undivided interest subdivision is a recreational vehicle park.

Laws Regulating Subdivisions. Laws that regulate subdivisions in California include the Subdivision Map Act, the Subdivided Lands Law, and the Interstate Land Sales Full Disclosure Act. The Subdivision Map Act is a "procedural" law, one that sets forth the procedures that must be followed to subdivide land. The Subdivided Lands Law is a "consumer protection" law, one that requires the subdivider to disclose certain information to those who purchase subdivision lots. The Interstate Land Sales Full Disclosure Act is a federal consumer protection law that applies to subdivision lots sold in interstate commerce.

Subdivision Map Act. The Subdivision Map Act establishes a set of procedures that must be followed before a subdivision can be created. It gives cities and counties the power to control the formation of subdivisions, and sets out rules for the exercise of that power. The purpose of the Subdivision Map Act is to ensure that new subdivisions comply with the local general plan. It also ensures that adequate public utilities are provided for each new subdivision. The act applies to all subdivisions of land with two or more parcels, but its most important provisions affect only subdivisions with five or more parcels.

When land is subdivided into five or more parcels, the subdivider must file a **tentative subdivision map** with the local planning agency. The tentative map includes the legal description of the property and shows the proposed lot boundaries, the location of utility easements and access roads, proposed street widths, the source of the water supply, and the provisions for control of flooding and geologic hazards. The planning agency sends copies of the map to other government agencies for their recommendations. These government agencies include transportation, health, and parks departments; school districts; city or county surveyors; and public utilities. The subdivider has the burden of demonstrating to these agencies that the off-site improvements, such as streets, curbs, sewers, and utilities, are adequate. Once these agencies report back to the planning agency, it can approve or reject the tentative map, or approve it on the condition that the subdivider take certain actions. For example, the planning agency may require the subdivider to dedicate some of the subdivision property for public streets.

When the planning agency approves a tentative map, the subdivider has 24 months to file a **final map**, showing the subdivision in its final form. The final map must bear the signatures of the owners and each public utility or other entity that considered the tentative map. No sale, lease, or contract for the sale or lease of any subdivided property is valid until a final map is filed.

Instead of tentative and final maps, a **parcel map** can be filed for subdivisions with two to four lots, and for condominiums and cooperatives. A parcel map does not have to be as detailed as a tentative subdivision map or final map.

Subdivided Lands Law. The Subdivided Lands Law requires a subdivider to disclose certain information to lot buyers. It applies to most subdivisions with five or more parcels. The five lots need not be contiguous if they are part of the same project.

The Subdivided Lands Law also applies to mobile home parks and planned developments with five or more lots; to condominiums, community apartment projects, and cooperatives with five or more units; and to some residential timeshare projects. Leases of apartments, offices, and stores within a building are exempt from the law. Subdivisions that are entirely within the limits of an incorporated city may also be exempt if the developer complies with certain rules. Also exempt are subdivisions with parcels that are 160 acres or larger.

Lots in a subdivision covered by the act cannot be sold, leased, or financed until the Real Estate Commissioner investigates the subdivision and issues a **final subdivision public report**. A public report is issued only if the subdivision meets the requirements set forth in the Subdivided Lands Law. A report will be denied:

1. if there is any evidence that the subdivision is unsuitable for the use proposed by the subdivider, or
2. if there is no assurance that the purchaser will get what he or she pays for.

For example, to obtain a final public report for a residential subdivision, the subdivider must be able to show that streets and other improvements will be completed and that there will be adequate drinking water and other utilities. The subdivider also must be able to demonstrate that any deposit money will be made secure, that there are satisfactory arrangements to clear any mechanic's liens or blanket mortgage liens (for instance, with the use of impound or escrow accounts), and that when the transaction is completed, title will be conveyed to the purchaser.

When the Commissioner has determined that a subdivision has met all legal requirements, a final subdivision public report will be issued. A public report includes the following information:

- the subdivider's name and the project's name, location, and size;
- the legal interest to be acquired by the purchaser;
- the procedure for handling the purchase money;
- the amount of any taxes and assessments;
- any private restrictions;
- any unusual costs the purchaser will have to bear;
- any hazards or adverse environmental factors; and
- any unusual or potentially harmful financial or conveyancing arrangements.

The public report must be given to anyone who requests it, and all prospective purchasers must receive a copy of the report before entering into a sales agreement. They must also sign a receipt proving that they received a copy of the report. That receipt must be kept by the subdivider for at least three years.

A final public report is valid for five years, unless a material change occurs in the subdivision. Material changes include physical changes to the subdivision itself (such as new street or lot lines), changes in the documents used to transfer or finance lots, the sale of five or more lots to one party, or new conditions that affect the value or use of lots.

Often, the Commissioner issues a **preliminary report** before issuing the final report. If the developer gives a prospective buyer a copy of a preliminary report, the buyer can reserve a lot in the subdivision. But until the buyer receives the final report, he or she has the right to back out and have any deposit refunded in full. Preliminary reports expire after one year, but may be renewed.

If a final public report is used for advertising purposes, it must be used in its entirety. A subdivider cannot, in an advertisement, refer to any improvements or facilities that do not actually exist, unless their completion is provided for with a bond. And an artist's rendering of the subdivision cannot be used in any advertisement unless it is described as such.

If the Commissioner discovers that a subdivider is violating any provisions of the Subdivided Lands Law, the Commissioner can stop the violations or sales of the lots with a **desist and refrain** order.

Out-of-State Subdivisions. If property in a subdivision located in another state is offered for sale in California, the subdivision must be registered with the California Department of Real Estate. Advertising and sales contracts must have disclaimers explaining that the DRE hasn't inspected or approved the subdivision.

ILSFDA. The **Interstate Land Sales Full Disclosure Act** (ILSFDA) is a federal consumer protection law concerning subdivisions offered for sale or lease in interstate commerce. It requires developers to register their projects with a division of the Department of Housing and Urban Development (HUD), and to disclose information to buyers. The law generally applies to subdivisions containing 25 or more vacant lots, although there are numerous exemptions.

Environmental Laws

The federal and state governments have enacted a number of laws aimed at preserving and protecting the physical environment, and many local governments have additional environmental regulations. These laws can have a substantial impact on the ways in which a property owner is allowed to use his or her land.

National Environmental Policy Act (NEPA). NEPA is a federal law that requires federal agencies to prepare an **environmental impact statement** (EIS) for governmental actions that would have a significant impact. NEPA also applies to private uses or developments that require the approval of a federal agency.

CERCLA. The Comprehensive Environmental Response, Compensation, and Liability Act, a federal law, concerns liability for environmental cleanup costs. In some cases, the current owners of contaminated property may be required to pay for cleanup, even if they did not cause the contamination.

Pollution Control Laws. Federal legislation sets national standards for air and water quality and requires the states to implement these objectives. Permits are required for the discharge of pollutants into the air or water.

California Environmental Quality Act (CEQA). This California law is similar to the National Environmental Policy Act. CEQA requires state or local agencies to prepare an **environmental impact report** (EIR) for any project (public or private) that may have a significant impact on the environment. An EIR is not required only if the public agency overseeing the project rules that it won't have significant adverse effects.

A public hearing is held for each EIR. Alternatives to the proposed action must be considered, and the developer may be required to make changes in the project to reduce its impact.

California Coastal Act. The Coastal Act established the Coastal Commission, which researches ways to protect the state's coastline and controls development along the coast. It has several regional divisions. No development is allowed in the coastal zone without a permit from the appropriate regional board.

Alquist-Priolo Act. Pursuant to the Alquist-Priolo Act, certain areas of the state are delineated as earthquake fault zones (sometimes called "special studies zones") on maps prepared by the state geologist. The zones follow traces of potentially active faults and are usually a quarter of a mile wide.

If property is located in a fault zone, any application for new development or construction generally must include a geologic report evaluating the property's earthquake risks. When property in a fault zone is sold, the seller and the seller's agent must inform buyers that the property is in such a zone.

Eminent Domain

As you've seen, the government can regulate the use of private property with a variety of laws—zoning ordinances, building codes, and so on. These laws are based on the police power, the government's power to regulate for the public health, safety, morals, and general welfare. Another governmental power that can be used to control land use is the power of **eminent domain**.

The power of eminent domain is the federal or state government's power to take private property for a public purpose upon payment of **just compensation** to the owner. A state government may delegate the power of eminent domain to local governments, and to private entities that serve the public, such as utility companies and railroads.

Fig. 5.2 *Police power vs. eminent domain*

	Police Power	Eminent Domain
Public purpose	Yes	Yes
Taking of property	No	Yes
Compensation required	No	Yes

Condemnation is the process by which the government exercises its power of eminent domain. When a particular property is needed for a public purpose, the government first offers to buy it from the owner. If the owner refuses to sell for the price offered, the government files a condemnation lawsuit. The court will order the property to be transferred to the government. The owner's only grounds for objection are that the intended use of the property is not a public use, or that the price offered is not just compensation. (Just compensation is usually defined as the fair market value of the property.)

A local government can use the power of eminent domain to implement its general plan. For example, to fulfill the plan's open space goals, several pieces of private property might be condemned for use as a public park.

It is important to understand the distinction between eminent domain and the police power. Eminent domain involves taking property away from the private owner, and the Constitution requires the government to pay the owner compensation. In an exercise of the police power, private property is regulated, but not taken away from the owner. The government is not required to compensate the owner for a proper exercise of the police power, even though the action (such as a zoning change) may significantly reduce the value of the property.

Taxation

Real property taxes affect property ownership. The taxes create liens, and if the property owner fails to pay the taxes, the government can sell the property to collect them. Real property taxation has always been a popular method of raising revenue because land has a fixed location, is relatively indestructible, and is essentially impossible to conceal. Thus, there is a high degree of certainty that the taxes will be collected.

In this section, we will discuss these three types of taxes on real property:

- general real estate taxes (also called ad valorem taxes),
- special assessments (also called improvement taxes), and
- the documentary transfer tax (also called an excise tax).

General Real Estate Taxes

General real estate taxes are levied to support the general operation and services of government. Public schools and police and fire protection are examples of government services paid for with general real estate tax revenues.

These taxes are levied by a number of governmental agencies, such as cities, counties, school districts, and water districts. Thus, a single property can be situated in five or six taxing districts.

Assessment. General real estate taxes are **ad valorem** taxes. That means the amount of tax owed depends on the value of the property. The valuation of property for purposes of taxation is called **assessment**. In California, property must be assessed by the county assessor at its **full cash value**, and as a general rule, the tax rate, as set by the county's Board of Supervisors, may not exceed **one percent** of the property's full cash value. (Proposition 13 governs property assessment and taxation in California.)

Protection from drastic tax increases is given to those who own the same home for a long period of time. The purchase price of a home becomes its **base value**. (If a home was last purchased prior to 1975, the property's 1975 value is its base value.) As long as the same person owns the property and no improvements are made, its assessed value cannot increase more than 2% per year. If the owner improves the property (by building a deck, for example), the assessed value may be increased by the amount the improvements add to the actual value.

The property's assessment is increased to the current full cash value only if there is a new owner or new construction on the property. When the property is sold or otherwise transferred, the new owner must file a **change in owner-ship statement** with the county recorder or assessor within 45 days of the transfer. Unless the transaction is exempt from reassessment on a change in ownership, the assessed value may be stepped up to the price paid or to the fair market value at the time of the transfer. That becomes the new base value.

If a property is transferred in the middle of a tax year, the new owner must pay a supplemental assessment for the remainder of the tax year. The supplemental assessment takes into account the difference between the previous assessed value and the new assessed value. A seller (or a seller's agent) is required to give a prospective buyer a notice explaining that the buyer may receive one or two supplemental tax bills, and that the buyer will be responsible for paying the additional taxes; the buyer's lender won't pay them out of the impound account maintained in connection with the buyer's loan.

Reassessment Exceptions. To avoid the harsh result of an increased assessment following a transfer of title when the property hasn't been sold or traded for profit, the law exempts several types of transfers from reassessment. The most significant exemptions include:

- transfers where the method of holding title is changed but the ownership isn't;
- certain transfers between parents and children; and
- transfers between spouses or registered domestic partners.

Also, when a homeowner who is over 55 or severely and permanently disabled sells his or her home and replaces it with another home in the same county, the assessed value of the old home can be used as the assessed value of the new home. The market value of the new home must be equal to or less than the market value of the old home, and the new home must be purchased within two years after the sale of the old one. A seller who purchases a replacement home in a different county may or may not be able to transfer the assessed value of the old home to the new home. That will depend on the laws of the county where the new home is located.

Property owners who are dissatisfied with the assessment of their property may appeal to the county. In some counties, appeals are handled by the Board of Supervisors. Larger counties have a separate Assessment Appeals Board (sometimes referred to as the board of equalization), which has the power to adjust the assessed value of property. Often, an

Fig. 5.3 Property tax dates

Real Property Taxes (Tax Year = July 1 – June 30)	
Taxes become lien	January 1
Taxes levied	by September 1
Tax bill mailed	by November 1
First installment due	November 1
First installment delinquent	December 10
Second installment due	February 1
Second installment delinquent	April 10

appeal is based on the property owner's claim that the property tax burden has been applied inconsistently, because similar properties in the neighborhood have been assessed differently.

Collection of Taxes. General real estate taxes are levied annually, on or before September 1 for each tax year. The tax year runs from July 1 through June 30 of the next calendar year. The tax lien attaches to the property on the previous January 1. So the lien for the July 2003–June 2004 tax year attached on January 1, 2003. Since the taxes are not levied until September, the specific amount of the tax lien isn't known when the lien attaches.

A tax bill is mailed to each property owner on or before November 1 of each year. The tax bill reflects the property's assessed value, less any exemptions to which the property owner is entitled. The assessed value is multiplied by the tax rate (no more than 1%), and the result is the amount of tax the property owner must pay.

An owner may pay his or her taxes in two installments, or may pay the total amount when the first installment is due. The first installment is due on November 1, covers the period from July through December, and is delinquent if not paid by 5:00 PM on December 10. The second installment is due February 1, covers the period from January through June, and is delinquent if not paid by 5:00 PM on April 10. A 10% penalty is added to any delinquent payment.

If the property taxes are not paid, the tax collector can foreclose on the tax lien. First a notice of impending default is published, and the property owner is informed of his or her opportunity to pay the taxes by June 30. If the taxes remain delinquent after June 30, the property is considered "in default" and a five-year redemption period begins to run. During this five-year period, the owner can keep possession of the property and has the opportunity to redeem it by paying the back taxes, interest, costs, and other penalties. If, after five years, the property has not been redeemed, it is deeded to the state. The tax collector can then sell the property at a tax sale and apply the proceeds to the tax debt. Any surplus from the sale is paid to the former owner or other parties who had an interest in the property.

Tax Exemptions. While the general rule is that all property is taxed at its full cash value, there are numerous total or partial exemptions. Property owned by the federal, state, or local government is totally exempt from taxation; so is most property that is used for religious, educational, charitable, or welfare purposes. There are also partial exemptions for owner-occupied homes and homes owned by veterans, senior citizens, and the disabled.

Special Assessments

Special assessments, also called local improvement taxes, are levied to pay for improvements that benefit particular properties, such as the installation of street lights or the widening of a street. Only the properties that benefit from the improvement are taxed, on the theory that the value of those properties is increased by the improvement. For instance, street improvements are assessed against each lot that benefits from the improvements on the basis of the front footage of the lot.

A special assessment is usually a one-time tax, although the property owners may be allowed to pay the assessment off in installments.

Like general real estate taxes, special assessments create liens against the taxed properties. If an owner fails to pay the assessment, the government can foreclose on the property.

Sometimes a city or county will create a special district to be in charge of a particular improvement, such as a street improvement project or an irrigation system. The district issues bonds to pay for the improvements. To pay off the bonds, the district taxes all of the property within the district. The assessment becomes a lien on all the taxed properties, and remains so until it is paid. Any obligations that are imposed on a property to pay for special improvements become part of the cost of the property, should the property be sold to another person.

California's Street Improvement Act of 1911 is commonly used to assess fees for street improvements. The act allows government entities to order the street improvements and bill the affected property owners. If the bills remain unpaid for more than 30 days, bonds will be issued to pay for the improvements. Funds raised under this act can be used to pay for streets, sidewalks, curbs, drainage systems, and other street improvements. The funds cannot be used to purchase the land needed for the original subdivision.

Here is a summary of the distinctions between general real estate taxes and special assessments:

1. General real estate taxes are levied to pay for ongoing government services, such as police protection. A special assessment is levied to pay for a specific improvement, such as adding sidewalks to a section of street.

2. General real estate taxes are levied against all taxable real property within a taxing district, for the benefit of the entire community. A special assessment, on the other hand, is levied against only those properties that benefit from the improvement in question.

3. General real estate taxes are levied every year. A special assessment is a one-time tax, levied only when a property is benefited by a public improvement.

Documentary Transfer Tax

An excise tax is levied on each sale of real property in California; it is called the **documentary transfer tax**. The tax is based on the property's selling price. As a general rule, the rate is fifty-five cents per $500 of value, or fraction thereof. (In certain cities, the rate is higher.)

Example: A house is sold for $202,200.

$$\$202,200 \div \$500 = 404.40$$
$$405 \times \$0.55 = \$222.75$$

The seller is required to pay $222.75 for the documentary transfer tax.

The documentary transfer tax does not apply to the amount of any loan the buyer is assuming or taking title subject to. If the buyer in the example above had assumed the seller's existing $125,200 trust deed, the tax would be due only on the $77,000 difference between the sales price and the assumed loan. The tax would then be only $84.70.

Chapter Summary

1. The police power—the government's power to adopt and enforce laws for the protection of the public health, safety, morals, and general welfare—is the constitutional basis for land use control laws.

2. A general plan is a county or city's comprehensive, long-term plan for development. A local government implements its general plan with zoning ordinances and other laws.

3. Zoning ordinances provide for certain exceptions to their rules: non-conforming uses, variances, and conditional uses. They also have procedures for rezones.

4. Building codes set standards for construction materials and practices, to protect the public. The codes are enforced through the building permit system.

5. California requires subdividers to comply with both the Subdivision Map Act and the Subdivided Lands Law. In certain cases, a subdivider may also have to comply with the Interstate Land Sales Full Disclosure Act, a federal law.

6. A number of federal and state environmental laws affect land use, including NEPA, CERCLA, CEQA, the California Coastal Act, and the Alquist-Priolo Act.

7. A government entity can use the power of eminent domain to implement its general plan. When property is taken under the power of eminent domain, the government must pay just compensation to the owner. (Compensation is not required when property is merely regulated under the police power.)

8. The government's power to tax also affects property ownership. General real estate taxes are levied each year to pay for ongoing government services. Special assessments are levied to pay for improvements that benefit specific properties. The documentary transfer tax must be paid on every sale of real property in California.

🔑 Key Terms

Police power—The power of state governments to regulate for the protection of the public health, safety, morals, and general welfare.

General plan—A comprehensive, long-term plan of development for a community, which is implemented by zoning and other laws.

Zoning—A method of controlling land use by dividing a community into zones for different types of uses.

Nonconforming use—A formerly legal use that does not conform to a new zoning ordinance, but is nonetheless allowed to continue.

Variance—An authorization to deviate from the rules in a zoning ordinance, granted because strict enforcement would cause undue hardship for the property owner.

Conditional use permit—A permit that allows a special use, such as a school or hospital, to operate in a neighborhood where it would otherwise be prohibited by the zoning.

Rezone—An amendment to a zoning ordinance; a property owner who feels his or her property has been zoned improperly may apply for a rezone.

Building codes—Regulations that set minimum standards for construction methods and materials.

Eminent domain—The government's power to take private property for public use, upon payment of just compensation to the owner.

Condemnation—The process of taking property pursuant to the power of eminent domain.

Subdivision—The division of one parcel of land into two or more parcels.

General real estate taxes—Taxes levied against real property annually to pay for general government services. They are based on the value of the property taxed (ad valorem).

Special assessment—A tax levied against property that benefits from a local improvement project, to pay for the project.

Documentary transfer tax—A tax levied when a piece of real property is sold. It is based on the selling price of the property.

Chapter Quiz

1. The police power is the government's power to:

   a) take private property for public use
   b) enact laws for the protection of the public health, safety, morals, and general welfare
   c) tax property to pay for police protection
   d) None of the above

2. Which of the following is likely to be controlled by a zoning ordinance?

   a) Use of the property
   b) Building height
   c) Placement of a building on a lot
   d) All of the above

3. Which of the following is NOT likely to be one of the goals of a land use control law?

   a) Ensuring that properties are put to their most profitable use
   b) Controlling growth and population density
   c) Ensuring that neighboring uses are compatible
   d) Preserving access to light and air

4. As a general rule, when a new zoning ordinance goes into effect, nonconforming uses:

   a) must comply with the new law within 90 days
   b) must shut down within 90 days
   c) will be granted conditional use permits
   d) are allowed to continue, but not to expand

5. An owner who feels that his or her property was improperly zoned should apply for a:

   a) conditional use permit
   b) variance
   c) rezone
   d) nonconforming use permit

6. A property owner is generally required to show undue hardship in order to obtain a:

   a) nonconforming use permit
   b) special exception permit
   c) rezone
   d) variance

7. Which of these is an example of a variance?

   a) Authorizing a hospital to be built in a residential zone
   b) Authorizing a structure to be built only 12 feet from the lot's boundary, although the zoning ordinance requires 15-foot setbacks
   c) Allowing a grocery store to continue in operation after the neighborhood is zoned residential
   d) Approving the subdivision of a parcel of land into two or more lots

8. Which of these is NOT an exercise of the police power?

   a) Condemnation
   b) Building code
   c) Zoning ordinance
   d) Subdivision regulations

9. Eminent domain differs from the police power in that:

   a) the government is required to compensate the property owner
   b) it can be exercised only by the state government, not a city or county government
   c) it affects only the use of the property, not the title
   d) the property must be unimproved

10. The Hancocks are planning to add a room onto their house. Before construction begins, they are probably required to:

   a) request a zoning inspection
   b) submit a proposal to the planning commission
   c) obtain a building permit
   d) All of the above

11. A special assessment is the same thing as:

   a) a general real estate tax
   b) an improvement tax
   c) a real estate excise tax
   d) a transfer tax

12. General real estate taxes are:

   a) used to support the general operation and services of government
   b) levied annually
   c) based on the value of the taxed property
   d) All of the above

13. Which of these is a state law that requires an environmental impact report to be prepared in certain circumstances?

   a) ILSFDA
   b) CERCLA
   c) CEQA
   d) None of the above

14. The documentary transfer tax is based on the property's:

   a) selling price
   b) fair market value
   c) current use
   d) highest and best use

15. Lots in a subdivision cannot be sold until:

   a) a final map is filed with the local planning agency
   b) a parcel map is filed with the Office of Interstate Land Sales
   c) a preliminary public report is issued by the Commissioner
   d) All of the above

Answer Key

1. b) The police power is the government's power to pass laws (such as zoning ordinances) for the protection of the public health, safety, morals, and general welfare.

2. d) Zoning ordinances typically control the height and placement of buildings as well as type of use.

3. a) Land use controls are not aimed at encouraging the most profitable use of particular properties. In some cases they prohibit more profitable uses that would be detrimental to the public health, safety, morals, or welfare.

4. d) A nonconforming use (a use established before new zoning rules go into effect, which does not comply with those rules) is ordinarily allowed to continue, but the use cannot be expanded, rebuilt after destruction, or resumed after abandonment.

5. c) A rezone is an amendment to the zoning ordinance, giving a particular area a new zoning designation.

6. d) A variance is granted when the property owner shows that strict enforcement of the zoning law would result in undue hardship.

7. b) A variance authorizes the improvement of property in a manner not ordinarily allowed by the zoning ordinance. Most variances permit only minor deviations from the rules.

8. a) Condemnation is an exercise of the power of eminent domain, not the police power.

9. a) When a government body takes property under the power of eminent domain, it is required to pay compensation to the owner. Compensation is not required if a property loses value due to regulation under the police power.

10. c) A building permit is generally required before an addition or remodeling project is begun, to ensure that the structure will comply with the building codes and zoning.

11. b) A special assessment is also called an improvement tax; it is levied to pay for a particular public improvement.

12. d) All of these statements concerning general real estate taxes are true.

13. c) CEQA is the California Environmental Quality Act. (CERCLA is a federal environmental law, and ILSFDA is a federal subdivision law.)

14. a) The documentary transfer tax is levied only when title to property is transferred, and it is based on the selling price.

15. a) A final map must be filed with the local planning agency before a subdivision lot can be sold.

Contract Law

Chapter Overview

Contracts are a significant part of the real estate business. Almost everyone has a basic understanding of what a contract is, but real estate agents need more than that. This chapter explains the requirements that must be met in order for a contract to be valid and binding; how a contract can be terminated; what is considered a breach of contract; and what remedies are available when a breach occurs.

Introduction

Real estate licensees deal with contracts on a daily basis: listing agreements, purchase and sale agreements, option agreements, and leases are all contracts. Thus, it is essential for a licensee to understand the basic legal requirements and effects of contracts.

Keep in mind, however, that a real estate licensee may not draft the original language for a contract. Anyone other than a lawyer who drafts a contract for someone else may be charged with the unauthorized practice of law.

Here is a general definition of a contract: an agreement between two or more competent persons to do or not do certain things in exchange for consideration. An agreement to sell a car, deliver lumber, or rent an apartment is a contract. And if it meets minimum legal requirements, it can be enforced in court.

Legal Classifications of Contracts

There are certain basic classifications that apply to any contract, no matter what type it is. Every contract is either express or implied, either unilateral or bilateral, and either executory or executed.

Express vs. Implied

An **express** contract is one that has been put into words. It may be written or oral. Each party to the contract has stated what he or she is willing to do and has been told what to expect from the other party. Most contracts are express. On the other hand, an **implied** contract, or contract by implication, is created by the actions of the parties, not by express agreement.

> **Example:** A written lease agreement expires, but the tenant continues to make payments and the landlord continues to accept them. Both parties have implied their consent to a new lease contract.

Unilateral vs. Bilateral

A contract is **unilateral** if only one of the contracting parties is legally obligated to perform. That party has promised to do a particular thing if the other party does something else. The other party has not promised to do anything and is not legally obligated to do anything.

Fig. 6.1 Contract classifications		
Express *Written or oral*	OR	**Implied** *Actions of the parties*
Unilateral *One promise*	OR	**Bilateral** *Two promises*
Executory *Not yet fully performed*	OR	**Executed** *Fully performed*

Example: In an open listing agreement, a seller promises to pay a real estate broker a commission if the broker finds a buyer for the property. The broker does not promise to try to find a buyer, but if he or she does, the seller is obligated to pay. An open listing agreement is a unilateral contract.

A **bilateral** contract is formed when each party promises to do something, so that both parties are legally obligated to perform. Most contracts are bilateral.

Example: In a purchase and sale agreement, the seller promises to transfer title to the buyer, and the buyer promises to pay the agreed price to the seller. This is a bilateral contract. Each party has made a promise, and both are obligated to perform.

Executory vs. Executed

An **executory** contract is one that has not yet been performed, or is in the process of being performed. An **executed** contract has been fully performed. With respect to contracts, the terms "executed" and "performed" mean the same thing. (Note that sometimes "executed" can mean "signed": when a contract is executed by the parties, it is signed by the parties. The context surrounding the term will indicate which meaning is intended.)

Elements of a Valid Contract

Four elements are needed for a valid and binding contract that will be enforced by a court:

1. legal capacity to contract,
2. mutual consent,
3. a lawful objective, and
4. consideration.

Capacity

The first requirement for a valid contract is that the parties have the legal capacity to enter into a contract. A person must be at least 18 years old to enter into a valid contract, and he or she must also be competent.

Age Eighteen. Eighteen years of age is sometimes referred to as the age of majority. Minors (those under the age of 18) do not have capacity to appoint agents or to enter into contracts. If a minor signs a contract, it is voidable by the minor; that is, it cannot be enforced against him or her.

> **Example:** A 16-year-old signs a contract to purchase a car. The car dealer cannot enforce the contract against the minor, although the minor could compel the dealer to honor the terms of the agreement.

The purpose of this rule is to prevent people from entering into legally binding agreements when they may be too young to understand the consequences.

In California, most types of contracts entered into by minors are voidable, as just discussed. However, real estate contracts entered into by minors are void. A purchase and sale agreement signed by a minor cannot be enforced by either party.

A minor who has been legally emancipated may enter into any type of contract. For example, a 17-year-old who is married is considered emancipated and may enter into a contract to buy a home. A minor can be emancipated in three ways: by marrying, by serving in the military, or by court order. When a minor who has been emancipated by court order enters into a sales transaction, copies of the emancipation documents should be given to the escrow company so it will know that the minor has the capacity to carry out the transaction.

Competent. A person must also be mentally competent to have capacity to contract. If a person has been declared incompetent by a court, any contract he or she signs is void. If a court declares someone incompetent after a contract was signed, but the party was probably incompetent when the contract was signed, the contract is voidable at the discretion of the court-appointed guardian.

A contract entered into by a person who is temporarily incompetent (for example, under the influence of alcohol or drugs) may be voidable if he or she takes legal action within a reasonable time after regaining mental competency. The fact that a person is receiving psychiatric treatment does not necessarily mean that he or she is incompetent.

Necessities Exception. There's an exception to these capacity rules. If a minor or an incompetent person contracts to buy necessities (such as food or medicine), he or she is required to pay the reasonable value of those items.

Representing Another. Often, one person has the capacity to represent another person or entity in a contract negotiation. For instance, the affairs of minors and incompetent persons are handled by parents or court-appointed guardians; corporations are represented by properly authorized officers; partnerships are represented by individual partners; deceased persons are represented by executors or administrators; and a competent adult (but not a minor) can appoint another competent adult to act on his or her behalf through a power of attorney. In each of these cases, the authorized representative can enter into a contract on behalf of the person represented.

Aliens. An alien has essentially the same property rights as a citizen and may acquire and convey property freely. However, aliens are subject to certain property transfer reporting requirements.

Convicts. Those convicted of crimes and serving time in prison are not automatically deprived of all of their civil rights. Generally, they do not forfeit their property, nor are they prevented from obtaining or transferring real property.

Mutual Consent

Mutual consent is the second requirement for a valid contract. Each party must consent to the agreement. Once someone has signed a contract, consent is presumed, so no contract should be signed until its contents are fully understood. A person can't use failure or inability to read an agreement as an excuse for nonperformance. An illiterate person should have a contract explained thoroughly by someone who is concerned with his or her welfare.

Mutual consent is sometimes called mutual assent, mutuality, or "a meeting of the minds." It is achieved through the process of **offer and acceptance**.

Offer. A contract offer shows the willingness of the person making it (the **offeror**) to enter into a contract under the stated terms. To be valid, an offer must meet two requirements.

1. It must express a willingness to contract. Whatever words make up the offer, they must clearly indicate that the offeror intends to enter into a contract.
2. It must be definite and certain in its terms. A vague offer that does not clearly state what the offeror is proposing is said to be illusory, and any agreement reached as a result is unenforceable.

Note that an advertisement that lists a property's price is not considered a contract offer; it is merely an invitation to negotiate.

Terminating an Offer. Sometimes circumstances change after an offer has been made, or perhaps the offeror has had a change of heart. If an offer terminates before it is accepted, no contract is formed. There are many things that can terminate an offer before it is accepted, including:

- revocation by the offeror,
- lapse of time,
- death or incompetence of the offeror,
- rejection of the offer, or
- a counteroffer.

The offeror can **revoke** the offer at any time until he or she is notified that the offer has been accepted. To effect a proper "offer and acceptance," the accepting party must not only accept the offer, but must also communicate that acceptance to the offeror before the offer is revoked. (See the discussion of acceptance, below.)

Many offers include a deadline for acceptance. If a deadline is set and acceptance is not communicated within the time allotted, the offer terminates automatically. If a time limit is not stated in the offer, a reasonable amount of time is allowed. What is reasonable is determined by the court if a dispute arises.

If the offeror dies or is declared incompetent before the offer is accepted, it is terminated.

A **rejection** also terminates an offer. Once the **offeree** (the person to whom the offer was made) rejects the offer, he or she cannot go back later and create a contract by accepting the offer.

Example: Valdez offers to purchase Carter's house for $385,000. Carter rejects the offer the next day. The following week, Carter changes her mind and decides to accept Valdez's offer. But her acceptance at this point does not create a contract, because the offer terminated with her rejection.

A **counteroffer** is sometimes called a qualified acceptance. It is actually a rejection of the offer and a tender of a new offer. Instead of either accepting or rejecting the offer outright, the offeree "accepts" with certain modifications. This happens when some, but not all, of the original terms are unacceptable to the offeree. When there is a counteroffer, the roles of the parties are reversed: the original offeror becomes the offeree and can accept or reject the revised offer. If he or she chooses to accept the counteroffer, there is a binding contract. If the counteroffer is rejected, the party making the counteroffer cannot go back and accept the original offer. The original offer was terminated by the counteroffer.

Example: Palmer offers to buy Harrison's property under the following conditions: the purchase price is $250,000, the closing date is January 15, and the downpayment is $25,000. Harrison agrees to all the terms but the closing date, which he wants to be February 15. By changing one of the terms, Harrison has rejected Palmer's initial offer and made a counteroffer. Now it is up to Palmer to either accept or reject Harrison's counteroffer.

Acceptance. An offer can be revoked at any time until acceptance has been communicated to the offeror. To create a binding contract, the offeree must communicate acceptance to the offeror in the manner and within the time limit stated in the offer (or before the offer is revoked). If no time or manner of acceptance is stated in the offer, a reasonable time and manner is implied.

The offeree's acceptance must also be free of any negative influences, such as fraud, undue influence, or duress. If an offer or acceptance is influenced by any of these negative forces, the contract is voidable by the injured party.

Fraud is misrepresentation of a material fact to another person who relies on the misrepresentation as the truth in deciding to enter into a transaction.

Fig. 6.2 Mutual consent is achieved through the process of offer and acceptance.

Offer
- Willingness to contract
- Definite and certain terms

Termination (No Mutual Consent)
- Revocation
- Lapse of time
- Death or incompetence of the offeror
- Rejection of the offer
- Counteroffer

Acceptance (Mutual Consent)
- By offeree
- Communicated to the offeror
- In specified manner
- Doesn't vary terms

- **Actual fraud** occurs when the person making the statement either knows the statement is false and makes it with an intent to deceive, or doesn't know whether or not the statement is true but makes it anyway. For example, a seller who conceals cracks in the basement and then tells the buyer that the foundation is completely sound is committing actual fraud. A promise that is made without any intent to keep it can also be considered actual fraud.
- **Constructive fraud** occurs when a person who occupies a position of confidence and trust, or who has superior knowledge of the subject matter, makes a false statement with no intent to deceive. For example, if a seller innocently points out incorrect lot boundaries, it may be constructive fraud.

Undue influence is using one's influence to pressure a person into making a contract, or taking advantage of another's distress or weakness of mind to induce him or her to enter into a contract.

Duress is compelling someone to do something—such as enter into a contract—against his or her will, with the use of force or constraint or the threat of force or constraint.

Lawful Objective

The third requirement for a valid contract is a lawful objective. Both the purpose of the contract and the consideration for the contract (discussed below) must be lawful. Examples of contracts with unlawful objectives are a contract requiring payment of an interest rate in excess of the state's usury limit, or a contract relating to unlawful gambling. If a contract does not have a lawful objective, it is void.

Sometimes contracts contain some lawful provisions and some unlawful provisions. In these situations, it may be possible to sever the unlawful portions of the contract and enforce the lawful portions.

> **Example:** Callahan and Baker enter into a contract for the purchase and sale of an apartment house. A clause in the contract prohibits the buyer from renting the apartments to persons of a certain race. The contract concerning the sale of the property would probably be enforceable, but the racially restrictive clause would be void because it is unlawful.

Consideration

The fourth element of a valid contract is **consideration**. Consideration is something of value exchanged by the contracting parties. It might be money, goods, or services, or a promise to provide money, goods, or services. Whatever form it takes, the consideration must be either a benefit to the party receiving it or a detriment to the party offering it. The typical real estate purchase and sale contract involves a promise by the purchaser to pay a certain amount of money to the seller at a certain time, and a promise by the seller to convey title to the purchaser when the price has been paid. Both parties have given and received consideration.

While consideration is usually the promise to do a particular act, it can also be a promise to not do a particular act. For example, Aunt Martha might promise to pay her nephew Charles $1,000 if he promises to stop smoking.

As a general rule, a contract is enforceable as long as the consideration has value, even though the value of the consideration exchanged is unequal. A contract to sell a piece of property worth $220,000 for $190,000 is enforceable. However, in cases where the disparity in value is quite large (for example, a contract to sell a piece of property worth $300,000 for $95,000), a court may refuse to enforce the contract. This is particularly likely to happen if the parties have unequal bargaining power (for example, if the buyer is a real estate developer and the seller is elderly, uneducated, and inexperienced in business).

Fig. 6.3 Real estate contract requirements

A Valid Real Estate Contract

- Capacity
- Mutual consent
- Lawful objective
- Consideration
- In writing

The Writing Requirement

For most contracts used in real estate transactions, there is a fifth requirement: they must be put into writing, as required by the statute of frauds.

The **statute of frauds** is a state law that requires certain types of contracts to be in writing and signed. Only the types of contracts covered by the statute of frauds have to be in writing; other contracts may be oral.

Each state has its own statute of frauds, and the requirements vary slightly from state to state. As a general rule, however, almost all of the contracts typically used in a real estate transaction are covered by the statute of frauds. In California, the statute of frauds applies to:

1. an agreement that is not to be performed within a year of its making;
2. any agreement for the sale or exchange of real property or an interest in real property;
3. a lease of real property that will expire more than one year after it was agreed to;
4. an agency agreement authorizing an agent to purchase or sell real property, or lease it for more than one year;
5. an agency agreement authorizing an agent to find a buyer or seller for real property, if the agent will receive compensation (a listing agreement); and
6. an assumption of a mortgage or deed of trust.

The "writing" required by the statute of frauds does not have to be in any particular form, nor does it have to be contained entirely in one document. A note or memorandum about the agreement or a series of letters will suffice, as long as the writing:

1. identifies the subject matter of the contract,
2. indicates an agreement between the parties and its essential terms, and
3. is signed by the parties to be bound.

If the parties fail to put a contract that falls under the statute of frauds in writing, the contract is usually unenforceable. However, occasionally a court will enforce an unwritten agreement. This might occur if there is both evidence that the contract exists and evidence of its terms, and if the party trying to enforce it has completely or substantially performed his or her contractual obligations. This is rare; the safest course is to put a contract in writing.

If a contract is partly printed and partly handwritten (like a filled-out contract form) and there's a conflict between the handwritten and printed portions, the handwritten portion takes precedence. It's presumed to be a more reliable indication of the parties' intent than the printed portion.

California has a special law that applies whenever someone in a trade or business negotiates certain types of contracts in Spanish, Chinese, Korean, Tagalog, or Vietnamese. Before the contract is executed, the businessperson must provide the other party (the consumer) with an unexecuted copy of it in the language that the negotiations took place in. The foreign language copy must contain every term and condition of the agreement. Among other types of contracts, this law applies to the negotiation of: loans for personal, family, or household purposes; "Article VII" loans (see Chapter 10); legal service fee agreements; and residential rental agreements for a period longer than one month. (Note that it doesn't apply to listing agreements or deposit receipts.)

Legal Status of Contracts

Four terms are used to describe the legal status of a contract: a contract is void, voidable, unenforceable, or valid. These terms have already been used in our discussion, and now we'll look more closely at what each one means.

Void

A void contract is no contract at all; it has no legal effect. This most often occurs because one of the essential elements, such as mutual consent or consideration, is completely lacking.

Example: Talbot signed a contract promising to deed some property to Worth, but Worth did not offer any consideration in exchange for Talbot's promise. Since the contract is not supported by consideration, it is void.

A void contract may be disregarded. Neither party is required to take legal action to withdraw from the agreement.

Fig. 6.4 Legal status of contracts

Type of Contract	Legal Effect	Example
Void	No contract at all	An agreement for which there is no consideration
Voidable	Valid until rescinded by one party	A contract entered into as a result of fraud
Unenforceable	One or both parties cannot sue to enforce	A contract after the limitations period expires
Valid	Binding and enforceable	An agreement that meets all the legal requirements

Voidable

A voidable contract appears to be valid, but has some defect giving one or both of the parties the power to withdraw from the agreement. For instance, a contract entered into as a result of fraud is voidable by the defrauded party.

Unlike a contract that is void from the outset, a voidable contract can't simply be ignored. Failure to take legal action within a reasonable time may result in a court declaring that the contract was ratified. (If the injured party decides to continue with the agreement, he or she may expressly ratify it.)

Unenforceable

An unenforceable contract is one that can't be enforced in court for one of the following reasons:

1. its contents cannot be proved,
2. the other party has a voidable contract, or
3. the statute of limitations has expired.

Contents Cannot Be Proved. This is most often a problem associated with oral agreements. Even if the law does not require a certain kind of contract to be written, it is a good idea to put it in writing because it avoids confusion and misunderstanding. Furthermore, even if a contract is in writing, the written agreement must clearly state all of the contract terms. Vaguely worded contracts are considered illusory and unenforceable.

One Party Has a Voidable Contract. If one party has a voidable contract, the other is left with an unenforceable contract. (Note that the party who has the voidable contract can enforce the contract against the other party.)

Statute of Limitations Expired. A statute of limitations is a law that sets a deadline for filing a lawsuit. Unless an injured party files suit before the deadline set by the applicable statute of limitations, his or her legal claim is lost forever. The purpose of a statute of limitations is to prevent lawsuits long after an event, when memories have faded and evidence has been lost.

Every state has a statute of limitations for contracts. If one of the parties to a contract fails to perform his or her obligations (breaches the contract), the other party must sue within a certain number of years after the breach. Otherwise, the limitations period will run out and the contract will become unenforceable.

In California, the statute of limitations generally requires lawsuits concerning written contracts to be filed within four years after their breach, and lawsuits concerning many oral contracts to be filed within two years after their breach.

The doctrine of **laches** is related to the concept of statutes of limitations. Laches is an equitable principle that courts can use to prevent someone from asserting a claim after an unreasonable delay. For instance, suppose a property owner knowingly stands by while a neighbor builds a house that encroaches a few feet onto his property. He then sues, demanding that it be torn down. Because the property owner's unreasonable delay caused the neighbor harm, the court may use the doctrine of laches to deny the requested remedy.

Valid

If an agreement has all the essential elements, can be proved in court, and is free of negative influences, it's a valid contract and a judge will enforce it.

Discharging a Contract

Once there is a valid, enforceable contract, it may be discharged by:

1. full performance, or
2. agreement between the parties.

Full Performance

Full performance means that the parties have performed all of their obligations; the contract is executed. For example, once the deed to the property has been transferred to the buyer, and the seller has received the purchase price, the purchase and sale agreement has been discharged by full performance.

Agreement Between the Parties

The parties to a contract can agree to discharge the contract in any of the following ways:

- rescission,
- cancellation,
- assignment, or
- novation.

Rescission. Sometimes the parties to a contract agree that they would be better off if the contract had never been signed. In such a case, they may decide to rescind the contract. A rescission is occasionally referred to as a "contract to destroy a contract."

The buyer and seller sign an agreement that terminates their previous agreement and puts them as nearly as possible back in the positions they were in before entering into the initial agreement. If any money or other consideration has changed hands, it will be returned.

In certain circumstances, a contract can be rescinded by court order (rather than by agreement between the parties). Court-ordered rescission is discussed later in this chapter.

Cancellation. A cancellation does not go as far as a rescission. The parties agree to terminate the contract, but previous acts are unaffected. For example, money that was paid prior to the cancellation is not returned.

When contracting to purchase real property, a buyer generally gives the seller a deposit to show that he or she is acting in good faith and intends to fulfill the terms of their agreement. This is called a **good faith deposit**, and the seller is entitled to keep it if the buyer defaults on the contract. If the buyer and seller agree to terminate the contract and the seller refunds the good faith deposit to the buyer, the contract has been rescinded. If the seller keeps the deposit, the contract has been canceled.

Assignment. Sometimes one of the parties to a contract wants to withdraw by assigning his or her interest in the contract to another person. As a general rule, a contract can be assigned to another unless a clause in the contract prohibits assignment. Technically, assignment does not discharge the contract. The new party (the assignee) assumes primary liability for the contractual obligations, but the withdrawing party (the assignor) is still secondarily liable.

Example: A buyer is purchasing a home on a land contract over a 15-year period. In the absence of any prohibitive language, she can sell the home, accept a cash downpayment, and assign her contract rights and liabilities to the new buyer. The new buyer would assume primary liability for the contract debt, but the original buyer would retain secondary liability.

One exception to the rule that a contract can be assigned unless otherwise agreed: a personal services contract can't be assigned without the other party's consent.

Example: A nightclub has a contract with a singer for several performances. The singer cannot assign her contract to another singer, because it is a personal services contract. The nightclub management has a right to choose who will be singing in their establishment.

Novation. The term "novation" has two generally accepted meanings. One type of novation is the substitution of a new party into an existing obligation. If a buyer under a real estate contract is released by the seller in favor of a new buyer under the same contract, there has been a novation. The first buyer is relieved of all liability connected with the contract.

Novation may also be the substitution of a new obligation for an old one. If a landlord and tenant agree to tear up a three-year lease in favor of a new ten-year lease, it is a novation.

Assignment vs. Novation. The difference between assignment and novation concerns the withdrawing party's liability. When a contract is assigned, there is continuing liability for the assignor. In a novation, on the other hand, the withdrawing party is released from liability, because he or she was replaced with an individual who was approved by the other party. Novation, unlike assignment, always requires the other party's consent.

Breach of Contract

A breach of contract occurs when one of the parties fails, without legal excuse, to perform any of the promises contained in the agreement. The injured party can seek a remedy in court only if the breach is a **material breach**. A breach is material when the promise that has not been fulfilled is an important part of the contract.

Many standard contract forms state that **"time is of the essence."** That phrase is used to warn the parties that timely performance is crucial and failure to meet a deadline would be a material breach. If one party misses a deadline, the other party may choose whether to proceed with the contract or use the time is of the essence clause as the basis for ending it.

When a breach occurs, there are four possible remedies available to the injured party:

- rescission,
- liquidated damages,
- damages, or
- specific performance.

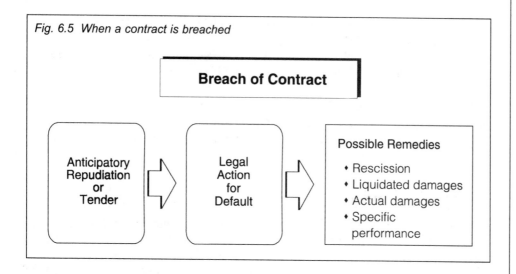

Fig. 6.5 *When a contract is breached*

Rescission

As previously explained, a rescission is a termination of the contract in which the parties are returned to their original positions. In the case of a purchase and sale agreement, the seller refunds the buyer's good faith deposit and the buyer gives up his or her equitable interest in the property. The rescission can be by agreement, or it can be ordered by a court at the request of one party when the other party has breached the contract.

Liquidated Damages

The parties to a contract sometimes agree in advance to an amount that will serve as full compensation to be paid in the event that one of the parties defaults. This sum is called liquidated damages.

Example: Able agrees to buy 25,000 hinges from Baker. They agree that if Baker cannot deliver the hinges to Able on time, Baker will pay Able $3,000 as full compensation. If Baker fails to deliver the hinges on time, Able will only receive $3,000 from Baker; she could not sue for any additional amount, even if her actual damages were greater than $3,000.

In a real estate transaction, the buyer's good faith deposit is often treated as liquidated damages. If the seller keeps the deposit and releases the buyer from the contract, the agreement is canceled. (Note that California has special rules that govern liquidated damages clauses in purchase and sale agreements. See Chapter 7.)

Damages

A damages award is an amount of money that the court orders the breaching party to pay the other party. Damages are generally intended to put the non-breaching party in the financial position he or she would have been in if the breaching party had fulfilled the terms of the contract.

Example: Suppose Able and Baker (from the example above) did not agree to any liquidated damages. Baker fails to deliver the hinges on time, and Able suffers $7,000 in damages because she must quickly purchase the hinges from another supplier at a higher price. Able can sue Baker for the $7,000 in damages.

Suppose a home seller breaches a purchase and sale agreement. The buyer has no good faith deposit to keep as liquidated damages, so he or she may choose to sue the seller for monetary compensation for any losses that resulted from the breach of contract.

Specific Performance

Specific performance is a legal action designed to compel a defaulting party to perform under the terms of the contract. For example, a court can order a seller to sign and deliver a deed to a buyer to complete a purchase.

Specific performance is usually available as a remedy only when monetary damages are not sufficient compensation. For example, when the purchase of real property is involved, the court might order specific performance because there is no other property that is just like the one the seller agreed to sell. Payment of damages would not enable the buyer to purchase another property exactly like it.

Note that if the consideration promised for the property is unreasonable, a court may refuse to order specific performance in the event of a breach.

Tender

A tender is an unconditional offer by one of the contract parties to perform his or her part of the agreement. It is frequently referred to as "an offer to make an offer good." A tender is usually made when it appears that the other party is going to default; it is necessary before legal action can be taken to remedy the breach of contract.

Example: A seller suspects that the buyer does not plan to complete the purchase, and he intends to sue the buyer if this happens. The seller must attempt to deliver the deed to the buyer as promised in the purchase and sale agreement. When the tender is made, if the buyer refuses to pay the agreed price and accept the deed, the buyer is placed in default and the seller may then file a lawsuit.

If a buyer has reason to believe the seller does not plan to complete the sale, the buyer tenders by attempting to deliver the full amount promised in the purchase and sale agreement to the seller. When the seller refuses to accept the money and deliver the deed, he or she is in default.

Sometimes there is an **anticipatory repudiation** by one of the parties. An anticipatory repudiation is a positive statement by the defaulting party indicating that he or she will not or cannot perform according to the terms of the agreement. When this happens, no tender is necessary as a basis for a legal action.

📖 Chapter Summary

1. A contract is an agreement between two or more competent persons to do or not do certain things in exchange for consideration. Every contract is either express or implied, either unilateral or bilateral, and either executory or executed.

2. For a contract to be valid and binding, the parties must have the legal capacity to contract, and there must be mutual consent (offer and acceptance), a lawful objective, and consideration. The statute of frauds requires real estate contracts to be in writing.

3. A contract may be void, voidable, unenforceable, or valid.

4. An existing contract can be discharged by full performance or by agreement between the parties. The parties can agree to terminate the contract by rescission or cancellation, or there can be an assignment or a novation.

5. A breach of contract occurs when a party fails, without legal excuse, to perform any material promise contained in the agreement. When a breach occurs, the four possible remedies are rescission, liquidated damages, damages, or specific performance.

🔑 Key Terms

Contract—An agreement between two or more competent persons to do or not do certain things in exchange for consideration.

Capacity—A person must be mentally competent and at least 18 years of age to have the capacity to contract.

Mutual consent—The agreement of both parties to the terms of the contract, effected by offer and acceptance.

Offer—A communication that shows the willingness of the person making it (the offeror) to enter into a contract, and that has definite and certain terms.

Acceptance—A communication showing the willingness of the offeree to be bound by the terms of the offer.

Counteroffer—A qualified acceptance. Technically, it is a rejection of the offer, with a new offer made on slightly different terms.

Fraud—The misrepresentation of a material fact to someone who relies on the misrepresentation as the truth in deciding whether to enter into a contract.

Undue influence—Pressuring someone or taking advantage of his or her distress to induce him or her to enter into a contract.

Duress—Compelling someone to enter into a contract with the use or threat of force or constraint.

Consideration—Something of value exchanged by the parties to a contract; either a benefit to the party receiving it or a detriment to the party offering it.

Statute of frauds—A state law that requires certain types of contracts (including most contracts related to real estate transactions) to be in writing and signed.

Valid—When a contract contains all of the required elements and is enforceable in court.

Void—When a contract lacks an essential element, so that it has no legal force or effect.

Voidable—When one of the parties can choose to rescind the contract, because of lack of capacity, fraud, etc.

Unenforceable—When a contract cannot be enforced in a court of law because its contents cannot be proved, or it is voidable by the other party, or the statute of limitations has expired.

Rescission—When a contract is terminated and any consideration given is returned, putting the parties as nearly as possible back into the position they were in prior to entering into the contract.

Cancellation—When a contract is terminated but previous contractual acts are unaffected.

Assignment—When one party transfers his or her rights and obligations under the contract to another party, but remains secondarily liable.

Novation—When one party is completely replaced with another, or one contract is completely replaced with another, and all liability under the original contract ends.

Liquidated damages—An amount that the parties agree in advance will serve as full compensation if one of them defaults.

Specific performance—A remedy for breach of contract in which the court orders the defaulting party to perform as agreed in the contract.

Tender—An unconditional offer by one of the parties to perform his or her part of the agreement, made when it appears that the other party is going to default.

Chapter Quiz

1. A contract can be valid and binding even though:

   a) it is not supported by consideration
   b) it does not have a lawful objective
   c) it is not put into writing
   d) there was no offer and acceptance

2. To have legal capacity to contract, a person must have:

   a) reached the age of majority
   b) been declared competent by a court
   c) a high school diploma or general equivalency certificate
   d) All of the above

3. An offer to purchase property would be terminated by any of the following, except:

   a) failure to communicate acceptance of the offer within the prescribed period
   b) revocation after acceptance has been communicated
   c) a qualified acceptance by the offeree
   d) death or insanity of the offeror

4. A counteroffer:

   a) terminates the original offer
   b) will result in a valid contract if accepted by the other party
   c) Both of the above
   d) None of the above

5. Tucker sends Johnson a letter offering to buy his property for $400,000 in cash, with the transaction to close in 60 days. Johnson sends Tucker a letter that says, "I accept your offer; however, the closing will take place in 90 days." Which of the following is true?

   a) Johnson's statement is not a valid acceptance
   b) Johnson's statement is a counteroffer
   c) There is no contract unless Tucker accepts the counteroffer
   d) All of the above

6. Which of these could be consideration for a contract?

   a) $163,000
   b) A promise to convey title
   c) A promise to not sell the property during the next 30 days
   d) All of the above

7. An executory contract is one that:

   a) is made by the executor of an estate for the sale of probate property
   b) has not yet been performed
   c) has been completely performed
   d) has been proposed but not accepted by either party

8. A void contract is one that:

   a) lacks an essential contract element
   b) needs to be rescinded by the injured party
   c) can be rescinded by agreement
   d) can no longer be enforced because the deadline set by the statute of limitations has passed

9. A voidable contract is:

   a) not enforceable by either party
   b) enforceable by the injured party
   c) void unless action is taken to rescind it
   d) None of the above

10. The statute of frauds is a law that requires:

   a) all contracts to be supported by consideration
   b) unlawful provisions to be severed from a contract
   c) certain contracts to be unilateral
   d) certain contracts to be in writing and signed

11. A contract can be discharged by all of the following except:

    a) novation
    b) performance
    c) cancellation
    d) breach

12. Brown and Murdock have a five-year contract. After two years, they agree to tear up that contract and replace it with a new ten-year contract. This is an example of:

    a) novation
    b) rescission
    c) duress
    d) specific performance

13. Graves and Chung are parties to a contract that doesn't prohibit assignment. If Chung assigns his interest in the contract to Stewart:

    a) Graves is not required to fulfill the contract
    b) Graves can sue for anticipatory repudiation
    c) Chung remains secondarily liable to Graves
    d) Chung is relieved of all further liability under the contract

14. A clause in the contract provides that if one party breaches, the other party will be entitled to $3,500 and cannot sue for more than that. This is a:

    a) just compensation provision
    b) compensation cap
    c) satisfaction clause
    d) liquidated damages provision

15. The McClures agreed to sell their house to Jacobsen, but then they breached the contract by refusing to go through with the sale. If Jacobsen wants a court order requiring the McClures to convey the house to her as agreed, she should sue for:

    a) damages
    b) specific performance
    c) liquidated damages
    d) rescission

Answer Key

1. c) Only certain types of contracts are required to be in writing, but all contracts require consideration, a lawful objective, and offer and acceptance.

2. a) A person has capacity to contract if he or she has reached the age of majority (in California, age 18) and is mentally competent. It isn't necessary to be declared competent by a court, however.

3. b) If the offeree accepts the offer before the offeror revokes it, a binding contract is formed.

4. c) A counteroffer terminates the original offer (operating as a rejection), but if the counteroffer is then accepted, a valid contract is formed.

5. d) All of the options are true statements.

6. d) Consideration is almost anything of value: money, goods, services, or a promise to do or not do something.

7. b) An executory contract has not yet been performed; an executed contract is one that has been fully performed.

8. a) A contract that lacks an essential element (such as consideration) is void. It has no legal force or effect, so there is nothing to rescind.

9. b) A voidable contract can be rescinded by the injured party.

10. d) The statute of frauds requires certain contracts to be in writing and signed by the party or parties to be bound.

11. d) Performance, cancellation, and novation are all ways of discharging a contract. Breach does not discharge the contract; the breaching party is liable to the other party.

12. a) Novation is the replacement of an existing contract with a new contract, or the replacement of a party to a contract with a new party.

13. c) A contract can be assigned unless otherwise agreed, but the assignor remains secondarily liable to the other party.

14. d) Liquidated damages is an amount the contracting parties agree in advance will be paid as full compensation if one of them breaches the contract.

15. b) If the court granted Jacobsen specific performance, the McClures would be ordered to convey the house as agreed in the contract (not merely to pay Jacobsen damages as compensation).

Types of Real Estate Contracts

Chapter Overview

In addition to understanding the basic principles of contract law, real estate agents must be familiar with the specific types of real estate contracts. This chapter describes several types of contracts related to real estate, including broker/salesperson agreements, listing agreements, deposit receipts, land contracts, options, and leases.

Broker/Salesperson Agreements

The type of contract a new real estate licensee is likely to encounter first is a **broker/salesperson agreement**. California law requires a broker to have a written employment agreement with each licensee who works for him or her. The agreement must be signed by both parties.

The agreement should include all the basic terms of the employment relationship, such as the duties of the parties, the amount and type of supervision to be exercised by the broker, the basis for the licensee's compensation, and the grounds for terminating the relationship. A copy of the CAR Independent Contractor Agreement form, which is commonly used to establish the broker/salesperson relationship, is shown in Figure 7.1. (Independent contractors are explained in Chapter 8.)

Listing Agreements

A **listing agreement** is a written employment contract between a property seller and a real estate broker. (A copy of the CAR Residential Listing Agreement form is shown in Figure 7.2.) The seller hires the broker to find a buyer who is ready, willing, and able to buy the property on the seller's terms. A listing agreement does not give the broker the authority to accept offers on behalf of the seller, or to transfer title to the seller's property.

Even though the listing agreement form is frequently filled out and signed by a salesperson working for the listing broker, the contract is between the seller and the broker (not the salesperson). Only a broker may directly contract with members of the public for brokerage services.

The standard form of payment for a real estate broker is the commission, also called a **brokerage fee**. The commission is usually computed as a percentage of the sales price (the price that the property is sold for), as opposed to the listing price.

In California, a broker cannot sue a seller to collect a commission unless they had a written listing agreement. (Note that an oral agreement between brokers to split a commission is enforceable, even though an oral listing agreement is not.) The broker must also have been properly licensed at the time the brokerage services were provided. In addition, the broker must have fulfilled the terms of the listing agreement that establish under what circumstances the seller is obligated to pay the broker a commission.

Fig. 7.1 Independent contractor agreement

CALIFORNIA ASSOCIATION OF REALTORS®

INDEPENDENT CONTRACTOR AGREEMENT
(Between Broker and Associate-Licensee)
(C.A.R. Form ICA, Revised 10/04)

This Agreement, dated _____ is made between _____
_____ ("Broker") and
_____ ("Associate-Licensee").
In consideration of the covenants and representations contained in this Agreement, Broker and Associate-Licensee agree as follows:

1. **BROKER:** Broker represents that Broker is duly licensed as a real estate broker by the State of California, ☐ doing business as _____
_____ (firm name), ☐ a sole proprietorship, ☐ a partnership, or ☐ a corporation.
Broker is a member of the _____
Association(s) of REALTORS®, and a subscriber to the _____ Multiple
Listing Service(s). Broker shall keep Broker's license current during the term of this Agreement.

2. **ASSOCIATE-LICENSEE:** Associate-Licensee represents that: (i) he/she is duly licensed by the State of California as a ☐ real estate broker,
☐ real estate salesperson, and (ii) he/she has not used any other names within the past five years, except _____
_____ . Associate-Licensee shall keep his/her license current during
the term of this Agreement, including satisfying all applicable continuing education and provisional license requirements.

3. **INDEPENDENT CONTRACTOR RELATIONSHIP:**
   A. Broker and Associate-Licensee intend that, to the maximum extent permissible by law: (i) This Agreement does not constitute an employment agreement by either party; (ii) Broker and Associate-Licensee are independent contracting parties with respect to all services rendered under this Agreement; and (iii) This Agreement shall not be construed as a partnership.
   B. Broker shall not: (i) restrict Associate-Licensee's activities to particular geographical areas or, (ii) dictate Associate-Licensee's activities with regard to hours, leads, open houses, opportunity or floor time, production, prospects, sales meetings, schedule, inventory, time off, vacation, or similar activities, except to the extent required by law.
   C. Associate-Licensee shall not be required to accept an assignment by Broker to service any particular current or prospective listing or parties.
   D. Except as required by law: (i) Associate-Licensee retains sole and absolute discretion and judgment in the methods, techniques, and procedures to be used in soliciting and obtaining listings, sales, exchanges, leases, rentals, or other transactions, and in carrying out Associate-Licensee's selling and soliciting activities, (ii) Associate-Licensee is under the control of Broker as to the results of Associate-Licensee's work only, and not as to the means by which those results are accomplished, (iii) Associate-Licensee has no authority to bind Broker by any promise or representation and (iv) Broker shall not be liable for any obligation or liability incurred by Associate-Licensee.
   E. Associate-Licensee's only remuneration shall be the compensation specified in paragraph 8.
   F. Associate-Licensee shall not be treated as an employee with respect to services performed as a real estate agent, for state and federal tax purposes.
   G. The fact the Broker may carry worker compensation insurance for Broker's own benefit and for the mutual benefit of Broker and licensees associated with Broker, including Associate-Licensee, shall not create an inference of employment.
   (Workers' Compensation Advisory: Even though Associate-Licensees may be treated as independent contractors for tax and other purposes, the California Labor and Workforce Development Agency considers them to be employees for workers' compensation purposes. According to this agency, **(i)** Broker must obtain workers' compensation insurance for Associate-Licensees and **(ii)** Broker, not Associate-Licensees, must bear the cost of workers' compensation insurance. Penalties for failure to carry workers' compensation include, among others, the issuance of stop-work orders and fines of up to $1,000 per agent, not to exceed $100,000 per company.)

4. **LICENSED ACTIVITY:** All listings of property, and all agreements, acts or actions for performance of licensed acts, which are taken or performed in connection with this Agreement, shall be taken and performed in the name of Broker. Associate-Licensee agrees to and does hereby contribute all right and title to such listings to Broker for the benefit and use of Broker, Associate-Licensee, and other licensees associated with Broker. Broker shall make available to Associate-Licensee, equally with other licensees associated with Broker, all current listings in Broker's office, except any listing which Broker may choose to place in the exclusive servicing of Associate-Licensee or one or more other specific licensees associated with Broker. Associate-Licensee shall provide and pay for all professional licenses, supplies, services, and other items required in connection with Associate-Licensee's activities under this Agreement, or any listing or transaction, without reimbursement from Broker except as required by law. Associate-Licensee shall work diligently and with his/her best efforts: (i) sell, exchange, lease, or rent properties listed with Broker or other cooperating Brokers; (ii) solicit additional listings, clients, and customers; and (iii) otherwise promote the business of serving the public in real estate transactions to the end that Broker and Associate-Licensee may derive the greatest benefit possible, in accordance with law. Associate-Licensee shall not commit any unlawful act under federal, state or local law or regulation while conducting licensed activity. Associate-Licensee shall at all times be familiar, and comply, with all applicable federal, state and local laws, including, but not limited to, anti-discrimination laws and restrictions against the giving or accepting a fee, or other thing of value, for the referral of business to title companies, escrow companies, home inspection companies, pest control companies and other settlement service providers pursuant to the California Business and Professions Code and the Real Estate Settlement Procedures Acts (RESPA). Broker shall make available for Associate-Licensee's use, along with other licensees associated with Broker, the facilities of the real estate office operated by Broker at _____
_____ and the facilities of any other office
locations made available by Broker pursuant to this Agreement.

ICA REVISED 10/04 (PAGE 1 OF 3)

Broker's Initials (_____) (_____)
Associate-Licensee's Initials (_____) (_____)

Reviewed by _____ Date _____

EQUAL HOUSING OPPORTUNITY

INDEPENDENT CONTRACTOR AGREEMENT (ICA PAGE 1 OF 3)

Reprinted with permission, California Association of REALTORS®. Endorsement not implied.

5. **PROPRIETARY INFORMATION AND FILES: (A)** All files and documents pertaining to listings, leads and transactions are the property of Broker and shall be delivered to Broker by Associate-Licensee immediately upon request or termination of this Agreement. **(B)** Associate-Licensee acknowledges that Broker's method of conducting business is a protected trade secret. **(C)** Associate-Licensee shall not use to his/her own advantage, or the advantage of any other person, business, or entity, except as specifically agreed in writing, either during Associate-Licensee's association with Broker, or thereafter, any information gained for or from the business, or files of Broker.

6. **SUPERVISION:** Associate-Licensee, within 24 hours (or ☐ _____) after preparing, signing, or receiving same, shall submit to Broker, or Broker's designated licensee: **(i)** All documents which may have a material effect upon the rights and duties of principals in a transaction, **(ii)** Any documents or other items connected with a transaction pursuant to this Agreement in the possession of or available to; Associate-Licensee and, **(iii)** All documents associated with any real estate transaction in which Associate-Licensee is a principal.

7. **TRUST FUNDS:** All trust funds shall be handled in compliance with the Business and Professions Code, and other applicable laws.

8. **COMPENSATION:**
   A. TO BROKER: Compensation shall be charged to parties who enter into a listing or other agreements for services requiring a real estate license:
   ☐ as shown in "Exhibit A" attached, which is incorporated as a part of this Agreement by reference, or
   ☐ as follows: _____
   _____
   _____
   Any deviation which is not approved in writing in advance by Broker, shall be: **(1)** deducted from Associate-Licensee's compensation, if lower than the amount or rate approved above; and, **(2)** subject to Broker approval, if higher than the amount approved above. Any permanent change in commission schedule shall be disseminated by Broker to Associate-Licensee.

   B. TO ASSOCIATE-LICENSEE: Associate-Licensee shall receive a share of compensation actually collected by Broker, on listings or other agreements for services requiring a real estate license, which are solicited and obtained by Associate-Licensee, and on transactions of which Associate-Licensee's activities are the procuring cause, as follows:
   ☐ as shown in "Exhibit B" attached, which is incorporated as a part of this Agreement by reference, or
   ☐ other: _____
   _____
   _____

   C. PARTNERS, TEAMS, AND AGREEMENTS WITH OTHER ASSOCIATE-LICENSEES IN OFFICE: If Associate-Licensee and one or more other Associate-Licensees affiliated with Broker participate on the same side (either listing or selling) of a transaction, the commission allocated to their combined activities shall be divided by Broker and paid to them according to their written agreement. Broker shall have the right to withhold total compensation if there is a dispute between associate-licensees, or if there is no written agreement, or if no written agreement has been provided to Broker.

   D. EXPENSES AND OFFSETS: If Broker elects to advance funds to pay expenses or liabilities of Associate-Licensee, or for an advance payment of, or draw upon, future compensation, Broker may deduct the full amount advanced from compensation payable to Associate-Licensee on any transaction without notice. If Associate-Licensee's compensation is subject to a lien, garnishment or other restriction on payment, Broker shall charge Associate-Licensee a fee for complying with such restriction.

   E. PAYMENT: (i) All compensation collected by Broker and due to Associate-Licensee shall be paid to Associate-Licensee, after deduction of expenses and offsets, immediately or as soon thereafter as practicable, except as otherwise provided in this Agreement, or a separate written agreement between Broker and Associate-Licensee. **(ii)** Compensation shall not to be paid to Associate-Licensee until both the transaction and file are complete. **(iii)** Broker is under no obligation to pursue collection of compensation from any person or entity responsible for payment. Associate-Licensee does not have the independent right to pursue collection of compensation for activities which require a real estate license which were done in the name of Broker. **(iv)** Expenses which are incurred in the attempt to collect compensation shall be paid by Broker and Associate-Licensee in the same proportion as set forth for the division of compensation (paragraph 8(B)). **(v)** If there is a known or pending claim against Broker or Associate-Licensee on transactions for which Associate-Licensee has not yet been paid, Broker may withhold from compensation due Associate-Licensee on that transaction amounts for which Associate-Licensee could be responsible under paragraph 14, until such claim is resolved. **(vi)** Associate-Licensee shall not be entitled to any advance payment from Broker upon future compensation.

   F. UPON OR AFTER TERMINATION: If this Agreement is terminated while Associate-Licensee has listings or pending transactions that require further work normally rendered by Associate-Licensee, Broker shall make arrangements with another associate-licensee to perform the required work, or Broker shall perform the work him/herself. The licensee performing the work shall be reasonably compensated for completing work on those listings or transactions, and such reasonable compensation shall be deducted from Associate-Licensee's share of compensation. Except for such offset, Associate-Licensee shall receive the compensation due as specified above.

9. **TERMINATION OF RELATIONSHIP:** Broker or Associate-Licensee may terminate their relationship under this Agreement at any time, with or without cause. After termination, Associate-Licensee shall not solicit: **(i)** prospective or existing clients or customers based upon company-generated leads obtained during the time Associate-Licensee was affiliated with Broker; **(ii)** any principal with existing contractual obligations to Broker; or **(iii)** any principal with a contractual transactional obligation for which Broker is entitled to be compensated. Even after termination, this Agreement shall govern all disputes and claims between Broker and Associate-Licensee connected with their relationship under this Agreement, including obligations and liabilities arising from existing and completed listings, transactions, and services.

Broker's Initials (_____) (_____)
Associate-Licensee's Initials (_____) (_____)

Reviewed by _____ Date _____

ICA REVISED 10/04 (PAGE 2 OF 3)

EQUAL HOUSING OPPORTUNITY

INDEPENDENT CONTRACTOR AGREEMENT (ICA PAGE 2 OF 3)

10. **DISPUTE RESOLUTION:**
  A. **Mediation:** Mediation is recommended as a method of resolving disputes arising out of this Agreement between Broker and Associate-Licensee.
  B. **Arbitration:** All disputes or claims between Associate-Licensee and other licensee(s) associated with Broker, or between Associate-Licensee and Broker, arising from or connected in any way with this Agreement, which cannot be adjusted between the parties involved, shall be submitted to the Association of REALTORS® of which all such disputing parties are members for arbitration pursuant to the provisions of its Bylaws, as may be amended from time to time, which are incorporated as a part of this Agreement by reference. If the Bylaws of the Association do not cover arbitration of the dispute, or if the Association declines jurisdiction over the dispute, then arbitration shall be pursuant to the rules of California law. The Federal Arbitration Act, Title 9, U.S. Code, Section 1, et seq., shall govern this Agreement.

11. **AUTOMOBILE:** Associate-Licensee shall maintain automobile insurance coverage for liability and property damage in the following amounts $ _____ /$ _____ . Broker shall be named as an additional insured party on Associate-Licensee's policies. A copy of the endorsement showing Broker as an additional insured shall be provided to Broker.

12. **PERSONAL ASSISTANTS:** Associate-Licensee may make use of a personal assistant, provided the following requirements are satisfied. Associate-Licensee shall have a written agreement with the personal assistant which establishes the terms and responsibilities of the parties to the employment agreement, including, but not limited to, compensation, supervision and compliance with applicable law. The agreement shall be subject to Broker's review and approval. Unless otherwise agreed, if the personal assistant has a real estate license, that license must be provided to the Broker. Both Associate-Licensee and personal assistant must sign any agreement that Broker has established for such purposes.

13. **OFFICE POLICY MANUAL:** If Broker's office policy manual, now or as modified in the future, conflicts with or differs from the terms of this Agreement, the terms of the office policy manual shall govern the relationship between Broker and Associate-Licensee.

14. **INDEMNITY AND HOLD HARMLESS:** Associate-Licensee agrees to indemnify, defend and hold Broker harmless from all claims, disputes, litigation, judgments, awards, costs and attorney's fees, arising from any action taken or omitted by Associate-Licensee, or others working through, or on behalf of Associate-Licensee in connection with services rendered or to be rendered pursuant to this Agreement. Any such claims or costs payable pursuant to this Agreement, are due as follows:

  ☐ Paid in full by Associate-Licensee, who hereby agrees to indemnify and hold harmless Broker for all such sums, or
  ☐ In the same ratio as the compensation split as it existed at the time the compensation was earned by Associate-Licensee
  ☐ Other: _____
  _____
  _____

  Payment from Associate-Licensee is due at the time Broker makes such payment and can be offset from any compensation due Associate-Licensee as above. Broker retains the authority to settle claims or disputes, whether or not Associate-Licensee consents to such settlement.

15. **ADDITIONAL PROVISIONS:** _____
  _____
  _____

16. **DEFINITIONS:** As used in this Agreement, the following terms have the meanings indicated:
  (A) "Listing" means an agreement with a property owner or other party to locate a buyer, exchange party, lessee, or other party to a transaction involving real property, a mobile home, or other property or transaction which may be brokered by a real estate licensee, or an agreement with a party to locate or negotiate for any such property or transaction.
  (B) "Compensation" means compensation for acts requiring a real estate license, regardless of whether calculated as a percentage of transaction price, flat fee, hourly rate, or in any other manner.
  (C) "Transaction" means a sale, exchange, lease, or rental of real property, a business opportunity, or a manufactured home, which may lawfully be brokered by a real estate licensee.

17. **ATTORNEY FEES:** In any action, proceeding, or arbitration between Broker and Associate-Licensee arising from or related to this Agreement, the prevailing Broker or Associate-Licensee shall be entitled to reasonable attorney fees and costs.

18. **ENTIRE AGREEMENT:** All prior agreements between the parties concerning their relationship as Broker and Associate-Licensee are incorporated in this Agreement, which constitutes the entire contract. Its terms are intended by the parties as a final and complete expression of their agreement with respect to its subject matter, and may not be contradicted by evidence of any prior agreement or contemporaneous oral agreement. This Agreement may not be amended, modified, altered, or changed except by a further agreement in writing executed by Broker and Associate-Licensee.

Broker:

_____
(Brokerage firm name)
By _____
Its ☐ Broker ☐ Office manager (check one)

_____
(Print name)

_____
(Address)

_____
(City, State, Zip)

_____
(Telephone)   (Fax)

Associate-Licensee:

_____
(Signature)

_____
(Print name)

_____
(Address)

_____
(City, State, Zip)

_____
(Telephone)   (Fax)

Published and Distrubuted by:
REAL ESTATE BUSINESS SERVICES, INC.
a subsidiary of the California Association of REALTORS®
525 South Virgil Avenue, Los Angeles, California 90020

Reviewed by _____ Date _____

ICA REVISED 10/04 (PAGE 3 OF 3)

INDEPENDENT CONTRACTOR AGREEMENT (ICA PAGE 3 OF 3)

Earning a Commission

A listing agreement can make payment of the broker's commission dependent on any lawful conditions that are mutually acceptable to the broker and the seller. For example, the seller might ask to include a "no sale, no commission" provision in the agreement. This would make the broker's commission payable only if the transaction actually closes and the seller receives full payment from the buyer. If this condition is not met due to circumstances beyond the seller's control (for example, because the buyer couldn't obtain financing), the commission need not be paid. On the other hand, if the condition is not met because of the bad faith or fraud of the seller, the broker is still entitled to the commission.

Unless otherwise agreed, however, certain standard rules are followed regarding payment of the broker's commission. These include the rules concerning a ready, willing, and able buyer, and those concerning the three types of listings.

Ready, Willing, and Able Buyer. As a general rule, a listing agreement obligates the seller to pay the listing broker a commission only if a **ready, willing, and able** buyer is found during the listing period.

Acceptable Offer. A buyer is considered "ready and willing" if he or she makes an offer that meets the seller's stated terms. In the listing agreement, the seller sets forth the terms on which he or she wants to sell the property: price, closing date, financing arrangements, etc. If a buyer makes an offer that matches those terms, the broker is usually entitled to the commission—even if the seller decides not to accept that offer after all.

When a buyer makes an offer on terms other than those set forth in the listing agreement, the seller can turn down the offer without becoming liable for the broker's commission. But if the seller accepts an offer, he or she generally is required to pay the broker's commission even if the offer did not match the terms set forth in the listing agreement.

Able to Buy. A ready and willing buyer is considered "able" if he or she has the capacity to contract and the financial ability to complete the purchase. The buyer must have enough cash to buy the property on the agreed terms, or else be eligible for the necessary financing.

Commission Without Closing. Generally, once a ready, willing, and able buyer has been found, the broker has earned the commission, whether or not the sale is ever completed. When failure to close is the seller's fault, the broker is still entitled to the commission (although the broker might decide not to demand payment). For example, once the seller accepts an offer, he or she still owes the broker a commission if the sale fails to close for any of these reasons:

- the seller has a change of heart and decides not to sell;
- the seller does not have marketable title;
- the seller is unable to deliver possession of the property to the buyer; or
- the seller and the buyer mutually agree to terminate their contract.

Unless specifically required by the listing agreement, it is not even necessary for the buyer and seller to execute a written purchase and sale agreement in order for the broker to be entitled to a commission. It is enough if the buyer and seller have reached an agreement as to the essential terms of the sale: the price, downpayment, loan term, interest rate, and amortization. If the seller

Fig. 7.2 Residential listing agreement

CALIFORNIA ASSOCIATION OF REALTORS®

RESIDENTIAL LISTING AGREEMENT - EXCLUSIVE
(Exclusive Authorization and Right to Sell)
(C.A.R. Form RLA, Revised 4/05)

1. **EXCLUSIVE RIGHT TO SELL:** _____ ("Seller")
   hereby employs and grants _____ ("Broker")
   beginning (date) _____ and ending at 11:59 P.M. on (date) _____ ("Listing Period")
   the exclusive and irrevocable right to sell or exchange the real property in the City of _____ ,
   County of _____ , Assessor's Parcel No._____ ,
   California, described as: _____ ("Property").

2. **ITEMS EXCLUDED AND INCLUDED:** Unless otherwise specified in a real estate purchase agreement, all fixtures and fittings that
   are attached to the Property are included, and personal property items are excluded, from the purchase price.
   ADDITIONAL ITEMS EXCLUDED: _____ .
   ADDITIONAL ITEMS INCLUDED: _____ .
   Seller intends that the above items be excluded or included in offering the Property for sale, but understands that: **(i)** the purchase
   agreement supersedes any intention expressed above and will ultimately determine which items are excluded and included in the
   sale; and **(ii)** Broker is not responsible for and does not guarantee that the above exclusions and/or inclusions will be in the purchase
   agreement.

3. **LISTING PRICE AND TERMS:**
   A. The listing price shall be: _____
   _____ Dollars ($ _____).
   B. Additional Terms: _____
   _____ .

4. **COMPENSATION TO BROKER:**
   **Notice: The amount or rate of real estate commissions is not fixed by law. They are set by each Broker
   individually and may be negotiable between Seller and Broker (real estate commissions include all
   compensation and fees to Broker).**
   A. Seller agrees to pay to Broker as compensation for services irrespective of agency relationship(s), either ☐ _____ percent
   of the listing price (or if a purchase agreement is entered into, of the purchase price), or ☐ $ _____ ,
   AND _____ , as follows:
   (1) If Broker, Seller, cooperating broker, or any other person procures a buyer(s) who offers to purchase the Property on the
   above price and terms, or on any price and terms acceptable to Seller during the Listing Period, or any extension.
   OR (2) If Seller, within _____ calendar days **(a)** after the end of the Listing Period or any extension, or **(b)** after any cancellation
   of this Agreement, unless otherwise agreed, enters into a contract to sell, convey, lease or otherwise transfer the Property
   to anyone ("Prospective Buyer") or that person's related entity: **(i)** who physically entered and was shown the Property
   during the Listing Period or any extension by Broker or a cooperating broker; or **(ii)** for whom Broker or any cooperating
   broker submitted to Seller a signed, written offer to acquire, lease, exchange or obtain an option on the Property. Seller,
   however, shall have no obligation to Broker under paragraph 4A(2) unless, not later than **3 calendar days** after the end of
   the Listing Period or any extension or cancellation, Broker has given Seller a written notice of the names of such
   Prospective Buyers.
   OR (3) If, without Broker's prior written consent, the Property is withdrawn from sale, conveyed, leased, rented, otherwise
   transferred, or made unmarketable by a voluntary act of Seller during the Listing Period, or any extension.
   B. If completion of the sale is prevented by a party to the transaction other than Seller, then compensation due under paragraph 4A
   shall be payable only if and when Seller collects damages by suit, arbitration, settlement or otherwise, and then in an amount
   equal to the lesser of one-half of the damages recovered or the above compensation, after first deducting title and escrow
   expenses and the expenses of collection, if any.
   C. In addition, Seller agrees to pay Broker: _____ .
   D. Seller has been advised of Broker's policy regarding cooperation with, and the amount of compensation offered to, other brokers.
   (1) Broker is authorized to cooperate with and compensate brokers participating through the multiple listing service(s) ("MLS"):
   (i) by offering MLS Brokers: either ☐ _____ percent of the purchase price, or ☐ $ _____ ;
   OR (ii) (if checked) ☐ as per Broker's policy.
   (2) Broker is authorized to cooperate with and compensate brokers operating outside the MLS as per Broker's policy.
   E. Seller hereby irrevocably assigns to Broker the above compensation from Seller's funds and proceeds in escrow. Broker may
   submit this Agreement, as instructions to compensate Broker pursuant to paragraph 4A, to any escrow regarding the Property
   involving Seller and a buyer, Prospective Buyer or other transferee.
   F. **(1)** Seller represents that Seller has not previously entered into a listing Agreement with another broker regarding the Property,
   unless specified as follows: _____ .
   (2) Seller warrants that Seller has no obligation to pay compensation to any other broker regarding the Property unless the
   Property is transferred to any of the following individuals or entities: _____
   _____
   (3) If the Property is sold to anyone listed above during the time Seller is obligated to compensate another broker: **(i)** Broker is
   not entitled to compensation under this Agreement; and **(ii)** Broker is not obligated to represent Seller in such transaction.

RLA REVISED 4/05 (PAGE 1 OF 3)

Seller acknowledges receipt of a copy of this page.
Seller's Initials (_____) (_____)

| Reviewed by _____ Date _____ |

EQUAL HOUSING OPPORTUNITY

RESIDENTIAL LISTING AGREEMENT - EXCLUSIVE (RLA PAGE 1 OF 3)

Reprinted with permission, California Association of REALTORS®. Endorsement not implied.

Property Address _____   Date: _____

5. **OWNERSHIP, TITLE AND AUTHORITY:** Seller warrants that: **(i)** Seller is the owner of the Property; **(ii)** no other persons or entities have title to the Property; and **(iii)** Seller has the authority to both execute this Agreement and sell the Property. Exceptions to ownership, title and authority are as follows: _____

6. **MULTIPLE LISTING SERVICE:** All terms of the transaction, including financing, if applicable, will be provided to the selected MLS for publication, dissemination and use by persons and entities on terms approved by the MLS. Seller authorizes Broker to comply with all applicable MLS rules. MLS rules allow MLS data to be made available by the MLS to additional Internet sites unless Broker gives the MLS instructions to the contrary. MLS rules generally provide that residential real property and vacant lot listings be submitted to the MLS within 48 hours or some other period of time after all necessary signatures have been obtained on the listing agreement. However, Broker will not have to submit this listing to the MLS if, within that time, Broker submits to the MLS a form signed by Seller (C.A.R. Form SEL or the locally required form) instructing Broker to withhold the listing from the MLS. Information about this listing will be provided to the MLS of Broker's selection unless a form instructing Broker to withhold the listing from the MLS is attached to this listing Agreement.

7. **SELLER REPRESENTATIONS:** Seller represents that, unless otherwise specified in writing, Seller is unaware of: **(i)** any Notice of Default recorded against the Property; **(ii)** any delinquent amounts due under any loan secured by, or other obligation affecting, the Property; **(iii)** any bankruptcy, insolvency or similar proceeding affecting the Property; **(iv)** any litigation, arbitration, administrative action, government investigation or other pending or threatened action that affects or may affect the Property or Seller's ability to transfer it; and **(v)** any current, pending or proposed special assessments affecting the Property. Seller shall promptly notify Broker in writing if Seller becomes aware of any of these items during the Listing Period or any extension thereof.

8. **BROKER'S AND SELLER'S DUTIES:** Broker agrees to exercise reasonable effort and due diligence to achieve the purposes of this Agreement. Unless Seller gives Broker written instructions to the contrary, Broker is authorized to order reports and disclosures as appropriate or necessary and advertise and market the Property by any method and in any medium selected by Broker, including MLS and the Internet, and, to the extent permitted by these media, control the dissemination of the information submitted to any medium. Seller agrees to consider offers presented by Broker, and to act in good faith to accomplish the sale of the Property by, among other things, making the Property available for showing at reasonable times and referring to Broker all inquiries of any party interested in the Property. Seller is responsible for determining at what price to list and sell the Property. **Seller further agrees to indemnify, defend and hold Broker harmless from all claims, disputes, litigation, judgments and attorney fees arising from any incorrect information supplied by Seller, or from any material facts that Seller knows but fails to disclose.**

9. **DEPOSIT:** Broker is authorized to accept and hold on Seller's behalf any deposits to be applied toward the purchase price.

10. **AGENCY RELATIONSHIPS:**
    A. **Disclosure:** If the Property includes residential property with one-to-four dwelling units, Seller shall receive a "Disclosure Regarding Agency Relationships" form prior to entering into this Agreement.
    B. **Seller Representation:** Broker shall represent Seller in any resulting transaction, except as specified in paragraph 4F.
    C. **Possible Dual Agency With Buyer:** Depending upon the circumstances, it may be necessary or appropriate for Broker to act as an agent for both Seller and buyer, exchange party, or one or more additional parties ("Buyer"). Broker shall, as soon as practicable, disclose to Seller any election to act as a dual agent representing both Seller and Buyer. If a Buyer is procured directly by Broker or an associate-licensee in Broker's firm, Seller hereby consents to Broker acting as a dual agent for Seller and such Buyer. In the event of an exchange, Seller hereby consents to Broker collecting compensation from additional parties for services rendered, provided there is disclosure to all parties of such agency and compensation. Seller understands and agrees that: **(i)** Broker, without the prior written consent of Seller, will not disclose to Buyer that Seller is willing to sell the Property at a price less than the listing price; **(ii)** Broker, without the prior written consent of Buyer, will not disclose to Seller that Buyer is willing to pay a price greater than the offered price; and **(iii)** except for (i) and (ii) above, a dual agent is obligated to disclose known facts materially affecting the value or desirability of the Property to both parties.
    D. **Other Sellers:** Seller understands that Broker may have or obtain listings on other properties, and that potential buyers may consider, make offers on, or purchase through Broker, property the same as or similar to Seller's Property. Seller consents to Broker's representation of sellers and buyers of other properties before, during and after the end of this Agreement.
    E. **Confirmation:** If the Property includes residential property with one-to-four dwelling units, Broker shall confirm the agency relationship described above, or as modified, in writing, prior to or concurrent with Seller's execution of a purchase agreement.

11. **SECURITY AND INSURANCE:** Broker is not responsible for loss of or damage to personal or real property, or person, whether attributable to use of a keysafe/lockbox, a showing of the Property, or otherwise. Third parties, including, but not limited to, appraisers, inspectors, brokers and prospective buyers, may have access to, and take videos and photographs of, the interior of the Property. Seller agrees: **(i)** to take reasonable precautions to safeguard and protect valuables that might be accessible during showings of the Property; and **(ii)** to obtain insurance to protect against these risks. Broker does not maintain insurance to protect Seller.

12. **KEYSAFE/LOCKBOX:** A keysafe/lockbox is designed to hold a key to the Property to permit access to the Property by Broker, cooperating brokers, MLS participants, their authorized licensees and representatives, authorized inspectors, and accompanied prospective buyers. Broker, cooperating brokers, MLS and Associations/Boards of REALTORS® are **not** insurers against injury, theft, loss, vandalism or damage attributed to the use of a keysafe/lockbox. Seller does (or if checked ☐ does not) authorize Broker to install a keysafe/lockbox. If Seller does not occupy the Property, Seller shall be responsible for obtaining occupant(s)' written permission for use of a keysafe/lockbox.

13. **SIGN:** Seller does (or if checked ☐ does not) authorize Broker to install a FOR SALE/SOLD sign on the Property.

14. **EQUAL HOUSING OPPORTUNITY:** The Property is offered in compliance with federal, state and local anti-discrimination laws.

15. **ATTORNEY FEES:** In any action, proceeding or arbitration between Seller and Broker regarding the obligation to pay compensation under this Agreement, the prevailing Seller or Broker shall be entitled to reasonable attorney fees and costs from the non-prevailing Seller or Broker, except as provided in paragraph 19A.

16. **ADDITIONAL TERMS:** _____
_____
_____
_____

Seller acknowledges receipt of a copy of this page.
Seller's Initials (_____) (_____)

RLA REVISED 4/05 (PAGE 2 OF 3)

Reviewed by _____ Date _____

RESIDENTIAL LISTING AGREEMENT - EXCLUSIVE (RLA PAGE 2 OF 3)

Property Address _____ Date: _____

17. MANAGEMENT APPROVAL: If an associate-licensee in Broker's office (salesperson or broker-associate) enters into this Agreement on Broker's behalf, and Broker or Manager does not approve of its terms, Broker or Manager has the right to cancel this Agreement, in writing, within **5 Days** after its execution.

18. SUCCESSORS AND ASSIGNS: This Agreement shall be binding upon Seller and Seller's successors and assigns.

19. DISPUTE RESOLUTION:

    A. MEDIATION: Seller and Broker agree to mediate any dispute or claim arising between them out of this Agreement, or any resulting transaction, before resorting to arbitration or court action, subject to paragraph 19B(2) below. Paragraph 19B(2) below applies whether or not the arbitration provision is initialed. Mediation fees, if any, shall be divided equally among the parties involved. If, for any dispute or claim to which this paragraph applies, any party commences an action without first attempting to resolve the matter through mediation, or refuses to mediate after a request has been made, then that party shall not be entitled to recover attorney fees, even if they would otherwise be available to that party in any such action. THIS MEDIATION PROVISION APPLIES WHETHER OR NOT THE ARBITRATION PROVISION IS INITIALED.

    B. ARBITRATION OF DISPUTES: (1) Seller and Broker agree that any dispute or claim in Law or equity arising between them regarding the obligation to pay compensation under this Agreement, which is not settled through mediation, shall be decided by neutral, binding arbitration, including and subject to paragraph 19B(2) below. The arbitrator shall be a retired judge or justice, or an attorney with at least 5 years of residential real estate law experience, unless the parties mutually agree to a different arbitrator, who shall render an award in accordance with substantive California Law. The parties shall have the right to discovery in accordance with Code of Civil Procedure §1283.05. In all other respects, the arbitration shall be conducted in accordance with Title 9 of Part III of the California Code of Civil Procedure. Judgment upon the award of the arbitrator(s) may be entered in any court having jurisdiction. Interpretation of this agreement to arbitrate shall be governed by the Federal Arbitration Act.

    (2) EXCLUSIONS FROM MEDIATION AND ARBITRATION: The following matters are excluded from mediation and arbitration hereunder: **(i)** a judicial or non-judicial foreclosure or other action or proceeding to enforce a deed of trust, mortgage, or installment land sale contract as defined in Civil Code §2985; **(ii)** an unlawful detainer action; **(iii)** the filing or enforcement of a mechanic's lien; and **(iv)** any matter that is within the jurisdiction of a probate, small claims, or bankruptcy court. The filing of a court action to enable the recording of a notice of pending action, for order of attachment, receivership, injunction, or other provisional remedies, shall not constitute a waiver of the mediation and arbitration provisions.

        "NOTICE: BY INITIALING IN THE SPACE BELOW YOU ARE AGREEING TO HAVE ANY DISPUTE ARISING OUT OF THE MATTERS INCLUDED IN THE 'ARBITRATION OF DISPUTES' PROVISION DECIDED BY NEUTRAL ARBITRATION AS PROVIDED BY CALIFORNIA LAW AND YOU ARE GIVING UP ANY RIGHTS YOU MIGHT POSSESS TO HAVE THE DISPUTE LITIGATED IN A COURT OR JURY TRIAL. BY INITIALING IN THE SPACE BELOW YOU ARE GIVING UP YOUR JUDICIAL RIGHTS TO DISCOVERY AND APPEAL, UNLESS THOSE RIGHTS ARE SPECIFICALLY INCLUDED IN THE 'ARBITRATION OF DISPUTES' PROVISION. IF YOU REFUSE TO SUBMIT TO ARBITRATION AFTER AGREEING TO THIS PROVISION, YOU MAY BE COMPELLED TO ARBITRATE UNDER THE AUTHORITY OF THE CALIFORNIA CODE OF CIVIL PROCEDURE. YOUR AGREEMENT TO THIS ARBITRATION PROVISION IS VOLUNTARY."

        "WE HAVE READ AND UNDERSTAND THE FOREGOING AND AGREE TO SUBMIT DISPUTES ARISING OUT OF THE MATTERS INCLUDED IN THE 'ARBITRATION OF DISPUTES' PROVISION TO NEUTRAL ARBITRATION."

Seller's Initials _____ / _____	Broker's Initials _____ / _____

20. ENTIRE AGREEMENT: All prior discussions, negotiations and agreements between the parties concerning the subject matter of this Agreement are superseded by this Agreement, which constitutes the entire contract and a complete and exclusive expression of their agreement, and may not be contradicted by evidence of any prior agreement or contemporaneous oral agreement. If any provision of this agreement is held to be ineffective or invalid, the remaining provisions will nevertheless be given full force and effect. This Agreement and any supplement, addendum or modification, including any photocopy or facsimile, may be executed in counterparts.

By signing below, Seller acknowledges that Seller has read, understands, accepts and has received a copy of this Agreement.

Seller _____ Date _____
Address _____ City _____ State _____ Zip _____
Telephone _____ Fax _____ E-mail _____

Seller _____ Date _____
Address _____ City _____ State _____ Zip _____
Telephone _____ Fax _____ E-mail _____

Real Estate Broker (Firm) _____
By (Agent) _____ Date _____
Address _____ City _____ State _____ Zip _____
Telephone _____ Fax _____ E-mail _____

Published and Distributed by:
REAL ESTATE BUSINESS SERVICES, INC.
a subsidiary of the California Association of REALTORS®
525 South Virgil Avenue, Los Angeles, California 90020

Reviewed by _____ Date _____

RLA REVISED 4/05 (PAGE 3 OF 3)

RESIDENTIAL LISTING AGREEMENT - EXCLUSIVE (RLA PAGE 3 OF 3)

backs out before the agreement is put into writing, the broker could still claim the commission.

Sometimes the seller and the broker disagree as to whether the buyer located by the broker was in fact ready, willing, and able. In California, a court will presume that the buyer was ready, willing, and able if a written purchase and sale agreement was signed. Since the seller accepted the buyer by entering into the contract, the seller has waived the right to claim that the buyer was unacceptable. This rule can be applied even if the buyer immediately defaulted because of financial inability to go through with the purchase.

On the other hand, if no contract has been signed and the agreement between the buyer and the seller is still at the unwritten stage when it falls through, the broker is not entitled to a commission unless he or she can prove that the buyer was financially able to perform the contract.

Types of Listing Agreements. The circumstances under which a seller is required to pay a broker's commission also depend on the type of listing agreement they have. The three basic types of listing agreements in current use are:

- the open listing,
- the exclusive agency listing, and
- the exclusive right to sell listing.

Open Listing. Under an open listing agreement, the seller is obligated to pay the broker a commission only if the broker was the **procuring cause** of the sale. The procuring cause is the person who was primarily responsible for bringing about the agreement between the parties. To be the procuring cause, a broker (or one of his or her salespersons) must have personally negotiated the offer from the ready, willing, and able buyer and communicated the offer to the seller.

An open listing is also called a non-exclusive listing, because a seller is free to give open listings to any number of brokers. If a seller signs two open listing agreements with two different brokers, and one of the brokers sells the property, only the broker who made the sale is entitled to a commission. The other broker is not compensated for his or her efforts. Or if the seller sells the property directly, without the help of either broker, then the seller does not have to pay any commission at all. The sale of the property terminates all outstanding listings.

The open listing arrangement has obvious disadvantages. If two competing brokers both negotiate with the person who ends up buying the property, there may be a dispute over which broker was the procuring cause of the sale. Also, because a broker with an open listing agreement is not assured of a commission when the property sells, he or she may not put as much effort into marketing the property, so it may take longer to sell. For the most part, open listing agreements are used only when a seller is unwilling to execute an exclusive listing agreement.

Exclusive Agency Listing. In an exclusive agency listing, the seller agrees to list with only one broker, but retains the right to sell the property him or herself without being obligated to pay the broker a commission. The broker is entitled to a commission if anyone other than the seller finds a buyer for the property, but not if the seller finds the buyer without the help of an agent.

In California, an exclusive agency listing must have a definite termination date; otherwise, the broker may be subject to disciplinary action (see Chapter 16).

Exclusive Right to Sell Listing. Under an exclusive right to sell listing, the seller agrees to list with only one broker, and that broker is entitled to a commission if the property sells during the listing term, regardless of who finds the buyer. Even if the seller makes the sale directly, the broker is still entitled to the commission.

In spite of the designation "exclusive right to sell," remember that this type of listing agreement does not actually authorize the broker to sell the property. As with the other types of listings, the broker is authorized only to submit offers to purchase to the seller.

The exclusive right to sell listing is preferred by most brokers, because it provides the most protection for the broker. It's the type of listing that is most commonly used.

Like an exclusive agency listing, an exclusive right to sell listing requires a definite termination date.

Due Diligence. There is a distinction between open and exclusive listings concerning the broker's contractual obligations. An open listing is usually a unilateral contract: the seller promises to pay the broker a commission if the broker finds a buyer, but the broker does not promise to make any effort to do so. If the broker does nothing at all, it is not a breach of contract.

On the other hand, an exclusive listing is usually a bilateral contract. In most exclusive listings, in exchange for the seller's promise to pay a commission no matter who finds a buyer (or if any agent finds a buyer), the broker promises to exercise due diligence and make a reasonable effort to find a buyer. If the seller can prove that the listing broker and salesperson did nothing to help sell the property, a court might not require the seller to pay the broker's commission.

Elements of a Listing Agreement

A listing agreement must have all of the essential elements of a valid contract that were discussed in the previous chapter, including competent parties, offer and acceptance, consideration, and a lawful purpose. Also, under the statute of frauds, a listing agreement must be in writing and must be signed by the seller. (If the property has more than one owner, only one of them has to sign the listing.) The broker usually also signs the listing agreement, although his or her signature is not strictly required. The broker gives implied consent to the terms of the agreement by starting to market the property.

If there is no written listing agreement, the broker cannot sue the seller for a commission, even though an oral agreement may have established an agency relationship between the broker and the seller (see Chapter 8).

At a minimum, a listing agreement should include provisions that:

- identify the property,
- set acceptable terms of sale,
- grant the broker authority,
- determine the broker's compensation, and
- state when the agreement will expire.

Property Description. A listing agreement must identify the seller's property. The street address is useful, but it may not be enough to identify the property with certainty. It's a good idea to attach a legal description of the property to the listing agreement as an exhibit. Any pages attached to a contract should be dated and initialed by the parties, to show that the attachments are intended to be part of the agreement.

Terms of Sale. A listing agreement should specify what the seller wants in the way of an offer. This includes how much money the seller wants for the property (the listing price) and any other terms of sale that matter to the seller. Any items that the seller wants to exclude from or include in the sale that would not otherwise be excluded or included should also be noted in the listing agreement.

As we explained earlier, the seller can reject any offer that doesn't meet the terms of sale described in the listing agreement, without becoming liable for a commission. However, if an offer is made that does meet those terms, and the seller rejects the offer, the broker may be entitled to a commission. Thus, it is very important for all of the essential terms of sale to be set forth clearly and fully in the listing agreement.

Broker's Authority. The listing agreement sets forth the broker's authority to find a buyer for the property. The broker is usually also given the authority to accept and hold good faith deposits on the seller's behalf. In the rare case where a broker is not given authority to accept deposits for the seller, if the prospective buyer gives the broker a deposit, then the broker is acting as an agent for the buyer in regard to the deposit. The seller would not be liable to the buyer if the broker were to lose or misappropriate the deposit.

Commission. A provision stating the rate or amount of the broker's commission is another key part of every listing agreement. The commission is usually computed as a percentage of the sales price. The commission rate or amount must be negotiable between the seller and the broker. In fact, it is a violation of state and federal antitrust laws for brokers to set uniform commission rates. Any discussion of commission rates among members of competing firms could give rise to a charge of price fixing (see Chapter 16).

A special law applies to listing agreements for one- to four-unit residential properties and mobile homes. If the broker uses a preprinted form for the listing agreement, it must state in boldface type that the amount or rate of the commission is not fixed by law and may be negotiated. The commission rate or amount cannot be printed in the form—it must be filled in for each transaction.

Sometimes the amount of the broker's commission is determined in an unusual way. Under a **net listing**, the seller stipulates the net amount of money he or she requires from the sale of the property. The broker then tries to sell the property for more than that net amount. When the property is sold, the seller receives the required net and the broker keeps any money in excess of that amount as the commission.

Example: The seller insists on getting $345,000 from the sale of her property. The broker sells the property for $378,000. $378,000 less the required $345,000 net equals $33,000. Thus, the broker's commission is $33,000. If the broker had sold the property for more, his commission would have been more. Likewise, if the broker had sold the property for less, his commission would have been less.

Net listings can be open, exclusive agency, or exclusive right to sell listings. Whatever the type, net listings carry the potential for abuse; an unscrupulous broker could easily use a net listing to take advantage of a seller. In California, a broker who uses a net listing must reveal the amount of his or her commission to the seller before the seller becomes committed to the transaction. Failure to do so may result in disciplinary action.

Payment. A broker's commission is typically paid with a check, but if the seller and the broker agree, the commission payment can take the form of a new promissory note, an assignment of an existing note, or an assignment of funds from the buyer to the seller.

Ordinarily, the commission is the only payment the broker receives. The broker does not present the seller with a bill for expenses incurred in selling the property, unless the seller specifically agreed to this arrangement in the listing agreement.

It should be noted that a salesperson may only receive a commission from the broker he or she is licensed under. The salesperson cannot accept any compensation from any other broker or agent, or directly from the seller. If the seller fails to pay the broker his or her commission, it is the broker who must sue the seller. The broker's salesperson cannot sue the seller, even though the salesperson is entitled to a portion of the broker's commission.

Safety Clauses. A safety clause (also called a protection clause or protection period clause) is found in most listing agreements. Under this type of provision, the broker is entitled to a commission if the seller sells the property after the listing term expires to any person the broker negotiated with during the listing term. This protects the broker from parties who conspire to deprive the broker of a commission by waiting until the listing has expired before they sign a purchase and sale agreement. The broker usually has to provide the seller with a list of the parties he or she negotiated with, and the list must be delivered to the seller on or before the listing's termination date. This lets the seller know whom he or she can sell the property to without becoming liable for a commission.

Termination Date. A listing agreement should include a termination date, the date on which the listing will expire and the broker's authority to act on the seller's behalf will end. This is especially important for an exclusive listing, because the seller is not really free to work with a different broker until the listing expires. As was mentioned earlier, in California every exclusive agency or exclusive right to sell listing agreement must have a definite termination date. This is a requirement of the Real Estate Law (see Chapter 16). Note that the law does not set either a minimum or a maximum limit on the length of the listing period.

Deposit Receipts

When a seller accepts a buyer's offer to purchase the property, they enter into a purchase and sale agreement. A purchase and sale agreement is a written contract between the buyer and seller that establishes all of the terms of the sale. In California, purchase and sale agreements are usually referred to as **deposit receipts**.

In most transactions, the buyer presents a written, signed offer to the seller along with a good faith deposit. The standard form used by the buyer to make the offer also serves as the buyer's receipt for the deposit. If the seller chooses to accept the offer, he or she signs the form, and the form then becomes the binding contract of sale.

The statute of frauds requires an agreement to buy and sell real property to be in writing. A copy of the CAR Residential Purchase Agreement form is shown in Figure 7.3.

The basic provisions of a deposit receipt are fairly simple. The deposit receipt:

- identifies the parties,
- describes the property,
- sets forth the price and method of payment, and
- sets the date for closing the transaction (when title and possession are transferred).

However, most deposit receipts are quite detailed. It's important for the deposit receipt to state all of the terms of the parties' agreement clearly and accurately. Who is required to do what and when depends on the terms of the deposit receipt.

Typical Provisions

A deposit receipt form typically includes the following types of provisions.

Identification of the Parties. Of course, the buyer(s) and seller(s) must be properly identified in the agreement. Everyone who has an ownership interest in the property must sign the contract, and each party must have the capacity to enter into a contract. Note that if the property is community property, both spouses must sign the deposit receipt for it to be enforceable.

Description of the Property. The deposit receipt must describe the property with certainty. As with the listing agreement, a full legal description of the property is not required. Even so, it is always a good practice to include the legal description. If it is too long to fit in the blanks on the form, a copy of the legal description should be initialed by the parties and attached to the deposit receipt as an exhibit.

Terms of Sale. The deposit receipt should set forth as clearly as possible all of the terms of the sale, such as the total sales price, the amount of the downpayment, the method of payment, and what items are included in or excluded from the sale.

Many deposit receipt forms include a preprinted checklist of the most common types of financing arrangements. But regardless of the form used, all of the financing arrangements should be fully described, including the type of loan, the principal amount, the interest rate, how the loan is amortized, the term of the loan, and the monthly payments. (Types of financing programs are discussed in Chapter 10.)

Conditions of Sale. Most deposit receipts are conditional. For example, it is common to condition a sale on the buyer's ability to obtain the necessary financing. If the buyer is unable to obtain the financing after making a good

Fig. 7.3 Residential purchase agreement

CALIFORNIA ASSOCIATION OF REALTORS®

**CALIFORNIA
RESIDENTIAL PURCHASE AGREEMENT
AND JOINT ESCROW INSTRUCTIONS**
For Use With Single Family Residential Property — Attached or Detached
(C.A.R. Form RPA-CA, Revised 1/06)

Date _____, at _____, California.

1. **OFFER:**
   A. **THIS IS AN OFFER FROM** _____ ("Buyer").
   B. **THE REAL PROPERTY TO BE ACQUIRED** is described as _____
   _____, Assessor's Parcel No. _____, situated in
   _____, County of _____, California, ("Property").
   C. **THE PURCHASE PRICE** offered is _____
   _____ Dollars $ _____.
   D. **CLOSE OF ESCROW** shall occur on _____ (date)(or ☐ _____ **Days** After Acceptance).
2. **FINANCE TERMS:** Obtaining the loans below **is a contingency** of this Agreement unless: **(i)** either 2K or 2L is checked below; or **(ii)** otherwise agreed in writing. Buyer shall act diligently and in good faith to obtain the designated loans. Obtaining deposit, down payment and closing costs **is not a contingency.** Buyer represents that funds will be good when deposited with Escrow Holder.
   A. **INITIAL DEPOSIT**: Buyer has given a deposit in the amount of ....$ _____
   to the agent submitting the offer (or to ☐ _____), by personal check
   (or ☐ _____), made payable to _____,
   which shall be held uncashed until Acceptance and then deposited within **3** business days after
   Acceptance (or ☐ _____), with
   Escrow Holder, (or ☐ into Broker's trust account).
   B. **INCREASED DEPOSIT**: Buyer shall deposit with Escrow Holder an increased deposit in the amount of ....$ _____
   within ____ **Days** After Acceptance, or ☐ _____.
   C. **FIRST LOAN IN THE AMOUNT OF** ....$ _____
   (1) NEW First Deed of Trust in favor of lender, encumbering the Property, securing a note payable at
   maximum interest of _____% fixed rate, or _____% initial adjustable rate with a maximum
   interest rate of _____%, balance due in _____ years, amortized over _____ years. Buyer
   shall pay loan fees/points not to exceed _____. (These terms apply whether the designated loan
   is conventional, FHA or VA.)
   (2) ☐ FHA ☐ VA: (The following terms only apply to the FHA or VA loan that is checked.)
   Seller shall pay _____% discount points. Seller shall pay other fees not allowed to be paid by
   Buyer, ☐ not to exceed $_____. Seller shall pay the cost of lender required Repairs
   (including those for wood destroying pest) not otherwise provided for in this Agreement, ☐ not to
   exceed $ _____. (Actual loan amount may increase if mortgage insurance premiums,
   funding fees or closing costs are financed.)
   D. **ADDITIONAL FINANCING TERMS:** ☐ Seller financing, (C.A.R. Form SFA); ☐ secondary financing, ...$ _____
   (C.A.R. Form PAA, paragraph 4A); ☐ assumed financing (C.A.R. Form PAA, paragraph 4B)
   _____
   _____
   E. **BALANCE OF PURCHASE PRICE** (not including costs of obtaining loans and other closing costs) in the amount of ...$ _____
   to be deposited with Escrow Holder within sufficient time to close escrow.
   F. **PURCHASE PRICE (TOTAL):** ....$ _____
   G. **LOAN APPLICATIONS:** Within **7** (or ☐ _____) **Days** After Acceptance, Buyer shall provide Seller a letter from lender or mortgage loan broker stating that, based on a review of Buyer's written application and credit report, Buyer is prequalified or preapproved for the NEW loan specified in 2C above.
   H. **VERIFICATION OF DOWN PAYMENT AND CLOSING COSTS:** Buyer (or Buyer's lender or loan broker pursuant to 2G) shall, within **7** (or ☐ _____) **Days** After Acceptance, provide Seller written verification of Buyer's down payment and closing costs.
   I. **LOAN CONTINGENCY REMOVAL: (i)** Within **17** (or ☐ _____) **Days** After Acceptance, Buyer shall, as specified in paragraph 14, remove the loan contingency or cancel this Agreement; **OR (ii)** (if checked) ☐ the loan contingency shall remain in effect until the designated loans are funded.
   J. **APPRAISAL CONTINGENCY AND REMOVAL:** This Agreement is (**OR,** if checked, ☐ is **NOT**) contingent upon the Property appraising at no less than the specified purchase price. If there is a loan contingency, at the time the loan contingency is removed (or, if checked, ☐ within **17** (or ____) **Days** After Acceptance), Buyer shall, as specified in paragraph 14B(3), remove the appraisal contingency or cancel this Agreement. If there is no loan contingency, Buyer shall, as specified in paragraph 14B(3), remove the appraisal contingency within **17** (or ____) **Days** After Acceptance.
   K. ☐ **NO LOAN CONTINGENCY** (If checked): Obtaining any loan in paragraphs 2C, 2D or elsewhere in this Agreement is NOT a contingency of this Agreement. If Buyer does not obtain the loan and as a result Buyer does not purchase the Property, Seller may be entitled to Buyer's deposit or other legal remedies.
   L. ☐ **ALL CASH OFFER** (If checked): No loan is needed to purchase the Property. Buyer shall, within **7** (or ☐ ____) **Days** After Acceptance, provide Seller written verification of sufficient funds to close this transaction.
3. **CLOSING AND OCCUPANCY:**
   A. Buyer intends (or ☐ does not intend) to occupy the Property as Buyer's primary residence.
   B. **Seller-occupied or vacant property:** Occupancy shall be delivered to Buyer at _____ AM/PM, ☐ on the date of Close Of Escrow; ☐ on _____; or ☐ no later than _____ **Days** After Close Of Escrow. (C.A.R. Form PAA, paragraph 2.) If transfer of title and occupancy do not occur at the same time, Buyer and Seller are advised to: **(i)** enter into a written occupancy agreement; and **(ii)** consult with their insurance and legal advisors.

RPA-CA REVISED 1/06 (PAGE 1 OF 8) Print Date

Buyer's Initials (_____)(_____)
Seller's Initials (_____)(_____)

Reviewed by _____ Date _____

EQUAL HOUSING OPPORTUNITY

CALIFORNIA RESIDENTIAL PURCHASE AGREEMENT (RPA-CA PAGE 1 OF 8)

Property Address: _____   Date: _____

C. **Tenant-occupied property: (i) Property shall be vacant** at least **5 (or ☐ _____) Days** Prior to Close Of Escrow, unless otherwise agreed in writing. **Note to Seller: If you are unable to deliver Property vacant in accordance with rent control and other applicable Law, you may be in breach of this Agreement.**

OR **(ii)** (if checked) ☐ **Tenant to remain in possession.** The attached addendum is incorporated into this Agreement (C.A.R. Form PAA, paragraph 3.);

OR **(iii)** (if checked) ☐ **This Agreement is contingent** upon Buyer and Seller entering into a written agreement regarding occupancy of the Property within the time specified in paragraph 14B(1). If no written agreement is reached within this time, either Buyer or Seller may cancel this Agreement in writing.

D. At Close Of Escrow, Seller assigns to Buyer any assignable warranty rights for items included in the sale and shall provide any available Copies of such warranties. Brokers cannot and will not determine the assignability of any warranties.

E. At Close Of Escrow, unless otherwise agreed in writing, Seller shall provide keys and/or means to operate all locks, mailboxes, security systems, alarms and garage door openers. If Property is a condominium or located in a common interest subdivision, Buyer may be required to pay a deposit to the Homeowners' Association ("HOA") to obtain keys to accessible HOA facilities.

4. **ALLOCATION OF COSTS** (If checked): Unless otherwise specified here, this paragraph only determines who is to pay for the report, inspection, test or service mentioned. If not specified here or elsewhere in this Agreement, the determination of who is to pay for any work recommended or identified by any such report, inspection, test or service shall be by the method specified in paragraph 14B(2).

A. **WOOD DESTROYING PEST INSPECTION:**

(1) ☐ Buyer ☐ Seller shall pay for an inspection and report for wood destroying pests and organisms ("Report") which shall be prepared by _____, a registered structural pest control company. The Report shall cover the accessible areas of the main building and attached structures and, if checked: ☐ detached garages and carports, ☐ detached decks, ☐ the following other structures or areas _____ _____. The Report shall not include roof coverings. If Property is a condominium or located in a common interest subdivision, the Report shall include only the separate interest and any exclusive-use areas being transferred and shall not include common areas, unless otherwise agreed. Water tests of shower pans on upper level units may not be performed without consent of the owners of property below the shower.

OR (2) ☐ **(If checked)** The attached addendum (C.A.R. Form WPA) regarding wood destroying pest inspection and allocation of cost is incorporated into this Agreement.

B. **OTHER INSPECTIONS AND REPORTS:**

(1) ☐ Buyer ☐ Seller shall pay to have septic or private sewage disposal systems inspected _____.
(2) ☐ Buyer ☐ Seller shall pay to have domestic wells tested for water potability and productivity _____.
(3) ☐ Buyer ☐ Seller shall pay for a natural hazard zone disclosure report prepared by _____.
(4) ☐ Buyer ☐ Seller shall pay for the following inspection or report _____.
(5) ☐ Buyer ☐ Seller shall pay for the following inspection or report _____.

C. **GOVERNMENT REQUIREMENTS AND RETROFIT:**

(1) ☐ Buyer ☐ Seller shall pay for smoke detector installation and/or water heater bracing, if required by Law. Prior to Close Of Escrow, Seller shall provide Buyer a written statement of compliance in accordance with state and local Law, unless exempt.
(2) ☐ Buyer ☐ Seller shall pay the cost of compliance with any other minimum mandatory government retrofit standards, inspections and reports if required as a condition of closing escrow under any Law. _____.

D. **ESCROW AND TITLE:**

(1) ☐ Buyer ☐ Seller shall pay escrow fee _____.
    Escrow Holder shall be _____.
(2) ☐ Buyer ☐ Seller shall pay for **owner's** title insurance policy specified in paragraph 12E _____.
    Owner's title policy to be issued by _____.
    (Buyer shall pay for any title insurance policy insuring Buyer's **lender**, unless otherwise agreed in writing.)

E. **OTHER COSTS:**

(1) ☐ Buyer ☐ Seller shall pay County transfer tax or transfer fee _____.
(2) ☐ Buyer ☐ Seller shall pay City transfer tax or transfer fee _____.
(3) ☐ Buyer ☐ Seller shall pay HOA transfer fee _____.
(4) ☐ Buyer ☐ Seller shall pay HOA document preparation fees _____.
(5) ☐ Buyer ☐ Seller shall pay the cost, not to exceed $ _____, of a one-year home warranty plan, issued by _____, with the following optional coverage: _____.
(6) ☐ Buyer ☐ Seller shall pay for _____.
(7) ☐ Buyer ☐ Seller shall pay for _____.

5. **STATUTORY DISCLOSURES (INCLUDING LEAD-BASED PAINT HAZARD DISCLOSURES) AND CANCELLATION RIGHTS:**

A. **(1)** Seller shall, within the time specified in paragraph 14A, deliver to Buyer, if required by Law: **(i)** Federal Lead-Based Paint Disclosures and pamphlet ("Lead Disclosures"); and **(ii)** disclosures or notices required by sections 1102 et. seq. and 1103 et. seq. of the California Civil Code ("Statutory Disclosures"). Statutory Disclosures include, but are not limited to, a Real Estate Transfer Disclosure Statement ("TDS"), Natural Hazard Disclosure Statement ("NHD"), notice or actual knowledge of release of illegal controlled substance, notice of special tax and/or assessments (or, if allowed, substantially equivalent notice regarding the Mello-Roos Community Facilities Act and Improvement Bond Act of 1915) and, if Seller has actual knowledge, an industrial use and military ordnance location disclosure (C.A.R. Form SSD).

(2) Buyer shall, within the time specified in paragraph 14B(1), return Signed Copies of the Statutory and Lead Disclosures to Seller.

(3) In the event Seller, prior to Close Of Escrow, becomes aware of adverse conditions materially affecting the Property, or any material inaccuracy in disclosures, information or representations previously provided to Buyer of which Buyer is otherwise unaware, Seller shall promptly provide a subsequent or amended disclosure or notice, in writing, covering those items. **However, a subsequent or amended disclosure shall not be required for conditions and material inaccuracies disclosed in reports ordered and paid for by Buyer.**

Buyer's Initials (_____)(_____)
Seller's Initials (_____)(_____)

RPA-CA REVISED 1/06 (PAGE 2 OF 8)

Reviewed by _____ Date _____

EQUAL HOUSING OPPORTUNITY

CALIFORNIA RESIDENTIAL PURCHASE AGREEMENT (RPA-CA PAGE 2 OF 8)

Property Address: _____   Date: _____

(4) If any disclosure or notice specified in 5A(1), or subsequent or amended disclosure or notice is delivered to Buyer **after the offer is Signed,** Buyer shall have the right to cancel this Agreement within **3 Days** After delivery in person, or **5 Days** After delivery by deposit in the mail, by giving written notice of cancellation to Seller or Seller's agent. (Lead Disclosures sent by mail must be sent certified mail or better.)

(5) Note to Buyer and Seller: Waiver of Statutory and Lead Disclosures is prohibited by Law.

B.   NATURAL AND ENVIRONMENTAL HAZARDS: Within the time specified in paragraph 14A, Seller shall, if required by Law: **(i)** deliver to Buyer earthquake guides (and questionnaire) and environmental hazards booklet; **(ii)** even if exempt from the obligation to provide a NHD, disclose if the Property is located in a Special Flood Hazard Area; Potential Flooding (Inundation) Area; Very High Fire Hazard Zone; State Fire Responsibility Area; Earthquake Fault Zone; Seismic Hazard Zone; and **(iii)** disclose any other zone as required by Law and provide any other information required for those zones.

C.   DATA BASE DISCLOSURE: Notice: Pursuant to Section 290.46 of the Penal Code, information about specified registered sex offenders is made available to the public via an Internet Web site maintained by the Department of Justice at www.meganslaw.ca.gov. Depending on an offender's criminal history, this information will include either the address at which the offender resides or the community of residence and ZIP Code in which he or she resides. (Neither Seller nor Brokers are required to check this website. If Buyer wants further information, Broker recommends that Buyer obtain information from this website during Buyer's inspection contingency period. Brokers do not have expertise in this area.)

6.   CONDOMINIUM/PLANNED UNIT DEVELOPMENT DISCLOSURES:

A.   SELLER HAS: 7 (or ☐ _____) Days After Acceptance to disclose to Buyer whether the Property is a condominium, or is located in a planned unit development or other common interest subdivision (C.A.R. Form SSD).

B. If the Property is a condominium or is located in a planned unit development or other common interest subdivision, Seller has **3 (or ☐ _____) Days** After Acceptance to request from the HOA (C.A.R. Form HOA): **(i)** Copies of any documents required by Law; **(ii)** disclosure of any pending or anticipated claim or litigation by or against the HOA; **(iii)** a statement containing the location and number of designated parking and storage spaces; **(iv)** Copies of the most recent 12 months of HOA minutes for regular and special meetings; and **(v)** the names and contact information of all HOAs governing the Property (collectively, "CI Disclosures"). Seller shall itemize and deliver to Buyer all CI Disclosures received from the HOA and any CI Disclosures in Seller's possession. Buyer's approval of CI Disclosures is a contingency of this Agreement as specified in paragraph 14B(3).

7.   CONDITIONS AFFECTING PROPERTY:

A. Unless otherwise agreed: **(i) the Property is sold (a) in its PRESENT physical condition as of the date of Acceptance and (b) subject to Buyer's Investigation rights; (ii)** the Property, including pool, spa, landscaping and grounds, is to be maintained in substantially the same condition as on the date of Acceptance; and **(iii)** all debris and personal property not included in the sale shall be removed by Close Of Escrow.

B.   SELLER SHALL, within the time specified in paragraph 14A, DISCLOSE KNOWN MATERIAL FACTS AND DEFECTS affecting the Property, including known insurance claims within the past five years, AND MAKE OTHER DISCLOSURES REQUIRED BY LAW (C.A.R. Form SSD).

C.   NOTE TO BUYER: You are strongly advised to conduct investigations of the entire Property in order to determine its present condition since Seller may not be aware of all defects affecting the Property or other factors that you consider important. Property improvements may not be built according to code, in compliance with current Law, or have had permits issued.

D.   NOTE TO SELLER: Buyer has the right to inspect the Property and, as specified in paragraph 14B, based upon information discovered in those inspections: (i) cancel this Agreement; or (ii) request that you make Repairs or take other action.

8.   ITEMS INCLUDED AND EXCLUDED:

A.   NOTE TO BUYER AND SELLER: Items listed as included or excluded in the MLS, flyers or marketing materials are **not** included in the purchase price or excluded from the sale unless specified in 8B or C.

B.   ITEMS INCLUDED IN SALE:

(1) All EXISTING fixtures and fittings that are attached to the Property;

(2) Existing electrical, mechanical, lighting, plumbing and heating fixtures, ceiling fans, fireplace inserts, gas logs and grates, solar systems, built-in appliances, window and door screens, awnings, shutters, window coverings, attached floor coverings, television antennas, satellite dishes, private integrated telephone systems, air coolers/conditioners, pool/spa equipment, garage door openers/remote controls, mailbox, in-ground landscaping, trees/shrubs, water softeners, water purifiers, security systems/alarms; and

(3) The following items: _____ .
_____

(4) Seller represents that all items included in the purchase price, unless otherwise specified, are owned by Seller.

(5) All items included shall be transferred free of liens and without Seller warranty.

C.   ITEMS EXCLUDED FROM SALE: _____
_____

9.   BUYER'S INVESTIGATION OF PROPERTY AND MATTERS AFFECTING PROPERTY:

A. Buyer's acceptance of the condition of, and any other matter affecting the Property, is a contingency of this Agreement as specified in this paragraph and paragraph 14B. Within the time specified in paragraph 14B(1), Buyer shall have the right, at Buyer's expense unless otherwise agreed, to conduct inspections, investigations, tests, surveys and other studies ("Buyer Investigations"), including, but not limited to, the right to: **(i)** inspect for lead-based paint and other lead-based paint hazards; **(ii)** inspect for wood destroying pests and organisms; **(iii)** review the registered sex offender database; **(iv)** confirm the insurability of Buyer and the Property; and **(v)** satisfy Buyer as to any matter specified in the attached Buyer's Inspection Advisory (C.A.R. Form BIA). Without Seller's prior written consent, Buyer shall neither make nor cause to be made: **(i)** invasive or destructive Buyer Investigations; or **(ii)** inspections by any governmental building or zoning inspector or government employee, unless required by Law.

B. Buyer shall complete Buyer Investigations and, as specified in paragraph 14B, remove the contingency or cancel this Agreement. Buyer shall give Seller, at no cost, complete Copies of all Buyer Investigation reports obtained by Buyer. Seller shall make the Property available for all Buyer Investigations. Seller shall have water, gas, electricity and all operable pilot lights on for Buyer's Investigations and through the date possession is made available to Buyer.

Buyer's Initials (_____)(_____)
Seller's Initials (_____)(_____)

Reviewed by _____ Date _____

RPA-CA REVISED 1/06 (PAGE 3 OF 8)

CALIFORNIA RESIDENTIAL PURCHASE AGREEMENT   (RPA-CA PAGE 3 OF 8)

Property Address: _____   Date: _____

10. REPAIRS: Repairs shall be completed prior to final verification of condition unless otherwise agreed in writing. Repairs to be performed at Seller's expense may be performed by Seller or through others, provided that the work complies with applicable Law, including governmental permit, inspection and approval requirements. Repairs shall be performed in a good, skillful manner with materials of quality and appearance comparable to existing materials. It is understood that exact restoration of appearance or cosmetic items following all Repairs may not be possible. Seller shall: **(i)** obtain receipts for Repairs performed by others; **(ii)** prepare a written statement indicating the Repairs performed by Seller and the date of such Repairs; and **(iii)** provide Copies of receipts and statements to Buyer prior to final verification of condition.

11. BUYER INDEMNITY AND SELLER PROTECTION FOR ENTRY UPON PROPERTY: Buyer shall: **(i)** keep the Property free and clear of liens; **(ii)** Repair all damage arising from Buyer Investigations; and **(iii)** indemnify and hold Seller harmless from all resulting liability, claims, demands, damages and costs. Buyer shall carry, or Buyer shall require anyone acting on Buyer's behalf to carry, policies of liability, workers' compensation and other applicable insurance, defending and protecting Seller from liability for any injuries to persons or property occurring during any Buyer Investigations or work done on the Property at Buyer's direction prior to Close Of Escrow. Seller is advised that certain protections may be afforded Seller by recording a "Notice of Non-responsibility" (C.A.R. Form NNR) for Buyer Investigations and work done on the Property at Buyer's direction. Buyer's obligations under this paragraph shall survive the termination of this Agreement.

12. TITLE AND VESTING:
   A. Within the time specified in paragraph 14, Buyer shall be provided a current preliminary (title) report, which is only an offer by the title insurer to issue a policy of title insurance and may not contain every item affecting title. Buyer's review of the preliminary report and any other matters which may affect title are a contingency of this Agreement as specified in paragraph 14B.
   B. Title is taken in its present condition subject to all encumbrances, easements, covenants, conditions, restrictions, rights and other matters, whether of record or not, as of the date of Acceptance except: **(i)** monetary liens of record unless Buyer is assuming those obligations or taking the Property subject to those obligations; and **(ii)** those matters which Seller has agreed to remove in writing.
   C. Within the time specified in paragraph 14A, Seller has a duty to disclose to Buyer all matters known to Seller affecting title, whether of record or not.
   D. At Close Of Escrow, Buyer shall receive a grant deed conveying title (or, for stock cooperative or long-term lease, an assignment of stock certificate or of Seller's leasehold interest), including oil, mineral and water rights if currently owned by Seller. Title shall vest as designated in Buyer's supplemental escrow instructions. THE MANNER OF TAKING TITLE MAY HAVE SIGNIFICANT LEGAL AND TAX CONSEQUENCES. CONSULT AN APPROPRIATE PROFESSIONAL.
   E. Buyer shall receive a CLTA/ALTA Homeowner's Policy of Title Insurance. A title company, at Buyer's request, can provide information about the availability, desirability, coverage, and cost of various title insurance coverages and endorsements. If Buyer desires title coverage other than that required by this paragraph, Buyer shall instruct Escrow Holder in writing and pay any increase in cost.

13. SALE OF BUYER'S PROPERTY:
   A. This Agreement is NOT contingent upon the sale of any property owned by Buyer.
   OR B. ☐ (If checked): The attached addendum (C.A.R. Form COP) regarding the contingency for the sale of property owned by Buyer is incorporated into this Agreement.

14. TIME PERIODS; REMOVAL OF CONTINGENCIES; CANCELLATION RIGHTS: The following time periods may only be extended, altered, modified or changed by mutual written agreement. Any removal of contingencies or cancellation under this paragraph must be in writing (C.A.R. Form CR).
   A. SELLER HAS: 7 (or ☐ _____) Days After Acceptance to deliver to Buyer all reports, disclosures and information for which Seller is responsible under paragraphs 4, 5A and B, 6A, 7B and 12.
   B. (1) BUYER HAS: 17 (or ☐ _____) Days After Acceptance, unless otherwise agreed in writing, to:
      (i) complete all Buyer Investigations; approve all disclosures, reports and other applicable information, which Buyer receives from Seller; and approve all matters affecting the Property (including lead-based paint and lead-based paint hazards as well as other information specified in paragraph 5 and insurability of Buyer and the Property); and
      (ii) return to Seller Signed Copies of Statutory and Lead Disclosures delivered by Seller in accordance with paragraph 5A.
      (2) Within the time specified in 14B(1), Buyer may request that Seller make repairs or take any other action regarding the Property (C.A.R. Form RR). Seller has no obligation to agree to or respond to Buyer's requests.
      (3) By the end of the time specified in 14B(1) (or 2I for loan contingency or 2J for appraisal contingency), Buyer shall, in writing, remove the applicable contingency (C.A.R. Form CR) or cancel this Agreement. However, if **(i)** government-mandated inspections/ reports required as a condition of closing; or **(ii)** Common Interest Disclosures pursuant to paragraph 6B are not made within the time specified in 14A, then Buyer has **5 (or ☐ _____) Days** After receipt of any such items, or the time specified in 14B(1), whichever is later, to remove the applicable contingency or cancel this Agreement in writing.
   C. CONTINUATION OF CONTINGENCY OR CONTRACTUAL OBLIGATION; SELLER RIGHT TO CANCEL:
      (1) Seller right to Cancel; Buyer Contingencies: Seller, after first giving Buyer a Notice to Buyer to Perform (as specified below), may cancel this Agreement in writing and authorize return of Buyer's deposit if, by the time specified in this Agreement, Buyer does not remove in writing the applicable contingency or cancel this Agreement. Once all contingencies have been removed, failure of either Buyer or Seller to close escrow on time may be a breach of this Agreement.
      (2) Continuation of Contingency: Even after the expiration of the time specified in 14B, Buyer retains the right to make requests to Seller, remove in writing the applicable contingency or cancel this Agreement until Seller cancels pursuant to 14C(1). Once Seller receives Buyer's written removal of all contingencies, Seller may not cancel this Agreement pursuant to 14C(1).
      (3) Seller right to Cancel; Buyer Contract Obligations: Seller, after first giving Buyer a Notice to Buyer to Perform (as specified below), may cancel this Agreement in writing and authorize return of Buyer's deposit for any of the following reasons: **(i)** if Buyer fails to deposit funds as required by 2A or 2B; **(ii)** if the funds deposited pursuant to 2A or 2B are not good when deposited; **(iii)** if Buyer fails to provide a letter as required by 2G; **(iv)** if Buyer fails to provide verification as required by 2H or 2L; **(v)** if Seller reasonably disapproves of the verification provided by 2H or 2L; **(vi)** if Buyer fails to return Statutory and Lead Disclosures as required by paragraph 5A(2); or **(vii)** if Buyer fails to sign or initial a separate liquidated damage form for an increased deposit as required by paragraph 16. **Seller is not required to give Buyer a Notice to Perform regarding Close of Escrow.**
      (4) Notice To Buyer To Perform: The Notice to Buyer to Perform (C.A.R. Form NBP) shall: **(i)** be in writing; **(ii)** be signed by Seller; and **(iii)** give Buyer at least **24 (or ☐ _____)** hours (or until the time specified in the applicable paragraph, whichever occurs last) to take the applicable action. A Notice to Buyer to Perform may not be given any earlier than **2 Days** Prior to the expiration of the applicable time for Buyer to remove a contingency or cancel this Agreement or meet a 14C(3) obligation.

Buyer's Initials (_____)(_____)
Seller's Initials (_____)(_____)

RPA-CA REVISED 1/06 (PAGE 4 OF 8)

Reviewed by _____ Date _____

EQUAL HOUSING OPPORTUNITY

CALIFORNIA RESIDENTIAL PURCHASE AGREEMENT (RPA-CA PAGE 4 OF 8)

Property Address: _____   Date: _____

D. EFFECT OF BUYER'S REMOVAL OF CONTINGENCIES : If Buyer removes, in writing, any contingency or cancellation rights, unless otherwise specified in a separate written agreement between Buyer and Seller, Buyer shall conclusively be deemed to have: **(i)** completed all Buyer Investigations, and review of reports and other applicable information and disclosures pertaining to that contingency or cancellation right; **(ii)** elected to proceed with the transaction; and **(iii)** assumed all liability, responsibility and expense for Repairs or corrections pertaining to that contingency or cancellation right, or for inability to obtain financing.

E. EFFECT OF CANCELLATION ON DEPOSITS: If Buyer or Seller gives written notice of cancellation pursuant to rights duly exercised under the terms of this Agreement, Buyer and Seller agree to Sign mutual instructions to cancel the sale and escrow and release deposits to the party entitled to the funds, less fees and costs incurred by that party. Fees and costs may be payable to service providers and vendors for services and products provided during escrow. **Release of funds will require mutual Signed release instructions from Buyer and Seller, judicial decision or arbitration award. A party may be subject to a civil penalty of up to $1,000 for refusal to sign such instructions if no good faith dispute exists as to who is entitled to the deposited funds (Civil Code §1057.3).**

15. FINAL VERIFICATION OF CONDITION: Buyer shall have the right to make a final inspection of the Property within **5 (or _____) Days** Prior to Close Of Escrow, NOT AS A CONTINGENCY OF THE SALE, but solely to confirm: **(i)** the Property is maintained pursuant to paragraph 7A; **(ii)** Repairs have been completed as agreed; and **(iii)** Seller has complied with Seller's other obligations under this Agreement.

16. LIQUIDATED DAMAGES: If Buyer fails to complete this purchase because of Buyer's default, Seller shall retain, as liquidated damages, the deposit actually paid. If the Property is a dwelling with no more than four units, one of which Buyer intends to occupy, then the amount retained shall be no more than 3% of the purchase price. Any excess shall be returned to Buyer. Release of funds will require mutual, Signed release instructions from both Buyer and Seller, judicial decision or arbitration award.
BUYER AND SELLER SHALL SIGN A SEPARATE LIQUIDATED DAMAGES PROVISION FOR ANY INCREASED DEPOSIT. (C.A.R. FORM RID)

Buyer's Initials _____/_____	Seller's Initials _____/_____

17. DISPUTE RESOLUTION:

A. MEDIATION: Buyer and Seller agree to mediate any dispute or claim arising between them out of this Agreement, or any resulting transaction, before resorting to arbitration or court action. Paragraphs 17B(2) and (3) below apply to mediation whether or not the Arbitration provision is initialed. Mediation fees, if any, shall be divided equally among the parties involved. If, for any dispute or claim to which this paragraph applies, any party commences an action without first attempting to resolve the matter through mediation, or refuses to mediate after a request has been made, then that party shall not be entitled to recover attorney fees, even if they would otherwise be available to that party in any such action. THIS MEDIATION PROVISION APPLIES WHETHER OR NOT THE ARBITRATION PROVISION IS INITIALED.

B. ARBITRATION OF DISPUTES: (1) Buyer and Seller agree that any dispute or claim in Law or equity arising between them out of this Agreement or any resulting transaction, which is not settled through mediation, shall be decided by neutral, binding arbitration, including and subject to paragraphs 17B(2) and (3) below. The arbitrator shall be a retired judge or justice, or an attorney with at least 5 years of residential real estate Law experience, unless the parties mutually agree to a different arbitrator, who shall render an award in accordance with substantive California Law. The parties shall have the right to discovery in accordance with California Code of Civil Procedure §1283.05. In all other respects, the arbitration shall be conducted in accordance with Title 9 of Part III of the California Code of Civil Procedure. Judgment upon the award of the arbitrator(s) may be entered into any court having jurisdiction. Interpretation of this agreement to arbitrate shall be governed by the Federal Arbitration Act.
(2) EXCLUSIONS FROM MEDIATION AND ARBITRATION: The following matters are excluded from mediation and arbitration: (i) a judicial or non-judicial foreclosure or other action or proceeding to enforce a deed of trust, mortgage or installment land sale contract as defined in California Civil Code §2985; (ii) an unlawful detainer action; (iii) the filing or enforcement of a mechanic's lien; and (iv) any matter that is within the jurisdiction of a probate, small claims or bankruptcy court. The filing of a court action to enable the recording of a notice of pending action, for order of attachment, receivership, injunction, or other provisional remedies, shall not constitute a waiver of the mediation and arbitration provisions.
(3) BROKERS: Buyer and Seller agree to mediate and arbitrate disputes or claims involving either or both Brokers, consistent with 17A and B, provided either or both Brokers shall have agreed to such mediation or arbitration prior to, or within a reasonable time after, the dispute or claim is presented to Brokers. Any election by either or both Brokers to participate in mediation or arbitration shall not result in Brokers being deemed parties to the Agreement.

"NOTICE: BY INITIALING IN THE SPACE BELOW YOU ARE AGREEING TO HAVE ANY DISPUTE ARISING OUT OF THE MATTERS INCLUDED IN THE 'ARBITRATION OF DISPUTES' PROVISION DECIDED BY NEUTRAL ARBITRATION AS PROVIDED BY CALIFORNIA LAW AND YOU ARE GIVING UP ANY RIGHTS YOU MIGHT POSSESS TO HAVE THE DISPUTE LITIGATED IN A COURT OR JURY TRIAL. BY INITIALING IN THE SPACE BELOW YOU ARE GIVING UP YOUR JUDICIAL RIGHTS TO DISCOVERY AND APPEAL, UNLESS THOSE RIGHTS ARE SPECIFICALLY INCLUDED IN THE 'ARBITRATION OF DISPUTES' PROVISION. IF YOU REFUSE TO SUBMIT TO ARBITRATION AFTER AGREEING TO THIS PROVISION, YOU MAY BE COMPELLED TO ARBITRATE UNDER THE AUTHORITY OF THE CALIFORNIA CODE OF CIVIL PROCEDURE. YOUR AGREEMENT TO THIS ARBITRATION PROVISION IS VOLUNTARY."

"WE HAVE READ AND UNDERSTAND THE FOREGOING AND AGREE TO SUBMIT DISPUTES ARISING OUT OF THE MATTERS INCLUDED IN THE 'ARBITRATION OF DISPUTES' PROVISION TO NEUTRAL ARBITRATION."

Buyer's Initials _____/_____	Seller's Initials _____/_____

Buyer's Initials (_____)(_____)
Seller's Initials (_____)(_____)

Reviewed by _____ Date _____

RPA-CA REVISED 1/06 (PAGE 5 OF 8)

EQUAL HOUSING OPPORTUNITY

CALIFORNIA RESIDENTIAL PURCHASE AGREEMENT (RPA-CA PAGE 5 OF 8)

Property Address: _____   Date: _____

18. PRORATIONS OF PROPERTY TAXES AND OTHER ITEMS: Unless otherwise agreed in writing, the following items shall be PAID CURRENT and prorated between Buyer and Seller as of Close Of Escrow: real property taxes and assessments, interest, rents, HOA regular, special, and emergency dues and assessments imposed prior to Close Of Escrow, premiums on insurance assumed by Buyer, payments on bonds and assessments assumed by Buyer, and payments on Mello-Roos and other Special Assessment District bonds and assessments that are now a lien. The following items shall be assumed by Buyer WITHOUT CREDIT toward the purchase price: prorated payments on Mello-Roos and other Special Assessment District bonds and assessments and HOA special assessments that are now a lien but not yet due. Property will be reassessed upon change of ownership. Any supplemental tax bills shall be paid as follows: **(i)** for periods after Close Of Escrow, by Buyer; and **(ii)** for periods prior to Close Of Escrow, by Seller. TAX BILLS ISSUED AFTER CLOSE OF ESCROW SHALL BE HANDLED DIRECTLY BETWEEN BUYER AND SELLER. Prorations shall be made based on a 30-day month.

19. WITHHOLDING TAXES: Seller and Buyer agree to execute any instrument, affidavit, statement or instruction reasonably necessary to comply with federal (FIRPTA) and California withholding Law, if required (C.A.R. Forms AS and AB).

20. MULTIPLE LISTING SERVICE ("MLS"): Brokers are authorized to report to the MLS a pending sale and, upon Close Of Escrow, the terms of this transaction to be published and disseminated to persons and entities authorized to use the information on terms approved by the MLS.

21. EQUAL HOUSING OPPORTUNITY: The Property is sold in compliance with federal, state and local anti-discrimination Laws.

22. ATTORNEY FEES: In any action, proceeding, or arbitration between Buyer and Seller arising out of this Agreement, the prevailing Buyer or Seller shall be entitled to reasonable attorney fees and costs from the non-prevailing Buyer or Seller, except as provided in paragraph 17A.

23. SELECTION OF SERVICE PROVIDERS: If Brokers refer Buyer or Seller to persons, vendors, or service or product providers ("Providers"), Brokers do not guarantee the performance of any Providers. Buyer and Seller may select ANY Providers of their own choosing.

24. TIME OF ESSENCE; ENTIRE CONTRACT; CHANGES: Time is of the essence. All understandings between the parties are incorporated in this Agreement. Its terms are intended by the parties as a final, complete and exclusive expression of their Agreement with respect to its subject matter, and may not be contradicted by evidence of any prior agreement or contemporaneous oral agreement. If any provision of this Agreement is held to be ineffective or invalid, the remaining provisions will nevertheless be given full force and effect. **Neither this Agreement nor any provision in it may be extended, amended, modified, altered or changed, except in writing Signed by Buyer and Seller.**

25. OTHER TERMS AND CONDITIONS, including attached supplements:
  A. ☑ Buyer's Inspection Advisory (C.A.R. Form BIA)
  B. ☐ Purchase Agreement Addendum (C.A.R. Form PAA paragraph numbers: _____) _____
  C. ☐ Statewide Buyer and Seller Advisory (C.A.R. Form SBSA)
  D. _____
    _____

26. DEFINITIONS: As used in this Agreement:
  A. **"Acceptance"** means the time the offer or final counter offer is accepted in writing by a party and is delivered to and personally received by the other party or that party's authorized agent in accordance with the terms of this offer or a final counter offer.
  B. **"Agreement"** means the terms and conditions of this accepted California Residential Purchase Agreement and any accepted counter offers and addenda.
  C. **"C.A.R. Form"** means the specific form referenced or another comparable form agreed to by the parties.
  D. **"Close Of Escrow"** means the date the grant deed, or other evidence of transfer of title, is recorded. If the scheduled close of escrow falls on a Saturday, Sunday or legal holiday, then close of escrow shall be the next business day after the scheduled close of escrow date.
  E. **"Copy"** means copy by any means including photocopy, NCR, facsimile and electronic.
  F. **"Days"** means calendar days, unless otherwise required by Law.
  G. **"Days After"** means the specified number of calendar days after the occurrence of the event specified, not counting the calendar date on which the specified event occurs, and ending at 11:59PM on the final day.
  H. **"Days Prior"** means the specified number of calendar days before the occurrence of the event specified, not counting the calendar date on which the specified event is scheduled to occur.
  I. **"Electronic Copy"** or **"Electronic Signature"** means, as applicable, an electronic copy or signature complying with California Law. Buyer and Seller agree that electronic means will not be used by either party to modify or alter the content or integrity of this Agreement without the knowledge and consent of the other.
  J. **"Law"** means any law, code, statute, ordinance, regulation, rule or order, which is adopted by a controlling city, county, state or federal legislative, judicial or executive body or agency.
  K. **"Notice to Buyer to Perform"** means a document (C.A.R. Form NBP), which shall be in writing and Signed by Seller and shall give Buyer at least 24 hours **(or as otherwise specified in paragraph 14C(4))** to remove a contingency or perform as applicable.
  L. **"Repairs"** means any repairs (including pest control), alterations, replacements, modifications or retrofitting of the Property provided for under this Agreement.
  M. **"Signed"** means either a handwritten or electronic signature on an original document, Copy or any counterpart.
  N. **Singular and Plural** terms each include the other, when appropriate.

Buyer's Initials (_____)(_____)
Seller's Initials (_____)(_____)

RPA-CA REVISED 1/06 (PAGE 6 OF 8)

Reviewed by _____ Date _____

CALIFORNIA RESIDENTIAL PURCHASE AGREEMENT (RPA-CA PAGE 6 OF 8)

Property Address: _____ Date: _____

27. AGENCY:

A. DISCLOSURE: Buyer and Seller each acknowledge prior receipt of C.A.R. Form AD "Disclosure Regarding Real Estate Agency Relationships."

B. POTENTIALLY COMPETING BUYERS AND SELLERS: Buyer and Seller each acknowledge receipt of a disclosure of the possibility of multiple representation by the Broker representing that principal. This disclosure may be part of a listing agreement, buyer-broker agreement or separate document (C.A.R. Form DA). Buyer understands that Broker representing Buyer may also represent other potential buyers, who may consider, make offers on or ultimately acquire the Property. Seller understands that Broker representing Seller may also represent other sellers with competing properties of interest to this Buyer.

C. CONFIRMATION: The following agency relationships are hereby confirmed for this transaction:
Listing Agent _____ (Print Firm Name) is the agent of (check one): ☐ the Seller exclusively; or ☐ both the Buyer and Seller.
Selling Agent _____ (Print Firm Name) (if not same as Listing Agent) is the agent of (check one): ☐ the Buyer exclusively; or ☐ the Seller exclusively; or ☐ both the Buyer and Seller. Real Estate Brokers are not parties to the Agreement between Buyer and Seller.

28. JOINT ESCROW INSTRUCTIONS TO ESCROW HOLDER:

A. The following paragraphs, or applicable portions thereof, of this Agreement constitute the joint escrow instructions of Buyer and Seller to Escrow Holder, which Escrow Holder is to use along with any related counter offers and addenda, and any additional mutual instructions to close the escrow: 1, 2, 4, 12, 13B, 14E, 18, 19, 24, 25B and 25D, 26, 28, 29, 32A, 33 and paragraph D of the section titled Real Estate Brokers on page 8. If a Copy of the separate compensation agreement(s) provided for in paragraph 29 or 32A, or paragraph D of the section titled Real Estate Brokers on page 8 is deposited with Escrow Holder by Broker, Escrow Holder shall accept such agreement(s) and pay out from Buyer's or Seller's funds, or both, as applicable, the Broker's compensation provided for in such agreement(s). The terms and conditions of this Agreement not set forth in the specified paragraphs are additional matters for the information of Escrow Holder, but about which Escrow Holder need not be concerned. Buyer and Seller will receive Escrow Holder's general provisions directly from Escrow Holder and will execute such provisions upon Escrow Holder's request. To the extent the general provisions are inconsistent or conflict with this Agreement, the general provisions will control as to the duties and obligations of Escrow Holder only. Buyer and Seller will execute additional instructions, documents and forms provided by Escrow Holder that are reasonably necessary to close the escrow.

B. A Copy of this Agreement shall be delivered to Escrow Holder within **3** business days after Acceptance (or ☐ _____). Buyer and Seller authorize Escrow Holder to accept and rely on Copies and Signatures as defined in this Agreement as originals, to open escrow and for other purposes of escrow. The validity of this Agreement as between Buyer and Seller is not affected by whether or when Escrow Holder Signs this Agreement.

C. Brokers are a party to the escrow for the sole purpose of compensation pursuant to paragraphs 29, 32A and paragraph D of the section titled Real Estate Brokers on page 8. Buyer and Seller irrevocably assign to Brokers compensation specified in paragraphs 29 and 32A, respectively, and irrevocably instruct Escrow Holder to disburse those funds to Brokers at Close Of Escrow or pursuant to any other mutually executed cancellation agreement. Compensation instructions can be amended or revoked only with the written consent of Brokers. Escrow Holder shall immediately notify Brokers: **(i)** if Buyer's initial or any additional deposit is not made pursuant to this Agreement, or is not good at time of deposit with Escrow Holder; or **(ii)** if Buyer and Seller instruct Escrow Holder to cancel escrow.

D. A Copy of any amendment that affects any paragraph of this Agreement for which Escrow Holder is responsible shall be delivered to Escrow Holder within **2** business days after mutual execution of the amendment.

29. BROKER COMPENSATION FROM BUYER: If applicable, upon Close Of Escrow, **Buyer** agrees to pay compensation to Broker as specified in a separate written agreement between Buyer and Broker.

30. TERMS AND CONDITIONS OF OFFER:

This is an offer to purchase the Property on the above terms and conditions. All paragraphs with spaces for initials by Buyer and Seller are incorporated in this Agreement only if initialed by all parties. If at least one but not all parties initial, a counter offer is required until agreement is reached. Seller has the right to continue to offer the Property for sale and to accept any other offer at any time prior to notification of Acceptance. Buyer has read and acknowledges receipt of a Copy of the offer and agrees to the above confirmation of agency relationships. If this offer is accepted and Buyer subsequently defaults, Buyer may be responsible for payment of Brokers' compensation. This Agreement and any supplement, addendum or modification, including any Copy, may be Signed in two or more counterparts, all of which shall constitute one and the same writing.

RPA-CA REVISED 1/06 (PAGE 7 OF 8)

Buyer's Initials (_____)(_____)
Seller's Initials (_____)(_____)

Reviewed by _____ Date _____

EQUAL HOUSING OPPORTUNITY

CALIFORNIA RESIDENTIAL PURCHASE AGREEMENT (RPA-CA PAGE 7 OF 8)

Property Address: _____   Date: _____

31. EXPIRATION OF OFFER: This offer shall be deemed revoked and the deposit shall be returned unless the offer is Signed by Seller and a Copy of the Signed offer is personally received by Buyer, or by _____, who is authorized to receive it by 5:00 PM on the third Day after this offer is signed by Buyer (or, if checked, ☐ by _____ (date), at _____ AM/PM).

Date _____   Date _____

BUYER _____   BUYER _____

_____   _____
(Print name)   (Print name)

_____
(Address)

32. BROKER COMPENSATION FROM SELLER:
   A. Upon Close Of Escrow, **Seller** agrees to pay compensation to Broker as specified in a separate written agreement between Seller and Broker.
   B. If escrow does not close, compensation is payable as specified in that separate written agreement.

33. ACCEPTANCE OF OFFER: Seller warrants that Seller is the owner of the Property, or has the authority to execute this Agreement. Seller accepts the above offer, agrees to sell the Property on the above terms and conditions, and agrees to the above confirmation of agency relationships. Seller has read and acknowledges receipt of a Copy of this Agreement, and authorizes Broker to deliver a Signed Copy to Buyer.
   ☐ (If checked) **SUBJECT TO ATTACHED COUNTER OFFER, DATED** _____.

Date _____   Date _____

SELLER _____   SELLER _____

_____   _____
(Print name)   (Print name)

_____
(Address)

(___/___)   **CONFIRMATION OF ACCEPTANCE:** A Copy of Signed Acceptance was personally received by Buyer or Buyer's authorized
(Initials)   agent on (date) _____ at _____ AM/PM. **A binding Agreement is created when a Copy of Signed Acceptance is personally received by Buyer or Buyer's authorized agent whether or not confirmed in this document. Completion of this confirmation is not legally required in order to create a binding Agreement; it is solely intended to evidence the date that Confirmation of Acceptance has occurred.**

REAL ESTATE BROKERS:
A. Real Estate Brokers are not parties to the Agreement between Buyer and Seller.
B. Agency relationships are confirmed as stated in paragraph 27.
C. If specified in paragraph 2A, Agent who submitted the offer for Buyer acknowledges receipt of deposit.
D. **COOPERATING BROKER COMPENSATION:** Listing Broker agrees to pay Cooperating Broker **(Selling Firm)** and Cooperating Broker agrees to accept, out of Listing Broker's proceeds in escrow: **(i)** the amount specified in the MLS, provided Cooperating Broker is a Participant of the MLS in which the Property is offered for sale or a reciprocal MLS; or **(ii)** ☐ (if checked) the amount specified in a separate written agreement (C.A.R. Form CBC) between Listing Broker and Cooperating Broker.

Real Estate Broker (Selling Firm) _____   License # _____
By _____   License # _____   Date _____
Address _____   City _____   State _____ Zip _____
Telephone _____ Fax _____   E-mail _____

Real Estate Broker (Listing Firm) _____   License # _____
By _____   License # _____   Date _____
Address _____   City _____   State _____ Zip _____
Telephone _____ Fax _____   E-mail _____

ESCROW HOLDER ACKNOWLEDGMENT:
Escrow Holder acknowledges receipt of a Copy of this Agreement, (if checked, ☐ a deposit in the amount of $ _____),
counter offer numbers _____ and _____, and agrees to act as Escrow Holder subject to paragraph 28 of this Agreement, any supplemental escrow instructions and the terms of Escrow Holder's general provisions.

Escrow Holder is advised that the date of Confirmation of Acceptance of the Agreement as between Buyer and Seller is _____

Escrow Holder _____   Escrow # _____
By _____   Date _____
Address _____
Phone/Fax/E-mail_____
Escrow Holder is licensed by the California Department of ☐ Corporations, ☐ Insurance, ☐ Real Estate. License # _____

(___/___)   **REJECTION OF OFFER:** No counter offer is being made. This offer was reviewed and rejected by Seller on
(Seller's Initials) _____ (Date)

Published and Distributed by:
REAL ESTATE BUSINESS SERVICES, INC.
a subsidiary of the California Association of REALTORS®
525 South Virgil Avenue, Los Angeles, California 90020

Reviewed by _____ Date _____

RPA-CA REVISED 1/06 (PAGE 8 OF 8)

CALIFORNIA RESIDENTIAL PURCHASE AGREEMENT (RPA-CA PAGE 8 OF 8)

faith effort to do so, he or she does not have to go through with the purchase, and does not have to forfeit the deposit.

Any and all conditions must be clearly stated in the deposit receipt. A provision setting forth a condition is called a **contingency clause**. A contingency clause should state exactly what must occur to fulfill the condition, and it should explain how one party is to notify the other when the condition has been fulfilled or waived. There should also be a time limit placed on the condition (for example, if the condition is not fulfilled by January 15, the contract is void). Finally, the contingency clause should explain the parties' rights in the event that the condition is not met or waived.

If a real estate licensee believes that a condition imposed in a deposit receipt may affect the date of closing or the date the buyer can take possession of the property, the licensee is required to explain that to the parties. Failure to do so is a violation of the California Real Estate Law and may lead to disciplinary action (see Chapter 16).

Condition of the Property. A deposit receipt may include a variety of provisions concerning the condition of the property. The seller may warrant the condition of certain elements (such as the roof, plumbing, or appliances) in the deposit receipt, or else may sell the property "as is." (Note that even if the property is sold "as is," there's a legal obligation to disclose all known material defects to the buyer. See Chapter 8.) The contract is also likely to address the buyer's right to inspect the property.

Disclosures. In a residential transaction, the deposit receipt often has a provision concerning the Transfer Disclosure Statement and other specific disclosures the seller may be required by law to provide (see Chapter 8). And certain required disclosures must be included in the contract itself; one example is a provision that explains how to access the "Megan's Law" database on the Internet. The database lists areas where registered sex offenders are residing.

Conveyance and Title. The deposit receipt should specify the type of deed that will be used to convey title to the buyer (ordinarily a grant deed). The contract usually also states that the title is free from undisclosed liens and encumbrances, and that the seller will pay for a title insurance policy protecting the buyer.

Escrow and Closing. It's a good idea for a deposit receipt to include the arrangements for escrow. At the very least, the agreement should set the closing date for the transaction. Both parties must agree to the identity of the escrow agent; one party can't choose the escrow agent without the other's consent.

Possession. Possession of the property is usually transferred to the buyer on the closing date, but other arrangements can be made in the deposit receipt. If possession will be transferred either before or after closing, the parties should execute a separate rental agreement called an **interim occupancy agreement**.

The Uniform Vendor and Purchaser Risk Act is a law that determines who suffers the loss when property subject to a contract of sale is damaged or destroyed. Under the terms of the law, until possession of the property is transferred to the buyer, the risk of loss is the seller's. For instance, if a house is destroyed by an earthquake the day before possession is transferred to the buyer, the seller bears the loss. Once possession is transferred to the buyer, however, the risk of loss is the buyer's.

The parties may choose to apportion the risk of loss differently by including a **risk clause** in the deposit receipt.

Time is of the Essence. Nearly all deposit receipts contain a "time is of the essence" clause (see Chapter 6). Thus, failure to meet any of the deadlines set in the agreement is a breach of contract.

Good Faith Deposit. The deposit receipt should not only acknowledge receipt of the good faith deposit, it should also explain the circumstances in which the deposit will be refunded to the buyer or forfeited to the seller. In many cases, the deposit is treated as liquidated damages (see Chapter 6). In a residential transaction, a liquidated damages provision in a deposit receipt must be in boldface type and must be initialed by the parties. And the amount of the liquidated damages may not exceed 3% of the purchase price.

It is common for a deposit receipt to provide that if the buyer defaults and the seller keeps the good faith deposit as liquidated damages, the broker is entitled to half of the amount retained by the seller (but no more than the broker would have collected if the transaction had closed).

The form of the deposit should be stated in the contract. A check is usual, but another form of payment—such as a promissory note—may be used. The form of the deposit must be disclosed to the seller before he or she accepts the offer.

Broker's Compensation. Many deposit receipts also provide for the payment of the broker's commission. In most cases, this provision is merely a reaffirmation of the commission agreement set forth in the listing agreement. But if the broker has risked working under an oral or implied listing agreement so far in the transaction, such a provision in the deposit receipt will satisfy the requirement for a written listing agreement, in case the broker needs to sue the seller for the commission.

Amendments

After the buyer and seller have signed the deposit receipt, the terms of the contract can only be modified in writing. All parties who signed the original agreement must sign the amendment, or it will be unenforceable. An amendment may also be referred to as a rider.

Don't confuse an amendment with an addendum. An amendment is a written modification that occurs after the parties have signed the deposit receipt. An addendum, on the other hand, is an attachment added to the agreement prior to signature.

Land Contracts

What we'll refer to as a **land contract** is also known by a number of other names: real estate contract, real property sales contract, conditional sales contract, installment sales contract, or contract for deed. Under a land contract, a buyer purchases property on an installment basis, rather than paying the seller the full purchase price all at once. The buyer takes possession of the property immediately, but the seller does not convey title to the buyer until the full price has been paid.

The California statute concerning land contracts provides this specific definition:

> "…an agreement wherein one party agrees to convey title to real property to another party upon the satisfaction of specified conditions set forth in the contract and which does not require conveyance of title within one year from the date of formation of the contract."

The parties to a land contract are usually referred to as the **vendor** (seller) and the **vendee** (buyer). The following example illustrates how a land contract works.

Example: Bender agrees to buy Jones's farm for $500,000, to be paid at the rate of $50,000 per year, plus 9% interest, for ten years. Jones (the vendor) allows Bender (the vendee) to take possession of the farm, and she promises to convey title to Bender when he has paid the full purchase price. Bender and Jones have entered into a land contract.

During the period in which the vendee is making payments on the contract, the vendor retains **legal title** to the property. The vendor does not deliver the deed to the vendee until the full purchase price has been paid. In the meantime, the vendee is said to have **equitable title** to the property. Equitable title is essentially the right to possess and enjoy the property while paying off the purchase price.

Rights and Responsibilities of the Parties

Both the vendor and the vendee have various rights and responsibilities under a land contract. The vendor retains legal title to the property and has the right to transfer or encumber the property without the vendee's consent. However, if legal title is transferred, the new owner takes title subject to the rights of the vendee under the land contract.

If the vendor creates any liens against the property, he or she must apply the vendee's contract payments to amounts due on the liens. For example, if the vendor owes an $800 monthly payment on a deed of trust, the vendor must apply the first $800 of the vendee's $1,000 monthly payment to that debt, instead of using the money for any other purpose. This protects the vendee from the possibility that the vendor will default on the lien and lose the property through foreclosure.

The vendor must pay off any liens before delivering the deed to the vendee. The vendor is required to deliver clear, marketable title when the vendee pays off the contract.

A land contract cannot be recorded unless the vendor's signature has been acknowledged. The vendor cannot prevent or prohibit the vendee from recording the contract.

If, for some reason, a land contract is not recorded, there are some additional statutory restrictions on the vendor's right to create liens. Unless the vendee consents to the liens, the vendor cannot encumber the property with liens that add up to more than the unpaid contract balance. And the monthly payments on those liens cannot total more than the vendee's monthly payment on the land contract.

The vendee's main responsibility is to make the required installment payments to the vendor. The vendee is generally also responsible for keeping the property insured and paying the property taxes.

In a land contract for residential property with four units or less, the vendor can prohibit prepayment only during the first 12 months following the sale. After that point, the vendee has the legal right to prepay any or all of the contract price. So if the vendee wants to pay off the entire balance of the contract price a year after entering into the contract, the vendor cannot refuse to accept the payment.

The vendee has the right to encumber the property, although few lenders are willing to make loans with a vendee's equitable interest as the only security. The vendee may sell his or her interest in the property by assigning the right to receive the deed when the contract price has been paid in full. (However, the vendee will remain responsible for making the contract payments unless the vendor releases the vendee from liability.) The vendee also has the right to devise (will) his or her interest.

Remedies for Default

If the vendee pays the purchase price in full, but the vendor fails to transfer legal title to the property, the vendee can sue for specific performance of the contract (see Chapter 6).

If the vendee defaults (for example, by failing to make the installment payments), the vendor can terminate the contract by sending the vendee the proper notice. The vendor must reimburse the vendee for the amount paid to the vendor under the contract. However, the vendee's reimbursement can be reduced by any damages that the vendor incurred, and by the fair market rental value of the property for the period the vendee was in possession.

> **Example:** Under a land contract, Porter paid Rollins $12,800 over a ten-month period. The rental value of the property for that period was $1,100 per month, or $11,000. Porter would be entitled to a reimbursement of only $1,800. ($12,800 − $11,000 = $1,800).

The vendee has the right to cure the default and reinstate the contract. And once the vendee has paid a substantial portion of the contract price, he or she gains a right of redemption.

If the vendee does not cure the default or redeem the property, then the vendor is entitled to retake possession. However, a recorded land contract is a cloud on the property's title; the vendor may need to obtain a quitclaim deed from the vendee or file a quiet title action to make the title marketable again.

Reasons for Using a Land Contract

A land contract is a security instrument that is used in conjunction with seller financing. The seller extends credit to the buyer and holds title to the property as security for the repayment of the debt. (See Chapter 9 for a detailed discussion of security instruments.) However, because of the vendee's rights of reinstatement, reimbursement, and redemption under a land contract, most people prefer to use deeds of trust in seller-financed transactions (see Chapter 9).

One exception is the Cal-Vet program, which regularly uses land contracts to finance home purchases by veterans (see Chapter 10).

Option Agreements

An **option agreement** is essentially a contract to make a contract. It is sometimes called a contract to keep an offer open. An option agreement creates a right to buy or lease a specified property for a fixed price within a set period of time. The parties to an option agreement are called the **optionor** (the one who grants the option right) and the **optionee** (the one who is granted the option right). In an option to purchase, the optionor is the seller and the optionee is the buyer.

Example: Alvarez is offering to sell his property for $620,000. Conners isn't yet sure that he wants to buy the property, but he doesn't want to lose the opportunity to do so. He asks Alvarez to give him a three-week option to purchase, and Alvarez agrees. They execute a written option agreement, and Conners pays Alvarez $750 as consideration for the option. The option gives Conners the right to buy the property at the stated price ($620,000) during the next three weeks, but does not obligate him to buy it at all.

The optionor is bound to keep the offer open for the period specified in the option agreement. He or she is not allowed to sell or lease the property to anyone other than the optionee until the option expires.

If the optionee decides to exercise the option (that is, to buy or lease the property on the stated terms), he or she must give written notice of acceptance to the optionor. If the optionee fails to exercise the option within the specified time, the option expires automatically.

Requirements for a Valid Option

Because an option is a contract, it must have all of the necessary elements of a contract, including consideration. The consideration may be a nominal amount—there's no set minimum. But some consideration must, in fact, pass from the optionee to the optionor; a mere statement of consideration in the agreement is not sufficient. (There is an exception to this rule for lease/option agreements, where the provisions of the lease are treated as sufficient consideration to support the option.)

An option agreement must be in writing; oral options are unenforceable. Furthermore, since an option to purchase anticipates that a sale may take place, the underlying terms of the sale (price, financing, etc.) should be spelled out in the option agreement.

Option Rights

The executed option gives the optionee a contract right, but does not create an interest in real property. An option is not a lien, and also cannot be used as security for a mortgage or a deed of trust.

If the optionor dies during the option period, that will not affect the rights of the optionee, who may still exercise the right to purchase or lease. The option contract is binding on the heirs and assignees of the optionor.

An option can be assigned, unless the agreement includes a provision prohibiting assignment. One exception to this rule is when the consideration paid by the optionee is in the form of an unsecured promissory note. In that case, the optionee must obtain the optionor's written permission before the option may be assigned.

Occasionally, when a real estate licensee takes a listing on a property, he or she also takes an option on the property. Before a licensee can exercise an option on a property that he or she has listed, the licensee must reveal to the seller, in writing, the full amount of the licensee's anticipated profit and get the seller's written consent to the amount of that profit.

Recording an Option

An option agreement may be recorded to give third parties constructive notice of the option. In that case, if the optionee exercises the option, his or her interest in the property will relate back to the date the option was recorded, taking priority over the rights of intervening third parties.

A recorded option that is not exercised creates a cloud on the optionor's title. The optionor should obtain a release from the optionee and record the release to remove the cloud.

Right of First Refusal

An option should not be confused with a **right of first refusal**, which gives a person the first opportunity to purchase or lease real property if and when it becomes available. For instance, a lease might give the tenant a right of first refusal to purchase the property if the landlord decides to sell it.

Once the property owner offers the property for sale or receives an offer to buy from a third party, the holder of the right of first refusal must be given a chance to match the offer. If he or she does not want the property or is unwilling to match the offer, the property may be sold to someone else.

Leases

A lease is both a method of conveyance and a contract. A lease conveys a less-than-freehold (leasehold) estate from the owner (the **landlord**) to the **tenant**. As we discussed in Chapter 2, the holder of a leasehold estate does not own the property, but rather has a right to exclusive possession of the property for a specified period of time. Sometimes the landlord and the tenant are said to be "in privity," which means they have a mutual interest in one property.

A lease contract is sometimes called a **rental agreement**. It sets out the rights and responsibilities of the two contracting parties, the landlord and the tenant. Note, however, that certain covenants and terms are implied by law in all leases, whether or not they are written in the agreement. These implied covenants (found in the California Landlord-Tenant Law) are discussed below.

Requirements for a Valid Lease

As with any contract, the parties to a lease must be competent and must mutually agree to its terms. Consideration (typically the rental payment) is also required. The amount of the rent and when it is due should be specified.

Under the statute of frauds, a lease must be in writing if it's for longer than one year, or if it won't be fully performed within one year after the contract is made. Any lease that should be in writing but is not creates a periodic tenancy.

A written lease must be signed by the landlord. Usually the tenant also signs the lease, but that isn't required. A tenant who takes possession of the property and pays rent is considered to have accepted the terms of the lease. Even so, it's best to have both parties sign. Also, since a lease is a contract pertaining to real property, an accurate legal description of the property should be included.

Landlord/Tenant Law

Use of the Premises. A tenant's use of the leased property is restricted by law to legal uses. Many landlords place additional restrictions on the use of the property, such as restricting commercial space to retail use. The restricting language must be clear, or the restrictions will be unenforceable. At a minimum, the lease should state that the premises are to be used only for the specified purpose and for no other. If there is no limitation in the lease, or if the language is not clearly restrictive, the tenant may use the premises for any legal purpose.

Payment of Rent. Most leases require the rent to be paid at the beginning of the rental period. However, if the lease doesn't specify when the rent is to be paid, it isn't due until the end of the rental period.

A landlord can't require a tenant to pay rent in cash unless the tenant has defaulted on the rent. After default, and upon written notice, the tenant may be required to make the next three payments (but no more) in cash.

A month-to-month tenant generally must be given 30 days' notice before a rent increase (or other change in lease terms) can take effect. For residential property with up to four units, if the rent increases more than 10% in a 12-month period, 60 days' notice is required.

Security Deposit. California law defines a security deposit as any payment, fee, deposit, or charge (including an advance payment of rent) paid by the tenant to secure the performance of the lease agreement. Such a payment is considered a security deposit no matter what the landlord and tenant call it.

The total security deposit for a residential lease can't exceed twice the monthly rental payment for unfurnished units, or three times the monthly payment for furnished units. But the landlord can demand a security deposit equal to six months' rent or more if the lease term is six months or longer.

Within three weeks after the termination of the lease, the landlord must return the deposit to the tenant, or send a letter explaining the reason for not returning any portion of the deposit. If the deposit or a written explanation is not given to the tenant within the three-week period, the landlord is liable for $600 in statutory damages, in addition to actual damages. The fact that a deposit is labeled "nonrefundable" (for example, "nonrefundable cleaning deposit") has no bearing on this requirement; the landlord must still return the payment or give a written explanation within three weeks.

Entry and Inspection. Most leases give the landlord the right to enter and inspect the leased premises during the lease term. California law provides that a residential landlord may enter the premises in an emergency, or in order to make repairs or improvements, perform other services, or show the premises to prospective buyers or tenants. Except in an emergency, the landlord is generally required to give the tenant 24 hours' notice. The entry must be during normal business hours unless the tenant consents to a different time.

Renewal. A lease may contain a provision that gives the tenant an option to renew the lease at the end of the term. Most renewal options require the tenant to give notice of his or her intention to exercise the option on or before a specific date.

To renew a lease, the parties often sign a renewal agreement. But a lease may be renewed by implication rather than express agreement. When the tenant makes a lease payment after the lease has expired, and the landlord accepts the payment, that can be considered an implied renewal of the lease. In this situation, the renewal term is the same as the term of the original lease, except that the renewal term may not exceed one year.

Repairs and Improvements. A tenant is not ordinarily required to make any repairs to the leased property. However, the tenant must return the property to the landlord in the same condition as it was in at the beginning of the lease term (though allowances are made for normal wear and tear). The landlord is typically responsible for making necessary repairs to the common areas, such as stairs, hallways, or elevators. A residential landlord is required to maintain the property in habitable condition (see below).

Neither the tenant nor the landlord is obligated to improve the property. The tenant may make improvements, which often can be removed by the tenant when the lease expires. (See Chapter 1 for a discussion of fixtures.)

Manager's Name and Address. If a residential property contains more than two rental units, the name and address of the manager of the rental units must be stated in the lease. Alternatively, this information may be posted in every elevator and in one other conspicuous place (or two conspicuous places if there are no elevators).

Transferring Leased Property

A landlord can sell the leased property during the term of the lease, but the buyer takes title subject to the lease. This means the buyer must honor the lease for the remainder of its term.

The tenant can also transfer his or her leasehold estate to another party, through assignment, subleasing, or novation. The tenant has the right to assign or sublease without the landlord's consent, unless the lease provides otherwise. A novation always requires the landlord's consent.

In an **assignment**, the tenant transfers the entire unexpired term of the lease.

Example: Landlord leases the premises to Tenant for a period starting January 1, 2003 and ending June 30, 2006. On July 1, 2003, Tenant leases the premises to the XYZ Corporation for a term starting July 1, 2003 and ending June 30, 2006. The agreement between Tenant and XYZ is an assignment, because the transfer is for the balance of the unexpired term.

The assignee becomes liable for paying the rent to the landlord (the original lessor) and the assignor (the original tenant) becomes secondarily liable for the rent. This means that the assignee has the primary responsibility for paying the rent, but the original tenant is not fully released from the duty to pay.

A **sublease** is a transfer of the leasehold estate for a period shorter than the unexpired term. The original tenant retains part of the leasehold estate.

Fig. 7.4 Transferring leased property

Assignment	Tenant transfers the entire unexpired term of the lease
Sublease	Tenant transfers less than the unexpired term of the lease
Novation	Lease is replaced with a new one, or one party is replaced by another party

Example: Landlord leases the premises to Tenant for a period starting January 1, 2003 and ending June 30, 2006. On July 1, 2003, Tenant leases the premises to a subtenant for a period starting July 1, 2003, through June 30, 2005, reserving the last year for himself. This agreement is a sublease because the tenant has transferred less than the balance of the lease term.

The subtenant (the new tenant) is liable for the rent to the original tenant, rather than to the landlord, and the original tenant is still liable to the landlord. This situation is sometimes referred to as a **sandwich lease**, because the original tenant is in the middle, sandwiched between the landlord and the subtenant.

A **novation** occurs when a new contract is created and the old contract is extinguished. When an existing lease is replaced either with a new lease between the same parties, or with a new lease between different parties, it has been novated. The purpose of a novation is to terminate the liability of the tenant under the original lease.

Termination of a Lease

A lease may be terminated before the end of its term in a variety of ways.

Surrender. A landlord and tenant may mutually agree to terminate a lease. This is called surrender.

Breach of Implied Covenant of Quiet Enjoyment. In every lease there is an implied covenant of quiet enjoyment. This is the landlord's implied promise that he or she will refrain from unlawfully interfering with the tenant's possession of the leased property, and that no third party will lawfully claim a right to possess the property. The tenant is guaranteed the exclusive possession and quiet enjoyment of the property.

The covenant of quiet enjoyment is breached when the tenant is wrongfully evicted from the leased property. There are two types of eviction: actual and constructive.

Actual eviction occurs when the landlord actually expels the tenant from the property. **Constructive eviction** occurs when the landlord causes or permits a substantial interference with the tenant's possession of the property. For example, failure to provide heat in the wintertime has been found to result in constructive eviction.

Breach of Implied Warranty of Habitability. In all residential leases, the landlord gives an implied guarantee that the premises meet all building and housing code regulations that affect health and safety on the premises. If the premises do not meet these criteria and the tenant notifies the landlord of the defective condition, then the landlord must correct the problem within certain time limits prescribed by statute. If the landlord fails to make the required repairs, the tenant can terminate the lease. Or if the landlord takes legal action to evict the tenant for nonpayment of rent, the tenant can use the uninhabitable condition of the premises as a defense.

Failure to Pay Rent. The tenant has a duty to pay rent as required by the terms of the lease. However, if the tenant fails to pay the rent, the leasehold estate is not automatically terminated. The landlord is required by statute to give notice of nonpayment to the tenant. If the tenant still fails to pay after receiving notice, the landlord may bring a court action for **unlawful detainer** to evict the tenant.

If the court finds the tenant in default, it may issue a **writ of possession**, which requires the tenant to move out peaceably or else be forcibly removed by the sheriff.

Although unlawful detainer actions are given priority on the court's docket, the process of legal eviction is often slow. However, landlords should be warned against taking matters into their own hands. A landlord who tries a "self-help" eviction (forcing the tenant out with threats, or by cutting off the utilities) instead of the legal process may end up defending a costly lawsuit.

Illegal or Unauthorized Use. If the tenant uses the premises in an illegal manner (in violation of the zoning code, for example), the landlord may demand that the tenant cease the illegal activity or leave the premises. Also, if the tenant uses the premises in a manner not authorized by the lease, the tenant has violated the agreement and the landlord may terminate the lease.

Destruction of the Premises. Unless there is a provision to the contrary, if the lease is for the use of the land and any buildings or other improvements on the land, or for the use of an entire building, the destruction of the building(s) will not terminate the lease. The destruction of a building does not prevent the use and enjoyment of the land, and therefore the purpose of the lease is not frustrated. The tenant is not relieved from the duty to pay the rent to the end of the rental period. If, however, the lease is only for a part of a building, such as an office, apartment, or commercial space, the destruction of the building frustrates the entire purpose of the lease, so the tenant will be released from the duty to pay rent.

Condemnation. Condemnation of property can also result in premature termination of a lease. (See Chapter 5 for a discussion of condemnation and the power of eminent domain.)

Types of Leases

There are five major types of leases: the fixed lease, the graduated lease, the percentage lease, the net lease, and the ground lease.

Sometimes called a "flat," "straight," or "gross" lease, a **fixed lease** provides for a fixed rental amount. The tenant is obligated to pay a fixed sum of money, and the landlord is obligated to pay all of the property's operating expenses: utilities, maintenance costs, taxes, and insurance. This type of lease is most commonly found in residential apartment rentals.

A **net lease** requires the tenant to pay the landlord a fixed rent, plus some or all of the operating expenses.

A **graduated lease** is similar to a fixed lease, but it provides for periodic increases in the rent, usually set at specific future dates and often based on the Consumer Price Index or a similar cost-of-living index. These increases are made possible by the inclusion of an **escalation clause**. This type of lease is also called a "step-up lease."

A **percentage lease** is common in the commercial setting, especially for properties located in shopping centers. The rent is based on a percentage of the gross or net income from the tenant's business. Typically, the lease provides for a minimum rent plus a percentage of the tenant's business income above a stated minimum.

When a tenant leases land and agrees to construct a building on that land, it is called a **ground lease**. Ground leases are common in metropolitan areas; they are usually long-term, in order to make the construction of buildings worth the tenant's while.

Chapter Summary

1. Brokers and their licensees must have written employment agreements (broker/salesperson agreements) that cover all of the basic terms of their relationship.

2. A property owner uses a listing agreement to hire a broker to find a buyer who is ready, willing, and able to buy the owner's property on the owner's terms. There are three different types of listing agreements: open listings, exclusive agency listings, and exclusive right to sell listings. The exclusive right to sell listing is the type most commonly used.

3. Listing agreements must include a property description, the terms of sale the property owner is willing to accept, the amount or rate of the commission, and the conditions under which the commission is earned. Most listing agreements also include a safety clause, which entitles the broker to a commission if the property is sold after the listing expires to anyone the broker negotiated with during the listing term.

4. A deposit receipt form serves as the buyer's offer to purchase, as the receipt for the buyer's good faith deposit, and, when it is signed by the seller, as the binding purchase and sale contract between the buyer and the seller. The deposit receipt must identify the parties, describe the property, and set forth the price, the method of payment, and the closing date.

5. Under a land contract, the buyer (vendee) purchases the property on an installment basis. The seller (vendor) retains legal title to the property while the contract is being paid off, but the vendee has the right to possess the property during that period. When the vendee has paid the full purchase price, the vendor delivers the deed to the vendee.

6. In an option to purchase, the optionee has a right to buy the property at a specified price (but is under no obligation to buy), and the optionor is not allowed to sell the property to anyone other than the optionee during the option period.

7. A landlord-tenant relationship is created with a lease. A lease must be in writing if it will not be fully performed within a year after the contract is made. A valid lease also requires consideration (usually the rental payment), the signature of the landlord, and a description of the property. Most leases include a security deposit requirement, a limitation on the use of the premises, and a clause allowing entry and inspection by the landlord.

Key Terms

Broker/salesperson agreement—A written employment agreement between a broker and a salesperson licensed to work under the broker.

Listing agreement—A written employment agreement between a property owner and a real estate broker, in which the owner hires the broker to find a buyer who is ready, willing, and able to buy the owner's property on the owner's terms.

Open listing—A type of listing that requires the property owner to pay a broker's commission only if the broker is the procuring cause of the sale.

Procuring cause—The real estate agent who is primarily responsible for bringing about a sale; the one who actually negotiates an agreement with the ready, willing, and able buyer.

Exclusive agency listing—A type of listing that requires the property owner to pay the broker a commission when the property is sold during the listing term by anyone other than the seller. If the seller finds the buyer, the broker is not entitled to a commission.

Exclusive right to sell listing—A type of listing that requires the property owner to pay the broker a commission if the property is sold during the listing term, no matter who sells the property.

Net listing—A type of listing in which the commission is any amount received from the sale over and above the "net" required by the seller.

Safety clause—A provision in a listing agreement that obligates the seller to pay a commission if the property is sold within a certain period after the listing expires to someone the broker negotiated with during the listing period. Also called a protection clause or protection period clause.

Deposit receipt—A binding contract between a buyer and a seller of real property, and also the receipt for the buyer's good faith deposit. Also called a purchase and sale agreement or contract of sale.

Contingency clause—A contract clause which provides that unless some specified event occurs, the contract is null and void.

Land contract—A contract for the sale of real property in which the buyer (vendee) pays the purchase price in installments. The vendee takes possession of the property immediately, but the seller (vendor) retains legal title until the full price has been paid.

Option agreement—An agreement that gives one party the right to buy or lease the other party's property at a set price for a certain period of time.

Lease—A contract in which one party (the tenant or lessee) pays the other (the landlord or lessor) rent in exchange for the possession of real estate. Also called a rental agreement.

Unlawful detainer—A court action brought by a landlord to evict a tenant.

Chapter Quiz

1. The type of listing that provides for payment of a commission to the listing broker regardless of who sells the property is a/an:

   a) open listing
   b) exclusive agency listing
   c) exclusive right to sell listing
   d) net listing

2. The type of listing that provides for the payment of a commission to the listing broker only if he or she was the procuring cause of the sale is a/an:

   a) open listing
   b) exclusive agency listing
   c) exclusive right to sell listing
   d) net listing

3. The type of listing that provides for the payment of a commission that consists of any proceeds from the sale over a specified amount is a/an:

   a) open listing
   b) exclusive agency listing
   c) exclusive right to sell listing
   d) net listing

4. The type of listing that provides for the payment of a commission to the listing broker if anyone other than the seller finds the buyer is a/an:

   a) open listing
   b) exclusive agency listing
   c) exclusive right to sell listing
   d) net listing

5. The listing broker has negotiated an offer from a ready, willing, and able buyer that matches the seller's terms of sale set forth in the listing agreement. Which of the following is true?

   a) The seller is required to accept the offer and pay the listing broker a commission
   b) The seller is required to accept the offer, but not required to pay the listing broker a commission
   c) The listing broker has earned the commission, whether or not the seller accepts the offer
   d) The listing broker has not earned the commission unless this is an exclusive agency listing

6. A safety clause provides that:

   a) the broker is entitled to a commission whether or not he or she is the procuring cause
   b) the buyer must share the cost of the broker's commission
   c) the seller warrants the safety of the premises
   d) the broker is entitled to a commission if the property is sold after the listing expires to someone the broker previously showed the property to

7. A deposit receipt serves as:

   a) the buyer's receipt for the good faith deposit
   b) the buyer's offer to purchase
   c) a binding contract between the buyer and the seller
   d) All of the above

8. A deposit receipt should state:

   a) only the purchase price, leaving the other terms to be worked out in the final contract
   b) the listing price as well as the purchase price
   c) the total purchase price, the method of payment, and the basic financing terms
   d) the seller's reasons for selling the property

9. A provision in the deposit receipt states that it will not be a binding contract unless the buyer can obtain financing. This provision is called:

   a) a contingency clause
   b) a defeasibility clause
   c) a bump clause
   d) an escrow clause

10. Under a land contract, the vendee initially gets:

    a) possession but not title
    b) title but not possession
    c) possession and title, but not the right to transfer ownership
    d) the right to novate the contract without the vendor's permission

11. To be binding, a lease must be signed by the:

    a) broker
    b) beneficiary
    c) landlord
    d) tenant

12. When leased property is sold, the lease:

    a) automatically terminates
    b) is breached by constructive eviction
    c) must be renegotiated by the tenant and the new owner
    d) is binding on the new owner

13. An oral lease may be valid if it is for less than:

    a) one year
    b) two years
    c) three years
    d) four years

14. You have a three-year lease on some commercial property. In the first year, your rental payment is $3,000 per month. In the second year, you must pay $3,400 a month, and in the third year, you must pay $3,800 a month. You have a:

    a) gross lease
    b) graduated lease
    c) triple lease
    d) straight lease

15. When a tenant assigns a lease, the assignee (new tenant) becomes:

    a) secondarily responsible for payment of the rent
    b) the subtenant
    c) primarily responsible for payment of the rent
    d) None of the above

👉 Answer Key

1. c) The exclusive right to sell listing obligates the seller to pay the listing broker a commission if the property sells during the listing period, regardless of who brings about the sale.

2. a) An open listing obligates the seller to pay a commission to the listing broker only if the broker was the procuring cause of the sale.

3. d) A net listing is a way of determining the amount of the commission, rather than the circumstances under which a commission is owed.

4. b) An exclusive agency listing obligates the seller to pay the listing broker a commission if any agent (anyone other than the seller) sells the property.

5. c) When the broker presents an offer from a ready, willing, and able buyer that matches the seller's terms of sale, the broker has earned the commission, whether or not the seller accepts the offer. The seller is under no obligation to accept the offer.

6. d) A safety clause entitles the broker to a commission if the property is sold within a certain time after the listing expires to someone the broker introduced to the property or negotiated with during the listing period.

7. d) The deposit receipt is used to set forth the buyer's offer, and it also serves as the receipt for the good faith deposit. If the seller signs the form, it becomes a binding contract.

8. c) A deposit receipt should state all of the terms of sale, including the total purchase price, the method of payment, and the terms on which the buyer will finance the purchase. It is the parties' final contract, not a preliminary agreement.

9. a) A provision that makes a deposit receipt contingent on the occurrence of a certain event is called a contingency clause.

10. a) Under a land contract, the vendee (buyer) gets possession of the land right away, but does not acquire title until the purchase price is paid in full.

11. c) Though it is wise to have both the landlord and the tenant sign the lease, only the landlord needs to sign in order for it to be valid. By taking possession of the leased property and paying the rent, a tenant is presumed to have accepted the lease terms.

12. d) The buyer takes title to the leased property subject to the existing lease, and must abide by its terms.

13. a) Leases need not be in writing if they will be fully performed within one year after the agreement is made.

14. b) Under a graduated lease, rental payments increase at specified times over the term of the lease.

15. c) An assignee has primary liability for paying the rent to the landlord. The original tenant retains secondary liability for the rent.

Real Estate Agency Law

🏘 Chapter Overview

Agency is a special legal relationship that involves certain duties and liabilities. The law of agency governs many aspects of a real estate agent's relationships with clients and customers. The first part of this chapter explains what an agency relationship is and how one is created, and then discusses agency duties and liabilities. The second part of this chapter describes the various types of agency relationships that are possible in real estate transactions. Agency disclosure requirements and the broker/salesperson relationship are also covered.

Introduction to Agency

We'll begin our discussion of real estate agency with some basic definitions and some information about the framework of agency law.

The Agency Relationship

An agency relationship arises when one person authorizes another to represent him or her, subject to his or her control, in dealings with third parties. The parties in an agency relationship are the **agent**, the person authorized to represent another, and the **principal**, the party who authorizes and controls the actions of the agent. Persons outside the agency relationship who seek to deal with the principal through the agent are called **third parties**.

There is usually an agency relationship between a property seller and the real estate broker with whom the seller has listed the property. The seller is the principal, who employs the broker to act as his or her agent. The broker/agent represents the seller/principal's interests in negotiations with potential buyers/third parties. The seller/principal is referred to as the broker's client.

A buyer may also have an agency relationship with a broker, who is hired to locate a particular kind of property and negotiate its purchase. The broker is the buyer's agent, and the buyer is that broker's principal.

There is also an agency relationship between a broker and the salespersons who work for the broker. In other words, a real estate salesperson is his or her broker's agent.

Agency Law

An agency relationship has significant legal implications. For a third party, dealing with the agent can be the legal equivalent of dealing with the principal. For instance, when an agent who is authorized to do so signs a document or makes a promise, it's as if the principal signed or promised. And in some cases, if the agent does something wrong, the principal may be held liable to third parties for harm resulting from the agent's actions.

Those rules are part of general agency law, a body of law that applies to agency relationships in nearly any context. For example, it governs the relationship between lawyer and client, or between trustee and beneficiary. It also applies to the relationship between a real estate agent and a home buyer or seller.

Creating an Agency Relationship

No particular formalities are required to create an agency relationship; the only requirement is the consent of both parties. Under general agency law, an agency relationship may be formed in four ways: by express agreement, by ratification, by estoppel, or by implication.

Express Agreement

Most agencies are created by express agreement: the principal appoints someone to act as his or her agent, and the agent accepts the appointment. The agreement does not need to be in writing in order to create a valid agency relationship.

The agency agreement also does not have to be supported by consideration. Agency rights, responsibilities, and liabilities arise even when the principal has no contractual obligation to compensate the agent for the services rendered.

For example, if a broker doesn't have a written listing agreement with a seller, the broker cannot sue the seller for compensation. Yet even without a written agreement, the broker still may be the seller's agent, with all of the duties and liabilities that agency entails.

Ratification

An agency is created by ratification when the principal gives approval after the fact to acts performed by:

- a person who is without authority to act for the principal, or
- an agent whose actions exceed the authority granted by the principal.

The principal may ratify unauthorized acts expressly, or by accepting the benefits of the acts. For example, if the principal accepts a contract offer negotiated by someone who wasn't authorized to negotiate on his or her behalf, the principal has ratified the agency.

Estoppel

Under the legal doctrine of estoppel, a person is not allowed to take a position that contradicts his or her previous conduct, if someone else has relied on the previous conduct. An agency can be created by estoppel when it would be unfair to a third party to deny the agent's authority, because the principal has allowed the third party to believe there was an agency relationship.

Implication

An agency may be created by implication when one person behaves toward another in a way that suggests or implies that he or she is acting as that other person's agent. If the other person reasonably believes that there is an agency relationship, and the supposed agent fails to correct that impression, he or she may owe the other person agency duties.

Although agency by implication resembles agency by estoppel, there's a significant difference between them. An agency by estoppel requires the principal to acknowledge that an agency relationship exists, to protect the interests of a third party. An agency by implication requires the agent to acknowledge that an agency relationship exists, to protect the principal's interests.

The Legal Effects of Agency

Once an agency relationship has been established, the principal is bound by acts of the agent that are within the scope of the agent's actual or apparent authority. Under general agency law, the principal may be held liable for harm caused by the agent's negligent or wrongful acts. In addition, the principal may be held to know information that is known to the agent. We will examine each of these legal effects of agency in turn.

Scope of Authority

The extent to which the principal can be bound by the agent's actions depends first of all on the scope of authority granted to the agent. In California, there are two basic types of agents:

- general agents, and
- special agents.

A **general agent** is authorized to handle all of the principal's affairs in one or more specified areas. He or she has the authority to conduct a wide range of activities on an ongoing basis on behalf of the principal. For example, a business manager who has the authority to handle personnel matters, enter into contracts, and manage the day-to-day operations of the business is considered to be a general agent.

A **special agent** has limited authority to do a specific thing or conduct a specific transaction. For instance, an attorney who is hired to litigate a specific legal matter, such as a person's divorce, is a special agent.

In most cases, a real estate broker is a special agent, because the broker has only limited authority. A seller hires a broker to find a buyer for a particular piece of property, and the broker is only authorized to negotiate with third parties, not to sign a contract on the seller's behalf. A real estate broker can be granted broader powers, but usually is not.

Actual vs. Apparent Authority

An agent may have actual authority to perform an action on the principal's behalf, or else may have only apparent authority.

Actual authority is authority granted to the agent by the principal, either expressly or by implication. Express actual authority is communicated to the agent in express terms, either orally or in writing. Implied actual authority is the authority to do what is necessary to carry out actions that were expressly authorized.

Example: When a seller lists property with a broker, the broker is given express actual authority to find a buyer for the property. Based on custom in the real estate industry, the broker also has the implied actual authority to delegate certain tasks to a licensed salesperson. In contrast, the authority granted to the broker does not imply the power to enter into a contract or execute a deed on the seller's behalf.

A person has **apparent authority** when he or she has no actual authority to act, but the principal negligently or deliberately allows it to appear that the person's actions are authorized. In other words, the principal's words or conduct lead a third party to believe that this person (the **apparent agent** or **ostensible agent**) has authority to act on behalf of the principal. This type of authority corresponds to an agency created by estoppel, which was explained earlier.

A principal is bound by acts performed within the scope of an ostensible agent's apparent authority. However, declarations of the agent alone cannot establish apparent authority; the principal must be aware of the declarations or acts and make no effort to deny that they are authorized.

A third party has a duty, when dealing with an agent, to make a reasonable effort to discover the scope of the agent's authority. The third party will not be able to hold the principal liable when an agent acts beyond the scope of his or her actual authority and the principal's conduct does not indicate approval of those acts. When a contract between the principal and a third party limits the agent's authority to make representations, the third party is on notice that any representations made by the agent beyond the written terms of the agreement are unauthorized and not binding on the principal.

Here is an example of what can happen when an agent exceeds the authority granted by the principal.

Example: Before signing the listing agreement, the seller crossed out the provision that authorized the broker to "receipt for deposits"—that is, to accept good faith deposits from prospective buyers on the seller's behalf. If the broker exceeds her authority and accepts a deposit check from a buyer, then she is acting not as the seller's agent, but as the buyer's agent, in regard to the deposit. If the broker misappropriated the buyer's deposit, it would be the buyer's loss. (If the broker had specific written authorization from the seller to accept deposits, the seller would have to bear the loss.)

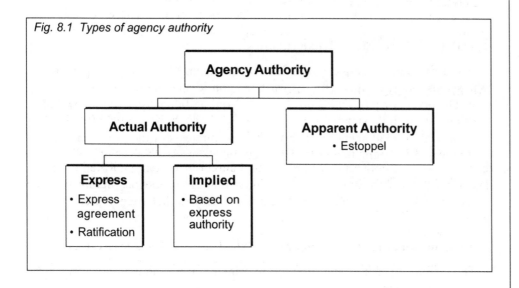

Fig. 8.1 Types of agency authority

Vicarious Liability

A **tort** is a negligent or intentional wrongful act involving breach of a duty imposed by law (as opposed to breach of a contractual duty). It is a mistake, accident, or misconduct that results in an injury or financial harm to another person. For example, negligent driving that results in an accident and injures another driver is a tort. Someone who commits a tort may be sued by the injured party and required to compensate him or her.

Under general agency law, a principal may be held liable for his or her agent's negligent or wrongful acts. This is referred to as **vicarious liability**. Thus, a real estate broker can be held liable for the acts of a salesperson who works for the broker. And a buyer or a seller can be held liable for the acts of his or her real estate broker.

Under the principle of vicarious liability, a buyer or a seller may also be held liable for the acts of a salesperson who is working for his or her broker. Unless an agent has no authority to employ other people to fulfill the terms of the agency, the principal may be legally responsible for the acts of the agent's agent. And a real estate broker is presumed to have the authority to employ a salesperson, because that's the standard practice in the industry. So a buyer or a seller can be held liable for a real estate salesperson's acts.

Imputed Knowledge

Under general agency law, a principal is considered to have notice of information that the agent has, even if the agent never actually tells the principal. In other words, the agent's knowledge is automatically imputed to the principal. As a result, the principal could be held liable for failing to disclose a problem to a third party, even if the agent never informed the principal of the problem.

Duties in an Agency Relationship

An agent owes certain duties to his or her principal, and both the agent and the principal have certain responsibilities to third parties.

The Agent's Duties to the Principal

An agency relationship is a **fiduciary** relationship. A fiduciary is a person who stands in a special position of trust and confidence in relation to someone else. The other party has a legal right to rely on the fiduciary, and the law holds the fiduciary to high standards of conduct.

As a fiduciary, an agent must serve the best interests of the principal. The agent owes the principal these fiduciary duties:

- reasonable care and skill,
- obedience and utmost good faith,
- accounting,
- loyalty, and
- disclosure of material facts.

These fiduciary duties are owed to the principal from the time the agency relationship begins, through the closing of the transaction.

Reasonable Care and Skill. An agent has a duty to use reasonable care and skill in the performance of his or her duties. If an agent claims to possess certain skills or abilities, the agent must act as a competent person having those skills and abilities would act. For example, a person who holds him or herself out as a real estate broker must exercise the care and skill that a competent broker would bring to the agency. If the broker (or the broker's salesperson) causes the principal harm due to carelessness or incompetence, the broker will be liable to the principal.

Obedience and Utmost Good Faith. The agent must obey the instructions of the principal and carry them out in good faith. The agent's acts must be in conformity with the purpose and intent of the instructions. A broker can be held liable for any loss caused by failure to obey the principal's instructions.

Accounting. The agent must account for any funds or other valuable items he or she receives on behalf of the principal. The agent is required to report to the principal on the status of those funds (called **trust funds**) and avoid mixing (**commingling**) them with his or her own money. In California, a real estate broker is required to deposit all trust funds in a special trust or escrow account to prevent improper use of the funds. California's trust fund requirements are discussed in Chapter 16.

Loyalty. The agency relationship is based on confidence, so loyalty is essential. The agent must place the principal's interests above the interests of a third party by refusing to reveal **confidential information**.

> **Example:** In negotiations with a prospective buyer, a seller's real estate agent should not reveal the seller's financial condition or willingness to accept less than the listing price, unless the seller has authorized such a disclosure.

Loyalty to the principal also means that the agent must not make any **secret profits** from the agency. For example, it is a breach of fiduciary duty for a broker to list a property for less than it is worth, secretly buy it through an intermediary, and then sell it for a profit. The California Real Estate Law prohibits a real estate agent from buying an interest in property from the principal (through a relative or friend, for example) without the full knowledge and consent of the principal.

Disclosure of Material Facts. The agent must inform the principal of any material facts that come to the agent's attention. Any fact that could influence the principal's judgment in the transaction must be revealed. For instance, if a seller's real estate agent discovers that a potential buyer is in a shaky financial situation, the agent must inform the seller, even if it means losing a sale and the subsequent commission.

It's important for an agent to remember that communication to the agent is deemed to be communication to the principal (this is the imputed knowledge rule we discussed earlier). If a third party provides information to the agent, in the eyes of the law the information has been provided to the principal, regardless of whether the agent actually told the principal. Thus, the principal may be held liable for failure to perform some required task the agent knew about but never communicated to the principal. However, the agent will in turn be liable to the principal for any loss caused by the failure to communicate information or disclose material facts.

A real estate agent representing a seller must be especially careful to avoid these disclosure problems:

- failure to present all offers,
- failure to inform the seller of the property's true value,
- failure to disclose any relationship between the agent and the buyer, and
- failure to reveal a dual agency.

A real estate agent must **present all offers** to the seller, regardless of how unacceptable a particular offer may appear to be. The principal, not the agent, decides whether or not to accept a particular offer. The agent should never hesitate to inform the principal of an offer, even if its acceptance would mean a smaller commission for the agent; the agent's first loyalty must be to the principal. Furthermore, an agent should present an offer even if the prospective buyer failed to submit a good faith deposit along with the offer.

A seller's agent is also required to inform the principal of the **property's true value**. It is not improper for a real estate agent to buy the principal's property with the principal's knowledge and consent, and then resell the property for a profit. But the agent must provide the principal with his or her estimate of the real value of the property before the property is sold. (Note that an ordinary buyer—an unlicensed person who is not acting as the seller's agent—is under no obligation to tell the seller that he or she plans to resell at a profit.)

The seller's agent must inform the principal if the agent has any **relationship with a buyer**—before the principal decides whether to accept the buyer's offer. If the buyer is a friend, relative, or business associate of the agent, or a company in which the agent has an interest, there may be a conflict of interest. The principal has a right to have this information when making his or her decision. The agent must also inform the principal if the agent plans to split the commission payment with the buyer.

In addition, the agent is required to reveal a **dual agency**. There is a dual agency when a real estate broker is employed by both the seller and the buyer in the same transaction. In most states, including California, dual agency is legal as long as the broker has fully informed and obtained the consent of both parties. However, a conflict of interest is inherent in a dual agency. A seller wants to get the highest possible price for the property, while the buyer wants to pay the lowest possible price. It is difficult, if not impossible, to adequately represent these two opposing interests simultaneously. Thus, a dual agency should be entered into with great caution, if at all.

To avoid some of the confusion regarding who is representing whom, many states require real estate brokers to provide sellers and buyers with an agency disclosure statement at some point before a binding purchase and sale agreement is entered into. California's agency disclosure rules are discussed later in this chapter.

The Agent's Duties to Third Parties

While agents owe utmost good faith and loyalty to their principals, this doesn't mean they can treat third parties with reckless disregard. In recent years, courts have held real estate agents to increasingly higher standards in their interactions with third parties.

A real estate agent owes a third party a duty of reasonable care and skill and a duty of good faith and fair dealing. In addition, in residential transactions there is a duty to inspect the property.

Reasonable Care and Skill. An agent must use reasonable care and skill in providing services to third parties as well as to the principal. If the agent's negligence or incompetence harms a third party, the agent may be liable.

Good Faith and Fair Dealing. Real estate agents must disclose all material facts about the property to the buyer, and they must avoid inaccuracies in their statements to prospective buyers. Any intentional material misrepresentation may constitute actual fraud, and even an unintentional misrepresentation may be considered constructive fraud or negligence. In either case, the buyer has the right to rescind the transaction and/or sue for damages.

Misrepresentations, which may be grounds for a lawsuit, should not be confused with mere opinions, predictions, or puffing. These are nonfactual or exaggerated statements that a buyer should realize he or she can't rely on. Since it isn't reasonable to rely on them, opinions, predictions, and puffing generally can't be the basis of a lawsuit.

> **Examples:**
>
> Opinion: "*I think this is the best buy on the market.*"
>
> Prediction: "*The properties in this neighborhood could double in value over the next ten years.*"
>
> Puffing: "*This is a dream house; it has a fabulous view.*"

It should be noted, however, that in California there is a growing tendency to treat these types of statements as representations of material facts. Unsophisticated buyers may rely on such statements and purchase property as a result of this reliance. All real estate agents should be wary of idle sales talk that could be construed as a statement of fact, such as the "prediction" given above of a property's dramatic increase in value.

Aside from avoiding misrepresentation, the seller and the seller's agent have a duty to disclose any known **latent defects** in the property to the buyer. A latent defect is one that is not discoverable by ordinary inspection.

> **Example:** The seller tells his real estate agent that the roof leaks in heavy rains. This is a latent defect that buyers who are shown the property in ordinary weather won't be able to see for themselves. The seller and the agent are legally required to disclose this problem.

There are some facts that do not have to be disclosed to a third party. State law specifically provides that a seller or a seller's real estate agent does not have to disclose that property was occupied by someone with AIDS. In fact, if a prospective buyer asks whether anyone with AIDS or HIV lived in a house, the agent should not answer the question. To do so could violate fair housing laws that prohibit discrimination based on disability (see Chapter 14).

California law also provides that a seller or a seller's agent need not disclose that someone died on the property more than three years earlier, no matter what the cause of death was. Naturally, though, if a prospective buyer asked about deaths on the property and the seller or the agent intentionally gave a false answer, they could be held liable for fraud.

Duty to Inspect. At one time, agents representing the seller were required only to pass on the seller's information about the property to prospective buyers; the law didn't require them to inspect the property and look for problems. Today, however, California law specifically imposes a duty of inspection on any agent who represents the seller of a one- to four-unit residential property, unless it's a new home in a subdivision offered for sale for the first time.

The agent must conduct a reasonably competent and diligent visual inspection of the property and disclose to prospective buyers any material information the inspection reveals. Stating that the property is for sale "as is" doesn't negate the agent's duty to inspect it and disclose material facts about its condition.

The agent is not required to inspect areas of the property that aren't reasonably accessible to visual inspection. In the case of a condominium or cooperative unit, the agent is only required to inspect the unit being sold. It should be noted that the agent's duty to inspect the property does not relieve buyers of the duty to use reasonable care to protect themselves.

Transfer Disclosure Statement. Any disclosures required as a result of an agent's property inspection are usually made in the appropriate section of the Real Estate Transfer Disclosure Statement, a form that must be presented to the prospective buyer in any transaction involving one- to four-unit residential property. The transfer disclosure statement is used to list the seller's disclosures concerning:

- what is included in the sale;
- any known defects in the property; and
- any other types of problems with the property, such as environmental hazards, structural changes made without appropriate permits, or neighborhood nuisances.

In addition, the form has separate sections to be filled out by the listing agent and the selling agent (the agent who obtains the buyer's offer). Each agent is required to make note of any material facts discovered in his or her own visual inspection of the property; the listing agent is also required to disclose material facts about the condition of the property learned from the seller. The selling agent is responsible for providing the completed disclosure statement to a prospective buyer.

It's important to remember that an agent should fill out only his or her own section of the form, not the seller's sections. Filling out those sections is the seller's responsibility. A sample Real Estate Transfer Disclosure Statement is shown in Figure 8.2.

The transfer disclosure statement should be delivered to the buyer as soon as possible. The law gives buyers three days from the time the disclosure statement is delivered (or five days from the time it is mailed) to rescind the purchase agreement, if they decide they don't want to purchase the property after all.

Some transactions involving one- to four-unit residential property do not require a transfer disclosure statement. These include transfers that occur as a result of a mortgage or deed of trust foreclosure, probate proceedings, divorce settlements, or other court orders. Sales of property in new subdivisions are also exempt.

Fig. 8.2 Transfer disclosure statement

CALIFORNIA
ASSOCIATION
OF REALTORS®

REAL ESTATE TRANSFER DISCLOSURE STATEMENT
(CALIFORNIA CIVIL CODE §1102, ET SEQ.)
(C.A.R. Form TDS, Revised 10/03)

THIS DISCLOSURE STATEMENT CONCERNS THE REAL PROPERTY SITUATED IN THE CITY OF _____
_____, COUNTY OF _____, STATE OF CALIFORNIA,
DESCRIBED AS _____.
THIS STATEMENT IS A DISCLOSURE OF THE CONDITION OF THE ABOVE DESCRIBED PROPERTY IN COMPLIANCE
WITH SECTION 1102 OF THE CIVIL CODE AS OF (date) _____. IT IS NOT A WARRANTY OF ANY
KIND BY THE SELLER(S) OR ANY AGENT(S) REPRESENTING ANY PRINCIPAL(S) IN THIS TRANSACTION, AND IS
NOT A SUBSTITUTE FOR ANY INSPECTIONS OR WARRANTIES THE PRINCIPAL(S) MAY WISH TO OBTAIN.

I. COORDINATION WITH OTHER DISCLOSURE FORMS

This Real Estate Transfer Disclosure Statement is made pursuant to Section 1102 of the Civil Code. Other statutes require disclosures,
depending upon the details of the particular real estate transaction (for example: special study zone and purchase-money liens on
residential property).

Substituted Disclosures: The following disclosures and other disclosures required by law, including the Natural Hazard Disclosure
Report/Statement that may include airport annoyances, earthquake, fire, flood, or special assessment information, have or will be made
in connection with this real estate transfer, and are intended to satisfy the disclosure obligations on this form, where the subject matter
is the same:

☐   Inspection reports completed pursuant to the contract of sale or receipt for deposit.
☐   Additional inspection reports or disclosures: _____
_____

II. SELLER'S INFORMATION

The Seller discloses the following information with the knowledge that even though this is not a warranty, prospective
Buyers may rely on this information in deciding whether and on what terms to purchase the subject property. Seller hereby
authorizes any agent(s) representing any principal(s) in this transaction to provide a copy of this statement to any person or
entity in connection with any actual or anticipated sale of the property.

**THE FOLLOWING ARE REPRESENTATIONS MADE BY THE SELLER(S) AND ARE NOT THE
REPRESENTATIONS OF THE AGENT(S), IF ANY. THIS INFORMATION IS A DISCLOSURE AND IS NOT
INTENDED TO BE PART OF ANY CONTRACT BETWEEN THE BUYER AND SELLER.**

Seller ☐ is ☐ is not occupying the property.

A. The subject property has the items checked below (read across):

☐ Range	☐ Oven	☐ Microwave
☐ Dishwasher	☐ Trash Compactor	☐ Garbage Disposal
☐ Washer/Dryer Hookups		☐ Rain Gutters
☐ Burglar Alarms	☐ Smoke Detector(s)	☐ Fire Alarm
☐ TV Antenna	☐ Satellite Dish	☐ Intercom
☐ Central Heating	☐ Central Air Conditioning	☐ Evaporator Cooler(s)
☐ Wall/Window Air Conditioning	☐ Sprinklers	☐ Public Sewer System
☐ Septic Tank	☐ Sump Pump	☐ Water Softener
☐ Patio/Decking	☐ Built-in Barbecue	☐ Gazebo
☐ Sauna		
☐ Hot Tub	☐ Pool	☐ Spa
☐ Locking Safety Cover*	☐ Child Resistant Barrier*	☐ Locking Safety Cover*
☐ Security Gate(s)	☐ Automatic Garage Door Opener(s)*	☐ Number Remote Controls ____
Garage: ☐ Attached	☐ Not Attached	☐ Carport
Pool/Spa Heater: ☐ Gas	☐ Solar	☐ Electric
Water Heater: ☐ Gas	☐ Water Heater Anchored, Braced, or Strapped*	
Water Supply: ☐ City	☐ Well	☐ Private Utility or
Gas Supply: ☐ Utility	☐ Bottled	Other_____
☐ Window Screens	☐ Window Security Bars ☐ Quick Release Mechanism on Bedroom Windows*	

Exhaust Fan(s) in _____ 220 Volt Wiring in _____ Fireplace(s) in _____
☐ Gas Starter _____ ☐ Roof(s): Type: _____ Age: _____ (approx.)
☐ Other: _____
Are there, to the best of your (Seller's) knowledge, any of the above that are not in operating condition? ☐ Yes ☐ No. If yes, then
describe. (Attach additional sheets if necessary): _____
_____

(*see footnote on page 2)

TDS REVISED 10/03 (PAGE 1 OF 3) Print Date

Buyer's Initials (_____)(_____)
Seller's Initials (_____)(_____)

Reviewed by _____ Date _____

EQUAL HOUSING
OPPORTUNITY

REAL ESTATE TRANSFER DISCLOSURE STATEMENT (TDS PAGE 1 OF 3)

Property Address: _____ Date: _____

B. Are you (Seller) aware of any significant defects/malfunctions in any of the following? ☐ Yes ☐ No. If yes, check appropriate
space(s) below.
☐ Interior Walls ☐ Ceilings ☐ Floors ☐ Exterior Walls ☐ Insulation ☐ Roof(s) ☐ Windows ☐ Doors ☐ Foundation ☐ Slab(s)
☐ Driveways ☐ Sidewalks ☐ Walls/Fences ☐ Electrical Systems ☐ Plumbing/Sewers/Septics ☐ Other Structural Components
(Describe: _____
_____
_____
_____)

If any of the above is checked, explain. (Attach additional sheets if necessary.): _____
_____
_____
_____
_____

*This garage door opener or child resistant pool barrier may not be in compliance with the safety standards relating to automatic reversing
devices as set forth in Chapter 12.5 (commencing with Section 19890) of Part 3 of Division 13 of, or with the pool safety standards of
Article 2.5 (commencing with Section 115920) of Chapter 5 of Part 10 of Division 104 of, the Health and Safety Code. The water heater
may not be anchored, braced, or strapped in accordance with Section 19211 of the Health and Safety Code. Window security bars may
not have quick release mechanisms in compliance with the 1995 edition of the California Building Standards Code.

C. Are you (Seller) aware of any of the following:
1. Substances, materials, or products which may be an environmental hazard such as, but not limited to, asbestos,
   formaldehyde, radon gas, lead-based paint, mold, fuel or chemical storage tanks, and contaminated soil or water
   on the subject property . . . . ☐ Yes ☐ No
2. Features of the property shared in common with adjoining landowners, such as walls, fences, and driveways,
   whose use or responsibility for maintenance may have an effect on the subject property . . . . ☐ Yes ☐ No
3. Any encroachments, easements or similar matters that may affect your interest in the subject property . . . . ☐ Yes ☐ No
4. Room additions, structural modifications, or other alterations or repairs made without necessary permits . . . . ☐ Yes ☐ No
5. Room additions, structural modifications, or other alterations or repairs not in compliance with building codes . . . ☐ Yes ☐ No
6. Fill (compacted or otherwise) on the property or any portion thereof . . . . ☐ Yes ☐ No
7. Any settling from any cause, or slippage, sliding, or other soil problems . . . . ☐ Yes ☐ No
8. Flooding, drainage or grading problems . . . . ☐ Yes ☐ No
9. Major damage to the property or any of the structures from fire, earthquake, floods, or landslides . . . . ☐ Yes ☐ No
10. Any zoning violations, nonconforming uses, violations of "setback" requirements . . . . ☐ Yes ☐ No
11. Neighborhood noise problems or other nuisances . . . . ☐ Yes ☐ No
12. CC&R's or other deed restrictions or obligations . . . . ☐ Yes ☐ No
13. Homeowners' Association which has any authority over the subject property . . . . ☐ Yes ☐ No
14. Any "common area" (facilities such as pools, tennis courts, walkways, or other areas co-owned in undivided
    interest with others) . . . . ☐ Yes ☐ No
15. Any notices of abatement or citations against the property . . . . ☐ Yes ☐ No
16. Any lawsuits by or against the Seller threatening to or affecting this real property, including any lawsuits alleging
    a defect or deficiency in this real property or "common areas" (facilities such as pools, tennis courts, walkways,
    or other areas co-owned in undivided interest with others) . . . . ☐ Yes ☐ No
If the answer to any of these is yes, explain. (Attach additional sheets if necessary.): _____
_____
_____
_____

Seller certifies that the information herein is true and correct to the best of the Seller's knowledge as of the date signed by the Seller.

Seller_____ Date _____

Seller_____ Date _____

TDS REVISED 10/03 (PAGE 2 OF 3)

Buyer's Initials (_____)(_____)

Reviewed by _____ Date _____   EQUAL HOUSING OPPORTUNITY

REAL ESTATE TRANSFER DISCLOSURE STATEMENT (TDS PAGE 2 OF 3)

Property Address: _____ Date: _____

III. AGENT'S INSPECTION DISCLOSURE
(To be completed only if the Seller is represented by an agent in this transaction.)

THE UNDERSIGNED, BASED ON THE ABOVE INQUIRY OF THE SELLER(S) AS TO THE CONDITION OF THE PROPERTY AND BASED ON A REASONABLY COMPETENT AND DILIGENT VISUAL INSPECTION OF THE ACCESSIBLE AREAS OF THE PROPERTY IN CONJUNCTION WITH THAT INQUIRY, STATES THE FOLLOWING:

☐ Agent notes no items for disclosure.

☐ Agent notes the following items: _____
_____
_____
_____
_____

Agent (Broker Representing Seller) _____ By _____ Date _____
                   (Please Print)   (Associate Licensee or Broker Signature)

IV. AGENT'S INSPECTION DISCLOSURE
(To be completed only if the agent who has obtained the offer is other than the agent above.)

THE UNDERSIGNED, BASED ON A REASONABLY COMPETENT AND DILIGENT VISUAL INSPECTION OF THE ACCESSIBLE AREAS OF THE PROPERTY, STATES THE FOLLOWING:

☐ Agent notes no items for disclosure.

☐ Agent notes the following items: _____
_____
_____
_____
_____

Agent (Broker Obtaining the Offer) _____ By _____ Date _____
                  (Please Print)   (Associate Licensee or Broker Signature)

V. BUYER(S) AND SELLER(S) MAY WISH TO OBTAIN PROFESSIONAL ADVICE AND/OR INSPECTIONS OF THE PROPERTY AND TO PROVIDE FOR APPROPRIATE PROVISIONS IN A CONTRACT BETWEEN BUYER AND SELLER(S) WITH RESPECT TO ANY ADVICE/INSPECTIONS/DEFECTS.

I/WE ACKNOWLEDGE RECEIPT OF A COPY OF THIS STATEMENT.

Seller _____ Date _____ Buyer _____ Date _____

Seller _____ Date _____ Buyer _____ Date _____

Agent (Broker Representing Seller) _____ By _____ Date _____
         (Please Print)   (Associate Licensee or Broker Signature)

Agent (Broker Obtaining the Offer) _____ By _____ Date _____
         (Please Print)   (Associate Licensee or Broker Signature)

SECTION 1102.3 OF THE CIVIL CODE PROVIDES A BUYER WITH THE RIGHT TO RESCIND A PURCHASE CONTRACT FOR AT LEAST THREE DAYS AFTER THE DELIVERY OF THIS DISCLOSURE IF DELIVERY OCCURS AFTER THE SIGNING OF AN OFFER TO PURCHASE. IF YOU WISH TO RESCIND THE CONTRACT, YOU MUST ACT WITHIN THE PRESCRIBED PERIOD.

A REAL ESTATE BROKER IS QUALIFIED TO ADVISE ON REAL ESTATE. IF YOU DESIRE LEGAL ADVICE, CONSULT YOUR ATTORNEY.

SURE TRAC
The System for Success™

Published by the
California Association of REALTORS®

| Reviewed by _____ Date _____ |

EQUAL HOUSING OPPORTUNITY

TDS REVISED 10/03 (PAGE 3 OF 3)

REAL ESTATE TRANSFER DISCLOSURE STATEMENT (TDS PAGE 3 OF 3)

Natural Hazards Disclosure. A Natural Hazards Disclosure Statement is used to disclose whether a property is in an area or zone that has been designated as especially subject to flooding, wildfires, or earthquakes. The disclosure must be based on maps drawn by state or federal authorities, not just the seller or agent's own knowledge.

Whether or not the property is in an earthquake fault zone, a buyer purchasing a home built before 1960 using light-frame construction must be given a Homeowner's Guide to Earthquake Safety. If improvements suggested in the booklet have not been made, that must be disclosed to the buyer.

Lead-based Paint Disclosures. Transactions that involve housing built before 1978 are subject to a federal law concerning lead-based paint, which is a health hazard to children. This law requires a seller or a landlord to disclose the location of any lead-based paint he or she is aware of in the home or in any common areas; provide a copy of any report concerning lead-based paint in the home, if it has been inspected; and give buyers or tenants a copy of a pamphlet on lead-based paint prepared by the U.S. Environmental Protection Agency.

In addition, buyers (though not tenants) must be offered at least a ten-day period in which to have the home tested for lead-based paint.

The purchase agreement or lease must include specific warnings and signed statements from the parties acknowledging that the requirements of this law were fulfilled. The acknowledgments must be kept for at least three years.

Breach of Duty

If a licensee breaches any duties owed to either a principal or a third party, it is considered a tort. (A tort, as we explained earlier, is a wrongful act resulting from a breach of a duty imposed by law.) The party injured by the tort, whether it is the principal or a third party, is then entitled to sue for redress.

The most common remedy in a tort suit is compensatory damages. A court will order the licensee to compensate the injured party for the financial loss the injured party suffered. This might include repaying any commission collected in a transaction. The injured party may also be allowed to rescind the transaction.

If a broker misrepresents property to a buyer, the buyer can sue the broker in a tort action. In addition, the buyer can sue the broker's principal, the seller. That's because, according to the principle of vicarious liability, a principal is liable for torts committed by the agent within the scope of his or her agency. So the seller could be held liable to the buyer even if the seller was not aware of the broker's misrepresentations. An innocent seller who has been held liable for the broker's misconduct could, in turn, sue the broker.

Most breaches of duty by a licensee are also violations of the California Real Estate Law. The Department of Real Estate may take disciplinary action against the licensee even if the injured party doesn't pursue a lawsuit. Disciplinary action may include fines as well as license suspension or revocation (see Chapter 16).

Terminating an Agency

Once an agency relationship has terminated, the agent is no longer authorized to represent the principal. Under general agency law, an agency may be terminated either by acts of the parties or by operation of law.

Termination by Acts of the Parties

The ways in which the parties can terminate an agency relationship include:

- mutual agreement,
- revocation by the principal, and
- renunciation by the agent.

Mutual Agreement. The parties may terminate the agency by mutual agreement at any time. If the original agreement was in writing, the termination agreement should also be in writing.

Principal Revokes. The principal may revoke the agency by firing the agent whenever he or she wishes. (Remember that an agency relationship requires the consent of both parties.) However, in some cases revoking an agency breaches a contractual agreement, and the principal may be liable for any damages suffered by the agent because of the breach.

An **agency coupled with an interest** cannot be revoked. An agency is coupled with an interest if the agent has a financial interest in the subject matter of the agency. For instance, if a real estate licensee co-owns a property with other people, and they've authorized him to represent them in selling the property, it's an agency coupled with an interest. The co-owners can't revoke it.

Agent Renounces. An agent can renounce the agency at any time. Like revocation, renunciation may be a breach of contract, in which case the agent could be liable for the principal's damages resulting from the breach. But since an agency contract is a personal services contract (the agent has agreed to provide personal services to the principal), the principal could not demand specific performance as a remedy. The courts will not force a person to perform personal services, because that would violate the constitutional prohibition against involuntary servitude.

Termination by Operation of Law

Several events terminate an agency relationship automatically, without action by either party. These events include:

- expiration of the agency term,
- fulfillment of the purpose of the agency,
- the death or incapacity of either party, and
- extinction of the subject matter.

Expiration of Agency Term. An agency terminates automatically when its term expires. If the agency agreement did not include an expiration date, it is deemed to expire within a reasonable time (which would vary, depending on the type of agency in question). If there is no expiration date, either party may terminate the agency without liability for damages, although the other party might be able to demand reimbursement for expenses incurred before the termination.

Fulfillment of Purpose. An agency relationship terminates when its purpose has been fulfilled. For example, if a broker is hired to sell the principal's property and the broker does so, the agency is terminated by fulfillment.

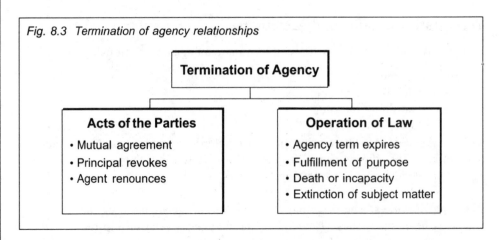

Fig. 8.3 Termination of agency relationships

Termination of Agency

Acts of the Parties	**Operation of Law**
• Mutual agreement	• Agency term expires
• Principal revokes	• Fulfillment of purpose
• Agent renounces	• Death or incapacity
	• Extinction of subject matter

Death or Incapacity. An agency is terminated before it expires if either the agent or the principal dies. Most states provide that the agency also terminates if either party becomes mentally incompetent. Generally, the agent has no authority to act after the death or incapacity of the principal, even if the agent is unaware of the principal's death or incapacity.

Extinction of Subject Matter. The subject matter of a real estate agency is the property in question. If the property is in any way extinguished (for example, sold or destroyed), the agency automatically terminates.

Real Estate Agency Relationships

A typical residential real estate transaction is likely to involve more than one real estate agent. Someone who wants to find a home in a particular area contacts a real estate broker's office in that area. One of the salespersons who works for that broker will interview the prospective buyer to find out what kind of a home he or she wants and can afford, and then will show the buyer various suitable properties. Most brokers belong to a multiple listing service, so the salesperson will show the buyer not only homes that are listed directly with his or her own broker, but also homes that are listed with other MLS members. If the buyer becomes interested in a particular home, negotiations for the purchase of that home will involve the listing agent as well as the salesperson who has been showing properties to the buyer.

Meanwhile, other real estate agents may be showing the same house to other prospective buyers. By the time the transaction closes, it may involve a listing broker, a listing salesperson, a selling broker, and a selling salesperson, in addition to other cooperating agents who showed the home to buyers who didn't want it or didn't offer enough for it.

Understanding the agency relationships in this transaction means understanding which party each of these real estate licensees is representing. As a first step, you should be familiar with all of the following terms.

- **Real estate agent:** Real estate agent is the generic term used to refer to real estate licensees. Real estate brokers are the only real estate agents who are authorized to represent a buyer or a seller directly; real estate salespersons act on behalf of their real estate brokers.

- **Client:** A client is a person who has engaged the services of an agent. A client may be a real estate seller, buyer, landlord, or tenant.

- **Customer:** In transactions where the agent is representing a seller or a landlord, third parties are sometimes referred to as customers. A customer may be a buyer or a tenant.

- **Listing agent:** Either the listing salesperson or the listing broker may be referred to as the listing agent. The listing salesperson is the salesperson who takes the listing on a home. (He or she may or may not be the one who eventually procures a buyer for the listed home.) The listing broker is the broker that the listing salesperson works for.

- **Selling agent:** Either the selling salesperson or the selling broker may be referred to as the selling agent. The selling salesperson is the salesperson who procures a buyer for a property. (He or she may or may not have taken the listing for the property sold.) The selling broker is the broker that the selling salesperson works for.

- **Cooperating agent:** A cooperating agent is a licensee who did not take the listing on the property and who attempts to find a buyer. (The cooperating agent who succeeds in procuring a buyer is then the selling agent.)

- **In-house sale:** A sale in which the buyer and the seller are brought together by salespersons working for the same broker.

- **Cooperative sale:** A sale in which the listing agent and the selling agent work for different brokers.

Agency Relationships: A Historical Perspective

In the 1980s, various organizations, including the Federal Trade Commission, the National Association of Realtors®, and the Association of Real Estate License Law Officials, conducted studies of agency representation in real estate transactions. Those organizations concluded that many real estate buyers and sellers were confused about which party the real estate agent represented. Buyers, in particular, appeared bewildered by the rules of real estate agency. They often thought the real estate agent that they were working with was representing them, when in fact the agent was almost always representing the seller.

Unilateral Offer of Subagency. This confusion was based on a standard provision found in most listing agreements. This provision stated that any member of the multiple listing service who found a buyer for a listed property automatically represented the seller. In other words, the selling broker was considered to be a **subagent** of the seller. (A subagent is an agent of an agent.) This listing provision was referred to as a "unilateral offer of subagency."

As long as this provision remained in listing agreements, it was difficult to enter into a buyer agency relationship. In order to represent a buyer in a particular MLS transaction, a licensee had to reject the offer of subagency in a timely fashion and then enter into a separate written agreement with the buyer. Thus, nearly all licensees represented the seller.

Inadvertent Dual Agency. Under these circumstances, it was easy for a buyer to mistakenly believe that the selling agent was acting as the buyer's agent, not the seller's. After all, the selling agent was working with the buyer on a continuous and usually friendly basis. The agent would often encourage the buyer's loyalty by going out of his or her way to meet the buyer's needs. As a result, the buyer often told the selling agent confidential information. Yet because the selling agent was representing the seller, he or she had a duty to pass along that confidential information to the seller. If the agent fulfilled that responsibility, the buyer might well be surprised and dismayed. But in many cases, the selling agent would let his or her natural desire to help the buyer interfere with the fiduciary duties owed to the seller. This confusion caused trouble for everyone, and sometimes resulted in the creation of an inadvertent dual agency.

> **Example:** Martinez was a salesperson working for Baker Realty. Over the course of several weeks, she showed the Greens many homes. Martinez liked the Greens and worked very hard to find them a good house. She gave them advice about purchasing a home and discussed their financial situation with them. Understandably, the Greens believed that Martinez was their agent. But Martinez did not have an agency agreement with the Greens, and that meant (under the traditional presumption) that she was acting in the capacity of a seller's agent.
>
> The Greens decided to make an offer on a house listed by Broker Rush. They were very excited about the house, and they told Martinez that they were willing to pay full price for it. Nevertheless, they wanted to start out with an offer that was $5,000 less than the listing price.
>
> If Martinez failed to disclose to the seller that the Greens were willing to pay the full listing price, it would be a breach of her duty of loyalty to the seller. However, her conduct had caused the Greens to believe that she was representing them. Thus, if Martinez did disclose this information to the seller, the Greens could claim that she had breached her duty of loyalty to them. And because she was inadvertently acting as agent for both parties, both could claim that she acted as a dual agent without their consent.

Cooperation and Compensation. In the 1990s, as new legal requirements and various other considerations made real estate transactions more complex, buyers became more interested in having their own agents to represent them. In response to the growing popularity of buyer agency, many multiple listing services replaced the unilateral offer of subagency in their listing agreements with a "cooperation and compensation" provision. Under the terms of this provision, other members of the MLS act only as cooperating agents, not as subagents. A cooperating agent is simply any member of the MLS who attempts to find a buyer; the listing agreement does not set any type of agency relationship for a cooperating agent. It becomes up to each individual cooperating agent to decide whether he or she will represent the seller or the buyer in a given transaction.

Disclosure Laws. In an effort to reduce confusion over agency representation, many states have passed agency disclosure laws—laws that require real estate agents to disclose to both the buyer and the seller which party they are representing in a transaction. (California's disclosure requirements are explained at the end of this chapter.) But even agency disclosures do not always prevent problems. Real estate agents must understand the consequences of the different types of agency relationships and learn to avoid the pitfalls that certain situations present.

Fig. 8.4 Types of real estate agency relationships

Types of Agency Relationships

There are few restrictions on which party a real estate agent may represent. Generally, the types of agency relationships can be divided into the following categories:

- seller agency,
- buyer agency, and
- dual agency.

Seller Agency. As we have seen, traditionally, real estate agents nearly always represented the seller. While buyer agency is now also common, seller agency is still the most prevalent type of real estate agency relationship.

Seller agency relationships are typically created with a listing agreement (discussed in Chapter 7). Under the terms of the listing agreement, the primary task of a seller's agent is to find a buyer for the seller's property at a price that is acceptable to the seller. To accomplish this, the seller's agent advises the seller about preparing the property for sale, helps the seller decide on the listing price, markets the property to advantage, and negotiates on the seller's behalf with selling agents and buyers.

A seller agency relationship can also be created by the words or conduct of the parties, although the broker will be prevented from suing for a commission if there is no written listing agreement. (See the discussion of implied agency earlier in this chapter.)

Seller's Agents and Buyers. Throughout a transaction, a seller's agent must use his or her best efforts to promote the interests of the seller. Yet the seller's agent may also provide some services to a prospective buyer. For example, the seller's agent may help a buyer who doesn't have his or her own agent fill out a purchase offer form and apply for financing. These services are considered to be in the best interests of the seller, and thus do not violate the agent's duties to the seller. Of course, the seller's agent must disclose to the buyer that he or she is acting as the seller's agent.

A seller's agent must be very careful to treat the buyer fairly, but the agent must not act as if he or she is representing the buyer. In other words, the agent must fully disclose all known material facts and answer the buyer's questions honestly. However, the agent should not give the buyer advice, such as suggesting how much to offer for the listed property.

Example: Harrison, who works for Broker Yates, recently listed Taylor's house. The listing price is $315,000, but Harrison has reason to believe that Taylor would accept an offer of $305,000. Harrison shows the listed house to Markham, who asks Harrison, "How low do you think the seller will go?" Harrison should make it clear to Markham that he is representing Taylor and cannot divulge confidential information to Markham. If he were to do so, Taylor could sue Harrison's broker for breach of agency duties.

The situation in which the problem of inadvertent dual agency is most likely to come up is when the listing agent (who always represents the seller) is the one who finds a buyer for the property. This is especially true if the listing agent has had a previous agency relationship with the buyer. It may be difficult for the agent to represent the seller's interests without feeling some loyalty to the buyer as well.

Example: After Harrison finds a buyer for Taylor's house, Taylor asks Harrison to help him find another home. Harrison shows Taylor one of his own listings, a house owned by a seller named Woods.

Under these circumstances, it would be easy for Taylor to think that Harrison is acting as his agent. However, because of the listing agreement with Woods, Harrison is the seller's agent, and he should emphasize this fact to Taylor. Taylor should be reminded that Harrison is obligated to disclose material information that Taylor tells him to the seller, and that in all negotiations Harrison will be representing the seller's best interests.

Buyer Agency. Many buyers are content with the traditional seller agency relationship, as long as it is fully disclosed. They use the services of a real estate agent because they want access to multiple listing inventory, complete and honest information about properties, and someone to present their offers to sellers. The seller agency relationship often satisfies those requirements nicely, and buyers do not have to commit to a buyer agency relationship to get the help they need. Quite often, however, buyers want more than the services a seller's real estate agent can provide to a customer. Some buyers want advice on property values and help in determining how much to offer for a particular house. They want someone to help them negotiate the terms of the sale and give them advice on confidential matters. For those buyers, a buyer agency relationship is usually the answer.

Advantages of Buyer Agency. The advantages of buyer agency include confidentiality and loyalty, objective advice, help with negotiations, and access to more homes.

A buyer's agent owes agency duties to the buyer, including the duties of confidentiality and loyalty. For many buyers, these two duties make up the most important advantage of buyer agency.

Example: Broker Mendez is helping Buyer Jackson find a home. He shows Jackson many houses, and there are two that interest her. One is a large fixer-upper selling for $345,000. The other is a small, newer house in mint condition selling for $330,000. Because Mendez must put Jackson's interests before his own, he advises her to purchase the smaller house because it better suits her needs. He does so even though he would earn a bigger commission if she bought the more expensive house.

Mendez advises Jackson to offer $324,900 for the $330,000 house. Jackson agrees to, although she tells Mendez that she is willing to pay the full listing price. Because

Mendez is Jackson's agent, he is obligated to keep that confidential. If he were the seller's agent, he would be required to disclose that information to the seller.

A buyer's agent can be relied upon to give the buyer objective advice about the pros and cons of purchasing a particular home. He or she will point out various issues the buyer should be aware of, such as energy costs, the need for future repairs, and property value trends. By contrast, a seller's agent will present the property in the most positive light and may use expert sales techniques to convince the buyer to sign on the dotted line.

Buyers often feel uncomfortable negotiating for a property, especially one they really want to buy. They may be afraid to make a mistake through ignorance, or they may feel pressured to make a high offer quickly before someone else snaps up the property. A buyer's agent can use his or her negotiating skills and intimate knowledge of the real estate market to help the buyer get the property on the best possible terms.

A buyer's agent may arrange to be compensated if the buyer purchases any home, even one that isn't listed with a broker. So a buyer's agent may pursue less traditional means of searching for properties, and show the buyer properties that are for sale by owner, properties with open listings, and properties in foreclosure or probate proceedings.

Creation of Buyer Agency. A buyer and a broker may enter into a buyer agency relationship by executing a written **representation agreement**. (An example is shown in Figure 8.5.) While the terms of buyer representation agreements vary, they generally include the following:

- the duration of the agency,
- the general characteristics of the property the buyer wants,
- the price range,
- the conditions under which a fee will be earned,
- who will pay the fee, and
- a description of the broker's duties.

Buyer's Agent's Compensation. There are a variety of ways in which a buyer's agent may be compensated. The three most common are:

- a retainer,
- a seller-paid fee, and/or
- a buyer-paid fee.

A **retainer** is a fee paid up front before services are provided. Some buyer's agents collect a retainer when they enter into a buyer agency relationship, to ensure that their services won't go entirely uncompensated. The retainer is usually nonrefundable, but it will be credited against any fee or commission that the agent becomes entitled to.

In many cases, a buyer's agent is paid by the seller through a **commission split**. The commission split is based on a provision found in most MLS listing agreements, whereby any cooperating broker who procures a buyer is entitled to the selling broker's portion of the commission, regardless of which party that cooperating broker represents. Note that the source of the agent's commission does not determine the identity of his or her principal; accepting a seller-paid fee does not create agency duties owed to the seller.

Fig. 8.5 Buyer representation agreement

**CALIFORNIA
ASSOCIATION
OF REALTORS®**

BUYER BROKER AGREEMENT - EXCLUSIVE
Right To Represent
(C.A.R. Form BBE, Revised 10/04)

1. **EXCLUSIVE RIGHT TO REPRESENT:** _____ ("Buyer")
    grants _____ ("Broker")
    beginning on (date) _____ and ending at: **(i)** 11:59 p.m. on (date) _____ , or
    (ii) completion of a resulting transaction, whichever occurs first ("Representation Period"), the exclusive and irrevocable right, on the
    terms specified in this Agreement, to represent Buyer in acquiring real property or a manufactured home. Broker agrees to exercise
    due diligence and reasonable efforts to fulfill the following authorizations and obligations. Broker will perform its obligations under
    this Agreement through the individual signing for Broker below, who is either Broker individually or an associate-licensee (an
    individual licensed as a real estate salesperson or broker who works under Broker's real estate license). Buyer agrees that Broker's
    duties are limited by the terms of this Agreement, including those limitations set forth in paragraphs 5 and 6.
2. **AGENCY RELATIONSHIPS:**
    A. **DISCLOSURE:** If the property described in paragraph 4 includes residential property with one-to-four dwelling units, Buyer
        acknowledges receipt of the "Disclosure Regarding Real Estate Agency Relationships" form prior to entering into this
        Agreement.
    B. **BUYER REPRESENTATION:** Broker will represent, as described in this Agreement, Buyer in any resulting transaction.
    C. **(1) POSSIBLE DUAL AGENCY WITH SELLER:** (C(1) APPLIES UNLESS C(2)(i) or (ii) is checked below.)
        Depending on the circumstances, it may be necessary or appropriate for Broker to act as an agent for both Buyer and a seller,
        exchange party, or one or more additional parties ("Seller"). Broker shall, as soon as practicable, disclose to Buyer any election
        to act as a dual agent representing both Buyer and Seller. If Buyer is shown property listed with Broker, Buyer consents to
        Broker becoming a dual agent representing both Buyer and Seller with respect to those properties. In event of dual agency,
        Buyer agrees that: **(a)** Broker, without the prior written consent of Buyer, will not disclose to Seller that the Buyer is willing to
        pay a price greater than the price offered; **(b)** Broker, without the prior written consent of Seller, will not disclose to Buyer that
        Seller is willing to sell property at a price less than the listing price; and **(c)** other than as set forth in (a) and (b) above, a dual
        agent is obligated to disclose known facts materially affecting the value or desirability of the Property to both parties.
        OR **(2) SINGLE AGENCY ONLY:** (APPLIES ONLY IF (i) or (ii) is checked below.)
        ☐ **(i) Broker's firm lists properties for sale:** Buyer understands that this election will prevent Broker from showing Buyer
        those properties that are listed with Broker's firm or from representing Buyer in connection with those properties. Buyer's
        acquisition of a property listed with Broker's firm shall not affect Broker's right to be compensated under paragraph 3. In any
        resulting transaction in which Seller's property is not listed with Broker's firm, Broker will be the exclusive agent of Buyer and
        not a dual agent also representing Seller.
        OR ☐ **(ii) Broker's firm DOES NOT list property:** Entire brokerage firm only represents buyers and does not list property. In any
        resulting transaction, Broker will be the exclusive agent of Buyer and not a dual agent also representing Seller.
    D. **OTHER POTENTIAL BUYERS:** Buyer understands that other potential buyers may, through Broker, consider, make offers on
        or acquire the same or similar properties as those Buyer is seeking to acquire. Buyer consents to Broker's representation of
        such other potential buyers before, during and after the Representation Period, or any extension thereof.
    E. **CONFIRMATION:** If the Property includes residential property with one-to-four dwelling units, Broker shall confirm the agency
        relationship described above, or as modified, in writing, prior to or coincident with Buyer's execution of a Property Contract.
3. **COMPENSATION TO BROKER:**
    **NOTICE: The amount or rate of real estate commissions is not fixed by law. They are set by each Broker
    individually and may be negotiable between Buyer and Broker (real estate commissions include all
    compensation and fees to Broker).**
    Buyer agrees to pay to Broker, irrespective of agency relationship(s), as follows:
    A. **AMOUNT OF COMPENSATION: (Check (1), (2) or (3). Check only one.)**
        ☐ **(1)** _____ percent of the acquisition price AND (if checked ☐) $ _____ .
    OR ☐ **(2)** $ _____ .
    OR ☐ **(3)** Pursuant to the compensation schedule attached as an addendum _____ .
    B. **BROKER RIGHT TO COMPENSATION:** Broker shall be entitled to the compensation provided for in paragraph 3A:
        (1) If Buyer enters into an agreement to acquire property described in paragraph 4, on those terms or any other terms
        acceptable to Buyer during the Representation Period, or any extension thereof.
        (2) If, within _____ **calendar days** after expiration of the Representation Period or any extension thereof, Buyer enters into
        an agreement to acquire property described in paragraph 4, which property Broker introduced to Buyer, or for which Broker
        acted on Buyer's behalf. The obligation to pay compensation pursuant to this paragraph shall arise only if, prior to or within
        3 (or ☐ _____) calendar days after expiration of this Agreement or any extension thereof, Broker gives Buyer a written
        notice of those properties which Broker introduced to Buyer, or for which Broker acted on Buyer's behalf.

Buyer and Broker acknowledge receipt of a copy of this page.
Buyer's Initials (_____) (_____)
Broker's Initials (_____) (_____)

**EQUAL HOUSING
OPPORTUNITY**

BBE REVISED 10/04 (PAGE 1 OF 4)

Reviewed by _____ Date _____

BUYER BROKER AGREEMENT – EXCLUSIVE (BBE PAGE 1 OF 4)

Buyer: _____ Date: _____

C. **PAYMENT OF COMPENSATION:** Compensation is payable:
   (1) Upon completion of any resulting transaction, and if an escrow is used, through escrow.
   (2) If acquisition is prevented by default of Buyer, upon Buyer's default.
   (3) If acquisition is prevented by a party to the transaction other than Buyer, when Buyer collects damages by suit, settlement or otherwise. Compensation shall equal one-half of the damages recovered, not to exceed the compensation provided for in paragraph 3A, after first deducting the unreimbursed expenses of collection, if any.

D. **BUYER OBLIGATION TO PAY COMPENSATION:** Buyer is responsible for payment of compensation provided for in this Agreement. **However, if anyone other than Buyer compensates Broker for services covered by this Agreement, that amount shall be credited toward Buyer's obligation to pay compensation.** If the amount of compensation Broker receives from anyone other than Buyer exceeds Buyer's obligation, the excess amount shall be disclosed to Buyer and if allowed by law paid to Broker, or (if checked) ☐ credited to Buyer, or ☐ other _____

E. Buyer hereby irrevocably assigns to Broker the compensation provided for in paragraph 3A from Buyer's funds and proceeds in escrow. Buyer agrees to submit to escrow any funds needed to compensate Broker under this Agreement. Broker may submit this Agreement, as instructions to compensate Broker, to any escrow regarding property involving Buyer and a seller or other transferor.

F. **"BUYER"** includes any person or entity, other than Broker, related to Buyer or who in any manner acts on Buyer's behalf to acquire property described in paragraph 4.

G. **(1)** Buyer has not previously entered into a representation agreement with another broker regarding property described in paragraph 4, unless specified as follows (name other broker here): _____
   _____
   (2) Buyer warrants that Buyer has no obligation to pay compensation to any other broker regarding property described in paragraph 4, unless Buyer acquires the following property(ies): _____ .
   (3) If Buyer acquires a property specified in G(2) above during the time Buyer is obligated to compensate another broker, Broker is neither: (i) entitled to compensation under this Agreement, nor (ii) obligated to represent Buyer in such transaction.

4. **PROPERTY TO BE ACQUIRED:**
Any purchase, lease or other acquisition of any real property or manufactured home described as follows:
_____
_____
_____
Price range: $ _____ to $ _____

5. **BROKER AUTHORIZATIONS AND OBLIGATIONS:**
   A. Buyer authorizes Broker to: **(i)** locate and present selected properties to Buyer, present offers authorized by Buyer, and assist Buyer in negotiating for acceptance of such offers; **(ii)** assist Buyer with the financing process, including obtaining loan pre-qualification; **(iii)** upon request, provide Buyer with a list of professionals or vendors who perform the services described in the attached Buyer's Inspection Advisory; **(iv)** order reports, and schedule and attend meetings and appointments with professionals chosen by Buyer; **(v)** provide guidance to help Buyer with the acquisition of property; and **(vi)** obtain a credit report on Buyer.

   B. For property transactions of which Broker is aware and not precluded from participating in by Buyer, Broker shall provide and review forms to create a property contract ("Property Contract") for the acquisition of a specific property ("Property"). With respect to such Property, Broker shall: **(i)** if the Property contains residential property with one-to-four dwelling units, conduct a reasonably competent and diligent on-site visual inspection of the accessible areas of the Property (excluding any common areas), and disclose to Buyer all facts materially affecting the value or desirability of such Property that are revealed by this inspection; **(ii)** deliver or communicate to Buyer any disclosures, materials or information received by, in the personal possession of or personally known to the individual signing for Broker below during the Representation Period; and **(iii)** facilitate the escrow process, including assisting Buyer in negotiating with Seller. Unless otherwise specified in writing, any information provided through Broker in the course of representing Buyer has not been and will not be verified by Broker. Broker's services are performed in compliance with federal, state and local anti-discrimination laws.

6. **SCOPE OF BROKER DUTY:**
   A. While Broker will perform the duties described in paragraph 5B, Broker recommends that Buyer select other professionals, as described in the attached Buyer's Inspection Advisory, to investigate the Property through inspections, investigations, tests, surveys, reports, studies and other available information ("Inspections") during the transaction. Buyer agrees that these Inspections, to the extent they exceed the obligations described in paragraph 5B, are not within the scope of Broker's agency duties. Broker informs Buyer that it is in Buyer's best interest to obtain such Inspections.

   B. Buyer acknowledges and agrees that Broker: **(i)** Does not decide what price Buyer should pay or Seller should accept; **(ii)** Does not guarantee the condition of the Property; **(iii)** Does not guarantee the performance, adequacy or completeness of inspections, services, products or repairs provided or made by Seller or others; **(iv)** Does not have an obligation to conduct an inspection of common areas, or offsite areas of the Property; **(v)** Shall not be responsible for identifying defects on the Property, in common areas or offsite unless such defects are visually observable by an inspection of reasonably accessible areas of the Property or are known to Broker; **(vi)** Shall not be responsible for inspecting public records or permits concerning the title or use of Property; **(vii)** Shall not be responsible for identifying the location of boundary lines or other items affecting title; **(viii)** Shall not be responsible for verifying square footage, representations of others or information contained in Investigation reports, Multiple Listing Service, advertisements, flyers or other promotional material; **(ix)** Shall not be responsible for providing legal or tax advice regarding any aspect of a transaction entered into by Buyer or Seller; and **(x)** Shall not be responsible for providing other advice or information that exceeds the knowledge, education and experience required to perform real estate licensed activity. Buyer agrees to seek legal, tax, insurance, title and other desired assistance from appropriate professionals.

Buyer and Broker acknowledge receipt of a copy of this page.
Buyer's Initials (_____) (_____)
Broker's Initials (_____) (_____)
Reviewed by _____ Date _____

BBE REVISED 10/04 (PAGE 2 OF 4)

BUYER BROKER AGREEMENT – EXCLUSIVE (BBE PAGE 2 OF 4)

Buyer: _____ Date: _____

C. Broker owes no duty to inspect for common environmental hazards, earthquake weaknesses, or geologic and seismic hazards. If Buyer receives the booklets titled "Environmental Hazards: A Guide for Homeowners, Buyers, Landlords and Tenants," "The Homeowner's Guide to Earthquake Safety," or "The Commercial Property Owner's Guide to Earthquake Safety," the booklets are deemed adequate to inform Buyer regarding the information contained in the booklets and, other than as specified in 5B above, Broker is not required to provide Buyer with additional information about the matters described in the booklets.

7. **BUYER OBLIGATIONS:**

A. Buyer agrees to timely view and consider properties selected by Broker and to negotiate in good faith to acquire a property. Buyer further agrees to act in good faith toward the completion of any Property Contract entered into in furtherance of this Agreement. Within **5 (or** ☐ _____ **) calendar days** from the execution of this Agreement, Buyer shall provide relevant personal and financial information to Broker to assure Buyer's ability to acquire property described in paragraph 4. If Buyer fails to provide such information, or if Buyer does not qualify financially to acquire property described in paragraph 4, then Broker may cancel this Agreement in writing. Buyer has an affirmative duty to take steps to protect him/herself, including discovery of the legal, practical and technical implications of discovered or disclosed facts, and investigation of information and facts which are known to Buyer or are within the diligent attention and observation of Buyer. Buyer is obligated to and agrees to read all documents provided to Buyer. Buyer agrees to seek desired assistance from appropriate professionals, selected by Buyer, such as those referenced in the attached Buyer's Inspection Advisory.

B. Buyer shall notify Broker in writing (C.A.R. Form BMI) of any material issue to Buyer, such as, but not limited to, Buyer requests for information on, or concerns regarding, any particular area of interest or importance to Buyer ("Material Issues").

C. **Buyer agrees to: (i) indemnify, defend and hold Broker harmless from all claims, disputes, litigation, judgments, costs and attorney fees arising from any incorrect information supplied by Buyer, or from any Material Issues that Buyer fails to disclose in writing to Broker, and (ii) pay for reports, Inspections and meetings arranged by Broker on Buyer's behalf.**

D. Buyer is advised to read the attached Buyer's Inspection Advisory for a list of items and other concerns that typically warrant Inspections or investigation by Buyer or other professionals.

8. **DISPUTE RESOLUTION:**

A. **MEDIATION:** Buyer and Broker agree to mediate any dispute or claim arising between them out of this Agreement, or any resulting transaction, before resorting to arbitration or court action, subject to paragraph 8B(2) below. Paragraph 8B(2) below applies whether or not the arbitration provision is initialed. Mediation fees, if any, shall be divided equally among the parties involved. If, for any dispute or claim to which this paragraph applies, any party commences an action without first attempting to resolve the matter through mediation, or refuses to mediate after a request has been made, then that party shall not be entitled to recover attorney fees even if they would otherwise be available to that party in any such action. THIS MEDIATION PROVISION APPLIES WHETHER OR NOT THE ARBITRATION PROVISION IS INITIALED.

B. **ARBITRATION OF DISPUTES: (1) Buyer and Broker agree that any dispute or claim in law or equity arising between them regarding the obligation to pay compensation under this Agreement, which is not settled through mediation, shall be decided by neutral, binding arbitration, including and subject to paragraph 8B(2) below. The arbitrator shall be a retired judge or justice, or an attorney with at least five years of residential real estate law experience, unless the parties mutually agree to a different arbitrator, who shall render an award in accordance with substantive California law. The parties shall have the right to discovery in accordance with Code of Civil Procedure §1283.05. In all other respects, the arbitration shall be conducted in accordance with Title 9 of Part III, of the California Code of Civil Procedure. Judgment upon the award of the arbitrator(s) may be entered in any court having jurisdiction. Interpretation of this agreement to arbitrate shall be governed by the Federal Arbitration Act.**

2) EXCLUSIONS FROM MEDIATION AND ARBITRATION: The following matters are excluded from mediation and arbitration hereunder: **(i)** a judicial or non-judicial foreclosure or other action or proceeding to enforce a deed of trust, mortgage, or installment land sale contract as defined in Civil Code §2985; **(ii)** an unlawful detainer action; **(iii)** the filing or enforcement of a mechanic's lien; **(iv)** any matter that is within the jurisdiction of a probate, small claims, or bankruptcy court; and **(v)** an action for bodily injury or wrongful death, or for any right of action to which Code of Civil Procedure §337.1 or §337.15 applies. The filing of a court action to enable the recording of a notice of pending action, for order of attachment, receivership, injunction, or other provisional remedies, shall not constitute a waiver of the mediation and arbitration provisions.

"NOTICE: BY INITIALING IN THE SPACE BELOW YOU ARE AGREEING TO HAVE ANY DISPUTE ARISING OUT OF THE MATTERS INCLUDED IN THE 'ARBITRATION OF DISPUTES' PROVISION DECIDED BY NEUTRAL ARBITRATION AS PROVIDED BY CALIFORNIA LAW AND YOU ARE GIVING UP ANY RIGHTS YOU MIGHT POSSESS TO HAVE THE DISPUTE LITIGATED IN A COURT OR JURY TRIAL. BY INITIALING IN THE SPACE BELOW YOU ARE GIVING UP YOUR JUDICIAL RIGHTS TO DISCOVERY AND APPEAL, UNLESS THOSE RIGHTS ARE SPECIFICALLY INCLUDED IN THE 'ARBITRATION OF DISPUTES' PROVISION. IF YOU REFUSE TO SUBMIT TO ARBITRATION AFTER AGREEING TO THIS PROVISION, YOU MAY BE COMPELLED TO ARBITRATE UNDER THE AUTHORITY OF THE CALIFORNIA CODE OF CIVIL PROCEDURE. YOUR AGREEMENT TO THIS ARBITRATION PROVISION IS VOLUNTARY."

"WE HAVE READ AND UNDERSTAND THE FOREGOING AND AGREE TO SUBMIT DISPUTES ARISING OUT OF THE MATTERS INCLUDED IN THE 'ARBITRATION OF DISPUTES' PROVISION TO NEUTRAL ARBITRATION."

Buyer's Initials _____ / _____ **Broker's Initials** _____ / _____

Buyer and Broker acknowledge receipt of a copy of this page.
Buyer's Initials (_____) (_____)
Broker's Initials (_____) (_____)
Reviewed by _____ Date _____

BBE REVISED 10/04 (PAGE 3 OF 4)

EQUAL HOUSING OPPORTUNITY

BUYER BROKER AGREEMENT – EXCLUSIVE (BBE PAGE 3 OF 4)

Buyer: _____ Date: _____

9. **TIME TO BRING LEGAL ACTION:** Legal action for breach of this Agreement, or any obligation arising therefrom, shall be brought no more than two years from the expiration of the Representation Period or from the date such cause of action may arise, whichever occurs first.

10. **OTHER TERMS AND CONDITIONS,** including **ATTACHED SUPPLEMENTS:** ☑ Buyer's Inspection Advisory (C.A.R. Form BIA)
_____
_____
_____
_____
_____

11. **ATTORNEY FEES:** In any action, proceeding or arbitration between Buyer and Broker regarding the obligation to pay compensation under this Agreement, the prevailing Buyer or Broker shall be entitled to reasonable attorney fees and costs, except as provided in paragraph 8A.

12. **ENTIRE AGREEMENT:** All understandings between the parties are incorporated in this Agreement. Its terms are intended by the parties as a final, complete and exclusive expression of their agreement with respect to its subject matter, and may not be contradicted by evidence of any prior agreement or contemporaneous oral agreement. This Agreement may not be extended, amended, modified, altered or changed, except in writing signed by Buyer and Broker. In the event that any provision of this Agreement is held to be ineffective or invalid, the remaining provisions will nevertheless be given full force and effect. This Agreement and any supplement, addendum or modification, including any copy, whether by copier, facsimile, NCR or electronic, may be signed in two or more counterparts, all of which shall constitute one and the same writing.

Buyer acknowledges that Buyer has read, understands, accepts and has received a copy of this Agreement.

Buyer _____ Date _____
Address _____ City _____ State _____ Zip _____
Telephone _____ Fax _____ E-mail _____

Buyer _____ Date _____
Address _____ City _____ State _____ Zip _____
Telephone _____ Fax _____ E-mail _____

Real Estate Broker (Firm) _____
By (Agent) _____ Date _____
Address _____ City _____ State _____ Zip _____
Telephone _____ Fax _____ E-mail _____

Published and Distributed by:
REAL ESTATE BUSINESS SERVICES, INC.
a subsidiary of the California Association of REALTORS®
525 South Virgil Avenue, Los Angeles, California 90020

Reviewed by _____ Date _____

BBE REVISED 10/04 (PAGE 4 OF 4)

BUYER BROKER AGREEMENT – EXCLUSIVE (BBE PAGE 4 OF 4)

Example: Helman lists his property with Broker Thurston and agrees to pay him a commission of 6% of the sales price. The listing agreement includes a clause that entitles any cooperating broker who procures a buyer to the selling broker's portion of the commission.

Broker Adams has a buyer agency agreement with Gray. Gray offers $450,000 for Helman's house and Helman accepts the offer.

When the transaction closes, Helman pays a $27,000 commission; $13,500 goes to Broker Thurston and $13,500 goes to Broker Adams.

Most buyer representation agreements provide for payment by means of a commission split when the buyer purchases a home that is listed through a multiple listing service. However, a buyer representation agreement may provide for a **buyer-paid fee** instead. The buyer-paid fee might be based on an hourly rate, in which case the agent is essentially a consultant. Alternatively, a buyer's agent may charge a percentage fee, so that the commission is a percentage of the purchase price. A third possibility is a flat fee—a specified sum that is payable if the buyer purchases a property found by the agent.

Some buyer agency agreements provide that the buyer's agent will accept a commission split if one is available, but the buyer will pay the agent a fee if the purchased property was unlisted (for example, if the property was for sale by owner).

Dual Agency. A dual agency relationship exists when an agent represents both the seller and the buyer in the same transaction. (In contrast, if an agent is representing only one of the parties, it is sometimes called single agency.) A dual agent owes fiduciary duties to both principals. Because the interests of the buyer and the seller usually conflict, it is difficult to represent both without being disloyal to one or both of them.

Example: Broker Kogawa represents both the buyer and the seller in a transaction. The seller informs Kogawa that she is in a big hurry to sell and will accept any reasonable offer. The buyer tells Kogawa that he is very interested in the house, and is willing to pay the full listing price. Should Kogawa tell the buyer of the seller's eagerness to sell? Should Kogawa tell the seller about the buyer's willingness to pay the full price?

In fact, it is really impossible for a dual agent to fully represent the interests of both parties. Thus, a more accurate name for dual agency is **limited dual agency**.

Disclosed Dual Agency. Dual agency is legal in California, even though it is generally discouraged. However, before acting as a dual agent, a broker must have the informed written consent of both parties to the transaction. Acting as a dual agent without full disclosure is a violation of the Real Estate Law, and will lead to disciplinary action. (See Chapter 16.) In fact, if a real estate licensee acts as a dual agent without full disclosure to one or both parties, neither party may have to pay the commission. Furthermore, either party could rescind the transaction.

Each party to a dual agency should be informed that he or she will not receive full representation. Certain facts must necessarily be withheld from each party; the dual agent cannot divulge confidential information about one party to the other party. Returning to the previous example, the dual agent must not tell the buyer the seller's bottom line price, nor tell the seller how much the buyer is willing to pay.

Statutory agency disclosure requirements are discussed in the next section of this chapter. Real estate agents should be particularly careful with their disclosures in the context of dual agency. Buyers and sellers, eager to get on with the business of buying and selling a home, may agree to a dual agency without really understanding what it means. They may accept the agent's explanation at face value and sign a disclosure form without question. Later, one party might feel that the agent breached his fiduciary duties. This kind of disappointment often leads to legal action.

Inadvertent Dual Agency. As we discussed earlier, a dual agency may be created unintentionally. In fact, many dual agency lawsuits involve an accidental or unintended dual agency in which the conduct of the seller's agent, or the personal relationship between the agent and the buyer, is such that an implied agency is created with the buyer. An agent's best protection against inadvertent dual agency is to comply carefully with the agency disclosure requirements and then act in accordance with the disclosure, never forgetting which party he or she is representing.

Agency Disclosure Requirements

To avoid some of the confusion about who is representing whom, California law requires real estate agents in residential transactions to make agency disclosures to their clients and customers. This requirement applies to transactions that involve property with one to four dwelling units.

The first step in the disclosure process is providing an **agency disclosure form** (see Figure 8.6). This form gives a clear explanation of the duties of a seller's agent, a buyer's agent, and a dual agent. An agent must give the parties the disclosure form and also have them sign a copy to acknowledge that they received it.

The listing agent must give a copy of the agency disclosure form to the seller before the seller signs the listing agreement. The selling agent must give a copy to each party as soon as practicable; the buyer must receive it before signing the offer to purchase, and the seller must receive it before the offer is presented. (If the selling agent is not dealing with the seller directly, the selling agent's disclosure form may be delivered to the seller by the listing agent or by certified mail.)

In addition to giving the parties the general disclosure form explaining the different types of real estate agency relationships, each agent is required to disclose whether he or she is representing only the seller, only the buyer, or both the seller and the buyer in this particular transaction. The agents must make their disclosures to the parties as soon as practicable. Each agent's disclosures must be confirmed in writing by having the parties sign an **agency confirmation statement** before or at the same time that they enter into a contract. An agency confirmation statement does not have to be a separate document; in most cases, the confirmation statements are included in the deposit receipt (see Chapter 7).

Fig. 8.6 Agency disclosure statement

**CALIFORNIA
ASSOCIATION
OF REALTORS®**

DISCLOSURE REGARDING
REAL ESTATE AGENCY RELATIONSHIPS
(As required by the Civil Code)
(C.A.R. Form AD, Revised 10/04)

When you enter into a discussion with a real estate agent regarding a real estate transaction, you should from the outset understand what type of agency relationship or representation you wish to have with the agent in the transaction.

SELLER'S AGENT

A Seller's agent under a listing agreement with the Seller acts as the agent for the Seller only. A Seller's agent or a subagent of that agent has the following affirmative obligations:
To the Seller:
   A Fiduciary duty of utmost care, integrity, honesty, and loyalty in dealings with the Seller.
To the Buyer and the Seller:
   (a) Diligent exercise of reasonable skill and care in performance of the agent's duties.
   (b) A duty of honest and fair dealing and good faith.
   (c) A duty to disclose all facts known to the agent materially affecting the value or desirability of the property that are not known to, or within the diligent attention and observation of, the parties.
An agent is not obligated to reveal to either party any confidential information obtained from the other party that does not involve the affirmative duties set forth above.

BUYER'S AGENT

A selling agent can, with a Buyer's consent, agree to act as agent for the Buyer only. In these situations, the agent is not the Seller's agent, even if by agreement the agent may receive compensation for services rendered, either in full or in part from the Seller. An agent acting only for a Buyer has the following affirmative obligations:
To the Buyer:
   A fiduciary duty of utmost care, integrity, honesty, and loyalty in dealings with the Buyer.
To the Buyer and the Seller:
   (a) Diligent exercise of reasonable skill and care in performance of the agent's duties.
   (b) A duty of honest and fair dealing and good faith.
   (c) A duty to disclose all facts known to the agent materially affecting the value or desirability of the property that are not known to, or within the diligent attention and observation of, the parties.
An agent is not obligated to reveal to either party any confidential information obtained from the other party that does not involve the affirmative duties set forth above.

AGENT REPRESENTING BOTH SELLER AND BUYER

A real estate agent, either acting directly or through one or more associate licensees, can legally be the agent of both the Seller and the Buyer in a transaction, but only with the knowledge and consent of both the Seller and the Buyer.

In a dual agency situation, the agent has the following affirmative obligations to both the Seller and the Buyer:
   (a) A fiduciary duty of utmost care, integrity, honesty and loyalty in the dealings with either the Seller or the Buyer.
   (b) Other duties to the Seller and the Buyer as stated above in their respective sections.

In representing both Seller and Buyer, the agent may not, without the express permission of the respective party, disclose to the other party that the Seller will accept a price less than the listing price or that the Buyer will pay a price greater than the price offered.

The above duties of the agent in a real estate transaction do not relieve a Seller or Buyer from the responsibility to protect his or her own interests. You should carefully read all agreements to assure that they adequately express your understanding of the transaction. A real estate agent is a person qualified to advise about real estate. If legal or tax advice is desired, consult a competent professional.

Throughout your real property transaction you may receive more than one disclosure form, depending upon the number of agents assisting in the transaction. The law requires each agent with whom you have more than a casual relationship to present you with this disclosure form. You should read its contents each time it is presented to you, considering the relationship between you and the real estate agent in your specific transaction.

This disclosure form includes the provisions of Sections 2079.13 to 2079.24, inclusive, of the Civil Code set forth on the reverse hereof. Read it carefully.

I/WE ACKNOWLEDGE RECEIPT OF A COPY OF THIS DISCLOSURE AND THE PORTIONS OF THE CIVIL CODE PRINTED ON THE BACK (OR A SEPARATE PAGE).

☐ BUYER ☐ SELLER _____ Date _____ Time _____ ☐ AM ☐ PM

☐ BUYER ☐ SELLER _____ Date _____ Time _____ ☐ AM ☐ PM

AGENT _____ By _____ Date _____
　　　　　　　　(Please Print)　　　　　　　　　　　　(Associate-Licensee or Broker Signature)

THIS FORM SHALL BE PROVIDED AND ACKNOWLEDGED AS FOLLOWS (Civil Code §2079.14):
● When the listing brokerage company also represents Buyer, the Listing Agent shall have one AD form signed by Seller and one signed by Buyer.
● When Buyer and Seller are represented by different brokerage companies, the Listing Agent shall have one AD form signed by Seller and the Buyer's Agent shall have one AD form signed by Buyer and one AD form signed by Seller.

The copyright laws of the United States (Title 17 U.S. Code) forbid the unauthorized reproduction of this form, or any portion thereof, by photocopy machine or any other means, including facsimile or computerized formats. Copyright © 1991-2004, CALIFORNIA ASSOCIATION OF REALTORS®, INC. ALL RIGHTS RESERVED.
THIS FORM HAS BEEN APPROVED BY THE CALIFORNIA ASSOCIATION OF REALTORS® (C.A.R.). NO REPRESENTATION IS MADE AS TO THE LEGAL VALIDITY OR ADEQUACY OF ANY PROVISION IN ANY SPECIFIC TRANSACTION. A REAL ESTATE BROKER IS THE PERSON QUALIFIED TO ADVISE ON REAL ESTATE TRANSACTIONS. IF YOU DESIRE LEGAL OR TAX ADVICE, CONSULT AN APPROPRIATE PROFESSIONAL.
This form is available for use by the entire real estate industry. It is not intended to identify the user as a REALTOR®. REALTOR® is a registered collective membership mark which may be used only by members of the NATIONAL ASSOCIATION OF REALTORS® who subscribe to its Code of Ethics.

Published and Distributed by:
REAL ESTATE BUSINESS SERVICES, INC.
a subsidiary of the California Association of REALTORS®
525 South Virgil Avenue, Los Angeles, California 90020

The System for Success™

Reviewed by _____ Date _____

EQUAL HOUSING
OPPORTUNITY

AD REVISED 10/04 (PAGE 1 OF 1)
DISCLOSURE REGARDING REAL ESTATE AGENCY RELATIONSHIPS (AD PAGE 1 OF 1)

Reprinted with permission, California Association of REALTORS®. Endorsement not implied.

The Broker/Salesperson Relationship

Finally, let's discuss the legal relationship between a real estate salesperson and the broker he or she works for. Under the terms of the California Real Estate Law (discussed in Chapter 16), a real estate salesperson cannot act directly as the agent of a principal in a real estate transaction. Rather, the salesperson acts as the agent of his or her broker, and it is the broker who acts as the principal's agent. (California statutes expressly state that a real estate salesperson is never a subagent of his or her broker's principal.)

For certain purposes, a real estate salesperson is classified either as the broker's **employee** or as an **independent contractor**. An independent contractor is hired to perform a particular job, and uses his or her own judgment to decide how the job should be completed. In contrast, an employee is hired to perform whatever tasks the employer requires, and is given instructions on how to accomplish each task. An employee is supervised and controlled much more closely than an independent contractor. Various employment and tax laws apply only when someone is hired as an employee, and not when someone is hired as an independent contractor.

A real estate broker is virtually always an independent contractor in relation to his or her principal (the buyer or the seller). When it comes to the relationship between a broker and a salesperson, however, the distinction between employee and independent contractor may be an issue.

Whether a salesperson is his or her broker's employee or an independent contractor depends on the degree of control the broker exercises over the salesperson. If the broker closely directs the activities of the salesperson and controls how the salesperson carries out his or her work, the salesperson may be considered an employee. For example, if the broker requires the salesperson to work on a set schedule, tells the salesperson when to go where, and decides what steps the salesperson should take in marketing each property, the salesperson is probably the broker's employee.

Most brokers exercise much less control over a salesperson's work than that. They generally focus on the end results—listings, closings, and satisfied clients—and not on the details of how the salesperson accomplishes those results. A broker usually isn't concerned with where the salesperson is or what he or she is doing at any given time. The salesperson is paid on the basis of results (by commission) rather than hours spent on the job. Thus, in most cases, a salesperson is an independent contractor, not the broker's employee.

If a salesperson were an employee, the broker would be required to withhold money from the salesperson's compensation to pay certain federal and state taxes (income tax, social security, unemployment insurance, and workers' compensation). An independent contractor, on the other hand, is responsible for paying his or her own social security and income taxes. (Note, however, that a broker may choose to carry workers' compensation insurance on his or her commissioned sales staff, as well as on salaried employees.)

The Internal Revenue Code provides that a real estate salesperson will be considered an independent contractor for federal income tax purposes if three conditions are met:

1. the individual is a licensed real estate salesperson;
2. substantially all of his or her compensation is based on commission rather than hours worked; and,

3. the services are performed under a written contract providing that the individual will not be treated as an employee for federal tax purposes.

Even when a salesperson is considered an independent contractor for federal income tax purposes, he or she may be treated as an employee under other laws. For example, the California Real Estate Law states that while a salesperson may be treated either as an independent contractor or an employee for tax purposes, that distinction will not affect the requirements or liabilities established in the Real Estate Law. Thus, whether a salesperson is an independent contractor or an employee, the broker is responsible for supervising the salesperson's actions, and the broker may be held liable for the salesperson's misconduct. (See Chapter 16.)

Chapter Summary

1. In an agency relationship, the agent represents the principal in dealings with third parties. An agent may be a general agent or a special agent, depending on the scope of authority granted.

2. Most agency relationships are created by express agreement (oral or written), but they can also be created by ratification, estoppel, or implication. Acts performed by an agent or an ostensible agent are binding on the principal if they fall within the scope of the agent's actual or apparent authority.

3. An agent owes fiduciary duties to the principal, including the duties of reasonable care and skill, obedience and utmost good faith, accounting, loyalty, and disclosure of material facts. The agent must inform the principal of all offers, the property's true value, any relationship between the agent and the buyer, and a dual agency.

4. An agent owes third parties the duties of reasonable care and skill and good faith and fair dealing. Neither the seller nor the seller's agent may misrepresent the property, and they must reveal any known latent defects to prospective buyers. In a residential transaction, an agent has the duty to visually inspect the property and reveal the results of that inspection to prospective buyers.

5. An agency relationship may be terminated by mutual agreement, revocation, renunciation, expiration, fulfillment of purpose, the death or incapacity of either party, or extinction of the subject matter.

6. A seller agency is usually created with a listing agreement. A salesperson who works for the seller's broker also works for the seller. If a cooperating agent is acting on the seller's behalf, he or she must be careful to avoid any actions that might give rise to an inadvertent agency relationship with the buyer.

7. Buyer's agents can provide special services to buyers, including access to more properties, expert advice, help with negotiating, and loyalty. Buyer agency relationships are generally created with a representation agreement. A buyer's agent may be paid by the buyer or the seller. If the agent is paid by the buyer, the fee may be in the form of a retainer, a commission, an hourly fee, or a flat rate.

8. Dual agency occurs when an agent represents both the seller and the buyer in the same transaction. Dual agencies are unlawful without the full, informed consent of both parties. Dual agencies may arise inadvertently, through the agent's actions.

9. California law requires real estate agents to disclose to the buyer and seller which party they represent. An agent must have the buyer and the seller sign an agency disclosure form and an agency confirmation statement before they sign the purchase and sale agreement.

10. For the purposes of certain tax and employment laws, a real estate salesperson may be classified either as his or her broker's employee, or as an independent contractor. In most cases, a salesperson is considered to be an independent contractor, even though the broker has legal responsibility for the salesperson's conduct.

🔑 Key Terms

Principal—The person who authorizes an agent to act on his or her behalf.

Agent—A person authorized to represent another in dealings with third parties.

Third party—A person seeking to deal with the principal through the agent.

Fiduciary—Someone who holds a special position of trust and confidence in relation to another.

Ratification—When the principal gives approval to unauthorized actions after they are performed, creating an agency relationship after the fact.

Estoppel—When the principal allows a third party to believe an agency relationship exists, so that the principal is estopped (legally precluded) from denying the agency.

Actual authority—Authority the principal grants to the agent either expressly or by implication.

Apparent authority—Where no actual authority has been granted, but the principal allows it to appear that the agent is authorized, and therefore is estopped from denying the agency. Also called ostensible authority.

Material facts—Information that has a substantial negative impact on the value of the property or on a party's ability to perform.

Secret profit—Any profit an agent receives as a result of the agency relationship and does not disclose to the principal.

Listing agent—The agent who takes the listing on a property, and who may or may not be the agent who procures a buyer.

Selling agent—The agent who procures a buyer for a property, and who may or may not have taken the listing.

Cooperating agent—Any agent other than the listing agent who attempts to find a buyer for a property.

In-house transaction—A sale in which the buyer and the seller are brought together by salespersons working for the same broker.

Cooperative transaction—A sale in which the buyer and the seller are brought together by salespersons who work for two different brokers.

Employee—Someone who works under the direction and control of another.

Independent contractor—A person who contracts to do a job for another, but retains control over how he or she will carry out the task, rather than following detailed instructions.

Chapter Quiz

1. An agency relationship can be created in any of the following ways, except:

   a) written agreement
   b) oral agreement
   c) ratification
   d) verification

2. An agency relationship requires:

   a) consideration
   b) the consent of both parties
   c) an enforceable contract
   d) None of the above

3. Garcia acted on behalf of Hilton without her authorization. At a later date, Hilton gave her approval to Garcia's actions. This is an example of:

   a) express agreement
   b) ratification
   c) estoppel
   d) assumption of authority

4. A seller lists his home with a broker at $290,000; he asks for a quick sale. When the listing broker shows the home to a buyer, he says the seller is financially insolvent and will take $275,000. The buyer offers $275,000 and the seller accepts. The broker:

   a) did not violate his duties to the seller, because the seller accepted the offer
   b) did not violate his duties to the seller, since he fulfilled the purpose of his agency
   c) violated his duties to the seller by disclosing confidential information to the buyer
   d) was unethical, but did not violate his duties to the seller, since he did not receive a secret profit

5. Stark lists his property with Bell, a licensed broker. Bell shows the property to her cousin, who decides he would like to buy it. Which of the following is true?

   a) Bell can present her cousin's offer to Stark, as long as she tells Stark that the prospective buyer is one of her relatives
   b) Bell violated her fiduciary duties to Stark by showing the property to one of her relatives
   c) It was not unethical for Bell to show the property to a relative, but it would be a violation of her duties if she presented her cousin's offer to Stark
   d) It is not necessary for Bell to tell Stark that the buyer is related to her, as long as he is offering the full listing price for the property

6. An agency relationship can be terminated by:

   a) renunciation without the principal's consent
   b) incapacity of either party
   c) extinction of the subject matter
   d) All of the above

7. A real estate agent tells potential buyers: "This is a great old house. They just don't make them like they used to." This statement would be considered:

   a) a misrepresentation
   b) actual fraud
   c) constructive fraud
   d) puffing

8. In most cases, a listing broker:

   a) is authorized to enter into contracts on behalf of the seller
   b) is considered a special agent
   c) Both of the above
   d) Neither of the above

9. Dual agency is:

   a) no longer legal in California
   b) legal as long as both principals consent to the arrangement in writing
   c) legal as long as the agent receives equal compensation from both principals
   d) encouraged by many professional associations as the best way of representing a client's interests

10. Able listed Glover's property. Able:

   a) cannot give a buyer any information about Glover's property without being considered a dual agent
   b) may give a buyer information about Glover's property without owing agency duties to the buyer
   c) must sign a disclaimer of liability if he presents a buyer's offer to purchase to Glover
   d) is a dual agent

11. A principal may be held liable for:

   a) the actions of his or her broker
   b) the actions of his or her broker's salesperson
   c) his or her own actions
   d) All of the above

12. Which one of the following is not a benefit of buyer agency?

   a) The buyer has access to more properties
   b) The buyer gets the benefit of objective advice
   c) Since the agent represents both parties, the buyer has access to information about the seller's bottom-line sales price
   d) The buyer gets help with negotiating the sales price

13. A buyer's agent:

   a) may not accept compensation paid by the seller
   b) must have a written listing agreement in order to be compensated
   c) may be paid through a commission split
   d) may not receive compensation that is based on the property's sales price

14. Disclosure of and consent to a dual agency:

   a) must be in writing
   b) is required only in an in-house transaction
   c) should come after the parties sign the purchase and sale agreement
   d) must be given to the buyer only after presenting the written offer to purchase

15. A dual agent must:

   a) keep each party's negotiating position confidential
   b) disclose all information to both parties, no matter how confidential
   c) act only as a facilitator, with no agency duties to either party
   d) refer all conflicts of interest to the Board of Equalization

👉 Answer Key

1. d) An agency relationship may be created by express agreement (written or oral), ratification, estoppel, or implication.

2. b) The consent of both parties is necessary to the creation of an agency relationship, but consideration is not. There does not have to be an enforceable contract between the principal and the agent.

3. b) An agency relationship is created by ratification when the principal gives approval to unauthorized actions after the fact.

4. c) The broker was disloyal to his principal and violated his fiduciary duties by disclosing confidential information to a third party.

5. a) A seller's real estate agent is required to tell the seller if the prospective buyer is related to the agent.

6. d) Any of the choices listed can terminate an agency relationship.

7. d) This is an example of puffing, an exaggerated statement that the buyers should realize they can't depend on.

8. b) A listing broker is usually a special agent, with limited authority to represent the principal in a particular transaction. A listing broker is ordinarily not authorized to sign contracts on behalf of the principal.

9. b) Dual agency is legal, but only if both the seller and the buyer are informed that the agent is representing both of them, and they both give their written consent to the arrangement.

10. b) A seller's agent can give a buyer information about the seller's property without becoming a dual agent.

11. d) A principal may be liable for his or her own actions and the actions of his or her broker and that broker's salesperson.

12. c) A buyer who retains his or her own agent does not get information about the seller's negotiating position.

13. c) Buyer's agents often accept a share of the commission that the listing broker receives from the seller. This arrangement does not create an agency relationship between the buyer's agent and the seller.

14. a) Disclosure of a dual agency must be in writing, and the parties' consent must also be in writing.

15. a) A dual agent must not disclose confidential information about one party to the other party. This includes information on each party's negotiating position.

Principles of Real Estate Financing

⌂⌂⌂⌂ Chapter Overview

Finance—lending and borrowing money—is essential to the real estate industry. If financing weren't available, buyers would have to pay cash for their property, and very few people could afford to do so. Thus, once a purchase and sale agreement has been signed, in most cases the next step is to arrange financing for the transaction. Real estate agents often help their clients and customers with this process, so they need a thorough understanding of real estate finance. This chapter starts with background information about real estate cycles, how the government influences real estate finance, and the secondary market. The chapter then goes on to explain how mortgages and other financing instruments work, the foreclosure process, and the various types of mortgage loans. The process of applying for a mortgage loan is covered in Chapter 10.

The Economics of Real Estate Finance

Nearly every buyer needs to borrow money in order to purchase real estate. Whether a particular buyer will be able to obtain a loan depends in part on his or her personal financial circumstances, and in part on national and local economic conditions. We're going to discuss real estate cycles and the government's role in the economy, to help you understand the economic factors that affect real estate lending.

From a lender's point of view, a loan is an investment. A lender loans money in the expectation of a return on the investment. The borrower will repay the money borrowed, plus interest; the interest is the lender's return.

As a general rule, investors demand a higher return on risky investments than they do on comparatively safe ones. That holds true for loan transactions; the greater the risk that the borrower won't repay the loan, the higher the interest rate charged. But the interest rate a lender charges on a particular loan also depends on market forces.

Real Estate Cycles

The real estate market is cyclical: it goes through active periods followed by slumps. These periodic shifts in the level of activity in the real estate market are called **real estate cycles**. Residential real estate cycles can be dramatic or moderate, and they can be local or regional. At any given time and place, there may be a buyer's market, where few people are buying and homes sit on the market for a long time, or there may be a seller's market, where many people are buying and homes sell rapidly.

These cycles obey the law of supply and demand. When demand for a product exceeds the supply (a seller's market), the price charged for the product tends to rise, and the price increase stimulates more production. As production increases, more of the demand is satisfied, until eventually the supply outstrips demand and a buyer's market is created. At that point, prices fall and production tapers off until demand catches up with supply, and the cycle begins again.

Real estate cycles are caused by changes in the supply of and demand for mortgage loan funds. The supply of mortgage funds depends on how much money investors have available and choose to invest in real estate loans. The demand for mortgage funds depends on how many people want to purchase real estate and can afford to borrow enough money to do so.

Interest rates represent the price of mortgage funds. They affect supply and demand, and they also fluctuate in response to changes in supply and demand. Interest is sometimes called the cost of money.

Generally, when mortgage funds are plentiful, interest rates are low. When funds are scarce, interest rates are high; this is called a **tight money market**. In a tight market, sellers may have to resort to offering to finance part of the purchase price in order to close a sale.

In a healthy economy, supply and demand are more or less in balance. This is the ideal; in reality, the forces affecting supply and demand are constantly changing, and so is the balance between them. But as long as supply and demand are reasonably close, the economy functions well. When supply far exceeds demand, or vice versa, the economy suffers.

Real estate cycles can be moderated, though not eliminated. Severe slumps can be prevented by factors that either help keep interest rates under control or directly affect the supply of mortgage funds. Federal economic policy plays a key role in moderating real estate cycles.

Interest Rates and Federal Policy

Economic stability is directly tied to the supply of and demand for money. If money is plentiful and can be borrowed cheaply (that is, interest rates are low), increased economic activity is usually the result. On the other hand, if funds are scarce and/or expensive to borrow, an economic slowdown will result.

Thus, manipulation of the availability and cost of money can do much to achieve economic balance. The federal government influences real estate finance, as well as the rest of the U.S. economy, through its **fiscal policy** and its **monetary policy**.

Fiscal Policy. Fiscal policy refers to the way in which the federal government manages its money. Congress and the President determine fiscal policy through tax legislation and the federal budget. The U.S. Treasury implements fiscal policy by managing tax revenues, expenditures, and the national debt.

When the federal government spends more money than it takes in, a shortfall called the **federal deficit** results. It is the Treasury's responsibility to borrow enough money to cover the deficit. It does this by issuing interest-bearing securities that are backed by the U.S. government and purchased by private investors. The securities can be issued for less than one year (Treasury bills), from one to five years (Treasury notes), or from five to ten years (Treasury certificates). Investors often prefer to invest in these government securities instead of other investments because they are comparatively low-risk.

When the government borrows money, it competes with private industry for available investment funds. Economists and politicians debate what impact this has on the economy. According to some, by draining the number of dollars in circulation, heavy government borrowing may lead to an economic slowdown. The greater the federal deficit, the more money the government has to borrow, and the greater the effect on the economy.

The government's taxation policies also affect the supply of and demand for money. As with the deficit, the effect of taxation on the economy is controversial. Basically, when taxes are low, taxpayers have more money to lend and invest. When taxes are high, taxpayers not only have less money to lend or invest, they also may be more likely to invest what money they do have in tax-exempt securities instead of taxable investments. Since real estate and real estate mortgages are taxable investments, this may have a significant impact on the real estate finance industry.

Monetary Policy. Monetary policy refers to the direct control the federal government exerts over the money supply and interest rates. The main goal of monetary policy is to keep the U.S. economy healthy.

Monetary policy is determined by the Federal Reserve, commonly called "the Fed." The Federal Reserve System, established in 1913, is the nation's central banking system. It is governed by the Federal Reserve Board and the board's chairman. It has twelve districts nationwide, with a Federal Reserve Bank in each district. Thousands of commercial banks across the country are members of the Federal Reserve.

The Fed is responsible for regulating commercial banks, and it also oversees implementation of the Truth in Lending Act (discussed in Chapter 10). But setting and implementing the government's monetary policy is perhaps the Fed's most important function.

The major objectives of monetary policy are high employment, economic growth, price stability, interest rate stability, and stability in financial and foreign exchange markets. Although these goals are interrelated, we are most concerned with the Federal Reserve policies that affect the availability and cost of borrowed money (interest rates), since those have the most direct impact on the real estate industry.

The Fed uses three tools to implement its monetary policy and influence the economy:

- key interest rates,
- reserve requirements, and
- open market operations.

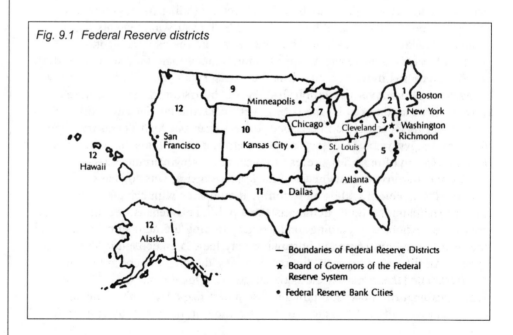

Fig. 9.1 Federal Reserve districts

Key Interest Rates. The Fed sets two interest rates, the federal funds rate and the discount rate. These are the interest rates charged when a bank borrows money, either from another bank or from a Federal Reserve Bank. When the Fed raises or lowers the interest rates that its member banks have to pay, the banks then raise or lower the interest rates they charge their customers. Lower interest rates tend to stimulate the economy, and higher rates tend to slow it down. The Fed may judge that a slower pace is desirable to keep price inflation in check.

Reserve Requirements. A commercial bank's reserve requirements are the percentages of deposits that the bank is required to maintain on deposit at the Federal Reserve Bank. Reserve requirements help prevent financial panics (a "run on the bank") by assuring depositors that their funds are safe and accessible; the bank will always have enough money available to meet unusual customer demand.

Reserve requirements also give the Fed some control over the growth of credit. By increasing reserve requirements, the Fed can reduce the amount of money banks have available to lend. On the other hand, a reduction in reserve requirements frees more money for investment or lending. So an increase in reserve requirements tends to decrease available loan funds and increase interest rates. Conversely, a decrease in reserve requirements tends to increase available loan funds and decrease interest rates.

Open Market Operations. The Fed also buys and sells government securities; these transactions are called open market operations. They are the Fed's chief method of controlling the money supply, and with the money supply, inflation and interest rates. Only money in circulation is considered part of the money supply, so actions by the Fed that put money into circulation increase the money supply, and actions that take money out of circulation decrease it.

When the Fed buys government securities from an investor, it increases the money supply, because the money it uses to pay for the securities goes into circulation. When the Fed sells government securities, the money the buyer uses to pay for the securities is taken out of circulation, decreasing the money supply. Interest rates tend to fall with increases in the money supply, and to rise with decreases in the money supply.

Other Agencies that Affect Finance. Aside from the Federal Reserve, there are a number of other federal agencies and programs that have some influence on real estate finance.

Federal Home Loan Bank System. The Federal Home Loan Bank System (FHLB) is made up of twelve regional, privately owned wholesale banks. The banks loan funds to FHLB members—local community lenders—and accept their mortgages and other loans as collateral. The FHLB, which is headed by the Federal Housing Finance Board, is active in promoting affordable housing.

Federal Deposit Insurance Corporation. The FDIC was created in 1933 to insure bank deposits against bank insolvency. It now includes two separate insurance funds, the Bank Insurance Fund and the Savings Association Insurance Fund. If a bank or savings and loan fails, the FDIC will step in to protect the institution's customers against the loss of their deposited funds, up to specified limits.

HUD. The Department of Housing and Urban Development (HUD) is a federal cabinet department. Among many other things, HUD's responsibilities include urban renewal projects, public housing, FHA-insured loan programs, and enforcement of the Federal Fair Housing Act (see Chapter 14). Ginnie Mae (discussed later in this chapter) and the Federal Housing Administration (discussed in Chapter 10) are both part of HUD.

Rural Housing Service. Formerly known as the Farmers Home Administration or FmHA, the Rural Housing Service is an agency within the Department of Agriculture. To help people living in rural areas purchase and improve their homes, the Rural Housing Service makes loans and grants and also guarantees loans made by lending institutions. In addition, it finances the construction of affordable housing in rural areas.

Farm Credit System. Originally developed by the federal government, the Farm Credit System is now a privately owned cooperative. It provides financial assistance to farmers, ranchers, and others in rural areas.

Real Estate Finance Markets

There are two "markets" that supply the funds available for real estate loans: the primary market and the secondary market. In addition to using monetary policy to control the money supply and interest rates, another way in which the federal government has helped moderate the severity and duration of real estate cycles is by establishing a strong, nationwide secondary market. The secondary market limits the adverse effects of local economic circumstances on real estate lending. We'll look first at the primary market, then at the secondary market.

Primary Market

The primary market is the local mortgage finance market, made up of the various lending institutions in a community. For example, if the Browns want to borrow money to finance the purchase of a home, they will seek a loan in the primary market, perhaps from a bank or a savings and loan.

The traditional source of funds for the primary market is the savings of individuals and businesses in the local area. For instance, a community savings and loan association is a typical lender in the primary market. It gets its funds from the savings deposits of members of the community. It will use the savings to make real estate loans to members of that same community.

The local economy has a significant effect on the amount of funds a local lender has available. When employment is high, consumers are more likely to borrow money for cars, vacations, or homes. Businesses expand and borrow to finance their growth. Banks and other lending institutions increase their lending activities to meet the demand, but at the same time, fewer people are saving. This decrease in deposits and corresponding increase in loan demand steadily depletes the funds available for lending. If local lenders could not attract money from other parts of the country to help meet the demand, their funds would be exhausted and the community's economy severely disrupted. The reverse is also true. When an area is in an economic slump, consumers are more inclined to save than to borrow. Businesses suspend plans for growth. The result is a drop in the demand for money, and the lending institutions' deposits grow.

From a lender's point of view, either too little or too much money on deposit is cause for concern. In the first case, with little money to lend, a lender's

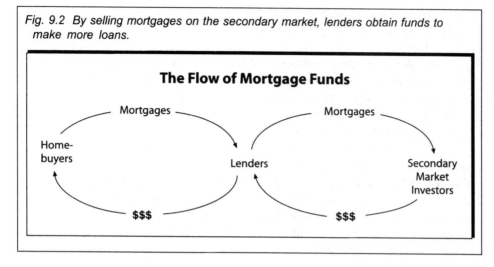

Fig. 9.2 *By selling mortgages on the secondary market, lenders obtain funds to make more loans.*

primary source of income is affected. In the second case, the lender is paying interest to its depositors, and if it is unable to reinvest the deposited funds quickly, it will lose money.

To get additional funds for real estate lending, a local lender may sell the mortgage loans it has already made. To do so, the lender will probably turn to the secondary market.

Secondary Market

The secondary market is a national market. It consists of private investors and government-sponsored agencies that buy and sell mortgages secured by real estate in all parts of the United States.

Buying and Selling Loans. Mortgage loans can be bought and sold just like other investments—stocks or bonds, for example. The value of a loan is influenced by the rate of return on the loan compared to the market rate of return, as well as the degree of risk associated with the loan (the likelihood of default). For instance, a **seasoned loan**—one with a history of several years of timely payments by the borrower—is less risky than a new, untested loan. As a result, a seasoned loan is worth more to an investor than a new loan for the same amount.

Investors generally buy mortgage loans at a discount, for less than their face value. However, if a borrower defaults on a loan purchased at a discount, the investor can still foreclose (force the sale of the property to recoup the amount of the debt) for the full face amount of the mortgage. For example, if an investor bought a $100,000 mortgage for $80,000 and the borrower immediately defaulted on the loan, the investor could foreclose for the full $100,000.

The availability of funds in the primary market (a local lender's ability to lend money to prospective borrowers) depends a great deal on the existence of the national secondary market. As explained above, a particular lender may have either too much or too little money to lend, depending on conditions in the local economy. It is the secondary market that provides balance by transferring funds from areas where there is an excess to areas where there is a shortage.

The secondary market has a stabilizing effect on local mortgage markets. Lenders are willing to commit themselves to long-term real estate loans even when local funds are scarce, because they can raise more funds by liquidating their loans on the secondary market.

Government-sponsored Agencies. The major players in the secondary market are three government-sponsored agencies:

- Fannie Mae,
- Freddie Mac, and
- Ginnie Mae.

Fannie Mae. The Federal National Mortgage Association (FNMA), often referred to as "Fannie Mae," started out as a federal agency in 1938. Its original purpose was to provide a secondary market for FHA-insured loans.

Fannie Mae has now been reorganized as a private corporation, but it is still chartered by the government and supervised by the Department of Housing and Urban Development (HUD). Fannie Mae now purchases conventional, FHA, and VA loans.

Freddie Mac. Congress created the Federal Home Loan Mortgage Corporation (FHLMC), nicknamed "Freddie Mac," in 1970. Its original purpose was to assist savings and loan associations (which had been hit particularly hard by a recession) by buying their conventional loans. Freddie Mac is now authorized to buy conventional, FHA, and VA loans from any type of lender. Like Fannie Mae, it is government-chartered and supervised by HUD.

Ginnie Mae. The Government National Mortgage Association (GNMA), nicknamed "Ginnie Mae," is one of the federal agencies that make up HUD. Among many other things, Ginnie Mae provides secondary market funds for government-insured loans made through the FHA and VA loan programs. (FHA and VA loans are discussed in Chapter 10.)

Uniform Underwriting Standards. Investors are willing to buy mortgage loans on the secondary market, without ever meeting the borrowers or seeing the properties, because the secondary market agencies have established uniform underwriting standards. Underwriting standards are the criteria lenders use to evaluate a loan applicant and the property offered as security, to determine if the loan would be a good investment or would involve too great a risk of default. (This is discussed in more detail in Chapter 10.) A lender generally cannot sell a mortgage on the secondary market unless the loan conforms to the secondary market's underwriting standards. The uniform standards impose a kind of quality control, assuring investors that the loans they're buying are reasonably safe investments.

Real Estate Finance Documents

Now let's turn to the legal aspects of a real estate finance transaction. Once a buyer has found a lender willing to finance his or her purchase on acceptable terms, the buyer is required to sign the finance documents. The legal documents used in conjunction with most real estate loans are the promissory note and a security instrument, which is either a mortgage or a deed of trust.

We'll look first at promissory notes, and then at security instruments and foreclosure procedures.

Promissory Notes

A promissory note is a written promise to repay a debt. One person loans another money, and the other signs a promissory note, promising to repay the loan (plus interest, in most cases). The borrower who signs the note is called the **maker**, and the lender is called the **payee**.

Basic Provisions. A promissory note states the loan amount (the **principal**), the amount of the payments, when and how the payments are to be made, and the maturity date—when the loan is to be repaid in full. The note also states the interest rate, and whether it is fixed or variable. (In some situations, the state usury law may prohibit the interest rate charged from exceeding a specified maximum.)

Naturally, the names of the borrowers will be listed on the promissory note. If each of the borrowers is to be individually liable for the entire loan amount, then the note will state that the borrowers are "jointly and severally" liable for the debt.

A promissory note in a real estate loan transaction does not need to contain a legal description of the property, because the note concerns only the debt, not the property. The legal description is instead included in the security instrument. Because the promissory note does not concern the property, it is ordinarily not recorded.

The note usually explains the consequences of a failure to repay the loan as agreed. Real estate lenders often protect themselves with late charges, acceleration clauses, and similar provisions; these will be discussed later in this chapter.

Sometimes a promissory note will provide that the borrower must keep a certain amount of money on deposit with the lender as a condition of the loan. The amount of money required to be on deposit is referred to as a compensating balance.

Fig. 9.3 Promissory note

Promissory Note

FOR VALUE RECEIVED, Maker promises to pay to the order of
_____ , or to Bearer,

THE SUM OF $_____ , paid as follows:
$_____ OR MORE per month starting _____ ,
including interest at _____% per annum.

ACCELERATION: In the event of default, Payee or Bearer can declare all sums due and payable at once.

_____
Maker/Borrower
Date: _____

Types of Notes. There are various types of promissory notes, classified according to the way the principal and interest are paid off. With a **straight note**, the periodic payments are interest only, and the full amount of the principal is due in a lump sum (called a balloon payment) when the loan term ends. With an **installment note**, the periodic payments include part of the principal as well as interest. If the installment note is **fully amortized**, the periodic payments are enough to pay off the entire loan, both principal and interest, by the end of the term. (Amortization is discussed in Chapter 10.)

Because the interest due on a loan is computed on the remaining principal balance, a straight note will cost the borrower more in interest over the life of the loan than an amortized loan. This is because the balance of an amortized loan is continually getting smaller; the amount of interest paid on the amortized loan is reduced with each payment.

Whether the payments are interest-only or amortized, the interest paid on a real estate loan is virtually always **simple interest**. In other words, it is computed annually on the remaining principal balance. (By contrast, compound interest is computed on the principal amount plus the accrued interest.)

Signing and Endorsing the Note. Though many copies of the note may be prepared, the maker (the borrower) signs only one copy. This is for the maker's protection. A promissory note is usually a **negotiable instrument**, which means the payee (the lender) has the option of assigning the debt to someone else by endorsing the note. (A note is endorsed to transfer the right to payment to another party in the same way that a check is endorsed. A check is another example of a negotiable instrument.) Having only one copy of the note signed by the maker ensures that the payee can assign the note to only one other party. If there were two or three signed copies, it would be possible to assign the note to two or three different parties, so that more than one could demand payment of the same debt from the maker. When the debt is paid off, the signed copy is returned to the maker marked "Paid."

To be negotiable, the note must state that it is payable either "to the order of" someone or "to bearer." To sell the note (at the secondary market level), the payee endorses it to a third party purchaser. If the purchaser buys the note for value, in good faith, and without notice of defenses against it, the purchaser is called a **holder in due course**.

If a note is endorsed to a specified person, it is called a special endorsement. Otherwise, the endorsement is said to be "in blank." The payee may also state that the endorsement is **without recourse** (or without warranty). This means that the matter of future payments is strictly between the maker and the third party purchaser; the original payee will not be liable to the holder in due course if the maker fails to pay as agreed. An endorsement without recourse is sometimes called a qualified endorsement.

Security Instruments

When someone borrows money to buy real estate, in addition to signing a promissory note in favor of the lender, he or she is also required to sign a security instrument. As we said earlier, the security instrument is either a mortgage or a deed of trust.

Relationship between Note and Security Instrument. It's important to understand the relationship between the promissory note and the security instrument. The promissory note is the borrower's binding promise to repay the loan. The security instrument is a contract that makes the real property collateral for the loan; it secures the loan by creating a lien on the property. If the borrower doesn't repay the loan as agreed,

Fig. 9.4 *Purpose of a security instrument*

Security Instrument
Mortgage or Deed of Trust

- Makes the borrower's property collateral for the loan
- Gives the lender the power to foreclose if the debt is not paid

the security instrument gives the lender the right to foreclose on the property.

A promissory note can be enforced even if it is not accompanied by a security instrument. If the borrower does not repay as agreed, then the lender can file a lawsuit and obtain a judgment against the defaulting borrower. But without a security instrument, the lender might have no way of collecting the judgment. For example, the borrower may have already sold all of his or her property, leaving nothing for the lender (now the judgment creditor) to obtain a lien against.

Title Theory vs. Lien Theory. To understand how security instruments work, it's useful to know how they developed. Historically, to protect the lender against default, a real estate borrower was required to transfer title to the property to the lender for the term of the loan. The borrower remained in possession of the property and had the full use of it, but the lender held title until the loan was paid off. If it wasn't paid off as agreed, the lender could take possession of the property.

This arrangement—in which title to property is given as collateral, but the borrower retains possession—is called **hypothecation**. When title is transferred only as collateral, unaccompanied by possessory rights, it is called legal title, bare title, or naked title. The property rights the borrower retains (without legal title) are referred to as equitable rights or equitable title.

In the United States today, the execution of a mortgage or a deed of trust is still regarded as a transfer of legal title to the lender in a handful of states. Those states are called "title theory" states. However, most states now follow "lien theory." According to lien theory, execution of a mortgage or a deed of trust only creates a lien against the property; it does not transfer title. The borrower retains full title to the property throughout the term of the loan, and the lender simply has the right to foreclose the lien if the borrower defaults.

California has a mixed approach. It is a lien theory state in regard to mortgages, but can be considered a title theory state in regard to deeds of trust. We'll explain this in more detail shortly.

There are actually not many differences between lending and foreclosure procedures in title theory and lien theory states now; the distinction is more theoretical than practical. Under either theory, the borrower will lose the property if the loan is not repaid.

Of course, personal property as well as real property may be used as collateral for a loan. When a borrower transfers possession of an item of personal property to a lender pending repayment of the loan, it is called a **pledge**. Alternatively, the borrower may retain possession of the personal property and give the lender a security interest in it. In that case, the borrower signs a document called a **security agreement**. A security agreement is the equivalent of a mortgage or deed of trust for personal property.

Mortgage vs. Deed of Trust. Now let's consider the two types of real property security instruments: mortgages and deeds of trust. Both are contracts in which a real property owner gives someone else a security interest in the property, usually as collateral for a loan. The most important difference between a mortgage and a deed of trust concerns the procedures for foreclosure if the borrower defaults. We will discuss the foreclosure process later in this chapter.

There are two parties to a mortgage: the **mortgagor** and the **mortgagee**. The mortgagor is the property owner and borrower. The mortgagee is the lender.

A deed of trust (sometimes called a trust deed) has three parties: the **trustor** or **grantor** (the borrower), the **beneficiary** (the lender), and the **trustee**. The trustee is a neutral third party who will handle the foreclosure process, if that proves necessary.

Foreclosure can be considerably easier with a deed of trust than with a mortgage, which makes deeds of trust popular with lenders. In California and a number of other states, deeds of trust are now much more widely used than mortgages.

The terminology used in a deed of trust has its roots in title theory. The document is called a "deed," and it conveys legal title to the trustee; the trustor has equitable title during the loan term. The trustee holds the deed "in trust" pending repayment of the debt. The trustee's title is inactive unless a default occurs. When the loan has been repaid, the trustee "reconveys" title to the trustor.

Recording. Whether it's a mortgage or a deed of trust, the lender should always record the security instrument immediately after the loan is made. The security instrument does not have to be recorded to create a valid lien on the property, but without recording only the lender and borrower would know the lien exists. Other parties who acquired an interest in the property without notice of the lender's security interest would not be subject to it, and subsequent liens would have priority over the lender's.

A real estate licensee who acts as a mortgage loan broker in a transaction is responsible for recording the security instrument. It generally must be recorded before the loan funds are disbursed, but can be recorded within ten days afterward with the written authorization of the lender.

Instruments as Personal Property. Note that even though it creates a lien against real property, a mortgage (or a deed of trust) is itself classified as personal property. A promissory note is also personal property.

Assignment. When a lender sells a mortgage or deed of trust to an investor, in addition to endorsing the promissory note, the lender executes a document called an assignment of mortgage (or deed of trust).

The investor may request an **offset statement** from the borrower. In an offset statement, the borrower confirms the status of the loan (the interest rate, principal balance, etc.) and describes any claims that could affect the investor's interest. The investor may also obtain a similar statement concerning the loan's status from the lender; this is called a **beneficiary's statement**.

Security Instrument Provisions

There is no standard mortgage or deed of trust form, but any security instrument must contain certain provisions and should contain certain others. For instance, every mortgage or deed of trust must contain the signature of the borrower. Most of the following provisions will be found in nearly every mortgage or deed of trust; some of them may also appear in the promissory note. In a few cases (noted below), there is a distinction between the type of provision found in a mortgage and the type found in a deed of trust.

Mortgaging or Granting Clause. Every security instrument is required to include a statement expressing what the instrument is designed to do, indicating that the property is being promised as security for the loan. This is sometimes called the mortgaging clause or (in a deed of trust) the granting clause. The clause may include the words "grant, bargain, sell, and convey," much like a deed, even if the transaction takes place in a lien theory state, where no actual transfer of title occurs.

Once a property has been promised as security for a loan, the borrower must get permission from the lender before making any changes that will affect either the value of the property (such as changing the boundaries of the lot) or the priority of the lien (such as entering into a debt consolidation agreement). Furthermore, the lender's lien will extend to any after-acquired title the borrower obtains in the property; for example, if the borrower improves the property, the lender's lien attaches to the improvements.

Property Description. Like a deed or any other document that transfers an interest in real estate, the security instrument must contain a complete and unambiguous description of the collateral property.

Taxes and Insurance. Security instruments invariably require the borrower to pay general real estate taxes, special assessments, and hazard insurance premiums when due. If the borrower were to allow the taxes to become delinquent or the insurance to lapse, the value of the lender's security interest could be severely diminished—by tax lien foreclosure or a fire, for example.

Acceleration Clause. An acceleration clause states that if the borrower defaults, the lender has the option of declaring the entire loan balance (all the principal still owed) due and payable immediately. Sometimes this is referred to as "calling the note." If the borrower fails to pay the balance as demanded, the lender can sue on the note or foreclose the lien.

An acceleration clause is likely to appear in both the promissory note and in the security instrument. Acceleration can be triggered by failure to make loan payments as agreed in the note, or by breach of a provision in the security instrument, such as failure to keep the property insured.

An acceleration clause that is included in a promissory note does not have any effect on the negotiability of the note, although it may make the note more attractive to investors.

Alienation Clause. An alienation clause is also called a **due-on-sale clause**. This provision gives the lender the right to accelerate the loan—demanding immediate payment of the entire loan balance, as described above—if the borrower sells the property or otherwise alienates an interest in it. (Alienation refers to any transfer of an interest in real estate. See Chapter 3.) An alienation clause does not prohibit the sale of the property, but it allows the lender to force the borrower to pay off the loan if the property is sold without the lender's approval.

Whether or not there is an alienation clause in the mortgage or deed of trust, sale of the property does not extinguish the lender's lien. If the loan is not paid off at closing, the purchaser can either assume the mortgage or deed of trust, or else take title subject to it.

In an **assumption**, the borrower sells the security property to a purchaser who agrees to "assume and pay the mortgage [or deed of trust] according to its terms." The purchaser becomes primarily liable to the lender for repayment of the loan, but the original borrower retains secondary liability in case the purchaser defaults.

By contrast, when a purchaser takes title **subject to** an existing mortgage or deed of trust (without assuming it), the original borrower remains fully liable for the debt. The purchaser is not personally liable to the lender, although in case of default the lender can still foreclose.

Even though the sale of the property doesn't extinguish the mortgage or deed of trust lien, lenders prefer to have the opportunity to approve or reject a prospective purchaser. Thus, most mortgages and deeds of trust include an alienation clause. When a lender evaluates a purchaser and concludes that he or she is creditworthy, the lender may agree to an assumption of the loan. The lender will usually charge an assumption fee, and may also raise the interest rate on the loan. In most cases, the lender will release the original borrower from any further liability; this is called a novation.

Late Payment Penalty. If a lender wants to impose penalties for late payments, the charges must be clearly defined in the finance documents. In California, when a loan is secured by a mortgage or deed of trust on a single-family, owner-occupied residence, the following restrictions on late charges apply. A late payment penalty cannot exceed: 1) six percent of the principal and interest installment due, or 2) five dollars, whichever is greater. A payment cannot be considered late unless it is paid at least ten days after the installment due date.

Note that late payment penalties are not considered interest on the loan, so they are not deductible on the borrower's income tax return.

Lock-in Clause. A lock-in clause prohibits the borrower from **prepaying** the loan—paying it off early, before payment is due. The borrower is "locked in" to the loan for the full term or for a specified number of years, so that the lender will not be deprived of interest it expects to collect. In California, the finance documents for loans on residential property with four units or less cannot contain lock-in clauses.

Prepayment Penalty. Sometimes a lender imposes a penalty if the borrower prepays the loan. For example, a promissory note might state, "The borrower may prepay up to 15% of the original loan amount during any twelve-month period without penalty. If the borrower prepays more than 15%, a prepayment fee equal to six months' interest on the excess will be charged."

A prepayment penalty is intended to compensate the lender for interest that it expected to collect, but won't be collecting because the borrower is paying the loan off early. The prepayment of a loan without a penalty does not in itself cause a direct loss to the lender, but the lender's profit on the loan will be less than expected.

A lender may be willing to waive a prepayment penalty if market interest rates are high. Under those circumstances, when borrowers prepay their loans, the lender can turn around and lend the same money at a higher rate.

California law places some restrictions on prepayment penalties for loans secured by owner-occupied residential property with four units or less. For these loans, the lender may charge prepayment penalties only during the first five years of the loan. There is also a limit on the amount of the prepayment penalties that may be charged during those first five years.

Today most mortgage loans made by institutional lenders do not have prepayment penalties. A mortgage loan without a prepayment penalty is sometimes referred to as an **open mortgage**. When prepayment is allowed without penalty, the promissory note usually contains a provision that states that the borrower can make the required payment "or more" on the specified payment date.

Subordination Clause. Occasionally a security instrument includes a subordination clause, which states that the instrument will have lower lien priority than another mortgage or deed of trust to be executed in the future. The clause makes it possible for a later security instrument to assume a higher priority position—usually first lien position—even though this earlier security instrument was executed and recorded first.

Subordination clauses are common in mortgages and deeds of trust that secure purchase loans for unimproved land, when the borrower is planning to get a construction loan later on. The construction lender will demand first lien position for its loan. Lien priority is ordinarily determined by recording date ("first in time is first in right"), but the subordination clause in the earlier land loan allows the later construction loan to have first lien position.

A subordination clause benefits the borrower, because it makes it easier for the borrower to obtain additional financing on the security property.

Defeasance Clause. A defeasance clause states that when the debt has been paid, the borrower will regain title and the security instrument will be canceled.

If the security instrument is a deed of trust, when the trustor has repaid the loan, the lien is removed by means of a **deed of reconveyance**, also called a reconveyance deed. Within 30 days after the loan payoff, the beneficiary (lender) is required to submit a request for reconveyance to the trustee. Within 21 days after receiving the request, the trustee is required to execute and record a deed of reconveyance.

If these requirements are not complied with, the trustor can ask a title insurance company to execute and record a deed of reconveyance (after proper notice to the trustee and beneficiary). The trustee or the beneficiary will be liable for any damages caused by the failure to record the deed of reconveyance, and will be subject to a statutory penalty of $500.

When a debt secured by a mortgage has been paid in full, a document called a **certificate of discharge** (or sometimes a "satisfaction of mortgage") is used to release the mortgage lien. The mortgagee must record the certificate of discharge within 30 days, or be subject to the penalties listed above.

Either a certificate of discharge or a deed of reconveyance may be referred to as a **lien release**. After a mortgage or deed of trust lien has been released, upon the written request of the borrower, the mortgagee or trustee is required to return the original note and security instrument to the borrower.

Foreclosure Procedures

If the borrower doesn't repay a secured loan as agreed, the lender may foreclose and collect the debt from the proceeds of a forced sale. Establishing the lender's right to foreclose is the basic purpose of a security instrument. There are different foreclosure procedures for mortgages and deeds of trust; in fact, that is the key difference between the two types of security instruments.

Mortgage Foreclosure. Mortgage foreclosures are sometimes called judicial foreclosures because they are carried out through the court system. Upon default, the lender files a lawsuit against the borrower in a court in the county where the collateral property is located. Any lienholders who have liens with lower priority than the mortgage (junior lienholders) are notified of the foreclosure action, so that they can take steps to protect their interests.

The lender will also record a **lis pendens**, which is a notice of a pending legal action (in this case, the foreclosure action) that could affect specified real property. A lis pendens makes the final court judgment binding on anyone who might acquire an interest in the property while the foreclosure action is pending.

When the complaint is heard in court, in the absence of unusual circumstances, the judge will issue a **decree of foreclosure**, ordering the property to be sold to satisfy the debt. The judge appoints a receiver to conduct the sale. The sale, which takes the form of a public auction, is sometimes referred to as a **sheriff's sale**.

Reinstatement. While the foreclosure action is pending, the borrower can cure the loan default by paying all the past due amounts, plus the costs and fees of the lawsuit. This is called **reinstatement**. When the loan is reinstated, all foreclosure proceedings are terminated, and the mortgage continues in full force and effect. Once the decree of foreclosure is issued, this right of reinstatement no longer exists.

Redemption. The borrower may have a second opportunity to reclaim his or her property. After the sheriff's sale, the borrower may, in some cases, **redeem** the property by paying off the entire debt, including interest, costs, and fees. The time period during which this **statutory right of redemption** exists varies. The redemption period continues for three months after the sale if the sale proceeds were enough to pay off the debt, plus interest, costs, and fees. The redemption period continues for one year after the sale date if the proceeds were not enough to pay off the full debt. However, if the lender waives its right to a deficiency judgment (discussed below) or is prohibited from obtaining a deficiency judgment, there is no right of redemption at all.

Certificate of Sale. When the property is sold subject to the statutory right of redemption, the successful bidder at the sheriff's sale receives a **certificate of sale** instead of a deed. The borrower is entitled to keep possession of the property during the redemption period, provided he or she pays reasonable rent to the holder of the certificate of sale. Only at the end of the redemption period is the certificate holder given a **sheriff's deed**, which transfers title and the right of possession of the property to the new owner.

The redemption period makes bidding at a mortgage foreclosure unappealing to many investors; understandably, they do not want to wait to gain title to the property. For this reason, there are often no outside bidders at a judicial foreclosure sale, and the lender acquires the property by bidding the amount the borrower owes. This is called **credit bidding**.

If there are outside bidders at the auction and the proceeds from the sale exceed the amount necessary to satisfy all valid liens against the property, the surplus belongs to the borrower.

Deficiency Judgments. If the proceeds of the foreclosure sale are insufficient to satisfy the debt, the lender can obtain a **deficiency judgment** against the borrower, unless the transaction is exempted by the anti-deficiency rules. A deficiency judgment is a personal judgment against the borrower for the difference between the amount owing on the debt and the net proceeds from the foreclosure sale.

The anti-deficiency rules prohibit deficiency judgments under the following circumstances:

1. when the foreclosure is by a trustee's sale (nonjudicial foreclosure);
2. when the security instrument is a purchase money mortgage given to the seller for all or part of the purchase price (seller financing);
3. when the security instrument is a mortgage given to a third-party lender to finance the purchase of an owner-occupied residential dwelling with four or fewer units; or
4. when the fair market value of the property exceeds the amount of the debt.

As you can see, a deficiency judgment would be prohibited after foreclosure of a typical home purchase loan.

Deed of Trust Foreclosure. A deed of trust foreclosure differs significantly from a mortgage foreclosure. Every deed of trust has a **power of sale** clause. If the borrower defaults, this provision authorizes the trustee to sell the property, through a process known as nonjudicial foreclosure. The trustee does not have to file a foreclosure lawsuit or get a judicial decree of foreclosure. Instead, the trustee can sell the property at an auction called a **trustee's sale**, and use the sale proceeds to pay off the debt owed to the lender (beneficiary). As with a sheriff's sale, if the trustee's sale results in a surplus, the excess amount belongs to the borrower.

Notices of Default and Sale. A nonjudicial foreclosure must be conducted in accordance with the procedures prescribed by statute. First, the trustee must record a **notice of default** in the county where the property is located, and also send a copy of the notice to the borrower and all lienholders. Three months after recording the notice of default, the trustee is required to publish a **notice of sale**, which must run in a newspaper of general circulation for at least 20

Fig. 9.5 *Comparison of mortgages and deeds of trust*

Security Instruments	
Mortgage	**Deed of Trust**
• Mortgagor and mortgagee • Judicial foreclosure • Reinstatement before decree of foreclosure • Redemption after sheriff's sale • Deficiency judgment allowed (subject to limitations)	• Trustor, beneficiary, and trustee • Nonjudicial foreclosure • Reinstatement before trustee's sale • No post-sale redemption • No deficiency judgment

days. In addition, the notice of sale must be recorded, posted on the security property, and sent to everyone who received a notice of default. The trustee's sale cannot take place until at least 20 days after the first date of publication of the notice of sale.

Reinstatement and Redemption. As with a mortgage foreclosure, the borrower under a deed of trust has a period in which he or she can reinstate the loan and stop the foreclosure proceedings. The borrower may reinstate the loan at any time from the notice of default up until five business days before the sale. This means the reinstatement period is at least three months and 15 days. The loan is reinstated by paying all past-due installments, plus costs and fees. If the loan is reinstated, the trustee cannot sell the property.

The borrower can also redeem the property by paying off the full balance of the loan plus costs at any time prior to the actual sale.

Trustee's Deed. The successful bidder at the trustee's sale receives a trustee's deed, which terminates all of the borrower's rights in the property. There is no post-sale redemption period or right of possession for the borrower, as there may be in a mortgage foreclosure.

The lender may bid at the sale, and is entitled to apply the amount due on the loan towards the bid. In other words, credit bidding is allowed.

Deficiency Judgments. If a lender forecloses on a deed of trust by means of a trustee's sale, its recovery is limited to the proceeds of the sale. The lender cannot bring any further action against the borrower, even if the sale proceeds do not cover the amount owing on the loan. A suit to recover such a deficiency is barred by the anti-deficiency rules discussed above. However, if the deed of trust is foreclosed judicially, a deficiency judgment may be possible.

Protection of Junior Lienholders. A trustee's sale under a deed of trust destroys not only the borrower's interest in the property, but also the interests of any junior lienholders (those with subordinate liens). To protect junior lienholders, the senior lienholder must send notices of default and sale to all junior lienholders who have recorded interests in the property. If the notices are not sent to a lienholder of record, that lienholder is not bound by the sale.

A junior lienholder can protect his or her interest by paying the delinquencies on the senior lien (curing the default) and adding the amount of these payments to the balance due under the junior lien. The junior lienholder may then foreclose his or her own lien. A purchaser at a junior lienholder's sale takes title to the property subject to any senior liens that may exist.

Comparison of Judicial and Nonjudicial Foreclosure. Many lenders prefer a deed of trust to a mortgage because it enables them to bypass court proceedings, which are often slow. Also, the trustee's sale is final; there is no statutory redemption period afterward. The disadvantage of a deed of trust from the lender's point of view is that after nonjudicial foreclosure, there is no right to a deficiency judgment. If the proceeds of the trustee's sale are insufficient to satisfy the debt, the lender takes a loss; the lender is not allowed to sue the borrower to make up the deficiency.

Deed in Lieu of Foreclosure. A defaulting borrower who doesn't have the resources to cure the default or redeem the foreclosed property may opt to give the lender a deed in lieu of foreclosure. The deed in lieu transfers title from the borrower to the lender; this satisfies the debt and stops foreclosure proceedings. A borrower might do this in order to protect his or her credit rating.

The lender takes title subject to any other liens that encumber the property. Thus, before accepting a deed in lieu, the lender will determine what other liens have attached to the property since the original loan was made.

Foreclosure vs. Bankruptcy. Although they can both happen to a person at the same time, foreclosure and bankruptcy are entirely separate legal procedures. A real property owner who is facing foreclosure is not necessarily also facing bankruptcy. And a property owner can declare bankruptcy without necessarily having his or her property foreclosed on.

Bankruptcy is a federal court procedure that enables a debtor to reduce, modify, or eliminate debts that have become unmanageable. If a mortgage or deed of trust borrower who is facing foreclosure files for bankruptcy, the foreclosure proceedings are temporarily stayed (put on hold). Any other actions by creditors are also stayed.

There are two types of consumer bankruptcy: Chapter 7 and Chapter 13. (A third type of bankruptcy, Chapter 11, applies only to businesses.) In Chapter 13, the debtor enters into a repayment plan to partially repay the creditors over time. The debtor is ordinarily allowed to keep his or her property.

In Chapter 7, most of the debtor's obligations are completely discharged. However, certain debts are non-dischargeable. These include child support, alimony, student loans, and federal income taxes for the three years previous to filing bankruptcy.

In exchange for the discharge, the Chapter 7 debtor is required to surrender all non-exempt property. Household goods and cars are exempt (with certain limits); life insurance, pensions, and public benefits are also exempt.

If the debtor owns a home, the homestead exemption will protect at least some of the debtor's equity. In California, the exemption amount is $50,000 for an individual, $75,000 for a head of household, and $150,000 for someone who is over 65 or disabled. If the debtor's equity is less than the applicable exemption amount and the mortgage payments are current, the debtor will be allowed to keep the home. If the debtor's equity is greater than the exemption amount, the home will be sold. (See Chapter 4 for more information about the homestead exemption.)

Types of Mortgage Loans

You will often hear "mortgage" or "deed of trust" coupled with an adjective that serves to describe the particular function of the security instrument or the circumstances in which it is used. For example, a "construction mortgage" is a mortgage used to secure a construction loan; a "blanket mortgage" is one that secures a loan with two or more parcels of property as collateral. Below are explanations of some of the most common of these terms. For the most part, we will use the term "mortgage" here, rather than the more cumbersome term "mortgage or deed of trust." In each case, however, a deed of trust could be (and today often would be) used instead of a mortgage.

First Mortgage. A first mortgage is simply any security instrument that holds first lien position; it has the highest lien priority. A second mortgage is one that holds second lien position, and so on.

Senior and Junior Mortgages. Any mortgage that has a higher lien position than another is called a senior mortgage in relation to that other one, which is called a junior mortgage. A first mortgage is senior to a second mortgage; a second mortgage is junior to a first mortgage, but senior to a third.

As explained in Chapter 4, lien priority matters in the event of a foreclosure, since the sale proceeds are used to pay off the first lien first. If any money remains, the second lien is paid, then the third, and so on, until the money is exhausted. Obviously, it is much better to be in first lien position than in third.

Purchase Money Mortgage. This term is used in two ways. Sometimes it means any mortgage loan used to finance the purchase of the property that is the collateral for the loan: a buyer borrows money to buy property and gives the lender a mortgage on that same property to secure the loan.

In other cases, "purchase money mortgage" is used more narrowly, to mean a mortgage that a buyer gives to a seller in a seller-financed transaction. Instead of paying the full price in cash at closing, the buyer gives the seller a mortgage on the property and pays the price off in installments. In such a situation, the seller is said to "take back" or "carry back" the mortgage.

> **Example:** The sales price is $240,000. The buyer makes a $24,000 downpayment and signs a note and purchase money mortgage in favor of the seller for $216,000. The buyer will pay the seller in monthly installments at 7% interest over 15 years.

In this narrower sense, a purchase money mortgage is sometimes called a **soft money mortgage**, because the borrower receives credit instead of actual cash. If a borrower gives a lender a mortgage and receives cash in return (as with a bank loan), it is called a **hard money mortgage**.

Swing Loan. It often happens that buyers are ready to purchase a new home before they've succeeded in selling their current home. They need funds for their downpayment and closing costs right away, without waiting for the proceeds from the eventual sale of the current home. In this situation, the buyers may be able to obtain a swing loan. A swing loan is usually secured by equity in the property that is for sale, and it will be paid off when that sale closes. A swing loan is also called a **gap loan** or a **bridge loan**.

Budget Mortgage. The monthly payment on a budget mortgage includes not just principal and interest on the loan, but one-twelfth of the year's property taxes and hazard insurance premiums as well. Most residential loans are secured by budget mortgages. This is the safest and most practical way for lenders to make sure the property taxes and insurance premiums are paid on time.

Package Mortgage. When personal property is included in the sale of real estate and financed along with the real estate with one loan, the security instrument is called a package mortgage. For example, if a buyer bought ovens, freezers, and other equipment along with a restaurant building, the purchase might be financed with a package mortgage.

Construction Mortgage. A construction mortgage is simply a mortgage that secures a construction loan. A construction loan (sometimes called an **interim loan**) is a temporary loan used to finance the construction of improvements on the land. When the construction is completed, the construction loan is replaced by permanent financing, which is called a **take-out loan**. A lender's promise to make a take-out loan at a later time when the borrower needs it is called a **standby loan commitment**.

If a construction loan has no specific maturity date (for example, if the loan is due "in five years"), the period of repayment begins to run on the date stated in the promissory note. For instance, if the loan term is five years and the note is dated January 10, but the loan funds are not disbursed until March 15, the five-year period begins running on January 10.

Construction loans can be profitable, but they are considered quite risky. Accordingly, lenders charge high interest rates and loan fees on construction loans, then supervise the progress of the construction. There is always a danger that the borrower will overspend on a construction project and exhaust the loan proceeds before construction is completed. If the borrower cannot afford to finish, the lender is left with a security interest in a partially completed project.

Lenders have devised a variety of plans for disbursement of construction loan proceeds that guard against overspending by the borrower. Perhaps the most common is the **fixed disbursement plan**. This calls for a series of predetermined disbursements, called **obligatory advances**, at various stages of construction. Interest begins to accrue with the first disbursement.

> **Example:** A construction loan agreement stipulates that the lender will release 10% of the proceeds when the project is 20% complete, and thereafter 20% draws will be available whenever construction has progressed another 20% toward completion.

The lender will often hold back 10% or more of the loan proceeds until the period for claiming mechanic's liens has expired, to protect against unpaid liens that could affect the marketability of the property. The construction loan agreement usually states that if a valid mechanic's lien is recorded, the lender may use the undisbursed portion of the loan to pay it off.

Blanket Mortgage. When a borrower mortgages more than one piece of real property as security for a single loan, it is called a blanket mortgage. For example, if one property does not provide sufficient collateral for a loan, another property that the borrower owns may be offered as additional collateral. The borrower will give the lender a blanket mortgage covering both properties.

Blanket mortgages are also used in subdivision development. For instance, a ten-acre parcel subdivided into twenty lots might be used to secure one loan made to the subdivider.

Blanket mortgages usually have a **partial release clause** (also called a partial satisfaction clause, or in a blanket deed of trust, a partial reconveyance clause). This provision requires the lender to release some of the security property from the blanket lien when specified portions of the overall debt have been paid off.

> **Example:** A ten-acre parcel subdivided into twenty lots secures a $1,500,000 loan. After selling one lot for $175,000, the subdivider pays the lender $150,000 and receives a release for the lot that is being sold. The blanket mortgage is no longer a lien against that lot, so the subdivider can convey clear title to the lot buyer.

A release schedule determines how much of the loan must be paid off in order to have a lot released from the blanket lien. The borrower typically has to pay off a larger share of the loan to release the first lots sold than to release the last lots sold. This arrangement helps protect the lender's security interest, since the best lots in a development often sell first.

Note that a mortgage is not the only type of lien that can be a blanket encumbrance. A contractor who provides labor or materials on more than one property owned by the same person can obtain a blanket mechanic's lien.

Participation Mortgage. A participation mortgage allows the lender to participate in the earnings generated by the mortgaged property, usually in addition to collecting interest payments on the principal. In some cases the lender participates by becoming a part-owner of the property. Participation loans are most common on large commercial projects where the lender is an insurance company or other large investor.

Shared Appreciation Mortgage. Real property ordinarily appreciates (increases in value) over time. Appreciation usually benefits only the property owner, by adding to his or her equity. With a shared appreciation mortgage, however, the lender is entitled to a specified share of the increase in the property's value.

Wraparound Mortgage. A wraparound mortgage is a new mortgage that includes or "wraps around" an existing first mortgage on the property. Wraparounds are generally used only in seller-financed transactions.

> **Example:** A home is being sold for $200,000; there is an existing $80,000 mortgage on the property. Instead of assuming that mortgage, the buyer merely takes title subject to it. The buyer gives the seller a $40,000 downpayment and a second mortgage for the remaining $160,000 of the purchase price. The $160,000 second mortgage is a wraparound mortgage. Each month, the buyer makes a payment on the wraparound to the seller, and the seller uses part of that payment to make the monthly payment on the underlying $80,000 mortgage.

Wraparound financing works only if the underlying loan does not contain an alienation clause (see the discussion earlier in this chapter). Otherwise the lender would require the seller to pay off the underlying loan at the time of sale. A wraparound arrangement should always be designed so that the underlying loan will be paid off before the wraparound, to ensure that the buyer's title will not still be encumbered with the seller's debt after the buyer has paid the full purchase price.

If the security instrument used for this type of financing arrangement is a deed of trust rather than a mortgage, it is called an **all-inclusive trust deed**.

Open-end Mortgage. An open-end mortgage sets a borrowing limit, but allows the borrower to reborrow, when needed, any part of the debt that has been repaid, without having to negotiate a new mortgage. The interest rate on the loan is usually a variable rate that rises and falls with market interest rates. The open-end mortgage is often used as a business tool by builders and farmers.

Graduated Payment Mortgage. A graduated payment mortgage allows the borrower to make smaller payments at first and gradually step up to larger payments. For example, the payments might increase annually for the first three to five years of the loan, and then remain level for the rest of the loan term. This arrangement can benefit borrowers who expect their earnings to increase during the next few years.

Growing Equity Mortgage. A growing equity mortgage, sometimes called a rapid payoff mortgage, is also beneficial to borrowers whose income is expected to increase. This type of mortgage uses a fixed interest rate throughout its term, but payments will increase according to an index or preset schedule. The amount of the increase is applied directly to the principal balance, thus allowing the borrower to pay off the loan more quickly.

Reverse Equity Mortgage. A reverse equity mortgage, sometimes called a reverse annuity mortgage, is designed to provide income to older homeowners. The owner borrows against the home's equity but will receive a monthly check from the lender, rather than making monthly payments. Typically, a reverse equity borrower must be over a certain age (for example, 62 or 65) and must own the home with little or no outstanding mortgage balance. The home usually must be sold when the owner dies in order to pay back the mortgage.

Refinancing. Borrowers who refinance their mortgage are actually obtaining an entirely new mortgage loan to replace the existing one. The funds from the refinance loan are used to pay off the existing loan.

Borrowers often choose to refinance when market interest rates drop; refinancing at a lower interest rate can result in substantial savings over the long run. Another situation in which a borrower is likely to refinance is when the payoff date of the existing mortgage is approaching and a large balloon payment will be required.

Land Contracts

Most real estate buyers finance their purchases with loans from an institutional lender. But as we've discussed, some transactions are financed by the seller; the seller extends credit to the buyer, accepting a downpayment and arranging to be paid over time, instead of requiring full payment at closing. In certain cases, a seller offers more favorable terms than institutional lenders (such as an exceptionally low interest rate), in order to attract a wider range of potential buyers and obtain a higher price for the property.

In a seller-financed transaction, the seller may ask the buyer to execute a mortgage or a deed of trust, just like an institutional lender. (As explained earlier, this is often called a purchase money mortgage loan.) Sellers also have the option of using a third type of security instrument: the **land contract**, also called a contract for deed, installment sales contract, real estate contract, or contract of sale.

The parties to a land contract are the **vendor** (the seller) and the **vendee** (the buyer). The vendee agrees to pay the purchase price (plus interest) in installments over a specified number of years. The vendee takes possession of the property right away, but the vendor retains legal title until the full price has been paid. In the meantime, the vendee has equitable title to the property. When the contract is finally paid off, the vendor delivers the deed to the vendee.

The rights and responsibilities of the buyer and seller under a land contract are discussed in detail in Chapter 7.

Chapter Summary

1. The federal government influences real estate finance directly and indirectly through its fiscal and monetary policy. The federal deficit may affect the availability of investment funds. The Federal Reserve Board uses key interest rates, reserve requirements, and open market operations to implement monetary policy, influencing the pace of economic growth and market interest rates.

2. The primary market is the local finance market, in which lenders make mortgage loans to borrowers. In the secondary market, mortgages are bought and sold by investors. The federal government created the major secondary market agencies (Fannie Mae, Freddie Mac, and Ginnie Mae) to help moderate local real estate cycles.

3. A promissory note is a written promise to repay a debt. For a real estate loan, the borrower is required to sign a negotiable promissory note along with a security instrument, which makes the borrower's property collateral for the loan.

4. The two main types of security instruments are mortgages and deeds of trust. The central difference between the two is that a deed of trust includes a power of sale clause, which allows the trustee to foreclose nonjudicially in the event of default.

5. Most security instruments include an acceleration clause and an alienation clause; some also have a late payment clause or a subordination clause. If there is no alienation clause, the loan can be assumed without the lender's consent.

6. A mortgage is foreclosed judicially. The borrower has the right to cure the default and reinstate the loan before the sheriff's sale, and a statutory right of redemption for a certain period afterwards. The lender may be entitled to a deficiency judgment.

7. A deed of trust can be foreclosed nonjudicially, by the trustee, which is usually much faster and less expensive than judicial foreclosure. Until shortly before the trustee's sale, the borrower has the right to cure the default and reinstate the loan. After the sale, the borrower has no right of redemption. The lender cannot obtain a deficiency judgment.

8. There are many different types of mortgage loans, including purchase money, swing, budget, package, construction, blanket, participation, shared appreciation, wraparound, open-end, graduated payment, growing equity, and reverse equity mortgages.

🔑 Key Terms

Federal Reserve Board—The body that regulates commercial banks and sets and implements the federal government's monetary policy; commonly called "the Fed."

Discount rate and federal funds rate—Two interest rates set by the Fed that have an effect on market interest rates.

Reserve requirements—The percentages of deposits commercial banks must keep on reserve with a Federal Reserve Bank.

Open market operations—The Fed's activities in buying and selling government securities.

Primary market—The local finance market, where individuals obtain loans (from banks, savings and loans, and other lenders).

Secondary market—The national finance market, where mortgages are bought and sold as investments.

Promissory note—A written promise to repay a debt.

Mortgage—A two-party security instrument that gives the lender (mortgagee) the right to foreclose on the security property by judicial process if the borrower (mortgagor) defaults.

Deed of trust—A three-party security instrument that includes a power of sale clause, allowing the trustee to foreclose nonjudicially if the borrower (trustor) fails to pay the lender (beneficiary) or otherwise defaults.

Acceleration clause—A provision in loan documents that gives the lender the right to demand immediate payment in full if the borrower defaults.

Alienation clause—A provision in a security instrument that gives the lender the right to accelerate the loan if the borrower transfers the property. Also called a due-on-sale clause.

Assumption—When a borrower sells the security property to a buyer who agrees to take on personal liability for repayment of the existing mortgage or deed of trust.

Defeasance clause—A provision giving the borrower the right to regain title to the security property when the debt is repaid.

Certificate of discharge—The document a mortgagee gives to the mortgagor when the mortgage debt is paid off, releasing the property from the lien. Also called a satisfaction of mortgage.

Deed of reconveyance—The document a trustee gives the trustor when the debt secured by a deed of trust is paid off, releasing the property from the lien.

Land contract—A contract between a seller (vendor) and a buyer (vendee) of real estate, in which the seller retains legal title to the property while the buyer pays off the purchase price in installments.

⌒⌒ Chapter Quiz

1. In a tight money market, when business is slow, a reduction in interest rates would be expected to cause:

    a) an increase in real estate sales
    b) more bank lending activity
    c) increased business activity
    d) All of the above

2. Which of the following actions by the Federal Reserve Board would tend to increase the money supply?

    a) Selling government securities on the open market
    b) Buying government securities on the open market
    c) Increasing the federal discount rate
    d) Increasing reserve requirements

3. Funds for single-family mortgage loans are supplied by:

    a) Fannie Mae
    b) savings and loan associations
    c) Both a) and b)
    d) Neither a) nor b)

4. With an installment note, the periodic payments:

    a) include both principal and interest
    b) are interest only
    c) are principal only
    d) are called balloon payments

5. A mortgage loan provision that permits the lender to declare the entire loan balance due upon default by the borrower is a/an:

    a) acceleration clause
    b) escalator clause
    c) forfeiture clause
    d) subordination clause

6. A mortgage loan provision that permits the lender to declare the entire loan balance due if the property is sold is a/an:

    a) escalator clause
    b) subordination clause
    c) alienation clause
    d) prepayment provision

7. After a sheriff's sale, the mortgagor has a specified period in which to redeem the property. This period is called the:

    a) lien period
    b) equitable redemption period
    c) statutory redemption period
    d) reinstatement period

8. After a trustee's sale, if there are any sale proceeds left over after paying off liens and foreclosure expenses, the money belongs to the:

    a) sheriff
    b) beneficiary
    c) trustee
    d) foreclosed owner

9. The document that a mortgagee gives a mortgagor after the debt has been completely paid off is called a:

    a) partial release
    b) certificate of discharge
    c) deed of reconveyance
    d) sheriff's deed

10. In a nonjudicial foreclosure, the borrower is entitled to:

    a) a statutory redemption period following the sheriff's sale
    b) a deficiency judgment
    c) a deed in lieu of foreclosure
    d) cure the default and reinstate the loan before the trustee's sale

11. When a buyer gives a mortgage to the seller rather than an institutional lender, it may be referred to as a:

   a) purchase money mortgage
   b) land contract
   c) shared appreciation mortgage
   d) reverse equity mortgage

12. A budget mortgage:

   a) is a loan made to a low-income borrower
   b) is a construction loan with a fixed disbursement plan
   c) is secured by personal property as well as real property
   d) has monthly payments that include taxes and insurance as well as principal and interest

13. The owner of five parcels of real property wants a loan. She offers all five parcels as security. She will be required to execute a:

   a) soft money mortgage
   b) participation mortgage
   c) package mortgage
   d) blanket mortgage

14. Victor is borrowing money to buy some land, and he plans to build a home on the property later on. To ensure that he will be able to get a construction loan when the time comes, Victor should make sure the mortgage he executes for the land loan includes a/an:

   a) lien waiver
   b) subordination clause
   c) acceleration clause
   d) wraparound clause

15. Under a fixed disbursement plan for a construction loan, the contractor is usually entitled to his or her final draw when:

   a) the project has been satisfactorily completed
   b) 80% of the work has been completed
   c) the building department issues a certificate of occupancy
   d) the period for claiming mechanic's liens expires

🖝 Answer Key

1. d) The Fed lowers interest rates in times of economic downturn in an attempt to stimulate the economy.

2. b) When the Fed buys government securities, it puts more money into circulation, which increases the money supply.

3. c) Mortgage money comes from the primary market (in the form of savings deposits) and from the secondary market (when investors like Fannie Mae buy mortgages).

4. a) An installment note involves periodic payments that include some of the principal as well as interest.

5. a) An acceleration clause gives the lender the right to declare the entire debt immediately due and payable if the borrower defaults.

6. c) An alienation clause allows the lender to accelerate the loan if the borrower transfers the security property without the lender's approval.

7. c) The statutory redemption period is the period of time after the sheriff's sale in which the borrower has the right to redeem the property by paying off the entire debt, plus costs.

8. d) Any excess proceeds from a foreclosure sale belong to the borrower—that is, to the foreclosed owner.

9. b) When the debt has been fully paid off, a mortgagee gives the mortgagor a certificate of discharge, releasing the property from the lien.

10. d) In the nonjudicial foreclosure of a deed of trust, the trustor is permitted to cure the default and reinstate the loan before the trustee's sale is held.

11. a) A mortgage given by a buyer to a seller is sometimes called a purchase money mortgage.

12. d) A budget mortgage payment includes a share of the property taxes and hazard insurance as well as principal and interest.

13. d) A blanket mortgage has more than one parcel of property as collateral.

14. b) A subordination clause in the mortgage for the land loan would give it lower priority than a mortgage executed later on for a construction loan. Lenders generally require first lien position for construction loans, because they are considered especially risky.

15. d) Construction lenders usually delay the final disbursement until no more mechanic's liens can be filed.

Applying for a Residential Loan

Chapter Overview

When it's time to arrange financing, a home buyer must shop for a loan and choose a lender. Next, the buyer fills out a loan application and supplies supporting documentation. Then the lender evaluates the application and decides whether or not to approve the loan. The first part of this chapter describes the different types of lenders in the primary market, explains loan fees, and discusses the Truth in Lending Act (a law that helps prospective borrowers compare loans) as well as state loan disclosure laws. The second part of the chapter covers the loan application form and the underwriting process. The last part of the chapter explains various features of a home purchase loan and provides an overview of the major residential finance programs: conventional loans, FHA-insured loans, VA-guaranteed loans, and Cal-Vet loans.

Choosing a Lender

Many home buyers look to their real estate agent for guidance in choosing a lender. Agents should be familiar with the lenders in their area and know how to help buyers compare the loans that different lenders are offering. We're going to discuss the various types of lenders that make home purchase loans, the fees that lenders charge, the Truth in Lending Act, and state finance disclosure laws.

Types of Mortgage Lenders

There are several major sources of residential financing in the primary market. Residential mortgage lenders include:

- savings and loans,
- commercial banks,
- savings banks,
- credit unions, and
- mortgage companies.

Savings and Loans. Savings and loan associations (S&Ls) are sometimes called "thrift institutions" or simply "thrifts." An S&L is chartered (authorized to do business) by either the federal government or a state government.

Savings and loans started out in the nineteenth century strictly as residential real estate lenders. Over the years they carried on their original function, investing the majority of their assets in purchase loans for single-family homes. By the mid-1950s, they dominated local residential mortgage markets, becoming the nation's largest single source of funds for financing homes.

Many factors contributed to the dominance of savings and loans; one of the most important was that home purchase loans had become long-term loans, usually having a 30-year term. S&Ls used individual savings—the savings deposits of their customers—as their main source of loan funds. Since most of the funds held by S&Ls were long-term deposits, S&Ls were comfortable making long-term home loans.

While savings and loans have branched out into different types of lending, they continue to focus on home mortgage loans. Yet S&Ls no longer dominate the residential finance market, because other types of lenders have become more involved in it.

Commercial Banks. A commercial bank is either a national bank, chartered by the federal government, or a state bank, chartered by a state government. Commercial banks are the largest source of investment funds in the United States. As their name implies, they were traditionally oriented toward commercial lending activities, supplying capital for business ventures and construction activities on a comparatively short-term basis.

In the past, residential mortgages were not a major part of commercial banks' business. That was partly because most of their deposits were demand deposits (checking accounts), and the government limited the amount of long-term investments the banks could make. But eventually banks began accepting more and more long-term deposits; demand deposits now represent a much smaller share of banks' total deposits than they once did.

While banks have continued to emphasize commercial loans, they have also diversified their lending, with a substantial increase in personal loans and home mortgages, especially to already-existing customers. They now have a significant share of the residential finance market.

Savings Banks. Savings banks started out in the nineteenth century offering financial services to small depositors, especially immigrants and members of the working class. They were called mutual savings banks (MSBs) because they were organized as mutual companies, owned by and operated for the benefit of their depositors (as opposed to stockholders).

Traditionally, MSBs were similar to savings and loans. They served their local communities. Their customers were individuals rather than businesses, and most of their deposits were savings deposits. Although the MSBs made many residential mortgage loans, they did not concentrate on them to the extent that S&Ls did. The MSBs were also involved in other types of lending, such as personal loans.

Today, savings banks can be organized as mutual companies or stock companies. Residential mortgages continue to be an important part of their business.

Credit Unions. Credit unions are depository institutions, like banks and S&Ls. But unlike banks and S&Ls, credit unions usually serve only members of a particular group, such as the members of a union or a professional association, or the employees of a large company.

Credit unions traditionally provided small personal loans to their members. In recent years, many credit unions have emphasized home equity loans, which are generally short-term. (A **home equity loan** is a mortgage on the borrower's equity in the home he or she already owns.) Some credit unions now make home purchase loans, and they're likely to expand that aspect of their business.

Mortgage Companies. Mortgage companies have been a rapidly growing force in residential lending. Unlike banks, S&Ls, and credit unions, mortgage companies are not depository institutions, so they don't lend out depositors' funds. Instead, they act as loan correspondents, intermediaries between large investors and home buyers applying for financing.

A **loan correspondent** lends an investor's money to buyers and then services the loans (collecting and processing the loan payments on behalf of the investor) in exchange for servicing fees. In some cases a bank or an S&L will act as a loan correspondent, but mortgage companies have specialized in this role.

Mortgage companies often act on behalf of large investors such as life insurance companies and pension funds. These investors control vast amounts of capital in the form of insurance premiums and employer contributions to employee pensions. This money generally isn't subject to sudden withdrawal, so it's well suited to investment in long-term mortgages. Since these large investors often operate on a national scale, they have neither the time nor the resources to understand the particular risks of local real estate markets or to deal with the day-to-day management of their loans. So instead of making loans directly to borrowers, insurance companies, pension plans, and other large investors hire local loan correspondents. Naturally, they prefer large, long-term commercial loans and stay away from high-risk, short-term construction loans.

Mortgage companies also borrow money from banks on a short-term basis and use the money to originate loans. They package the loans and sell them to the secondary market agencies and other private investors. Using short-term financing to make loans before selling them to permanent investors is referred to as **warehousing**.

Banks and S&Ls generally keep some of the loans they make "in portfolio," instead of selling them to investors. In contrast, mortgage companies do not keep any of the loans they make. The loans are either made on behalf of an investor or else sold to an investor.

Mortgage companies are sometimes called mortgage bankers. The term "mortgage banker" should not be confused with "mortgage broker." A mortgage broker simply negotiates loans, bringing borrowers together with lenders in exchange for a commission. Once the loan has been arranged, the mortgage broker's involvement ends. Mortgage bankers, on the other hand, originate loans on behalf of an investor and then service the loans to the end of their terms, in exchange for servicing fees. Although mortgage companies may act as mortgage brokers, for the most part they are mortgage bankers.

Private Lenders. Real estate limited partnerships, real estate investment trusts (see Chapter 2), and other types of private investment groups put a great deal of money into real estate. They often finance large residential developments and commercial ventures such as shopping centers and office buildings. They do not offer loans to individual home buyers, however.

From the home buyer's point of view, the most important type of private lender is the home seller. Sometimes sellers provide all of the financing for the purchase of their homes, and it's quite common for sellers to supplement the financing their buyers obtain from an institutional lender. In fact, sellers are the most common source of second (or junior) mortgages for home purchases. Sellers are an especially important source of financing when institutional loans are hard to come by or market interest rates are high.

Comparing Types of Lenders. At one time, financial institutions in the United States were quite specialized. It was almost as if each type of institution had its own function—its own types of deposits, its own types of services, and its own types of loans. That is no longer true. Federal deregulation of financial institutions in the 1980s removed a number of restrictions that applied to certain types of institutions; for example, limits on the maximum interest rates they could pay their depositors were lifted. This caused the historical differences between lenders to gradually fade. To a great extent, all of the major depository institutions can now be regarded as "financial supermarkets," offering a wide range of services and loans.

There still are differences between the types of institutions, in terms of lending habits and government regulations, but these generally will not affect a loan applicant who wants to finance the purchase of a home.

Loan Costs

For the majority of buyers, the primary consideration in choosing a lender is how much the loan they need is going to cost. While the interest rate has the greatest impact, lenders impose other charges that can greatly affect the cost of a loan. Most important among these are origination fees and discount points. Both are often simply grouped together as "points." The term "point" is short for "percentage point." A point is one percentage point (one percent) of the loan amount. For example, on a $90,000 loan, one point would be $900; six points would be $5,400.

Origination Fees. A loan origination fee is designed to pay administrative costs the lender incurs in processing a loan; it is sometimes called a service fee, an administrative charge, or simply a loan fee. An origination fee is charged in virtually every residential loan transaction. It is a closing cost, paid when the transaction closes, and it is usually paid by the buyer.

> **Example:** The buyer is borrowing $100,000, and the lender is charging 1.5 points (1.5% of the loan amount) as an origination fee. The buyer will pay this $1,500 fee to the lender at closing.

Discount Points. Discount points are used to increase the lender's yield, or profit, on the loan. By charging discount points, the lender not only gets interest throughout the loan term, it collects an additional sum of money up front, when the loan is funded. As a result, the lender is willing to make the loan at a lower interest rate than it would have without the discount points. In effect, the lender is paid a lump sum at closing so the borrower can avoid paying more interest later. A lower interest rate also translates into a lower monthly payment.

Discount points are not charged in all loan transactions, but they have become increasingly common. The number of points charged usually depends on how the loan's interest rate compares to market interest rates; typically, a lender that offers an especially low rate charges more points to make up for it.

As a rule of thumb, it generally takes about six discount points to increase the lender's yield on a 30-year loan by 1%. So a lender offering an interest rate 1% below market might charge six points to make up the difference. This rule of thumb gives only a rough estimate, however.

In some cases, the seller is willing to pay the discount points on the buyer's loan in order to help the buyer qualify for financing. Even when the lender is not charging discount points, the seller may offer to pay points to make the loan more affordable. This type of arrangement is called a **buydown**: the seller pays the lender points to "buy down" the interest rate on the buyer's loan.

Rate Lock-ins. A prospective borrower may want to have the interest rate quoted by the lender "locked in" for a specified period. Unless the interest rate is locked in, the lender can change it at any time until the transaction closes. If market interest rates are rising, the lender is likely to increase the interest rate on the loan. That could cost the borrower a lot of money over the long term, or else actually price the borrower out of the transaction altogether.

On the other hand, locking in the interest rate is generally not desirable when market interest rates are expected to go down. A lender will typically charge the borrower the locked-in rate even if market rates drop in the period before closing.

Most lenders charge the borrower a fee to lock in the interest rate. The fee is typically applied to the borrower's closing costs if the transaction closes. If the lender rejects the borrower's application, the fee is refunded; it will be forfeited to the lender, though, if the borrower withdraws from the transaction.

Truth in Lending Act

An origination fee, discount points, and other charges may increase the cost of a mortgage loan significantly. They also make it more difficult to compare the cost of loans offered by different lenders. For example, suppose one lender charges 7% interest, a 1% origination fee, and no discount points, while another charges 6.75% interest, a 1% origination fee, and two discount points. It isn't easy to tell at a glance which of these loans will cost the borrower more in the long term. (The second loan is just slightly less expensive.)

The Truth in Lending Act (TILA) is a federal consumer protection law that addresses this problem of comparing loan costs. The act requires lenders to disclose the complete cost of credit to consumer loan applicants, and also regulates the advertisement of consumer loans. The Truth in Lending Act is implemented by **Regulation Z**, a regulation adopted by the Federal Reserve Board. TILA is enforced by the Federal Trade Commission.

Loans Covered by TILA. A loan is a **consumer loan** if it is used for personal, family, or household purposes. A consumer loan is covered by the Truth in Lending Act if it is to be repaid in more than four installments, or is subject to finance charges, and is either:

- for $25,000 or less, or
- secured by real property.

Thus, any mortgage loan is covered by the Truth in Lending Act as long as the proceeds are used for personal, family, or household purposes (such as buying a home or sending children to college).

Loans Exempt from TILA. The Truth in Lending Act applies only to loans made to natural persons, so loans made to corporations or organizations aren't covered. Loans for business, commercial, or agricultural purposes are also exempt. So are loans in excess of $25,000, unless the loan is secured by real property. (Real estate loans for personal, family, or household purposes are covered regardless of the loan amount.) Most seller financing is exempt, because extending credit isn't in the seller's ordinary course of business.

Fig. 10.1 Truth in Lending Act disclosure form

TRUTH-IN-LENDING DISCLOSURE STATEMENT REQUIRED BY FEDERAL RESERVE REGULATIONS Z	
	LOAN NUMBER
DATE 19	
TYPE OF LOAN	LOAN TERM YEARS
PROPERTY LOCATION	

BORROWER(S)

ANNUAL PERCENTAGE RATE The cost of your credit as a yearly rate	FINANCE CHARGE The dollar amount your credit will cost you	AMOUNT FINANCED The amount of credit provided to you or on your behalf	TOTAL OF PAYMENTS The amount you will have paid after you have paid all payments as scheduled
%	$	$	$

Notice to Borrower(s): In compliance with Truth-In-Lending Law you are receiving a Good Faith Estimate of Settlement Charges in lieu of an itemization statement.

Your Payment Schedule will be:

	Number of Payments	Amount of Payments	When Payments Are Due	Number of Payments	Amount of Payments	When Payments Are Due
		$			$	
Monthly Beginning		$			$	
		$			$	
Date		$			$	

☐ This loan has a **Demand Feature.**

☐ Your loan contains a **Variable Rate Feature.** Disclosures about the Variable Rate have been provided to you earlier.
   Your ARM Loan ☐ has ☐ does not have a **Conversion Feature.** (The option to convert your ARM loan to a Fixed Rate Mortgage loan.) If choose to convert to a Fixed Rate mortgage loan, your new interest rate will not be higher than _____ %, which is the Maximum Rate.

☐ **Variable Rate not applicable.**

☐ **Insurance:** The following insurance is required: ☐ Property Insurance ☐ Flood Insurance
   You may obtain insurance from an agent of your choice, provided they are acceptable to this lender.
   ☐ Property Insurance is available through the lender at a cost of $_____ for a one year term.
   ☐ Flood Insurance is available through the lender at a cost of $_____ for a one year term.
   ☐ Credit Life Insurance or Disability Insurance are not required.
   ☐ Credit Life Insurance and/or Disability Insurance are not provided.
   ☐ Credit Life Insurance and/or Disability Insurance are not available through this lender.
   ☐ Credit Life is available at a cost of $_____ for a _____ term. (X _____)
   ☐ Disability Insurance is available at a cost of $_____ for a _____ term. (X _____)

Security: You are giving a Security Interest ☐ in the property being purchased ☐ other accounts you have with us
other (describe) _____

Late Charge: If your payment is _____ days late, you will be required to pay a Penalty charge of _____% of your payment.

Prepayment: If you pay this loan early, you ☐ will ☐ will not have to pay a penalty
and you ☐ may ☐ will not be entitled to a refund of a part of the finance charge.

Assumption: Someone buying your property ☐ may, subject to conditions ☐ may not assume the remainder of your loan on the Original terms.

☐ This is an assumption of an existing loan. The interest rate for the term of the loan will not exceed ____%, which is the maximum rate.
☐ Filing Fees $_____

☐ This is an **Early Disclosure** and all dates and numerical disclosures are estimates except for late payment disclosures.
☐ This is your **Final Disclosure**

NOTE: See your contract documents for any additional information about nonpayment. default, any required repayment in full before the scheduled date and prepayment refunds and penalties.

(e) means an-estimate _____

I/we acknowledge receipt of a completed copy of this disclosure statement.

X _____ Date _____ 19 ____ X _____
Borrower   *Co-Borrower*

Disclosure Requirements. The primary disclosures that the Truth in Lending Act requires a lender or credit arranger to make to a loan applicant are the total finance charge and the annual percentage rate.

The **total finance charge** is the sum of all fees and charges the borrower pays in connection with the loan. In addition to the interest on the loan, all of the following would be included in the total finance charge: origination fee, discount points paid by the borrower, finder's fees, service fees, and mortgage insurance premiums.

In real estate loan transactions, appraisal fees, credit report charges, and points paid by the seller are not included in the total finance charge.

The **annual percentage rate** (APR) expresses the total cost of the loan as an annual percentage of the loan amount. This key figure enables a prospective borrower to compare loans much more accurately than the interest rate alone. The APR is sometimes referred to as the effective rate of interest, as opposed to the nominal rate (the interest rate stated on the face of the promissory note).

In a residential mortgage transaction, within three days after receiving a written loan application, the lender or credit arranger must give the applicant a **disclosure statement** listing good faith estimates of the finance charges. Among other information, the disclosure statement should state whether the borrower will be charged a prepayment penalty if the loan is paid off early.

Home Equity Loans. The Truth in Lending Act has a special rule for home equity loans. When the security property is the borrower's existing principal residence, the act gives the borrower a right of rescission: the borrower may rescind the loan agreement up until three days after signing it, receiving the disclosure statement, or receiving notice of the right of rescission, whichever comes latest. If the borrower never receives the disclosure statement or the notice, the right of rescission does not expire for three years. (Remember that this right applies only to home equity loans. There is no right of rescission for a loan financing or refinancing the purchase or construction of the borrower's principal residence.)

Advertising Under TILA. The Truth in Lending Act strictly controls advertising of credit terms. Its advertising rules apply to anyone who advertises consumer credit, not just lenders and credit arrangers. For example, a real estate broker advertising financing terms for a listed home has to comply with TILA and Regulation Z.

It is always legal to state the cash price or the annual percentage rate in an ad. But if any other particular loan terms (such as the downpayment or the interest rate) are stated in the ad, then all of the rest of the terms must also be included. For example, if an ad says, "Assume VA loan at 9% interest," it will violate the Truth in Lending Act if it does not go on to reveal the APR, the downpayment, and all the terms of repayment. However, general statements such as "low downpayment," "easy terms," or "affordable interest rate" do not trigger the full disclosure requirement.

California Finance Disclosure Requirements

The typical home buyer is considerably less knowledgeable about residential financing than the typical lender. And without all of the necessary information, the buyer may not be able to make the best financial choices. This is why the state has passed laws to help ensure that home buyers get the information they need to make an informed decision about financing. These laws include the Mortgage Loan Broker Law and the Seller Financing Disclosure Law.

Mortgage Loan Broker Law. Real estate agents often help buyers obtain financing. This assistance may go beyond simply helping the buyer apply to one institutional lender. In some cases, it's necessary to get loans from two or more lenders to raise enough cash to close the transaction. An agent who negotiates a loan for compensation is considered to be acting as a mortgage loan broker.

California's **Mortgage Loan Broker Law** is also known as the Necessitous Borrower Act, the Real Property Loan Law, or Article VII of the Real Estate Law. It regulates real estate agents who act as loan brokers and requires them to give borrowers a disclosure statement. And for loans secured by residential property, the law restricts the size of the fees and commissions paid by the borrower or received by the loan broker. The following is only a brief overview of a few of the law's key provisions.

Disclosure Statement. The disclosure statement required by the Mortgage Loan Broker Law must be on a form approved by the Real Estate Commissioner (an example is shown in Figure 10.2). It discloses all of the costs involved in obtaining the loan, and the actual amount the borrower will receive after all of the costs and fees are deducted from the loan. The borrower must receive the statement before signing the note and security instrument, or within three days of the lender's receipt of the borrower's loan application, whichever is earlier.

A disclosure statement is required whenever a real estate agent negotiates a loan or performs services for borrowers or lenders in connection with a loan. It is required for loans secured by commercial property as well as for residential loans. The disclosure statement must be kept on file by the real estate agent for at least three years.

Commissions, Costs, and Terms. The Mortgage Loan Broker Law limits the commissions and costs that a real estate agent may charge the borrower for arranging an "Article VII loan" secured by residential property with one to four units. An Article VII loan is either:

- a first deed of trust for less than $30,000, or
- a junior deed of trust for less than $20,000.

For these loans, the maximum commissions the loan broker can charge are:

- for a first deed of trust:
  - 5% of the principal if the loan term is less than three years, or
  - 10% of the principal if the loan term is three years or more.
- for a junior deed of trust:
  - 5% of the principal if the term is less than two years,
  - 10% of the principal if the term is at least two years, but less than three years, or
  - 15% of the principal if the term is three years or more.

The costs of making these loans (such as the appraisal and escrow fees) cannot exceed 5% of the loan amount, or $390, whichever is greater. But the costs charged to the borrower must never exceed $700 and must not exceed the actual costs.

Balloon Payments. The Mortgage Loan Broker Law also prohibits balloon payments in Article VII loans that are to be paid off in less than three years.

Fig. 10.2   Mortgage loan disclosure statement

MORTGAGE LOAN DISCLOSURE STATEMENT
(BORROWER)

**(As required by the Business and Professions Code §10241
and Title 10, California Administrative Code, §2840)**

_____

(Name of Broker/Arranger of Credit)

_____

(Business Address of Broker)

I. SUMMARY OF LOAN TERMS
   A. PRINCIPAL AMOUNT . . . . $ _____
   B. ESTIMATED DEDUCTIONS FROM PRINCIPAL AMOUNT
      1. Costs and Expenses (See Paragraph III-A). . . . . $ _____
     *2. Broker Commission/Organization Fee (See Paragraph III-B). . . . . $ _____
      3. Lender Origination Fee/Discounts (See Paragraph III-B) . . . . $ _____
      4. Additional compensation will/may be received from lender not deducted from loan proceeds.
        □ YES $ _____(if known) or □ NO
      5. Amount to be Paid on Authorization of Borrower (See Paragraph III). . . . . $ _____
   C. ESTIMATED CASH PAYABLE TO BORROWER (A less B) . . . . $ _____

II. GENERAL INFORMATION ABOUT LOAN
   A. If this loan is made, Borrower will be required to pay the principal and interest at _____% per year, payable
      as follows: _____ payments of $ _____
          (number of payments)   (monthly/quarterly/annually)
      and a **FINAL/BALLOON** payment of $ _____ to pay off the loan in full.

   **NOTICE TO BORROWER: IF YOU DO NOT HAVE THE FUNDS TO PAY THE BALLOON PAYMENT WHEN IT
   COMES DUE, YOU MAY HAVE TO OBTAIN A NEW LOAN AGAINST YOUR PROPERTY TO MAKE THE
   BALLOON PAYMENT. IN THAT CASE, YOU MAY AGAIN HAVE TO PAY COMMISSIONS, FEES AND EXPENSES
   FOR THE ARRANGING OF THE NEW LOAN. IN ADDITION, IF YOU ARE UNABLE TO MAKE THE MONTHLY
   PAYMENTS OR THE BALLOON PAYMENT, YOU MAY LOSE THE PROPERTY AND ALL OF YOUR EQUITY
   THROUGH FORECLOSURE. KEEP THIS IN MIND IN DECIDING UPON THE AMOUNT AND TERMS OF THIS
   LOAN.**

   B. This loan will be evidenced by a promissory note and secured by a deed of trust on property identified as (street
      address or legal description):
      _____
      _____

   C. 1. Liens presently against this property (do not include loan being applied for):

Nature of Lien	Priority	Lienholder's Name	Amount Owing
_____	_____	_____	_____
_____	_____	_____	_____
_____	_____	_____	_____

      2. Liens that will remain against this property after the loan being applied for is made or arranged (include loan
        being applied for):

Nature of Lien	Priority	Lienholder's Name	Amount Owing
_____	_____	_____	_____
_____	_____	_____	_____
_____	_____	_____	_____

   NOTICE TO BORROWER: Be sure that you state the amount of all liens as accurately as possible. If you contract
   with the broker to arrange this loan, but it cannot be arranged because you did not state these liens correctly, you
   may be liable to pay commissions, fees and expenses even though you do not obtain the loan.

Borrower acknowledges receipt of copy of this page.

Borrower's Initials (_____)(_____)

EQUAL HOUSING
OPPORTUNITY

Reviewed by

Broker or Designee _____ Date _____

MORTGAGE LOAN DISCLOSURE STATEMENT (MS-11 PAGE 1 OF 3)

Property Address: _____   Date: _____

   D. If Borrower pays all or part of the loan principal before it is due, a PREPAYMENT PENALTY computed as follows may be charged:

_____
_____
_____

   E. Late Charges: ☐ YES, see loan documents   or   ☐ NO
   F. The purchase of credit life or credit disability insurance by a borrower is not required as a condition of making this loan.
   G. Is the real property which will secure the requested loan an "owner-occupied dwelling?" ☐ YES____ or ☐ NO____
                                                                           (Borrower initial opposite YES or NO)

An "owner-occupied dwelling" means a single dwelling unit in a condominium or cooperative or residential building of four or fewer separate dwelling units, one of which will be owned and occupied by a signatory to the mortgage or deed of trust for this loan within 90 days of the signing of the mortgage or deed of trust.

III. DEDUCTIONS FROM LOAN PROCEEDS
   A. Estimated Maximum Costs and Expenses of Arranging the Loan to be Paid Out of Loan Principal:

	PAYABLE TO	
	Broker	**Others**
1. Appraisal fee	_____	_____
2. Escrow fee	_____	_____
3. Title insurance policy	_____	_____
4. Notary fees.	_____	_____
5. Recording fees	_____	_____
6. Credit investigation fees	_____	_____
7. Other costs and expenses:		
_____	_____	_____
_____	_____	_____
Total Costs and Expenses	$ _____	

  *B. Compensation. . . . . $ _____
      1. Brokerage Commission/Origination Fee . . . . $ _____
      2. Lender Origination Fee/Discounts . . . . $ _____
   C. Estimated Payment to be Made out of Loan Principal on Authorization of Borrower

	PAYABLE TO	
	Broker	**Others**
1. Fire or other hazard insurance premiums	_____	_____
2. Credit life or disability insurance premiums (see Paragraph II-F)	_____	_____
3. Beneficiary statement fees	_____	_____
4. Reconveyance and similar fees	_____	_____
5. Discharge of existing liens against property:		
_____	_____	_____
_____	_____	_____
6. Other:		
_____	_____	_____
_____	_____	_____
_____	_____	_____
Total to be Paid on Authorization of Borrower	$ _____	

If this loan is secured by a first deed of trust on dwellings in a principal amount of less than $30,000 or secured by a junior lien on dwellings in a principal amount of less than $20,000, the undersigned licensee certifies that the loan will be made in compliance with Article 7 of Chapter 3 of the Real Estate Law.

*This loan **may / will / will not** (delete two) be made wholly or in part from broker-controlled funds as defined in Section 10241(j) of the Business and Professions Code.

REVISION DATE 10/2000   Print Date
MS-11 (PAGE 2 OF 3)

Borrower acknowledges receipt of copy of this page.
Borrower's Initials (_____)(_____)

EQUAL HOUSING OPPORTUNITY

Reviewed by
Broker or Designee _____ Date _____

MORTGAGE LOAN DISCLOSURE STATEMENT (MS-11 PAGE 2 OF 3)

Property Address: _____   Date: _____

*NOTICE TO BORROWER: This disclosure statement may be used if the Broker is acting as an agent in arranging the loan by a third person or if the loan will be made with funds owned or controlled by the broker. If the Broker indicates in the above statement that the loan "may" be made out of Broker-controlled funds, the Broker must notify the borrower prior to the close of escrow if the funds to be received by the Borrower are in fact Broker-controlled funds.

_____   _____
Name of Broker   Broker Representative
_____   _____
License Number   License Number
_____ OR _____
Signature of Broker   Signature

The Department of Real Estate License Information phone number is _____.

NOTICE TO BORROWER:

DO NOT SIGN THIS STATEMENT UNTIL YOU HAVE READ AND UNDERSTAND ALL OF THE INFORMATION IN IT. ALL PARTS OF THE FORM MUST BE COMPLETED BEFORE YOU SIGN.

Borrower hereby acknowledges the receipt of a copy of this statement.

DATED _____   _____
                                            (Borrower)

                                            _____
                                            (Borrower)

Broker Review: Signature of Real Estate Broker after review of this statement.

DATED _____   _____
                                            Real Estate Broker or Assistant Pursuant to Section 2725

Published and Distributed by:
REAL ESTATE BUSINESS SERVICES, INC.
a subsidiary of the CALIFORNIA ASSOCIATION OF REALTORS®
525 South Virgil Avenue, Los Angeles, California 90020

Reviewed by _____
Broker or Designee _____ Date _____

REVISION DATE 10/2000   Print Date
MS-11 (PAGE 3 OF 3)

MORTGAGE LOAN DISCLOSURE STATEMENT (MS-11 PAGE 3 OF 3)

And when the property is an owner-occupied home, a balloon payment is prohibited if the loan term is less than six years. (These rules don't apply to seller financing, however.) For the purposes of this law, a balloon payment is one that is more than twice as large as the smallest payment required by the loan agreement.

Seller Financing Disclosure Law. The Seller Financing Disclosure Law is also called the Residential Purchase Money Loan Disclosure Law. When a seller carries back a purchase money loan on residential property, California law requires certain disclosures to be made to both the buyer and the seller if an "arranger of credit" is involved. An arranger of credit, for the purposes of this law, is anyone (other than the buyer or seller) who:

- is involved in negotiating the credit agreement,
- participates in preparing the documents, or
- is directly or indirectly compensated for arranging for the financing or the property sale that is facilitated by the financing.

There is an exception for escrow agents and for attorneys representing either party—these are not considered arrangers of credit. But if an attorney or a real estate agent is a party to the transaction, he or she is considered an arranger of credit if neither party is represented by a real estate agent.

Coverage of the Law. The disclosure law applies when the seller gives the buyer credit for all or part of the purchase price, if:

1. the property is residential with one to four units,
2. the credit arrangements involve a finance charge or provide for more than three payments (not including the downpayment), and
3. an arranger of credit is involved.

A transaction is exempt if it is already covered by other disclosure laws, such as the Truth in Lending Act, the Real Estate Settlement Procedures Act, or the Mortgage Loan Broker Law.

Disclosure Requirements. When this disclosure law applies to a transaction, the required disclosures must be made before the buyer signs the note or the security instrument. The seller must make disclosures to the buyer, and the buyer must make disclosures to the seller. The arranger of credit is responsible for ensuring that each party discloses all required information to the other.

The statute contains a long list of required disclosures. Here are some of them:

1. the terms of the note and the security instrument;
2. a description of the terms and conditions of senior encumbrances (such as a first trust deed the buyer will be assuming);
3. whether the financing will result in a balloon payment (if so, the buyer must be warned that it may be difficult to obtain refinancing to cover the balloon payment); and
4. employment, income, and credit information about the buyer, or else a statement that the arranger of credit has made no representation regarding the buyer's creditworthiness.

An example of a disclosure form that could be used to comply with the Seller Financing Disclosure Law is shown in Figure 10.3.

Fig. 10.3   Seller financing disclosure statement

**CALIFORNIA
ASSOCIATION
OF REALTORS®**

SELLER FINANCING ADDENDUM AND DISCLOSURE
(California Civil Code §§2956-2967)
(C.A.R. Form SFA, Revised 10/02)

This is an addendum to the ☐ Residential Purchase Agreement, ☐ Counter Offer, or ☐ Other _____
_____, ("Agreement"), dated _____,
On property known as _____ ("Property"),
between _____ ("Buyer"),
and _____ ("Seller").
Seller agrees to extend credit to Buyer as follows:

1. **PRINCIPAL; INTEREST; PAYMENT; MATURITY TERMS:** ☐ Principal amount $ _____, interest at _____%
   per annum, payable at approximately $ _____ per ☐ month, ☐ year, or ☐ other _____,
   remaining principal balance due in _____ years.
2. **LOAN APPLICATION; CREDIT REPORT:** Within 5 (or ☐ _____) **Days** After Acceptance: **(a)** Buyer shall provide Seller a completed
   loan application on a form acceptable to Seller (such as a FNMA/FHLMC Uniform Residential Loan Application for residential one to four
   unit properties); and **(b)** Buyer authorizes Seller and/or Agent to obtain, at Buyer's expense, a copy of Buyer's credit report. Buyer shall
   provide any supporting documentation reasonably requested by Seller. Seller, after first giving Buyer a Notice to Buyer to Perform, may
   cancel this Agreement in writing and authorize return of Buyer's deposit if Buyer fails to provide such documents within that time, or if
   Seller disapproves any above item within **5 (or ☐ _____) Days** After receipt of each item.
3. **CREDIT DOCUMENTS:** This extension of credit by Seller will be evidenced by: ☐ Note and deed of trust; ☐ All-inclusive
   note and deed of trust; ☐ Installment land sale contract; ☐ Lease/option (when parties intend transfer of equitable title);
   OR ☐ Other (specify) _____
   **THE FOLLOWING TERMS APPLY ONLY IF CHECKED. SELLER IS ADVISED TO READ ALL TERMS, EVEN THOSE NOT
   CHECKED, TO UNDERSTAND WHAT IS OR IS NOT INCLUDED, AND, IF NOT INCLUDED, THE CONSEQUENCES THEREOF.**
4. ☐ **LATE CHARGE:** If any payment is not made within _____ **Days** After it is due, a late charge of either $ _____,
   or _____% of the installment due, may be charged to Buyer. **NOTE:** On single family residences that Buyer intends to occupy,
   California Civil Code §2954.4(a) limits the late charge to no more than 6% of the total installment payment due and requires a
   grace period of no less than 10 days.
5. ☐ **BALLOON PAYMENT:** The extension of credit will provide for a balloon payment, in the amount of $ _____,
   plus any accrued interest, which is due on _____ (date).
6. ☐ **PREPAYMENT:** If all or part of this extension of credit is paid early, Seller may charge a prepayment penalty as follows (if
   applicable): _____. Caution: California Civil Code
   §2954.9 contains limitations on prepayment penalties for residential one-to-four unit properties.
7. ☐ **DUE ON SALE:** If any interest in the Property is sold or otherwise transferred, Seller has the option to require immediate
   payment of the entire unpaid principal balance, plus any accrued interest.
8.* ☐ **REQUEST FOR COPY OF NOTICE OF DEFAULT:** A request for a copy of Notice of Default as defined in California Civil
   Code §2924b will be recorded. **If Not,** Seller is advised to consider recording a Request for Notice of Default.
9.* ☐ **REQUEST FOR NOTICE OF DELINQUENCY:** A request for Notice of Delinquency, as defined in California Civil Code §2924e,
   to be signed and paid for by Buyer, will be made to senior lienholders. **If not,** Seller is advised to consider making a Request for
   Notice of Delinquency. Seller is advised to check with senior lienholders to verify whether they will honor this request.
10.* ☐ **TAX SERVICE:**
   A. If property taxes on the Property become delinquent, tax service will be arranged to report to Seller. **If not,** Seller is
      advised to consider retaining a tax service, or to otherwise determine that property taxes are paid.
   B. ☐ Buyer, ☐ Seller, shall be responsible for the initial and continued retention of, and payment for, such tax service.
11. ☐ **TITLE INSURANCE:** Title insurance coverage will be provided to **both** Seller and Buyer, insuring their respective interests
   in the Property. **If not,** Buyer and Seller are advised to consider securing such title insurance coverage.
12. ☐ **HAZARD INSURANCE:**
   A. The parties' escrow holder or insurance carrier will be directed to include a loss payee endorsement, adding Seller to
      the Property insurance policy. **If not,** Seller is advised to secure such an endorsement, or acquire a separate
      insurance policy.
   B. Property insurance **does not** include earthquake or flood insurance coverage, unless checked:
      ☐ Earthquake insurance will be obtained; ☐ Flood insurance will be obtained.
13. ☐ **PROCEEDS TO BUYER:** Buyer will receive cash proceeds at the close of the sale transaction. The amount received will be
   approximately $_____, from _____ (indicate source of
   proceeds). Buyer represents that the purpose of such disbursement is as follows: _____.
14. ☐ **NEGATIVE AMORTIZATION; DEFERRED INTEREST:** Negative amortization results when Buyer's periodic payments are
   less than the amount of interest earned on the obligation. Deferred interest also results when the obligation does not
   require periodic payments for a period of time. In either case, interest is not payable as it accrues. This accrued interest
   will have to be paid by Buyer at a later time, and may result in Buyer owing more on the obligation than at its origination.
   The credit being extended to Buyer by Seller will provide for negative amortization or deferred interest as indicated below.
   (Check A, B, or C. CHECK ONE ONLY.)
   ☐ **A.** All negative amortization or deferred interest shall be added to the principal _____
      (e.g., annually, monthly, etc.), and thereafter shall bear interest at the rate specified in the credit documents (compound interest);
   OR ☐ **B.** All deferred interest shall be due and payable, along with principal, at maturity;
   OR ☐ **C.** Other _____.

*(For Paragraphs 8-10) In order to receive timely and continued notification, Seller is advised to record appropriate notices and/or to
notify appropriate parties of any change in Seller's address.

Buyer's Initials (_____)(_____)
Seller's Initials (_____)(_____)

| Reviewed by _____ Date _____ |

**EQUAL HOUSING
OPPORTUNITY**

SELLER FINANCING ADDENDUM AND DISCLOSURE   (SFA PAGE 1 OF 3)

Property Address: _____   Date: _____

15. ☐ **ALL-INCLUSIVE DEED OF TRUST; INSTALLMENT LAND SALE CONTRACT:** This transaction involves the use of an all-inclusive (or wraparound) deed of trust or an installment land sale contract. That deed of trust or contract shall provide as follows:
   A. In the event of an acceleration of any senior encumbrance, the responsibility for payment, or for legal defense is: _____ _____ ; OR ☐ **Is not** specified in the credit or security documents.
   B. In the event of the prepayment of a senior encumbrance, the responsibilities and rights of Buyer and Seller regarding refinancing, prepayment penalties, and any prepayment discounts are: _____ ; OR ☐ **Are not** specified in the documents evidencing credit.
   C. Buyer will make periodic payments to _____ (Seller, collection agent, or any neutral third party), who will be responsible for disbursing payments to the payee(s) on the senior encumbrance(s) and to Seller. **NOTE:** The Parties are advised to designate a neutral third party for these purposes.

16. ☐ **TAX IDENTIFICATION NUMBERS:** Buyer and Seller shall each provide to each other their Social Security Numbers or Taxpayer Identification Numbers.

17. ☐ **OTHER CREDIT TERMS** _____

18. ☐ **RECORDING:** The documents evidencing credit (paragraph 3) will be recorded with the county recorder where the Property is located. **If not,** Buyer and Seller are advised that their respective interests in the Property may be jeopardized by intervening liens, judgments, encumbrances, or subsequent transfers.

19. ☐ **JUNIOR FINANCING:** There will be additional financing, secured by the Property, junior to this Seller financing. Explain: _____

20. **SENIOR LOANS AND ENCUMBRANCES:** The following information is provided on loans and/or encumbrances that will be **senior** to Seller financing. **NOTE:** The following are estimates, unless otherwise marked with an asterisk (*). If checked: ☐ A separate sheet with information on additional senior loans/encumbrances is attached

	1st	2nd
A. Original Balance	$ _____	$ _____
B. Current Balance	$ _____	$ _____
C. Periodic Payment (e.g. $100/month):	$ _____	$ _____ / ____
Including Impounds of:	$ _____	$ _____ / ____
D. Interest Rate (per annum)	_____ %	_____ %
E. Fixed or Variable Rate:	_____	_____
If Variable Rate: Lifetime Cap (Ceiling)	_____	_____
Indicator (Underlying Index)	_____	_____
Margins	_____	_____
F. Maturity Date	_____	_____
G. Amount of Balloon Payment	$ _____	$ _____
H. Date Balloon Payment Due	_____	_____
I. Potential for Negative Amortization? (Yes, No, or Unknown)	_____	_____
J. Due on Sale? (Yes, No, or Unknown)	_____	_____
K. Pre-payment penalty? (Yes, No, or Unknown)	_____	_____
L. Are payments current? (Yes, No, or Unknown)	_____	_____

21. **BUYER'S CREDITWORTHINESS:** (CHECK EITHER A OR B. Do not check both.) In addition to the loan application, credit report and other information requested under paragraph 2:
   A. ☐ No other disclosure concerning Buyer's creditworthiness has been made to Seller;
OR B. ☐ The following representations concerning Buyer's creditworthiness are made by Buyer(s) to Seller:

Borrower _____	**Co-Borrower** _____
1. Occupation _____	1. Occupation _____
2. Employer _____	2. Employer _____
3. Length of Employment _____	3. Length of Employment _____
4. Monthly Gross Income _____	4. Monthly Gross Income _____
5. Other _____	5. Other _____

22. **ADDED, DELETED OR SUBSTITUTED BUYERS:** The addition, deletion or substitution of any person or entity under this Agreement or to title prior to close of escrow shall require Seller's written consent. Seller may grant or withhold consent in Seller's sole discretion. Any additional or substituted person or entity shall, if requested by Seller, submit to Seller the same documentation as required for the original named Buyer. Seller and/or Brokers may obtain a credit report, at Buyer's expense, on any such person or entity.

Buyer's Initials (_____)(_____)
Seller's Initials (_____)(_____)

SFA REVISED 10/02 (PAGE 2 OF 3)

Reviewed by _____ Date _____

EQUAL HOUSING OPPORTUNITY

SELLER FINANCING ADDENDUM AND DISCLOSURE (SFA PAGE 2 OF 3)

Property Address: _____   Date: _____

23. CAUTION:

  A. If the Seller financing requires a balloon payment, Seller shall give Buyer written notice, according to the terms of Civil Code §2966, at least 90 and not more than 150 days before the balloon payment is due if the transaction is for the purchase of a dwelling for not more than four families.

  B. If **any** obligation secured by the Property calls for a balloon payment, Seller and Buyer are aware that refinancing of the balloon payment at maturity may be difficult or impossible, depending on conditions in the conventional mortgage marketplace at that time. There are no assurances that new financing or a loan extension will be available when the balloon prepayment, or any prepayment, is due.

  C. If **any** of the existing or proposed loans or extensions of credit would require refinancing as a result of a lack of full amortization, such refinancing might be difficult or impossible in the conventional mortgage marketplace.

  D. In the event of default by Buyer: (1) Seller may have to reinstate and/or make monthly payments on any and all senior encumbrances (including real property taxes) in order to protect Seller's secured interest; (2) Seller's rights are generally limited to foreclosure on the Property, pursuant to California Code of Civil Procedure §580b; and (3) the Property may lack sufficient equity to protect Seller's interests if the Property decreases in value.

If this three-page Addendum and Disclosure is used in a transaction for the purchase of a dwelling for not more than four families, it shall be prepared by an Arranger of Credit as defined in California Civil Code §2957(a). (The Arranger of Credit is usually the agent who obtained the offer.)

_____

Arranger of Credit - (Print Firm Name)   By _____   Date _____

Address _____   City _____   State _____   Zip _____

Phone _____   Fax _____

BUYER AND SELLER ACKNOWLEDGE AND AGREE THAT BROKERS: (A) WILL NOT PROVIDE LEGAL OR TAX ADVICE; (B) WILL NOT PROVIDE OTHER ADVICE OR INFORMATION THAT EXCEEDS THE KNOWLEDGE, EDUCATION AND EXPERIENCE REQUIRED TO OBTAIN A REAL ESTATE LICENSE; OR (C) HAVE NOT AND WILL NOT VERIFY ANY INFORMATION PROVIDED BY EITHER BUYER OR SELLER. BUYER AND SELLER AGREE THAT THEY WILL SEEK LEGAL, TAX AND OTHER DESIRED ASSISTANCE FROM APPROPRIATE PROFESSIONALS. BUYER AND SELLER ACKNOWLEDGE THAT THE INFORMATION EACH HAS PROVIDED TO THE ARRANGER OF CREDIT FOR INCLUSION IN THIS DISCLOSURE FORM IS ACCURATE. BUYER AND SELLER FURTHER ACKNOWLEDGE THAT EACH HAS RECEIVED A COMPLETED COPY OF THIS DISCLOSURE FORM.

Buyer _____   Date _____
                    (signature)

Address _____   City _____   State _____   Zip _____

Phone _____   Fax _____   E-mail _____

Buyer _____   Date _____
                    (signature)

Address _____   City _____   State _____   Zip _____

Phone _____   Fax _____   E-mail _____

Seller _____   Date _____
                    (signature)

Address _____   City _____   State _____   Zip _____

Phone _____   Fax _____   E-mail _____

Seller _____   Date _____
                    (signature)

Address _____   City _____   State _____   Zip _____

Phone _____   Fax _____   E-mail _____

SURE TRAC
The System for Success™

Published by the
California Association of REALTORS®

Reviewed by _____ Date _____

EQUAL HOUSING
OPPORTUNITY

SFA REVISED 10/02 (PAGE 3 OF 3)

SELLER FINANCING ADDENDUM AND DISCLOSURE (SFA PAGE 3 OF 3)

The Loan Application Process

Once a buyer has compared loan costs and selected a lender, the next step is applying for the loan. The buyer fills out a loan application form and provides the lender with supporting documentation. The application is then submitted to the lender's underwriting department, which evaluates the application and ultimately approves or rejects the proposed loan.

Preapproval

Traditionally, buyers would first find the house that they wanted and then apply for a loan. In recent years, however, getting **preapproved** for a mortgage loan has become a common practice. To get preapproved, a prospective buyer submits a loan application to a lender before starting to house-hunt. If the lender approves the application, the buyer is preapproved for a specified maximum loan amount.

Preapproval lets the buyer know in advance, before shopping, just how expensive a house he or she can afford. If a house meets the lender's standards and is in the established price range, the buyer will be able to buy it. This spares the buyer the disappointment of initially choosing a house that turns out to be too expensive and having the loan request turned down. Preapproval also helps streamline the closing process once the buyer has found the right house.

The Application Form

A mortgage loan application form asks the prospective borrower for detailed information about his or her finances. The lender requires this information because it wants its loans to be profitable investments. A loan is unlikely to be profitable if the borrower doesn't have the financial resources to make the payments reliably, or if the borrower has a habit of defaulting on debts. The application helps the lender identify and turn down potential borrowers who are likely to create collection problems.

Most mortgage lenders use a standard residential loan application form developed by Fannie Mae and Freddie Mac. The form requires all of the following information.

Personal Information. In addition to basic information such as address and social security number, loan applicants must also supply certain personal information that has some bearing on their financial condition. This includes the applicant's age, education, marital status, and number of dependents.

Housing Expense. The applicant is asked how much he or she currently spends on housing. This will be the applicant's monthly rent or monthly house payment. In addition to principal and interest, the house payment would include property taxes, homeowner's insurance, any mortgage insurance, and any homeowner's association dues.

Employment. The application form asks the name of the applicant's current employer, what type of business it is, the applicant's position and title, and how many years the applicant has spent at that job and in that line of work. If the applicant has been with his or her current employer for less than two years, information about previous employment is required.

Income. A loan applicant should list all of his or her sources of income. In regard to employment income, this includes not only the applicant's salary or wages, but also bonuses and commissions. Dividends, interest, pension payments, and income from any other sources should be listed as well. The lender will verify the applicant's employment income by contacting the employer, and will require the applicant to submit documentation of other income sources along with the application.

Assets and Liabilities. The loan application form calls for a list of the applicant's assets, which may include money in bank accounts, stocks and bonds, life insurance, real estate, retirement funds, automobiles, and other personal property. The applicant must also list liabilities, which may include credit card debts, car loans, real estate loans, alimony or child support payments, and unpaid taxes. The lender will verify the applicant's asset and liability information (for example, by sending a verification form to the financial institutions where the applicant has accounts).

Underwriting the Loan

Once a loan application has been submitted and the information has been verified, the loan is ready for underwriting. **Loan underwriting** is the process of evaluating both the applicant and the property he or she wants to buy to determine whether they meet the lender's minimum standards. The person who conducts the evaluation is called a loan underwriter or credit underwriter.

In theory, a lender is free to set its own underwriting standards, taking virtually any risks it likes. In practice, however, most lenders apply standards set by the major secondary market agencies (or in the case of an FHA or VA loan, standards set by the FHA or VA).

Qualifying the Buyer. In evaluating a loan applicant's financial situation, an underwriter must consider many factors. These factors fall into three main groups: income, net worth, and credit history.

Income. A primary consideration for the underwriter is whether the loan applicant's monthly income is enough to cover the proposed monthly mortgage payment in addition to all of the applicant's other expenses. So the underwriter needs to determine how much income the applicant has.

Not all income is equal in an underwriter's eyes, however. To be taken into account in deciding whether the applicant qualifies for the loan, the income must meet standards of quality and durability. In other words, it must be from a dependable source, such as an established business, and it must be likely to continue for some time. Income that meets the tests of quality and durability is generally referred to as the loan applicant's **stable monthly income**.

For example, a regular salary from permanent employment would count as stable monthly income, and so would Social Security retirement benefits. On the other hand, neither overtime pay from a permanent job nor wages from a temporary job would be considered stable monthly income, because they could not be relied upon to continue.

Once the underwriter has calculated the loan applicant's stable monthly income, the next step is to measure its adequacy: Is the stable monthly income enough so that the applicant can afford the proposed monthly mortgage payment? To answer this question, underwriters use **income ratios**. The rationale behind the ratios is that if a borrower's expenses exceed a certain percentage of his or her monthly income, the borrower may have a difficult time making the payments on the loan.

There are two types of income ratios:

- A **housing expense to income ratio** measures the proposed monthly mortgage payment against the applicant's stable monthly income.

- A **debt to income ratio** measures all of the applicant's monthly obligations (the proposed mortgage payment, plus car payments, child support payments, etc.) against the stable monthly income.

For these calculations, the monthly mortgage payment includes principal, interest, taxes, and insurance (often abbreviated PITI). Each ratio is expressed as a percentage; for example, a loan applicant's housing expense to income ratio would be 29% if her proposed mortgage payment represented 29% of her stable monthly income. Whether that ratio would be considered too high would depend on the lender and on the type of loan applied for.

Net Worth. An individual's net worth is determined by subtracting total personal liabilities from total personal assets. According to Fannie Mae, "accumulation of net worth is a strong indication of creditworthiness." A loan applicant who has built up a significant net worth from earnings, savings, and other investments clearly has the ability to manage financial affairs.

Getting an idea of the loan applicant's financial skills is not the only reason for investigating his or her net worth, however. The underwriter needs to make sure that the applicant has sufficient funds to cover the downpayment, the closing costs, and other expenses incidental to the purchase of the property.

In addition, a loan applicant is often required to have cash reserves left over after closing. This provides some assurance that the applicant would be able to handle financial emergencies, such as unexpected bills or a temporary interruption of income, without defaulting on the mortgage.

Credit History. In addition to evaluating a loan applicant's income and net worth, the underwriter also analyzes the applicant's credit history, using a credit report obtained from a credit reporting agency. The credit report indicates how reliably the applicant has paid bills and other debts, and whether there have been any severe problems such as bankruptcy or foreclosure.

Many underwriters use **credit scores** to help assess how likely it is that a loan applicant will default on the proposed loan. A credit reporting agency calculates an individual's credit score using the credit report and a statistical model that correlates different types of negative credit information with actual loan defaults.

Credit problems can be an indication of financial irresponsibility, but in some cases they result from a personal crisis such as loss of a job, divorce, or hospitalization. A loan applicant with a poor credit history should explain any extenuating circumstances to the lender.

According to California law, a consumer credit reporting agency must give consumers a copy of their credit information upon request. If a credit agency fails to do so, a consumer may sue the credit agency for actual damages, punitive damages of up to $5,000, and the cost of the legal action.

Qualifying the Property. In addition to deciding whether the buyer is a good risk, the underwriter also has to consider whether the property that the buyer wants to purchase is a good risk. After all, the property is acting as the security for the loan. Is the property worth enough to serve as collateral for the loan amount in question? In other words, if foreclosure became necessary, would the property sell for enough money to pay off the loan? To answer these questions, the underwriter relies on an appraisal report commissioned by the lender. The appraisal provides an expert's estimate of the property's value. (Appraisal is discussed in Chapter 11.)

Loan Commitment. Once the underwriting analysis has been completed, a report summarizing the characteristics of the prospective borrower, the property, and the proposed loan is prepared. This summary, sometimes called a **mortgage evaluation**, is submitted to a loan committee, which will make the final decision on whether to approve the loan. If the committee's decision is favorable, the lender issues a **loan commitment**, agreeing to make the loan on specified terms.

Basic Loan Features

In this section of the chapter, we'll look at the basic features of a home mortgage loan. These include the loan term, the amortization, the loan-to-value ratio, a secondary financing arrangement (in some cases), and a fixed or adjustable interest rate. A lender is likely to present a home buyer with a number of options concerning these various loan features. For example, the buyer may be offered a choice between a 30-year loan and a 15-year loan, and between a fixed-rate loan and an adjustable-rate loan. Each of these choices has an impact on how large a loan the buyer will qualify for, and ultimately on how expensive a home the buyer can purchase.

Loan Term

A mortgage loan's term (also known as the repayment period) has a significant impact on both the monthly mortgage payment and the total amount of interest paid over the life of the loan. The longer the term, the lower the monthly payment, and the more interest paid.

Since the 1930s, the standard term for a mortgage loan has been 30 years. This long repayment period makes the monthly payments affordable, which reduces the risk of default.

Although 30-year loans continue to predominate, 15-year loans have also become popular. A 15-year loan has higher monthly payments than a comparable 30-year loan, but the 15-year loan offers substantial savings for the borrower in the long run. Lenders frequently offer lower interest rates on 15-year loans, because the shorter term means less risk for the lender. And the borrower will save thousands of dollars in total interest charges over the life of the loan (see

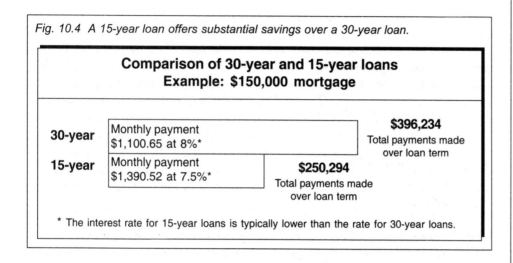

Fig. 10.4 A 15-year loan offers substantial savings over a 30-year loan.

Comparison of 30-year and 15-year loans
Example: $150,000 mortgage

30-year | Monthly payment $1,100.65 at 8%*

$396,234
Total payments made over loan term

15-year | Monthly payment $1,390.52 at 7.5%*

$250,294
Total payments made over loan term

* The interest rate for 15-year loans is typically lower than the rate for 30-year loans.

Figure 10.4). A 15-year loan also offers free and clear ownership of the property in half the time.

However, the monthly payments for a 15-year loan are significantly higher, and in some cases a much larger downpayment would be necessary to reduce the monthly payments to a level the borrower can afford.

> **Example:** Bob has a choice between a 30-year loan at 7.5% and a 15-year loan at 7%. Based on his stable monthly income, he can afford to make monthly principal and interest payments of $2,000. This is enough to amortize a $286,000 loan at 7.5% over 30 years, but it will amortize only about $222,500 at 7% over 15 years. In other words, Bob could qualify for a $286,000 loan under the 30-year plan, but will qualify for only $222,500 if he chooses the 15-year option. The difference between the two loan amounts would have to be made up with a larger downpayment.

Amortization

Most mortgage loans are **fully amortized**. A fully amortized loan is repaid within a certain period of time by means of regular payments that include a portion for principal and a portion for interest. As each payment is made, the appropriate amount of principal is deducted from the debt and the remainder of the payment, which is the interest, is retained by the lender as earnings or profit. With each payment, the amount of the debt is reduced and the interest due with the next payment is recalculated based on the lower balance. The total payment remains the same throughout the term of the loan, but every month the interest portion of the payment is reduced and the principal portion is increased. (See Figure 10.5.) The final payment pays off the loan completely; the principal balance is zero and no further interest is owed.

> **Example:** A $190,000 loan at 7.25% interest can be fully amortized over a 30-year term with monthly principal and interest payments of $1,296.13. If the borrower pays $1,296.13 each month, then the loan will be fully repaid (with interest) after 30 years.

There are two alternatives to fully amortized loans: partially amortized loans and interest-only loans. A **partially amortized** loan requires regular payments of both interest and principal, but those payments are not enough to repay all of

Fig. 10.5 Payments for a fully amortized loan

Example: $190,000 loan @ 7.25%, 30-year term, monthly payments

Payment No.	Beginning Balance	Total Payment	Interest Portion	Principal Portion	Ending Balance
1	$190,000.00	$1,296.13	$1,147.92	$148.22	$189,851.78
2	$189,851.78	$1,296.13	$1,147.02	$149.11	$189,702.67
3	$189,702.67	$1,296.13	$1,146.12	$150.01	$189,552.65
4	$189,552.65	$1,296.13	$1,145.21	$150.92	$189,401.73
5	$189,401.73	$1,296.13	$1,144.30	$151.83	$189,249.90

the principal; the borrower is required to make a large balloon payment (the remaining principal balance) at the end of the loan term.

Example: A $190,000 partially amortized mortgage calls for regular monthly payments of $1,296.13 for principal and interest, with a loan term of five years. Because the monthly payments are more than enough to cover the interest on the loan, some of the principal will be repaid during the five-year term. But since it would take 30 years to fully repay the loan at this rate, a substantial amount of principal (roughly $179,000) will still be unpaid after five years. This amount will be due as a balloon payment. To pay it, the borrower will have to refinance the property or come up with the funds from some other source.

With an **interest-only** loan, the borrower's regular payments during the loan term cover the interest accruing on the loan, without paying any of the principal off. The entire principal amount—the amount originally borrowed—is due at the end of the term.

Example: A five-year, $190,000, interest-only loan at 7.25% interest requires monthly payments of $1,147.92, the amount needed to cover the monthly interest accruing on the loan. At the end of the five-year term, the borrower owes the lender the full amount of the principal ($190,000).

Alternatively, an interest-only loan may allow the borrower to make interest-only payments for a specified period at the beginning of the loan term; at the end of this period, the borrower must begin making amortized payments that will pay off all of the principal and interest by the end of the term. This financing arrangement has become popular in areas where housing costs are high.

Loan-to-Value Ratios

The loan-to-value ratio (LTV) for a particular transaction expresses the relationship between the loan amount and the value of the property. The lower the LTV, the smaller the loan amount and the bigger the downpayment.

Example: If a lender makes an $80,000 loan secured by a home appraised at $100,000, the loan-to-value ratio is 80%. The loan amount is 80% of the property's value, and the buyer makes a 20% downpayment. If the lender loaned $75,000 secured by the same property, the LTV would be 75% and the downpayment would be 25%.

The downpayment represents the borrower's initial investment or **equity** in the property. (A property owner's equity is the difference between the property's market value and the amount of the liens against it.) So the lower the loan-to-value ratio, the greater the borrower's equity. Appreciation of the property benefits the borrower, since any increase in the property's value increases the borrower's equity interest.

The loan-to-value ratio affects the degree of risk involved in the loan—both the risk of default and the risk of loss in the event of default. A borrower who has a substantial investment (equity) in the property will try harder to avoid foreclosure; and when foreclosure is necessary, the lender is more likely to recover the entire debt if the LTV is relatively low. If a lender made a loan with a 100% LTV, it would recover the outstanding loan balance and all of its costs in a foreclosure sale only if property values had appreciated and the property sold for considerably more than its original purchase price. This is because the foreclosure process itself costs the lender a substantial amount of money.

The higher the LTV, the greater the lender's risk. So lenders use loan-to-value ratios to set maximum loan amounts.

Example: If a lender's maximum LTV for a certain type of loan is 75%, and the property's appraised value is $100,000, then $75,000 is the maximum loan amount.

Lenders actually base the maximum loan amount on the sales price or the appraised value, whichever is less. Thus, if the $100,000 property in the example above was selling for $95,000, the maximum loan amount would be $71,250 (75% of $95,000).

Many lenders have special rules for high-LTV loans because of the extra risk they pose. We'll discuss these rules later in the chapter.

Secondary Financing

Sometimes a buyer obtains two mortgage loans at once: a primary loan to pay for most of the purchase price, and a second loan to pay part of the downpayment or closing costs required for the first loan. This supplementary second loan is called **secondary financing**. Secondary financing may come from an institutional lender, the seller, or a private third party.

In most cases, the primary lender will allow secondary financing only if it complies with certain requirements. For example, the borrower must be able to qualify for the combined payment on the first and second loans. The borrower usually has to make a minimum downpayment out of his or her own funds. And the second loan must be payable at any time, without a prepayment penalty.

Fixed and Adjustable Interest Rates

A fixed-rate loan is repaid over its term at an unchanging rate of interest. For example, the interest rate is set at 6.75% when the loan is made, and the borrower pays 6.75% interest on the unpaid principal throughout the loan term.

When market interest rates are relatively low and stable, fixed-rate loans work well for borrowers and lenders. But in periods when market rates are high and volatile, neither borrowers nor lenders are comfortable with fixed-rate loans. High interest rates price many borrowers out of the market. And if market rates are fluctuating rapidly, lenders prefer not to tie up their funds for long periods at a set interest rate.

A type of loan that addresses both of these issues is the **adjustable-rate mortgage** (ARM), sometimes called a variable-rate loan. An ARM permits the lender to periodically adjust the loan's interest rate so that it accurately reflects changes in the cost of money. With an ARM, it is the borrower who is affected by interest rate fluctuations. If rates climb, the borrower's monthly payment goes up; if they decline, the payment goes down. Because the ARM shifts this risk to the borrower, lenders usually charge a lower interest rate for an ARM than for a fixed-rate loan.

How an ARM Works. With an ARM, the borrower's interest rate is determined initially by the cost of money at the time the loan is made. Once the rate has been set, it's tied to one of several widely recognized indexes, and future interest adjustments are based on the upward and downward movements of the index.

Index and Margin. An **index** is a published statistical rate that is a reliable indicator of changes in the cost of money. Examples include the one-year Treasury bill index and the Eleventh District cost of funds index. At the time a loan is made, the lender selects the index it prefers, and thereafter the loan's interest rate will rise and fall with the rates reported for the index.

Since the index reflects the lender's cost of money, it is necessary to add a **margin** to the index to ensure sufficient income for administrative expenses and profit. The lender's margin is usually 2% or 3%, or somewhere in between. The index plus the margin equals the interest rate charged to the borrower.

Example:

5.25%	Current index value
+ 2.00%	Margin
7.25%	Borrower's interest rate

It is the index that fluctuates during the loan term and causes the borrower's interest rate to increase and decrease; the lender's margin remains constant.

Adjustment Periods. The borrower's interest rate is not adjusted every time the index changes. Each ARM has a rate adjustment period, which determines how often its interest rate is adjusted. A rate adjustment period of one year is the most common.

An ARM also has a payment adjustment period, which determines how often the borrower's monthly mortgage payment is increased or decreased (reflecting changes in the interest rate). For most ARMs, payment adjustments are made at the same intervals as rate adjustments.

Caps. One problem associated with ARMs is a phenomenon known as "payment shock." If market interest rates rise rapidly, so will an ARM's index, which could lead to a sharp increase in the interest rate the lender charges the borrower. Of course, a higher interest rate translates into a higher monthly payment. If the payment increases so dramatically that the borrower can no longer afford it, it's called payment shock.

To protect borrowers from payment shock and themselves from default, lenders impose caps on their ARMs. An interest rate cap limits how much the lender can raise the interest rate on the loan, even if the index goes way up. A mortgage payment cap limits how much the lender can increase the monthly payment.

Negative Amortization. If an ARM has certain features, payment increases may not keep up with increases in the loan's interest rate, so that the monthly payments do not cover all of the interest owed. The lender usually handles this by adding the unpaid interest to the loan's principal balance; this is called **negative amortization**. Ordinarily, a loan's principal balance declines steadily, although gradually. But negative amortization causes the principal balance to go up instead of down. The borrower may owe the lender more money than he or she originally borrowed. Today, lenders generally structure their ARMs to avoid negative amortization.

Residential Financing Programs

Residential financing programs can be divided into two main groups: conventional loans and government-sponsored loans. In this section, we'll look first at conventional loans, and then at the most important loan programs sponsored by the government: the FHA-insured loan program, the VA-guaranteed loan program, and the Cal-Vet loan program. As you'll see, each program has its own qualifying standards and its own rules concerning the downpayment and other aspects of the loan.

Conventional Loans

A conventional loan is simply any institutional loan that is not insured or guaranteed by a government agency. For example, FHA-insured and VA-guaranteed loans are not conventional loans, because they are backed by a government agency.

The rules for conventional loans presented here reflect the criteria established by the secondary market agencies that purchase conventional loans, Fannie Mae and Freddie Mac (see Chapter 9). When a loan does not meet secondary market criteria it is considered **nonconforming** and cannot be sold to the major secondary market agencies. Today, most lenders want to be able to sell their loans on the secondary market, so they tailor their standards for conventional loans to match those set by Fannie Mae or Freddie Mac.

Conventional LTVs. For decades, the standard conventional loan-to-value ratio has been 80% of the appraised value or sales price of the home, whichever is less. Lenders feel confident that a borrower who makes a 20% downpayment with his or her own funds is unlikely to default; the borrower has too much to lose. And even if the borrower were to default, a foreclosure sale would be likely to generate at least 80% of the purchase price.

While 80% is the standard LTV for a conventional loan, it is not the maximum. Most lenders allow loan-to-value ratios up to 95%, and loans with 97% or even 100% LTVs are also available. The loans are classified by LTV, and different rules may apply to each category. A loan is classified as an 80% loan if the LTV is 80% or less, as a 90% loan if the LTV is over 80% but not more than 90%, as a 95% loan if the LTV is over 90% but not more than 95%, and so on.

Example: A home has been appraised at $100,000, which is also the sales price. The buyers have $18,000 to use as a downpayment, and the lender has agreed to loan them $82,000, the balance of the price. The LTV for this loan is 82%. Since the LTV is over 80% but not more than 90%, the loan will be treated as a 90% loan.

Because the lender's risk is greater when the borrower's downpayment is smaller, lenders require borrowers to obtain private mortgage insurance for any conventional loan with an LTV over 80%. (Private mortgage insurance is discussed below.) Some lenders also charge higher interest rates and larger loan fees for conventional loans with higher LTVs.

The rules for loans with LTVs over 90% tend to be especially strict. Some lenders require these loans to have a fixed interest rate, because there's a greater risk of default with an adjustable-rate mortgage. And many apply more stringent underwriting standards to high-LTV loans, so that it's harder for a buyer to qualify for a loan with such a low downpayment.

Owner-Occupancy. Unless the borrower is making an unusually large downpayment—over the standard 20%—owner-occupancy is usually required for a conventional loan. That is, the borrower must intend to occupy the home purchased with the loan, as opposed to renting it out to tenants. Owner-occupants are considered less likely to default than non-occupant borrowers.

Private Mortgage Insurance. Private mortgage insurance (PMI) is designed to protect lenders from the greater risk of high LTV loans; PMI makes up for the reduced borrower equity. PMI is usually required on conventional loans with downpayments of less than 20%.

When insuring a loan, the mortgage insurance company actually assumes only a portion of the risk of default. It does not insure the entire loan amount, but rather the upper portion of the loan. The amount of coverage varies; typically it is 20% to 25% of the loan amount.

Example: 20% coverage

$100,000	Sales price
× 90%	LTV
$90,000	90% loan
× 20%	Amount of coverage
$18,000	Amount of policy

In the event of default and foreclosure, the lender, at the insurer's option, will either sell the property and make a claim for reimbursement of actual losses (if any) up to the amount of the policy, or relinquish the property to the insurer and make a claim for actual losses up to the policy amount. Losses incurred by the lender take the form of unpaid interest, property taxes and hazard insurance, attorney's fees, and the cost of preserving the property during the period of foreclosure and resale, as well as the expense of selling the property itself.

Conventional Qualifying Standards. Fannie Mae and Freddie Mac's underwriting standards include detailed guidelines for evaluation of a conventional loan applicant's income, net worth, and credit history. To determine whether the applicant's stable monthly income is sufficient, an underwriter often calculates both a housing expense to income ratio and a total debt to income ratio.

> **Example:** Suppose the lender's maximum housing expense to income ratio is 28% and maximum debt to income ratio is 36%. If a loan applicant's housing expense to income ratio is 27% (under the lender's limit), but her debt to income ratio is 38% (over the lender's limit), then the lender probably won't approve the loan unless there are special considerations.

In some cases, the underwriter considers only the total debt to income ratio. Because the debt to income ratio takes all of the applicant's monthly obligations into account, it is considered a more reliable indicator of creditworthiness than the housing expense to income ratio.

Note that some lenders apply lower maximum income ratios to qualify applicants for conventional loans with loan-to-value ratios over 90%, to make up for the greater risk posed by a high-LTV loan.

Some lenders require an applicant for a conventional loan to have the equivalent of two months' mortgage payments in reserve after making the downpayment and paying all their closing costs. For loans with LTVs over 90%, a lender might require three months' mortgage payments in reserve.

Assumption. Most conventional loan agreements include an alienation clause, so the borrower can't sell the property and arrange for the buyer to assume the loan without the lender's permission. Typically, the lender will evaluate the buyer with the same qualifying standards that it applies in a new loan transaction. If the lender approves the assumption, it will charge an assumption fee, and it may also adjust the interest rate to the prevailing rates at that time.

FHA-Insured Loans

The Federal Housing Administration (FHA) was created by Congress in 1934 as part of the National Housing Act. The purpose of the act, and of the FHA, was to generate new jobs through increased construction activity, to exert a stabilizing influence on the mortgage market, and to promote the financing, repair, improvement, and sale of real estate nationwide. An additional by-product of the FHA housing program was the establishment of minimum housing construction standards.

Today the FHA is part of the U.S. Department of Housing and Urban Development (HUD). Its primary function is insuring mortgage loans; the FHA compensates lenders who make loans through its programs for losses that result from borrower default. The FHA does not build homes or make loans.

In effect, the FHA serves as a giant mortgage insurance agency. Its insurance program, known as the **Mutual Mortgage Insurance Plan**, is funded with premiums paid by FHA borrowers.

Under the plan, lenders who have been approved by the FHA to make insured loans either submit applications from prospective borrowers to the local FHA office for approval or, if authorized by the FHA to do so, perform the underwriting functions themselves. Lenders who are authorized to underwrite their own FHA loan applications are called direct endorsers.

Lenders who don't underwrite their own FHA loans forward applications to the local FHA office for underwriting and approval. Note that the FHA does not accept applications directly from borrowers; they must begin by applying to a lender such as a bank or a mortgage company for an initial loan commitment, sometimes called a conditional commitment.

As the insurer, the FHA is liable to the lender for the full amount of any losses resulting from the borrower's default and a subsequent foreclosure. In exchange for insuring a loan, the FHA regulates many of the terms and conditions on which the loan is made.

Characteristics of FHA Loans. The typical FHA-insured loan has a 30-year term, although the borrower may have the option of a shorter term (as short as 15 years). The property purchased with an FHA loan must be the borrower's primary residence.

A lender must charge a 1% origination fee on an FHA loan, and may also charge discount points. The discount points can be paid either by the borrower or by the seller.

FHA loans have a number of features that distinguish them from conventional loans. Here are the most significant differences:

1. **Less stringent qualifying standards.** It is easier to qualify for an FHA loan than for a conventional loan.
2. **Lower interest rates.** Lenders typically charge lower interest rates on FHA loans, because the FHA insurance reduces the lender's risk. The FHA used to set interest rates for the loans it insured, but now the rate is determined in the standard way, by negotiation between the lender and the borrower.
3. **Low downpayments.** The downpayment required for an FHA loan is often considerably less than it would be for a comparable conventional loan.
4. **Minimum cash investment.** The FHA requires the borrower to make a minimum cash investment of at least 3% of the property's sales price. But most closing costs paid by the borrower, as well as the borrower's downpayment, count toward meeting this requirement. (Note, however, that discount points paid by the borrower do not count.)
5. **Mortgage insurance required on all loans.** Regardless of the size of the downpayment, mortgage insurance is required on all FHA-insured loans.

FHA Loan Amounts. FHA programs are primarily intended to help low- and middle-income home buyers. So HUD sets maximum loan amounts, limiting the size of loans that can be insured under a particular program. Maximum loan amounts vary from one place to another because they are based on median housing costs in each area. An area where housing is expensive has a higher maximum loan amount than a low-cost area.

The size of an FHA loan is limited not only by the maximum loan amount for the area, but also by the FHA's loan-to-value rules. The LTV limit that applies to a particular transaction depends on the appraised value or sales price of the home being purchased. For most transactions, the LTV can be over 97%; in some, it can be over 98%. As a result, the amount of cash an FHA borrower needs at closing can be much less than a conventional borrower would need for the same purchase.

FHA Qualifying Standards. As with any institutional mortgage loan, the underwriting for an FHA-insured loan involves the analysis of the applicant's income, net worth, and credit history. But the FHA's underwriting standards are not as strict as the Fannie Mae/Freddie Mac standards used for conventional loans. The FHA standards make it easier for low- and middle-income home buyers to qualify for a mortgage.

Income. Just as with a conventional loan, an underwriter evaluating an application for an FHA loan will apply two ratios to determine the adequacy of the applicant's income. However, the FHA's maximum income ratios are higher than the ones typically set for conventional loans. This means that an FHA borrower's mortgage payment and other monthly obligations can be a larger percentage of his or her income than a conventional borrower's.

Although the FHA loan program is targeted toward low- and middle-income buyers, there is no maximum income level. A person with a high income could qualify for an FHA loan, as long as the requested loan didn't exceed the maximum loan amount for the area.

Funds for Closing. At closing, an FHA borrower must have sufficient funds to cover the minimum cash investment, any discount points he or she has agreed to pay, and certain other closing costs. An FHA borrower is usually not required to have reserves after closing.

FHA Insurance Premiums. Mortgage insurance premiums for FHA loans are commonly referred to as the **MIP**. For most programs, an FHA borrower pays both a one-time premium and annual premiums. The one-time premium may be paid at closing, or else financed along with the loan amount and paid off over the loan term.

Assumption of FHA Loans. FHA loans made before 1990 can be assumed without the lender's approval, if the seller does not need a release of liability. Loans made since then can be assumed only by a buyer who meets FHA underwriting standards. The buyer must intend to occupy the home as his or her primary residence.

VA-Guaranteed Loans

The VA-guaranteed home loan program was established to help veterans finance the purchase of their homes with affordable loans. VA financing offers many advantages over conventional financing and has few disadvantages.

Eligibility for VA Loans. Eligibility for a VA home loan is based on length of continuous active service in the U.S. armed forces. The minimum requirement varies from **90 days** to **24 months**, depending on when the veteran served. (Longer periods are required for peacetime service than for wartime service.) Eligibility may also be based on longtime service in the national guard or reserves. Military personnel who receive a dishonorable discharge are not eligible for VA loans.

A veteran's surviving spouse may be eligible for a VA loan if he or she has not remarried and the veteran was killed in action or died of service-related injuries. A veteran's spouse may also be eligible if the veteran is listed as missing in action or is a prisoner of war.

Application Process. An eligible veteran will be issued a **Certificate of Eligibility** by the U.S. Department of Veterans Affairs (the VA). To apply for a VA loan, the applicant must present the certificate to an institutional lender. The lender will process the veteran's loan application and forward it to the VA. Note that the Certificate of Eligibility is not a guarantee that the veteran will qualify for a loan.

The property that the veteran wants to purchase must be appraised in accordance with VA guidelines. The appraised value is set forth in a document called a **Certificate of Reasonable Value** (CRV).

When a lender approves a VA loan, the loan is guaranteed by the federal government. If the borrower defaults, the VA will reimburse the lender for part or all of its loss. The loan guaranty works essentially like mortgage insurance; it protects the lender against a large loss if the borrower fails to repay the loan.

Characteristics of VA Loans. A VA loan can be used to finance the purchase or construction of a single-family residence or a multifamily residence with up to four units. The veteran must intend to occupy the home. (In the case of a multifamily property, the veteran must occupy one of the units.)

VA-guaranteed loans are attractive to borrowers for several reasons, including the following:

- Unlike most loans, a typical VA loan does not require a downpayment. The loan amount can be as large as the sales price or appraised value, whichever is less. In other words, the loan-to-value ratio can be 100%.
- The VA does not set a maximum loan amount or impose any income restrictions. (VA loans are not limited to low- or middle-income buyers.)
- VA underwriting standards are less stringent than either conventional or FHA qualifying standards.
- VA loans do not require mortgage insurance.

Traditionally, the interest rate for VA loans was set by the VA, but that's no longer the case. The interest rate for a VA loan is now negotiated between the lender and the borrower in the usual way. It's typically a fixed rate, but in some cases an adjustable rate is an option.

A lender may charge discount points on a VA loan. At one time, VA borrowers were not allowed to pay discount points themselves, so any points charged had to be paid by the seller or a third party. That rule no longer applies; the borrower may pay the points.

VA Guaranty. The government's guaranty of a VA loan significantly reduces the lender's risk of loss in case of default. Without the guaranty, a lender would be very reluctant to make a no-downpayment loan.

Like private mortgage insurance, the VA guaranty covers only part of the loan amount, up to a maximum set by the government. The maximum guaranty amount is increased periodically. The amount of the guaranty available to a particular veteran is sometimes called the vet's "entitlement."

Because the guaranty amount is limited, a large loan amount presents some risk for the lender. Many lenders require the VA borrower to make at least a small downpayment if the loan amount exceeds a certain limit. This is a limit set by the lender, however, not by the VA.

Reinstatement. If a veteran sells property he or she financed with a VA loan and repays the loan in full from the proceeds of the sale, the veteran is entitled to a full reinstatement of guaranty rights for future use. However, because of the owner-occupancy requirement, the veteran must demonstrate a need for new housing in order to obtain a new VA loan.

Substitution of Entitlement. If a home purchased with a VA loan is sold and the loan is assumed instead of repaid, the veteran's entitlement can be restored under certain circumstances. The buyer who assumes the loan must be an eligible veteran and agree to substitute his or her entitlement for the seller's. The loan payments must be current, and the buyer must be an acceptable credit risk. If these conditions are met, the veteran can formally request a substitution of entitlement from the VA.

Note that a VA loan can be assumed by a non-veteran who meets the VA's standards of creditworthiness. But the entitlement of the veteran seller will not be restored if the buyer assuming the loan is not a veteran.

Qualifying Standards. Lenders must follow guidelines established by the VA to evaluate a VA loan applicant's creditworthiness. The VA's rules for income analysis are quite different from those used for conventional or FHA loans.

Instead of using both a housing expense to income ratio and a total debt to income ratio, the VA uses only a total debt to income ratio. The VA's maximum debt to income ratio is considerably higher than the maximum permitted for a conventional loan.

In addition to the total debt to income ratio, the underwriter will also consider the veteran's **residual income**. This is calculated by subtracting the proposed mortgage payment, all other recurring obligations, and certain taxes from the veteran's gross monthly income. The veteran's residual income must meet the VA's minimum requirements, which vary based on the region of the country where the veteran lives, family size, and the size of the proposed loan.

Overall, the VA's qualifying standards are much more liberal than the Fannie Mae/Freddie Mac rules. A buyer who would be considered marginal for a conventional loan might easily qualify for a VA loan—as long as he or she is an eligible veteran.

Cal-Vet Loans

The state of California also offers attractive loans to eligible veterans. Its program is called the California Veterans Farm and Home Purchase Program. The loans are commonly called Cal-Vet loans. A Cal-Vet loan may be used to purchase either a farm or a single-family home (including a mobile home or a condominium unit). The California Department of Veterans Affairs processes, originates, and services the loans until they are paid in full.

The Cal-Vet program works very differently from the federal VA guaranty program. Under the Cal-Vet program, the state actually purchases and takes title to the home desired by a veteran applicant. The state then sells the property to the applicant under a land contract. The state retains title to the property throughout the contract term. During this period the veteran has an equitable interest in the property.

Eligibility. To be eligible for a Cal-Vet loan, veterans generally must have been honorably discharged and have served at least 90 days of active duty. (At one time, wartime service was required, but that's no longer true.) Veterans discharged before 90 days because of a service-connected disability are also eligible.

In addition, current service members are eligible for a Cal-Vet loan after 90 days of active duty. Members of the California National Guard or the U.S. Reserves are eligible if they've served at least one year of a six-year obligation.

A veteran's surviving spouse may obtain a Cal-Vet loan if the veteran died as a result of injuries sustained in the line of duty, is designated as missing or as a prisoner of war, or died after applying for a Cal-Vet loan.

Restrictions. Some Cal-Vet loans are subject to the following restrictions:

- the borrower must either be a first-time homebuyer or purchasing a home in an area targeted as economically distressed;
- the purchase price of the property can't exceed a specified limit that's based on average prices in the area; and
- the borrower's family income can't exceed a specified limit that varies depending on family size and the county where the property is located.

Keep in mind that these restrictions don't apply to all applicants. Someone interested in a Cal-Vet loan should check with the California Department of Veterans Affairs to determine whether they apply in his or her case.

Occupancy. The borrower or his or her immediate family must occupy the property within 60 days after signing a Cal-Vet contract. Transferring, encumbering, or leasing the property is prohibited without permission.

Characteristics of Cal-Vet Loans. An application for a Cal-Vet loan can be submitted directly to the Department of Veterans Affairs or to a mortgage broker expressly authorized to handle Cal-Vet loans.

Term. The standard contract term for a Cal-Vet loan is 30 years, although the borrower may choose to pay the loan off sooner than that. Cal-Vet loans can be prepaid at any time without penalty.

Loan Amount. A Cal-Vet loan can't exceed the maximum loan amount set by the state ($521,250 in 2006).

Guaranty or PMI. Although the state sells the property to the veteran under a land contract, the state obtains either a federal VA guaranty or private mortgage insurance to protect its interest, unless there's a downpayment of 20% or more.

Downpayment and LTV. If the Cal-Vet loan has a VA guaranty, no downpayment is required. Otherwise, a downpayment of at least 3% is usually required, so that the maximum loan-to-value ratio is 97%. Secondary financing is allowed, but the total amount borrowed can't exceed the appraised value.

Funding Fee or PMI Premium. To pay for the VA guaranty or the PMI coverage, the borrower is usually charged a fee of between 1.25% and 2% of the loan amount, depending on the size of the downpayment.

Other Fees. The borrower must pay a $50 application fee, an appraisal fee (typically $400), and a 1% origination fee, but doesn't pay any discount points.

Interest Rate. The state sets a below-market interest rate for Cal-Vet loans. The rate may vary over the loan term, but can't increase more than 0.5%.

Life Insurance. A new Cal-Vet borrower under age 62 is required to purchase life insurance through the Cal-Vet program. If the borrower dies, the Cal-Vet loan will be paid off out of the insurance proceeds.

Assumption. Cal-Vet loans cannot be assumed.

📖 Chapter Summary

1. Real estate lenders in the primary market include savings and loan associations, commercial banks, savings banks, mortgage companies, credit unions, and private lenders.

2. Lenders charge an origination fee to cover their administrative costs, and sometimes charge discount points to increase the yield on the loan. One point is 1% of the loan amount.

3. The Truth in Lending Act applies to any consumer loan that is secured by real property. It requires lenders and credit arrangers to give loan applicants a disclosure statement about loan costs. It also regulates how financing information is presented in advertising. California's finance disclosure laws include the Mortgage Loan Broker Law and the Seller Financing Disclosure Law.

4. In qualifying a buyer for a real estate loan, an underwriter examines the buyer's income, net worth, and credit history to determine if he or she can be expected to make the proposed monthly mortgage payments. Income ratios measure the adequacy of the buyer's stable monthly income.

5. The traditional loan term for a mortgage loan is 30 years, but 15-year loans are also available. A 15-year loan requires higher payments than a comparable 30-year loan, but it saves the borrower thousands of dollars in interest.

6. Most mortgage loans are fully amortized, but partially amortized loans and interest-only loans are also available.

7. The loan-to-value ratio for a particular transaction expresses the relationship between the loan amount and the property's appraised value or sales price, whichever is less. The higher the loan-to-value ratio, the greater the lender's risk.

8. Secondary financing may be used to cover part of the downpayment and closing costs required for the primary loan. A secondary financing arrangement must comply with rules set by the primary lender.

9. The interest rate on a mortgage loan may be either fixed or adjustable. An ARM's interest rate is tied to an index, and it is adjusted at specified intervals to reflect changes in the index.

10. A conventional loan is an institutional loan that is not insured or guaranteed by the government. Conventional loans are often classified by loan-to-value ratio (as 80% loans, 90% loans, 95% loans, and so on). Private mortgage insurance is required for loans with LTVs over 80%.

11. FHA-insured loans are distinguished from conventional loans by less stringent qualifying standards, lower downpayments, and less cash needed for closing. The maximum loan amount available for an FHA loan depends on housing costs in the area where the property is located. FHA mortgage insurance is required on all FHA loans.

12. Eligible veterans may obtain a VA-guaranteed home loan. No down-payment is required for a VA loan. There is no maximum loan amount, although there is a maximum guaranty amount. The qualifying standards for a VA loan are considerably less stringent than the standards for conventional or FHA loans.

13. Advantages of the Cal-Vet loan program include low downpayment requirements, minimal loan fees, and low interest rates.

O━┓ Key Terms

Mortgage company—A type of lender that is not a depository institution and that makes and services loans on behalf of large investors. Sometimes called a mortgage banker.

Mortgage broker—An individual or company that arranges loans between borrowers and investors, but does not service the loans.

Point—One percent of the amount of a loan.

Origination fee—A fee that a lender charges to cover the administrative costs of processing a loan.

Discount points—A fee that a lender may charge to increase the yield on the loan, over and above the interest rate.

Annual percentage rate (APR)—Under the Truth in Lending Act, the relationship of the total finance charge to the loan amount, expressed as an annual percentage.

Loan underwriting—Evaluating the creditworthiness of the buyer and the value of the property to determine if a loan should be approved.

Stable monthly income—Income that satisfies the lender's standards of quality and durability.

Income ratios—Percentages used to determine whether a loan applicant's stable monthly income is sufficient.

Housing expense to income ratio—A percentage that measures a loan applicant's proposed mortgage payment against his or her stable monthly income.

Debt to income ratio—A percentage that measures all of a loan applicant's monthly obligations (including the proposed mortgage payment) against the stable monthly income. Also called a total debt service to income ratio.

Net worth—An individual's total personal assets minus his or her total personal liabilities.

Fully amortized loan—A loan that is repaid by the end of its term by means of regular principal and interest payments.

Loan-to-value ratio (LTV)—The relationship between the loan amount and the property's appraised value or sales price, whichever is less.

Secondary financing—A second loan to help pay the downpayment or closing costs associated with the primary loan.

Fixed-rate loan—A loan repaid over its term at an unchanging rate of interest.

Adjustable-rate mortgage (ARM)—A loan that allows the lender to periodically adjust the loan's interest rate to reflect changes in the cost of money.

Index—A published rate that is a reliable indicator of the current cost of money.

Margin—The difference between the index value on an ARM and the interest rate the borrower is charged.

Negative amortization—When unpaid interest is added to the loan balance.

Conventional loan—Any institutional loan that is not insured or guaranteed by a government agency.

Nonconforming loan—A loan that does not meet the underwriting standards of the major secondary market agencies.

PMI—Private mortgage insurance; insurance designed to protect lenders from the greater risks of high-LTV conventional loans.

MIP—The mortgage insurance premiums required for FHA-insured loans.

Certificate of Eligibility—The document that establishes a veteran's eligibility to apply for a VA home loan.

Certificate of Reasonable Value—The document issued when a home is appraised in connection with the underwriting of a VA loan.

Residual income—The amount of monthly income a VA borrower has left over after deducting monthly expenses and taxes.

∞ Chapter Quiz

1. A mortgage company:

   a) arranges loans but does not service them
   b) services loans but does not make them
   c) is the same as a mortgage broker
   d) is sometimes called a mortgage banker

2. To increase its yield on a loan, the lender is charging 2% of the loan amount, to be paid at closing. This charge is called:

   a) the origination fee
   b) PMI
   c) the index
   d) discount points

3. The Truth in Lending Act and Regulation Z:

   a) place restrictions on how much a lender can charge for a consumer loan
   b) require lenders to give loan applicants a disclosure statement concerning loan costs
   c) prohibit lenders from advertising specific financing terms
   d) All of the above

4. A loan's APR expresses the relationship between:

   a) the total finance charge and the loan amount
   b) the interest rate on the loan and the discount rate
   c) the downpayment and the total finance charge
   d) the monthly payment and the interest rate

5. After determining the quantity of the loan applicant's stable monthly income, the underwriter measures the adequacy of the income using:

   a) the consumer price index
   b) income ratios
   c) credit scoring
   d) federal income tax tables

6. Fifteen-year mortgages typically have all of the following disadvantages, except:

   a) a higher interest rate
   b) higher monthly payments
   c) a larger downpayment
   d) All of these are disadvantages of a 15-year mortgage

7. A house was appraised for $403,000 and its sales price is $400,000. If the loan-to-value ratio is 90%, how much is the loan amount?

   a) $322,400
   b) $360,000
   c) $362,700
   d) $393,000

8. With an adjustable-rate mortgage, the interest rate:

   a) is adjusted at specified intervals, and so is the payment amount
   b) is adjusted monthly, and so is the payment amount
   c) increases and decreases, but the payment amount remains the same
   d) may increase periodically, but does not decrease

9. Unpaid interest added to the loan balance is referred to as:

   a) payment shock
   b) partial amortization
   c) negative amortization
   d) prequalification

10. For conventional loans, private mortgage insurance is required when the loan-to-value ratio is:

    a) 75% or higher
    b) 90% or higher
    c) over 95%
    d) over 80%

11. For conventional loans, some lenders require
the borrower to have:

   a) at least two months' mortgage payments
   in reserve
   b) secondary financing for the downpayment
   c) residual income that meets minimum
   requirements
   d) a 3% margin to provide for emergencies

12. The FHA:

   a) makes loans
   b) insures loans
   c) buys and sells loans
   d) All of the above

13. All of the following statements about FHA
loans are true, except:

   a) No downpayment is required
   b) The borrower is usually not required to
   have reserves after closing
   c) Mortgage insurance is required on all loans
   d) The borrower must occupy the property
   as his or her primary residence

14. A VA loan can be assumed:

   a) only by an eligible veteran
   b) only by an eligible veteran who agrees to a
   substitution of entitlement
   c) by any buyer who passes the credit check
   d) by any buyer, without regard to creditworthiness

15. All of the following statements about Cal-Vet
loans are true, except:

   a) The veteran purchases the property from
   the state under a land contract
   b) The veteran may be required to obtain life
   insurance
   c) The loan can be paid off early without
   penalty
   d) The veteran must apply within five years
   after discharge from the military

Answer Key

1. d) A mortgage company is sometimes called a mortgage banker. Mortgage companies make loans and also service loans on behalf of investors.

2. d) Discount points are a percentage of the loan amount paid at closing to increase the lender's yield on the loan.

3. b) TILA and Regulation Z require lenders to disclose loan costs to loan applicants, but they do not restrict how much a lender can charge in connection with a loan. And while these laws regulate how financing terms are presented in advertising, they do not prohibit advertisement of financing terms.

4. a) The APR is the annual percentage rate, which indicates the relationship between the total finance charge and the loan amount.

5. b) Income ratios are used to measure the adequacy or sufficiency of a loan applicant's stable monthly income.

6. a) Fifteen-year mortgages usually have lower interest rates than 30-year mortgages.

7. b) The loan amount is $360,000, because the loan-to-value ratio is based on the appraised value or the sales price, whichever is less. $400,000 × 90% = $360,000.

8. a) Both the interest rate and the payment amount for an ARM are adjusted at specified intervals. The rate and the payment amount may increase or decrease to reflect changes in the index.

9. c) Negative amortization is unpaid interest that is added to the loan balance.

10. d) When the LTV of a conventional loan is more than 80%, PMI is required.

11. a) To qualify for a conventional loan, the borrower may be required to have at least two months' mortgage payments in reserve.

12. b) The FHA only insures loans made by institutional lenders. It does not make loans itself, nor does it buy and sell loans on the secondary market.

13. a) A downpayment is required for an FHA loan.

14. c) A VA loan can be assumed by any buyer, whether or not he or she is an eligible veteran. The buyer is required to pass a credit check, however.

15. d) Applying for a Cal-Vet loan within five years after discharge isn't a requirement of the program.

Real Estate Appraisal

Chapter Overview

The foundation of each real estate transaction is the value placed on the property in question. The value of a home affects its selling price, its financing terms, its rental rate, its income tax consequences, its property tax assessment, and its insurance coverage. It is important to know what the property is worth aside from any emotional or subjective value placed on it by the buyer or seller. An estimate or opinion of value is called an appraisal. This chapter examines what is meant by the term "value" and explains the various methods appraisers use to estimate value.

Introduction to Appraisal

An **appraisal** is an estimate or an opinion of value. It usually takes the form of a written statement, called an **appraisal report**, setting forth the appraiser's opinion of the value of a piece of property as of a given date. An appraisal is sometimes called a **valuation**.

Purpose and Function of an Appraisal

In appraisal terminology, a distinction is made between the purpose and the function of an appraisal. The basic **purpose** of an appraisal is to estimate value; in most cases the appraiser is estimating the property's market value (which is defined later in this chapter). The **function** of an appraisal refers to the reason the appraisal is being made. For example, an appraisal's function may be to help a seller decide on a fair listing price, or to help a buyer determine how much to pay for a property. Most often, the function of an appraisal is to help a lender decide whether the property a buyer has chosen is suitable security for a loan, and if so, what the maximum loan amount should be.

In addition to helping to determine a fair price or a maximum loan amount, an appraiser's services are regularly required in order to:

- identify raw land's highest and best use;
- estimate a property's value for purposes of taxation;
- establish rental rates;
- estimate the relative values of properties being exchanged;
- determine the amount of hazard insurance coverage necessary;
- estimate remodeling costs or their contribution to value;
- help establish just compensation in a condemnation proceeding; or
- estimate the value of properties involved in the liquidation of estates, corporate mergers and acquisitions, or bankruptcies.

The Appraiser-Client Relationship

An appraiser can be self-employed or work for a bank, a savings and loan, a mortgage company, a private corporation that has an active real estate department, or a government agency. An appraiser who is hired to appraise property for a fee is called a **fee appraiser**.

The person who employs the appraiser is the client. The appraiser is the client's agent. A principal/agent relationship exists and the laws of agency apply (see Chapter 8). Because of the fiduciary relationship that exists between the appraiser and his or her client, an appraiser has a duty of confidentiality and should discuss the results of the appraisal process only with the client. Duties imposed by the agency relationship also require an appraiser to disclose in the appraisal report any interest he or she has in the property being appraised. And if the appraiser is not sure whether to classify a particular item as real or personal property, or is uncertain about any other aspect of the property, that information should also be included in the appraisal report.

An appraiser's fee is determined in advance, based on the expected difficulty of the appraisal and the amount of time it is likely to take. The fee cannot be calculated as a percentage of the appraised value of the property, nor can it be based on the client's satisfaction with the appraiser's findings.

Licensing and Certification of Appraisers

The state of California licenses and certifies appraisers. Although the state does not require all appraisers to be licensed or certified, under federal law only appraisals prepared by state-licensed or certified appraisers in accordance with the Uniform Standards of Professional Appraisal Practice can be used in "federally related" loan transactions. The Uniform Standards are guidelines adopted by the Appraisal Foundation, a nonprofit organization. (An appraiser who fails to abide by these standards in order to defraud a federally insured lender could be found guilty of a felony.) The majority of real estate loans are federally related, since the category includes loans made by any bank or savings and loan association that is regulated or insured by the federal government. Transactions for $250,000 or less are exempt from this requirement, however.

Note that for the purposes of the California appraisal licensing law, the definition of an appraisal does not include opinions of value given by real estate licensees in the ordinary course of their real estate activities. For instance, a competitive market analysis prepared by a real estate agent for a listing presentation would not be considered an appraisal.

In California, the Office of Real Estate Appraisers examines appraisers and issues licenses. There are four levels of appraisal licenses.

1. **Certified General Real Estate Appraisers** may appraise any type of real property. This license requires 180 hours of appraisal-related education and 3,000 hours of appraisal experience, including 1,500 hours of appraising non-residential properties. The appraisal experience must have been gained over at least 30 months. An applicant for this type of license must pass the Uniform State Certified General Real Property Appraiser Examination.

2. **Certified Residential Real Estate Appraisers** may appraise any one- to four-unit residential property, and any non-residential property with a value up to $250,000. This requires 120 hours of appraisal education and at least 2,500 hours of appraisal experience obtained over at least 30 months. An applicant must pass the Uniform State Certified Residential Real Property Appraiser Examination.

3. An appraiser with a **Residential License** may appraise any one- to four-unit residential property with a transaction value up to $1 million, and any non-residential property with a value up to $250,000. This license requires 90 hours of appraisal education and at least 2,000 hours of appraisal experience (or 1,000 hours of experience for a holder of a valid California real estate broker license). An applicant must pass the Uniform State Residential Licensed Real Property Appraiser Examination.

4. An appraiser with a **Trainee License** must work under the technical supervision of a licensed appraiser and may assist on any appraisal that falls within the scope of the supervising appraiser's license. This license requires 15 hours of instruction and passage of the Uniform State Residential Licensed Real Property Appraiser Examination.

An appraisal license is valid for two years. To renew an appraisal license, an appraiser must complete 14 hours of instruction per year. Continuing education documentation must be submitted every four years.

Value

Value is a term with many meanings. One common definition is "the present worth of future benefits." Value may also be defined as the ability of an item or service to command other items or services in exchange, or as the relationship between a desired thing and the person who desires it. Value is usually measured in terms of money.

For a product to have value, it must have certain characteristics, called the elements of value:

1. utility,
2. scarcity,
3. demand, and
4. transferability.

A product must render a service or fill a need in order to have value; this is called utility. But utility must exist in conjunction with the other elements of value or the product has no economic value. For example, air has great utility, but it's universally available; because it lacks scarcity, it has no economic value.

Generally, the scarcer an item is, the greater its value. For instance, if diamonds were to become much more plentiful, their value would decline.

Demand is also an essential part of value. There is demand for an item if it produces a desire to own. And there is **effective demand** when that desire is coupled with purchasing power.

Of course, if an item cannot be transferred from one party to another, it will not have any economic value. Transferability refers to the ability to transfer possession and control of the rights that constitute ownership of property.

Types of Value

For appraisal purposes, value falls into two general classifications: **value in use** and **value in exchange**. Value in use is the subjective value placed on a property by a particular person, while value in exchange is the objective value of a property as viewed by the average person. Value in use and value in exchange may be quite different, depending on the circumstances.

> **Example:** A large, expensive, one-bedroom home, designed, built, and occupied by its owner, would undoubtedly be worth more to the owner than to the average buyer. Most buyers would look at the property objectively and expect more than one bedroom for the price.

Market Value. Value in exchange, more commonly called market value, is the more significant of the two types of value. Estimating a property's market value is the purpose of most appraisals.

Here is the most widely accepted definition of market value, taken from the Uniform Standards of Professional Appraisal Practice:

> *The most probable price which a property should bring in a competitive and open market under all conditions requisite to a fair sale, the buyer and seller each acting prudently and knowledgeably, and assuming the price is not affected by undue stimulus.*

Notice that according to this definition, market value is the *most probable* price (not "the highest price") that the property *should bring* (not "will bring"). Appraisal is a matter of estimation and likelihood, not certainty.

The Federal Housing Administration offers this succinct explanation of market value: "The price which typical buyers would be warranted in paying for the property for long-term use or investment, if they were well informed and acted intelligently, voluntarily, and without necessity."

Market Value vs. Market Price. There is an important distinction between market value and market price. Market price is the price actually paid for a property, regardless of whether the parties to the transaction were informed and acting free of unusual pressure. Market value is what should be paid if a property is purchased and sold under all the conditions requisite to a fair sale. These conditions include an open and competitive market, prudent and informed parties, and no undue stimulus (that is, no unusual pressure to sell or buy immediately). A sale made under those conditions is called an **arm's length transaction**.

Principles of Value

Of the major forces that influence our attitudes and behavior, four interact to create, support, or erode property values:

- social ideals and standards,
- economic fluctuations,
- government regulations, and
- physical and environmental factors.

A change in attitudes regarding family size and the emergence of the two-car family are examples of social forces that affect the value of homes (in this case, homes with one-car garages or too many bedrooms). Economic forces include employment levels, interest rates, and any other factors that affect the community's purchasing power. Government regulations, such as zoning ordinances, serve to promote, stabilize, or discourage the demand for property. Physical and environmental factors, such as climate, earthquakes, and flood control measures, can also have an impact on property values.

All four of these forces affect value independently of the owner's efforts. For instance, an economic force such as inflation will cause a property's value to increase, even though the owner has done nothing at all to improve the property. When the value of a property increases due to outside forces, the increase is referred to as an **unearned increment**.

Over the years, appraisers have developed a reliable body of principles, referred to as the **principles of value**, that take these forces into account and guide appraisers in making decisions in the valuation process. Note that these principles are valid no matter which appraisal method is used to arrive at an estimate of value.

Principle of Highest and Best Use. Highest and best use refers to the most profitable use of a piece of property, the use that will provide the greatest net return over a period of time. Net return usually refers to net income, but it cannot always be measured in terms of money. With residential properties, for example, net return might manifest itself in the form of amenities—the pleasure and satisfaction derived from living on the property.

Determining the highest and best use may be a simple matter of confirming that deed restrictions or an existing zoning ordinance limit the property to its present use. Often the present use of a property is its highest and best use. But change is constant, and a warehouse site that was once profitable might now generate a greater net return as a parking lot.

Principle of Change. The principle of change holds that real estate values are constantly in flux, moving up and down in response to changes in the various social, economic, governmental, and environmental forces that affect value. A property's value also changes as the property itself improves or deteriorates. A property that was worth $500,000 last year may be worth $530,000 today, and its value is likely to change in the coming year as well. Because value is always

Fig. 11.1 Principle of highest and best use

Highest and Best Use (Alternative Use Considerations)		
	Annual Income	**Estimated Value**
Present Use: Warehouse	$38,560 (actual)	$350,000
Alternative Use 1: Parking lot	$33,600 (estimated)	$302,000
Alternative Use 2: Gas station	$41,000 (estimated)	$368,000
Alternative Use 3: Triplex	$28,600 (estimated)	$264,000

subject to change, an estimate of value must be tied to a given date, called the **effective date** of the appraisal.

Related to the principle of change is the idea that property has a four-phase life cycle: **integration**, **equilibrium**, **disintegration**, and **rejuvenation**. Integration (also called growth or development) is the early stage, when the property is being developed. Equilibrium is a period of stability, when the property undergoes little, if any, change. Disintegration is a period of decline, when the property's economic usefulness is near an end and constant upkeep is necessary. And rejuvenation (also known as revitalization) is a period of renewal, when the property is reborn, often with a different highest and best use.

Rejuvenation or revitalization of a property can take different forms. If a building is restored to good condition without being changed, it's called **rehabilitation**; if the floor plan or style are altered, it's called **remodeling**. And an entire neighborhood can be rejuvenated by **redevelopment**, such as an urban renewal project in which rundown buildings are demolished and replaced.

Every property has both a physical and an economic life cycle. A property's **economic life** (also called its useful life) is the period when the land and its improvements are profitable. The economic or useful life almost always ends before the physical life. The appraiser must recognize and take into account which stage of the life cycle a property is in when estimating its present worth.

Principle of Anticipation. It is the future, not the past, that is important to appraisers. Knowing that property values change, an appraiser asks: What is happening to this property? What is its future? How do prospective buyers view its potential? The appraiser must be aware of the social, economic, and governmental factors that will affect the future value of the property.

Value is created by the anticipated future benefits of owning a property. It is future benefits, not past benefits, that arouse a desire to own.

Anticipation can help or hurt value, depending on what informed buyers and sellers expect to happen to the property in the future. They usually expect property values to increase, but in certain situations they anticipate that values will decline, as when the community is experiencing a severe recession.

Principle of Supply and Demand. The principle of supply and demand affects almost every commodity, including real estate. Values tend to rise as demand increases and supply decreases, and diminish when the reverse is true. It is not so much the demand for or supply of real estate in general that affects values, but the demand for or supply of a particular type of property. For instance, a generally depressed community may have one or two very attractive, sought-after neighborhoods. The value of these homes remains high, no matter what the general trend is for the rest of the community.

Principle of Substitution. This principle states that no one will pay more for a property than they would have to pay for an equally desirable substitute property, provided there would be no unreasonable delay in acquiring that substitute. Explained another way, the principle of substitution holds that if two properties for sale are equally desirable (whether in terms of their use, their design, or the income they generate), the least expensive will be in greater demand. The principle of substitution is the basis of all three methods of appraisal (discussed below).

Principle of Conformity. The maximum value of land is achieved when there is an acceptable degree of social and economic conformity in the area. Conformity should be reasonable, not carried to an extreme.

In a residential appraisal, one aspect of conformity the appraiser considers is similarity in the size, age, and quality of the homes in the neighborhood. Nonconformity can work to the benefit or to the detriment of the nonconforming home. The value of a home of much lower quality than those around it is increased by its association with the higher quality homes; this is the principle of **progression.**

> **Example:** A small, unkempt home surrounded by large, attractive homes will be worth more in this neighborhood than it would be if it were situated in a neighborhood of other small homes in poor condition.

Conversely, the value of a large, expensive home in a neighborhood of small, inexpensive homes will suffer because of its surroundings; this is the principle of **regression**.

Principle of Contribution. Contribution refers to the value an improvement adds to the overall value of the property. Some improvements will add more value than the expense of making them; others will cost more than they contribute to value.

A remodeled basement ordinarily will not contribute its cost to the value of the home. On the other hand, the addition of a second bathroom may increase a home's value by more than the cost of installing it.

Principle of Competition. Competition may have a dramatic impact on the value of property, especially income property. For example, if one convenience store in a neighborhood is extremely profitable, its success is very likely to bring a competing convenience store into the area. This competition will probably mean lower profits for the first store (as some of its customers begin doing business with the second store), and lower profits will reduce the property's value.

Principle of Balance. This principle maintains that the maximum value of real estate is achieved when the **agents in production—labor, coordination, capital,** and **land**—are in proper balance with each other.

To see whether the agents in production are in proper balance, the appraiser deducts a dollar figure that can be attributed to each agent from the property's gross earnings. First, the appraiser deducts the wages (labor) that are paid as a part of the property's operating costs. Next, the appraiser deducts the cost of the management (coordination). The third item deducted is the expense of principal and interest (capital), which represents the funds invested in the building and equipment. The **surplus productivity**—whatever earnings remain after the first three productive agents have been deducted—is credited to the land for its part in the production of the gross income.

The amount credited to the land will reflect the land's value under its present use. If an imbalance exists and too much of the gross earnings are attributed to the land, the buildings are probably an underimprovement and the land is not serving its highest and best use. If too little income is credited to the land, the buildings are probably an overimprovement and, again, the land is not serving its highest and best use.

The Appraisal Process

Properly done, the appraisal process is orderly and systematic. While there is no official procedure, appraisers generally carry out the appraisal process in the following manner.

1. **Define the problem.** Each client wants an appraiser to solve a specific problem: to estimate the value of a particular property as of a particular date and for a particular purpose. The first step in the appraisal process is to define the problem to be solved. This involves identifying the subject property—what property and which aspect(s) of it are to be appraised. Typically, the appraiser considers all of the elements of real property: the land and its improvements, all of the rights that go along with land ownership, and the utility of the proper-ty. (The value of land and its improvements together is called the **improved value**.) The appraiser must also establish the function of the appraisal and how the client intends to use it. Unless instructed to do otherwise, the appraiser will estimate the property's value as of the date the appraisal is performed.

2. **Determine what data is needed and where it can be found.** The data that the value estimate will be based on is divided into two categories: general and specific.

    General data concerns matters outside the subject property that affect its value. It includes population trends, prevailing economic circumstances, zoning, and proximity to shopping, schools, and transportation, as well as the condition and quality of the neighbor-hood. **Specific data** concerns the subject property itself. The apprais-er will gather information about the title, the buildings, and the site. (General and specific data will be discussed in more detail in the next section of the chapter.)

3. **Gather and verify the general data.**
4. **Gather and verify the specific data.**
5. **Select and apply the valuation method(s).** In some cases, the appraiser will approach the problem of estimating value three different

---

Fig. 11.2 *The appraisal process*

Steps in the Appraisal Process

1. Define the problem
2. Determine data needed
3. Gather and verify general data
4. Gather and verify specific data
5. Select and apply valuation methods
   - Sales comparison approach
   - Cost approach
   - Income approach
6. Reconciliation and final estimate
7. Issue appraisal report

ways: with the sales comparison approach, the cost approach, and the income approach. In other cases, he or she will use only the method that seems most appropriate for the problem to be solved. Whether one, two, or three approaches are used is a matter of judgment.

Sometimes a particular method cannot be used. Raw land, for example, cannot be appraised using the cost approach. A public library, on the other hand, must be appraised by the cost method because it does not generate income and no market exists for it.

6. **Reconcile value indicators for the final value estimate.** The figures yielded by each of the three approaches are called value indicators; they give indications of what the property is worth, but are not final estimates themselves.

The appraiser will take into consideration the purpose of the appraisal, the type of property being appraised, and the reliability of the data gathered for each of the three approaches. He or she will place the greatest emphasis on the approach that seems to be the most reliable indication of value.

7. **Issue appraisal report.** The formal presentation of the value estimate and an explanation of what went into its determination are made in the form of an appraisal report.

Gathering Data

Once the appraiser knows what property he or she is to appraise and what the purpose of the appraisal is, the appraiser begins to gather the necessary data. As mentioned above, data is broken down into general data (about the neighborhood and other external influences) and specific data (about the subject property itself).

General Data

General data includes both general economic data about the community and information about the subject property's neighborhood.

Economic Trends. The appraiser examines economic trends for hints as to the direction the property's value might take in the future. A trend is a series of related developments that form a pattern. Economic trends can take shape at the local, regional, national, or international level, although local trends have the most significant impact on a property's value. Generally, prosperous conditions tend to have a positive effect on property values; economic declines have the opposite effect.

Economic forces include population growth shifts, employment and wage levels (purchasing power), price levels, building cycles, personal tax and property tax rates, building costs, and interest rates.

Neighborhood Analysis. A property's value is inevitably tied to its surrounding neighborhood. A neighborhood is a residential, commercial, industrial, or agricultural area that contains similar types of properties. Its boundaries are

Fig. 11.3 Neighborhood data form

NEIGHBORHOOD DATA FORM

Property adjacent to:
NORTH_____*Plum Boulevard, garden apartments*_____
SOUTH_____*Cherry Boulevard, single-family residences*_____
EAST _____*14th Avenue, single-family residences*_____
WEST_____*12th Avenue, single-family residences*_____

Population: ☐ increasing   ☐ decreasing   ☑ stable

Stage of Life Cycle: ☐ integration ☑ equilibrium ☐ disintegration ☐ rebirth

Tax Rate: ☐ higher   ☐ lower   ☑ same as competing areas

Services: ☑ police   ☑ fire   ☑ garbage   ☐ other

Average family size:____*3.5*____
Predominant occupations:_____*white collar, skilled tradesman*_____

Distance from:
Commercial areas _____*3 miles*_____
Primary schools _____*6 blocks*_____
Secondary schools _____*1 mile*_____
Recreational areas _____*2 miles*_____
Cultural areas _____*3 miles*_____
Places of worship _____*Methodist, Catholic, Baptist*_____
Public transportation _____*Bus stops nearby, excellent service*_____
Freeways/highways _____*10 blocks*_____

Typical Properties	%	Age	Price Range	% Owner-Occupied
vacant lots	0			
single-family residences	80%	10 years	$380,000-395,000	93%
2- to 4-unit apartments	15%	15 years		
over 4-unit apartments	5%	5 years		
non-residential	0			

Nuisances in neighborhood (odors, noise, etc.) _____*none*_____
Hazards in neighborhood (chemical storage, pollution, etc.) _____*none*_____

determined by physical barriers (such as highways and bodies of water), land use patterns, the age or value of homes or other buildings, and the economic status of the residents.

Neighborhoods are continually changing and, like the individual properties that make them up, they have a four-phase life cycle of integration, equilibrium, disintegration, and rejuvenation. When evaluating the future of a neighborhood, the appraiser must consider its physical, social, and economic characteristics, and also governmental influences.

Here are some of the specific factors appraisers look at when gathering data about a residential neighborhood:

1. **Percentage of home ownership.** Is there a high degree of owner-occupancy or do rental properties predominate? Owner-occupied neighborhoods are generally better maintained and less susceptible to deterioration.

2. **Vacant homes and lots.** An unusual number of vacant homes or lots suggests a low level of interest in the area, which has a negative effect on property values. On the other hand, significant construction activity in a neighborhood signals strong interest in the area.

3. **Conformity.** The homes in a neighborhood should be reasonably similar to one another in style, age, size, and quality. Strictly enforced zoning and private restrictions promote conformity and protect property values.

4. **Changing land use.** Is the neighborhood in the midst of a transition from residential use to some other type of use? If so, the properties may be losing their value.

5. **Contour of the land.** Mildly rolling topography is preferred to terrain that is either monotonously flat or excessively hilly.

6. **Streets.** Wide, gently curving streets and cul-de-sacs (short dead-end streets) are more appealing than narrow or straight streets. Streets should be hard surfaced and well maintained.

7. **Utilities.** Is the neighborhood adequately serviced by electricity, water, gas, sewers, telephones, and cable TV?

8. **Nuisances.** Nuisances in or near a neighborhood (odors, eyesores, industrial noises or pollutants, or exposure to unusual winds, smog, or fog) hurt property values.

9. **Prestige.** Is the neighborhood considered prestigious, in comparison to others in the community? If so, that will increase property values.

10. **Proximity.** How far is it to traffic arterials and to important points such as downtown, employment centers, and shopping centers?

11. **Schools.** What schools serve the neighborhood? Are they highly regarded? Are they within walking distance? The quality of a school or school district can make a major difference in property values in a residential neighborhood.

12. **Public services.** Is the neighborhood properly serviced by public transportation, police, and fire units?

13. **Government influences.** Does zoning in and around the neighborhood promote residential use and insulate the property owner from nuisances? How do property tax rates compare with those of other areas nearby? High property taxes may discourage new construction.

Fig. 11.4 Site data form

SITE DATA FORM

Address: _____ 10157 - 13th Avenue _____

Legal Description: _see attached description_

Size _50' x 200'_   Shape _Rectangular_

Square Feet _10,000_   Street Paving _Asphalt_

Landscaping _professional_ Topsoil _good_

Drainage _good_   Frontage _good_

☐ corner lot   ☑ inside lot

Utilities: ☑ water ☑ telephone   **Improvements:** ☑ sidewalks
☑ gas ☑ sewers ☑ electricity   ☑ curb ☑ alleys ☑ driveway
☑ storm drains

Specific Data

Specific data has to do with the property itself. Often the appraiser will evaluate the site (the land and utilities) and the improvements to the site separately. For example, where properties are being assessed for tax purposes, most states require the assessments to show the distribution of value between land and its improvements. Another reason for appraising the land separately is to see if it is worth too much or too little compared to the value of the improvements. Where an imbalance exists, the land is not serving its highest and best use. The primary purpose of site analysis is to determine highest and best use.

Site Analysis. A thorough site analysis calls for accumulation of a good deal of data concerning the property's physical characteristics, as well as factors that affect its use or the title. A site's physical characteristics include all of the following:

1. **Width.** This refers to the lot's measurements from one side boundary to the other. Width can vary from front to back, as in the case of a pie-shaped lot on a cul-de-sac.
2. **Frontage.** Frontage is the length of the front boundary of the lot, the boundary that abuts a street or a body of water. The amount of frontage is often a more important consideration than width because it measures the property's accessibility, or its access to something desirable.
3. **Area.** Area is the size of the site, usually measured in square feet or acres. Comparisons between lots often focus on the features of frontage and area.

    Commercial land (especially retail property) is usually valued in terms of frontage; that is, it is worth a certain number of dollars per front foot. Industrial land, on the other hand, tends to be valued in terms of square feet or acreage. Residential lots are measured both ways: by square feet or acreage in most instances, but by front foot when the property abuts a lake or river, or some other desirable feature.

Occasionally, newly subdivided land is measured in "commercial acres." A **commercial acre** is the buildable portion of an acre that remains after part of the land has been dedicated for streets, sidewalks, and parks.

4. **Depth.** Depth is the distance between a site's front boundary and its rear boundary. Greater depth (more than the norm) can mean greater value, but it doesn't always. For example, suppose Lot 1 and Lot 2 have the same amount of frontage along a lake, but Lot 2 is deeper; Lot 2 is not necessarily more valuable than Lot 1. The additional square footage of Lot 2 might simply be considered **excess land**.

   Each situation must be analyzed individually. Even when greater depth or less depth affects value, the increase or decrease in value usually isn't proportional to the increase or decrease in depth.

   There are various rules of thumb concerning the relationship between depth and value. One of the most common is the 4-3-2-1 rule, which states that the front quarter of a lot holds 40% of its overall value; the second quarter holds 30%; the next quarter holds 20%; and the back quarter holds only 10% of the value. Because it's less accessible, the rear portion of a lot is less useful.

   In certain situations a **depth table** is used to evaluate how a lot's depth affects its value. This is a table of mathematical factors that can be multiplied by the front foot value of a standard lot to estimate the value of a lot with a specified depth. Depth tables are not considered accurate enough for most appraisal purposes. However, tax assessors sometimes use depth tables when valuing commercial property for tax purposes.

   Under certain circumstances, combining two or more adjoining lots to achieve greater width, depth, or area will make the larger parcel more valuable than the sum of the values of its component parcels. The increment of value that results when two or more lots are combined to produce greater value is called **plottage**. The process of assembling lots to increase their value is most frequently part of industrial or commercial land development.

5. **Shape.** Lots with uniform width and depth (such as rectangular lots) are almost always more useful than irregularly shaped lots. This is true for any kind of lot—residential, commercial, or industrial.

6. **Topography.** A site is generally more valuable if it is aesthetically appealing. Rolling terrain is preferable to flat, monotonous land. On the other hand, if the site would be costly to develop because it sits well above or below the street or is excessively hilly, then that lessens its value.

7. **Utilities.** Site analysis includes an investigation into the availability and cost of utility connections. Remote parcels lose value because the cost of bringing utility lines to the site is high or even prohibitive.

8. **Site in relation to area.** How a lot is situated in relation to the surrounding area influences its value. For instance, a retail store is often worth more if it is located on a corner, because it enjoys more exposure and its customers have access from two different streets. The effect the corner location has on the value of a business site is called **corner influence**.

By contrast, a corner location has a negative effect on the value of a residential property. That's because a corner lot is more exposed to through traffic than a lot in the middle of the block. Similarly, the lots inside a subdivision are considered more desirable than the ones on the perimeter, next to the arterial streets.

Building Analysis. The improvements to the site must also be analyzed, along with any special amenities. (**Amenities** are attractive features such as a nice view or beautiful landscaping.) Of course, the functional utility of a home depends on the needs and desires of its occupants, but there are some primary considerations that apply to most homes. These include:

1. **Construction quality.** Is the quality of the materials and workmanship good, average, or poor?
2. **Age/condition.** How old is the home? Is its overall condition good, average, or poor? If the foundation shows signs of cracking, or doors and windows don't close properly, an appraiser may recommend a soil engineer's report to check the soil stability.
3. **Size of house (square footage).** The outside dimensions of a home are used to calculate its square footage. The square footage includes the improved living area, but not the garage, basement, and porches. Commercial buildings, including warehouses, are also measured in terms of square feet.
4. **Orientation**. Orientation refers to how a building is positioned on the property in relation to views, privacy, and exposure to wind, sunlight, and noise.
5. **Basement.** A functional basement, especially a finished basement, contributes to value. (As we mentioned earlier, however, the amount a finished basement contributes to value is often not enough to recover the cost of the finish work.)
6. **Interior layout.** Is the floor plan functional and convenient? It should not be necessary to pass through a public room (such as the living room) to reach other rooms, or to pass through one of the bedrooms to reach another.
7. **Number of rooms.** The appraiser adds up the total number of rooms in the house, excluding the bathrooms and (usually) any basement rooms.
8. **Number of bedrooms.** The number of bedrooms has a major impact on value. For instance, if all else is equal, a two-bedroom home is worth considerably less than a three-bedroom home.
9. **Number of bathrooms.** A full bath is a lavatory (wash basin), toilet, and bathtub, with or without a shower; a three-quarters bath is a lavatory, toilet, and shower (no tub); a half bath is a lavatory and toilet only. The number of bathrooms can have a noticeable effect on value.
10. **Air conditioning.** The presence or absence of an air conditioning system is important in hot regions.
11. **Energy efficiency.** With spiraling energy costs, an energy-efficient home is more valuable than a comparable one that is not. Energy-efficient features such as double-paned windows, good insulation, and weather stripping increase value.

Fig. 11.5 Building data form

BUILDING DATA FORM

Address: _____ *10157 - 13th Avenue* _____

Age: _____ *7 yrs.* _____   Square feet: _____ *1,350* _____

Number of rooms: _*7*_   Quality of construction: _*excellent*_

Style: _*ranch*_

	Good	Bad	Fair
Exterior (general condition)	✔		
Foundation (slab/bsmt./(crawl sp.))	✔		
Exterior (brick/(frame)/veneer/stucco/aluminum)	✔		
Garage ((attached)/detached/single/double)	✔		
(Patio)/porch/shed/other	✔		
Interior (general condition)	✔		
Walls ((drywall)/wood/plaster)	✔		
Ceilings	✔		
Floor (wood/tile/(carpet)/concrete)	✔		
Electrical wiring	✔		
Heating ((electrical)/gas/oil/other)	✔		
Air conditioning	✔		
Fireplace(s) one	✔		
Kitchen	✔		
Bathroom(s) two	✔		
Bedroom(s) three	✔		

Additional amenities _____ *none* _____

Design advantages _____ *convenient, sunny kitchen* _____

Design flaws _____ *none* _____

Energy efficiency _____ *insulation, weather-stripping, storm windows, heat pump* _____

	Living Rm.	Dining Rm.	Ktchn.	Bdrm.	Bath	Family Rm.
Basement						
1st Floor	✔	✔	✔	✔	✔	
2nd Floor						
Attic						

Depreciation:

Deferred Maintenance _____ *normal wear* _____

Functional Obsolescence _____ *none* _____

External Obsolescence _____ *none* _____

12. **Garage/carport.** As a general rule, an enclosed garage is considered better than a carport. How many cars can the garage accommodate? Is there work or storage space in addition to parking space? Is it possible to enter the home directly from the garage or carport, protected from the weather?

Methods of Appraisal

Once the appraiser has accumulated the necessary general and specific data, he or she will begin applying one or more of the three methods of appraising property:

- the sales comparison approach,
- the cost approach, and
- the income approach.

Different types of properties lend themselves to different appraisal methods. For example, appraisers rely most on the sales comparison method in valuing older residential properties and vacant land. Churches and public buildings, such as libraries or courthouses, aren't sold on the open market, nor do they generate income, so the cost approach is invariably used. On the other hand, the income approach is usually the most reliable method for appraising an apartment complex.

Sales Comparison Approach to Value

The sales comparison approach (also known as the market data approach) is the best method for appraising residential property, and the most reliable method for appraising raw land. It involves comparing the subject property to similar properties that have recently sold, which are referred to as **comparable sales** or **comparables**. The appraiser gathers pertinent information about comparables and makes feature-by-feature comparisons with the subject property. The appraiser then translates his or her findings into an estimate of the market value of the subject property. Appraisers use this method whenever possible because the sales prices of comparables—which reflect the actions of informed buyers and sellers in the marketplace—are excellent indicators of market value.

An appraiser needs at least three reliable comparable sales to have enough data to evaluate a residential property. It is usually possible to find three good comparables, but when it isn't (for instance, if the market is inactive), the appraiser will turn to the alternative appraisal methods—the cost approach and the income approach.

Elements of Comparison. To determine whether a particular sale can legitimately be used as a comparable sale, the appraiser will check the following aspects of the transaction, which are known as the primary elements of comparison.

Date of Comparable Sale. A comparable sale should be recent, within the past six months if possible. Recent sales give a more accurate indication of what is happening in the marketplace today. If the market has been inactive and there are not three legitimate comparable sales from the past six months, then the appraiser can go back further. (Comparable sales over one year old are generally not acceptable, however.) When using a comparable more than six months old, it is necessary to make adjustments for the time factor, allowing for inflationary or deflationary trends or any other forces that have affected prices in the area.

Example: A comparable residential property sold ten months ago for $280,000. Local property values have risen by 5% over the past ten months. The comparable property, then, should be worth approximately 5% more than it was worth ten months ago.

$280,000	Value ten months ago
× 105%	Inflation factor
$294,000	Approximate present value

Location of Comparable Sale. Whenever possible, comparables should be selected from the neighborhood where the subject property is located. In the absence of any legitimate comparables in the neighborhood, the appraiser can look elsewhere, but the properties selected should at least come from comparable neighborhoods.

If a comparable selected from an inferior neighborhood is structurally identical to the subject property, it is probably less valuable; conversely, a structurally identical comparable in a superior neighborhood is probably more valuable than the subject property. It is generally conceded that location contributes more to the value of real estate than any other characteristic. A high-quality property cannot overcome the adverse effects on value that a low-quality neighborhood causes. On the other hand, the value of a relatively weak property is enhanced by a stable and desirable neighborhood.

Physical Characteristics. To qualify as a comparable, a property should have physical characteristics (construction quality, design, amenities, etc.) that are similar to those of the subject property. When a comparable has a feature that the subject property lacks, or lacks a feature that the subject property has, the appraiser will adjust the comparable's price.

Example: One of the comparables the appraiser is using is quite similar to the subject property overall, but there are several significant differences. The subject property has a two-car garage, while the comparable has only a one-car garage. Based on experience, the appraiser estimates that space for a second car adds approximately $6,000 to the value of a home in this area. The comparable actually sold for $345,500. The appraiser will add $6,000 to that price, to estimate what the comparable would have been worth with a two-car garage.

On the other hand, the comparable has a fireplace and the subject property does not. The appraiser estimates that a fireplace adds approximately $1,400 to the value of a home. She will subtract $1,400 from the comparable's price, to estimate what the comparable would have sold for without a fireplace.

After adjusting the comparable's price up or down for each difference in this way, the appraiser can identify what the comparable would have sold for if it had been identical to the subject property. When the appraiser repeats this process for each comparable, the value of the subject property becomes evident.

Terms of Sale. The terms of sale can affect the price a buyer will pay for a property. Attractive financing concessions (such as seller-paid discount points or seller financing with an especially low interest rate) can make a buyer willing to pay a higher price than he or she would otherwise be willing to pay.

An appraiser has to take into account the influence the terms of sale may have had on the price paid for a comparable property. If the seller offered the property on very favorable terms, there is a good chance the sales price did not represent the true market value of the comparable.

Under the Uniform Standards of Professional Appraisal Practice, an appraiser giving an estimate of market value must state whether it's the most probable price:

1. in terms of cash;
2. in terms of financial arrangements equivalent to cash; or
3. in other precisely defined terms.

If the estimate is based on financing with special conditions or incentives, those terms must be clearly set forth, and the appraiser must estimate their effect on the property's value. Market data supporting the value estimate (comparable sales) must be explained in the same way.

Arm's Length Transaction. Last but not least, a comparable sale can be relied on as an indication of what the subject property is worth only if it was an arm's length transaction. That is, both the buyer and seller were informed of the property's attributes and deficiencies, both were acting free of unusual pressure, and the property was offered for sale on the open market for a reasonable length of time.

Thus, the appraiser must investigate the circumstances of each comparable sale to determine whether the price paid was influenced by a condition that would render it unreliable as an indication of value. For example, if the property sold only days before a scheduled foreclosure sale, the sales price may have reflected the pressure under which the seller was acting. Or if the buyer and seller were relatives, it's possible that the price was less than it would have been between two strangers. Or if the home sold the same day it was listed, it may have been underpriced. In each of these cases, there is reason to suspect that the sales price did not reflect the property's true value, so the appraiser would not use the transaction as a comparable sale.

Comparing Properties and Making Adjustments. A proper comparison between the subject property and each comparable is essential to an accurate estimate of value. The more similar the properties, the easier the comparison. A comparable property that is the same design and in the same condition as the subject property, on a very similar site in the same neighborhood, which sold under typical financing terms the previous month, will give an excellent indication of the market value of the subject property. However, except perhaps in a new subdivision where the houses are nearly identical, the appraiser usually cannot find such ideal comparables. There are likely to be at least some significant differences between the comparables and the subject property. So, as you've seen, the appraiser has to make adjustments, taking into account differences in time, location, physical characteristics, and terms of sale, in order to arrive at an **adjusted selling price** for each comparable.

It stands to reason that the more adjustments an appraiser has to make, the less reliable the resulting estimate of value will be. These adjustments are an

Fig. 11.6 Comparable sales comparison chart

Comparable Sales Comparison Chart					
	Subject Property	Comparables			
		1	2	3	4
Sales price		$391,750	$396,500	$387,000	$388,500
Location	quiet street				
Age	7 yrs.				
Lot size	50'x200'				
Construction	frame			+6,000	
Style	ranch				
Number of Rooms	7		−5,000		
Number of Bedrooms	3				
Number of Baths	2	+3,500			+3,500
Square feet	1,350				
Exterior	good				
Interior	good				
Garage	1 car attached				
Other improvements		−4,000			
Financing					
Date of sale		−3,000	−3,000		
Net Adjustments		−3,500	−8,000	+6,000	+3,500
Adjusted Price		$388,250	$388,500	$393,000	$392,000

inevitable part of the sales comparison approach, but appraisers try to keep them to a minimum by selecting the best comparables available.

The appraiser bases his or her estimate of the subject property's value on the adjusted prices of the comparables, but the value estimate is never merely an average of those prices; careful analysis is required. Also note that the original cost of the subject property (how much the current owners paid for it) is irrelevant to the appraisal process.

Use of Listings. When comparable sales are scarce (as when the market is just emerging from a dormant period), the appraiser may compare the subject property to properties that are presently listed for sale. The appraiser must keep in mind, however, that listing prices tend to be high and often represent the ceiling of the market value range. The appraiser might also use prices offered by buyers (but not accepted by the sellers), though these can be difficult to confirm, since records of offers aren't always kept. Offers are usually at the low end of the value range. Actual market value is typically somewhere between offers and listing prices.

Note that assessed values set for tax purposes are never used in place of comparable sales.

Cost Approach to Value

The cost approach is based on the premise that the value of a property is limited by the cost of replacing it. (This is the principle of substitution: if the asking price for a home was more than it would cost to build a new one just like it, no one would buy it.) The estimate of value arrived at through the cost approach usually represents the upper limits of the property's value.

The cost approach involves estimating how much it would cost to replace the subject property's existing buildings, then adding to that the estimated value of the site on which they rest. Because the cost approach involves estimating the value of land and buildings separately, then adding the estimates together, it is sometimes called the **summation method**.

There are three steps to the cost approach:

1. Estimate the cost of replacing the improvements.
2. Estimate and deduct any accrued depreciation.
3. Add the value of the lot to the depreciated value of the improvements.

It is important to distinguish between replacement cost and reproduction cost. **Reproduction cost** is the cost of constructing an exact duplicate—a replica—of the subject building, at current prices. **Replacement cost**, on the other hand, is the current cost of constructing a building with a utility equivalent to the subject's—that is, a building that can be used in the same way. Reproduction cost and replacement cost may be the same if the subject property is a new home. But if the structure is older and was built with the detailed workmanship and expensive materials of earlier times, then the reproduction cost and the replacement cost will be quite different. So the appraiser must base his or her estimate of value on the replacement cost. The reproduction cost would be prohibitive, and it would not represent the current market value of the improvements.

Estimating Replacement Cost. The replacement cost of a building can be estimated in three different ways:

1. the square foot method,
2. the unit-in-place method, and
3. the quantity survey method.

Square Foot. The simplest way to estimate replacement cost is the square foot method (also known as the **comparative cost** method). By analyzing the average cost per square foot of construction for recently built comparable homes, the appraiser can calculate the square foot cost of replacing the subject home. The number of square feet in a home is determined by measuring the outside dimensions of each floor of the structure.

To calculate the cost of replacing the subject property's improvements, the appraiser multiplies the estimated cost per square foot by the number of square feet in the subject.

Example: The subject property is a ranch-style house with a wooden exterior, containing 1,600 square feet. Based on an analysis of the construction costs of three recently built homes of comparable size and quality, the appraiser estimates that it would cost $89.38 per square foot to replace the home.

1,600	Square feet
× $89.38	Cost per square foot
$143,008	Estimated cost of replacing improvements

Of course, a comparable structure (or "benchmark" building) is unlikely to be exactly the same as the subject property. Variations in design, shape, and grade of construction will affect the square-foot cost, either moderately or substantially. When recently built comparable homes are not available, then the appraiser relies on current cost manuals to estimate the basic construction costs.

Unit-in-Place. The unit-in-place method involves estimating the cost of replacing specific components of the building, such as the floors, roof, plumbing, and foundation. For example, one of the estimates might be a certain number of dollars per one hundred square feet of roofing. Another component estimate would be a certain amount per cubic yard of concrete for an installed foundation. Then the appraiser adds all of the estimates together to determine the replacement cost of the structure itself.

Quantity Survey. The quantity survey method involves a detailed estimate of the quantities and prices of construction materials and labor, which are added to the indirect costs (building permit, survey, etc.) for what is generally regarded as the most accurate replacement cost estimate. Because it's complex and time consuming, this method is generally used only by experienced contractors and price estimators.

Estimating Depreciation. When the property being appraised is a used home, the presumption is that it is less valuable than a comparable new home; it has depreciated in value. So after estimating replacement cost—which indicates what the improvements would be worth if they were new—the appraiser's next step is to estimate depreciation. **Depreciation** is a loss in value due to any cause.

Don't confuse an appraiser's approach to depreciation with an accountant's approach to depreciation. While an accountant is concerned with book depreciation for tax purposes, appraisers are concerned with actual losses in the value of real property.

Always keep in mind that it is only the property improvements that depreci-

Fig. 11.7 Calculating value using the cost approach

Cost Approach

Replacement cost of improvements
− Depreciation of improvements
+ Value of land
_____
Value of subject property

Fig. 11.8 A house with four bedrooms and just one bath loses value due to functional obsolescence.

ate, not the land. An appraiser regards land as indestructible; it does not lose value.

Types of Depreciation. Value can be lost as a result of physical wear and tear (**deferred maintenance**); functional inadequacies, often caused by age or poor design (**functional obsolescence**); and factors outside the property, such as a deteriorating neighborhood or poor access to important areas like downtown and employment centers (**external obsolescence**).

Deferred maintenance includes any type of physical deterioration (wear and tear, decay, cracks, etc.) and structural defects. Deferred maintenance is measured in terms of how much it would cost to correct it. It is the easiest form of depreciation to spot, and also the easiest to estimate.

The second type of depreciation, **functional obsolescence**, is a loss in value due to functional inadequacies such as a poor floor plan (a bedroom connects to the living room), unappealing design (massive cornices on the outside of the building), outdated fixtures (an old stove and no dishwasher), or too few bathrooms in relation to the number of bedrooms.

Functional obsolescence results whenever a building lacks functional utility. A building's functional utility is its ability to fulfill the desires of its occupants or users; it includes attractiveness as well as actual usefulness.

Deferred maintenance and functional obsolescence may be either **curable** or **incurable**. Depreciation is considered curable if the cost of correcting it could be recovered in the sales price when the property is sold. Depreciation is incurable if it is impossible to correct, or if it would cost so much to correct that it would be impractical to do so.

External obsolescence (also referred to as economic obsolescence) is the last type of depreciation. It is caused by conditions outside the property itself, such as zoning changes, neighborhood deterioration, traffic problems, or exposure to nuisances, like noise from airport flight patterns. Identifying external obsolescence is the primary purpose of an appraiser's neighborhood analysis. Since external obsolescence is beyond a property owner's control, it is virtually always incurable.

Note that more value is typically lost due to functional and external obsolescence than to deferred maintenance.

Methods of Estimating Depreciation. Accurately estimating how much depreciation has accrued is the most difficult phase of the cost approach. In many cases, depreciation estimates are highly subjective, and they are never any more reliable than the judgment and skill of the appraiser who is making them.

The various methods of estimating depreciation are divided into indirect methods and direct methods. **Indirect methods** include the capitalization method and the market data method, and **direct methods** include the straight-line method and the engineering method.

When applying the **capitalization method** to estimate depreciation, the appraiser uses the income approach to value (discussed below) to estimate the current value of the building. This figure, which is called the capitalized value, should be lower than the appraiser's replacement cost estimate, since the replacement cost indicates what the building would be worth if it were new. The difference between the replacement cost and the capitalized value is the amount of depreciation that has accrued.

Example:

$300,000	Replacement cost
− 270,000	Capitalized value
$30,000	Depreciation

With the **market data method**, the appraiser uses the market data (sales comparison) approach to estimate the current value of the building. Again, the appraiser subtracts this value estimate from the replacement cost estimate, and the difference is the depreciation.

The **straight-line method** of estimating depreciation is the easiest method to apply. The appraiser estimates what the useful life (economic life) of the building would be if it were new. He or she then divides the estimated useful life into the building's replacement cost to determine how much depreciation would occur each year, assuming the improvements lose value evenly over the years. The amount of annual depreciation is then multiplied by the age of the building.

It should be noted that when an appraiser considers the age of a property, he or she is concerned with its **effective age**, rather than its actual chronological age. The effective age depends on how long the appraiser believes the structure will remain productive in its present use. If, in the appraiser's opinion, a 75-year-old building has 33 productive years ahead of it, and similar buildings typically have a 40-year useful life, then the building's effective age would be seven years old, rather than 75 years old. (Remember that a building's physical life is typically longer than its useful life. That's why the axiom "More buildings are torn down than fall down" is true.)

The following example shows how the straight-line method of estimating depreciation works.

Example: After estimating that a building's replacement cost is $400,000, the appraiser uses the straight-line method to estimate how much the building has depreciated. Based on her knowledge of similar structures, she concludes that the building's useful life is 40 years. By dividing the replacement cost by the useful life, the appraiser determines that the value of the building decreases by $10,000 each year because of depreciation ($400,000 ÷ 40 years = $10,000 per year).

Suppose the appraiser decides that the building has a remaining useful life of 33 years. Its effective age is therefore seven years. The appraiser multiplies $10,000 (the annual depreciation figure) by seven (the building's effective age) to arrive at the estimated amount of depreciation. $10,000 × 7 = $70,000. Therefore, the depreciated value of the building is $330,000 ($400,000 − $70,000 = $330,000).

Straight-line depreciation can also be expressed as a percentage of the building's useful life. The appraiser can divide the useful life (40 years) into the building's replacement cost new (100% of its value) to determine the percentage of its original value it will lose each year (100% ÷ 40 = 2.5% per year).

The straight-line method is sometimes called the **age-life method** because the depreciation estimate is based on a building's effective age in relation to a typical economic life.

The **engineering method** of estimating depreciation, sometimes called the **observed condition method**, calls for the appraiser to inspect the structure, making observations about actual depreciation. The conclusions are entirely a matter of the appraiser's judgment and skill. Generally, the observed condition method of estimating depreciation is considered the most reliable.

Adding Land Value. The last step in the replacement cost process is to add the value of the land to the depreciated value of the improvements. The value of the land is usually estimated by the sales comparison method. Prices recently paid for lots similar to the subject lot are compared and used as indications of what the subject lot is worth. (Site valuation is discussed later in this chapter.)

Income Approach to Value

The income method of appraisal, also known as the capitalization method, is based on the idea that there is a relationship between the income a property generates (its productivity) and its market value to an investor. In effect, the income method seeks to determine the present value of a property's future income.

Gross Income. When using the income method, the appraiser first finds the property's gross income. He or she does this by estimating the rent the property would bring in if it were presently available for lease on the open market. What it would earn on the open market is called the **economic rent**, as distinguished from what it is actually earning now, which is called the **contract rent** or **historical rent**. Contract rent can be used to gauge the property's earnings potential. A pattern of rent increases or decreases is a strong indication of whether the contract rent is above or below the economic rent.

The property's economic rent is also called its **potential gross income** or **gross scheduled income**. This is what it could earn if it were fully occupied and all rents owed were collected. But it is unrealistic to expect a rental property to be fully occupied throughout its productive life; vacancies must be expected. Also, there are going to be tenants who do not pay their rent. So the appraiser must make a deduction from potential gross income to allow for occasional vacancies and unpaid rents. Called a **bad debt and vacancy factor**, this deduction is expressed as a percentage of the potential gross income. For example, the appraiser might deduct 5% from potential gross income as a bad debt and vacancy factor. Once the bad debt and vacancy factor is deducted, the appraiser is left with a more reliable income figure, called **effective gross income**.

Operating Expenses. From the effective gross income, the appraiser deducts the expenses connected with operating the building. They fall into three classifications: fixed expenses, maintenance expenses, and reserves for replacement.

- **Fixed expenses:** Real estate taxes and hazard insurance.
- **Maintenance expenses:** Services for tenants, utilities, supplies, cleaning, administration costs, building employee wages, and repairs.
- **Reserves for replacement:** Regular allowances set aside to replace structures and equipment that are expected to wear out, such as roofs, heating equipment, air conditioners, and (in a residential building) kitchen ranges and refrigerators.

The income that is left when operating expenses are deducted from effective gross income is called **net income**. It is net income that is capitalized to determine the property's value.

Some expenses, such as the owner's income taxes, depreciation reserves, and mortgage payments (called **debt service**) are not deducted from the effective gross income to arrive at the net income. These are not considered operating expenses from an appraisal standpoint.

Capitalization. The process of converting net income into a meaningful value is called capitalization. The mathematical procedure is expressed in this formula:

$$\text{Annual Net Income} \div \text{Capitalization Rate} = \text{Value}$$

Example: The property's net income is $45,700 and the capitalization rate is 11%. According to the capitalization formula, the property's value is $415,455.

$$\$45,700 \div 0.11 = \$415,455$$

The capitalization rate is the rate of return an investor (a potential purchaser) would want to receive on the money he or she invests in the property (the purchase price). When the investor chooses the rate of return, it is plugged into the formula shown above. By dividing the net income by the desired rate of return, the investor can determine how much he or she can pay for the property and still realize that desired return.

Example: The property's annual net income is $25,000 and the investor's desired return is 9.5%.

$$\$25,000 \div 9.5\% = \$263,160$$

The investor can pay up to $263,160 for a property earning $25,000 net income and realize her desired yield of 9.5%.

Recapture. As general rule, a capitalization rate must take into consideration both the investor's desired rate of return on the investment and the return of the investment. Interest is a **return on** an investment. This is the investor's profit on the amount of money he or she has invested in the purchase of the property. The **return of** an investment is the investor's ability to recoup the purchase price of the property at the end of his or her term of ownership. This return of the investment is also called **recapture**.

The portion of the purchase price attributable to the land need not be recaptured during the investment period because land is indestructible and its value can be recovered when the property is sold. The improvements, however, are assets that will wear out. Because the purchase price of the improvements will not be recovered when the property is sold, most investors insist on including in their capitalization rate a provision for recapturing their original investment.

In other words, a recapture provision is included in anticipation of future depreciation accrual. A capitalization rate that provides for both interest and recapture is called an **overall rate**.

> **Example:** Ted bought a small apartment building for $1,250,000. The land is worth $500,000 and the building is worth $750,000. The building has a remaining economic life of 30 years. Ted expects a 10% return on his investment. He also wants the value of the building ($750,000) to be repaid over the 30-year economic life. That works out to $25,000 a year, or 2% of the purchase price annually. This 2% return of his investment, added to his 10% return on the investment, results in an overall rate of 12%.

Selecting a Capitalization Rate. To appraise property using the income approach, the appraiser tries to determine the capitalization rate that investors generally demand for similar properties under current market conditions.

There are a number of methods an appraiser can use to determine an appropriate capitalization rate for a property. For instance, the appraiser could analyze recent sales of comparable income properties and assume that the subject property would have a capitalization rate similar to theirs. This is known as the **direct comparison method**.

Another method of selecting a capitalization rate is the **band of investment method**, which takes into account prevailing mortgage interest rates that would apply to the investor's loan, in addition to the rate of return required on the investor's equity investment.

The third method used to select a rate is the **summation method**. With this method, the appraiser builds a capitalization rate for the subject property by considering the four component parts of a capitalization rate, assigning an appropriate percentage to each component, and then adding them together to reach the total rate. Here are the four components:

1. **Safe rate**—the rate paid on secure investments such as savings accounts or long-term government bonds.
2. **Risk rate**—the portion of the rate designed to compensate the investor for the hazards that are peculiar to the investment; this component increases or decreases according to the degree of risk involved.
3. **Nonliquidity rate**—the extra return an investor will expect from a nonliquid investment such as real estate.
4. **Management rate**—the part of the rate that compensates the owner/investor for managing the investment and reinvesting the money the investment yields.

Regardless of the method used for selecting a capitalization rate, two very important considerations are the quality and durability of the investment property's income. **Quality** (how reliable the tenants are) and **durability** (how long the income can be expected to last) influence the risk factor. The greater the risk, the higher the capitalization rate and the lower the property's value. On the other hand, the smaller the risk, the lower the capitalization rate and the higher the value.

Capitalization Methods. After the appraiser has calculated the subject property's net income and chosen a capitalization rate, the final step in the income approach is capitalizing the property's income to arrive at an estimate of value. At this point, depending on the situation, the appraiser uses one of three capitalization methods. These are the building residual technique, the land residual technique, and the property residual technique.

In the first two of these methods, the land and the building are valued separately. The capitalization methods are called residual techniques because they involve capitalizing a **residual**, which means something that's left over.

The first step in the **building residual technique** is to value the land separately from the building. The appraiser then deducts from the property's annual net income the portion of the income that must be attributable to the land to justify its value. What remains (what's left over) is the income to be credited to the building. The final step is to divide the net income attributable to the building by an appropriate overall capitalization rate to find the value of the building.

The building residual method is most reliable when land values are relatively stable and can be determined easily (because of an abundance of comparable sales and market data). It is also used when appraising older buildings where depreciation is difficult to measure.

In the **land residual technique**, the building is appraised separately. Then the net income that must be attributable to the building is deducted to arrive at the net income to be credited to the land. The land's earnings are then capitalized to determine the land's value. (Note that the capitalization rate used in this step is only an interest rate, with no recapture provision, because land does not depreciate.)

The land residual technique is used when the land value cannot be estimated by the sales comparison method because of an absence of comparable sales. It is also used when the building the land supports is new and represents its highest and best use.

With the **property residual technique**, land and building are treated as one. This method is applied when it is difficult or impractical to apply the land residual or building residual technique.

Gross Income Multipliers. Residences generally aren't thought of as income-producing properties, so traditional income analysis techniques do not apply. If a residential appraiser uses an income method at all, he or she will use a simplified version called the **gross income multiplier method**. As a rule, this method is applied only when appraising rental homes. It's sometimes called the **gross rent multiplier method**, since rents are typically the only form of income generated by rental homes.

In the gross income multiplier method, the appraiser looks at the relationship between a rental property's income and the price paid for the property.

Example:

Sales price:	$275,000
Monthly rent:	$1,815
Conclusion:	The monthly rent is equal to 0.66% of the sales price; the sales price is approximately 150 times the monthly rent.

Monthly rents may run about 1% of selling prices in one market, and more or less in another. A market exists where specific rental properties compete with each other for tenants. For competitive reasons, rents charged for similar properties tend to be much alike within the same market. As a result, if one rental property has a monthly income that is 1% of its sales price, comparable properties will have similar income-to-price ratios.

A monthly multiplier is established by dividing the sales price by the monthly rental income. An annual multiplier is calculated by dividing the sales price by the annual rental income.

Example:

Sales Price		Monthly Rent		Monthly Multiplier
$275,000	÷	$1,815	=	151.52

Sales Price		Annual Rent		Annual Multiplier
$275,000	÷	$21,780	=	12.63

After locating at least four comparable residential rental properties, the appraiser can determine their gross income multipliers (either monthly or annual—it's a matter of the appraiser's preference) by dividing the rents into their respective selling prices.

Example:

Comp No.	Sales Price	Monthly Rent	Monthly Multiplier
1	$264,500	$1,800	146.94
2	$276,525	$1,825	151.52
3	$268,300	$1,850	145.03
4	$280,750	$1,895	148.15

The appraiser uses the multipliers of the comparables to determine an appropriate multiplier for the subject property, taking into account the similarities and differences between the properties. Then the appraiser multiplies the rent that the subject property is generating by the chosen multiplier for a rough estimate of its value as income-producing property.

The principal weakness of the gross income multiplier method is that it is based on gross income figures and does not take into account vacancies or operating expenses. If two rental homes have the same rental income, the gross income multiplier method would indicate they are worth the same amount; but if one is older and has higher maintenance costs, the net return to the owner would be less, and so would be the value of the property.

If possible, the appraiser should use the subject property's economic rent as opposed to the contract rent (the rent the owner is actually receiving) in calculating the gross income multiplier.

Example: The owner leased the home two years ago for $1,850 a month, and the lease contract has another year to go. Market rents have risen sharply over the past two years, so that the property could now command a much higher rent—probably about $2,200 a month. If the appraiser were to use the $1,850 contract rent in the gross income multiplier method instead of the $2,200 economic rent, it would distort the estimate of value.

Site Valuation

An appraiser may be asked to value unimproved property (also referred to as raw land). And when appraising improved property, an appraiser may be called upon to appraise the site and the buildings separately (for instance, when property is being assessed for tax purposes). Occasionally, an appraiser is asked to appraise a property on which there is a building that needs to be torn down. In that case, the appraiser will need to appraise the site at its highest and best use, and then deduct the cost of removing the structure.

There are four main ways to appraise a site:

1. the sales comparison method,
2. the land residual technique,
3. the distribution method, and
4. the development method.

Sales Comparison Method. The sales comparison approach is the method of site valuation preferred by most appraisers, because it reflects the actions of informed buyers and sellers in the marketplace. With this method, the appraiser uses the sales prices of vacant sites that have recently sold and that are similar to the subject property's site to arrive at an estimate of its value.

Land Residual Technique. The land residual technique, which we discussed earlier, is site valuation by the income approach. It is used for improved property. The appraiser determines the income attributable to the land, then calculates the value of the land by capitalizing its income.

Distribution Method. In the distribution method—also called allocation or abstraction—the appraiser analyzes recent sales of improved properties to determine what percentage of their sales prices involved land costs. If the lots typically account for 18% to 20% of the cost of the properties, the appraiser might conclude that the portion of the subject property's overall value attributable to the land is about 18% to 20%.

The distribution method is not as reliable as the sales comparison method. Its principal weakness is that in many cases there are no consistent land-to-property value ratios on which the appraiser can rely.

Development Method. Also called the anticipated use method, this valuation technique is applied fairly often. It is used to value vacant land when the highest and best use of the land is for subdivision and development. In this method, the appraiser estimates the future value of the developed lots, and then subtracts the costs of development to arrive at the current value of the land.

Reconciliation and Final Estimate of Value

Throughout the appraisal process, the appraiser is gathering facts on which he or she will base the ultimate conclusion, the final estimate of the property's value. In many cases, the facts require nothing beyond simple verification; their meaning is self-evident. In other instances, they require expert interpretation.

Appraisers refer to the assembly and interpretation of all the facts that influence a property's value as **reconciliation**. Nowhere in the appraisal process does the appraiser's experience and judgment play a more critical role.

The final value estimate is not simply the average of the results yielded by the three appraisal methods—sales comparison, cost, and income. Rather, it is the figure that represents the appraiser's expert opinion of the subject property's value after all the data have been assembled and analyzed.

Once the appraiser has determined the final estimate of value, he or she presents it to the client in an appraisal report. The two most common types of reports are the narrative report and the form report. A **narrative report** is a thorough, detailed, written presentation of the facts and reasoning behind the appraiser's estimate of value. The property value is usually stated in the section of the narrative report that discusses the purpose of the appraisal. A **form report** is a brief, standard form used by lending institutions and government agencies (e.g., the FHA and VA), presenting only the key data and the appraiser's conclusions. This is the most common type of appraisal report. The first two pages of the standard form report for residential appraisals are shown in Figure 11.9; these are the pages that set forth the appraiser's data and sales comparison analysis. (Subsequent pages present the cost approach and income approach analysis, if any, and the appraiser's certification of the report.)

Fig. 11.9 Uniform Residential Appraisal Report form

Uniform Residential Appraisal Report
File #

The purpose of this summary appraisal report is to provide the lender/client with an accurate, and adequately supported, opinion of the market value of the subject property.

SUBJECT

Property Address		City		State	Zip Code
Borrower	Owner of Public Record			County	

Legal Description

Assessor's Parcel #	Tax Year	R.E. Taxes $
Neighborhood Name	Map Reference	Census Tract

Occupant ☐ Owner ☐ Tenant ☐ Vacant   Special Assessments $ ☐ PUD HOA $ ☐ per year ☐ per month

Property Rights Appraised ☐ Fee Simple ☐ Leasehold ☐ Other (describe)

Assignment Type ☐ Purchase Transaction ☐ Refinance Transaction ☐ Other (describe)

Lender/Client	Address

Is the subject property currently offered for sale or has it been offered for sale in the twelve months prior to the effective date of this appraisal? ☐ Yes ☐ No

Report data source(s) used, offering price(s), and date(s).

CONTRACT

I ☐ did ☐ did not analyze the contract for sale for the subject purchase transaction. Explain the results of the analysis of the contract for sale or why the analysis was not performed.

Contract Price $ Date of Contract   Is the property seller the owner of public record? ☐ Yes ☐ No Data Source(s)

Is there any financial assistance (loan charges, sale concessions, gift or downpayment assistance, etc.) to be paid by any party on behalf of the borrower? ☐ Yes ☐ No
If Yes, report the total dollar amount and describe the items to be paid.

NEIGHBORHOOD

Note: Race and the racial composition of the neighborhood are not appraisal factors.

Neighborhood Characteristics			One-Unit Housing Trends				One-Unit Housing		Present Land Use %	
Location ☐ Urban	☐ Suburban	☐ Rural	Property Values ☐ Increasing	☐ Stable	☐ Declining		PRICE	AGE	One-Unit	%
Built-Up ☐ Over 75%	☐ 25–75%	☐ Under 25%	Demand/Supply ☐ Shortage	☐ In Balance	☐ Over Supply		$ (000)	(yrs)	2-4 Unit	%
Growth ☐ Rapid	☐ Stable	☐ Slow	Marketing Time ☐ Under 3 mths	☐ 3–6 mths	☐ Over 6 mths		Low		Multi-Family	%
Neighborhood Boundaries							High		Commercial	%
							Pred.		Other	%

Neighborhood Description

Market Conditions (including support for the above conclusions)

SITE

Dimensions	Area	Shape	View

Specific Zoning Classification   Zoning Description

Zoning Compliance ☐ Legal ☐ Legal Nonconforming (Grandfathered Use) ☐ No Zoning ☐ Illegal (describe)

Is the highest and best use of the subject property as improved (or as proposed per plans and specifications) the present use? ☐ Yes ☐ No If No, describe

Utilities	Public	Other (describe)		Public	Other (describe)	Off-site Improvements—Type	Public	Private
Electricity	☐	☐	Water	☐	☐	Street	☐	☐
Gas	☐	☐	Sanitary Sewer	☐	☐	Alley	☐	☐

FEMA Special Flood Hazard Area ☐ Yes ☐ No FEMA Flood Zone   FEMA Map #   FEMA Map Date

Are the utilities and off-site improvements typical for the market area? ☐ Yes ☐ No If No, describe

Are there any adverse site conditions or external factors (easements, encroachments, environmental conditions, land uses, etc.)? ☐ Yes ☐ No If Yes, describe

IMPROVEMENTS

General Description	Foundation	Exterior Description materials/condition	Interior materials/condition
Units ☐ One ☐ One with Accessory Unit	☐ Concrete Slab ☐ Crawl Space	Foundation Walls	Floors
# of Stories	☐ Full Basement ☐ Partial Basement	Exterior Walls	Walls
Type ☐ Det. ☐ Att. ☐ S-Det./End Unit	Basement Area sq. ft.	Roof Surface	Trim/Finish
☐ Existing ☐ Proposed ☐ Under Const.	Basement Finish %	Gutters & Downspouts	Bath Floor
Design (Style)	☐ Outside Entry/Exit ☐ Sump Pump	Window Type	Bath Wainscot
Year Built	Evidence of ☐ Infestation	Storm Sash/Insulated	Car Storage ☐ None
Effective Age (Yrs)	☐ Dampness ☐ Settlement	Screens	☐ Driveway # of Cars
Attic ☐ None	Heating ☐ FWA ☐ HWBB ☐ Radiant	Amenities ☐ Woodstove(s) #	Driveway Surface
☐ Drop Stair ☐ Stairs	☐ Other Fuel	☐ Fireplace(s) # ☐ Fence	☐ Garage # of Cars
☐ Floor ☐ Scuttle	Cooling ☐ Central Air Conditioning	☐ Patio/Deck ☐ Porch	☐ Carport # of Cars
☐ Finished ☐ Heated	☐ Individual ☐ Other	☐ Pool ☐ Other	☐ Att. ☐ Det. ☐ Built-in

Appliances ☐ Refrigerator ☐ Range/Oven ☐ Dishwasher ☐ Disposal ☐ Microwave ☐ Washer/Dryer ☐ Other (describe)

Finished area **above** grade contains: Rooms   Bedrooms   Bath(s)   Square Feet of Gross Living Area Above Grade

Additional features (special energy efficient items, etc.)

Describe the condition of the property (including needed repairs, deterioration, renovations, remodeling, etc.).

Are there any physical deficiencies or adverse conditions that affect the livability, soundness, or structural integrity of the property? ☐ Yes ☐ No If Yes, describe

Does the property generally conform to the neighborhood (functional utility, style, condition, use, construction, etc.)? ☐ Yes ☐ No If No, describe

Uniform Residential Appraisal Report

File #

| There are | comparable properties currently offered for sale in the subject neighborhood ranging in price from $ | | | | to $ | | |
| There are | comparable sales in the subject neighborhood within the past twelve months ranging in sale price from $ | | | | to $ | | |

FEATURE	SUBJECT	COMPARABLE SALE # 1		COMPARABLE SALE # 2		COMPARABLE SALE # 3	
Address							
Proximity to Subject							
Sale Price	$		$		$		$
Sale Price/Gross Liv. Area	$ sq. ft.	$ sq. ft.		$ sq. ft.		$ sq. ft.	
Data Source(s)							
Verification Source(s)							
VALUE ADJUSTMENTS	DESCRIPTION	DESCRIPTION	+(-) $ Adjustment	DESCRIPTION	+(-) $ Adjustment	DESCRIPTION	+(-) $ Adjustment
Sale or Financing Concessions							
Date of Sale/Time							
Location							
Leasehold/Fee Simple							
Site							
View							
Design (Style)							
Quality of Construction							
Actual Age							
Condition							
Above Grade	Total Bdrms. Baths	Total Bdrms. Baths		Total Bdrms. Baths		Total Bdrms. Baths	
Room Count							
Gross Living Area	sq. ft.	sq. ft.		sq. ft.		sq. ft.	
Basement & Finished Rooms Below Grade							
Functional Utility							
Heating/Cooling							
Energy Efficient Items							
Garage/Carport							
Porch/Patio/Deck							
Net Adjustment (Total)		☐ + ☐ -	$	☐ + ☐ -	$	☐ + ☐ -	$
Adjusted Sale Price of Comparables		Net Adj. % Gross Adj. %	$	Net Adj. % Gross Adj. %	$	Net Adj. % Gross Adj. %	$

I ☐ did ☐ did not research the sale or transfer history of the subject property and comparable sales. If not, explain

My research ☐ did ☐ did not reveal any prior sales or transfers of the subject property for the three years prior to the effective date of this appraisal.

Data source(s)

My research ☐ did ☐ did not reveal any prior sales or transfers of the comparable sales for the year prior to the date of sale of the comparable sale.

Data source(s)

Report the results of the research and analysis of the prior sale or transfer history of the subject property and comparable sales (report additional prior sales on page 3).

ITEM	SUBJECT	COMPARABLE SALE # 1	COMPARABLE SALE # 2	COMPARABLE SALE # 3
Date of Prior Sale/Transfer				
Price of Prior Sale/Transfer				
Data Source(s)				
Effective Date of Data Source(s)				

Analysis of prior sale or transfer history of the subject property and comparable sales

Summary of Sales Comparison Approach

Indicated Value by Sales Comparison Approach $

Indicated Value by: Sales Comparison Approach $ Cost Approach (if developed) $ Income Approach (if developed) $

This appraisal is made ☐ "as is", ☐ subject to completion per plans and specifications on the basis of a hypothetical condition that the improvements have been completed, ☐ subject to the following repairs or alterations on the basis of a hypothetical condition that the repairs or alterations have been completed, or ☐ subject to the following required inspection based on the extraordinary assumption that the condition or deficiency does not require alteration or repair:

Based on a complete visual inspection of the interior and exterior areas of the subject property, defined scope of work, statement of assumptions and limiting conditions, and appraiser's certification, my (our) opinion of the market value, as defined, of the real property that is the subject of this report is $, as of   , which is the date of inspection and the effective date of this appraisal.

Chapter Summary

1. An appraisal is an estimate or an opinion of value. Most real estate appraisals concern a property's market value, the price it is likely to bring on the open market in an arm's length transaction.

2. Appraisers have developed many "principles of value" that guide them in the valuation process. These include the principles of highest and best use, change, anticipation, supply and demand, substitution, conformity, contribution, competition, and balance.

3. The steps in the appraisal process include defining the problem, determining what data is needed and where it can be found, gathering and verifying general and specific data, selecting and applying the valuation methods, reconciling the value indicators, and issuing the appraisal report.

4. General data concerns factors outside the subject property itself that influence the property's value. The appraiser gathers general data by evaluating economic and social trends and by performing a neighborhood analysis. Specific data (about the subject property itself) is gathered through site analysis and building analysis.

5. In the sales comparison approach to value (which is the most important method of appraisal for residential properties), the appraiser compares the subject property to comparable properties that were sold recently, and uses the adjusted selling prices of the comparables to estimate the value of the subject property.

6. In the cost approach, the appraiser estimates the cost of replacing the improvements, deducts any depreciation, and adds the estimated value of the land to arrive at an estimate of the value of the whole property. Depreciation takes the form of deferred maintenance, functional obsolescence, and external obsolescence. Land does not depreciate.

7. In the income approach to value, the appraiser divides the property's net income by a capitalization rate to estimate its value to an investor. The appraiser first estimates the property's potential gross income (economic rent), then deducts a bad debt and vacancy factor to determine the effective gross income, then deducts operating expenses to determine net income. The gross income multiplier method is a simplified version of the income approach that is sometimes used in appraising residential rental properties.

8. The methods used for site valuation (appraising raw land, or appraising a site separately from its improvements) are the sales comparison method, the land residual technique, the distribution method, and the development method.

🔑 Key Terms

Market value—The most probable price that a property should bring in a competitive and open market under all conditions requisite to a fair sale, the buyer and seller each acting prudently and knowledgeably, and assuming the price is not affected by undue stimulus.

Arm's length transaction—A transaction in which both parties have full knowledge of the property's merits and shortcomings, neither party is acting under unusual pressure, and the property has been exposed on the open market for a reasonable length of time.

Highest and best use—The most profitable use of the property; the one that provides the greatest net return over time.

Principle of change—Real property is in a constant state of change. It goes through a four-phase life cycle of integration, equilibrium, disintegration, and rejuvenation.

Principle of substitution—No one will pay more for a piece of property than they would have to pay for an equally desirable substitute.

Sales comparison approach—The method of appraisal in which the appraiser compares the subject property to recently sold comparable properties.

Cost approach—The method of appraisal in which the appraiser estimates the replacement cost of the building, deducts depreciation, and adds the value of the site.

Depreciation—Loss in value due to any cause.

Deferred maintenance—Depreciation caused by wear and tear; physical deterioration.

Functional obsolescence—Depreciation caused by functional inadequacies or outmoded design.

External obsolescence—Depreciation caused by forces outside the property, such as neighborhood decline or proximity to nuisances. Also called economic obsolescence.

Income approach—The method of appraising property in which net income is converted into value by use of a capitalization rate.

Effective gross income—Potential gross income less a bad debt and vacancy factor.

Net income—Effective gross income less operating expenses.

Capitalization rate—The rate of return an investor wants on his or her investment in the property.

Economic rent—The rent that a property would earn on the open market if it were currently available for rent, as distinguished from the rent it is actually earning now (the contract rent).

Chapter Quiz

1. An appraisal is:

   a) a scientific determination of a property's value

   b) a property's average value, as indicated by general and specific data

   c) an estimate of a property's value as of a specific date

   d) a mathematical analysis of a property's value

2. The focus of most appraisals is the subject property's:

   a) market value

   b) market price

   c) sales price

   d) value in use

3. A property's highest and best use is:

   a) the use that will generate the greatest net return

   b) the best use it could be put to if there were no zoning or other restrictions

   c) the use that best promotes the public health, safety, and welfare

   d) the use that is best suited to the present owner's plans

4. The earliest phase of a property's life cycle, when it is being developed, is called:

   a) substitution

   b) regression

   c) integration

   d) disintegration

5. Developers have announced plans to build a multimillion dollar shopping center next door to a vacant commercial lot you own. Property values in the area will tend to increase as a result of this announcement. This is an example of the principle of:

   a) highest and best use

   b) supply and demand

   c) substitution

   d) anticipation

6. The owner of an apartment building has asked an appraiser to determine if it would make financial sense to put in a swimming pool for the tenants' use. The appraiser will be most concerned with the principle of:

   a) regression

   b) substitution

   c) conformity

   d) contribution

7. If someone were to build a high-quality home costing $450,000 in a neighborhood where all of the other homes were valued at around $175,000, the expensive home would suffer a loss in value. This illustrates the principle of:

   a) regression

   b) supply and demand

   c) progression

   d) aversion

8. An appraiser gathers general data in a:

   a) site analysis

   b) building analysis

   c) neighborhood analysis

   d) None of the above

9. The sales comparison approach would almost certainly be much more important than the other two methods (the cost approach and the income approach) in the appraisal of:

a) a six-unit apartment building
b) an industrial building
c) a shopping center
d) a single-family home

10. A residential appraiser looking for good comparables is most likely to consider homes that:

a) have not changed hands within the past three years
b) are currently listed for sale
c) were sold within the past six months
d) were listed for less than they eventually sold for

11. In which of the following situations would the sales comparison method of appraisal be least reliable?

a) When all of the comparables are in the same price range
b) In an inactive real estate market
c) When some of the comparables are located in another neighborhood
d) When the subject property is in better condition than the comparables

12. When applying the sales comparison method to appraise a single-family home, an appraiser would never use as a comparable a similar home that:

a) sold over six months age
b) sold recently but is located in another neighborhood
c) was sold by owners who were forced to sell because of financial difficulties
d) is situated on a corner lot

13. When using the replacement cost approach, which of the following would be least important?

a) Current construction cost per square foot
b) Rental cost per square foot
c) Depreciation
d) Estimated land value

14. An appraiser is applying the cost approach in valuing an elegant building that was built in 1894. Which of the following is most likely to be true?

a) The building's replacement cost is the same as its reproduction cost
b) The building's replacement cost is a better indicator of its market value than its reproduction cost
c) The building's reproduction cost is a better indicator of its market value than its replacement cost
d) The building's replacement cost is much greater than its reproduction cost

15. In the income approach to value, which of the following is not considered to be one of the property's operating expenses?

a) General real estate taxes
b) Maintenance expenses
c) Reserves for replacement
d) Mortgage payments

☞ Answer Key

1. c) An appraisal is only an estimate or opinion of value, and it is valid only in regard to a specified date.

2. a) An appraiser is usually asked to determine the subject property's market value (or value in exchange).

3. a) The highest and best use is the use that would produce the greatest net return over time, given the current zoning and other restrictions on use.

4. c) Integration is the period during which the property is being developed.

5. d) This is an example of the principle of anticipation, which holds that value is created by the expectation of future benefits to be derived from owning a property.

6. d) The appraiser will be concerned with the principle of contribution. Will the proposed improvement—the swimming pool—contribute enough to the property's value (in the form of higher rents from tenants, and, ultimately, net income to the owner) to justify the expense of installing it?

7. a) The principle of regression holds that association with properties of much lower quality reduces a property's value.

8. c) General data is data concerning factors outside the subject property itself that affect the property's value. A neighborhood analysis involves collection of general data, whereas the site and building analyses involve collection of specific data about the subject property itself.

9. d) In the appraisal of single-family homes, the sales comparison approach is given the most weight.

10. c) A sales comparison appraisal of residential property is usually based on the sales prices of homes that sold within the past six months.

11. b) There is little data available in an inactive market. (However, the appraiser can use comparable sales that took place up to one year earlier, if he or she determines the rate of appreciation or depreciation and adjusts the prices accordingly.)

12. c) Forced sales are never used as comparables for appraisal purposes. Comparable sales must be arm's length transactions, where neither party was acting under unusual pressure.

13. b) The cost method involves estimating the current cost of construction, subtracting the amount of accrued depreciation, then adding back in the estimated value of the land. How much the property rents for is irrelevant to the cost approach.

14. b) The cost of producing a replica of an old building at current prices (reproduction cost) is invariably much higher than the cost of constructing a building with the equivalent utility using modern materials (replacement cost). Reproduction cost is not a good indicator of an old building's market value.

15. d) The mortgage payments—referred to as the property's debt service—are not considered operating expenses for the purposes of the income approach.

Closing Real Estate Transactions

Chapter Overview

The real estate agent's job doesn't end when the parties sign the purchase and sale agreement. Many matters must be taken care of before the sale can be finalized, and the service provided by the real estate agent during the closing process is just as important as the agent's marketing efforts before the sale. Guiding the parties through closing prevents unnecessary delays and earns the agent a reputation for professionalism. Every real estate agent should be familiar with escrow procedures and the allocation of closing costs. This chapter explains the purpose of escrow and the steps involved in closing. It also discusses how settlement statements work, how closing costs are allocated and prorated, income tax aspects of closing, and the requirements of the federal Real Estate Settlement Procedures Act.

Introduction

Once a purchase and sale agreement has been signed and all of the contingencies (such as arranging financing) have been satisfied, preparations are made to finalize the transaction. Finalizing a real estate transaction is called **closing** or **settlement**.

The closing process varies considerably from one state to another. In some states, all of the parties involved in the transaction get together to sign and exchange documents and transfer funds. In many other states (including California), the closing process is handled by a neutral third party, through the creation of an escrow.

Escrow

Escrow is an arrangement in which money and documents are held by a neutral third party (the **escrow agent**) on behalf of the buyer and the seller until the transaction is ready to close. The escrow agent is a dual agent, representing both the buyer and the seller, with fiduciary duties to both parties (see the discussion of dual agency in Chapter 8).

The parties usually give the escrow agent written **escrow instructions**, which determine under what conditions and at what time the agent will distribute the money and documents to the proper parties. The escrow instructions are a bilateral contract between the buyer and the seller. Neither party may choose the escrow agent or set the terms and conditions of escrow without the consent of the other party.

The escrow instructions ordinarily reflect the contingencies and other requirements for the transaction that were set forth in the purchase and sale agreement. If there is a conflict between the terms of the purchase and sale agreement and the escrow instructions, the escrow agent is usually supposed to comply with the later of the two contracts—the escrow instructions.

The purpose of escrow is to ensure that the seller receives the purchase price, the buyer receives clear title to the property, and the lender's security interest in the property is perfected. Escrow protects each party from the other's change of mind. For example, if the seller suddenly doesn't want to sell the property as agreed, he or she can't just refuse to deliver the deed to the buyer. Once a deed has been given to an escrow agent, if the buyer fulfills all of the conditions specified in the escrow instructions and deposits the purchase price into escrow, the escrow agent is required to deliver the deed to the buyer. An added advantage of escrow is convenience: the parties do not have to be present to close the transaction.

Escrow Services

Escrow agents perform a wide variety of services to prepare a transaction for closing. Most escrow closings involve all of the following steps:

- obtaining a title report from the title insurance company;
- ordering inspections;
- paying off existing loans secured by the property;
- preparing documents, such as the deed;
- depositing funds from the buyer (and seller if necessary);
- obtaining title insurance policies;
- requesting the funding of the buyer's loan;
- prorating expenses and allocating closing costs;
- preparing a Uniform Settlement Statement;
- recording documents; and
- disbursing funds and delivering documents.

However, the escrow agent's services are usually quite limited in nature. For example, while an escrow agent would contact a structural pest control company to order an inspection called for in the purchase agreement, the escrow agent would not discuss the results of the inspection with the company or authorize necessary repairs. That would be up to the parties.

Termination of Escrow

Escrow terminates when the transaction closes. Alternatively, it will terminate if the terms of the escrow instructions have not been fulfilled by the scheduled closing date (or if no closing date has been set, within a reasonable time). As a general rule, escrow can be terminated earlier only if the buyer and seller mutually consent to the termination. Neither party can terminate the escrow unilaterally, without the other's consent. Nor does the death or incapacity of either party terminate the escrow.

Example: The seller deposits a properly executed deed into escrow and dies shortly afterward. If the buyer fulfills the terms of the escrow instructions, the transaction will still close, in spite of the death of the seller.

Sometimes if a transaction fails to close, there is a dispute between the buyer and seller over which of them is entitled to funds or other items that were placed into escrow. If the parties are unable to resolve the dispute, the escrow agent should file an **interpleader** action, turning the matter over to a court. The court will decide which party is the rightful owner of the items in escrow. It is not the escrow agent's role to arbitrate a dispute between the parties.

Escrow Agents

Title companies are the most common escrow agents in northern California. In the southern part of the state, independent escrow companies also close a large number of transactions. Many institutional lenders have their own escrow departments, to close their own loan transactions.

California's Escrow Law requires all escrow companies to be licensed by the state Department of Corporations. Only corporations may be licensed as escrow companies; individuals are not eligible. Banks, savings and loans, insurance companies, title companies, attorneys, and real estate brokers are exempt from this licensing requirement, because they are regulated by other agencies.

Note that real estate brokers are only exempt from the escrow licensing requirement while engaged in activities that require a real estate license and that occur in the course of a real estate transaction in which the broker is an agent or a party. This exemption allows brokers to provide escrow services to their clients, and they may charge a fee for these services. The exemption does not permit brokers to operate as escrow agents for transactions in which they have no bona fide interest other than that of providing escrow services.

Closing Costs and Settlement Statements

Most real estate transactions involve a wide variety of costs in addition to the purchase price: inspection fees, title insurance charges, loan fees, and so on. These are known as **closing costs**. Some of these closing costs are paid by the buyer, and some are paid by the seller. Some are paid by one party to the other; for example, the buyer may have to reimburse the seller for property taxes the seller already paid. Other closing costs are paid by one of the parties to a third party; for instance, the seller may be required to pay a pest inspector's fee.

There are also other payments to be made in connection with closing. For example, the seller often has to pay off an existing mortgage or other liens. Who is required to pay how much to whom at closing can be a complicated matter.

So for each transaction, the escrow agent prepares a **settlement statement**. A settlement statement (also known as a closing statement) sets forth all of the financial aspects of the transaction in detail. It shows exactly how much the buyer will have to pay at closing, and exactly how much the seller will take away from closing. A simplified example of a settlement statement is shown in Figure 12.1.

Preparing a Settlement Statement

The items listed on the settlement statement are either **debits** or **credits**. A debit is a charge payable *by* a particular party; the purchase price is a debit to the buyer, for example, and the sales commission is a debit to the seller. Credits are items payable *to* a party; the buyer is credited for his or her new loan, and the seller for the purchase price.

Preparing a settlement statement involves little more than determining what charges and credits apply to a given transaction and making sure each one is allocated to the right party. When allocating expenses, an escrow agent is generally guided by the terms of the purchase and sale agreement or the escrow

Fig. 12.1 Simplified settlement statement

	Buyer		Seller	
	Debits	**Credits**	**Debits**	**Credits**
Purchase price	175,000.00			175,000.00
Deposit		8,750.00		
Documentary transfer tax			192.50	
Sales commission			12,250.00	
Payoff of seller's loan			92,950.00	
Assumption of seller's loan				
New loan		140,000.00		
Seller financing				
Owner's title insurance			120.00	
Lender's title insurance	456.00			
Origination/assumption fee	2,100.00			
Discount points				
Property taxes				
In arrears				
Paid in advance	684.50			684.50
Hazard insurance				
Assumption of policy				
New policy	260.00			
Interest				
Payoff of seller's loan			382.86	
Assumption				
New loan (prepaid)	161.08			
Reserve account				
Payoff of seller's loan				286.05
Assumption				
Credit report	40.00			
Appraisal	275.00			
Survey				
Pest inspection and repairs			150.00	
Personal property				
Recording fees	50.00		25.00	
Escrow fee	147.00		147.00	
Balance due from buyer		30,423.58		
Balance due to seller			69,753.19	
TOTALS	179,173.58	179,173.58	175,970.55	175,970.55

instructions. The allocation can also be determined by custom (local or general), provided the custom doesn't conflict with the terms of the parties' contract. For example, in most places the buyer usually pays the cost of an appraisal, so that cost would ordinarily be charged to the buyer at closing. But if the seller agreed in the purchase and sale agreement to pay the appraisal fee, custom would be disregarded and the expense would be a debit to the seller at closing.

Of course, neither custom nor the agreement between the parties can be followed if they are contrary to local, state, or federal law.

Although a real estate agent may not necessarily ever be called upon to prepare a formal settlement statement, every agent should know what closing costs are likely to be involved in a transaction and how they are customarily allocated. The buyer and the seller may want to negotiate about the allocation of particular costs, and in any case they are entitled to know the full extent of their costs before signing a contract. A real estate agent should be able to prepare a good estimate of closing costs for each party.

Guide to Settlement Statements

The double entry accounting method is used for settlement statements, so each party has a credit column and a debit column. The sum of the buyer's credits must equal the sum of the buyer's debits. And the sum of the seller's credits must equal the sum of the seller's debits. Think of the settlement statement as a check register for a bank account. Debits are like checks written against the account, and credits are the equivalent of deposits into the account. When the transaction closes, the balance in each party's account should be zero.

When an item is payable by one party to the other, it will appear on the settlement statement as a debit to the paying party and as a credit to the party paid. An obvious example is the purchase price, which is debited to the buyer and credited to the seller.

If an item is paid by one of the parties to a third party, it appears on the settlement statement in the paying party's debit column, and it does not appear in the other party's columns at all. For example, the seller is customarily charged for the documentary transfer tax, which is paid to the county treasurer. The tax is a debit to the seller, but it is not a credit to the buyer.

Similarly, certain items are shown as a credit to one party, but not as a debit to the other. The seller's reserve account is a case in point. If the sale calls for the payoff of the seller's existing mortgage, any property tax, insurance, or other reserves held by the seller's lender are refunded. They are a credit to the seller, but not a debit to the buyer.

Settlement Charges. Here is a list of the items that appear on the settlement statements for most standard residential transactions.

Purchase Price. Paid by the buyer to the seller, the purchase price is listed as a debit to the buyer and a credit to the seller.

Good Faith Deposit. In most transactions, the buyer gives the seller a good faith deposit when the purchase and sale agreement is signed. If the transaction closes, the deposit is applied to the purchase price. Since the buyer has already paid the deposit, it appears on the settlement statement as a credit to the buyer. And since the full purchase price has already been debited to the buyer and credited to the seller, no entry is made on the seller's side of the statement.

Sales Commission. The real estate broker's commission is normally paid by the seller, so it is entered as a debit to the seller.

New Loan. If the buyer secures a new loan to finance part or all of the sale, the loan amount is listed as a credit to the buyer. Like the deposit, the buyer's loan is part of the purchase price already credited to the seller, so no entry is made on the seller's side of the statement.

Assumed Loan. If the buyer assumes the seller's existing loan, it is part of the money used to finance the transaction, so (like a new loan) it is credited to the buyer. The assumed loan balance is a debit to the seller.

Seller Financing. If the seller accepts a mortgage or deed of trust from the buyer for part of the purchase price, that shows up in the buyer's credit column, just like an institutional loan. At the same time, a seller financing arrangement reduces the amount of cash the seller will receive at closing, so it is listed as a debit to the seller.

If the property is sold under a land contract, the contract price (less the downpayment) is credit extended by the seller. It reduces the seller's net at closing and is used by the buyer to finance the purchase, so it is a debit to the seller and a credit to the buyer.

Payoff of Seller's Loan. If the seller has a loan to pay off, the escrow agent requests a **beneficiary's statement** from the seller's lender. This document states the loan's remaining principal balance. The loan payoff is a debit to the seller. No entry is made on the buyer's side of the settlement statement.

Prepayment Penalty. A prepayment penalty is a charge the seller's lender may impose on the seller for paying the loan off before the end of its term. It would be a debit to the seller on the settlement statement.

Seller's Reserve Account. As was mentioned earlier, the seller often has reserves on deposit with the lender to cover certain expenses connected with the property. These expenses, sometimes referred to as the **recurring costs**, include property taxes and insurance, and in some cases assessments, home-owners or condominium association fees, or other periodic charges. (The principal and interest payments on the mortgage are not considered part of the recurring costs, however.) During the loan term, the lender requires the borrower to make regular payments toward the recurring costs, and these payments are kept in a **reserve account** (also called an **impound account** or **escrow account**). The lender uses the funds in the reserve account to pay the taxes, insurance, and other charges when they come due.

When the seller's loan is paid off, the unused balance in the reserve account is refunded to the seller. It appears as a credit on the seller's side of the settlement statement. If the buyer is assuming the loan and the reserve account, the reserves would appear as a credit to the seller and a debit to the buyer.

Appraisal Fee. The appraisal is usually required by the buyer's lender, so the fee is ordinarily a debit to the buyer.

Credit Report. The buyer's lender charges the buyer for the credit investigation, so this is also a debit to the buyer.

Survey. Sometimes a lender requires a survey as a condition for making the loan. Unless otherwise agreed, the cost of the survey is a debit to the buyer.

Origination Fee. This is the lender's one-time charge to the borrower for setting up the loan (see Chapter 10). It's a debit to the buyer.

Discount Points. The discount points are a debit to the buyer, unless the seller has agreed to pay for a buydown (again, see Chapter 10). In that case, the points are a debit to the seller.

Assumption Fee. A lender charges an assumption fee when the buyer is assuming the seller's existing loan. The assumption fee is a debit to the buyer.

Owner's Title Insurance Premium. In northern California, the buyer usually pays the premium for the owner's title insurance policy (which protects the buyer); in southern California, the seller usually pays it.

Lender's Title Insurance Premium. The lender requires the buyer to provide an extended coverage policy to protect the lender's lien priority. The premium for this policy is a debit to the buyer, unless otherwise agreed.

Sale of Personal Property. If the seller is selling the buyer some personal property along with the real property, the price of these items should be credited to the seller and debited to the buyer. (The seller should sign a bill of sale to be delivered to the buyer at closing along with the deed.)

Inspection Fees. The cost of an inspection is allocated by agreement between the parties. For example, the buyer might agree to pay for the cost of a pest inspection, while the seller agrees to pay for repairs if the inspection shows that any are necessary.

Hazard Insurance Policy. The lender generally requires the buyer to pay for one to three years of hazard insurance coverage in advance. This is a debit to the buyer.

Documentary Transfer Tax. This is a tax imposed on every sale of real property in California (see Chapter 5). It is also called the **excise tax**. It is customarily paid by the seller, so it would usually be listed in the seller's debit column.

Attorney's Fees. A buyer or seller who is represented by an attorney in the transaction is responsible for his or her own attorney's fees. On the settlement statement, the fees will show up as a debit to the appropriate party.

Recording Fees. The fees for recording the various documents involved in the transaction are usually charged to the party who benefits from the recording. For example, the fees for recording the deed and the new mortgage or deed of trust are debits to the buyer; the fee for recording a satisfaction of the old mortgage is a debit to the seller.

Escrow Fee. Also called a settlement fee or closing fee, the escrow fee is the escrow agent's charge for his or her services. The buyer and the seller commonly agree to split the escrow fee; in that case, half the fee will be debited to each party.

Prorations. There are, of course, certain periodic expenses connected with ownership of real estate, including property taxes, hazard insurance premiums, and mortgage interest payments. As a general rule, the seller is responsible for these expenses during his or her period of ownership, but not beyond. In preparing a settlement statement, the escrow agent checks to see whether the seller will be current, in arrears, or paid in advance with respect to these expenses on the closing date. The escrow agent then **prorates** the expenses, determining what share of them the seller is responsible for. To prorate an expense is to divide and allocate it proportionately, according to time, interest, or benefit.

If, in regard to a particular expense, the seller will be in arrears on the closing date, the amount that he or she owes is entered as a debit on the settlement statement. If the seller has paid in advance, he or she is entitled to a partial refund, which appears as a credit on the statement. If the expense is one that will continue after closing (as in the case of property taxes), the buyer is responsible for it once his or her period of ownership begins. That will show up on the buyer's side of the settlement statement as a credit (if the seller is in arrears) or as a debit (if the seller has paid in advance).

The first step in prorating an expense is to divide it by the number of days it covers to determine the **per diem** (daily) rate. So an annual expense would be divided by 365 days (366 in a leap year); the per diem rate would be $1/365$th of the annual amount. A monthly expense would be divided by the number of days in the month in question (28, 29, 30, or 31).*

The next step is to determine the number of days during which a particular party is responsible for the expense. The final step is to multiply that number of days by the per diem rate, to arrive at the share of the expense that party is responsible for. Examples appear below. (See Chapter 17 for further discussion of proration calculations.)

Property Taxes. The seller is responsible for property taxes up to the day of closing; the buyer is responsible for them on the day of closing and thereafter. If the seller has already paid the property taxes for the year, he or she is entitled to a prorated refund at closing. On the settlement statement, this will appear as a credit to the seller and a debit to the buyer. (Note: In California, the property tax year runs from July 1 to June 30.)

> **Example:** Sharon is selling her house to Ben. The transaction will close January 2. This year the property taxes on the house are $2,190. The escrow agent calculates the per diem rate by dividing the property tax figure by 365, the number of days in the year.
>
> $$\$2,190 \div 365 = \$6.00 \text{ per diem}$$
>
> Sharon, the seller, is responsible for the property taxes through January 1—in other words, for the first 185 days of the year. The buyer, Ben, is responsible for the taxes from January 2 forward—the remaining 180 days in the year.
>
> Sharon has already paid the full year's taxes, so at closing she'll be entitled to a credit for the share that is Ben's responsibility. The escrow agent multiplies the number of days for which Ben is responsible by the per diem rate to determine the amount Ben will owe Sharon at closing.
>
> $$\$6.00 \times 180 = \$1,080$$
>
> This $1,080 will appear as a credit on the seller's side of the settlement statement, and as a debit on the buyer's side of the statement.

If the taxes are in arrears, the amount the seller should have paid for the period before closing will be a debit to the seller on the settlement statement.

Hazard Insurance. Hazard insurance is usually paid for well in advance. At closing, the seller is entitled to a refund for the unused portion of the policy. For example, if the seller has paid the premium for the year, and there are three months left in the year, the seller is entitled to a refund of one-fourth of the

* It was once a common practice to simplify proration calculations by using a 360-day year and 30-day months (regardless of how many days there actually were in a particular month or year). But now that calculators are so widely available, most closing agents use the exact number of days in the year or month in question. Also, note that in order for the result of a proration to be completely accurate, the per diem rate must be calculated to an accuracy of at least 4 decimal places for monthly amounts, and 5 decimal places for annual amounts. Here again, calculators make this a painless process.

premium. This would show up as a credit to the seller on the settlement statement. If the buyer is going to assume the policy, the seller will be credited and the buyer will be debited for the appropriate amount.

Interest on Seller's Loan. Interest on a real estate loan is almost always paid in arrears. In other words, the interest accruing during a given month is paid as part of the next month's payment. For instance, a loan payment due on September 1 includes the interest that accrued during August. If a transaction closes in the middle of the payment period, the seller owes the lender some interest.

> **Example:** The closing date is August 15. Although the seller made a payment on her loan on August 1, that payment did not include any of the interest that is accruing during August. At closing, the seller will owe the lender interest for the period from August 1 through August 15. The escrow agent prorates the interest, charging the seller only for those days, rather than the whole month's interest. The prorated amount is entered on the settlement statement as a debit to the seller.
>
> If the buyer assumes the loan, his first payment will be due September 1, and it will pay all of the interest for August. The seller will be debited for the interest owed up to August 15, and the buyer will be credited for the same amount.

Prepaid Interest on Buyer's Loan. Another expense that the escrow agent prorates (one that does not concern the seller) is the interest on the buyer's new mortgage loan. As a general rule, the first payment date of a new loan is not the first day of the month immediately following closing, but rather the first day of the next month after that.

> **Example:** The buyer is financing the purchase with a new institutional loan. Closing takes place on January 23. The buyer is not required to make a payment on the new loan on February 1. Instead, the first payment is not due until March 1.

Even though the first payment isn't due for an extra month, interest begins accruing on the loan on the closing date. As was explained above, the first regular payment will cover the interest for the preceding month. So if the transaction closes on January 23, the first payment will be due on March 1, and that payment will cover the interest accrued in February. However, it will not cover the interest accrued between January 23 and January 31. Instead, the lender requires the buyer to pay the interest for those nine days in January at closing. This is called **prepaid interest** or **interim interest**. It will appear as a debit to the buyer on the settlement statement.

> **Example:** The buyer is borrowing $430,000 at 7% interest to finance the purchase. The annual interest on the loan during the first year will be $30,100 ($430,000 × 7% = $30,100). The escrow agent divides that annual figure by 365 to determine the per diem interest rate.
>
> $$\$30,100 \div 365 = \$82.47 \text{ per diem}$$
>
> There are nine days between the closing date (January 23) and the first day of the following month, so the lender will expect the buyer to prepay nine days' worth of interest at closing.
>
> $$\$82.47 \times 9 \text{ days} = \$742.23 \text{ prepaid interest}$$
>
> The escrow agent will enter $742.23 as a debit to the buyer on the settlement statement.

Rent. So far we've only discussed prorated expenses. In some transactions, there is also income to be prorated at closing. If the property generates rental income and the tenants have paid for some period beyond the closing date, the seller is debited and the buyer credited for the rent paid in advance. If the rent is paid in arrears, the seller will be credited for the amount due up to closing, and the buyer will be debited for the same amount.

Note that tenants' security deposits are not prorated. The seller must transfer all of the deposits to the buyer, since the leases will continue after closing.

Cash at Closing. As we said earlier, on a settlement statement the sum of one party's credits should equal the sum of that same party's debits, so that the final balance in each party's "account" is zero. In order for the statement to work this way, it must list the amount of cash that the buyer will have to bring to closing, and also the amount of cash the seller will take away from closing.

Balance Due from Buyer. Add up all of the buyer's credits, then add up all of the buyer's debits. Subtract the buyer's credits from the buyer's debits to find the balance due, which is the amount of cash the buyer will have to pay at closing. Enter this amount as a credit for the buyer. Now the buyer's credits column should add up to exactly the same amount as the buyer's debits column.

Balance Due to Seller. Add up all of the seller's credits, then add up all of the seller's debits. Subtract the seller's debits from the seller's credits. The result is the amount of cash the seller will receive at closing (if any). Enter this amount as a debit if credits exceed debits, but as a credit if debits exceed credits. Now the seller's credits column should add up to exactly the same amount as the seller's debits column.

Note that the buyer's two column totals must match each other, and the seller's two column totals must match each other. However, the buyer's column totals do not have to match the seller's column totals. Although they might conceivably match in a particular transaction, in most transactions they do not.

Income Tax Aspects of Closing

Nearly all real estate transactions have tax implications for the parties (see Chapter 13) and, naturally, it is up to each party to fulfill his or her own tax obligations. However, there are certain requirements related to income taxes that must be taken care of when a transaction closes.

1099-S Reporting

An escrow agent (or other closing agent) must report every sale of real property to the Internal Revenue Service. Form 1099-S is used to report the seller's name and social security number and the gross proceeds from the sale. The escrow agent may not charge an extra fee for filling out the 1099-S.

The escrow agent has primary responsibility for 1099-S reporting. If the escrow agent fails to report the sale to the IRS, the mortgage lender is required to do so. If the mortgage lender also fails to report the sale, it becomes the real estate broker's responsibility to do so.

FIRPTA

The Foreign Investment in Real Property Tax Act (FIRPTA) was passed in 1980 to help prevent foreign investors from evading their tax liability on income generated from the sale of real estate. It requires a property buyer to determine whether the seller is a U.S. citizen. If not, the buyer must withhold 10% of the net proceeds of the sale and forward that amount to the IRS. Payment must be made within ten days after the transfer date. (In most cases, the escrow agent handles these requirements on behalf of the buyer.) Certain types of transactions, including some residential transactions, are exempt from FIRPTA.

California Withholding Law

California also has a state law that requires escrow agents to withhold funds for tax purposes. To comply with this law, an escrow agent must withhold 3.33% of the total sales price from the seller and send the funds to the Franchise Tax Board. For an individual seller, this requirement applies if the seller's last known address is outside of California (even if the seller is a U.S. citizen). However, the transaction is exempt if the property sold was the seller's principal residence, or if the sales price was $100,000 or less. If the seller is a company or organization rather than an individual, the withholding requirement may apply even if the seller has a California address, unless the seller qualifies for a specific exemption from the withholding law.

Real Estate Settlement Procedures Act

The Real Estate Settlement Procedures Act (**RESPA**), a federal law, was passed in 1974. It affects how closing is handled in most residential transactions financed with institutional loans. The law has two main goals:

- to provide borrowers with information about their closing costs, to help them become better shoppers for settlement services; and
- to eliminate kickbacks and referral fees that unnecessarily increase the costs of settlement.

Transactions Covered by RESPA

RESPA applies to "federally related" loan transactions. A loan is federally related if:

1. it will be secured by a mortgage or deed of trust against:
   - property on which there is (or on which the loan proceeds will be used to build) a dwelling with four or fewer units;
   - a condominium unit or a cooperative apartment;
   - a lot with (or on which the loan proceeds will be used to place) a mobile home; and
2. the lender is federally regulated, has federally insured accounts, is assisted by the federal government, makes loans in connection with a federal program, sells loans to Fannie Mae, Ginnie Mae, or Freddie Mac, or makes real estate loans totaling more than $1,000,000 per year.

In short, the act applies to almost all institutional lenders and to most residential loans.

Exemptions. RESPA does not apply to the following loan transactions:

- a loan used to purchase 25 acres or more;
- a loan primarily for a business, commercial, or agricultural purpose;
- a loan used to purchase vacant land, unless there will be a one- to four-unit dwelling built on it or a mobile home placed on it;
- temporary financing, such as a construction loan; or
- an assumption for which the lender's approval is neither required nor obtained.

Note that RESPA also does not apply to seller-financed transactions, since they are not federally regulated.

RESPA Requirements

RESPA has these requirements for federally related loan transactions:

1. Within three days after receiving a written loan application, the lender must give all loan applicants:
   - a copy of a **booklet about settlement procedures**, prepared by HUD, which explains RESPA, closing costs, and the settlement statement;
   - a **good faith estimate of closing costs** (see Figure 12.2), which must also include information about any provider of settlement services (such as a particular title insurance company or escrow agent) that the lender requires the borrower to use; and
   - a **mortgage servicing disclosure statement**, which discloses whether the lender intends to service the loan or transfer it to another lender.
2. The closing agent (whoever handles closing, whether it's an escrow agent, an employee of the lender, a real estate broker, a lawyer, etc.) must itemize all loan settlement charges on a **Uniform Settlement Statement** form (discussed below).
3. If the borrower will have to make deposits into an escrow account (a reserve or impound account) to cover taxes, insurance, and other recurring costs, the lender cannot require excessive deposits (more than necessary to cover the expenses when they come due).
4. A lender or a provider of settlement services (such as a title company) may not:
   - pay kickbacks or referral fees to anyone for referring customers;
   - accept unearned fees—that is, fees for settlement services that were not actually provided; or
   - charge a fee for the preparation of the Uniform Settlement Statement, an escrow account statement, or the disclosure statement required by the Truth in Lending Act.
5. The seller may not require the buyer to use a particular title company.

Fig. 12.2 Good faith estimate of closing costs

GOOD FAITH ESTIMATE

Date: _____

Borrower: _____

Property Address: _____

This gives an **ESTIMATE** of most of the charges you will have to pay at the settlement of your loan. The figures shown **AS ESTIMATES**, are subject to change. The figures are computed on an estimated value of $_____, a loan amount of $ _____ an interest rate of _____%, a term of _____ and a LTV of _____%.

_____ owner occupied   _____ non-owner occupied   Loan Type _____

<small>Unless otherwise discussed rates and fees are not locked in.</small>

ESTIMATED CLOSING COSTS

801	Loan Origination Fee _____%	_____
802	Discount _____	_____
803	Appraisal Fee	_____
804	Borrower Credit Report(s)	_____
808	Document Preparation Fee/Underwriting Fee	_____
810	Tax Registration	_____
812	Processing Fee	_____
1101	Escrow Fee	_____
1106	Flood Determination Letter/Courier/Fed. Express	_____
1108	Title Insurance Premium	_____
1201	Recording Fees	_____
	Total Closing Costs	$ _____

PREPAID ITEMS AND RESERVES

901	Interim Interest _____ Days @ $ _____	_____
902	Mortgage Insurance Premium	_____
902	Hazard Insurance Premium (12 months to be prepaid)	_____
1001	Hazard Insurance Reserve _____ mos. @ $_____	_____
1002	Mortgage Insurance Reserve _____ mos. @ $ _____	_____
1004	Property Tax Reserve for _____mos. @ $ _____	_____
	Total Prepaids and Reserves to be paid at closing	$ _____

ESTIMATED MONTHLY PAYMENT

Principal & Interest	$_____
Property Tax	$_____
Hazard Insurance	$_____
Mortgage Insurance	$_____
Total Estimated Monthly Payment	$_____

ESTIMATED CASH REQUIRED AT CLOSING

Sales Price/Cost to Build/Payoff	$_____
Closing Costs	$_____
Prepaid Items & Reserves	$_____
Sub-Total	$_____
Less Earnest Money	$_____
Less Good Faith Deposit	$_____
Less Standby Takeout Fee	$_____
Less Seller Contributions	$_____
Less Loan Amount	$_____
Est. Cash Req. at Closing	$_____

The above is for information only and is not a loan commitment.

The information provided below reflects estimates of the charges which you are likely to incur at the settlement of your loan. The fees listed are estimate - the actual charges may be more or less. Your transaction may not involve a fee for every item listed. The numbers listed beside the estimates generally correspond to the numbered lines contained in the HUD-1 settlement statement which you will be receiving at settlement. The HUD-1 settlement statement will show you the actual cost for items paid at settlement.

An applicant, by signing this Good Faith Estimate, acknowledges receipt of HUD Booklet outlining settlement costs.

An applicant for an Adjustable Rate Mortgage, by signing this Good Faith Estimate, acknowledges receipt of the booklet entitled, "Consumer Handbook on Adjustable Rate Mortgages".

_____   _____
                                                                                     DATE

_____   _____
                                                                                     DATE

Prepared by: _____   _____
                                                                                     DATE

Uniform Settlement Statement

The closing agent must provide completed Uniform Settlement Statement forms to the borrower, the seller, and the lender on or before the closing date. (The borrower may sign a written waiver of the right to receive the form by closing, in which case it must be provided to the parties as soon as practicable after closing.) If the borrower requests it, the closing agent must allow the borrower to inspect the statement one business day before closing.

A copy of the Uniform Settlement Statement form is shown in Figure 12.3. It does not have the same format as the simplified settlement statement shown earlier in this chapter (with buyer's credit and debit columns and seller's credit and debit columns side by side), but it presents the same information.

On the Uniform Settlement Statement, each party's closing costs are itemized on the back of the form (that is, on the second page shown here), with the buyer's costs in the left column and the seller's costs in the right column. Each party's costs are added up, and the total is transferred to the front of the form. The buyer's total costs are entered on line 103, and the seller's total costs are entered on line 502.

On the front of the Uniform Settlement Statement form, lines 101 through 120 correspond to the "Buyer's Debits" column on the simplified version. Lines 201 through 301 correspond to the "Buyer's Credits" column. Lines 401 through 420 are the equivalent of the "Seller's Credits" column, and lines 501 through 601 represent the "Seller's Debits" column. The amount of cash the buyer must bring to closing is shown on line 303, and the amount of cash the seller will receive at closing is shown on line 603.

Fig. 12.3 Uniform Settlement Statement

A. **Settlement Statement**	**U.S. Department of Housing and Urban Development**	OMB Approval No. 2502-0265

B. Type of Loan

1. ☐ FHA 2. ☐ FmHA 3. ☐ Conv. Unins.
4. ☐ VA 5. ☐ Conv. Ins.

6. File Number:	7. Loan Number:	8. Mortgage Insurance Case Number:

C. Note: This form is furnished to give you a statement of actual settlement costs. Amounts paid to and by the settlement agent are shown. Items marked "(p.o.c.)" were paid outside the closing; they are shown here for informational purposes and are not included in the totals.

D. Name & Address of Borrower:	E. Name & Address of Seller:	F. Name & Address of Lender:

G. Property Location:	H. Settlement Agent:	
	Place of Settlement:	I. Settlement Date:

J. Summary of Borrower's Transaction		**K. Summary of Seller's Transaction**	
100. Gross Amount Due From Borrower		**400. Gross Amount Due To Seller**	
101. Contract sales price		401. Contract sales price	
102. Personal property		402. Personal property	
103. Settlement charges to borrower (line 1400)		403.	
104.		404.	
105.		405.	
Adjustments for items paid by seller in advance		**Adjustments for items paid by seller in advance**	
106. City/town taxes to		406. City/town taxes to	
107. County taxes to		407. County taxes to	
108. Assessments to		408. Assessments to	
109.		409.	
110.		410.	
111.		411.	
112.		412.	
120. Gross Amount Due From Borrower		**420. Gross Amount Due To Seller**	
200. Amounts Paid By Or In Behalf Of Borrower		**500. Reductions In Amount Due To Seller**	
201. Deposit or earnest money		501. Excess deposit (see instructions)	
202. Principal amount of new loan(s)		502. Settlement charges to seller (line 1400)	
203. Existing loan(s) taken subject to		503. Existing loan(s) taken subject to	
204.		504. Payoff of first mortgage loan	
205.		505. Payoff of second mortgage loan	
206.		506.	
207.		507.	
208.		508.	
209.		509.	
Adjustments for items unpaid by seller		**Adjustments for items unpaid by seller**	
210. City/town taxes to		510. City/town taxes to	
211. County taxes to		511. County taxes to	
212. Assessments to		512. Assessments to	
213.		513.	
214.		514.	
215.		515.	
216.		516.	
217.		517.	
218.		518.	
219.		519.	
220. Total Paid By/For Borrower		**520. Total Reduction Amount Due Seller**	
300. Cash At Settlement From/To Borrower		**600. Cash At Settlement To/From Seller**	
301. Gross Amount due from borrower (line 120)		601. Gross amount due to seller (line 420)	
302. Less amounts paid by/for borrower (line 220)	( )	602. Less reductions in amt. due seller (line 520)	( )
303. Cash ☐ From ☐ To Borrower		**603. Cash** ☐ To ☐ From Seller	

Section 5 of the Real Estate Settlement Procedures Act (RESPA) requires the following: • HUD must develop a Special Information Booklet to help persons borrowing money to finance the purchase of residential real estate to better understand the nature and costs of real estate settlement services; • Each lender must provide the booklet to all applicants from whom it receives or for whom it prepares a written application to borrow money to finance the purchase of residential real estate; • Lenders must prepare and distribute with the Booklet a Good Faith Estimate of the settlement costs that the borrower is likely to incur in connection with the settlement. These disclosures are manadatory.

Section 4(a) of RESPA mandates that HUD develop and prescribe this standard form to be used at the time of loan settlement to provide full disclosure of all charges imposed upon the borrower and seller. These are third party disclosures that are designed to provide the borrower with pertinent information during the settlement process in order to be a better shopper.

The Public Reporting Burden for this collection of information is estimated to average one hour per response, including the time for reviewing instructions, searching existing data sources, gathering and maintaining the data needed, and completing and reviewing the collection of information.

This agency may not collect this information, and you are not required to complete this form, unless it displays a currently valid OMB control number.

The information requested does not lend itself to confidentiality.

Previous editions are obsolete   Page 1 of 2   form **HUD-1** (3/86)
                                                                       ref Handbook 4305.2

L. Settlement Charges

		Paid From Borrowers Funds at Settlement	Paid From Seller's Funds at Settlement
700. Total Sales/Broker's Commission based on price $ @ % =			
Division of Commission (line 700) as follows:			
701. $ to			
702. $ to			
703. Commission paid at Settlement			
704.			
800. Items Payable In Connection With Loan			
801. Loan Origination Fee %			
802. Loan Discount %			
803. Appraisal Fee to			
804. Credit Report to			
805. Lender's Inspection Fee			
806. Mortgage Insurance Application Fee to			
807. Assumption Fee			
808.			
809.			
810.			
811.			
900. Items Required By Lender To Be Paid In Advance			
901. Interest from to @$ /day			
902. Mortgage Insurance Premium for months to			
903. Hazard Insurance Premium for years to			
904. years to			
905.			
1000. Reserves Deposited With Lender			
1001. Hazard insurance months@$ per month			
1002. Mortgage insurance months@$ per month			
1003. City property taxes months@$ per month			
1004. County property taxes months@$ per month			
1005. Annual assessments months@$ per month			
1006. months@$ per month			
1007. months@$ per month			
1008. months@$ per month			
1100. Title Charges			
1101. Settlement or closing fee to			
1102. Abstract or title search to			
1103. Title examination to			
1104. Title insurance binder to			
1105. Document preparation to			
1106. Notary fees to			
1107. Attorney's fees to			
(includes above items numbers:)			
1108. Title insurance to			
(includes above items numbers:)			
1109. Lender's coverage $			
1110. Owner's coverage $			
1111.			
1112.			
1113.			
1200. Government Recording and Transfer Charges			
1201. Recording fees: Deed $; Mortgage $; Releases $			
1202. City/county tax/stamps: Deed $; Mortgage $			
1203. State tax/stamps: Deed $; Mortgage $			
1204.			
1205.			
1300. Additional Settlement Charges			
1301. Survey to			
1302. Pest inspection to			
1303.			
1304.			
1305.			
1400. Total Settlement Charges (enter on lines 103, Section J and 502, Section K)			

Chapter Summary

1. After a purchase and sale agreement has been signed, the next stage of the transaction is the closing process. Closing is often handled through escrow, an arrangement in which money and documents are held by a neutral third party (the escrow agent) on behalf of the buyer and the seller, and distributed when all of the conditions in the escrow instructions have been fulfilled.

2. The escrow agent prepares a settlement statement, detailing all of the charges payable by (debits) and payable to (credits) each of the parties at closing. Who pays which closing costs may be determined by agreement or by local custom. Certain expenses must be prorated as of the closing date.

3. Certain requirements related to income taxes must be fulfilled when a real estate transaction closes. These include the 1099-S reporting requirement and the requirements of FIRPTA and the California Withholding Law.

4. RESPA applies to almost all residential loan transactions involving institutional lenders. It requires a lender to give a loan applicant a good faith estimate of closing costs within three days after a written loan application is submitted. RESPA also requires the closing agent to complete a Uniform Settlement Statement and have it available to the buyer one day before closing, if the buyer asks to see it in advance.

Key Terms

Closing—The final stage of a real estate transaction, in which documents are signed and delivered and funds are transferred. Also called settlement.

Escrow—An arrangement in which money and documents are held by a neutral third party on behalf of the buyer and the seller.

Escrow agent—A neutral third party who holds money and documents in trust and carries out the closing process. Also called a closing agent.

Escrow instructions—A bilateral contract between the buyer and the seller that tells the escrow agent how to proceed and states the conditions each party must fulfill before the transaction can close.

Settlement statement—A statement that sets forth all of the financial aspects of a real estate transaction in detail and indicates how much cash each party will be required to pay or will receive at closing.

Debit—A charge payable by a party, either to the other party or to a third party.

Credit—A charge payable to a party, either by the other party or by a third party.

Reserve account—Funds on deposit with a lender to pay the property taxes, insurance premiums, and other recurring costs when due.

Prorate—To divide and allocate an expense proportionately, according to time, interest, or benefit, determining what share of it a particular party is responsible for.

Prepaid interest—Interest on the buyer's new mortgage loan that the lender requires to be paid at closing, covering the period from the closing date through the last day of the month.

Uniform Settlement Statement—The settlement statement form that closing agents are required to use in transactions covered by the Real Estate Settlement Procedures Act.

Chapter Quiz

1. Which of the following would not be prorated at closing in the sale of a rental property?

   a) Prepaid property taxes
   b) Interest on seller's existing loan
   c) Security deposit
   d) Interest on buyer's new loan

2. Every debit on the buyer's side of the settlement statement is a charge that:

   a) will be paid to the buyer at closing
   b) must be paid by the buyer at closing
   c) the buyer must pay to the seller at closing
   d) the seller must pay to the buyer at closing

3. On a settlement statement, the purchase price will be listed as:

   a) a debit to the buyer
   b) a debit to the seller
   c) Both of the above
   d) Neither of the above

4. The transaction is closing on September 16. The seller has already paid the annual premium for hazard insurance, and the buyer will not be assuming the policy. On the settlement statement, part of the insurance premium will be listed as:

   a) a debit to the buyer and a credit to the seller
   b) a debit to the seller and a credit to the buyer
   c) a credit to the buyer
   d) a credit to the seller

5. How does the buyer's good faith deposit show up on a settlement statement?

   a) It is listed as a debit on the buyer's side of the statement, and as a credit on the seller's side of the statement
   b) It is listed as a credit on the buyer's side of the statement, but it is not listed on the seller's side because it is included in the purchase price
   c) It is listed as a credit on the seller's side of the statement, but it is not listed on the buyer's side because it will be refunded at closing
   d) It is listed as a debit on both the buyer's side and the seller's side of the statement

6. When a buyer assumes a mortgage, how does the mortgage balance appear on the settlement statement?

   a) Only as a credit to the seller
   b) Only as a debit on the seller's side of the statement
   c) As a credit to the buyer and a debit to the seller
   d) As a credit to the seller and a debit to the buyer

7. Which of the following is ordinarily one of the seller's closing costs?

   a) Sales commission
   b) Credit report fee
   c) Appraisal fee
   d) Origination fee

8. Which of the following is ordinarily one of the buyer's closing costs?

   a) Sales commission
   b) Lender's title insurance premium
   c) Documentary transfer tax
   d) None of the above

9. On a settlement statement, prepaid interest would usually appear as a:

a) seller's debit
b) buyer's credit
c) seller's credit
d) buyer's debit

10. The Matsons are selling their home. They are current on their mortgage payments, having made their most recent payment on May 1. They will be paying off their mortgage when the sale closes on May 17. At closing, the Matsons will probably be:

a) entitled to a refund of the mortgage interest accruing in May
b) required to pay the mortgage interest accruing in May
c) entitled to a refund of the prepayment penalty
d) required to pay part of the mortgage interest that accrued in April

11. A settlement statement:

a) is given to the buyer but not the seller
b) sets out the items to be paid by each party
c) is given only to the buyer's lender
d) is required only in transactions closed by independent escrow companies

12. When an item is prorated it means that:

a) it is deleted from the cost of the sale
b) it is calculated on the basis of a particular time period
c) it is not paid until closing
d) the escrow agent must pay the fee

13. Under RESPA, a loan is considered federally related if:

a) it will be used to finance the purchase of real property
b) the property has up to four dwelling units
c) the lender is federally regulated
d) All of the above

14. Under FIRPTA:

a) a foreign investor can never buy or sell property without special authorization
b) if a seller is not a U.S. citizen, the escrow agent will have to deduct 10% of the net sale proceeds and send it to the IRS
c) escrow agents must notify the real estate broker if the buyer is a foreign investor
d) a foreign investor purchasing property in the U.S. must pay an additional 10% over and above the purchase price and submit it to the IRS

15. For an additional $300, the seller has agreed to include her refrigerator as a part of the real property transaction. In addition to the deed, the seller should sign a/an:

a) bill of sale
b) Uniform Settlement Statement
c) appraisal report
d) voucher

👉 Answer Key

1. c) Security deposits are not prorated at closing; they are simply transferred to the buyer of the rental property.

2. b) A debit on the buyer's side of the statement is a charge that the buyer must pay. In some cases, it is a charge that the buyer must pay to the seller (a refund for taxes paid in advance, for example), but in other cases the buyer owes it to a third party (the loan fee paid to the lender, for example).

3. a) The purchase price is a debit to the buyer and a credit to the seller.

4. d) The seller is entitled to a refund for the insurance he or she paid in advance, and this will show up as a credit on the seller's side of the settlement statement. Since the buyer is not assuming the policy, the seller's insurance is not listed on the buyer's side of the statement.

5. b) The good faith deposit is a credit to the buyer, since it has already been paid. It does not appear on the seller's side of the statement, because the full purchase price is listed as a credit to the seller, and the deposit is included in the price.

6. c) A loan the buyer uses to finance the transaction is listed as a credit to the buyer, whatever its source. When the financing comes through the seller—either through an assumption of the seller's loan, or through seller financing—it is a debit to the seller as well as a credit to the buyer.

7. a) The seller almost always pays the real estate broker's commission. The other expenses listed relate to the buyer's loan, and they are ordinarily paid by the buyer.

8. b) The buyer is usually required to pay the premium for the lender's extended coverage title insurance policy.

9. d) Prepaid interest—interest on a new loan to cover the period from the closing date through the last day of the month—is one of the buyer's debits.

10. b) Because mortgage interest is paid in arrears—the month after it accrues—at closing the sellers will be required to pay the interest that has accrued during May. (Their May 1 mortgage payment included the interest that accrued in April.)

11. b) A settlement statement sets forth the items that must be paid by each party, and also the items that must be paid to each party.

12. b) Prorating an expense is allocating it on the basis of a particular time period, such as a certain number of days.

13. d) All of these are elements of a federally related loan under RESPA.

14. b) In a transaction subject to FIRPTA, if the seller is not a U.S. citizen, the escrow agent is required to deduct 10% of the net sale proceeds and send it to the IRS.

15. a) A bill of sale is used to transfer title to personal property.

Income Taxation and Real Estate

Chapter Overview

Almost every business transaction has tax consequences, and real estate transactions are no exception. Not only are there taxes that arise at the time of sale (such as the documentary transfer tax discussed in Chapter 5), there are also income tax ramifications for the parties involved. This chapter provides an overview of how federal income taxation affects the transfer and ownership of real estate. It explains some income tax terminology, discusses certain types of transactions that receive special treatment, and also covers tax deductions available to real estate owners.

Basic Taxation Concepts

As you almost certainly know, in the United States the federal government taxes the income of individuals and businesses on an annual basis. Before discussing how the transfer or acquisition of real estate can affect the federal income taxes a seller or buyer is required to pay, we need to explain some basic terms and concepts.

Progressive Tax

A tax may be "proportional," "regressive," or "progressive," depending on how its burden is distributed among taxpayers. A tax is proportional if the same tax rate is applied to all levels of income. A tax is regressive if the rate applied to higher levels of income is lower than the rate applied to lower levels. Our federal income tax is a **progressive** tax. This means that the more a taxpayer earns in a given tax year, the higher his or her tax rate will be. In other words, someone who earns a large income is generally required not just to pay more taxes than someone who earns a small income, but to pay a greater percentage of his or her income in taxes.

Tax rates increase in uneven steps called **tax brackets**. An additional dollar earned by a given taxpayer may be taxed at a higher rate than the dollar earned just before it, because it crosses the line into a higher bracket. But the additional dollar earned will not increase the tax the taxpayer is required to pay on dollars previously earned. The term **marginal tax rate** refers to the rate that will apply to the next dollar that a taxpayer earns.

Income

When asked about their income, many people tend to think only in terms of the wages or salary they earn at a job. The Internal Revenue Service (IRS) takes a much broader view of income, however. It regards any economic benefit realized by a taxpayer as part of his or her income, unless it is a type of benefit specifically excluded from income by the tax code. (The concept of realization is discussed below.)

Deductions and Tax Credits

The tax code authorizes certain expenses to be deducted from income. For example, if a business loses money in a particular tax year, the owner may be allowed to deduct the loss. A taxpayer who is entitled to a deduction can subtract a specified amount from his or her income before it is taxed. By reducing the amount of income that is taxed, the deduction also reduces the amount of tax the taxpayer owes.

In contrast to deductions, tax credits are subtracted directly from the amount of tax owed. The taxpayer's income is added up, the tax rate is applied, and then any applicable tax credits are subtracted to determine how much the taxpayer will actually have to pay.

The federal government often uses deductions and tax credits to implement social and economic policy. For example, allowing homeowners to deduct mortgage interest from their taxable income helps make home ownership much more affordable. (The mortgage interest deduction is explained later in this chapter.)

Gains and Losses

The sale or exchange of an asset (such as real estate) nearly always results in either a gain or a loss. Gains are treated as income, so any gain is taxable unless the tax code specifically says otherwise. On the other hand, a loss may be deducted from income only if the deduction is specifically authorized by the tax code.

Most deductible losses are losses incurred in a trade or business or in transactions entered into for profit. A business entity (such as a corporation) can deduct all of its losses. An individual taxpayer can deduct a loss only if it was incurred in connection with:

1. the taxpayer's trade or business,
2. a transaction entered into for profit, or
3. a casualty loss or theft of the taxpayer's property.

No deduction is allowed for a loss suffered on the sale of the taxpayer's principal residence or other real property owned for personal use.

Capital Gains and Losses. A gain or loss on the sale of an asset held for personal use or as an investment is considered a **capital gain** or a **capital loss**. Capital gains and capital losses are netted against each other. If there is a net gain, it is taxed as a capital gain. Capital gains receive favorable tax treatment: the maximum tax rate applied to most capital gains is considerably lower than the rate for ordinary income.

On the other hand, there is a limit on the deductibility of capital losses. No more than $3,000 in net capital losses can be deducted in a single tax year. Capital losses in excess of the limit may be carried forward and deducted in future years.

Remember that losses on personal use property are not deductible, so they are not netted against capital gains.

Business and Rental Property. Gains and losses on the sale of real property used in a business or held for the production of income (rental property) are treated somewhat differently from gains and losses on the sale of personal use and investment property. If business property or rental property is owned for more than one year and then sold, a gain on the sale is treated as a capital gain. But a loss on the sale is deductible as an ordinary loss rather than a capital loss.

This is an advantage, because the $3,000 annual limit on the deduction of capital losses does not apply. The full amount of the loss can be deducted in the year it is incurred.

Note that losses resulting from the operation of a rental property are also deductible as ordinary losses. For example, suppose a rental house was vacant for most of the year and the annual operating expenses added up to more than the rent received. The owner of the house could deduct this lost income as an ordinary loss.

Basis

For income tax purposes, a property owner's **basis** in the property is his or her investment in it. If a taxpayer sells an asset, the basis is the maximum amount that he or she can receive in payment for the asset without realizing a gain. To determine gains and losses, it is necessary to know the taxpayer's basis in the property in question.

Initial Basis. In most cases, a taxpayer's **initial basis** (also called cost basis or unadjusted basis) is equal to the original cost of acquisition—that is, how much it cost to acquire the property. A person who paid $280,000 for a rental house plus $14,000 in closing costs has an initial basis of $294,000 in the property. He or she could turn around and sell the house for $294,000 without having to report a gain to the IRS.

Adjusted Basis. The initial basis may be increased or decreased to arrive at an **adjusted basis**, which reflects capital expenditures and any allowable depreciation or cost recovery deductions. **Capital expenditures** are expenditures made to improve the property, such as money a homeowner spends on adding a new room or remodeling the kitchen. Capital expenditures increase the value of the property or significantly extend its useful life. They are added to the initial basis in calculating the adjusted basis.

> **Example:** Greene buys a duplex as a rental property for $345,000 plus $11,000 in closing costs. Four years later, she spends $45,000 on improvements to the property, remodeling the bathrooms and the kitchens in both units. After Greene makes these capital expenditures, her adjusted basis in the duplex property is $401,000.

Maintenance expenses, such as repainting, replacing a broken window, or having the roof cleaned, are not capital expenditures. Maintenance expenses do not affect basis.

For certain types of property, a taxpayer's initial basis is also adjusted to take into account depreciation or cost recovery deductions, which will be discussed later in this chapter. These deductions are subtracted from the initial basis in calculating the adjusted basis.

        Initial basis (acquisition cost)
+   Capital expenditures
−   Depreciation/Cost recovery deductions
        Adjusted basis

Realization

Not every gain is immediately taxable. A gain is not considered taxable income until it is **realized**. Ownership of an asset involves gain if the asset is appreciating in value. But for tax purposes, a gain is realized only when a sale or exchange occurs; the gain is then separated from the asset.

> **Example:** Referring back to the example given above, suppose that during Greene's six years of ownership property values have been increasing steadily. Her improved duplex (which she bought for $356,000 and invested another $45,000 in) now has a market value of $489,000.
>
> Greene has enjoyed an economic gain or benefit: she now owns property that is worth $88,000 more than what she put into it. However, that $88,000 is not realized—and therefore is not treated as income subject to taxation—until she sells the duplex.

The gain or loss realized on a transaction is the difference between the net sales price (called the **amount realized** in the tax code) and the adjusted basis of the property:

Amount realized (net sales price)
− Adjusted basis
———————————————
Gain or loss

In calculating the amount realized, the sales price includes money or other property received in exchange for the property, plus the amount of any mortgage debt that is eliminated. This means that if the buyer takes the property subject to the seller's mortgage or assumes it, the amount of that debt is treated as part of the sales price for tax purposes.

The selling expenses (such as the brokerage commission and the seller's other closing costs) are deducted from the sales price to arrive at the amount realized.

Money received
+ Market value of other property received
+ Mortgage debt disposed of
− Selling expenses
———————————————
Amount realized (net sales price)

Recognition and Deferral

A gain is said to be **recognized** in the year it is taxed. A gain will be recognized in the year it is realized, unless there is a specific exception in the tax code that allows the taxpayer to defer payment of taxes on the gain until a later tax year or a later transaction, or exclude payment of taxes altogether. For example, the tax code permits an individual selling his or her rental property on an installment basis to defer taxation of part of the gain to the year in which it is actually received (rather than the year the sale takes place). The tax code provisions that allow recognition of a gain to be deferred are called "nonrecognition provisions."

Nonrecognition provisions that apply to real estate transactions (including the rule already mentioned concerning installment sales) are discussed in detail later in this chapter.

Classifications of Real Property

Whether a particular type of real estate transaction qualifies for special tax treatment depends on the type of property involved. The tax code divides real property into the following classes:

1. principal residence property,
2. personal use property,
3. unimproved investment property,
4. property held for the production of income,
5. property used in a trade or business, and
6. dealer property.

Principal Residence Property. This is the home the taxpayer owns and occupies as his or her primary dwelling. It may be a single-family home, a duplex, a condominium unit, a cooperative apartment, or a mobile home. If the taxpayer owns two homes and lives in both of them, the one in which he or she lives most of the time is the principal residence. A taxpayer cannot have two principal residences at the same time.

Personal Use Property. Real property that a taxpayer owns for personal use, other than the principal residence, is classified as personal use property. A second home or a vacation cabin belongs in this category.

Unimproved Investment Property. Unimproved investment property is vacant land that produces no rental income. The land is held simply as an investment, in the expectation that it will appreciate in value.

Property Held for Production of Income. Property held for the production of income includes residential, commercial, and industrial property that is used to generate rental income for the owner.

Property Used in a Trade or Business. This category includes land and buildings that the taxpayer owns and uses in his or her trade or business, such as a factory owned by the manufacturer, or a small building the owner uses for his or her own retail business.

Dealer Property. This is property held primarily for sale to customers rather than for long-term investment. If a developer subdivides land for sale to the public, the lots will usually be included in this classification until they are sold.

Nonrecognition Transactions

As was explained earlier, when a nonrecognition provision in the tax code applies to a particular transaction, the taxpayer is not required to pay taxes on a gain in the year it is realized. The real estate transactions that are covered by nonrecognition provisions include:

- installment sales,
- involuntary conversions,
- sales of low-income housing, and
- "tax-free" exchanges.

Keep in mind that nonrecognition provisions do not completely exclude the gain from taxation, but merely defer the tax consequences to a later tax year. These are not really "tax-free" transactions. The realized gain is simply recognized and taxed in a subsequent year.

Installment Sales

The tax code considers a sale to be an **installment sale** if less than 100% of the sales price is received in the year of sale. Nearly all seller-financed transactions are installment sales. Installment sale reporting allows the taxpayer/seller to defer recognition of part of the gain to the year(s) in which it is actually received. In effect, taxes are paid only on the portion of the profit received each year; the gain is prorated over the term of the installment contract. Installment sale reporting is permitted for all classes of property, except that dealer property is eligible only under special conditions.

In installment sales, the gain recognized in any given year is calculated based on the ratio of the gross profit to the contract price. The **gross profit** is the difference between the sales price and the adjusted basis.

To calculate the gross profit, take the seller's adjusted basis at the time of sale, add the amount of the commission and other selling expenses, and subtract this sum from the sales price.

Fig. 13.1 Eligibility for installment sale reporting

Installment Sale Reporting

1. Less than 100% of sales price received in year of sale

2. All classifications of real property eligible except dealer property

> **Example:** Once again, we'll use Greene as an example. Her basis in her duplex was $401,000. She sold the property for $489,000. She had to pay a $29,000 commission and $8,200 in other selling expenses.

$489,000	Sales price

$401,000	Seller's basis
+ 37,200	Commission and selling expenses
$438,200	Adjusted basis

$489,000	Sales price
− 438,200	Adjusted basis
$50,800	Gross profit

The next step is to compare the gross profit to the contract price to arrive at the **gross profit ratio**. The contract price is the total amount of all principal payments the buyer will pay the seller. In most cases, unless the buyer assumes an existing loan, the contract price is the same as the sales price.

> **Example:**
>
> | Gross Profit | ÷ | Contract Price | = | Gross Profit Ratio |
> |---|---|---|---|---|
> | $50,800 | ÷ | $489,000 | = | 10% |

The gross profit ratio is applied to the principal payments received in each year to determine how much of the principal is gain to be taxed that year. Note that the gross profit ratio is not applied to the interest the buyer pays the seller; all of the interest payments are treated as taxable income in the year received.

If the seller in the example above received a $48,900 downpayment, $2,500 in principal installment payments, and $30,500 in interest the first year, the taxable income would be calculated as follows:

$48,900	Downpayment
+ 2,500	Installment principal payments
$51,400	Total principal payments
$51,400	Total principal payments
× 10%	Gross profit ratio
$5,140	Recognized gain
+ 30,500	Interest income
$35,640	Total taxable income

If the buyer assumes or takes subject to a mortgage that is larger than the seller's basis in the property, the excess is treated as payment received from the buyer. If the property is subject to recapture provisions because of depreciation or cost recovery deductions (discussed later in this chapter), the amount recaptured is also treated as a payment received in the year of sale.

Involuntary Conversions

An involuntary conversion occurs when an asset is turned into cash without voluntary action on the part of the owner: the asset is condemned, destroyed, stolen, or lost, and the owner receives a condemnation award or insurance proceeds. Since the award or proceeds usually represent the property's replacement cost or market value, the owner often realizes a gain on an involuntary conversion.

However, recognition of a gain on an involuntary conversion can be deferred if the taxpayer uses the money received to replace the property within the replacement period set by the IRS. Generally, the replacement period lasts for two years after the end of the tax year in which the gain was realized; for business or income property, the period is three years. Recognition of the gain is deferred only to the extent that the condemnation award or insurance proceeds are reinvested in the replacement property. Any part of the gain that is used for purposes other than purchase of replacement property will be taxed as income.

Sales of Low-Income Housing

A taxpayer who owns certain qualified low-income housing may sell it and reinvest the proceeds in similar housing within one year without recognizing a gain on the sale. Gain that is not reinvested in similar property is recognized in the year of the sale.

"Tax-Free" Exchanges

Section 1031 of the tax code concerns property exchanges. Section 1031 exchanges are commonly called "tax-free" exchanges, but they're really just tax-deferred exchanges. If unimproved investment property, income property, or property used in a trade or business is exchanged for **like-kind** property, recognition of any realized gain will be deferred. A principal residence, personal use property, and dealer property are not eligible for this type of deferral.

Tax-free exchanges are used to reduce or eliminate current tax expenses. And a taxpayer may be able to acquire property in an exchange that would be impossible to buy with the after-tax proceeds from the sale of the old property.

The property the taxpayer receives in the exchange must be like-kind—that is, the same kind as the property given. This requirement refers to the general nature of the properties rather than their quality. Most real estate is considered to be of like kind for the purposes of the exchange deferral, without regard to whether it is improved, unimproved, residential, commercial, or industrial. For example, if a taxpayer exchanges a strip shopping center for an apartment complex, the transaction can qualify as a tax-free exchange. Both of the exchanged properties must be located in the United States to be considered like-kind property.

If nothing other than like-kind property is received in the exchange, no gain or loss is recognized in the year of the exchange. However, anything other than like-kind property that the taxpayer receives is called **boot** and recognized in the year of the exchange. In a real estate exchange, boot might be cash, stock, other types of personal property, or **debt relief**—the difference between mortgage balances.

Example: A taxpayer exchanges a property with a mortgage debt of $220,000 for one with a mortgage debt of $200,000. The taxpayer has received $20,000 in boot because of the reduction in debt (regardless of whether there has been a formal assumption of the loan). The taxpayer may be required to pay taxes on a gain of $20,000, just as if she had received $20,000 in cash along with the real property.

The following example shows how a taxpayer's actual gain and recognized gain are calculated in an exchange transaction involving boot.

Example: Taxpayer A is exchanging a small office building for Taxpayer B's commercial property. Taxpayer A's building is valued at $1,860,000 and has an adjusted basis of $1,744,000. Its mortgage has a remaining balance of $1,340,000.

Taxpayer B is giving Taxpayer A real property worth $1,804,000 with a mortgage balance of $1,305,000, plus $21,000 in cash. The debt relief for Taxpayer A is $35,000 ($1,340,000−$1,305,000= $35,000).

Fig. 13.2 Eligibility for tax-free exchanges

"Tax-Free" Exchanges

1. Only property held for production of income, property used in a trade or business, or unimproved investment property is eligible.
2. Must be exchanged for like-kind property.
3. Boot is taxed in the year it is received.

Here's how Taxpayer A's gain would be calculated:

$1,804,000   Like-kind property
    35,000   Debt relief (boot)
+ 21,000   Cash (boot)
$1,860,000   Total value of property and boot received
– 1,744,000   Adjusted basis of Taxpayer A's former property
  $116,000   Actual (realized) gain

So Taxpayer A is receiving property and boot worth $1,860,000 and realizing a $116,000 gain on the transaction. However, only the portion of the realized gain that is attributable to boot is taxable in the year the exchange takes place. Thus, Taxpayer A's recognized gain is $56,000 ($35,000 debt relief + $21,000 cash = $56,000 total boot). Taxation of the rest of the gain ($60,000) is deferred.

Note that boot is taxable only to the extent of the gain. If the boot received exceeded the taxpayer's realized gain on the transaction, then only the amount of the gain would be taxed, not the full amount of the boot.

The taxpayer's basis in the property exchanged is transferred to the property he or she receives. If nothing other than like-kind property is exchanged, no adjustments are necessary. But if the exchange involved boot, the basis must be adjusted for any boot that was paid or received, and for any gain or loss that was recognized because of the boot.

Keep in mind that under certain circumstances, an exchange of real property may be a tax-deferred transaction for one of the parties but not for the other. For example, suppose Taxpayer A trades his principal residence for a rental home owned by Taxpayer B. Both A and B are planning to use their new properties as rental homes. This can't be a tax-free exchange for Taxpayer A, because a principal residence isn't eligible. But this is a tax-free exchange for Taxpayer B, who has traded one income property for another.

An agent who arranges a tax-free exchange may receive compensation from both of the parties.

Exclusion of Gain from the Sale of a Principal Residence

We will discuss only one exclusion from capital gains taxation, the one that will be of greatest interest to most homeowners: the exclusion of gain on the sale of a principal residence.

Until May 1997, an individual who sold his or her principal residence was often eligible for the "rollover" deferral of taxation. The seller was allowed to defer taxation of the gain if the sale proceeds were used within two years to buy another residence. And a seller who was 55 or older could take advantage of a one-time exclusion of gain from the sale of the principal residence, even if the gain was not invested in a new residence. The 1997 tax bill replaced both of these tax benefits with a single, less complicated exclusion from taxation.

Amount of Gain Excluded. Under current law, a taxpayer may exclude the entire gain on the sale of his or her principal residence, up to $250,000 if the taxpayer is filing a single return, or $500,000 if the taxpayer is married and filing a joint return.

Example:

$275,000	Amount realized (after selling costs)
− 80,000	Seller's basis in home
$195,000	Gain realized

Whether filing singly or jointly, the seller will be able to exclude the entire amount of gain—$195,000—from taxation.

If the amount of the gain on the sale of the home exceeds the $250,000 or $500,000 limit, the amount in excess of the limit will be taxed at the capital gains rate.

Example:

$375,000	Amount realized (after selling costs)
− 70,000	Seller's basis in home
$305,000	Gain realized

If the seller is filing a single return, only $250,000 of the $305,000 gain will be excluded from taxation. The seller will have to pay capital gains taxes on the $55,000 that exceeded the exclusion limit.

Eligibility. To qualify for this exclusion, the seller must have both owned and used the property as a principal residence for at least two years during the previous five-year period. Because of this rule, this exclusion is available only once every two years.

Note that if the sellers are married and filing a joint return, only one spouse has to meet the ownership test, but both spouses must meet the use test. If only one spouse meets both the ownership test and the use test, the maximum exclusion the married couple can claim is $250,000, even if they file a joint return.

If the seller owned and used the property as a principal residence for less than two years because of special circumstances (for example, if he or she sold the home after only a year because of a change in health or employment), the seller may be able to claim a reduced exclusion.

Deductions Available to Property Owners

As was explained earlier, a deduction is subtracted from a taxpayer's income before the tax rate is applied. The income tax deductions allowed to real property owners are a significant benefit of ownership. There are deductions for:

- depreciation and cost recovery,
- uninsured casualty and theft losses,
- repairs,
- real property taxes,
- mortgage interest, and
- points paid to a mortgage lender.

Depreciation and Cost Recovery Deductions

What used to be called depreciation deductions in the tax code are now called cost recovery deductions, but they are essentially the same thing. They permit a taxpayer to recover the cost of an asset used for the production of income or used in a trade or business. They cannot be taken in connection with a principal residence, personal use property, unimproved investment property, or dealer property.

Depreciable Property. In general, only property that wears out and will eventually have to be replaced is **depreciable**—that is, eligible for depreciation or cost recovery deductions. For example, apartment buildings, business or factory equipment, and commercial fruit orchards all have to be replaced, so they are depreciable. But land does not wear out, so it is not depreciable.

Time Frame. The entire expense of acquiring an asset cannot be deducted in the year it is incurred (although that is permitted with many other business expenses, such as wages, supplies, and utilities). However, the expense can be deducted over a number of years; for most real estate, the recovery period is between 15 and 31½ years. The length of the recovery period is a reflection of legislative policy and has little, if any, relationship to the actual length of time that the property will be economically useful. The whole field of depreciation and cost recovery deductions has been subject to frequent modification by Congress.

Effect on Basis. As we said in the discussion of basis at the beginning of the chapter, any allowable depreciation or cost recovery deductions reduce the taxpayer's adjusted basis in the property. Note that this reduction occurs whether or not the taxpayer actually takes the deduction. If the deduction was allowable—that is, the taxpayer was entitled to take it—the basis will be reduced. By reducing the basis, these deductions affect the taxpayer's eventual gain or loss on resale of the property.

Fig. 13.3 Tax-deferred transactions

Eligibility for Favorable Income Tax Treatment			
	Installment Sale	"Tax-Free" Exchange	Depreciation Deductions
Principal Residence	Yes	No	No
Personal Use	Yes	No	No
Unimproved Investment	Yes	Yes	No
Trade or Business	Yes	Yes	Yes
Income	Yes	Yes	Yes
Dealer	No	No	No

Uninsured Casualty or Theft Loss Deductions

When property is damaged or stolen and the loss is not covered or is only partially covered by insurance, the property owner is generally permitted to deduct the uninsured loss from taxable income. To calculate the amount of the deductible loss, first subtract the estimated fair market value of the property after the loss from its estimated value before the loss. Compare this reduction in value to the owner's adjusted basis in the property. From the lower of the two figures, subtract any insurance reimbursement that the owner has received or will receive. For most types of property, the result is the amount of the deductible loss.

Example: Ramirez owned property worth $975,000, with an adjusted basis of $714,000. After the property was damaged in a flood, its value dropped to $830,000. This represented a reduction in value of $145,000:

$975,000	Value before flood damage
− 830,000	Value after flood damage
$145,000	Reduction in value

Ramirez's insurance company paid her only $110,000, so she suffered an uninsured casualty loss. To calculate how much of the loss Ramirez will be able to deduct from her taxable income, use the reduction in value ($145,000), since that figure is less than Ramirez's adjusted basis ($714,000).

$145,000	Reduction in value
− 110,000	Insurance reimbursement
$35,000	Deductible loss

For personal use property (including a principal residence), the amount of the deductible loss is reduced by some additional calculations. After going through the steps described above, subtract $100 from the loss. Next, subtract 10% of the taxpayer's adjusted gross income. The result is the taxpayer's deductible loss for personal use property.

Example: Return to the previous example, but now suppose that the property is Ramirez's home. Start where the previous calculation left off, subtract $100, and then subtract 10% of Ramirez's adjusted gross income, which is $95,000.

$35,000	Uninsured loss
100	Subtracted from loss
− 9,500	10% of adjusted gross income
$25,400	Deductible loss

Thus, Ramirez will be able to deduct $25,400 from her taxable income for this casualty loss concerning personal use property.

If a taxpayer has more than one casualty loss for personal use property in a given tax year, $100 must be subtracted from each loss. However, 10% of the adjusted gross income is subtracted from the total amount of those losses, not from each loss.

Repair Deductions

For most types of real property, expenditures for repairs are deductible in the year paid. A repair expense is one incurred to keep the property in ordinary, efficient, operating condition.

Repair expenses are not deductible for principal residences or other personal use property. This includes expenditures for maintenance, upkeep, and ordinary wear and tear, and it also includes condominium assessments.

For any type of real property, repair expenses should not be confused with capital expenditures. As explained earlier, capital expenditures add to the value of the property and frequently prolong its economic life. Capital expenditures are not deductible in the year made, but rather are added to the taxpayer's basis. The resulting increase in the basis will affect the gain or loss on the eventual sale of the property. It will also increase the allowable depreciation or cost recovery deductions if the property is eligible for those.

Property Tax Deductions

General real estate taxes are deductible for any type of property. Special assessments for repairs or maintenance are deductible, but those for improvements (such as new sidewalks) are not.

Mortgage Interest Deductions

For most property, interest paid on a mortgage or deed of trust is usually completely deductible. However, there are some limitations on interest deductions for personal residences (which are the only allowable consumer interest deductions).

A taxpayer may deduct interest payments on mortgage debt of up to $1,000,000 used to buy, build, or improve a first or second residence. In addition, interest on a home equity loan of up to $100,000 can be deducted without regard to the purpose of the loan. When the loan amount exceeds these limits, the interest on the excess is not deductible.

Occasionally a condominium project borrows money by mortgaging the common areas, and the unit owners are required to pay a share of the mortgage payment. In that case, a unit owner may deduct the interest portion of his or her share from taxable income.

Deductibility of Points and Other Loan Costs

The IRS considers points paid to a lender in connection with a new loan (including discount points and the origination fee) to be prepaid interest, and the borrower is generally allowed to deduct them. This is true even if the points were paid by the seller on the borrower's behalf. (The borrower's basis in the property must be reduced by the amount of the seller-paid points.)

Note that fees a lender charges to cover specific services are not deductible, even if the lender refers to them as points. This includes, for example, appraisal fees, document preparation fees, and mortgage insurance premiums.

If a seller paying off a loan is required to pay a prepayment penalty, the amount of the penalty is usually deductible. For tax purposes, a prepayment penalty is treated as a form of interest.

Rental Payment Deductions

Finally, we should mention one deduction connected with real estate that concerns not property owners but tenants. Rent paid for property used in a trade or business is deductible as a business expense. However, rent paid for property not used in a trade or business (such as rent for a home) is not deductible.

California Income Tax

In addition to the federal income tax, there is a California state income tax. California income tax laws are substantially the same as the provisions of the Internal Revenue Code. For example, with limited exceptions, the California statutes simply refer to the federal law for such items as the definitions of gross income, adjusted gross income, itemized deductions, and taxable income. There is a different standard deduction under state law for those who do not itemize and, of course, the tax rates on taxable income are different. As with federal law, the state income tax is a progressive tax with higher rates imposed on higher income levels. Income tax brackets and the standard deduction are adjusted for inflation by the California Franchise Tax Board each year based on the California Consumer Price Index.

Chapter Summary

1. Any economic benefit realized by a taxpayer is treated as part of his or her income, unless there is a specific provision of the tax code that excludes it from income. The tax code provides for certain deductions from income before the tax rate is applied, and also for tax credits, which are subtracted from the amount of tax owed.

2. A gain or a loss is realized when an asset is sold. A gain is recognized (taxed) in the year it is realized, unless a nonrecognition or exclusion provision in the tax code applies.

3. A taxpayer's initial basis in property is the amount he or she originally invested in it. To determine the adjusted basis, capital expenditures are added to the initial basis, and allowable cost recovery deductions are subtracted from it. The taxpayer's gain or loss is the difference between the amount realized and the adjusted basis.

4. In the tax code, real property is classified as principal residence property, personal use property, unimproved investment property, property held for the production of income, property used in a trade or business, or dealer property.

5. The tax code's nonrecognition provisions for real property transactions allow taxation of gain to be deferred in installment sales, involuntary conversions, sales of certain low-income housing, and "tax-free" exchanges. There is also an exclusion of up to $250,000 (or $500,000 if filing jointly) of gain allowed on the sale of a principal residence.

6. The tax deductions available to property owners include cost recovery deductions (only for income property and property used in a trade or business); uninsured casualty or theft loss deductions; repair deductions (not for principal residences or personal use property); deduction of property taxes; deduction of mortgage interest; and deduction of points. There are some limits on the mortgage interest deduction for personal residences.

🔑 Key Terms

Income—Any economic benefit realized by a taxpayer that is not excluded from income by the tax code.

Deduction—An expense that can be used to reduce taxable income.

Marginal tax rate—The tax rate that applies to the next dollar that a taxpayer earns.

Basis—A taxpayer's investment in his or her property for income tax purposes.

Initial basis—The original acquisition cost of a property; how much it cost to acquire the property. Also called the cost basis or the unadjusted basis.

Adjusted basis—The initial basis plus capital expenditures and minus allowable depreciation or cost recovery deductions.

Realization—A gain or a loss is realized when it is separated from the asset. This separation generally occurs when the asset is sold.

Recognition—A gain is said to be recognized when it is taxable. It is recognized in the year it is realized, unless recognition is deferred by the tax code.

Installment sale—A sale in which less than 100% of the sales price is received in the year of sale.

Involuntary conversion—When property is converted to cash without the voluntary action of the owner, as when property is destroyed and the owner receives insurance proceeds.

Cost recovery deductions—Deductions from the taxpayer's income to allow the cost of an asset to be recovered. These are allowed only for depreciable property that is held for the production of income or used in a trade or business. Also called depreciation deductions.

Repair expenses—Money spent on repairs to keep property in ordinary, efficient operating condition.

Capital expenditures—Money spent on improvements to property, which add to its value or prolong its economic life.

Tax-free exchange—When like-kind property is exchanged, allowing taxation of the gain to be deferred. Also called a Section 1031 exchange.

Like-kind property—In a tax-free exchange, property received that is of the same kind as the property transferred. Any two pieces of real estate are considered to be of like kind.

Boot—Something given or received in a tax-free exchange that is not like-kind property, such as cash.

/OܠO Chapter Quiz

1. A homeowner's basis would be adjusted to reflect:

   a) cost recovery deductions
   b) expenses incurred to keep the property in good repair
   c) mortgage interest paid
   d) the cost of installing a deck

2. A married couple bought a home for $250,000. After living in the home for three years, they sold it for only $246,000. How much of this loss can they deduct on their federal income tax return?

   a) The full $4,000 loss
   b) Only $3,000
   c) Only $2,000
   d) None of it

3. Which of the following could the owner of unimproved investment property deduct on his or her federal income tax return?

   a) A loss on the sale of the property
   b) The depreciation of the land
   c) Cost recovery deductions
   d) Any of the above

4. Which of the following exchanges could not qualify as a "tax-free" exchange?

   a) An office building for a hotel
   b) An apartment house for a warehouse
   c) Timber land for farm equipment
   d) A city lot for a ranch

5. Under the federal income tax code, income is always taxed in the year it is:

   a) realized
   b) recognized
   c) recovered
   d) deferred

6. Ortega just sold his principal residence. After subtracting his selling costs, the amount of gain realized was $163,000. Ortega will be allowed to exclude the entire amount of the gain from taxation only if:

   a) he is married and is filing a joint return
   b) he has never claimed this exclusion before, since it can only be used once in a lifetime
   c) the gain is not considered capital gain
   d) he owned and occupied the property as his principal residence for two of the previous five years

7. Torrence owns a triplex. She paid $550,000 for it, including her closing costs. The allowable cost recovery deductions for the property have amounted to $20,000, Torrence has spent $50,000 on capital improvements, and the market value of the property has risen by 15%. What is Torrence's adjusted basis?

   a) $600,000
   b) $620,000
   c) $580,000
   d) $530,000

8. Gillespie is buying a home that will be his principal residence. He is financing the purchase with a $300,000 mortgage loan. How much of the interest that he pays on the loan can he deduct from his income?

   a) All of it
   b) Up to $100,000 in interest
   c) 50%
   d) None of it

9. The Wongs are selling some property on a five-year contract. Their gross profit ratio on the sale is 15%. This year, they will receive $4,775 in interest and $1,675 in principal. With installment sale reporting, approximately how much of that will be recognized and included in the Wongs' taxable income for this year?

   a) $251
   b) $967
   c) $2,391
   d) $5,026

10. Sherrick is selling a lot for $72,000. Her adjusted basis in the property is $56,000. In addition to the 6% commission she'll be paying her real estate broker, she will also have to pay $2,500 in closing costs. For federal income tax purposes, what is the gain Sherrick will realize in this transaction?

   a) $6,820
   b) $9,180
   c) $16,000
   d) $22,820

☞ Answer Key

1. d) The cost of installing a deck is a capital expenditure, which would be added to the taxpayer's basis. Remember that personal residences do not qualify for depreciation or cost recovery deductions.

2. d) A loss on the sale of a personal residence is never deductible.

3. a) If the owner loses money on the sale of the property, he or she may be able to deduct that loss. Depreciation and cost recovery deductions are not allowed for unimproved investment property, because land is not depreciable.

4. c) The like-kind property requirement means that real estate must be exchanged for other real estate.

5. b) Income is taxed when it is recognized. It is often recognized in the same year it is realized, but that is not true if a nonrecognition provision applies.

6. d) To qualify for the exclusion from taxation, the taxpayer must have both owned and used the property as a principal residence for two of the previous five years.

7. c) The initial basis, plus the capital expenditures, less the allowable cost recovery deductions, equals an adjusted basis of $580,000.

$550,000 + $50,000 - $20,000 = $580,000

(Ignore the increase in market value; it does not affect the taxpayer's basis.)

8. a) A taxpayer can deduct all of the interest paid on a loan of up to $1,000,000 used to purchase a first or second personal residence.

9. d) Multiply the principal payments by the gross profit ratio to determine the amount of principal that will be recognized this year. Then add that to the entire amount of interest received (all of the interest is taxable).

$1,675 \times 15\% = $251.25 + $4,775 = $5,026.25

10. b) Sherrick will realize a $9,180 gain in the transaction. First subtract her selling expenses (the commission and closing costs) from the sales price to determine the amount realized; then subtract her adjusted basis from the amount realized to determine the gain.

$72,000 \times 6\% = $4,320 \text{ commission}

$4,320 + $2,500 \text{ costs} = $6,820

$72,000 - $6,820 = $65,180 \text{ (amount realized)}

$65,180 - $56,000 = $9,180 \text{ (gain realized)}

Civil Rights and Fair Housing

Chapter Overview

Unfair discrimination is prohibited in almost all real estate transactions by federal and state law. With limited exceptions, it is illegal for either property owners or real estate professionals to discriminate. In this chapter, we will cover several federal antidiscrimination laws, including the Civil Rights Act of 1866, the Federal Fair Housing Act, and the Americans with Disabilities Act. We will also discuss various state laws that prohibit discrimination in housing as well as in other real estate transactions.

Introduction

Over the years, various civil rights laws have been enacted to achieve one major goal: the freedom of choice. In the context of real estate, freedom of choice means that all types of people with similar financial resources should have equal access to the same types of housing. Anyone with the requisite income, net worth, and credit history should be able to choose a home or apartment in any affordable neighborhood, regardless of race, national origin, gender, or other similar characteristics.

Today, civil rights laws are an integral part of the real estate profession. The importance of the right to equal housing is well established, and real estate professionals must be familiar with both federal and state laws that prohibit discrimination.

The Civil Rights Act of 1866

This law states that "all citizens of the United States shall have the same right, in every state and territory as is enjoyed by white citizens thereof to inherit, purchase, lease, sell, hold and convey real and personal property." The act prohibits any discrimination based on race or ancestry.

Enacted immediately after the Civil War, the act was largely ignored for almost a century. In the 1960s, during the civil rights movement, the act was challenged as an unconstitutional interference with private property rights. But the U.S. Supreme Court upheld the act in the landmark case of *Jones v. Mayer*, decided in 1968. The court ruled that the 1866 act "prohibits all racial discrimination, private or public, in the sale and rental of property," and that the act is constitutional based on the 13th Amendment to the U.S. Constitution, which prohibits slavery.

Someone who has been discriminated against in violation of the Civil Rights Act of 1866 can sue in federal court. The court could issue an injunction ordering the defendant to stop discriminating or to take affirmative steps to correct the violation. This might involve an order requiring the defendant to sell or lease the property to the plaintiff. The court could also order the defendant to pay the plaintiff actual damages (compensatory damages) to compensate for financial losses, humiliation, and suffering caused by the discrimination. In addition, the defendant might be ordered to pay punitive damages (an additional sum to punish the defendant for wrongdoing).

The Civil Rights Act of 1964

The Civil Rights Act of 1964 was one of the first attempts made by the federal government to implement fair housing ideals. The act prohibited discrimination based on race, color, religion, or national origin in many programs and activities for which the federal government offered financial assistance. Unfortunately, the effect of the act was extremely limited, because most FHA and VA loans were not covered. In fact, it is estimated that less than 1% of all houses purchased were covered by the act. It was not until the Civil Rights Act of 1968 that major progress was made towards fair housing.

The Federal Fair Housing Act

Contained in Title VIII of the Civil Rights Act of 1968, the Fair Housing Act is intended to provide fair housing opportunity throughout the United States. This law makes it illegal to discriminate on the basis of **race, color, religion, sex, national origin, disability**, or **familial status** in the sale or lease of residential property or in the sale or lease of vacant land for the construction of residential buildings. The law also prohibits discrimination in advertising, lending, real estate brokerage, and other services in connection with residential real estate transactions. However, unlike the 1866 Civil Rights Act, the Fair Housing Act does not apply to nonresidential transactions, such as those involving commercial or industrial properties.

Exemptions

While the Fair Housing Act applies to the majority of residential real estate transactions, there are four types of transactions that are exempt from it.

1. The law does not apply to the sale or rental of a single-family home by its owner, provided that:
   - the owner does not own more than three such homes;
   - no real estate broker or agent is employed in the transaction; and
   - no discriminatory advertising is used.

   If the owner isn't the most recent occupant of the home, he or she may use this exemption only once every 24 months.

2. The law does not apply to the rental of a unit or a room in a dwelling with up to four units, provided that:
   - the owner occupies one of the units as his or her residence;
   - no real estate broker or agent is employed; and
   - no discriminatory advertising is used.

   (This is sometimes called the **Mrs. Murphy exemption**.)

3. In dealing with their own property in noncommercial transactions, religious organizations or societies or affiliated nonprofit organizations may limit occupancy to or give preference to their own members, provided that membership isn't restricted on the basis of race, color, or national origin.

Fig. 14.1 Fair housing poster

U.S. Department of Housing and Urban Development

**EQUAL HOUSING
OPPORTUNITY**

We Do Business in Accordance With the Federal Fair Housing Law

(The Fair Housing Amendments Act of 1988)

> # It is Illegal to Discriminate Against Any Person Because of Race, Color, Religion, Sex, Handicap, Familial Status, or National Origin

- ■ In the sale or rental of housing or residential lots

- ■ In advertising the sale or rental of housing

- ■ In the financing of housing

- ■ In the provision of real estate brokerage services

- ■ In the appraisal of housing

- ■ Blockbusting is also illegal

Anyone who feels he or she has been discriminated against may file a complaint of housing discrimination:
   1-800-669-9777 (Toll Free)
   1-800-927-9275 (TDD)

**U.S. Department of Housing and
Urban Development
Assistant Secretary for Fair Housing and
Equal Opportunity
Washington, D.C. 20410**

Previous editions are obsolete

form HUD-928.1A(8-93)

4. Private clubs with lodgings that aren't open to the public and that aren't operated for a commercial purpose may limit occupancy to or give preference to their own members.

These limited exemptions apply very rarely. Remember, the 1866 Civil Rights Act prohibits discrimination based on race or ancestry in any property transaction regardless of any exemptions available under the Fair Housing Act. In addition, there is no exemption for any transaction involving a real estate licensee.

Prohibited Acts

The Fair Housing Act prohibits any of the following acts if they are done on the basis of race, color, religion, sex, national origin, handicap, or familial status:

- refusing to rent or sell residential property after receiving a bona fide offer;
- refusing to negotiate for the sale or rental of residential property, or otherwise making it unavailable;
- changing the terms of sale or lease for different potential buyers or tenants;
- using advertising that indicates a preference or intent to discriminate;
- representing that property is not available for inspection, sale, or rent when it is in fact available;
- using discriminatory criteria when making a housing loan;
- limiting participation in a multiple listing service or similar service;
- coercing, intimidating, threatening, or interfering with anyone on account of his or her enjoyment, attempt to enjoy, or encouragement or assistance to others in enjoying the rights granted by the Fair Housing Act.

Also prohibited are the discriminatory practices known as blockbusting, steering, and redlining.

- **Blockbusting** occurs when someone tries to induce homeowners to list or sell their properties by predicting that members of another race (or disabled persons, persons of a particular ethnic background, etc.) will be moving into the neighborhood, and that this will have undesirable consequences such as lower property values. The blockbuster then profits by purchasing the homes at reduced prices or (in the case of a real estate agent) by collecting commissions on the induced sales. Blockbusting is also known as **panic selling** or **panic peddling**.

  Example: An African-American family recently moved into an all-white neighborhood. XYZ Realty immediately began calling all the homeowners in the neighborhood. XYZ's salespeople warned the homeowners of the following: several African-American families were planning on moving into the neighborhood, city police predicted a significant increase in crime in the neighborhood, property values would drop dramatically, and within months homeowners would find it difficult to sell their properties to anyone at any price. Because of these "facts" made up by XYZ agents, several homeowners immediately listed their homes with XYZ Realty. XYZ Realty is guilty of blockbusting.

- **Steering** refers to channeling prospective buyers or tenants toward or away from specific neighborhoods based on their race (or religion, national origin, etc.) in order to maintain or change the character of those neighborhoods.

  Example: The salespeople at PQR Realty are "encouraged" to show Hispanic buyers only properties in the city's predominantly Hispanic neighborhood. Non-Hispanic buyers aren't shown properties there, except by specific request. This is done on the principle that Hispanic buyers would be more "comfortable" living in the Hispanic neighborhood and non-Hispanic buyers would be "uncomfortable" there. PQR Realty is guilty of steering.

- **Redlining** is the refusal to make a loan because of the racial or ethnic composition of the neighborhood in which the security property is located.

  Example: Buyer Jones applies to Community Savings for a loan to purchase a home located in the Cherrywood neighborhood. Cherrywood is a predominantly minority neighborhood. Community Savings rejects the loan, because it fears that property values in Cherrywood may suffer in the future because of possible racial tension. Community Savings is guilty of redlining.

The prohibition against redlining is enforced through the **Home Mortgage Disclosure Act of 1975**, which requires large institutional lenders to file an annual report of all mortgage loans made. The loans are categorized according to the locations of the properties, which makes it easier to discover cases of redlining.

Handicap and Familial Status

Originally, the Fair Housing Act did not prohibit discrimination based on handicap or familial status; these classifications were added to the law in 1988.

Handicap. Under the Fair Housing Act, it is illegal to discriminate against someone because he or she has a physical disability or mental impairment that substantially limits one or more major life activities. This includes people suffering from chronic alcoholism, mental illness, or AIDS. But the act does not protect those who are a direct threat to the health or safety of others, or who are currently using controlled substances.

A residential landlord must allow a disabled tenant to make reasonable modifications to the property at the tenant's expense, so long as the modifications are necessary for the tenant's full use and enjoyment of the premises. (The tenant can be required to restore the premises to their original condition at the end of the tenancy, however.) Landlords must also make reasonable exceptions to their rules to accommodate disabled tenants. For example, even if they don't allow pets, they can't refuse to rent to someone with a guide dog.

There are special wheelchair accessibility rules that apply to newer residential construction with four or more units.

Familial Status. Discrimination on the basis of familial status refers to discrimination against a person because he or she has a child (under 18 years old) living with him or her. Parents, legal guardians, pregnant women, and those in the process of obtaining custody of a child are protected against discrimination on the basis of their familial status.

While the Fair Housing Act does not override local laws limiting the number of occupants permitted in a dwelling, it is unlawful for anyone to discriminate in selling, renting, or lending money to buy residential property because the applicant is pregnant or lives with a child. "Adults only" apartment or condominium complexes are forbidden, as are complexes divided into "adult" and "family" areas.

However, the law includes an exemption for properties that qualify as "housing for older persons." Children can be excluded from properties that fit into one of the following categories:

1. properties developed under a government program to assist the elderly;
2. properties intended for and solely occupied by persons 62 years old or older; or
3. properties intended for older persons and designed to meet their physical and social needs, if at least 80% of the units are occupied by at least one person who is 55 years old or older.

Enforcement

The Fair Housing Act is enforced by the Department of Housing and Urban Development (HUD), through its Office of Fair Housing and Equal Opportunity. An aggrieved person may file a complaint with HUD or may file a lawsuit in federal or state court. If a complaint is filed with HUD, the agency will investigate the complaint and attempt to confer with the parties in order to reconcile their differences and persuade them to abide by the law.

If this doesn't resolve the dispute and the claims are found to have merit, an administrative hearing will be held, unless either party chooses to have the case decided in federal court instead. In an administrative hearing, HUD attorneys litigate the case on behalf of the complainant. If the case goes from HUD to federal court, the U.S. Attorney General's office litigates for the complainant.

When someone is held to have violated the Fair Housing Act, the administrative law judge or the court may issue an injunction ordering the violator to stop the discriminatory conduct or to take affirmative steps to correct a violation. The violator may also be ordered to pay actual damages and attorney's fees to the complainant. Actual damages may include compensation for humiliation suffered as a result of discrimination, as well as for financial losses. A federal court can order the violator to pay punitive damages to the complainant. An administrative law judge can impose a civil penalty; the maximum penalty ranges from $11,000 for a first offense up to $60,000 for subsequent offenses.

In states such as California, where the state fair housing laws are very similar to the federal law, HUD may refer complaints to the equivalent state agency (e.g., the California Department of Fair Employment and Housing).

Federal Fair Lending Laws

Real estate agents and sellers are not the only ones who must avoid discriminatory activities. There are federal laws designed to eliminate discrimination in lending. They include:

*   the Federal Fair Housing Act (discussed above),
*   the Equal Credit Opportunity Act, and
*   the Home Mortgage Disclosure Act.

The Fair Housing Act prohibits discrimination in home loans and other aspects of residential financing. It does not apply to any other credit transactions.

The **Equal Credit Opportunity Act** (ECOA) applies to all consumer credit, including residential real estate loans. Consumer credit is credit that is extended to an individual (not a corporation or business) for personal, family, or household purposes. The act prohibits lenders from discriminating based on race, color, religion, national origin, sex, marital status, age (as long as the applicant is of legal age), or because the applicant's income is derived partly or wholly from public assistance.

The **Home Mortgage Disclosure Act** is a way of learning whether lenders are fulfilling their obligation to serve the housing needs of the communities where they are located. The act facilitates the enforcement of federal laws against redlining.

Under the Home Mortgage Disclosure Act, institutional lenders in metropolitan areas with assets of over $28 million must make annual reports on residential mortgage loans (both purchase and improvement loans) that were originated or purchased during the fiscal year. The information is categorized as to number and dollar amount, type of loan (FHA, VA, other), and geographic location by census tract or county (for small counties with no established census tracts). The reports disclose areas where few or no home loans have been made and alert investigators to potential redlining.

Equal Access to Facilities

The **Americans with Disabilities Act** (ADA), which became effective in January of 1992, is a federal law that was passed to ensure that disabled persons have equal access to public facilities. The ADA requires any business or other facility open to the public to be accessible to the disabled.

Under the ADA, no one can be discriminated against on the basis of disability in any place of public accommodation. **Public accommodation** is defined to include any private entity with facilities open to the public, as long as the operation of the facilities affects commerce. A **disability** is defined as any physical or mental impairment that substantially limits one or more of the individual's major life activities.

Real estate offices are considered to be public accommodations, along with hotels, restaurants, retail stores, shopping centers, banks, and the offices of attorneys, accountants, and doctors.

To ensure the accessibility of public accommodations, the ADA requires each of the following to be accomplished, as long as it is "readily achievable":

- Both architectural and communication barriers must be removed so that goods and services are accessible to the disabled.
- Auxiliary aids and services must be provided so that no disabled person is excluded, denied services, segregated, or otherwise treated differently from other individuals.
- New commercial construction must be accessible to the disabled, unless structurally impractical.

For example, the owner of a commercial building with no elevator may have to install automatic entry doors and a buzzer at street level so that customers of a second-floor business can ask for assistance. A commercial building owner might also be required to alter the height of a pay phone to make it accessible to someone in a wheelchair, add grab bars to restroom stalls, and take a variety of other steps to make the building's facilities accessible.

California Antidiscrimination Legislation

Not only must real estate agents, sellers, and landlords comply with the federal laws we've covered, they must also comply with state laws that prohibit discrimination. In California, the Unruh Civil Rights Act, the Fair Employment and Housing Act, the Housing Financial Discrimination Act, and the real estate license law all include provisions designed to promote fair housing within the state.

Unruh Civil Rights Act

California's Unruh Civil Rights Act states that all persons are entitled to the full use of any services provided by a business establishment, regardless of race, color, religion, ancestry, national origin, sex, disability, medical condition, or age. In transactions related to housing, business establishments are also not allowed to discriminate based on sexual orientation, marital status, familial status, or source of income.

The act prohibits a broker from discriminating in the performance of his or her work, since a brokerage firm is a business establishment. A broker cannot refuse a listing or turn away a prospective buyer for discriminatory reasons.

Apartment houses, condominium owners' associations, and other real estate developments are considered business establishments under the Unruh Act. Thus, the act makes it unlawful for most condominium or apartment complexes to have a "No Children" rule. However, "senior citizen" developments may require at least one member of each household to be at least 62 or older, and may exclude those younger than 45. Remember that this state law must be interpreted in conjunction with the federal rules concerning housing for older persons, discussed above. The state law may be applied to give more protection against age discrimination than federal law, but not to give less protection.

Someone held to have violated the Unruh Act will be required to pay the injured party's actual damages and attorney's fees. In addition, the violator may have to pay up to three times the amount of actual damages or $4,000, whichever is more.

Fair Employment and Housing Act

The Fair Employment and Housing Act is also known as the **Rumford Act**. It generally prohibits all housing discrimination in California based on race, color, religion, sex, sexual orientation, marital status, national origin, ancestry, familial status, source of income, or disability.

It is unlawful for any owner, lessor, assignee, managing agent, real estate broker or salesperson, or any business establishment to discriminate in selling or leasing any housing accommodation. The law specifically prohibits a seller or

---

Fig. 14.2 Antidiscrimination legislation

Legislation	Prohibits Discrimination
Civil Rights Act of 1866	Based on race
Civil Rights Act of 1964	In some federal programs
Federal Fair Housing Act	In sale, lease, or financing of housing
Americans with Disabilities Act	Based on disability
Unruh Civil Rights Act	By any business establishment
Fair Employment and Housing Act	By owners, lessors, agents, lenders
Housing Financial Discrimination Act	By lenders in residential transactions

---

landlord from asking about the race, color, religion, sex, sexual orientation, marital status, national origin, ancestry, familial status, or disability of any prospective buyer or tenant. A real estate licensee should refuse to answer such a question from a seller or lessor.

The Fair Employment and Housing Act also specifically prohibits anyone from advertising housing for sale or rent in discriminatory terms. This includes any ad that suggests a preference for a particular group, such as a landlord's ad indicating a preference for women or married couples as tenants.

The act also prohibits discrimination in the financing of housing. Under the act, it is unlawful for any bank, mortgage company, or other financial institution to discriminate against any person because of his or her race, color, religion, sex, sexual orientation, marital status, national origin, ancestry, familial status, source of income, or disability.

The act doesn't apply to the rental of a portion of a single-family owner-occupied home to one boarder, or to accommodations operated by nonprofit religious, fraternal, or charitable organizations.

Housing discrimination complaints are submitted to the Department of Fair Employment and Housing. The complaints are investigated by the department's staff. If it appears that a violation has occurred, the department first tries to persuade the violator to stop or correct the violation. If those efforts fail, the department will issue an accusation and the Fair Employment and Housing Commission will hold a hearing on the accusation.

If found guilty, the violator may be ordered to:

- sell or lease the housing in question to the injured party, if it is still available;
- sell or lease similar property to the injured party, if available; or
- provide financial assistance or other benefits previously denied.

In addition, the violator may be required to pay the injured party actual damages, plus a civil penalty ranging from $10,000 up to $50,000.

Housing Financial Discrimination Act

This law requires a lender to make lending decisions based on the merits of the borrower and the security property, rather than on the fact that the property is in a particular neighborhood. A lender cannot refuse to lend money simply because the borrower wishes to purchase a home in an Asian or Hispanic neighborhood, for example.

The California Housing Financial Discrimination Act (which is sometimes called the **Holden Act**) states that it is against California's public policy to deny mortgage loans or to impose stricter terms on loans because of neighborhood characteristics unrelated to the creditworthiness of the borrower or the value of the real property.

Under this act, financial institutions may not:

- discriminate in the provision of financial assistance to purchase, construct, rehabilitate, improve, or refinance housing on the basis of the characteristics of the neighborhood surrounding the property, unless the lender can demonstrate that such consideration is necessary to avoid an unsound business practice;
- consider the racial, ethnic, religious, or national origin composition of the neighborhood surrounding the property; or
- discriminate in the provision of financial assistance for housing on the basis of race, color, religion, sex, marital status, national origin, or ancestry.

Real Estate Law and Regulations

Both the California Real Estate Law and the Real Estate Commissioner's regulations prohibit discriminatory behavior by licensees. Licensees who engage in discriminatory behavior are subject to disciplinary action, and may have their licenses suspended or revoked. (See Chapter 16.)

Brokers have the duty to supervise their affiliated licensees and take reasonable steps to make sure they are familiar with the requirements of both federal and state laws prohibiting discrimination.

Discriminatory Restrictive Covenants

At one time in the United States it was quite common for a property's deed or a subdivision's CC&Rs to include a restrictive covenant prohibiting the sale or lease of the property to non-whites or non-Christians. These discriminatory restrictions were generally considered legal and enforceable until the Supreme Court decided the case of *Shelley v. Kraemer* in 1948. The court ruled that it was unconstitutional—a violation of the 14th Amendment—for state courts or federal courts to be involved in the enforcement of racially restrictive covenants. As a result of the decision, those covenants became legally unenforceable.

Today, although discriminatory restrictive covenants still appear in some older documents, it is a violation of both federal and state laws to attempt to enforce or comply with them. If such a restriction is included in a new deed, the restriction is unenforceable, but it does not affect the conveyance.

Chapter Summary

1. Discrimination in real estate transactions is prohibited by the Civil Rights Act of 1866, the Federal Fair Housing Act, and California antidiscrimination statutes.

2. The Civil Rights Act of 1866 prohibits all discrimination based on race or ancestry in the sale and rental of property. The Civil Rights Act of 1964 prohibits discrimination in programs and services for which the federal government provided financial assistance.

3. The Federal Fair Housing Act goes farther than the Civil Rights Acts of 1866 and 1964 by prohibiting discrimination based on race, color, religion, sex, national origin, handicap, or familial status. However, it applies only to transactions involving residential property.

4. Three specifically prohibited acts under the Federal Fair Housing Act are blockbusting, steering, and redlining. Blockbusting is attempting to obtain listings or arrange sales by predicting the entry of minorities into the neighborhood and implying that this will cause a decline in the neighborhood. Steering is the channeling of buyers or renters to specific neighborhoods based on race or other protected characteristics. Redlining is the refusal, for discriminatory reasons, to make loans on properties located in particular areas.

5. Several federal laws prohibit discrimination in credit transactions: the Federal Fair Housing Act, the Equal Credit Opportunity Act, and the Home Mortgage Disclosure Act.

6. The Americans with Disabilities Act guarantees equal access to public accommodations regardless of physical or mental disability.

7. California state law prohibits discrimination not just in housing, but also in employment, credit transactions, and other types of business activities. There are only limited exemptions.

8. Discriminatory restrictive covenants in a deed or a subdivision's declaration of restrictions are illegal. A conveyance of property is not affected by a discriminatory restriction; the restriction itself is simply unenforceable.

🔑 Key Terms

Blockbusting—Attempting to induce homeowners to list or sell their homes by predicting that members of another race or ethnic group, or people with a disability, will be moving into the neighborhood. Also called panic selling.

Steering—Channeling prospective buyers or tenants toward or away from particular neighborhoods based on their race, religion, or national origin, in order to maintain or change the character of the neighborhoods.

Redlining—Refusing to make a loan because of the racial or ethnic composition of the neighborhood in which the security property is located.

Familial status—A category including persons who have children (under 18 years old) living with them. It also includes someone who is pregnant or is in the process of securing custody of a child.

Disability—A physical disability or mental impairment that substantially limits one or more major life activities.

Public accommodation—A public or private entity with facilities open to the public, if operation of the facilities affects commerce.

Chapter Quiz

1. When a real estate agent channels prospective buyers away from a particular neighborhood because of their race, it is called:

   a) blockbusting
   b) steering
   c) redlining
   d) clipping

2. Rental of a room in an owner-occupied dwelling is exempt from the Federal Fair Housing Act if the dwelling contains:

   a) two or more units
   b) three units or less
   c) less than five units
   d) six units or more

3. A real estate broker is helping the Jacksons sell their single-family home. Can this transaction be exempt from the Federal Fair Housing Act?

   a) Yes, as long as the Jacksons own no more than three single-family homes
   b) Yes, as long as no discriminatory advertising is used
   c) No, because a real estate agent is involved
   d) No, the act applies to all residential sales transactions, without exception

4. The Gardenia Village condominium has a "no kids" rule. This is not a violation of the Federal Fair Housing Act:

   a) if the condo qualifies as "housing for older persons" under the terms of the law
   b) if no discriminatory advertising is used
   c) because age discrimination is not prohibited by the law
   d) because condominiums aren't covered by the law

5. Title VIII of the Civil Rights Act of 1968 precludes:

   a) discrimination in housing
   b) discrimination in lending
   c) Both a) and b)
   d) Neither a) nor b)

6. Blockbusting is an acceptable practice:

   a) only under the supervision of real estate licensees
   b) only when approved by either HUD or the Justice Department
   c) under no circumstances
   d) only if the seller and buyer mutually agree

7. A deed restriction created in 1920 that prohibits the sale of property to a non-Caucasian person until after 2015 is:

   a) valid until all the property owners agree to eliminate the restriction
   b) enforceable
   c) unenforceable
   d) covered by title insurance

8. The Home Mortgage Disclosure Act helps to enforce the prohibition against:

   a) redlining
   b) steering
   c) blockbusting
   d) None of the above

9. A landlord who is subject to the provisions of the Federal Fair Housing Act must:

   a) permit a disabled tenant to make reasonable modifications to the property at the tenant's expense
   b) make reasonable exceptions to the landlord's rules to accommodate disabled tenants
   c) Both a) and b)
   d) Neither a) nor b)

10. Under California law, it would be permissible for a landlord to refuse to rent to a prospective tenant because the tenant:

a) has a child
b) is blind
c) cannot afford the rent
d) All of the above

11. The Unruh Civil Rights Act prohibits discriminatory activities by:

a) lenders only
b) real estate agents only
c) all real estate–related businesses
d) any business entity

12. Which of the following is not covered by the Federal Fair Housing Act?

a) A commercial property
b) An eight-unit multifamily dwelling
c) A triplex listed for sale with a real estate broker
d) A vacant lot intended for residential construction

13. A developer who intended to rent housing in a particular development only to persons 45 years of age or over would be in violation of the:

a) Civil Rights Act of 1866
b) Civil Rights Act of 1964
c) Federal Fair Housing Act
d) Americans with Disabilities Act

14. Under the Americans with Disabilities Act:

a) real estate firms are exempt
b) real estate firms may discriminate against the disabled when taking listings, if appropriate
c) real estate firms must be accessible to the disabled
d) only individual real estate agents are prohibited from discriminating against the disabled

15. The California Housing Financial Discrimination Act prohibits:

a) redlining
b) steering
c) blockbusting
d) panic selling

👉 Answer Key

1. b) Channeling prospective buyers or tenants away from (or toward) certain neighborhoods based on their race, religion, or national origin is called steering. It is a violation of the Federal Fair Housing Act.

2. c) The Fair Housing Act exemption for rentals applies to owner-occupied dwellings with up to four units.

3. c) No residential transaction in which a real estate agent is employed is exempt from the Federal Fair Housing Act.

4. a) The Federal Fair Housing Act does not allow apartment houses and condominiums to discriminate on the basis of familial status unless the complex qualifies as "housing for older persons."

5. c) Title VIII of the 1968 Civil Rights Act (better known as the Federal Fair Housing Act) prohibits discriminatory practices when selling, renting, advertising, or financing housing.

6. c) Blockbusting is a discriminatory practice entirely prohibited by the Federal Fair Housing Act.

7. c) A deed containing such a provision is valid, but the restriction is unenforceable.

8. a) The Home Mortgage Disclosure Act helps to enforce the prohibition against redlining by requiring large institutional lenders to file an annual report of all mortgage loans made during that year. Loans are categorized according to location, alerting investigators to areas of possible redlining.

9. c) The Fair Housing Act requires a residential landlord to allow a disabled tenant to make reasonable modifications to the property. The landlord must also make reasonable exceptions to the rules to accommodate a disabled tenant.

10. c) It is permissible for a landlord to reject an applicant because he or she cannot afford the rent.

11. d) The Unruh Civil Rights Act prohibits discriminatory activities by business entities.

12. a) The Federal Fair Housing Act applies to residential properties, not commercial or industrial properties.

13. c) The developer's age limit would violate the Federal Fair Housing Act. Senior housing is permitted, but 45 is not the cutoff age.

14. c) Under the provisions of the ADA, real estate firms must take reasonable actions necessary to make their accommodations accessible to the disabled.

15. a) This California law (also known as the Holden Act) prohibits redlining.

Chapter 15

Real Estate Construction, Ownership, and Investment

Chapter Overview

In bringing a buyer and seller together, the real estate agent must be a "jack of all trades." Not only must he or she be familiar with property values, contracts, and financing, the agent must also be familiar with the rudiments of residential construction, the advantages of buying a home, the elements to look for in a home, and the benefits of investing in real estate. This chapter briefly describes some aspects of residential construction, focusing on wood frame construction. Then the chapter goes on to discuss the relative merits of renting or buying a home, and the factors to consider when choosing a home— either as a residence or as an investment. The final section of the chapter is an introduction to real estate investment.

Construction

A real estate agent is not a home inspector or an architect, and should not give clients and customers the impression that he or she is an expert in residential construction. However, California law does impose a duty on all licensees to visually inspect the homes they sell. Furthermore, most homebuyers rely on their real estate agents for some advice on the structural quality of a particular home. Thus, agents must be able to evaluate the basic soundness of a home's construction. This preliminary evaluation should be supplemented, whenever necessary, with the opinions of professional inspectors, especially with respect to structural integrity and the safety and suitability of the plumbing and electrical components of the building.

In order to evaluate the basic soundness of a home, real estate agents should be familiar with the following aspects of residential construction:

- architectural styles,
- local building codes and regulations,
- the role of the architect,
- plans and specifications, and
- construction methods and terminology.

Architectural Styles

Homes come in a variety of architectural styles. The quality of a home's construction is not determined by its style (although the style may affect the cost of constructing the home). No one style is inherently more desirable than another. The value of each particular style depends on the personal preference of the homebuyer.

Several common architectural styles are illustrated in Figure 15.1. Of course, many homes have their own unique style, or are combinations of two or more styles. Split-level, Spanish, California ranch, and modern (sometimes called contemporary) are popular architectural styles in California.

Split-level homes have visually attractive designs and make effective use of hilly terrains. Spanish-style homes are one- or two-story homes with white or pastel stucco exteriors and red tile roofs; they look cool and comfortable in

Fig. 15.1 Architectural styles

southern California's heat. Modern-style homes usually incorporate large windows and glass doors, and are designed with an open interior. Because of the flexibility of modern home designs, they are well suited for building on hillsides or other difficult sites. California ranch homes have one story and low-pitched or flat roofs. The exterior may be wood, masonry, or stucco.

A one-story ranch home is the simplest to construct and maintain. However, it requires more land in relation to living space than a two-story or split-level home. Thus, a one-story home may be uneconomical where land is at a premium. Split-level construction is more expensive, but it is popular because it effectively utilizes land with varying topography. Two-story construction is the most economical per square foot of living space, since twice as much living space is provided with one foundation, one roof, and the same amount of land. The inconvenience of stairs and exterior maintenance on the upper story are the primary drawbacks of two-story homes.

Building Codes and Regulations

Local building codes prescribe the types of materials that must be used in residential construction, the acceptable methods of construction, and the number and placement of such items as electrical outlets, plumbing fixtures, and windows. The size and placement of a building on its lot are also governed by building codes and other local regulations.

These codes and regulations promote some degree of uniformity in construction. The construction guidelines assure a homebuyer that the home's quality meets at least minimum requirements. This is especially important in regard to safety issues. For example, a home's ability to resist fire or earthquake damage is of vital importance to both the homeowner and the surrounding community. (See Chapter 5 for a discussion of the local government's authority to enact and enforce building codes.)

Key sources of information regarding local regulations are local planning and building departments, architects, and construction contractors.

The Role of the Architect

The architect is the construction industry professional that the real estate agent is most likely to meet. Most people think of an architect as a person who designs buildings, but a good architect will also provide a range of other services throughout the construction process.

Under a standard contract, an architect will first work with the owner to develop a design that fulfills the owner's needs. Next, the architect will prepare more detailed drawings, describing all of the components of the building, along with an estimate of the probable cost of construction. When the design has been approved by the owner, the architect will draw up the official plans and specifications and will help the owner get bids from contractors and permits from government agencies.

Finally, the architect acts as the owner's representative throughout the actual construction phase, visiting the site to inspect the work, approving periodic payments to the contractor, and interpreting the plans and specifications.

Plans and Specifications

Plans and specifications are the technical drawings and text that explain in detail how a building is to be constructed. The **plans** are drawings of the vertical and horizontal cross-sections of the building. They show the placement of foundations, floors, walls, roofs, doors, windows, fixtures, and wiring. The **specifications** are the text that accompanies the plans, prescribing the type of materials to be used and the required quality of workmanship. Plans and specifications are usually prepared by an architect and take the form of blueprints.

Wood Frame Construction

The most common type of home construction is the wood frame building. It is popular because of its low cost, ease and speed of construction, and flexibility of design. One-story, two-story, and split-level homes can all be wood frame homes.

Because wood frame buildings are so common, this is the type of construction we will focus on here. The construction of a wood frame building is illustrated in the following diagrams, and a glossary of construction terms is provided for use in conjunction with these diagrams.

Elements of Wood Frame Construction. It is easier to judge the quality of a home with some knowledge of the elements of construction. The materials required for each element are usually specified by local building codes. The following are the basic elements of residential wood frame construction.

Foundation. Virtually all modern building foundations are made with reinforced concrete. Concrete has the advantages of low cost, plasticity, and high compressive strength. When concrete is reinforced by steel bars or mesh, it also has good tensile strength (resistance to bending or cracking).

The wider part of the base of a foundation wall is called a **footing**. It supports the weight of the structure. A **sill plate** is a board that is attached to the top of the concrete foundation. The framing of the house rests on the sill plate.

Framing. The framing is usually constructed of wooden boards and dimensional lumber, although the use of metal framing is becoming more common in some areas. Lumber is classified as either "green" or "dry," depending on its moisture content. Dry lumber is considered superior to green lumber for framing because it is less prone to warpage—the deformity in shape caused by uneven shrinking.

The size and length of framing members varies,

Fig. 15.2 Foundation and framing

Top Plates
Lap Top Plates
Window Header
Stud
Window Sill
Header Joist
Sole Plate
Subfloor
Stringer Joist
Anchored Sill Plate
Foundation Wall
Space Block

Fig. 15.3 Residential construction details

CONSTRUCTION DETAILS

1. CROSS BRIDGING
2. SECOND FLOOR JOISTS
3. ROOF RAFTERS
4. COLLAR BEAM
5. RIDGE BOARD
6. PLASTER BASE, LATH AND PLASTER WALLS
7. CROSS BRACING
8. FLASHING AND COUNTER FLASHING
9. BRICK CHIMNEY
10. TIGHT ROOF SHEATHING (ALL OTHER COVERINGS)
11. SPACED 1" x 4" SHEATHING (WOOD SHINGLES)
12. ROOFING FELT
13. FINISH ROOFING (SHINGLE)
14. SOFFIT OR CORNICE
15. FACIA OF CORNICE
16. FIRE STOPS
17. VERTICAL BOARD AND BATTEN SIDING

18. RIBBON PLATE
19. FACIA BOARD
20. LEADER HEAD OR CONDUCTOR HEAD
21. LEADER, DOWNSPOUT OR CONDUCTOR
22. STAIR STRINGER
23. MAIN STAIR TREADS AND RISERS
24. ENTRANCE DOOR SILL
25. CONCRETE STOOP
26. FIRST FLOOR JOISTS
27. BASEMENT POST
28. CINDERFILL
29. BOILER OR FURNACE
30. BASEMENT CONCRETE FLOOR
31. DAMPER CONTROL
32. ASH DUMP
33. CLEANOUT DOOR
34. BASEBOARDS
35. GIRDER

36. FRAME PARTITION
37. POST
38. FOOTING
39. SUB-FLOORING, DIAGONAL
40. FOUNDATION WALL
41. PLATE ANCHOR BOLT
42. DRAIN TILE
43. TERMITE SHIELD
44. SILL PLATE
45. GRAVEL FILL
46. GRADE LINE
47. BASEMENT AREAWAY
48. SOLE PLATE
49. CORNER BRACING
50. FINISH FLOOR
51. INSULATION, BATTS
52. WALL SIDING
53. WALL BUILDING PAPER
54. GUTTER
55. WALL SHEATHING, DIAGONAL

Fig. 15.4 Methods of roof framing

Fig. 15.5 Roof styles

depending upon their particular application as girders, joists, studs, rafters, and so on. The parallel boards used to support the load of the floor and ceiling are called joists. Vertical members called studs are attached to the sole plate, which is a horizontal board that rests on the floor joists. (See Figure 15.2.)

Walls serve two purposes. They provide structural support and they separate the interior space into individual rooms. The walls that provide support are called **load-bearing walls**. Load-bearing walls support a vertical load, such as a second floor or the roof. (See Figure 15.4.) Load-bearing walls are usually built to be stronger than non-load bearing walls, and they are rarely moved during remodeling.

Exterior Sheathing and Siding. Exterior sheathing is the covering applied to the outside of the frame. The most common form of exterior sheathing is plywood panels that are four feet wide by eight feet long. Plywood serves an additional function by adding shear strength to the walls. Shear strength is the capacity of a wall to resist a sideways racking force, and it is normally provided by corner bracing in the frame.

Exterior siding is the visible finish layer applied to the outside of the building. It may be plywood, boards, vinyl siding, shingles, or other materials. The two most important characteristics of siding are its resistance to weathering and its aesthetic appeal.

Interior Sheathing. This is the covering applied to the inside of the frame, on the walls and ceilings. In the past, the most common form of sheathing was lath and plaster, a cement-like mixture applied over a matrix of wood strips attached to the frame. Modern buildings use drywall construction for interior sheathing. The term "drywall" is used because there is no need to add water to the material before application. Drywall products usually come in large sheets (like plywood) and are fastened to the frame with glue, nails, or screws. Sheetrock and wallboard are two common drywall products. The joints between panels are hidden by covering them with a strip of tape imbedded in a plaster-like filler. This process is called "taping" the joints.

Roofing. The structural part of the roof is composed of the ridge board (the highest structural member of the house), rafters, and plywood or boards laid perpendicular to the rafters. This sheathing is then covered with a tar-impregnated paper called roofing felt. The final layer of roofing may be wood shingles, tiles, or composition roofing (tar-like shingles or rolls of material). Sometimes hot tar is simply interspersed with more layers of felt; this is called a "built-up" roof. Flashing (metal sheeting) is installed on top of the roofing material around chimneys and other openings to prevent water seepage.

Floor Covering. The strength of the floor is provided by tongue-and-groove floor boards or plywood attached to the floor joists, which is called the subflooring. The subflooring is then covered with finished flooring, which may be carpet, tile, linoleum, hardwood strips, or other material.

Plumbing. The plumbing includes drain pipes, supply pipes, and fixtures. The drain pipes are made of cast iron, concrete, or plastic. The supply pipes are made of galvanized steel, copper, or plastic. Plumbing fixtures are either cast iron or pressed steel that is coated with enamel or fiberglass.

Electrical. Most modern wiring is in the form of cable, which is an insulated cord-like material containing two or more strands of copper or aluminum wire. The electrical cables are enclosed in metal or plastic piping called conduit.

The electrical cables run in circuits from a supply source (a fuse box or, more commonly, a breaker panel) to the various outlets for plugs or light

Fig. 15.6 Construction terms

Glossary of Construction Terms

Anchor bolts—Bolts embedded in concrete, used to hold structural members in place.

Areaway—An open space around a basement window or doorway that provides light, ventilation, and access.

Beam—A principal structural member used between posts, columns, or walls.

Bearing wall or partition—A wall or partition that supports a vertical load in addition to its own weight.

Board—Lumber that is less than two inches thick.

Bridging—Pieces fitted in pairs from the bottom of one floor joist to the top of adjacent joists, and crossed to distribute the floor load.

BTU—British Thermal Unit; a measure of heating capacity.

Built-up roof—A roof composed of several layers of rag felt, saturated with pitch or asphalt.

Cased opening—An interior opening without a door that is finished with jambs and trim.

Caulk—To seal cracks and joints to make them waterproof.

Collar beam—A beam connecting rafters at a point considerably above the wall plate.

Column—An upright supporting member, circular or rectangular in shape.

Conduit—A pipe or tube, usually metal, in which wiring is installed.

Corner braces—Diagonal braces set into studs to reinforce corners of frame structures.

Counterflashing—Flashing used on chimneys at the roof line to cover shingle flashing and prevent the entry of moisture.

Crawl space—A space between the ground and the first floor that is used for access.

Dimensional lumber—Lumber that is two to five inches thick and up to twelve inches wide.

Dormer—A projecting structure built out from a sloping roof.

Drywall—Materials used for wall covering that do not need to be mixed with water before application (e.g., sheetrock).

Eaves—The margin or lower part of a roof that projects over an exterior wall.

Fascia—A wooden member nailed to the ends of projecting rafters.

Fire stop—A block or stop used in a wall between studs to prevent the spread of fire and smoke.

Flashing—Sheet metal or other material used in roof and wall construction to prevent rain or other water from entering.

Flue—The space in a chimney through which smoke, gas, or fumes rise.

Footing—The spreading course at the base of a foundation wall, pier, or column.

Framing—The timber structure of a building that gives it shape and strength. It includes the wall, floors, ceilings, and roof.

Gable—That portion of a wall contained between the slopes of a roof.

Glazing—The process of installing glass into sashes and doors.

Gutter—A wooden or metal trough attached to the edge of a roof to collect and conduct water from rain and melting snow.

Header—A horizontal structural member that supports the load over an opening, such as a window or door.

Hip roof—A roof that rises from all four sides of the building.

Interior trim—A general term for all the molding, casing, baseboards, and other trim items applied inside the building.

Insulation—Any material highly resistant to heat transmission that is used to reduce the rate of heat flow.

Jamb—The top and two sides of a door or window frame that contact the door or sash.

Joist—One of a series of parallel framing members used to support floor and ceiling loads.

Lath—Material fastened to the frame of a building to act as a base for plaster.

Molding—A narrow strip of wood used to conceal surface or angle joints, or as an ornamentation.

Partition—An interior wall that subdivides space within a building.

Pier—A column of masonry used to support other structural members.

Pilaster—A part of a wall that projects not more than one-half of its own width beyond the outside or inside face of a wall.

Pitch—Inclination or slope.

Plan—A drawing representing any one of the cross-sections of a building.

Plaster—A mixture of lime, cement, and sand used to cover inside or outside wall surfaces.

Plate—The horizontal member of a wall frame to which the studs are attached.

Rafter—One of a series of structural members of a roof.

Reinforced concrete—Concrete poured around steel bars or steel meshwork, in such a manner that the two materials act together to resist force.

Riser—The vertical stair member between two consecutive stair treads.

R-value—A measure of resistance to heat transfer.

Sheathing—Structural covering; boards or prefabricated panels that are attached to the exterior studding or rafters.

Siding—The finish covering of the outside walls of a frame building.

Sill—The lowest member of the frame of a structure, usually horizontal, resting on the foundation. Also, the lower member of a window or exterior door frame.

Specifications—A written document stipulating the quality of materials and workmanship required for a job.

Stud—One of a series of vertical wood or metal structural members in walls and partitions. In most modern frame buildings, the studs are set 16 inches apart.

Subfloor—Boards or panels laid directly on floor joists, over which a finished floor will be laid.

Timber—A piece of lumber five inches or larger in its least dimension.

Trim—The finish materials in a building (moldings, etc.).

Trimmer—The stud into which a header is framed; it adds strength to the side of the opening.

Truss—A structural unit, usually triangular in shape, which provides rigid support over wide spans.

Weephole—A small hole in the foundation wall to drain water to the outside.

fixtures. A breaker panel is a series of circuit breakers that automatically shut off the current in a circuit under overload conditions. Most outlets supply 110 volts of power, except for certain outlets designed for major appliances (ranges, water heaters, dryers, etc.), which supply 220 volts.

Heating, Ventilating, and Air Conditioning (HVAC). These systems are composed of heating and/or cooling appliances that serve warm, cool, or fresh air to the rooms of a house through a series of galvanized sheet metal tubes called ducts. The ducts open at various places in the building called registers. The registers may be closed off independently in order to direct the heat or air conditioning to areas where it is needed.

HVAC systems sometimes have an energy-efficient ratio (EER) rating. The higher the EER, the more efficient the system.

Insulation is used to make HVAC systems less costly to run. Insulation is material that is resistant to the transfer of heat. It comes in batts or rolls, or in loose form, and it is inserted between wall studs and between the joists of floors and ceilings. Insulation also comes in sheets that can be secured to the sheathing of the structure. The effectiveness of insulating materials is gauged by an "R-value." The higher the R-value, the more resistant the material is to the transfer of heat, and the better it is for insulation purposes. Local building codes require insulation with a minimum R-value to be used in all new construction. When insulation is adequate, the inside surface of an exterior wall will be about the same temperature as the surface of an interior wall.

Structural Pest Problems. One major problem with wood frame buildings is their susceptibility to damage by wood-eating insects, especially termites. Several techniques are used to minimize the possibility of termite damage:

- the ground under and around the building may be treated with a chemical that keeps termites away from the foundation;
- lumber that is in contact with the soil or the foundation, such as sills or beams, may be treated with a chemical to prevent termites from gaining access to the frame of the building; and
- metal shields may be inserted between the foundation and the superstructure to physically prevent termites from reaching the wood.

It is always a good idea to have a licensed structural pest control inspector examine a home before a sale closes. In fact, lenders in California typically require such an inspection. (And in some termite-prone parts of the state, pest control inspections are also required by the FHA and VA.) The inspector will provide a complete report on the structural soundness of the building, listing any defects caused by moisture and fungus or by insects.

A pest control inspection is usually ordered by a seller when the property is first listed. A copy of the inspection report must be given to the party that ordered the inspection within ten working days. Real estate agents should make sure the buyer gets a copy of the report as soon as is practical. The report must be filed with the state Structural Pest Control Board and a copy of it must be kept for two years.

Ordinarily, unless the parties agree otherwise, the seller is required to pay for having existing pest problems corrected, but not for work to prevent infestation. Instead, the buyer pays for any preventive work.

To Rent or to Buy?

Real estate agents are often asked to discuss the relative advantages and disadvantages of renting versus buying a place to live. Some considerations are primarily emotional, such as security, pride of ownership, and the freedom to have pets or to remodel according to personal preference. These types of considerations cannot be evaluated objectively by a third party—their importance can be measured only by the prospective homebuyer. However, other elements of comparison are largely financial, and a real estate agent can help a prospective homebuyer evaluate these elements objectively.

Advantages of Renting

The advantages of renting over buying can be briefly summarized:

- renting requires less financial commitment and risk;
- renting gives the tenant greater mobility; and
- renting carries with it fewer responsibilities.

Financial Commitment. Compared to the funds necessary to buy a home, the initial cash outlay to rent a home or an apartment is quite modest. In most cases, a security deposit and one or two months of prepaid rent is sufficient. Even in conjunction with low-downpayment financing, the cash required to purchase a home (the amount of the downpayment, loan fees, and closing costs) normally far exceeds the cost of moving into an apartment or a rental home. Furthermore, at least for the first few years, the monthly rental payment is likely to be substantially less than a monthly mortgage payment.

Financial Risk. Renters have little financial investment in their rented premises and the neighborhood in which they live. Therefore, there is little financial risk in renting. If the property values in a neighborhood decline and the neighborhood becomes run down or otherwise undesirable, renters can simply give the required notice—or wait until the lease expires—and move away. A homeowner in the same neighborhood runs the risk of losing some or all of his or her investment in the property.

Mobility. It is faster, easier, and cheaper for a renter to move than for a homeowner to move. A renter has only to give the required notice or wait until the lease expires before he or she can move out. Even if a renter has to leave abruptly, any deposit or prepaid rent that may be forfeited is almost sure to be less than the cost of selling one home and buying another. Selling a home is a lengthy and expensive process, taking at least a few months and costing about 10% of the home's value.

Maintenance and Repairs. An owner is responsible for maintaining the property and making any needed repairs. For a renter, the cost of maintenance and repairs is simply included in the rent. The renter usually has no direct responsibility for doing maintenance work and making repairs. Also, a renter does not face the burden of sudden large expenditures for unexpected repairs.

Amenities. In many cases, renters enjoy the use of recreational facilities, such as swimming pools and tennis courts, that are beyond the financial reach of most homeowners.

Advantages of Buying

For many people, buying instead of renting affords both the subjective advantages of security and personal satisfaction and the financial advantages of equity appreciation and tax deductions.

Security. A homeowner enjoys a certain amount of security in knowing that he or she can continue to live in the home as long as the mortgage payments are made. A renter has no real security beyond the term of the lease. When the lease expires, or when the landlord gives the required notice, a renter will have to find another place to live.

Privacy and Freedom from Restrictions. In most cases, a homeowner enjoys greater privacy than a renter and has greater freedom to use the property. An owner can redecorate or remodel the home to suit his or her own taste, and can keep pets or engage in other activities that are prohibited by many rental agreements.

Monthly Payments. A homeowner's monthly mortgage payment usually starts out higher than the rental payment for equivalent lodging. However, over time, rents usually rise at a faster rate than mortgage payments. This is especially true if the mortgage has a fixed interest rate. In that case, payments usually increase slowly as the property tax and insurance portions of the mortgage payments increase. If the mortgage loan has an adjustable interest rate, payments may increase rapidly if interest rates rise, but they will decrease if interest rates go down. Thus, it is quite possible for a monthly rental payment to eventually exceed a monthly mortgage payment.

Investment Appreciation. Although it is impossible to predict whether or how much a particular home will appreciate in value, over the last several decades average home values have increased at a rate that is higher than the average inflation rate. Typically, a homeowner enjoys an increase in home equity—and thus an increase in net worth—as his or her home appreciates in value. For a renter, in contrast, the appreciation of property values is likely to mean a rent increase.

Tax Advantages. For the homeowner, federal income tax laws allow tax deductions for property taxes and for mortgage interest. The interest paid on a loan secured by a personal residence is the only type of consumer interest that is eligible for deduction from federal income taxes. Also, at least part of the gain realized on the sale of most principal residences is never taxed at all. An equivalent tax benefit is simply not available to those who rent their principal residence. (See Chapter 13 for a more complete discussion of income taxes and real estate ownership.)

Comparison of Renting and Buying

Many real estate agents use worksheets to compare the net costs of renting and buying. Worksheet forms take into account not only the monthly mortgage or rental payments, but also the homeowner's increases in equity and the benefit of income tax deductions. These worksheets demonstrate to prospective buyers that the overall cost of buying a home is often less than the cost of renting.

A simplified example of such a worksheet form is shown in Figure 15.7. This worksheet has been filled in with data for a proposed purchase of a $250,000 home, with the buyer making a 10% downpayment and obtaining a $225,000 loan at a fixed annual interest rate of 7%. (These figures were chosen to keep the example simple; the $250,000 price is too low to be realistic in many California communities.) Closing costs bring the total cash requirement for the purchase up to $32,500. Taxes, homeowner's insurance, the annual appreciation rate for local property values, and the buyers' income tax bracket have all been estimated. The total estimated monthly payment, including principal and interest, property taxes, homeowner's insurance, and the monthly renewal premium for private mortgage insurance, is approximately $1,967.

The monthly cost of buying the home on these terms is compared with the cost of renting comparable housing at a monthly rent of $1,300. At first glance, a comparison of the monthly mortgage payment of $1,967 to the monthly rental payment of $1,300 would seem to give the advantage to renting, especially considering the substantial amount of cash required for the purchase. However, an analysis of all of the economic benefits of home ownership results in a lower net cost for the home purchase, even when taking into account the interest lost on the money spent for the downpayment and closing costs.

To begin with, part of the monthly mortgage payment goes to amortize the loan. These payments to principal are typically recovered when the home is sold. For a $225,000 loan with a 30-year term, the average monthly amortization would be $625 ($225,000 ÷ 360 months = $625). Of course, in the early years of the loan term a much smaller portion of each payment would go to principal, and in the later years a larger portion of the monthly payment would go to principal.

Next, some portions of the payment—the interest and the property taxes—are tax deductible. In this case, the average monthly interest is $872 (again, in the early years a larger portion would go to interest, and in the later years a smaller portion would go to interest), and the monthly property tax payment is $317, for a total of $1,189 in tax-deductible items. If the buyer is in the 28% income tax bracket, that would represent a tax savings of about $333 per month ($1,189 × .28 = $332.92).

Finally, the home is likely to appreciate in value and give the purchaser a return on his or her investment as well as a place to live. Even at the modest rate of appreciation used in this example, 3% per year, the appreciation return is substantial. On $250,000, it would be $7,500 per year, or about $625 per month.

After taking into account all of the economic benefits of buying, the net effective cost of buying is only $384 per month.

Fig. 15.7 *Comparison of renting and buying*

Comparison of Estimated Net Cost of Renting and Buying

Buying

Purchase price	$250,000
Cash required (downpayment and closing costs)	$32,500
Loan amount	$225,000
Loan term	30 years
Interest rate	7%
Property taxes	$3,800
Homeowner's insurance premium	$900
Property appreciation rate (estimated)	3%
Income tax bracket	28%

Out of pocket costs:
Monthly payment

Principal and interest		$1,497
Property taxes		317
Homeowner's insurance		75
Other monthly expenses (PMI)		+ 78
Total monthly payment		$1,967
less:		
Average monthly principal amortization		− 625
Tax benefit		
Average interest portion of payment	872	
Property tax portion of payment	317	
Other	+ 0	
Total deductible items	$1,189	
Monthly value of tax deduction		− 333
Effective monthly cost of ownership		$1,009
less:		
Average monthly appreciation		− 625
Monthly Net Cost of Buying		**$384**

Renting

Out-of-pocket costs:	
Monthly rent	$1,300
less:	
Interest from savings not used for purchase ($32,500 @ 4%)	− 108
Monthly Net Cost of Renting	**$1,192**

The monthly rental is $1,300, with no federal income tax deductions and no benefits to the renter if the property appreciates in value. The renter would be able to obtain some interest or other investment yield on the $32,500 not used for a downpayment and closing costs. In this example, a yield of 4% is used, giving the renter a monthly benefit of $108 and a net effective cost of renting of $1,192 per month.

It should be emphasized that this example is based on estimates and assumptions that are subject to change. A change in interest rates, property tax rates, or the tax law would significantly alter the income tax benefits of buying. Also, the average monthly principal and interest portions would be different for a buyer who intended to own the home for less than the full 30-year amortization term. Perhaps most importantly, a change in the rate of appreciation would have a great impact on the final net cost of home ownership. However, worksheets of this type serve a useful purpose in displaying the benefits of home ownership that can offset what first appears to be the higher cost of buying a home.

Factors to Consider When Choosing a Home

When a real estate agent shows a home to a buyer, both the buyer and the seller often rely on the agent to point out the positive features of that home. So it is important that real estate agents understand what considerations are important to most homebuyers. These features have an impact on both the property's subjective attractiveness to a homebuyer and the property's objective value as estimated by an appraiser. (Appraisal is discussed in Chapter 11.)

Neighborhood Considerations

Since the surrounding neighborhood greatly influences the overall desirability of a home and also has a great impact on value, careful consideration should be given to neighborhood characteristics.

Percentage of Home Ownership. Are most of the homes owner-occupied, or is there a large percentage of rental properties? Neighborhoods that are predominantly owner-occupied are generally better maintained, less susceptible to loss in value, and more likely to appreciate in value.

Conformity. Values are protected if there is a reasonable degree of homogeneity in the neighborhood. This includes homogeneity of styles, ages, prices, sizes, and quality of structures.

Changing Land Use. Does the neighborhood land use appear stable, or are there indications of a transition from residential to some other type of land use?

Street and Sidewalks. Do the neighborhood streets have good access to traffic arterials? If a property does not front on a publicly dedicated and maintained street, the buyer should ask whether there is an enforceable road maintenance agreement signed by the property owners.

What is the condition of the driveway, street, and sidewalks? Are there street lights and fire hydrants on the block? Are there sanitary and/or storm sewers?

If so, have they already been paid for, or is there a special assessment against the properties in the neighborhood?

Availability of Utilities and Public Services. Are all of the typical utilities available, including water, electricity, gas, sewers, telephones, and other desirable services, such as television and internet cable? Are the telephone and power lines above ground or is there underground wiring? Is the neighborhood adequately served by public transportation, police, and fire protection?

School District. In what primary and secondary school districts is the neighborhood located? How far away are the schools? Are they within walking distance? The quality of the local schools or school district can make a major difference in value and can be an extremely important basis of decision for many buyers with school-age children.

Social Services. Are there places of worship, hospitals or health care facilities, and other social services nearby?

Overall Neighborhood Values. Does it appear that the overall condition and values in the neighborhood are stable, increasing, or decreasing?

The Home

Of course, the home itself—its size, condition, and amenities—should be reviewed with the prospective buyer.

Site/View. First, the agent should look at the lot on which the house is located. What is the size and shape of the lot? Rectangular lots are usually more desirable than odd or irregularly shaped parcels. Is the lot on the corner? Is it level, gently sloping, or steep? Unusually steep lots present a danger of soil instability. Does it appear that water runoff and drainage are good? What is the quality and extent of the landscaping? If the home is new, has any landscaping (such as the lawn, shrubbery, and trees) already been done, or will the buyer have to do it all? The cost of new landscaping can be quite a bit more than many homebuyers realize.

Is there a view? In many areas, a view can increase the value of the lot substantially and add greatly to the property's appeal.

Exterior Appearance. How old is the house, and when was it last painted? What is the age and condition of the roof and flashing, gutters, downspouts, siding, windows, doors, and weather stripping? Thin or curled shingles, cracked, blistered, or peeling paint, and rusted or sagging gutters and downspouts are indications that costly repairs may soon be needed. Does the foundation appear to be in good shape, or are there cracks or other evidence of settling? If there is no basement, are the vents and crawlspace adequate?

Plumbing and Electrical Systems. If it is not a new home, what is the age of the plumbing and electrical systems? Is the plumbing copper, plastic, or some combination of materials? Is the water pressure adequate? Do the electrical service panel and existing outlets indicate there is sufficient electrical service to the home? Do the electrical and plumbing systems, or as much of them as can be seen, appear to be in good condition?

Heating, Ventilating, and Air Conditioning. What type of heating system does the home have: electric, gas, or oil; forced air, floor furnaces, baseboard heaters? What is the type and size of the water heater? If there is air conditioning, is it a central system or window units? If it is not a new home, what is the age and apparent condition of the heating, hot water, and air conditioning systems? Is the present owner aware of any problems, inadequacies, or defects?

Garage/Carport. Generally, a garage is better than a carport. What is the size of the garage or carport—single, double, or triple? Is there work or storage space in addition to space for parking? Is there an entrance, protected from the weather, directly from the garage or carport into the home?

Attic/Basement. Is there an attic or a basement? If so, what type of access is there from the rest of the home? Is there room for storage or work space? Would it be possible to convert all or part of the basement into additional bedrooms or living area?

Energy-Efficient Features. Escalating energy costs have created an increased demand for energy-efficient homes. Examples of energy-efficient features include clock-controlled thermostats, insulation-wrapped water heaters, insulated ducts and pipes in unheated areas, adequate insulation for floors, walls, and attic, and weather stripping for doors and windows. In some areas, solar water and space heating equipment is popular.

Overall Interior Design. A real estate agent should know some of the features of a well-designed, efficient floor plan. For instance, it should not be necessary to pass through the living room to reach other rooms, or to go through one of the bedrooms to reach another.

Other design considerations include the number of bedrooms, closets, and bathrooms—is there a sufficient number and size for the square footage of the home? Is there a separate dining room, or is the dining area part of the kitchen or living room? Is there sufficient work space in the kitchen and laundry room, and is there storage space for cleaning and gardening tools? Are there enough windows and natural light, especially in the kitchen and other work or recreational spaces?

Considerations for Individual Rooms. Individual rooms have certain features that are important to their comfort and efficient use.

- **Living Room/Family Room.** How large are the living room and the family or recreation room (if any)? Is the shape of each room and the available wall space adequate for the furniture that will be placed in it?
- **Dining Room or Area.** Is the dining area convenient to the kitchen, large enough in relation to the size of the home, and able to accommodate the number of people who will be eating there?

- **Kitchen.** Is the kitchen convenient to an outside entrance and to the garage or carport? Is there adequate counter and cabinet space? What is the quality and condition of the kitchen cabinets? What is the type, quality, and condition of the kitchen floor? Are any of the appliances going to be included in the sale? If so, are they large enough, of good quality, and in good repair?
- **Bedrooms.** Is the number of bedrooms and their size adequate for the family? The size of the master bedroom is especially important. Are the closets large enough? It is better for the bedrooms to be located apart from the family room, living room, kitchen, and other work or recreational spaces.
- **Bathrooms.** There should be at least two bathrooms if the home has more than two bedrooms. In many areas, particularly in newer homes, a private bathroom off the master bedroom is standard. What is the type and condition of the tile or other wall and floor coverings? Are there windows or ceiling fans to provide adequate ventilation?

Design Deficiencies. Here is a brief list of some of the most common design deficiencies that homebuyers should watch out for:

- the front door opens directly into the living room;
- there is no front hall closet;
- the back door is difficult to reach from the kitchen, or from the driveway or garage;
- there is no comfortable area in or near the kitchen where the family can eat;
- the dining room is not easily accessible from the kitchen;
- the stairway is off of a room rather than in a hallway or foyer;
- bedrooms and baths are visible from the living room or foyer;
- the family room (or rec room) is not visible from the kitchen;
- there is no access to the basement from outside the house;
- the bedrooms are not separated by a bathroom or closet wall (for soundproofing); and
- outdoor living areas are not accessible from the kitchen.

Investing in Real Estate

After buying a home, many people become interested in purchasing real estate as an investment. They realize that while the value of real estate fluctuates, property that is in good condition and that is located in a good neighborhood will usually increase in value in the long run. (A word of caution: real estate agents should not act as investment counselors; they should always refer clients to an accountant, attorney, or investment specialist for investment advice.)

An investment is an asset that is expected to generate a **return** (a profit). A return on an investment can take various forms, including interest, dividends, or appreciation in value. An asset appreciates in value because of inflation, and may also appreciate because of a rising demand for the asset. For example, a parcel of prime vacant land appreciates in value as developable land becomes increasingly scarce.

Types of Investments

Investments can be divided into two general categories: ownership investments and debt investments. With **ownership investments**, the investor takes an ownership interest in the asset. Real estate and stocks are examples of ownership investments. The return on ownership investments usually takes the form of dividends or appreciation (or both in some cases). Ownership investments are sometimes called **equities**.

A **debt investment** is essentially a loan that an investor makes to an entity. For example, a bond is a debt owed to an investor by a government entity or corporation. The investor lends the entity money for a set period of time, and in return the entity promises to repay the money on a specific date (the maturity date) along with a certain amount of interest.

Investors often choose to diversify their investments—that is, they choose to invest in a variety of different types of investments. The mix of investments owned by an individual or company, plus any cash reserves, is referred to as a **portfolio**.

Note that for tax purposes, investment income (such as interest, dividends, or rent) is sometimes distinguished from earned income (salaries, wages, or self-employment income).

Investment Characteristics

An investor considers any investment in terms of three potential advantages: liquidity, safety, and total return on the investment (sometimes called **yield**). These three characteristics are interrelated. For example, liquidity and safety generally go together. On the other hand, for a high return an investor often sacrifices safety or liquidity, or both.

A **liquid asset** is one that can be converted into cash quickly. Money in a bank account is extremely liquid: to convert it into cash, the investor need only present the bank with a withdrawal slip or check. Mutual funds, stocks, and bonds are less liquid—they take a little longer (perhaps a week or so) to convert into cash. Other items, such as jewelry or coin collections, are not considered liquid at all, because an investor might have to wait months to exchange those assets for cash. Real estate is not considered a liquid asset.

Liquid investments do not offer very high returns. In general, the more liquid the asset, the lower the return. For example, the money in your wallet is the most liquid asset you can have, but it earns no return (interest) at all. Money in a savings account is a little less liquid—you have to go to the bank to withdraw it—but it offers only a modest return, in the form of a low rate of interest. By contrast, real estate can offer a very high rate of return, but it is not at all liquid.

The most liquid investments are generally considered the safest. With liquid assets, there is little risk of losing the asset itself. Money in the bank is both liquid and safe. Since your deposit is insured by the federal government (up to $100,000), there is little chance of losing your investment. Other, less liquid types of investments, such as gold or real estate, are not as safe. For example, a property owner might be forced to sell when real estate values are low, and as a result lose a good portion of his or her original investment in the property.

Investments that are both safe and liquid offer the lowest returns. In a sense, investors "pay" for safety and liquidity with a low return. Savings accounts and certificates of deposit, both safe investments, offer low returns. Mutual funds, gold, and real estate can generate high returns, but at a considerable risk to the investor. For some types of assets, such as real estate, the safety of the investment will increase if the investor can afford to keep the investment for a long period of time. For example, if an investor does not need to cash out his or her investment in real estate for ten or fifteen years, chances are good that the investor will reap a high return. This is true because the investor will have more control over when to sell the asset, and will be able to take full advantage of healthy market conditions.

Example: Jeanne and Harold each invest $20,000 in rental homes in the same year. One year later, Jeanne desperately needs some cash and is forced to sell her rental home at a loss. She ends up with only $17,000 of her original $20,000 investment.

Harold, on the other hand, keeps his rental home for twelve years. He's in no hurry to sell his property, so he can wait for optimal market conditions. He sells at the peak of a real estate cycle, when property values are high. Because Harold could afford to choose when he sold the property, he walked away from the transaction with $60,000, a very healthy return on his original $20,000 investment.

Advantages of Investing in Real Estate

People invest in real estate for many reasons. The advantages of investing in real estate can be broken down into three general categories:

- appreciation,
- leverage, and
- cash flow.

In addition, real estate investment has certain tax benefits.

Appreciation. Appreciation refers to an increase in a property's value due to changes in the economy or other outside factors. Although real estate values may fluctuate, over a period of several years real estate usually increases in value at a rate equal to or higher than the rate of inflation. Thus, real estate is considered an effective hedge against inflation. And when buildable property becomes scarce, the value of properties in prime locations increases even more rapidly.

Appreciation causes a property owner's equity to increase. **Equity** is the difference between the value of the property and the liens against it, so an increase in the property's value increases the owner's equity in the property. Also, each monthly mortgage payment increases the owner's equity, in proportion to the reduction of the principal amount of the loan. Equity adds to an owner/investor's net worth and can also be used to secure a home equity loan. So even though real estate is not considered a liquid asset, equity in real estate can be used to generate cash funds.

Leverage. Real estate investors can take advantage of leverage, which is defined as using borrowed money to invest in an asset. If the asset appreciates, then the investor earns money on the money borrowed as well as the money he or she invested.

Example: Martin purchases a rental home for $315,000. He makes a $63,000 down-payment and borrows the rest of the purchase price. The rent generated by the property covers all the expenses of operating the property, plus the mortgage payment and income taxes. The property appreciates at 3% per year for five years. At the end of the five years, Martin sells the property for $365,000. He's made a $50,000 profit on his $63,000 investment. This averages out to a 15.8% annual return over the five-year period. The property appreciated at 3% per year, but because he invested only 20% of the purchase price, Martin was able to generate a 15.8% return on his investment.

Cash Flow. Many real estate investments generate a positive cash flow, as well as appreciate in value. Cash flow is defined as spendable income—the amount of money left after all the property's expenses have been paid, including operating costs, mortgage payments, and taxes. When a real estate investment generates a positive cash flow, the investor's monthly income increases. Thus, a real estate investment can increase both the investor's net worth (through appreciation) and his or her income (through positive cash flow).

Another way in which a property can generate cash flow is through a **sale-leaseback** arrangement. In a sale-leaseback, the owner of a building (typically a commercial property) sells the building to an investor, but then leases the property back from the investor and continues to use it. The money generated by the sale can be used for expansion, acquiring inventory, or investment elsewhere. At the same time, the seller can deduct the rent paid to lease the property from his or her income taxes as a business expense. Sometimes a sale-leaseback arrangement also includes a **buyback** agreement, in which it's agreed that the seller will buy the property back for its fair market value after a certain number of years.

Investors sometimes use the term "cash on cash," which refers to a property's first year cash flow divided by the initial investment. It pinpoints the ratio between cash invested (equity) and cash received.

Tax Benefits. The tax benefits of real estate investment include reducing taxes with deductions for depreciation, mortgage interest, and operating expenses, and deferring taxes with tax-free exchanges and installment sales. The income tax implications of real estate ownership are discussed in Chapter 13.

Disadvantages of Investing in Real Estate

Of course, real estate investments can be a mixed blessing. There are some disadvantages to real estate investments that must be considered carefully.

First of all, expert advice is often required to invest in real estate. Investing in real estate is a lot more complicated than putting money in a savings account or a mutual fund. It is also more time-consuming. Not only does the initial purchase take time and effort, but the property must be managed after it is purchased. Rental rates must be set, tenants found, rents collected, and maintenance and repairs completed. Even if the investor decides to hire a property manager to manage the property, there are many decisions that must be made by the investor.

As we discussed earlier, real estate investments are not liquid. Time is required to convert real estate into cash. Furthermore, there are substantial risks involved in investing in real estate. There is no guarantee that the investor will not lose some or all of his or her downpayment. For instance, there is always the chance that the property's value may decline because of a local economic trend.

> **Example:** On a national scale, property values are keeping pace with inflation. However, Lumbertown relies solely on the timber industry and the local lumber mill for employment. The local mill shuts down and the town is economically crippled. Even though real estate is usually a good investment, property values in Lumbertown will decline rapidly.

Also, the income generated by a property may not be enough to cover the expenses of operating the property. A negative cash flow may force the investor to sell the property quickly, for less than he or she paid for it.

Choices When Investing in Real Estate

There are two different ways to invest in real estate. One way is to purchase the property as an individual investor. The other way is to invest in real estate indirectly, through real estate investment syndicates, real estate investment trusts, real estate mortgage investment conduits, or mortgage-backed securities.

A **real estate investment syndicate** is created when people or companies form a business entity (syndicate) in order to purchase and develop a piece of real estate. The syndicate may take the form of a partnership, a corporation, a trust, or a limited liability company.

A **real estate investment trust** (REIT) is an investment company that takes the form of a trust. If the requirements set forth in the tax code are met, an REIT can take advantage of special tax benefits. (REITs are discussed in Chapter 2.)

A **real estate mortgage investment conduit** (REMIC) is a special business entity that is formed for tax purposes. To qualify for special tax treatment, a substantial amount of a REMIC's investments must be in qualified mortgage loans. Like an REIT, a REMIC is subject to complicated legal restrictions.

Investors may also purchase **mortgage-backed securities** issued by one of the secondary market agencies, such as Fannie Mae or Freddie Mac. (The secondary market is discussed in Chapter 9.)

Types of Properties. An investor who decides to purchase real property directly must first decide what type of property to invest in, and then which particular piece of property to purchase.

There are many types of real estate for an investor to choose from. There are residential properties (including single-family homes, duplexes, triplexes, four-plexes, and apartment buildings), office properties, retail properties, and industrial parks. Of course, an investor might choose to purchase vacant land and develop it, or simply hold onto it to reap the benefits of appreciation.

The investor should consider whether a potential investment will require property management. A commercial property or a multifamily residential property may require on- or off-site management, either by the investor or by a professional property manager.

Most real estate investors start out by purchasing residential property. The first choice is often a single-family home or duplex.

There are many advantages to investing in a rental house. Rental houses are more affordable for the beginning investor than other types of income property. They are scarce in many communities, so they are often easy to rent. Single-family homes often attract stable tenants, such as single professionals or young families. Rental houses are usually easier to sell than other income property, in case the investor needs to liquidate. Also, single-family homes can be managed easily by the owner. Two- to four-unit residential properties have many of these same advantages. In addition, the investor may choose to live in one of the units of a duplex, triplex, or four-plex, which makes management even easier.

Qualities to Look For. Purchasing rental properties is often simpler than purchasing a home—it is a business decision rather than an emotional decision. When a family purchases a home, it looks for a house that fits its lifestyle and satisfies its emotional needs. On the other hand, a rental house usually has to meet only a few requirements: it should be in good condition, it should be located in a good neighborhood, it should contain enough square footage to satisfy the average tenant, and the design should not be so unconventional that it would alienate the average tenant.

The location of a rental property should appeal to its potential tenants, which typically include blue collar workers, single people, people pursuing careers, elderly people, and young families. The neighborhood should have easy access to employment centers, transportation, shopping, and schools. A rental house will have extra appeal if it is located near a college, hospital, or shopping center.

The structural components of the property should be in good condition. This will attract better tenants and eliminate the need for costly upkeep and repairs. The foundation is critical; are there any cracks, breaks, bulges, or shifts? The age and condition of the heating, wiring, and plumbing systems should be examined. Are they expensive to maintain or repair? What about the insulation? Will the tenant be faced with large electricity or gas bills?

Once an investor has found a suitable property in a good location, he or she will be ready to begin managing the property (perhaps with the help of a professional property manager) and learning first hand about how real estate investments work.

Property Management. A real estate investor may need to hire a property manager to oversee day-to-day operations of a large property. The duties of a property manager can include maintaining the property, performing repairs and periodic property inspections, handling tenant complaints, collecting rents, showing vacant units, and acting as a liaison between tenants and the owner. Under California law, a residential property with more than 15 units must have a resident manager (one who lives on the premises).

A property manager may be paid a flat fee or a commission. The commission could be a percentage of gross receipts, of new leases, or of the rent expected over the lease term.

📖 Chapter Summary

1. To accurately assess the value of a home, a real estate agent needs to be able to judge the quality of the construction. It is important to be familiar with common construction techniques and materials, and to have some understanding of the technical systems (plumbing, wiring, heating, and cooling). Knowing how to read plans and specifications can be very useful, especially when dealing with new construction.

2. A real estate agent is often asked to compare buying a home to renting one. The advantages of renting include less financial commitment and risk, fewer maintenance responsibilities, greater mobility, and facilities a homeowner often could not afford. The advantages of buying include security, satisfaction in ownership, privacy, and freedom from restrictions. Although a mortgage payment is typically much larger than a rental payment, property appreciation, equity, and tax deductions make buying less expensive than renting over the long run.

3. In addition to judging construction quality, a real estate agent helping a customer choose a home should evaluate the neighborhood, the site, and the exterior and interior design.

4. After purchasing a home, some people decide to venture into real estate investment. The advantages of real estate investment include appreciation, leverage, cash flow, and tax benefits. The disadvantages include the time required to choose and manage property, the fact that real estate investments are not liquid, and the risk of losing the investment.

🔑 Key Terms

Plans—Detailed technical drawings of the vertical and horizontal cross-sections of a building, used as a guide in its construction.

Specifications—Text that accompanies the plans of a building, describing the types of materials and the standards of workmanship to be used in the construction.

Investment—An asset that is expected to generate a return (a profit).

Portfolio—The mix of investments (plus cash reserves) owned by an individual or company.

Liquidity—An asset's ability to be converted into cash quickly.

Appreciation—When an asset increases in value. Appreciation may be due to inflation, or it may occur because the asset is becoming scarcer or demand for it is increasing.

Equity—The difference between the value of a property and the liens against it.

Leverage—Using borrowed money to invest in an asset. If the asset appreciates, the investor earns money on the borrowed funds as well as the funds he or she invested.

Cash flow—Spendable income; the amount of money left after all of the property's expenses have been paid, including operating costs, mortgage payments, and taxes.

Real estate investment syndicate—A group of people or companies who join together to purchase and develop a piece of real estate.

Real estate investment trust (REIT)—A trust that invests exclusively in real estate and real estate mortgages and qualifies for special tax treatment.

Real estate mortgage investment conduit (REMIC)—A special business entity that must invest a substantial amount of its funds in qualified mortgage loans to receive special tax treatment.

Chapter Quiz

1. In building construction, standards of construction quality are assured through:

   a) the planning commission
   b) zoning ordinances
   c) building codes
   d) None of the above

2. All of the following are likely to go up eventually; which of them will probably increase the most gradually?

   a) A rental payment
   b) A fixed-rate mortgage payment
   c) An adjustable-rate mortgage payment
   d) All of the above will increase at the same rate

3. All of the following lots contain the same area. Which would generally be considered the most desirable?

   a) A rectangular lot with a gentle slope
   b) A triangular lot with a steep slope
   c) A triangular lot with a gentle slope
   d) A level T-shaped lot

4. Which of the following is considered a drawback in a floor plan?

   a) A door leads directly from the kitchen to the garage
   b) The front door leads directly into the living room
   c) The separate dining room is right next to the kitchen
   d) The bedrooms are isolated from the kitchen and family room

5. The value of a home is enhanced if:

   a) there are rental properties in the neighborhood as well as owner-occupied homes
   b) there are retail businesses as well as homes on the block
   c) strict zoning laws have made the lots and houses in the neighborhood similar to one another
   d) All of the above

6. When comparing a mortgage payment to a rental payment, all of the following should be taken into account except:

   a) the landlord's equity in the rental property
   b) appreciation of the homeowner's property
   c) the federal tax deduction for mortgage interest
   d) whether the mortgage interest rate is fixed or adjustable

7. A house with many horizontal projections and vertical lines, and with large areas of glass, is classified as:

   a) contemporary
   b) ranch
   c) colonial
   d) Spanish

8. Which of the following is an advantage of renting, as opposed to owning, a home?

   a) Security and stability
   b) Appreciation
   c) Federal tax deduction
   d) Mobility

9. Which of the following is not drywall material?

   a) Wallboard
   b) Plywood
   c) Sheetrock
   d) Plaster

10. R-value is a term used in reference to:

   a) a type of loan
   b) a zoning classification
   c) a government agency
   d) insulation

11. The mix of investments owned by an individual or company is known as:

   a) a portfolio
   b) leverage
   c) yield
   d) equity

12. Martinson's investments consist of $10,000 in a money market account, $5,000 in a savings account, and $12,000 in certificates of deposit. Martinson's main investment concern is probably:

   a) a high return
   b) liquidity
   c) safety
   d) Both b) and c)

13. A major disadvantage of investing in real estate is:

   a) the use of leverage to increase returns
   b) lack of liquidity
   c) uniformly low returns
   d) the fact that a constantly increasing supply decreases values

14. Stocks, real estate, and investment in an REIT all have what in common?

   a) They are all considered liquid investments
   b) They are all very safe investments
   c) They all provide safe, but low, returns
   d) They are all ownership investments

15. The difference between the value of real property and the liens against it is:

   a) equity
   b) leverage
   c) yield
   d) cash flow

👉 **Answer Key**

1. c) Building codes are local ordinances that set standards for construction quality.

2. b) A fixed-rate mortgage payment will increase very gradually, as property taxes and mortgage insurance premiums go up.

3. a) Rectangular lots are preferred to odd-shaped lots because more of the area can be used efficiently. Steeply sloping lots are often difficult to build on and are unstable, so level land or a gentle slope is preferable.

4. b) It is a disadvantage to have the front door open directly into the living room (rather than into an entry hall), since it is then necessary to pass through the living room to get to the rest of the house. All of the other design features listed are considered advantages.

5. c) While few people would like all of the houses on their street to be identical, a reasonable degree of conformity is considered desirable and enhances the value of the homes.

6. a) The landlord's equity in the rental property is not likely to have much effect on the rental payment. However, appreciation, mortgage rates, and federal and state income tax deductions do affect how mortgage payments compare to rental payments.

7. a) The house described is contemporary, or modern, in design. One of the main features of contemporary houses is many large windows.

8. d) It is much easier and less expensive to move out of a rental than to sell a home and buy a new one. All of the other answers are advantages of owning a home.

9. d) Drywall material (unlike plaster) does not require the addition of water during construction.

10. d) R-value is a measure of insulating capacity.

11. a) A portfolio is the mixture of investments (and cash reserves) held by a person or entity.

12. d) All of these types of investments are both relatively liquid and relatively safe.

13. b) The lack of liquidity is a serious disadvantage of investing in real estate. The use of leverage is one of the benefits of investing in real estate.

14. d) Stocks and real estate (either owned directly or through a real estate investment trust) are both considered ownership investments.

15. a) The difference between the value of real estate and the liens against it is the owner's equity.

California Real Estate License Law

Chapter Overview

In California, the real estate profession is closely regulated by the state government. Both real estate licensing requirements and the day-to-day responsibilities of real estate agents are set forth in the Real Estate Law. This chapter discusses the various requirements of the Real Estate Law and how the law is administered. It also explains how antitrust laws affect real estate agents.

Administration of the Real Estate Law

California's **Real Estate Law** is contained in sections 10000 to 10580 of the Business and Professions Code. This law was passed to regulate the real estate profession and protect the public from incompetent, unethical, or dishonest real estate agents. The Real Estate Law is administered by the **Department of Real Estate**, a division of the California Business and Transportation Agency. The Real Estate Law is enforced by the chief officer of the Department of Real Estate, the **Real Estate Commissioner**.

Real Estate Commissioner

The Real Estate Commissioner's job is to implement and enforce the provisions of the Real Estate Law so as to give the maximum protection possible to those who deal with real estate licensees. The Commissioner is given many broad powers to accomplish this end.

Authority. The Commissioner has the power to adopt, amend, or repeal regulations necessary to enforce the Real Estate Law. These regulations have the force and effect of law. The Commissioner's regulations can be found in sections 2705 to 3109 of Title 10 in the California Code of Regulations.

The Commissioner also has the authority to:

- investigate non-licensees alleged to be performing activities for which a license is required;
- screen and qualify applicants for a license;
- investigate complaints against licensees; and
- regulate some aspects of the sale of subdivisions, franchises, and real property securities.

Furthermore, the Commissioner may:

- hold formal hearings to determine issues involving a licensee, a license applicant, or a subdivider and, after such a hearing, suspend, revoke, or deny a license or stop sales in a subdivision;
- bring actions for injunctions and claims for restitution on behalf of those injured by licensees who violate the Real Estate Law; and
- bring actions to stop trust fund violations.

The Real Estate Commissioner is advised on legal matters by the state Attorney General. However, it is the duty of the district attorney of each county to prosecute those who violate the Real Estate Law within that county.

Qualifications. The Real Estate Commissioner is appointed by the Governor and serves at his or her pleasure. To qualify for the position of Real Estate Commissioner, a person must have been a real estate broker, actively engaged in business for five years in California, or must have related experience associated with real estate activity in California for five of the previous ten years. The Commissioner (as well as any of his or her employees) is prohibited from engaging in professional real estate activities, and from having an interest in any real estate firm.

Fig.16.1 Commissioner's powers and duties

California Real Estate Commissioner

- Adopts and amends regulations to implement Real Estate Law
- Screens and qualifies real estate license applicants
- Issues, renews, or denies licenses
- Investigates complaints against licensees and enforces Real Estate Law
- Regulates some aspects of subdivisions, franchises, and real property securities

Real Estate Licenses

A common way of regulating an industry or profession is to require its members to be licensed. The state can try to control a licensed person's competence and professional activities by requiring education, testing, and recordkeeping, and by enforcing ethical standards.

When a License is Required

The Real Estate Law requires certain people to be licensed before they can engage in real estate activities: anyone who is acting, advertising, or appearing to act as a real estate broker or real estate salesperson must have a real estate license.

Definition of Real Estate Broker. A real estate broker is a person who does or negotiates to do certain acts on behalf of another, for compensation or in the expectation of compensation. These acts include:

1. selling, buying, leasing, or collecting rents from, or buying, selling, or exchanging leases on, real property or business opportunities (**exception:** a resident apartment manager, who manages the apartment complex in which he or she lives);
2. filing applications for the purchase or lease of federal land;
3. soliciting borrowers or lenders, negotiating loans, performing services in connection with loans, or buying, selling, or exchanging obligations secured by real property or business opportunities;

4. listing, advertising, or offering real property or business opportunities for sale, lease, exchange, or financing;
5. engaging as a principal in the business of buying for resale, selling, or exchanging eight or more real property securities (e.g., sales contracts or promissory notes) within one year; and
6. collecting an advance fee to promote the sale or lease of real property or business opportunities by advertising, by listing with a broker's association, or in some other way.

Fig.16.2 Types of licensees

Broker

- Individual, corporation, or partnership
- Authorized to operate brokerage and represent clients

Affiliated Licensees

- Work with and represent broker
- Cannot represent principal directly

Definition of Salesperson. A real estate salesperson is someone who is employed by a broker to do one or more of the acts listed above. It should be noted that a salesperson's license permits real estate activity only while in the employ of and under the control and supervision of a broker. A real estate salesperson cannot act directly for a principal in a real estate transaction.

Furthermore, a salesperson may receive compensation only from his or her own employing broker. Clients and cooperating brokers may not pay the salesperson directly. Instead, they pay the salesperson's employing broker, who then pays the salesperson.

In some cases a broker chooses to work for another broker instead of operating his or her own brokerage. Such a broker (who may be called an **associate broker**) has basically the same rights and limitations as a salesperson.

Penalties for Unlicensed Activities. The penalty for doing any of the acts listed above without a real estate broker's or salesperson's license is a fine of up to $10,000 and/or six months' imprisonment for an individual, or a fine of up to $50,000 for a corporation.

Note that it is unlawful for a broker to employ or compensate any unlicensed person for performing acts that require a salesperson's license. A broker who does so will be subject to disciplinary action and could have his or her license suspended or revoked.

When a License is Not Required

There are several important exceptions to the licensing requirements. These exceptions are meant to exclude those who are acting on their own behalf, those who are regulated by another agency (such as licensed securities brokers), and those who are merely performing clerical functions. The exceptions include:

1. those acting on their own behalf with respect to their own property;
2. a corporate officer acting on behalf of a corporation, or a general partner acting on behalf of a partnership, with respect to property owned, leased, or to be purchased or leased by the corporation or partnership;

3. a person acting under a duly recorded power of attorney from the owner of the property;
4. attorneys in the performance of their duties;
5. persons acting under court order (e.g., a receiver in bankruptcy or a trustee);
6. a trustee under a deed of trust;
7. with respect to real property securities transactions:
   a. employees of banks, savings and loan associations, insurance companies, or credit unions;
   b. licensed personal property brokers (e.g., finance companies);
8. with respect to business opportunity transactions, a licensed securities broker or dealer;
9. any cemetery authority that is authorized to do business in California, or its authorized agent;
10. persons performing clerical functions and not discussing the price, terms, or condition of the property;
11. the manager of a hotel, motel, or trailer park; and
12. persons who negotiate for the use of property for photographic purposes.

License Qualifications

Several qualifications must be met before a person can obtain a real estate license. By imposing these qualifications, particularly the education requirements, the state tries to ensure at least a minimum level of competence for all real estate professionals.

Salesperson's Qualifications. To obtain a salesperson's license, an applicant must:

1. be at least eighteen years old;
2. be honest and truthful;
3. pass the qualifying exam;
4. apply on the prescribed form;
5. pay the license fee;
6. be fingerprinted;
7. provide his or her social security number to the Department of Real Estate;
8. submit proof of legal presence (documentation showing that he or she is in the United States legally); and
9. complete nine semester units of education:
   a. One course, real estate principles, must be enrolled in before taking the examination and completed before applying for a license.
   b. Two more courses must be completed either before the original license is issued, or within 18 months of licensure. One course must be real estate practice, and the other must be chosen from the following: legal aspects of real estate, real estate appraisal, real estate financing, real estate economics or accounting, business law, escrow, property management, real estate office administration, mortgage loan brokering and lending, common interest developments, or computer applications in real estate. (Note: If the required education isn't completed within 18 months of licensure, the license is automatically suspended.)

Broker's Qualifications. To obtain a broker's license, an applicant must:

1. have two years of experience as a real estate licensee within the past five years;
2. be at least eighteen years old;
3. be honest and truthful;
4. pass the qualifying exam;
5. apply on the prescribed form;
6. pay the license fee;
7. be fingerprinted;
8. provide his or her social security number to the Department of Real Estate;
9. submit proof of legal presence (documentation showing that he or she is in the United States legally); and
10. complete 24 semester units (eight courses) of education:
    a. The following five courses must be completed: real estate practice, real estate appraisal, legal aspects of real estate, real estate financing, and either real estate economics or general accounting.
    b. The other three courses are chosen from this list: advanced legal aspects of real estate, advanced appraisal, advanced financing, real estate principles, property management, escrow, business law, real estate office administration, mortgage loan brokering and lending, common interest developments, or computer applications in real estate.

The experience requirement (item one on the list above) may be waived if the applicant either has the equivalent of two years of general real estate experience, or else has a degree from a four-year college or university in a course of study that included specialization in real estate. To obtain this type of waiver, an applicant must submit a written petition to the Department of Real Estate.

License Application and Term

License applicants must apply for their licenses within one year of the date of passing the exam (not the date of notice of passage). Brokers' and salespersons' licenses must be renewed every four years.

License Renewals. Licenses are renewed by completing the continuing education requirements (discussed below), applying to the Department of Real Estate, and paying the appropriate fees. The licensee does not have to take another examination. The renewal application must be postmarked prior to midnight of the expiration date to prevent the license from expiring. However, the renewal application may not be filed earlier than 90 days before the expiration date.

A renewal applicant who has not already submitted proof of legal presence in the United States to the Department of Real Estate will be required to do so at the time of renewal. (Resident aliens who don't have permanent status are required to submit proof of legal presence every time they renew their licenses.)

Late Renewal. A license that has expired within the previous two years may be renewed without examination, at the Commissioner's discretion. The licensee must file a renewal application and pay a late renewal fee. If the license is not renewed within the two-year grace period, all license rights are lost. This means that in order to be licensed again, the former licensee must meet all the requirements for original license applicants, including passing the qualifying exam again.

Late renewal is not allowed for a licensee whose initial license expires before he or she has completed the two courses (real estate practice and an elective) that are required within 18 months of licensure.

Continuing Education. A real estate license cannot be renewed unless the licensee fulfills the continuing education requirement. A special form that confirms attendance at the required courses must accompany the renewal application.

Initial Renewal. A salesperson renewing his or her license for the first time after it was issued must have completed four separate three-hour courses, one in each of these mandatory subjects: ethics, agency, trust fund handling, and fair housing. Thus, a total of 12 hours of continuing education is required.

The first time a broker's license is renewed, the broker must have taken a total of 45 hours of continuing education during the previous four years, including:

1. twelve hours of mandatory courses, consisting of four separate three-hour courses, one in each of the mandatory subjects (ethics, agency, trust fund handling, and fair housing);
2. at least 18 hours of courses designated as consumer protection courses; and
3. the remaining 15 hours in courses designated either as consumer protection courses or as consumer service courses (courses related to business skills that enable the licensee to competently serve customers).

Subsequent Renewals. For all subsequent renewals after the initial renewal, a salesperson or broker must have completed a total of 45 hours of continuing education during the previous four years, including the following courses:

1. a six-hour combined survey course covering the mandatory subjects (ethics, agency, trust fund handling, and fair housing);
2. at least 18 hours of consumer protection courses; and
3. the remaining 15 hours in consumer protection or consumer service courses.

Upcoming Changes in Continuing Education Requirements. As you can see, ethics, agency, trust fund handling, and fair housing are mandatory subjects for every license renewal. Legislation that will become effective on July 1, 2007 has added risk management to the list of mandatory subjects. The first time a licensee renews his or her license after July 1, 2007 (whether it's that licensee's initial renewal or a subsequent renewal), he or she will be required to have completed a three-hour risk management course. For later renewals, risk management will be incorporated into the combined survey course, which will be expanded from six hours to eight hours.

Once these new rules go into effect, the initial renewal of a salesperson's license will require a total of 15 hours (instead of 12 hours) of continuing education. However, the total hours required for subsequent renewals of a salesperson's license or for any renewal of a broker's license will not be increased; the requirement will still be 45 hours.

Exemption. A licensee 70 years old or older is not required to fulfill the continuing education requirement if he or she has been a real estate licensee in good standing in California for at least 30 years. The licensee must submit proof that he or she qualifies for this exemption to the Department of Real Estate.

Miscellaneous License Provisions

Location of Licenses. Brokers are required to keep the licenses of all of the salespersons they employ. All real estate licenses (including the broker's) must remain in the broker's main office.

Transfer of Salesperson's License. If a salesperson transfers employment from one broker to another, the Commissioner must be notified. The new broker must submit a notification form to the Department of Real Estate within five days after the salesperson enters his or her employment.

Termination of Employment. If a salesperson quits or is discharged by his or her broker, the broker is required to return the salesperson's license certificate to the salesperson within three business days.

Discharge for Disciplinary Cause. If a salesperson is discharged for conduct that is grounds for disciplinary action, the employing broker must file a certified written statement of facts with the Commissioner. If the broker fails to do so, his or her own license could be suspended or revoked.

Termination of Broker's License. If a broker's license is suspended or revoked, the licenses of all of the broker's salespersons are automatically canceled. The salespersons may transfer their licenses to other brokers.

If a broker's license expires, the salespersons' licenses are immediately placed on non-working status; the broker can reactivate them after renewing his or her own license.

Change of Name or Address. When a broker changes his or her office name or address, the broker must forward written notice to the Department of Real Estate within one business day. When the change occurs, the certificate can be corrected by the licensee.

To cancel or add a branch office, the broker must file a special form. Each branch office requires a separate license.

Fictitious Names. A real estate broker may obtain a license under a fictitious business name, unless the name:

1. is misleading or would constitute false advertising;
2. implies a partnership or corporation that does not exist;
3. includes the name of a real estate salesperson;
4. violates provisions of the law; or
5. is the name formerly used by a licensee whose license has since been revoked.

A fictitious business name statement must be filed with the clerk of the county where the business is located. In addition, the statement must be published at least once a week for four weeks in a newspaper in the county. An **affidavit** (a written statement sworn before a notary public) showing the publication must also be submitted to the county clerk. The statement expires five years after December 31 of the year it is initially filed.

Child Support Delinquency. The Department of Real Estate cannot issue or renew a license if the applicant's name appears on a list (provided by the California Department of Social Services) of persons who have not complied with a court order concerning child support payments. Also, if a current licensee's name appears on the list and is not removed within 150 days, the Department of Real Estate may suspend his or her license.

Special Licenses and Activities

Special real estate licenses are available for particular kinds of license applicants or in special circumstances. There are also some special activities that require only a real estate broker's license.

Corporate Licenses. A real estate license can be issued to a corporation. At least one corporate officer must be designated to act as the broker under the corporate brokerage license. That officer must also be individually licensed as a broker, and can only act as a broker with respect to the corporate brokerage.

Partnerships. While there is no "partnership license," a partnership may perform acts for which a broker's license is required, provided that every partner through whom the partnership acts is a licensed real estate broker.

Restricted Licenses. The Commissioner will sometimes issue a restricted license to replace a license that has been suspended or revoked. The restricted license is, in effect, a probationary license. It may have a limited term, restrict the licensee to certain types of activities, require employment by a particular broker or the filing of a surety bond, or impose other limitations.

Mineral, Oil, and Gas Transactions. Brokers are no longer required to have a special mineral, oil, and gas license or permit. Only a real estate license is required for transactions involving mineral, oil, or gas rights.

Real Property Securities Dealers. A real property securities dealer is a person engaged in the business of selling or reinvesting funds in real property securities. A real property securities dealer must have a real estate license, and in certain circumstances may also be required to have a special permit.

Prepaid Rental Listing Service. A prepaid rental listing service provides prospective tenants with listings of residential property available for rent. Tenants are charged a fee before or at the same time that the listing service provides the listings. The listing service is not involved in negotiating leases or rental agreements.

Licensed real estate brokers may operate a prepaid rental listing service without an additional license or a special permit. Other individuals or companies must obtain a prepaid rental listing service license from the Department of Real Estate.

Out-of-State Subdivisions. In order for a licensee to sell lots in an out-of-state subdivision, the subdivision must first be registered with the Department of Real Estate.

A real estate broker licensed in California can engage in transactions involving out-of-state property, as long as he or she remains physically in California. A California broker may also split a commission with an out-of-state broker.

Business Opportunities

A business opportunity is the sale or lease of a business, typically including inventory, fixtures, lease assignments, and goodwill. Listing a business opportunity or representing a buyer of a business opportunity requires a real estate license, even if there is no real property involved. If shares of stock in a corporation are involved in the sale, the agent may also need a securities license.

One common type of business opportunity is a **franchise agreement**, where the purchaser (franchisee) buys the right to sell goods under a brand name and marketing system offered by the franchisor in exchange for a franchise fee. A franchise may be sold by a real estate licensee, a securities licensee, or any person registered for that purpose with the Commissioner of Corporations.

Sales of business opportunities are subject to California sales and use taxes, since they involve the transfer of personal property. A buyer of a wholesale or retail business must obtain a Certificate of Clearance from the state Board of Equalization, certifying that the seller has paid his or her sales tax in full; otherwise, the buyer may have **successor's liability** for the seller's unpaid sales taxes and be required to pay them. To start operating the business, the buyer will have to obtain a seller's permit from the Board of Equalization.

Business opportunity buyers must also comply with the **Uniform Commercial Code**, which imposes certain requirements on bulk sales. A **bulk sale** is a sale, not in the ordinary course of the seller's business, of more than half of the seller's inventory. A buyer who is interested in a bulk sale must notify the seller's creditors by recording a notice of intent to buy with the county recorder, sending a notice of the purchase to the county tax collector by certified or registered mail, and publishing a notice in the local newspaper. If this notice requirement is not met, the buyer may become liable to the seller's creditors.

A sale of a business opportunity may also include the transfer of an alcoholic beverage license. Licenses authorizing the sale of alcoholic beverages are issued by the Department of Alcoholic Beverage Control, which first investigates the applicant and the proposed location before issuing a license. Notice of an application to sell alcoholic beverages must be posted on the proposed premises. An on-sale liquor license is one that may, subject to approval, be transferred from person to person or premises to premises. During the first five years after its issuance, an on-sale license may not be resold for more than $6,000, the cost of the initial application.

In a sale of a business opportunity, a bill of sale is typically used, since the sale usually involves the transfer of personal property. The bill of sale must contain the names of the transferor and transferee, the location of the business, and a description of the personal property, including any fixtures and equipment and the trade name. If the sale also involves real property, two sales agreements might be used, one for the real property and one for the personal property.

Escrow is typically used in a business opportunity transaction. Often, two separate escrows will be used, one for the real property involved and one for the personal property.

Disciplinary Action

Any law designed to regulate an industry will fail if its provisions are ignored by those who are supposed to be regulated. So the Real Estate Commissioner is empowered to enforce the Real Estate Law by investigating and disciplining licensees who violate its provisions.

Disciplinary Procedures

The Commissioner is required to investigate the actions of a licensee when someone makes a written complaint. The Commissioner may also investigate a licensee on his or her own motion, even when no formal complaint has been made. The investigation usually consists of getting statements from witnesses and the licensee; checking bank records, title company records, and public records; and perhaps calling an informal meeting of everyone concerned.

If it appears that a violation of the law has occurred, an **accusation** is filed. An accusation is a written statement of the charges against the accused licensee. The accusation must be filed within three years of the allegedly unlawful act, unless the act involved fraud, misrepresentation, or a false promise. In that case, an accusation must be filed within one year after discovery by the injured party or within three years after the act (whichever is later), but in no case can it be filed more than ten years after the act.

The licensee is served with the accusation. A date is set for an **administrative hearing**; an administrative law judge will hear the case. The accused licensee is also given an explanation of his or her rights at the hearing.

The licensee may appear at the hearing with or without an attorney. Testimony is taken under oath, and a record is made of the proceedings. The administrative judge then makes a proposed decision based on his or her findings. The Commissioner may accept or reject the proposed decision in making his or her own formal decision. If the evidence at the hearing substantiates the charges against the licensee, his or her license will be suspended or revoked, and he or she may not apply for reinstatement for one year. The licensee may petition for reconsideration, and also has the right to appeal the formal decision to superior court.

If it is in the public interest, the Commissioner may impose a fine rather than suspend or revoke a license. The amount of the monetary penalty cannot exceed $250 for each day the license would have been suspended, up to $10,000.

If a person obtains a license through fraud, misrepresentation, deceit, or material misstatements of fact, the license can be suspended without a hearing. This power of the Commissioner expires 90 days after the license is issued, and the suspension is effective only until a hearing is held and the Commissioner makes a formal decision.

Imposition of a fine or other disciplinary penalty by the Commissioner does not protect a licensee from criminal prosecution or from liability in a civil suit. This criminal or civil liability would not be considered "double jeopardy."

Grounds for Disciplinary Action

The grounds for suspending, revoking, or denying a license are set forth in the Real Estate Law; the main list can be found in Sections 10176 and 10177 of the Business and Professions Code. While the licensing and license renewal requirements discussed in the first part of this chapter attempt to ensure the licensee's minimum competence, it is this list of acts or omissions that sets the standard for the licensee's day-to-day behavior.

The grounds for disciplinary action include all of the following actions and conduct:

1. Making a substantial misrepresentation (deliberately or negligently making a false statement of fact, or failing to disclose a material fact to a principal).

2. Making a false promise that is likely to persuade someone to do or refrain from doing something.

3. Embarking on a continued and flagrant course of misrepresentation or false promises.

4. Acting as a dual agent without the knowledge or consent of all of the parties involved.

5. Commingling your own money or property with money or property you received or are holding on behalf of a client or customer (trust funds).

6. Failing to put a definite termination date in an exclusive listing agreement.

7. Making an undisclosed amount of compensation on a transaction (a secret profit).

8. If you have a listing agreement that includes an option to purchase the listed property, exercising the option without revealing to the principal in writing the amount of profit to be made and obtaining the principal's written consent.

9. Acting in any way, whether specifically prohibited by statute or not, that constitutes fraud or dishonest dealing.

10. Getting a purchaser's written agreement to buy a business opportunity property and to pay a commission, without first obtaining the written authorization of the property owner (a listing agreement).

11. Failing to comply with the law that requires a real property transfer disclosure statement in certain transactions.

12. Acquiring or renewing a license by fraud, misrepresentation, or deceit.

13. Being convicted of a felony or a misdemeanor involving moral turpitude.

14. False advertising.

15. Willfully disregarding or violating the Real Estate Law or the Commissioner's regulations.

16. Willfully using the term "Realtor®" or any trade name of a real estate organization that you are not actually a member of.

17. Having a real estate license denied, revoked, or suspended in another state for actions that would be grounds for denial, revocation, or suspension in California.

18. Performing license activities negligently or incompetently.

19. As a broker, failing to exercise reasonable supervision over the activities of your salespersons.

20. Using government employment to gain access to private records, and improperly disclosing their confidential contents.

21. Violating the terms of a restricted license.

22. Using "blockbusting" tactics: soliciting business on the basis of statements regarding race, color, sex, religion, ancestry, marital status, or national origin.

23. Violating the Corporations Code or the Franchise Investment Law.

24. When selling property in which you have a direct or indirect ownership interest, failing to disclose the nature and extent of that interest to a buyer.

25. Having a final judgment entered against you in a civil suit for fraud, misrepresentation, or deceit in regard to a real estate transaction.

26. As a broker, failing to notify the Commissioner in writing of the discharge of any salesperson based on his or her violation of the license law or regulations.

27. Committing fraud in an application for the registration of a mobile home, failing to provide for the delivery of a properly endorsed certificate of ownership of a mobile home from the seller to the buyer, or participating in the sale or disposal of a stolen mobile home.

28. Failing to include a licensee designation and your employing broker's name in advertisements (placing "blind ads").

29. As a broker, failing to notify the buyer and the seller, in writing, of the property's selling price within one month after the sale closes, unless escrow issues a closing statement.

30. Employing or compensating an unlicensed person for any act that requires a license.

31. Failing to give a copy of any contract to the person signing it at the time of signing.

32. Accepting compensation for referring a customer to any of these types of companies: escrow, pest control, home warranty, or title insurer.

Examples of Unlawful Conduct

The Department of Real Estate's *Reference Book* lists examples of unlawful conduct that would be grounds for disciplinary action. It is divided into two parts: unlawful conduct in sale, lease, and exchange transactions, and unlawful conduct in loan transactions. This list is reprinted here in full.

Examples of Unlawful Conduct—Sale, Lease, or Exchange. In a sale, lease, or exchange transaction, conduct such as the following may result in license discipline under Sections 10176 or 10177 of the Business and Professions Code:

1. Knowingly making a substantial misrepresentation of the likely value of real property to:
   a) Its owner either for the purpose of securing a listing or for the purpose of acquiring an interest in the property for the licensee's own account.
   b) A prospective buyer for the purpose of inducing the buyer to make an offer to purchase the real property.

2. Representing to an owner of real property when seeking a listing that the licensee has obtained a bona fide written offer to purchase the property, unless at the time of the representation the licensee has possession of a bona fide written offer to purchase.

3. Stating or implying to an owner of real property during listing negotiations that the licensee is precluded by law, by regulation, or by the rules of any organization, other than the broker firm seeking the listing, from charging less than the commission or fee quoted to the owner by the licensee.

4. Knowingly making substantial misrepresentations regarding the licensee's relationship with an individual broker, corporate broker, or franchised brokerage company or that entity's/person's responsibility for the licensee's activities.

5. Knowingly underestimating the probable closing costs in a communication to the prospective buyer or seller of real property in order to induce that person to make or to accept an offer to purchase the property.

6. Knowingly making a false or misleading representation to the seller of real property as to the form, amount and/or treatment of a deposit toward the purchase of the property made by an offeror.

7. Knowingly making a false or misleading representation to a seller of real property, who has agreed to finance all or part of a purchase price by carrying back a loan, about a buyer's ability to repay the loan in accordance with its terms and conditions.

8. Making an addition to or modification of the terms of an instrument previously signed or initialed by a party to a transaction without the knowledge and consent of the party.

9. A representation made as a principal or agent to a prospective purchaser of a promissory note secured by real property about the market value of the securing property without a reasonable basis for believing the truth and accuracy of the representation.

10. Knowingly making a false or misleading representation or representing, without a reasonable basis for believing its truth, the nature and/or condition of the interior or exterior features of a property when soliciting an offer.

11. Knowingly making a false or misleading representation or representing, without a reasonable basis for believing its truth, the size of a parcel, square footage of improvements or the location of the boundary lines of real property being offered for sale, lease or exchange.

12. Knowingly making a false or misleading representation or representing to a prospective buyer or lessee of real property, without a reasonable basis to believe its truth, that the property can be used for certain purposes with the intent of inducing the prospective buyer or lessee to acquire an interest in the real property.

13. When acting in the capacity of an agent in a transaction for the sale, lease or exchange of real property, failing to disclose to a prospective purchaser or lessee facts known to the licensee materially affecting the value or desirability of the property, when the licensee has reason to believe that such facts are not known to nor readily observable by a prospective purchaser or lessee.

14. Willfully failing, when acting as a listing agent, to present or cause to be presented to the owner of the property any written offer to purchase

received prior to the closing of a sale, unless expressly instructed by the owner not to present such an offer, or unless the offer is patently frivolous.

15. When acting as the listing agent, presenting competing written offers to purchase real property to the owner in such a manner as to induce the owner to accept the offer which will provide the greatest compensation to the listing broker without regard to the benefits, advantages and/or disadvantages to the owner.

16. Failing to explain to the parties or prospective parties to a real estate transaction for whom the licensee is acting as an agent the meaning and probable significance of a contingency in an offer or contract that the licensee knows or reasonably believes may affect the vacating of the property by the seller or its occupancy by the buyer.

17. Failing to disclose to the seller of real property in a transaction in which the licensee is an agent for the seller the nature and extent of any direct or indirect interest that the licensee expects to acquire as a result of the sale. (The licensee should disclose to the seller: prospective purchase of the property by a person related to the licensee by blood or marriage; purchase by an entity in which the licensee has an ownership interest; or purchase by any other person with whom the licensee occupies a special relationship where there is a reasonable probability that the licensee could be indirectly acquiring an interest in the property.)

18. Failing to disclose to the buyer of real property in a transaction in which the licensee is an agent for the buyer the nature and extent of a licensee's direct or indirect ownership interest in such real property: e.g., the direct or indirect ownership interest in the property by a person related to the licensee by blood or marriage; by an entity in which the licensee has an ownership interest; or by any other person with whom the licensee occupies a special relationship.

19. Failing to disclose to a principal for whom the licensee is acting as an agent any significant interest the licensee has in a particular entity when the licensee recommends the use of the services or products of such entity.

Examples of Unlawful Conduct—Loan Transactions. Conduct such as the following when soliciting, negotiating or arranging a loan secured by real property or the sale of a promissory note secured by real property may result in license discipline:

1. Knowingly misrepresenting to a prospective borrower of a loan to be secured by real property or to an assignor/endorser of a promissory note secured by real property that there is an existing lender willing to make the loan or that there is a purchaser for the note, for the purpose of inducing the borrower or assignor/endorser to utilize the services of the licensee.

2. Knowingly making a false or misleading representation to a prospective lender or purchaser of a loan secured directly or collaterally by real property about a borrower's ability to repay the loan in accordance with its terms and conditions.

3. Failing to disclose to a prospective lender or note purchaser information about the prospective borrower's identity, occupation, employment, income and credit data as represented to the broker by the prospective borrower.

4. Failing to disclose information known to the broker relative to the ability of the borrower to meet his or her potential or existing contractual obligations under the note or contract, including information known about the borrower's payment history on an existing note, whether the note is in default or the borrower in bankruptcy.

5. Knowingly underestimating the probable closing costs in a communication to a prospective borrower or lender of a loan to be secured by a lien on real property for the purpose of inducing the borrower or lender to enter into the loan transaction.

6. When soliciting a prospective lender to make a loan to be secured by real property, falsely representing or representing without a reasonable basis to believe its truth, the priority of the security, as a lien against the real property securing the loan, i.e., a first, second or third deed of trust.

7. Knowingly misrepresenting in any transaction that a specific service is free when the licensee knows or has a reasonable basis to know that it is covered by a fee to be charged as part of the transaction.

8. Knowingly making a false or misleading representation to a lender or assignee/endorsee of a lender of a loan secured directly or collaterally by a lien on real property about the amount and treatment of loan payments, including loan payoffs, and the failure to account to the lender or assignee/ endorsee of a lender as to the disposition of such payments.

9. When acting as a licensee in a transaction for the purpose of obtaining a loan, and in receipt of an advance fee from the borrower for this purpose, failure to account to the borrower for the disposition of the advance fee.

10. Knowingly making a false or misleading representation about the terms and conditions of a loan to be secured by a lien on real property when soliciting a borrower or negotiating the loan.

11. Knowingly making a false or misleading representation or representing, without a reasonable basis for believing its truth, when soliciting a lender or negotiating a loan to be secured by a lien on real property, about the market value of the securing real property, the nature and/or condition of the interior or exterior features of the securing real property, its size or the square footage of any improvements on the securing real property.

As you can see, there are many grounds for disciplinary action in California. These provisions are the state's attempt to prevent unscrupulous behavior by real estate licensees. However, suspending a real estate license after the fact does not help someone who lost money because of a licensee's unlawful actions. Of course, the injured party has a right to sue the licensee in a civil court, but what if the licensee has no money or other assets? In that case, a civil judgment would be worthless. Under those circumstances, the state has provided an additional means of redress, through the Real Estate Fund.

The Real Estate Fund

All license fees go to the State Treasury and are then credited to a fund called the **Real Estate Fund**. Some of the money in the Real Estate Fund is then disbursed to other accounts. Up to 8% of the money is credited to an **Education and Research Account**, and is then used to advance real estate education and research projects. Up to 12% of the money in the Real Estate Fund is credited to the **Recovery Account**. The purpose of the Recovery Account is to reimburse those injured by real estate licensees.

When an injured party gets a civil judgment (or arbitration award) against a licensee based on the licensee's intentional fraud, misrepresentation, or deceit or conversion of trust funds, the injured party can apply to the Recovery Account for payment of the judgment. The injured party must be able to show that the licensee has no funds or assets that could be seized to pay the judgment.

The Recovery Account will pay up to $20,000 for losses in a single transaction and up to $100,000 for losses caused by one licensee. Once payment is made from the Recovery Account on behalf of a licensee, his or her license is automatically suspended as of the day of payment. The license can't be reinstated until the amount disbursed from the Recovery Account is fully repaid, with interest. Even bankruptcy does not release the licensee from this obligation.

Trust Funds

The most common cause of disciplinary action is the mishandling of trust funds. This is largely due to confusion as to what trust funds are and what is to be done with them. However, California law is very specific about how trust funds are to be handled, and it is imperative for licensees to be thoroughly acquainted with the rules and regulations governing trust funds.

Definition of Trust Funds

The first step toward properly handling trust funds is learning to recognize them. Simply stated, trust funds are money or other valuables in the possession of a licensee that belong to someone else. Trust funds can be cash, a check, a promissory note, or any other item of personal property. The licensee merely holds the money or property on behalf of another party (usually a client or customer) while a real estate transaction is in progress. The Department of Real Estate's *Reference Book* provides this definition of trust funds:

> *Money or other things of value received by a broker or salesperson on behalf of a principal or any other person, and which are held for the benefit of others in the performance of any acts for which a real estate license is required.*

The most common example of trust funds is the good faith deposit that a buyer gives to the broker along with the buyer's offer to purchase real property. The broker holds the deposit "in trust" while the seller decides whether or not to accept the buyer's offer.

Advance fees are also considered trust funds. These are fees that a seller may pay in advance to defray costs associated with a listing, such as marketing and advertising expenses.

Other types of funds, such as real estate commissions, general operating funds, or rent from a broker's own real estate, are not trust funds, because the broker is not holding them on behalf of someone else.

Handling Trust Funds

Because trust funds belong to someone else, licensees must manage them carefully. Licensees violate not only the license law, but also their fiduciary duties as agents, if they fail to handle trust funds properly.

When a broker accepts trust funds from a client or customer, he or she must deposit them into:

1. a neutral escrow account,
2. the hands of the principal, or
3. a trust account maintained by the broker in a bank or other recognized depository.

The trust funds must be deposited no later than three business days following the receipt of the funds. If the funds are deposited into escrow or the hands of the principal rather than into the broker's trust account, the transfer must be noted in the broker's trust fund records.

If trust funds are given to a salesperson instead of directly to the broker, the salesperson must immediately deliver the funds to the broker, or, if so directed by the broker, to one of the three places listed above.

There is one exception to these rules. When a broker receives a deposit check from a buyer, the broker can hold the check uncashed before the buyer's offer is accepted, if:

1. the check is not negotiable by the licensee, or the buyer has given written instructions that the check is not to be deposited or cashed until the offer is accepted; and
2. the seller is informed (before or when the offer is presented) that the check is being held.

Once the offer is accepted, the broker can continue to hold the uncashed check only if he or she receives written authorization from the seller to do so.

Trust funds must stay in the trust account until their owner directs otherwise. While the owner of the trust funds is usually easy to identify, it should be noted that the ownership of trust funds may change as the real estate transaction progresses. For example, the ownership of a good faith deposit varies depending on whether or not the buyer's offer has been accepted. Before acceptance, the funds belong to the buyer and must be handled according to his or her instructions. After acceptance, however, ownership is not so clear-cut, and the funds must be handled as follows:

- A check held uncashed by the broker before acceptance of the offer may continue to be held uncashed only on written authorization from the seller.
- The check may be given to the seller only if both parties so provide in writing.
- No part of the deposit money can be refunded without the express written permission of the seller.

If a transaction falls through after the good faith deposit has been deposited into escrow or a broker's trust account, there may be a dispute over the money; the buyer and seller may each feel entitled to it. In this situation, the escrow agent or broker who holds the funds in trust may file an **interpleader** action, turning the matter over to a court. The court will decide which party is the rightful owner of the funds.

Trust Accounts

The primary reason for maintaining a separate account for trust funds is to avoid **commingling**. Commingling means mixing trust funds with personal funds. A broker must never put trust funds into his or her general account. Likewise, the broker must never put his or her own funds into a trust account. This is true even if careful records are kept of the deposits and withdrawals.

Commingling should not be confused with **conversion**, which is the actual misappropriation of a party's funds for the broker's own purposes. Conversion is a basis for theft charges under the California penal code. Theft may also include removing a piece of real or personal property, or defrauding another person of money, labor, or real or personal property.

The prohibition against commingling makes it more difficult for a broker to "borrow" trust funds. The prohibition also protects trust funds from any legal action that might be taken against the broker.

> **Example:** Suppose a broker dies, or is sued by a client. The broker's general account could very well be frozen during the course of the probate or lawsuit. If trust funds were kept in the broker's general account, they would be unavailable to the client until the probate was completed or the lawsuit concluded.

Also, if trust funds were placed in the broker's general account, a judgment creditor might be able to seize those funds along with the broker's own funds.

Shortages or Overages. The total amount of funds in the trust account must always equal the broker's aggregate trust fund liability. The process of comparing the trust fund balance to the sum of individual transactions is called **reconciliation**. When reconciled, the trust account balance must equal the total of the balances due to individual clients and customers.

If the trust account balance is less than the total liability, there is a **trust fund shortage**. Such a shortage is a violation of the Real Estate Commissioner's regulations. If the trust account balance is greater than the total liability, there is a **trust fund overage**.

Fig.16.3 Rules for handling trust funds

Handling Trust Funds

- Must be deposited within three days following receipt.

- Salesperson must deliver funds to broker or deposit in trust account.

- Check for good faith deposit can be held uncashed before buyer's acceptance under certain circumstances.

- Broker must not commingle his or her own funds with trust funds.

This is also a violation of the regulations, since non-trust funds cannot be commingled with trust funds.

A broker should always make sure that a check deposited into the trust account has cleared before disbursing any funds against the check. If funds are disbursed and the check has not cleared, or the check bounces, a trust fund shortage will occur.

Exceptions to Commingling Rule. There are two exceptions to the rule against commingling.

1. The broker must pay the service charges on the trust account out of his or her general funds. The broker can have up to $200 of personal funds in a trust account for this purpose. However, it is better to have the bank deduct the trust account service fees directly from the broker's general account.

2. Sometimes a broker is entitled to deduct his or her commission from trust funds. In this case, the broker should promptly transfer the commission out of the trust account into his or her general account. However, if it is not practical to transfer the commission immediately, it can stay in the trust account for up to 25 days.

   The broker should never pay personal obligations out of the trust account, even if the payments are a draw against the broker's commission. The earned commission must be transferred to the broker's general account before it can be used to pay personal obligations.

Account Requirements. A trust account must be opened in the broker's name as it appears on the broker's license, in a recognized financial institution in California. The account must be specifically designated as a trust account, with the broker as trustee. The financial institution cannot require prior written notice before allowing withdrawals from the account.

The trust account cannot be an interest-bearing account, with one exception: at the request of the trust fund owner, the broker can deposit the trust funds into a separate interest-bearing trust account, as long as the broker discloses how the interest is calculated, who pays the service charges, and how the interest is to be paid. The broker may not receive any of the interest.

Withdrawals. Withdrawals from a trust account generally require the signature of the broker (or in the case of a corporation licensed as a broker, the signature of the designated broker-officer). However, a broker may also authorize the following individuals to withdraw trust funds:

1. a salesperson or associate broker employed by the broker; or
2. any unlicensed employee, provided that he or she is covered by a fiduciary bond equal to the total amount held in trust.

While a broker can authorize other people to withdraw trust funds, he or she cannot delegate responsibility for the funds. The broker is always accountable for any trust fund violation, even if the violation was caused by the negligence or irresponsibility of an employee.

Trust Fund Records

It is very important to keep proper records of all trust funds, including trust fund checks that are held uncashed, trust funds that are sent directly to escrow, and trust funds that have been released to the owner. Thorough trust fund records enable the broker to prepare accurate accountings for clients, to calculate the amounts owed to clients at any given time, and to see if there is an imbalance in the trust account. The broker should reconcile his or her trust account records on a monthly basis.

A broker can use one of two types of accounting systems to keep track of trust funds: a simple columnar system or an alternative system that complies with general accounting practices. Regardless of which method is used, the accounting system must show the following:

1. all trust fund receipts and disbursements with pertinent details in chronological order;
2. the balance of each trust account based on all recorded transactions;
3. all receipts and disbursements affecting each client or customer's account in chronological order; and
4. the balance owing to each beneficiary based on recorded transactions.

Columnar System. If a broker chooses to use the columnar recordkeeping system, there are three types of records he or she must keep:

1. **A record of all trust funds received and disbursed.** This record is used to list all trust funds deposited to and disbursed from the trust account. It must include the following information:
   a. the date the funds were received;
   b. from whom they were received;
   c. the amount received;
   d. the date of deposit;
   e. for disbursements, the party to whom the funds were paid;
   f. the amount paid out;
   g. the check number and date; and
   h. the daily balance of the bank account.

2. **A record for each client/customer or transaction.** This record lists the funds received from or for each client or customer. It must include the following information:
   a. the date of the deposit;
   b. the amount of the deposit;
   c. the name of the payee or the payor;
   d. for funds paid out, the check number, date, and amount; and
   e. the daily balance of the individual account.

3. **A record of trust funds received but not deposited into the trust account.** This record must show:
   a. the date the funds were received;
   b. the form of the payment;
   c. the amount received;
   d. a description of any property received in lieu of funds;
   e. where the funds were forwarded to; and
   f. the date of disposition.

General Accounting Practices System. If a broker uses a system that complies with generally accepted accounting practices, that system must include a journal, a cash ledger, and beneficiary records for each trust account.

1. **Journal.** A journal is a daily chronological record of trust fund receipts and disbursements that shows:
   a. all trust fund transactions in chronological order;
   b. enough information to identify the transaction (e.g., date, amount received, name of payee, etc.); and
   c. the total receipts and total disbursements at least once a month.

2. **Cash ledger.** This shows, usually in summary form, the increases and decreases in the trust account and the resulting account balance.

3. **Beneficiary ledger.** A beneficiary ledger must be maintained for each client or customer, or for each transaction or series of transactions. It shows, in chronological order, the details of all receipts and disbursements relating to the individual account, and the resulting account balance.

All trust fund records are subject to inspection by the Commissioner. The broker must keep copies of all trust records (including canceled checks) for each transaction for three years. The three-year period begins on the date the transaction closes, or on the date of the listing if the transaction does not close.

Documentation Requirements

In addition to trust fund records, the Department of Real Estate also requires brokers to keep all of the documents connected with a real estate transaction. These documents include:

- listings;
- purchase and sale agreements;
- rent collection receipts;
- bank deposit slips;
- canceled checks;
- supporting papers for checks, such as invoices, escrow statements, or receipts;
- agency disclosure statements;
- transfer disclosure statements; and
- property management agreements.

These documents must be kept for at least three years, beginning with the date of closing (or the date of listing, if the transaction doesn't close), and they must be available for inspection by the Commissioner. If there is sufficient cause, these records may be audited.

The following documents must be kept for four years instead of three: real property security statements, and disclosure statements given to noninstitutional lenders or trust deed purchasers.

Copies Given to Signators

Whenever a broker or salesperson prepares a document for signature, he or she must deliver a copy of the document to the person signing it when the signature is obtained. This rule applies to listing agreements, purchase and sale agreements, contract addenda, and property management agreements.

Broker's Review of Documentation

Brokers are responsible for supervising their salespersons, and failure to do so is grounds for disciplinary action. The broker's supervisory responsibilities include reviewing any documents prepared by a salesperson that may have a material effect on the rights or obligations of a party to a transaction.

Broker-Salesperson Agreements

Whenever a broker hires a real estate salesperson, there must be a written agreement that documents their employment relationship. The broker must keep the agreement on file at the broker's office, and then retain the agreement for three years after the relationship is terminated.

Advertising Regulations

Real estate licensees need to be aware of the laws that regulate advertising—not just those that pertain specifically to real estate, but also more general rules, such as the prohibition against false advertising. A violation of state laws against false advertising is a misdemeanor; it's also a violation of the Real Estate Law.

Blind Ads

The most important rule that brokers and salespersons must be aware of is the prohibition against **blind ads**. An advertisement published by a licensee must include the name of the broker submitting the ad and indicate that it was placed by a licensee. (This rule doesn't apply when a licensee advertises his or her own property for sale, since that isn't an act for which a real estate license is required.)

Internet Advertising

Brokers who advertise or provide information about real estate services on the Internet or the Web are required to comply with a rule concerning contact with specific customers. There must be procedures in place to ensure that only a real estate licensee (or someone exempt from the licensing requirement) responds to inquiries from customers or otherwise contacts customers.

Advertising Loans and Notes

California imposes additional regulations on a licensee's advertisements for loans secured by real property. Any ad of this type must receive prior approval from the Department of Real Estate before it is published. Naturally, any ad that is misleading or deceptive will not be approved.

Ads for loans may not use a phrase like "guaranteed" without explaining how the loan is secured. They also may not imply that a loan can or will be approved over the telephone; that any government agency has endorsed the licensee's business activities; or that loans are available on terms more favorable than those generally available in the community, unless the advertiser can show that those terms would be available without undisclosed restrictions or conditions.

Similar regulations apply to ads concerning the resale of promissory notes. For instance, an advertisement may not guarantee a yield on a note other than the interest rate specified in the note unless it also includes the amount of the discount. (The discount is the difference between the outstanding note balance and the sales price of the note.)

Inducements

Sometimes a gift, prize, or rebate will be offered as an **inducement**, either for attending a sales presentation or for purchasing property. (Inducements are always forbidden as part of loan transactions.) If attendance at a sales presentation is required to obtain a gift, that must be disclosed in the advertisement or solicitation. Any other conditions for receiving gifts or prizes must also be disclosed. Note that if an inducement is given to one of the parties in a transaction, it is a material fact that must be disclosed to all of the parties.

Do Not Call Registry

Licensees who solicit business by making "cold calls" to strangers must comply with the Federal Trade Commission's telemarketing rules. It's against the law to make this type of call to someone whose name appears on the National "Do Not Call" Registry, so licensees must check the registry before placing calls.

Antitrust Laws and Their Effect on Licensees

In addition to the Real Estate Law, federal antitrust laws impose certain restrictions on a real estate agent's behavior towards clients, customers, and other agents.

Federal antitrust laws are not new: the **Sherman Act** was passed in 1890, well over a century ago. The Sherman Act prohibits any agreement that has the effect of restraining trade, including conspiracies. A **conspiracy** occurs when two or more business entities participate in a common scheme, the effect of which is the restraint of trade.

At the foundation of antitrust laws is the notion that free enterprise is a part of our democratic society, and that competition is good for both the economy and society as a whole. While many people associate antitrust laws with big steel mills and telephone companies, in 1950 antitrust laws were held to apply to the real estate industry. In a landmark case, the United States Supreme Court held that mandatory fee schedules, established and enforced by a real estate board, violated the Sherman Act (*United States v. National Association of Real Estate Boards*).

If a real estate agent violates antitrust laws, he or she may be subject to both civil and criminal actions. If an individual is found guilty of violating the Sherman Act, he or she can be fined up to one million dollars and/or sentenced to ten years' imprisonment. If a corporation is found guilty of violating the Sherman Act, it can be fined up to one hundred million dollars.

The activities that are prohibited by antitrust laws can be grouped into three main categories:

- price fixing (fixing commission rates),
- group boycotts, and
- tie-in arrangements.

Price Fixing

Price fixing is defined as the cooperative setting of prices or price ranges by competing firms. To avoid the appearance of price fixing, two agents from different brokerages should never discuss their commission rates. It is a discussion between competing agents that is dangerous—a broker can discuss commission rates with his or her own salespeople. One exception to this general prohibition is that two competing brokers may discuss a commission split (the division of the commission between the listing broker and the selling broker) in a cooperative sale.

Even a casual announcement that a broker is planning on raising his or her commission rates could lead to antitrust problems.

> **Example:** Broker Wood goes to a dinner given by his local MLS. He is called on to discuss current market conditions and, in the middle of his speech, he announces that he is going to raise his commission rate, no matter what anyone else does. This statement could be viewed as an invitation to conspire to fix prices. If any other MLS members raise their rates in response to his announcement, they can be held to have accepted Wood's invitation to conspire.

Brokers must understand that they do not have to actually consult with each other to be charged with conspiring to fix commission rates. The kind of scenario described in the previous example is enough to lead to an antitrust lawsuit.

Publications that appear to fix prices are prohibited as well. Any MLS or other association that publishes "recommended" or "going" rates for commissions could be sued.

Group Boycotts

A group boycott is an agreement between two or more real estate brokers to exclude other brokers from fair participation in real estate activities.

> **Example:** Becker and Jordan are both brokers. Over lunch together, they discuss the business practices of a third broker, Harley. Becker says she thinks Harley is dishonest. Jordan agrees. He says that he's decided not to do business with Harley. He avoids Harley whenever possible, and just doesn't call back if Harley calls to ask about a listed property. He suggests that Becker should do the same. Jordan and Becker could be found guilty of a conspiracy to boycott.

If a broker feels another broker is dishonest or unethical, he or she may choose not to do business with him or her. However, that broker cannot encourage other brokers to do the same.

The purpose of group boycotts is to hurt or destroy a competitor, and they are automatically unlawful under antitrust laws.

Tie-in Arrangements

A tie-in arrangement is defined as "an agreement to sell one product, only on the condition that the buyer also purchases a different (or tied) product..."

Example: Brown is a subdivision developer. Tyson, a builder, wants to buy a lot. Brown tells Tyson that he will sell him a lot only if Tyson enters into a list-back agreement. In other words, Tyson must sign a contract promising that after he builds a house on the lot, he will list the improved property with Brown.

Tie-in arrangements are automatically violations of the antitrust laws. (Note that list-back agreements only violate antitrust laws if they are a required condition of the sale. Two parties may mutually agree on a list-back agreement without violating antitrust laws.)

Avoiding Antitrust Violations. There are several ways to prevent possible antitrust violations. Brokers should:

- always establish their fees and other listing policies independently, without consulting competing firms;
- never use listing forms that contain preprinted commission rates;
- never imply to a client that the commission rate is fixed or non-negotiable, or refer to a competitor's commission policies when discussing commission rates;
- never discuss their business plans with competitors;
- never tell clients or competitors that they won't do business with a competing firm, or tell them not to work with that firm because of doubts about its competence or integrity; and
- train their licensees to be aware of what may constitute an antitrust law violation.

Chapter Summary

1. The California Real Estate Law requires those engaging in real estate activities to be licensed, and then regulates the actions of licensees. The purpose of the Real Estate Law is to protect members of the public who deal with real estate agents.

2. The Real Estate Commissioner implements the provisions of the Real Estate Law by enacting regulations, investigating the activities of licensees, and taking disciplinary action against those who violate the Real Estate Law.

3. The Real Estate Law determines who is required to have a real estate license and sets forth the licensing requirements for brokers and salespersons.

4. The Real Estate Law and related regulations also establish standards of lawful conduct and specify the grounds for disciplinary action.

5. It is essential for a licensee to know the rules concerning trust funds. Trust funds generally must be deposited into a trust account or a neutral escrow, or delivered to the principal, within three business days after they are received.

6. Brokers are required to keep trust account and transaction records for at least three years.

7. Antitrust laws prohibit price fixing, group boycotts, and tie-in arrangements. Real estate brokers must be especially careful to avoid discussing commission rates with competing brokers.

🔑 Key Terms

Real Estate Law—A California statute that governs the licensing and business practices of real estate agents.

Department of Real Estate—The government agency that administers the Real Estate Law.

Real estate broker—A person who is licensed to represent others for compensation in real estate transactions.

Real estate salesperson—A person who is licensed to work for and represent a broker in real estate transactions.

Real Estate Fund—A special account into which all license fees are placed.

Recovery Account—An account funded by license fees, used to reimburse those injured by the unlawful acts of real estate licensees.

Trust funds—Funds held by a broker on behalf of clients or customers.

Commingling—The mingling of trust funds with a broker's personal or business funds.

Trust account—A bank account held in a broker's name and specially designated for trust funds. A trust account is used to keep trust funds segregated from the broker's personal or business funds.

Price fixing—The cooperative setting of prices by competing firms.

Group boycott—An agreement between two or more real estate brokers to exclude other brokers from fair participation in real estate activities.

Tie-in arrangement—An agreement to sell one product only on the condition that the buyer also purchases a different product.

Chapter Quiz

1. Someone applying to renew his or her real estate license usually must have completed _____ hours of approved courses within the four-year period preceding license renewal.

   a) 15
   b) 20
   c) 45
   d) 90

2. A corporation may engage in the real estate brokerage business if the officer acting for the corporation:

   a) is a licensed salesperson
   b) is given the proper authority from the Corporations Commissioner
   c) is a licensed broker
   d) is the president of the corporation

3. Commingling is:

   a) the same as embezzlement
   b) mixing personal funds with trust funds
   c) any dishonest behavior related to trust funds
   d) paying a commission to a non-licensed person

4. Brokers must retain copies of all listings, purchase and sale agreements, and trust records for:

   a) one year
   b) two years
   c) three years
   d) four years

5. Withdrawals cannot be made from a broker's trust account by:

   a) a salesperson in the broker's employ who has been authorized by the broker
   b) the broker's secretary, who has been authorized by the broker and is covered by a fiduciary bond
   c) a corporate officer of a corporation licensed as a broker
   d) the unlicensed, unbonded spouse of a broker who has been authorized by the broker

6. The Recovery Account will pay a maximum of _____ per transaction.

   a) $20,000
   b) $40,000
   c) $100,000
   d) There is no limit

7. The bill of sale used in a business opportunity transaction must contain all of the following, except:

   a) names of transferor and transferee
   b) description of the personal property
   c) location of the business
   d) names and addresses of any creditors

8. A broker's trust account records:

   a) can be kept by a columnar method
   b) must be kept in a safe deposit box at a financial institution in California
   c) can be kept by the principal
   d) should be discarded one year after the transaction closes

9. A broker may keep an earned commission in a trust account for no more than:

   a) one day
   b) seven days
   c) 25 days
   d) 60 days

10. It is legal for a broker to place a good faith deposit:

    a) in a trust account
    b) in a neutral escrow
    c) in the hands of the broker's principal
    d) Any of the above

11. The maximum amount of a broker's own funds allowed in his or her trust account is:

    a) none
    b) $50
    c) $200
    d) $500

12. The commission rate a listing broker can charge on a sale is determined by:

    a) the Real Estate Commissioner
    b) the seller and the broker
    c) the multiple listing service
    d) the buyer and the seller

13. A broker's license:

    a) must be carried by the broker at all times
    b) should be kept in a safe place, such as a home safe or a safe deposit box at a bank
    c) must be kept in the broker's main office
    d) is kept in the field office of the Department of Real Estate nearest the broker's main office

14. A salesperson's license is valid for:

    a) two years
    b) three years
    c) four years
    d) five years

15. The funds that support the Recovery Account come from:

    a) interest accruing on trust accounts
    b) a surcharge on fines from real estate criminal convictions
    c) private donations
    d) real estate license fees

16. Trust funds must be deposited into a broker's trust account:

    a) within three business days following receipt of the funds
    b) within 30 days of receipt of the funds
    c) by the broker's certified public accountant
    d) within three days after the transaction closes

17. Applicants for a broker's license must have:

    a) three years' experience as a real estate licensee
    b) 24 semester units of real estate education
    c) a sponsoring broker willing to testify to the applicant's honesty
    d) All of the above

18. A resident apartment manager who manages the apartment complex he or she lives in:

    a) must have a real estate salesperson's license
    b) need not have a real estate license
    c) must be supervised by a real estate licensee
    d) must register with the Department of Real Estate

19. All of the following are grounds for disciplinary action except:

    a) commingling
    b) failing to put a termination date in an exclusive listing
    c) negotiating with a seller to establish the commission rate
    d) failing to supervise a salesperson

20. Trust funds:

   a) are always money, never items of personal property
   b) may be put into the broker's general account, as long as scrupulous records of the deposits and withdrawals are kept
   c) can be given to the Real Estate Commissioner for deposit
   d) must never be deposited into the broker's general account

👉 Answer Key

1. c) Except for salespersons renewing their licenses for the first time, license renewal applicants must have completed 45 hours of continuing education during the four years prior to renewal.

2. c) Under a corporate license, any officer designated to represent the corporation in real estate brokerage activities must also be licensed as a broker.

3. b) Mixing personal funds with trust funds is called commingling.

4. c) Most records must be kept for three years.

5. d) Withdrawals may not be made without the signature of the broker or of an authorized licensee, corporate officer, or bonded employee.

6. a) The Recovery Account will pay up to $20,000 per transaction to satisfy an unpaid judgment against a licensee.

7. d) In the sale of a business opportunity, the bill of sale must contain the names of the transferor and transferee, the location of the business, and a description of the personal property.

8. a) The broker's trust fund records can be kept by a columnar method.

9. c) Earned commissions should be withdrawn as soon as possible, but may remain in the trust account for up to 25 days if necessary.

10. d) A good faith deposit may be placed in a trust account or in a neutral escrow, or be given to the principal.

11. c) A broker may keep up to $200 in a trust account to cover service charges.

12. b) Commissions are negotiated between the broker and the client/seller.

13. c) A broker's license must be displayed at the broker's main office.

14. c) A salesperson's license must be renewed every four years.

15. d) Up to 12% of all real estate license fees go into the Recovery Account.

16. a) Trust funds must be deposited in a trust account no later than three business days after receipt of the funds.

17. b) Broker applicants must complete 24 semester units (eight courses) of real estate education.

18. b) A resident apartment manager need not be licensed.

19. c) Brokers are free to negotiate their commissions with sellers. (In fact, it is grounds for disciplinary action to lead a seller to believe the commission rate is set by regulation.)

20. d) Trust funds must never be deposited into the broker's general account. This would be commingling, which is grounds for disciplinary action.

Chapter 17

Real Estate Math

I. Solving Math Problems
   A. Four-step approach
      1. read the question
      2. write down the formula
      3. substitute
      4. calculate
   B. Decimal numbers
      1. converting fractions
      2. converting percentages
      3 decimal calculations
II. Area Problems
   A. Squares and rectangles
   B. Triangles
   C. Odd shapes
III. Volume Problems
IV. Percentage Problems
   A. Solving percentage problems
   B. Commission problems
   C. Loan problems
      1. interest
      2. principal balance
   D. Profit or loss problems
   E. Capitalization problems
V. Tax Assessment Problems
VI. Seller's Net Problems
VII. Proration Problems
   A. Property taxes
   B. Insurance premiums
   C. Rent
   D. Mortgage interest

Chapter Overview

Real estate agents use math constantly: to calculate their commissions, to determine the square footage of homes they are listing or selling, to prorate closing costs, and so on. Electronic calculators make all of these tasks much easier than they once were, but it is still necessary to have a basic grasp of the math involved. This chapter provides step-by-step instructions for solving a wide variety of real estate math problems.

Solving Math Problems

We're going to begin our discussion of real estate math with a simple approach to solving math problems. Master this four-step process, and you'll be able to solve most math problems you are likely to encounter.

1. Read the question

The most important step is to thoroughly read and understand the question. You must know what you are looking for before you can successfully solve any math problem. Once you know what you want to find out (for example, the area, the commission amount, or the total profit), you'll be able to decide which formula to use.

2. Write down the formula

Write down the correct formula for the problem you need to solve. For example, the area formula is *Area = Length × Width*, which is abbreviated $A = L \times W$. Formulas for each type of problem are presented throughout this chapter, and there is a complete list at the end of the chapter.

3. Substitute

Substitute the relevant numbers from the problem into the formula. Sometimes there are numbers in the problem that you will not use. It's not unusual for a math problem to contain unnecessary information, which is why it is very important to read the question first and determine what you are looking for. The formula will help you distinguish between the relevant and irrelevant information given in the problem.

In some problems you will be able to substitute numbers into the formula without any additional steps, but in other problems one or more preliminary steps will be necessary. For instance, you may have to convert fractions to decimals.

4. Calculate

Once you have substituted the numbers into the formula, you are ready to perform the calculations to find the unknown—the component of the formula that was not given in the problem. Most of the formulas have the same basic form: $A = L \times W$. The problem will give you two of the three numbers (or information to enable you to find two of the numbers) and then you will either have to divide or multiply to find the third number, which is the solution to the problem.

Whether you'll multiply or divide is determined by which component in the formula is the unknown. For example, the formula $A = L \times W$ may be converted into two other formulas. All three formulas are equivalent, but they are put into different forms depending on the element to be discovered.

▸ If the quantity A (the area) is unknown, then the following formula is used.

$$\begin{array}{r} Length \\ \times\ Width \\ \hline Area \end{array} \quad \text{or} \quad A = L \times W$$

The number L is **multiplied** by W. The product of L multiplied by W is A.

▸ If the quantity L (the length) is unknown, the following formula is used.

$$Width\overline{)Area}^{\ Length} \quad \text{or} \quad L = A \div W$$

The number A is **divided** by W. The quotient of A divided by W is L.

▸ If the quantity W (the width) is unknown, the following formula is used.

$$Length\overline{)Area}^{\ Width} \quad \text{or} \quad W = A \div L$$

The number A is **divided** by L. The quotient of A divided by L is W.

Thus, the formula $A = L \times W$ may be used three different ways depending on which quantity is unknown. For the examples below, assume the area of a rectangle is 800 square feet, the length is 40 feet, and the width is 20 feet.

$A = L \times W$	$L = A \div W$	$W = A \div L$
$A = 40' \times 20'$	$L = 800\ Sq.\ Ft. \div 20'$	$W = 800\ Sq.\ Ft. \div 40'$
$\begin{array}{r} 40' \\ \times\ 20' \\ \hline 800 \end{array}$ Sq. Ft.	$20'\overline{)800}^{\ 40'}$ Sq. Ft.	$40'\overline{)800}^{\ 20'}$ Sq. Ft.

After you've substituted the numbers given in the problem into the formula, you might have trouble deciding whether you're supposed to multiply or divide. It may help to compare your equation to the very familiar calculation $2 \times 3 = 6$. If the unknown component of your equation is in the same position as the 6 in $2 \times 3 = 6$, then you need to multiply the two given numbers to find the unknown.

If the unknown component is in the 2 position or the 3 position, you need to divide. You'll divide the given number in the 6 position by the other given number to find the unknown.

$$? \times 3 = 6 \quad becomes \quad 3\overline{)6}^{\,2} \qquad \bigg| \qquad 2 \times\ ? = 6 \quad becomes \quad 2\overline{)6}^{\,3}$$

Now let's apply the four-step approach to an example. Suppose a room is 10 feet wide and 15 feet long. How many square feet does it contain?

1. **Read the question**. This problem asks you to find the square footage or area of a rectangular room. So you'll need the area formula for a rectangle.

2. **Write down the formula**. *Area = Length × Width*

3. **Substitute**. Substitute the numbers given in the problem into the formula. The length of the rectangle measures 15 feet, and the width measures 10 feet. *A = 15′ × 10′*

4. **Calculate**. Multiply *Length* times *Width* to get the answer.

$$\begin{array}{r} 15' \\ \times 10' \\ \hline 150 \ \ Sq.\ Ft. \end{array}$$

Thus, *A = 150*. The area of the room is 150 square feet.

Suppose the problem gave you different pieces of information about the same room: the area is 150 square feet and it's 10 feet wide. How long is the room? Again, follow the four-step approach.

1. **Read the question**. You're asked to find the length or width of a rectangle. You'll need the area formula again.

2. **Write down the formula**. *Area = Length × Width*

3. **Substitute**. Substitute the numbers given in the problem into the formula. *150 = L × 10*

4. **Calculate**. The length of the rectangle is the unknown. Thus, the basic area formula is converted into a division problem to find the quantity *L*.

$$10'\overline{)150} \ Sq.\ Ft. \quad \begin{array}{c} 15' \end{array}$$

The quotient of 150 divided by 10 is 15. The length of the rectangle, or of the room, is therefore 15 feet.

Decimal Numbers

To carry out a calculation, it's easier to work with decimal numbers than with fractions or percentages. So if a problem presents you with fractions or percentages, you'll usually convert them into decimal numbers.

Converting Fractions. To convert a fraction into decimal form, divide the top number of the fraction (the numerator) by the bottom number of the fraction (the denominator).

Example: To change ¾ into a decimal, divide the top number, 3, by the bottom number, 4.

$$4\overline{)3.00} \quad \begin{array}{c} .75 \end{array}$$

Example: To convert ²/₃ into a decimal, divide the top number, 2, by the bottom number, 3.

$$3\overline{)2.00} \quad .66667$$

If you don't already know them, it's useful to memorize the decimal equivalents of the most common fractions:

¼ = .25

½ = .5

¾ = .75

Converting Percentages. To solve a problem involving a percentage, you'll first convert the percentage into a decimal number, then convert the decimal answer back into percentage form.

To convert a percentage to a decimal, remove the percent sign and move the decimal point two places to the left. It may be necessary to add a zero.

Example:

98% becomes .98

5% becomes .05

32.5% becomes .325

17.5% becomes .175

To convert a decimal into a percentage, do just the opposite. Move the decimal point two places to the right and add a percent sign.

Example:

.15 becomes 15%

.08 becomes 08%

.095 becomes 09.5%

The percent key on a calculator performs the conversion of a percentage to a decimal number automatically. On most calculators, you can key in the digits and press the percent key, and the calculator will display the percentage in decimal form.

Decimal Calculations. Calculators handle decimal numbers in exactly the same way as whole numbers. If you enter a decimal number into the calculator with the decimal point in the correct place, the calculator will do the rest. But if you're working without a calculator, you'll need to apply the following rules.

To add or subtract decimals, put the numbers in a column with their decimal points lined up.

Example: To add 3.75, 14.62, 1.245, 679, 1,412.8, and 1.9, put the numbers in a column with the decimal points lined up as shown below, then add them together.

$$
\begin{array}{r}
3.75 \\
14.62 \\
1.245 \\
679.0 \\
1,412.8 \\
+ \quad 1.9 \\
\hline
2,113.315
\end{array}
$$

To multiply decimal numbers, first do the multiplication without worrying about the decimal points. Then put a decimal point into the answer in the correct place. The answer should have as many decimal places (that is, numbers to the right of its decimal point) as the total number of decimal places in the numbers that were multiplied. So count the decimal places in the numbers you are multiplying and put the decimal point the same number of places to the left in the answer.

Example: Multiply 24.6 times 16.7. The two numbers contain a total of two decimal places.

$$
\begin{array}{r}
24.6 \\
\times \ 16.7 \\
\hline
410.82
\end{array}
$$

In some cases, it will be necessary to include one or more zeros in the answer to have the correct number of decimal places.

Example: Multiply .2 times .4. There is a total of two decimal places.

$$
\begin{array}{r}
.2 \\
\times .4 \\
\hline
.08
\end{array}
$$

A zero has to be included in the answer in order to move the decimal point two places left.

To divide by a decimal number, move the decimal point in the denominator (the number you're dividing the other number by) all the way to the right. Then move the decimal point in the numerator (the number that you're dividing) the same number of places to the right. (In some cases it will be necessary to add one or more zeros to the numerator in order to move the decimal point the correct number of places.)

Example: Divide 26.145 by 1.5. First move the decimal point in 1.5 all the way to the right (in this case, that's only one place). Then move the decimal point in 26.145 the same number of places to the right.

$$26.145 \div 1.5 \text{ becomes } 261.45 \div 15$$

Now divide.

$$
\begin{array}{r}
17.43 \\
15\overline{)261.45}
\end{array}
$$

Remember, these steps are unnecessary if you're using a calculator. If the numbers are keyed in correctly, the calculator will automatically give you an answer with the decimal point in the correct place.

Area Problems

A real estate agent often needs to calculate the area of a lot, a building, or a room. Area is usually stated in square feet or square yards. The formula to be used for the calculation depends on the shape of the area in question. It may be a square, a rectangle, a triangle, or some combination of those shapes.

Squares and Rectangles

As stated earlier, the formula for finding the area of a square or a rectangle is $A = L \times W$.

Example: If a rectangular room measures 15 feet along one wall and 12 feet along the adjoining wall, how many square feet of carpet would be required to cover the floor?

1. **Read the question.** You're being asked to find the area (the square footage) of a rectangle.

2. **Write down the formula.** $A = L \times W$

3. **Substitute.** $A = 15' \times 12'$

4. **Calculate.** Since the quantity A is unknown, multiply L times W for the answer.

$$\begin{array}{r} 15' \\ \times 12' \\ \hline 180 \text{ Sq. Ft.} \end{array}$$

180 square feet of carpet are needed to cover the floor.

Now take the problem one step further. If carpet is on sale for $12 per square yard, how much would it cost to carpet the room?

1. **Read the question.** You're first being asked to determine how many square feet there are in a square yard, and then to determine how many square yards there are in 180 square feet. A square yard is a square that measures one yard on each side. There are three feet in a yard.

2. **Write down the formula.** $A = L \times W$

3. **Substitute.** $A = 3' \times 3'$

4. **Calculate.** Since the quantity A is the unknown, multiply L times W.

$$\begin{array}{r} 3' \\ \times 3' \\ \hline 9 \text{ Sq. Ft.} \end{array}$$

So there are 9 square feet in a square yard. Now divide 180 by 9 to see how many square yards there are in 180 square feet.

$$\begin{array}{r} 20 \ Sq.Yd. \\ 9\overline{)180} \ Sq.Ft. \end{array}$$

Now multiply the number of square yards (20) by the cost per square yard ($12).

$$\begin{array}{r} 20 \ \textit{Square yards} \\ \times \ \$12 \ \textit{Per yard} \\ \hline \$240 \ \textit{Cost to carpet room} \end{array}$$

Triangles

The formula for finding the area of a triangle is:

$$\begin{array}{r} \textit{Height} \\ \times \ \frac{1}{2} \ \textit{Base} \\ \hline \textit{Area} \end{array} \qquad \text{or} \qquad \textit{Area} = \frac{1}{2} \ \textit{Base} \times \textit{Height}$$

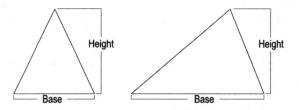

Example: If commercial building lots in a certain neighborhood are selling for approximately $5 per square foot, approximately how much should the lot pictured below sell for?

1. **Write down the formula.** $A = \frac{1}{2} B \times H$

2. **Substitute.** Area = $55'$ ($\frac{1}{2}$ of 110) $\times 75'$

3. **Calculate.**

$$\begin{array}{r} 75' \\ \times \ 55' \\ \hline 4,125 \ \textit{Sq. Ft.} \end{array}$$

The order of multiplication doesn't matter. You can multiply 110 times 75 and then divide it in half. Or you can divide 110 by 2 and then multiply the result by 75. Or you can divide 75 by 2 and then multiply the result by 110. Whichever way you do it, the answer will be the same.

	Step 1	**Step 2**	**Answer**
a)	$\begin{array}{r} 110 \\ \times\ 75 \\ \hline 8,250 \end{array}$	$\begin{array}{r} 4,125 \\ 2\overline{)8,250} \end{array}$	*4,125 Sq. Ft.*
b)	$\begin{array}{r} 55 \\ 2\overline{)110} \end{array}$	$\begin{array}{r} 55 \\ \times\ 75 \\ \hline 4,125 \end{array}$	*4,125 Sq. Ft.*
c)	$\begin{array}{r} 37.75 \\ 2\overline{)75} \end{array}$	$\begin{array}{r} 37.5 \\ \times\ 110 \\ \hline 4,125 \end{array}$	*4,125 Sq. Ft.*

The lot contains 4,125 square feet. If similar lots are selling for about $5 per square foot, this lot should sell for about $20,625.

$$\begin{array}{r} 4,125 \quad \textit{Square feet} \\ \times\ \$5 \quad \textit{Per square foot} \\ \hline \$20,625 \quad \textit{Selling price} \end{array}$$

Odd Shapes

The best approach to finding the area of an odd-shaped figure is to divide it up into squares, rectangles, and triangles. Find the areas of those figures and add them all up to arrive at the area of the odd-shaped lot, room, or building in question.

Example: If the lot pictured below is leased on a 50-year lease for $3 per square foot per year, with rental payments made monthly, how much would the monthly rent be?

First, divide the lot up into rectangles and triangles.

The next step is to find the area of each of the following figures. The height of the triangle is determined by adding together the 70 foot border of the small rectangle and the 40 foot border of the large rectangle, as shown above.

First, find the area of the triangle.

1. **Write down the formula.** *A = ½ Base × Height*

2. **Substitute.** *A = 32.5′ (½ of 65′) × 110′*

3. **Calculate.**

$$\begin{array}{r} 32.5' \\ \times\ 110' \\ \hline 3{,}575\ \textit{Sq. Ft.} \end{array}$$

Then, find the area of the large rectangle.

1. **Write down the formula.** *A = Length × Width*

2. **Substitute.** *A = 110′ × 60′*

3. **Calculate.**

$$\begin{array}{r} 110' \\ \times\ 60' \\ \hline 6{,}600\ \textit{Sq. Ft.} \end{array}$$

Next, find the area of the small rectangle.

1. **Write down the formula.** *A = Length × Width*

2. **Substitute.** *A = 70′ × 50′*

3. **Calculate.**

$$\begin{array}{r} 50' \\ \times\ 70' \\ \hline 3{,}500\ \textit{Sq. Ft.} \end{array}$$

Finally, add the three areas together to find the area of the entire lot.

$$
\begin{array}{r}
3,575 \\
6,600 \\
+\ 3,500 \\
\hline
13,675 \ \textit{Total square feet}
\end{array}
$$

The lot contains 13,675 square feet. At \$3 per square foot per year, the annual rent would be \$41,025.

$$
\begin{array}{r}
13,675 \quad \textit{Square feet} \\
\times\ \$3 \quad \textit{Rent per square foot} \\
\hline
\$41,025 \quad \textit{Annual rent}
\end{array}
$$

The monthly rental payment would be one-twelfth of the annual rent.

$$
\begin{array}{r}
\$3,418.75 \\
\hline
12)\overline{\$41,025}
\end{array}
$$

Thus, the monthly rental payment for this odd-shaped lot is \$3,418.75.

Volume Problems

Occasionally you may need to calculate the volume of a three-dimensional space. Volume is usually stated in cubic feet or cubic yards. A formula for calculating volume can be stated as: *Volume = Length × Width × Height*, or $V = L \times W \times H$. It's the same as the area formula, except it has one added element: H, the height of the space being measured.

Example: The floor of a storage unit measures 13 feet 6 inches by 20 feet, and it has a 12-foot ceiling. What is the volume of the unit in cubic yards?

1. **Write down the formula.** $V = L \times W \times H$

2. **Substitute.** $V = 20' \times 13.5' \times 12'$

3. **Calculate.**

<u>Step 1</u>

$$
\begin{array}{r}
20' \\
\times\ 13.5' \\
\hline
270 \quad \textit{Square feet}
\end{array}
$$

<u>Step 2</u>

$$
\begin{array}{r}
270 \quad \textit{Square feet} \\
\times\ 12' \\
\hline
3,240 \quad \textit{Cubic feet}
\end{array}
$$

4. **Now convert the cubic feet into cubic yards.** As you saw earlier, a square yard measures 3 feet by 3 feet, or 9 square feet. A cubic yard measures 3 feet by 3 feet by 3 feet, or 27 cubic feet. Divide the volume of the storage area in cubic feet by 27 to find the volume in cubic yards.

$$
\begin{array}{r}
120 \quad \textit{Cubic yards} \\
\hline
27)\overline{3,240} \quad \textit{Cubic feet}
\end{array}
$$

The volume of the storage space is 120 cubic yards.

Percentage Problems

Many real estate math problems involve percentages. This includes problems about brokerage commissions, interest on mortgage loans, property appreciation or depreciation, and capitalization.

Solving Percentage Problems

To solve percentage problems, you'll usually convert the percentage into a decimal number, calculate, and then convert the answer back into percentage form. As explained earlier, a percentage is converted into a decimal number by removing the percent sign and moving the decimal point two places to the left. If the percentage is a single digit (for example, 7%), it will be necessary to add a zero (.07). To convert a decimal number into a percentage, you reverse those steps: move the decimal point two places to the right and add the percent sign.

In a math problem, whenever something is expressed as a percentage "of" another number, that indicates that you should multiply that other number by the percentage. For instance, what is 75% of $40,000?

<u>**Step 1**</u>

75% becomes .75

<u>**Step 2**</u>

$$\begin{array}{r} \$40,000 \\ \times\ .75 \\ \hline \$30,000 \end{array}$$

Percentage problems basically ask you to find a part of a whole. The whole is a larger figure, such as a property's sales price. The part is a smaller figure, such as a broker's commission. The general formula might be stated thus: *A percentage of the whole equals the part.* This can be written as an equation.

$$\dfrac{\begin{array}{c} Whole \\ \times\ Percentage \end{array}}{Part} \qquad \text{or} \qquad Part = Whole \times Percentage$$

Example: A house is listed for sale at a price of $172,000, with an agreement to pay the broker a commission of 6% of the sales price. The property sells for $170,000. How much is the commission?

1. **Write down the formula.** $P = W \times \%$

2. **Substitute.** Change the percentage into a decimal number: 6% becomes .06.
   $P = \$170,000 \times .06$

3. **Calculate.**

   $$\begin{array}{rl} \$170,000 & Sales\ price \\ \times\ \ .06 & Commission\ rate \\ \hline \$10,200 & Commission \end{array}$$

The broker's commission is $10,200.

In some percentage problems, the part is given and you're asked to calculate either the whole or the percentage. For those problems, you'll need to rearrange the percentage formula into a division problem. If the whole is the unknown, divide the part by the percentage.

$$\overset{\textstyle Whole}{Percentage \overline{)\, Part}} \qquad \text{or} \qquad Whole = Part \div Percentage$$

If the percentage is the unknown, divide the part by the whole:

$$\overset{\textstyle Percentage}{Whole \overline{)\, Part}} \qquad \text{or} \qquad Percentage = Part \div Whole$$

Notice that in either case, you'll be dividing the value of the part by either the whole (to determine the percentage) or by the percentage (to determine the whole).

Commission Problems

Like the example above, most commission problems can be solved with the general percentage formula.

$$\begin{array}{r} Whole \\ \times\, Percentage \\ \hline Part \end{array} \qquad \text{or} \qquad Part = Whole \times Percentage$$

The percentage is the commission rate, and the whole is the amount that the commission is based on. In most problems, this will be the sales price of a piece of property. The part is the amount of the commission.

Example: A listing agreement provides for a commission of 7% of the sales price to be paid to the broker. If the broker has agreed to pay the salesperson 60% of the commission, how much will the salesperson receive if the property sells for $145,000?

1. **Write down the formula.** $P = W \times \%$

2. **Substitute.** Change the percentage to a decimal number: 7% becomes .07.
   $P = \$145,000 \times .07$

3. **Calculate.** The part is the unknown quantity, so the percentage is multiplied by the whole.

   $$\begin{array}{rl} \$145,000 & \textit{Sales price} \\ \times\, .07 & \textit{Commission rate} \\ \hline \$10,150 & \textit{Total commission} \end{array}$$

The total commission is $10,150. The salesperson is entitled to 60% of the total commission. Apply the percentage formula again to determine the amount of the salesperson's share.

1. **Write down the formula.** $P = W \times \%$

2. **Substitute.** Convert the percentage to a decimal number: 60% becomes .60.
   $P = \$10,150 \times .60$

3. **Calculate.**

$10,150 *Total commission*
× .60   *Salesperson's percentage*
$6,090 *Salesperson's share*

The following example illustrates another form that commission problems can take.

Example: A listing agreement provided for a two-tiered commission based on the property's sales price. The commission would be 7% of the first $100,000 and 5% of any amount over $100,000. If the commission was $8,250, what was the sales price?

1. **Read the question.** You're given the commission rates and the amount of the commission, and then asked to find the sales price. Your first step in the process is to find out how much of the commission amount is attributable to the first $100,000 of the sales price.

2. **Write down the formula.** $P = W \times \%$

3. **Substitute,** converting the percentage to a decimal. $P = \$100,000 \times .07$

4. **Calculate.**

$100,000
× .07
$7,000

So $7,000 of the commission is based on the first $100,000 of the sales price. Next, subtract to find the amount of the rest of the commission.

$8,250 *Total commission*
− 7,000 *Commission from first $100,000*
$1,250

Now you know that out of the total commission, $1,250 is attributable to the part of the sales price in excess of $100,000. You can use that figure along with the second-tier commission rate (5% of the amount over $100,000) to determine by how much the sales price exceeded $100,000.

1. **Write down the formula.** $P = W \times \%$

2. **Substitute,** converting the percentage to a decimal. $\$1,250 = W \times .05$

3. **Calculate.** The quantity W (the whole) is the unknown. To isolate the unknown, the basic formula must be turned into a division problem. The part divided by the percentage equals the whole.

$$.05\overline{)\,\$1,250} = \$25,000$$

This shows that the portion of the sales price in excess of $100,000 amounted to $25,000. Thus, the total sales price is $100,000 plus $25,000, or $125,000.

Loan Problems

Loan problems include interest problems and principal balance problems. These can be solved using the general percentage formula, *Part = Whole × Percentage*. Here, the part is the amount of the interest, the whole is the loan amount or principal balance, and the percentage is the interest rate.

Example: Henry borrows $5,000 for one year and agrees to pay 7% interest. How much interest will he be required to pay?

1. **Write down the formula.** $P = W \times \%$

2. **Substitute.** $P = \$5,000 \times .07$

3. **Calculate.**

$$\begin{array}{rl}
\$5,000 & \textit{Loan amount} \\
\times .07 & \textit{Interest rate} \\
\hline
\$350 & \textit{Interest}
\end{array}$$

Henry will pay $350 in interest.

Interest Rates. Interest rates are expressed as annual rates—a certain percentage per year. Some problems present you with monthly, quarterly, or semi-annual interest payments instead of the annual amount. In that case, you'll need to multiply the payment amount stated in the problem to determine the annual amount before you substitute the numbers into the formula.

Example: If $450 in interest accrues on a $7,200 interest-only loan in six months, what is the annual interest rate?

1. **Read the question.** You're asked to find the annual interest rate, but the interest amount given in the problem ($450) accrued in only six months. The annual interest amount would be double that, or $900.

2. **Write down the formula.** $P = W \times \%$

3. **Substitute.** For the part (the interest amount), be sure to use the annual figure, $900. $\$900 = \$7,200 \times Percentage$

4. **Calculate.** Rearrange the formula to isolate the unknown (in this case, the percentage). The part is divided by the whole to determine the percentage.

$$\begin{array}{r}
.125 \\
\$7,200\overline{)\$900}
\end{array}$$

Convert the decimal number back into a percentage: .125 becomes 12.5%. Thus, the annual interest rate is 12½%.

Principal Balance. Some loan problems ask you to determine a loan's current principal balance at a certain point in the loan term.

Example: A home loan has monthly payments of $625, which include principal and 9% interest and $47.50 per month for tax and insurance reserves. If $27.75 of the June 1 payment was applied to the principal, what was the outstanding principal balance during the month of May? (Mortgage interest is paid in arrears, so the June payment includes the interest that accrued during May.)

1. **Write down the formula**. $P = W \times \%$. Once again, in this context the part is the amount of interest, the whole is the loan balance, and the percentage is the interest rate.

2. **Substitute**. First, find the interest portion of the payment by subtracting the reserves and the principal portion.

$$
\begin{array}{rl}
\$625.00 & \textit{Total June payment} \\
47.50 & \textit{Reserves} \\
-\ 27.75 & \textit{Principal} \\
\hline
\$549.75 & \textit{Interest portion of payment}
\end{array}
$$

Next, multiply the interest portion by 12 to determine the annual interest amount.

$$
\begin{array}{r}
\$549.75 \\
\times\ 12 \\
\hline
\$6,597
\end{array}
$$

Now substitute the annual interest amount and rate into the formula. $\$6,597 = W \times .09$

3. **Calculate**. Rearrange the formula to isolate the unknown, W. This is a divison problem.

$$
.09\overline{)\,\$6,597\,}\ \ ^{\$73,300}
$$

The outstanding principal balance for May was $73,300.

Profit or Loss Problems

Profit or loss problems ask you to compare the cost or value of a piece of property at an earlier point in time with its cost or value at a later point. They can be solved using a variation on the percentage formula. Instead of *Part = Whole × Percentage*, the formula is stated like this:

$$
\begin{array}{c}
\textit{Then} \\
\underline{\times\ \textit{Percentage}} \\
\textit{Now}
\end{array}
\quad \text{or} \quad \textit{Now} = \textit{Then} \times \textit{Percentage}
$$

The Then spot in the formula is for the value or cost of the property at an earlier time specified in the problem. The Now spot is for the value or cost at a later time. The percentage is 100% plus the percentage of profit or minus the percentage of loss.

The idea is to express the value of the property after a profit or loss (Now) as a percentage of the property's value before the profit or loss (Then). If there is no profit or loss, the Now value is exactly 100% of the Then value, because the value has not changed. If there is a profit, the Now value will be greater than 100% of the Then value, since the value has increased. If there is a loss, the Now value will be less than 100% of the Then value.

Example: Bonnie bought a house five years ago for $150,000 and sold it this year for 30% more than she paid for it. What did she sell it for?

1. **Write down the formula.** *Now = Then × %*

2. **Substitute.** To get the percentage, you must add the percentage of profit to or subtract the percentage of loss from 100%. In this case there is a profit, so you add 30% to 100%, then convert it to a decimal number. 130% becomes 1.30. *Now = $150,000 × 1.30*

3. **Calculate.**

$$\begin{array}{r} \$150{,}000 \\ \times\ 1.30 \\ \hline \$195{,}000 \end{array}$$

Bonnie sold her house for $195,000.

Example: Paul sold his house this year for $210,000. He paid $262,500 for it two years ago. What was the percentage of loss?

1. **Write down the formula.** *Now = Then × %*

2. **Substitute.** *$210,000 = $262,500 × %*

3. **Calculate.** The percentage is the unknown quantity; thus, the formula is rearranged to isolate the percentage.

$$\begin{array}{r} .80 \text{ or } 80\% \\ \$262{,}500\overline{)\$210{,}000} \end{array}$$

The Now value is 80% of the Then value. Subtract 80% from 100% to find the percentage of loss.

$$\begin{array}{r} 100\% \\ -\ 80\% \\ \hline 20\%\ \ Loss \end{array}$$

Paul took a 20% loss on the sale of his house.

Let's look at another example, except this time there is a profit instead of a loss.

Example: Martha bought her home six years ago for $125,800. She sold it recently for $140,900. What was her percentage of profit?

1. **Write down the formula.** *Now = Then × %*

2. **Substitute.** *$140,900 = $125,800 × %*

3. **Calculate.** Once again, the percentage is the unknown quantity; thus, the formula is rearranged to isolate the percentage.

$$\begin{array}{r} 1.12 \text{ or } 112\% \\ \$125{,}800\overline{)\$140{,}900} \end{array}$$

The Now value is approximately 112% of the Then value. Subtract 100% from 112%, and you determine Martha received 100% of what she paid for it, plus a 12% profit.

Let's try to solve one last variation of this type of problem.

Example: Ken sold his duplex for $280,000, which represents a 16% profit over what he paid for it five years ago. What did Ken originally pay for the property?

1. **Write down the formula.** *Now = Then × %*

2. **Substitute.** *$280,000 = Then × 116%*

3. **Calculate.** In this instance, the unknown is the price Ken originally paid for the duplex; so you isolate the Then part of the equation.

$$1.16 \overline{)\begin{array}{c} \$241,379.31 \\ \$280,000 \end{array}}$$

The price paid by Ken was $241,379.31.

Some profit or loss problems involve appreciation or depreciation that has accrued at an annual rate over a specified number of years. You solve this type of problem by applying the Then and Now formula one year at a time.

Example: A property that is currently worth $174,000 has depreciated 3% per year for the past four years. How much was it worth four years ago?

1. **Write down the formula.** *Now = Then × %*

2. **Substitute.** Because the property is worth 3% less than it was one year ago, the percentage is 97% (100% − 3% = 97%). *$174,000 = Then × .97*

3. **Calculate.** Rearrange the formula to isolate the unknown, the Then value.

$$.97 \overline{)\begin{array}{c} \$179,381.44 \\ \$174,000 \end{array}}$$

The property was worth $179,381.44 one year ago. Apply the formula to $179,381.44 to determine the property's value two years ago. Repeat the process twice more to find the value four years ago.

$$\$179,381.44 \div .97 = \$184,929.31$$
$$\$184,929.31 \div .97 = \$190,648.77$$
$$\$190,648.77 \div .97 = \$196,545.12$$

The property was worth about $196,545 four years ago.

Capitalization Problems

Capitalization problems involve the capitalization approach to value, a method of real estate appraisal that is discussed in detail in Chapter 11.

The capitalization formula is another variation on the percentage formula. Instead of *Part = Whole × Percentage*, the formula is stated like this:

$$\frac{Value}{Income} \times Capitalization\ Rate \quad or \quad Income = Value \times Capitalization\ Rate$$

The value here is an investment property's value, or the purchase price an investor should be willing to pay for the property in order to obtain a specified rate of return.

The specified rate of return is the capitalization rate. This is the percentage of return the investor desires on the investment. The desired rate of return varies according to many factors. A higher desired rate of return will mean a higher capitalization rate and a lower value for the property.

The income in the capitalization formula is the annual net income produced by the investment property.

Example: A property produces an annual net income of $26,000. If an investor desires an 11% rate of return, what should he pay for the property?

1. **Write down the formula.** $I = V \times \%$

2. **Substitute.** *$26,000 = V × .11*

3. **Calculate.** Rearrange the formula to isolate the unknown, *V*.

$$.11\overline{)\,\$26,000}\ \ ^{\$236,363.64}$$

The investor should be willing to pay approximately $236,364 for the property.

Example: If a property is valued at $100,000 using an 8% capitalization rate, what would its value be using a 10% capitalization rate? First, apply the capitalization formula to determine the property's annual net income.

1. **Write down the formula.** $I = V \times \%$

2. **Substitute.** *I = $100,000 × .08*

3. **Calculate.**

$$
\begin{array}{ll}
\$100,000 & Value \\
\underline{\times\ .08} & Capitalization\ rate \\
\$8,000 & Annual\ net\ income
\end{array}
$$

The net income is $8,000 annually. Now substitute that figure into the formula to find the value at a 10% capitalization rate.

4. **Substitute.** *$8,000 = V × .10*

5. **Calculate.** Rearrange the formula to isolate the unknown quantity, *V*.

$$.10\overline{)\,\$8,000}\ \ ^{\$80,000}$$

So the value of the same property using a 10% capitalization rate is $80,000, compared to $100,000 at the 8% rate. As you can see, a higher capitalization rate applied to the same net income results in a lower value for the property.

In some problems, it's necessary to deduct a bad debt/vacancy factor and operating expenses from gross income to arrive at the net income.

Example: A ten-unit apartment building has six units that rent for $800 per month and four units that rent for $850 per month. Allow 5% for vacancies and uncollected rent. Operating expenses include: annual property taxes of $7,200, monthly utilities of $2,475, and maintenance expenses of approximately $13,600 per year. The owner has an outstanding mortgage balance of $257,000 at 8% interest, with monthly payments of $2,150. If an investor requires a 7.5% rate of return, how much should she offer for the property?

1. **Write down the formula.** $I = V \times \%$

2. **Substitute.** Remember that the income referred to in the capitalization formula is annual net income. Thus, it's necessary to calculate the annual net income before substituting. The first step in that process is calculating the annual gross income.

$$\$800 \times 12 \ months = \quad \$9,600/year \times 6 \ units = \$57,600$$
$$\$850 \times 12 \ months = \$10,200/year \times 4 \ units = \underline{\$40,800}$$
$$\$98,400$$

The gross income is $98,400 per year.

Next, calculate the bad debt/vacancy factor and deduct it from the gross income to find the effective gross income. The bad debt/vacancy factor is 5% of the gross income.

$$\$98,400 \quad Gross \ income$$
$$\underline{\times \ .05}$$
$$\$4,920 \quad Bad \ debts \ and \ vacancies$$

Thus, the loss to be expected from uncollected rents and vacancies is $4,920 per year.

$$\$98,400 \quad Gross \ income$$
$$\underline{- \ 4,920} \quad Bad \ debts \ and \ vacancies$$
$$\$93,480 \quad Effective \ gross \ income$$

The operating expenses must be deducted from the effective gross income to arrive at the net income. Remember, since you are trying to find annual net income, all the expenses must be annual also. The operating expenses add up as follows:

$$\$7,200 \quad Property \ taxes$$
$$\$29,700 \quad Utilities \ (at \ \$2,475 \ per \ month)$$
$$\underline{+ \ \$13,600} \quad Maintenance$$
$$\$50,500 \quad Annual \ operating \ expenses$$

The annual operating expenses are $50,500. (The mortgage payments are not treated as operating expenses. See Chapter 11.) Subtract the operating expenses from the effective gross income to determine the annual net income.

$93,480 *Effective gross income*
– 50,500 *Annual operating expenses*
$42,980 *Annual net income*

Now, substitute the net income and the cap rate into the formula $I = V \times \%$.
$42,980 = V \times .075$

3. **Calculate**. Rearrange the formula to isolate the unknown quantity, V.

$$.075 \overline{)\begin{array}{c} \$573,067 \\ \$42,980 \end{array}}$$

The investor should be willing to pay approximately $573,067 for the property.

Example: Continuing with the previous example, if an investor paid $750,000 for the apartment building, what capitalization rate was used? (Assume that the property's income and operating expenses were the same.)

1. **Write down the formula.** $V \times \% = I$

2. **Substitute**. You already know the net income from the preceding problem.
    $42,980 = \$750,000 \times \%$

3. **Calculate**. Isolate the unknown quantity, the capitalization rate.

$$\$750,000 \overline{)\begin{array}{c} .0573 \text{ or } 5.73\% \\ \$42,980 \end{array}}$$

The investor used a capitalization rate of approximately 5.7%.

A capitalization problem may give you the property's **operating expense ratio** (O.E.R.). The O.E.R. is the percentage of the gross income that is used to pay the annual operating expenses. The remainder is the annual net income.

Example: The property's annual gross income is $480,000, and its O.E.R. is 79%. If an investor wants a 10½% return, how much is the property worth to her?

1. **Write down the formula.** $I = V \times \%$

2. **Substitute**. Calculate the annual operating expenses using the operating expense ratio. Then subtract the operating expenses from the gross income to arrive at the annual net income.

    $480,000 \times .79 = \$379,200$ *Annual operating expenses*
    $480,000 - \$379,200 = \$100,800$ *Annual net income*

Now substitute the income and the cap rate into the formula. $100,800 = V \times .105$

3. **Calculate**. Rearrange the formula to isolate the unknown, V.

$$.105 \overline{)\begin{array}{c} \$960,000 \text{ } Value \\ \$100,800 \end{array}}$$

The investor should be willing to pay $960,000 for the property.

Tax Assessment Problems

Many tax assessment problems can be solved using this formula: *Tax = Assessed Value × Tax Rate*. You may first have to determine the assessed value before you can carry out the rest of the calculations. Assessed value is a property's value for taxation purposes.

Example: According to the tax assessor, the property's market value is $292,300. The applicable assessment ratio is 85%. If the tax rate is 3%, how much is the annual tax amount?

1. **Multiply** the market value by the assessment ratio to determine the assessed value of the property. *$292,300 × 85% = $248,455 Assessed value*

2. **Substitute** the assessed value and the tax rate into the formula. *Tax = $248,455 × .03*

3. **Calculate**.

   $248,455 Assessed value
   × .03 Tax rate
   $7,453.65 Annual taxes

The annual taxes for this property are $7,453.65.

In some problems, the tax rate is not stated as a percentage of the assessed value. Instead, it is expressed as a dollar amount per hundred or per thousand dollars of assessed value.

Example: A property with an assessed value of $173,000 is taxed at a rate of $2.35 per hundred dollars of assessed value. How much is the annual tax amount?

1. **Divide** $173,000 by 100 to determine how many hundred dollar increments there are in the assessed value:

   1,730 $100 increments
   100)$173,000

2. **Multiply** the number of hundred dollar increments by the tax rate to calculate the annual tax amount.

   1,730 $100 increments
   × $2.35 Tax rate
   $4,065.50 Annual taxes

The annual tax is $4,065.50.

In other problems, the tax rate is expressed as a specified number of mills per dollar of assessed value. A mill is one-tenth of one cent (.001). Ten mills equals one cent, and 100 mills equals 10 cents.

Example: The property's market value is $310,000 and the assessment ratio is 70%. The tax rate is 21 mills per dollar of assessed value. How much is the annual tax amount?

1. **Multiply** the market value by the assessment ratio to find the assessed value.

$310,000 *Market value*
× .70 *Assessment ratio*
$217,000 *Assessed value*

2. **Multiply** the assessed value by the tax rate to determine the tax. In decimal form, 21 mills is .021.

$217,000 *Assessed value*
× .021 *Tax rate*
$4,557 *Annual tax*

The annual tax is $4,557.

Seller's Net Problems

In a seller's net problem, you're told that a seller wants to take away a specified net amount from closing, after paying the broker's commission and other closing costs. You're then asked to calculate how much the property will have to sell for if the seller is to receive the desired net.

Example: The seller wants to net $50,000 from the sale of her home. She will have to pay off her mortgage balance, which is approximately $126,500, and pay $1,560 for repairs, $2,015 for other closing costs, and a 7% broker's commission. What's the minimum sales price that will net the seller $50,000?

1. **Add** the seller's desired net to the costs of sale, excluding the commission.

$50,000 *Seller's net*
126,500 *Mortgage*
1,560 *Repairs*
+ 2,015 *Closing costs*
$180,075 *Total*

$180,075 is the amount that must be left to the seller after the commission has been paid, if she is to be able to pay all of the listed expenses and still have $50,000 left over.

2. **Subtract** the commission rate from 100%. *100% – 7% = 93%*

3. **Divide** the total from step one by the percentage from step two. Since the commission rate will be 7% of the sales price, the seller's net plus the other costs will have to equal 93% of the sales price.

$193,629 *Selling price*
.93)$180,075

The property will have to sell for approximately $193,629 for the seller to net $50,000.

Proration Problems

Proration is the allocation of an expense between two or more parties. As was explained in Chapter 12, prorations are required in real estate closings, where a variety of expenses are prorated based on the closing date.

There are basically three steps in the proration process:

1. Calculate the per diem (daily) rate of the expense.
2. Determine the number of days for which one person is responsible for the expense.
3. Multiply the per diem rate by the number of days to determine the share of the expense that one party is responsible for.

$$\begin{array}{r} Day \\ \times\ Rate \\ \hline Share \end{array} \qquad \text{or} \qquad Share = Rate \times Days$$

To determine the per diem rate of an annual expense, divide the amount of the expense by 365 days, or 366 in a leap year. Some problems will instruct you to divide by 360 days instead, to simplify the calculation. (A 360-day year is sometimes referred to as a banker's year, as opposed to a calendar year.)

To determine the per diem rate of a monthly expense when you are prorating on the basis of a calendar year, divide the amount of the expense by the number of days in that particular month. Alternatively, to simplify the calculation, you may be instructed to base your prorations on a banker's year, which means that every month has 30 days, including February.

We'll present you with a series of examples concerning the proration of various expenses: property taxes, hazard insurance, rent, and mortgage interest. See Chapter 12 for more information about these expenses.

Property Tax Prorations

Property taxes are an annual expense. At closing, the taxes may or may not have been paid yet. If they've already been paid, the buyer will owe the seller a share of the taxes. If they haven't been paid, the seller will owe the buyer a share. Either way, the proration process is essentially the same.

Example: The closing date is February 3, and the seller has already paid the annual property taxes, which were $2,045. At closing, the seller is entitled to a credit for the tax amount covering the period from February 3 through June 30 (the tax year begins on July 1). The same amount will be a debit for the buyer. How much will the buyer owe the seller for the property taxes? Use a 360-day year with 30-day months for your calculations.

1. **Calculate the per diem rate** for the property taxes, using a 360-day year.

$$\begin{array}{r} \$5.68 \ \ Per\ diem \\ 360\overline{)\$2,045} \end{array}$$

2. **Count the number of days** that the buyer is responsible for, using 30-day months.

> *28 days   February 3 through 30*
> *30 days   March*
> *30 days   April*
> *30 days   May*
> *+ 30 days   June*
> *148 days*

3. **Substitute** the rate and number of days into the formula ($S = R \times D$), then calculate.

> *148   Days*
> *× $5.68   Per diem*
> *$840.64   Credit to seller*

At closing, the buyer will be debited $840.64 and the seller will be credited $840.64 for the property taxes from February 3 through the end of the tax year.

In the following example, the taxes haven't been paid yet. You're given the seller's share of the taxes and asked to calculate the annual tax amount.

Example: The seller hasn't paid any portion of the annual taxes. The closing is scheduled for September 21. At closing, the seller will owe the buyer $663.60 for the taxes. How much was the annual tax bill? This time, use a 365-day year and exact-day months in your calculations. The buyer's responsibility for the taxes begins on the day of closing.

1. **Write down the formula.** $S = R \times D$

2. **Substitute.** First add up the number of days that the seller is responsible for.

> *31 days   July*
> *31 days   August*
> *+ 20 days   September*
> *82 days*

Substitute the seller's share and the number of days into the formula.
$663.60 = R × 82

3. **Calculate.** Rearrange the formula to isolate the unknown, *R*.

> *$8.09   Per diem*
> *82)$663.60*

The per diem rate is $8.09. Multiply that by 365 to arrive at the annual tax amount.

> *365   Days*
> *× $8.09   Per diem*
> *$2,953   Annual taxes*

The annual taxes were $2,953.

Insurance Prorations

A seller is entitled to a refund from the hazard insurance company for any prepaid insurance coverage extending beyond the closing date.

Example: The Morgans are selling their house, and the transaction is closing on May 12. They paid an annual hazard insurance premium of $810 that provides coverage through the end of October. If the insurance company does not charge the sellers for the day of closing, how much of the premium will be refunded to them? Base your calculations on a 360-day year.

1. **Calculate the per diem rate** for the insurance, using a 360-day year.

$$360\overline{)\$810} \quad \$2.25 \text{ Per diem}$$

2. **Add up the number of days** the sellers are owed a refund for, using 30-day months.

$$
\begin{array}{rl}
19 \text{ days} & May \\
30 \text{ days} & June \\
30 \text{ days} & July \\
30 \text{ days} & August \\
30 \text{ days} & September \\
+ 30 \text{ days} & October \\
\hline
169 \text{ days} &
\end{array}
$$

3. **Substitute** the rate and number of days into the formula ($S = R \times D$), then calculate.

$$
\begin{array}{rl}
169 & Days \\
\times \ \$2.25 & Per\ diem \\
\hline
\$380.25 & Credit\ to\ seller
\end{array}
$$

The insurance company will refund $380.25 to the sellers.

Rent Prorations

If the property being sold is rental property, the seller will owe the buyer a prorated share of any rent that has been paid in advance.

Example: A ten-unit apartment building is being sold, with the closing scheduled for April 23. Four of the units rent for $1,500 per month, and the other six rent for $1,200 per month. All of the tenants paid their April rent on time. What share of the prepaid rents will the seller owe the buyer at closing?

1. **Determine the total amount** of rent owed for April.

$$
\begin{array}{l}
\$1,500 \times 4 = \$6,000 \\
\$1,200 \times 6 = \$7,200 \\
\$6,000 + \$7,200 = \$13,200
\end{array}
$$

2. **Calculate the per diem rate** for the month of April.

$$30\overline{)\$13,200} \quad \$440 \text{ Per diem}$$

3. **Determine the number of days** of rent the buyer is entitled to, beginning on the closing date. April 23 through April 30 is eight days.

4. **Substitute** and **calculate**.

$440   *Per diem*
× 8   *Days*
$3,520   *Prorated rent*

The seller will owe the buyer $3,520 in prepaid rents at closing.

Mortgage Interest Prorations

Two different types of mortgage interest prorations are necessary in most transactions, one for the seller and one for the buyer. The seller typically owes a final interest payment on the loan he is paying off.

Example: The remaining balance on the seller's mortgage is $317,550, and the interest rate is 8%. The closing date is set for July 6. Because mortgage interest is paid in arrears, the mortgage payment that the seller paid on July 1 covers the interest that accrued during June. At closing, the seller owes the lender interest covering July 1 through the closing date. How much will that interest payment be? Base your calculations on a calendar year.

1. First calculate the annual interest, using the percentage formula.

   a) **Write down the formula**. *Payment = Loan balance × Interest*

   b) **Substitute**. *P = $317,550 × .08*

   c) **Calculate**.

   $317,550   *Loan amount*
   × .08   *Interest rate*
   $25,404   *Annual interest*

2. Next, find the per diem rate of the expense. Divide the annual rate by 365.

   $69.60 *Per diem*
   365)$25,404

3. Determine the number of days the seller owes interest for. The lender will charge the seller interest for the day of closing. Thus, the seller owes interest for six days, from July 1 through July 6.

4. Finally, substitute the numbers into the proration formula ($S = R \times D$) and calculate.

   $69.60   *Per diem*
   × 6   *Days*
   $417.60   *Final interest payment*

At closing, the seller will be required to make a final interest payment of $417.60.

The buyer also owes some mortgage interest at closing. This is prepaid interest (interim interest) on the buyer's new loan. Prepaid interest covers the closing date through the last day of the month in which closing takes place.

Example: The principal amount of the buyer's new loan is $230,680. The interest rate is 8%. The transaction closes on June 22. How much prepaid interest will the buyer's lender require the buyer to pay at closing? Base your calculations on a 365-day year.

1. Use the percentage formula to calculate the annual amount of interest.

   a) **Write down the formula**. *Payment = Loan Balance × Interest rate*

   b) **Substitute**. *P = $230,680 × 8%*

   c) **Calculate**.

$$\begin{array}{r} \$230,680 \\ \times\,.08 \\ \hline \$18,454.40 \end{array}$$

2. Find the per diem rate of the expense. Divide the annual rate by 365.

$$\begin{array}{r} \$50.56 \;\; Per\,diem \\ 365\overline{)\$18,454.40} \end{array}$$

3. Determine the number of days the buyer is responsible for. In prepaid interest prorations, the buyer pays for the day of closing. There are nine days: June 22, 23, 24, 25, 26, 27, 28, 29, and 30.

4. Substitute the daily rate and number of days into the proration formula *(S = R × D)* and calculate.

$$\begin{array}{r} \$50.56 \;\; Per\,diem \\ \times\,9 \;\; Days \\ \hline \$455.04 \;\; Prepaid\ interest \end{array}$$

The buyer's interest charge would be $455.04.

Chapter Summary

Converting fractions to decimals:
Divide numerator (top number) by denominator (bottom number).

Converting percentages to decimals:
Move decimal point two places to the left and drop the percent sign.

Converting decimals to percentages:
Move decimal point two places to the right and add a percent sign.

Area formula for squares and rectangles:
Area = Length × Width
A = L × W

Area formula for triangles:
Area = ½ Base × Height
A = ½ B × H

Volume formula:
Volume = Length × Width × Height
V = L × W × H

Percentage formula:
Part = Whole × Percentage
P = W × %

Profit or loss formula:
Now = Then × %

Capitalization formula:
Income = Rate × Value
I = V × %

Proration formula:
Share = Daily Rate × Number of Days
S = R × D

1. Find annual or monthly amount;

2. Find daily rate;

3. Determine number of days; and

4. Substitute and calculate.

Chapter Quiz

1. Christine and Tom bought a house one year ago for $168,500. If property values in their neighborhood are increasing at an annual rate of 7%, what is the current market value of their house?

   a) $180,295
   b) $184,270
   c) $195,980
   d) $198,893

2. A home just sold for $183,500. The listing broker charged the seller a 6½% commission. The listing broker will pay 50% of that amount to the selling broker, and 25% to the listing salesperson. How much will the listing salesperson's share of the commission be?

   a) $11,927
   b) $5,963
   c) $3,642
   d) $2,982

3. A rectangular lot that has a 45-foot frontage and contains 1,080 square yards has a depth of:

   a) 63 feet
   b) 216 feet
   c) 188 feet
   d) 97 feet

4. An acre contains 43,560 square feet. What is the maximum number of lots measuring 50 feet by 100 feet that can be created from a one-acre parcel?

   a) Six
   b) Seven
   c) Eight
   d) Nine

5. Felicia sold a client's building for $80,000 and received a commission of $5,600. What was her commission rate?

   a) 6.5%
   b) 7%
   c) 7.5%
   d) 8%

6. Jake bought a lot for $5,000 and later sold it for $8,000. What was his percentage of profit?

   a) 60%
   b) 75%
   c) 80%
   d) 85%

7. Diane wants to purchase an income property that has an annual net income of $16,000. If she wants at least an 8% return on her investment, what is the most she should pay for the property?

   a) $150,000
   b) $175,000
   c) $195,000
   d) $200,000

8. George purchases a building for $85,000. The building generates a yearly net income of $5,100. What is his rate of return?

   a) 5.5%
   b) 6%
   c) 6.5%
   d) 7%

9. How many square yards are there in a rectangle that measures 75 × 30 feet?

   a) 6,750
   b) 2,250
   c) 750
   d) 250

10. Mike is purchasing an apartment building. The closing date is September 15, and the seller has already collected the monthly rents in the amount of $13,960 for September. At closing, the seller will have to pay Mike a prorated share of the September rents, which will amount to approximately:

a) $612
b) $931
c) $7,445
d) $9,035

11. A triangular lot has a 40-foot base and a 30-foot height. What is the area of the lot?

a) 500 square feet
b) 600 square feet
c) 750 square feet
d) 650 square feet

12. What is the decimal equivalent of five-eighths (5/8)?

a) .625
b) .0825
c) 1.58
d) 1.60

13. Kay has obtained a $112,000 loan at 8.5% interest, to finance the purchase of a home. At closing, the lender will require her to prepay interest for April 26 through April 30. Assuming that the closing agent uses a 365-day year for the proration, how much will that prepaid interest amount to?

a) $64.35
b) $104.32
c) $130.40
d) $1,403.84

14. The Binghams are selling their house and paying off the mortgage at closing. The remaining principal balance on the mortgage at closing will be $168,301.50. They will also have to pay interest that accrued over the 7-day period between their last mortgage payment and the closing date. If the annual interest rate on the Binghams' mortgage was 10%, how much will they have to pay in interest at closing? (Use a 365-day year for the proration.)

a) $85.21
b) $322.77
c) $409.86
d) $694.41

15. Carol has just paid $460,000 for a building that will bring her a 9.75% return on her investment. What is the building's annual net income?

a) $34,965
b) $36,750
c) $41,220
d) $44,850

☞ Answer Key

1. a) The current market value of Christine and Tom's house is approximately $180,295. The question asks you to determine the current value of the house based on its earlier value, so the applicable formula is *Then × % = Now*. Here, the value has increased by 7%, so the appropriate percentage is 107% (100% + 7%), or 1.07 (as a decimal). *$168,500 × 1.07 = $180,295.*

2. d) The listing salesperson will get $2,982. This is a percentage question with two parts. First multiply the sales price by the broker's commission rate to determine the full commission. *$183,500 × .065 = $11,927.50.* Then multiply that number by 25% to determine the listing salesperson's share: *$11,927.50 × .25 = $2,981.88*

3. b) The depth of the lot is 216 feet. The question asks you to determine the length of one of the sides of a rectangle, so the applicable formula is *Area = Length × Width, A = L × W.*

     First convert the area from square yards to square feet, so that it is in the same unit of measurement as the frontage. A square yard is a square that measures 3 feet on each side, or 9 square feet (3 × 3 = 9). Thus, 1,080 square yards is 9,720 square feet (*1,080 × 9 = 9,720*).

     Now substitute the numbers you have into the formula. *9,720 = 45 × L.* Isolate the unknown quantity, H, by changing to another version of the same formula: *L = 9,720 ÷ 45.*

     Divide the area, 9,720 square feet, by the width, 45 feet, to determine the length of the rectangle: *9,720 ÷ 45 = 216 feet.*

4. c) There are eight 50' × 100' lots in an acre, with one somewhat smaller lot left over. Use the area formula to determine the area of a 50' × 100' lot. *A = 50 × 100 = 5,000 square feet.* Thus, each lot will have an area of 5,000 square feet. Now divide the total number of square feet in the acre by the area of each lot: *43,560 ÷ 5,000 = 8.71.*

5. b) Felicia's commission rate was 7%. Use the percentage formula, *Part = Whole × Percentage, P = W × %.* You know the part ($5,600) and the total ($80,000), so switch the formula to isolate the percentage, then substitute and calculate.

     P ÷ W = %

     $5,600 ÷ $80,000 = %

     $5,600 ÷ $80,000 = .07. Thus, the commission rate was 7%.

6. a) Jake's profit on the sale of the lot was 60%. The question asks you to determine what percentage of the original price (the Then value) the sales price (the Now value) represents. So use the formula *Now = Then × %*, switching it around to isolate the unknown quantity, the percentage:

     Now ÷ Then = %

     $8,000 ÷ $5,000 = 1.60 = 160%

     The Now value is 160% of the Then value—in other words, 60% more than the Then value. Thus, Jake's profit on the sale was 60%.

7. d) Diane could pay $200,000 for the property and get an 8% return on that investment. This is a capitalization problem, so use the capitalization formula, *Income = Rate × Value, I = R × V*. You know the net income ($16,000) and the capitalization rate (8%), so switch the formula to isolate the unknown quantity, V:

$I \div R = V$

$16,000 \div .08 = $200,000$

8. b) George has a 6% return on his investment. This problem calls for the capitalization formula again, but this time it's the rate that is unknown. Switch the formula to isolate the rate, R:

$I \div V = R$

$5,100 \div $85,000 = .06 = 6\%$

9. d) There are 250 square yards in a 75' × 30' rectangle. The area formula, A = B × H, will give you the area in square feet: *75 × 30 = 2,250 square feet*. Then you must convert that figure to square yards. There are 9 square feet in a square yard, so divide 2,250 by 9: *2,250 ÷ 9 = 250 square yards*.

10. c) Mike, the buyer, is entitled to approximately $7,445 in rent for the period from the closing date through September 30. The proration formula is *Share = daily Rate × number of Days, S = R × D*. First determine the per diem rate for the rents by dividing the total amount by the number of days in the month: *$13,960 ÷ 30 = $465.33*. Next, determine the number of days for which the buyer is entitled to the rent: September 15 through 30 is 16 days. Finally, multiply the rate by the number of days to find the buyer's share: *$465.33 × 16 = $7,445*.

11. b) The area of the lot is 600 square feet. Since the lot is triangular, the appropriate area formula is Area = ½ Base × Height, A = ½ B × H. Here, the base is 40 feet, so ½ the base is 20 feet. 20 feet × 30 feet = 600 square feet.

12. a) The decimal equivalent of 5/8 is .625. To determine this, divide the numerator of the fraction (the top number, 5) by the denominator (the bottom number, 8). *5 ÷ 8 = .625*.

13. c) The prepaid interest will be $130.40. First determine the annual interest, using the percentage formula: *Part = Whole × Percentage, P = W × %*. The principal (the whole) is $112,000 and the rate (the percentage) is 8.5%. *$112,000 × .085 = $9,520*. Next, divide the annual interest by 365 to determine the per diem rate. *$9,520 ÷ 365 = $26.08*. Multiply the per diem rate by the number of days for which Kay is responsible for this expense—five days. *$26.08 × 5 = $130.40*.

14. b) The Binghams will have to pay $322.77 in interest at closing. To find the annual interest amount, use the percentage formula, *P = W × %. $168,301.50 × .10 = $16,830.15*. Divide that figure by 365 to determine the per diem rate: *$16,830.15 ÷ 365 = $46.11*. Finally, multiply the per diem rate by the number of days: *$46.11 × 7 days = $322.77*.

15. d) The building's annual net income is $44,850. Use the capitalization formula, *Income = Rate × Value; .0975 × $460,000 = $44,850*.

The definitions given here explain how the listed terms are used in the real estate field. Some of the terms have additional meanings, which can be found in a standard dictionary.

AAA Tenant—A nationally known tenant with the highest credit rating, whose name would lend prestige to the property.

Abandonment—Failure to occupy and use property, which may result in a loss of rights.

Abrogate—To repeal, annul, nullify, abolish, or otherwise bring to an end by official or formal action.

Absolute Fee—*See*: Fee Simple.

Abstract of Judgment—A document summarizing the essential provisions of a court judgment which, when recorded, creates a lien on the judgment debtor's real property.

Abstract of Title—*See*: Title, Abstract of.

Abut—To touch, border on, be adjacent to, or share a common boundary with.

Acceleration Clause—A provision in a promissory note or security instrument allowing the lender to declare the entire debt due immediately if the borrower breaches one or more provisions of the loan agreement. Also referred to as a call provision.

Acceptance—1. Agreeing to the terms of an offer to enter into a contract, thereby creating a binding contract. 2. Taking delivery of a deed from the grantor.

Acceptance, Qualified—*See*: Counteroffer.

Accession—The acquisition of title to additional property by its annexation to real estate already owned. This can be the result of human actions (as in the case of fixtures) or natural processes (such as accretion and reliction).

Accord and Satisfaction—An agreement to accept something different from (and usually less than) what the contract originally called for.

Accretion—A gradual addition to dry land by the forces of nature, as when waterborne sediment is deposited on waterfront property.

Accrued Items of Expense—Expenses that have been incurred but are not yet due or payable. In a settlement statement, the seller's accrued expenses are credited to the buyer.

Acknowledgment—When a person who has signed a document formally declares to an authorized official (usually a notary public) that he or she signed voluntarily. The official can then attest that the signature is voluntary and genuine.

Acquisition Cost—The amount of money a buyer was required to expend in order to acquire title to a piece of property. In addition to the purchase price, this might include closing costs, legal fees, and other expenses.

Acre—An area of land equal to 43,560 square feet, or 4,840 square yards, or 160 square rods.

Actual Age—*See*: Age, Actual.

Actual Authority—*See*: Authority, Actual.

Actual Eviction—*See*: Eviction, Actual.

Actual Notice—*See*: Notice, Actual.

ADA—Americans with Disabilities Act.

Addendum—A paragraph attached to a purchase and sale agreement or other contract that contains additional provisions.

Adjacent—Nearby, next to, bordering, or neighboring; may or may not be in actual contact.

Adjustable-Rate Mortgage—*See*: Mortgage, Adjustable-Rate.

Adjusted Basis—*See*: Basis, Adjusted.

Adjustment Period—The interval at which an adjustable-rate mortgage borrower's interest rate or monthly payment is changed.

Administrative Agency—A government agency (federal, state, or local) that administers a complex area of law and policy, adopting and enforcing detailed regulations that have the force of law. For example, the California Department of Real Estate is the administrative agency charged with regulating the real estate profession.

Administrative Law Judge—An official appointed to decide cases in which an individual is in conflict with the rules and regulations of an administrative agency. For example, a disciplinary hearing against a real estate agent accused of violating the Real Estate Law would ordinarily be conducted by an administrative law judge.

Administrator—A person appointed by the probate court to manage and distribute the estate of a deceased person, when no executor is named in the will or there is no will.

Ad Valorem—A Latin phrase that means "according to value," used to refer to taxes that are assessed on the value of property.

Adverse Possession—Acquiring title to real property that belongs to someone else by taking possession of it without permission, in the manner and for the length of time prescribed by statute.

Affiant—One who makes an affidavit.

Affidavit—A sworn statement made before a notary public (or other official authorized to administer an oath) that has been written down and acknowledged.

Affiliated Licensee—An associate broker or salesperson who is employed by a broker.

Affirm—1. To confirm or ratify. 2. To make a solemn declaration that is not under oath.

After-Acquired Title—*See*: Title, After-Acquired.

Age, Actual—The age of a structure from a chronological standpoint (as opposed to its effective age); how many years it has actually been in existence.

Age, Effective—The age of a structure as indicated by its condition and remaining usefulness (as opposed to its actual age). Good maintenance may increase a building's effective age, and poor maintenance may decrease it; for example, a 50-year-old home that has been well maintained might have an effective age of 15 years, meaning that its remaining usefulness is equivalent to that of a 15-year-old home.

Agency—A relationship of trust created when one person (the principal) grants another (the agent) authority to represent the principal in dealings with third parties.

Agency, Apparent—When third parties are given the impression that someone who has not been authorized to represent another is that person's agent, or else given the impression that an agent has been authorized to perform acts which are in fact beyond the scope of his or her authority. Also called ostensible agency.

Agency, Dual—When an agent represents both parties to a transaction, as when a broker represents both the buyer and the seller.

Agency, Exclusive—*See*: Listing, Exclusive.

Agency, Ostensible—*See*: Agency, Apparent.

Agency Confirmation Statement—A written statement that indicates which party a real estate agent is representing. It must be signed by both the buyer and the seller before they enter into a residential transaction.

Agency Disclosure Form—A form that explains the duties of a seller's agent, a buyer's agent, and a dual agent. It must be signed by both the buyer and the seller before they enter into a residential transaction.

Agency Law—The body of legal rules that govern the relationship between agent and principal, imposing fiduciary duties on the agent and also imposing liability for the agent's actions on the principal.

Agent—A person authorized to represent another (the principal) in dealings with third parties.

Agent, Closing—The person who handles the closing process on behalf of the parties to a real estate transaction. It may be an independent escrow agent, an employee of the lender or the title company, the real estate broker, or a lawyer.

Agent, Dual—*See*: Agency, Dual.

Agent, Escrow—A neutral third party who holds funds, documents, or other valuables on behalf of the parties to a transaction, releasing these items to the parties only when certain conditions in the escrow instructions have been fulfilled.

Agent, General—An agent authorized to handle all of the principal's affairs in one area or in specified areas.

Agent, Gratuitous—An agent who does not have a legal right to claim compensation for his or her services (such as a broker who does not have a written employment contract with the seller).

Agent, Listing—A broker who has a listing agreement with a seller, or a salesperson representing the listing broker. The listing agent may or may not turn out also to be the selling agent, the one who negotiates an acceptable offer from the buyer.

Agent, Selling—The real estate agent who writes and presents the offer to purchase that the seller accepts. The selling agent may or may not also be the listing agent, but is considered to be an agent of the seller unless otherwise agreed.

Agent, Special—An agent with limited authority to do a specific thing or conduct a specific transaction.

Agent, Universal—An agent authorized to do everything that can be lawfully delegated to a representative.

Agents in Production—The elements necessary to generate income and establish a value in real estate: labor, coordination, capital, and land.

Age of Majority—*See*: Majority, Age of.

Agreement—*See*: Contract.

Air Lot—A parcel of property above the surface of the earth, not containing any land; for example, a condominium unit on the third floor.

Air Rights—The right to undisturbed use and control of the airspace over a parcel of land; may be transferred separately from the land.

Alienation—The transfer of ownership or an interest in property from one person to another, by any means.

Alienation, Involuntary—Transfer of an interest in property against the will of the owner, or without action by the owner, occurring through operation of law, natural processes, or adverse possession.

Alienation, Voluntary—When an owner voluntarily transfers an interest to someone else.

Alienation Clause—A provision in a security instrument that gives the lender the right to declare the entire loan balance due immediately if the borrower sells or otherwise transfers the security property. Also called a due-on-sale clause.

All-Inclusive Trust Deed—*See*: Mortgage, Wraparound.

Allodial System—A system of individual ownership of land (as opposed to the feudal system, in which the sovereign owned all of the land).

Alluvion—The solid material deposited along a riverbank or shore by accretion. Also called alluvium.

Alquist-Priolo Act—A California law that requires geologic reports when residences are built in certain areas of the state.

ALTA—American Land Title Association, a nationwide organization of title insurance companies. An extended coverage title policy is sometimes referred to as an ALTA policy.

Amendment—A supplementary agreement changing one or more terms of a contract, which must be signed by all of the parties to the original contract. Also called a contract modification.

Amenities—Features of a property that contribute to the pleasure or convenience of owning it, such as a fireplace, a beautiful view, or its proximity to a good school.

Americans with Disabilities Act—A federal law requiring facilities that are open to the public to ensure accessibility to disabled persons, which may include making architectural modifications.

Amortization, Negative—The addition of unpaid interest to the principal balance of a loan, thereby increasing the amount owed.

Amortize—To gradually pay off a debt with installment payments that include both principal and interest. *See also*: Loan, Amortized.

Annexation—Attaching personal property to real property, so that it becomes part of the real property (a fixture) in the eyes of the law.

Annexation, Actual—The physical attachment of personal property to real property, so that it becomes part of the real property.

Annexation, Constructive—The association of personal property with real property in such a way that the law treats it as a fixture, even though it is not physically attached. For example, a house key is constructively annexed to the house.

Annual Percentage Rate (APR)—All of the charges that a borrower will pay for the loan (including the interest, loan fee, discount points, and mortgage insurance costs), expressed as an annual percentage of the loan amount.

Annuity—A sum of money received in a series of payments at regular intervals (often annually) over a period of time.

Anticipation, Principle of—An appraisal principle which holds that value is created by the expectation of benefits to be received in the future.

Anticipatory Repudiation—Action taken by one party to a contract to inform the other party, before the time set for performance, that he or she does not intend to fulfill the contract.

Anti-deficiency Rules—Laws that prohibit a secured lender from suing the borrower for a deficiency judgment in certain circumstances (for example, after nonjudicial foreclosure of a deed of trust).

Appeal—When one of the parties to a lawsuit asks a higher court to review the judgment or verdict reached in a lower court.

Appellant—The party who files an appeal because he or she is dissatisfied with the lower court's decision. Also called the petitioner.

Appellee—In an appeal, the party who did not file the appeal. Also called the respondent.

Apportionment—A division of property (as among tenants in common when the property is sold or partitioned) or liability (as when responsibility for closing costs is allocated between the buyer and seller) into proportionate, but not necessarily equal, parts.

Appraisal—An estimate or opinion of the value of a piece of property as of a particular date. Also called valuation.

Appraiser—One who estimates the value of property, especially an expert qualified to do so by training and experience.

Appreciation—An increase in value; the opposite of depreciation.

Appropriation—Taking property or reducing it to personal possession, to the exclusion of others.

Appropriation, Prior—A system of allocating water rights, under which a person who wants to use water from a certain lake or river is required to apply for a permit. A permit has priority over other permits that are issued later. *Compare*: Riparian Rights.

Appropriative Rights—The water rights of a person who holds a prior appropriation permit.

Appurtenances—Rights that go along with ownership of a particular piece of property, such as air rights or mineral rights. They are ordinarily transferred with the property, but may, in some cases, be sold separately.

Appurtenances, Intangible—Rights that go with ownership of a piece of property that do not involve physical objects or substances; for example, an access easement (as opposed to mineral rights).

Appurtenant Easement—*See*: Easement Appurtenant.

APR—*See*: Annual Percentage Rate.

Area—1. Locale or region. 2. The size of a surface, usually in square units of measure, such as square feet or square miles.

ARM—*See*: Mortgage, Adjustable-Rate.

Arm's Length Transaction—1. A transaction in which both parties are informed of the property's merits and shortcomings, neither is acting under unusual pressure, and the property has been exposed on the open market for a reasonable length of time. 2. A transaction in which there is no pre-existing family or business relationship between the parties.

Arranger of Credit—A real estate licensee or attorney who arranges a transaction where credit is extended by a seller of residential property.

Artificial Person—A legal entity, such as a corporation, that the law treats as an individual with legal rights and responsibilities; as distinguished from a natural person, a human being. Sometimes called a legal person.

Assemblage—Combining two or more adjoining properties into one tract.

Assessment—The valuation of property for purposes of taxation.

Assessor—An official who determines the value of property for taxation.

Asset—Anything of value that a person owns.

Assets, Capital—Assets held by a taxpayer other than: (1) property held for sale to customers; and (2) depreciable property or real property used in the taxpayer's trade or business. Thus, real property is a capital asset if it is used for personal use or for profit.

Assets, Liquid—Cash and other assets that can be readily turned into cash (liquidated), such as stock.

Assets, Section 1231—Properties used in a trade or business or held for the production of income (a reference to Section 1231 in the federal income tax code).

Assign—To transfer rights (especially contract rights) or interests to another.

Assignee—One to whom rights or interests have been assigned.

Assignment—1. A transfer of contract rights from one person to another. 2. In the case of a lease, the transfer by the original tenant of his or her entire leasehold estate to another. *Compare*: Sublease.

Assignment of Contract and Deed—The instrument used to substitute a new vendor for the original vendor in a land contract.

Assignor—One who has assigned his or her rights or interest to another.

Assumption—Action by a buyer to take on personal liability for paying off the seller's existing mortgage or deed of trust.

Assumption Fee—A fee paid to the lender, usually by the buyer, when a mortgage or deed of trust is assumed.

Attachment—Court-ordered seizure of property belonging to a defendant in a lawsuit, so that it will be available to satisfy a judgment if the plaintiff wins. In the case of real property, an attachment creates a lien.

Attachments, Man-Made—*See*: Fixture.

Attachments, Natural—Plants growing on a piece of land, such as trees, shrubs, or crops. *See*: Emblements; Fructus Industriales; Fructus Naturales.

Attestation—The act of witnessing the execution of an instrument, such as a deed or will.

Attorney General—The principal legal advisor for state government, including legal advisor to the Department of Real Estate on matters regarding license law.

Attorney in Fact—Any person authorized to represent another by a power of attorney; not necessarily a lawyer (an attorney at law).

Attractive Nuisance—A property feature that is dangerous and inviting to children, and a potential source of liability for the property owner.

Auditing—Verification and examination of records, particularly the financial accounts of a business or other organization.

Authority, Actual—Authority actually given to an agent by the principal, either expressly or by implication.

Authority, Apparent—Authority to represent another that someone appears to have and that the principal is estopped from denying, although no actual authority has been granted.

Authority, Express—Actual authority that the principal has expressly given to his or her agent, either orally or in writing.

Authority, Implied—An agent's authority to do everything reasonably necessary to carry out the principal's express orders.

Avulsion—1. A sudden (not gradual) tearing away of land by the action of water. 2. A sudden shift in a watercourse.

Bad Debt/Vacancy Factor—A percentage deducted from a property's potential gross income to determine the effective gross income, estimating the income that will probably be lost because of vacancies and tenants who don't pay.

Balance, Principle of—An appraisal principle which holds that the maximum value of real estate is achieved when the agents in production (labor, coordination, capital, and land) are in proper balance with each other.

Balance Sheet—*See*: Financial Statement.

Balloon Payment—A payment on a loan (usually the final payment) that is significantly larger than the regular installment payments.

Bankruptcy—1. A situation resulting when the liabilities of an individual, corporation, or firm exceed the assets. 2. Declaration by a court that an individual, corporation, or firm is insolvent, with the result that the assets and debts are administered under bankruptcy laws.

Barter—To exchange or trade one commodity or piece of property for another without the use of money.

Base Line—In the government survey system, a main east-west line from which township lines are established. Each principal meridian has one base line associated with it.

Basis—A figure used in calculating a gain on the sale of real estate for federal income tax purposes. Also called cost basis.

Basis, Adjusted—The owner's initial basis in the property, plus capital expenditures for improvements, and minus any allowable depreciation or cost recovery deductions.

Basis, Initial—The amount of the owner's original investment in the property; what it cost to acquire the property, which may include closing costs and certain other expenses, as well as the purchase price.

Bearer—Whoever has possession of a negotiable instrument. *See*: Endorsement in Blank.

Bench Mark—A surveyor's mark at a known point of elevation on a stationary object, used as a reference point in calculating other elevations in a surveyed area; often a metal disk set into cement or rock.

Beneficiary—1. One for whom a trust is created and on whose behalf the trustee administers the trust. 2. The lender in a deed of trust transaction. 3. One entitled to receive real or personal property under a will; a legatee or devisee.

Bequeath—To transfer personal property to another by will.

Bequest—Personal property (including money) that is transferred by will.

Betterment—An improvement to real property that is more extensive than ordinary repair or replacement and that increases the value of the property.

Bilateral Contract—*See*: Contract, Bilateral.

Bill of Sale—A document used to transfer title to personal property from one person to another.

Binder—1. An agreement to consider a deposit as evidence of the potential buyer's good faith when he or she makes an offer to buy a piece of real estate. 2. An instrument providing immediate insurance coverage until the regular policy is issued. 3. Any payment or preliminary written statement intended to make an agreement legally binding until a formal contract has been drawn up.

Blind Ad—An advertisement placed by a real estate licensee that does not include the broker's name.

Block—In a subdivision, a group of lots surrounded by streets or unimproved land.

Blockbusting—Attempting to induce owners to list or sell their homes by predicting that members of another race or ethnic group, or people suffering from some disability, will be moving into the neighborhood. This violates antidiscrimination laws. Also called panic selling.

Blue Laws—Statutes or ordinances restricting the transaction of business or other activities on Sundays and certain holidays.

Blue Sky Laws—Laws that regulate the promotion and sale of securities in order to protect the public from fraud.

Board of Directors—The body responsible for governing a corporation on behalf of the shareholders, which oversees the corporate management.

Bona Fide—In good faith; genuine; not fraudulent.

Bond—1. A written obligation, usually interest-bearing, to pay a certain sum at a specified time. 2. Money put up as a surety, protecting someone against failure to perform, negligent performance, or fraud.

Bond, Completion—A bond posted by a contractor to guarantee that a project will be completed satisfactorily and free of liens. Also called a performance bond.

Bonus—An extra payment, over and above what is strictly due.

Boot—In a tax-free exchange, something given or received that is not like-kind property; for example, in an exchange of real property, if one party gives the other cash in addition to real property, the cash is boot.

Boundary—The perimeter or border of a parcel of land; the dividing line between one piece of property and another.

Bounds—Boundaries. *See*: Metes and Bounds Description.

Branch Manager—An associate broker designated by a firm's primary broker to manage the operations of a branch office.

Breach—Violation of an obligation, duty, or law; especially an unexcused failure to perform a contractual obligation.

Breach of Contract—An unexcused failure to perform a contractual obligation.

Broker, Associate—A person who has qualified as a broker, but is affiliated with another broker.

Broker, Cooperating—A broker who belongs to a multiple listing service and helps sell a property that is listed with another member of the service (the listing broker). Like the listing broker, the cooperating broker represents the seller unless otherwise agreed.

Broker, Designated—A corporate officer or general partner who is authorized to act as the broker for a licensed corporation or partnership.

Broker, Fee—A real estate broker who allows another person to use his or her license to operate a brokerage, in violation of the license law.

Broker, Listing—A broker who has a listing agreement with a property seller (in contrast to a cooperating broker from the multiple listing service, who may help sell the property and share the listing broker's commission, but does not have a contract directly with the seller).

Broker, Real Estate—One who is licensed to represent members of the public in real estate transactions for compensation.

Brokerage—A real estate broker's business.

Brokerage Fee—The commission or other compensation charged for a real estate broker's services.

Buffer—An undeveloped area separating two areas zoned for incompatible uses.

Building Codes—Regulations that set minimum standards for construction methods and materials.

Building Restrictions—Rules concerning building size, placement, or type; they may be public restrictions (in a zoning ordinance, for example) or private restrictions (CC&Rs, for example).

Bulk Transfer—The sale of all or a substantial part of the merchandise, equipment, or other inventory of a business, not in the ordinary course of business.

Bulk Transfer Law—A law requiring a seller who negotiates a bulk transfer (usually in connection with the sale of the business itself) to furnish the buyer with a list of creditors and a schedule of the property being sold, and to notify creditors of the impending transfer.

Bump Clause—A provision in a purchase and sale agreement that allows the seller to keep the property on the market while waiting for a contingency clause to be fulfilled. If the seller receives another good offer in the meantime, he or she can require the buyer either to waive the contingency clause or terminate the contract.

Bundle of Rights—The rights inherent in ownership of property, including the right to use, lease, enjoy, encumber, will, sell, or do nothing with the property.

Business Opportunity—A business that is for sale.

Buydown—The payment of discount points to a lender to reduce (buy down) the interest rate charged to the borrower; especially when a seller pays discount points to help the buyer/borrower qualify for financing.

California Coastal Act—A California law designed to protect and control development along the California coastline.

California Environmental Quality Act (CEQA)—A California law that is designed to protect the state's environment. It is similar to the National Environmental Policy Act.

California Mobile Home Code—A set of state laws that regulate mobile home sales practices.

California Veterans Farm and Home Purchase Program—A state-sponsored residential finance program designed to provide inexpensive home and farm loans to veterans. Often referred to as Cal-Vet.

Call—In a metes and bounds description, a specification that describes a segment of the boundary. For example, "south 15° west 120 feet" is a call.

Call Provision—*See*: Acceleration Clause.

Cal-Vet—*See*: California Veterans Farm and Home Purchase Program.

Cancellation—Termination of a contract without undoing acts that have already been performed under the contract. *Compare*: Rescission.

Cap—A limit on how much a lender may raise an adjustable rate mortgage's interest rate or monthly payment per year.

Capacity—The legal ability or competency to perform some act, such as enter into a contract or execute a deed or will.

Capital—Money (or other forms of wealth) available for use in the production of more money.

Capital Assets—Assets held by a taxpayer other than: 1) property held for sale to customers in the ordinary course of the taxpayer's business; and 2) depreciable property or real property used in the taxpayer's trade or business. Thus, real property is a capital asset if it is owned for personal use or for profit.

Capital Expenditures—Money spent on improvements and alterations that add to the value of the property and/or prolong its life.

Capital Gain—Profit realized from the sale of a capital asset. If the asset was held for more than one year, it is a long-term capital gain; if the asset was held for one year or less, it is a short-term capital gain.

Capital Improvement—Any improvement that is designed to become a permanent part of the real property or that will have the effect of significantly prolonging the property's life.

Capitalization—A method of appraising real property by converting the anticipated net income from the property into the present value. Also called the income approach to value.

Capitalization Rate—A percentage used in capitalization (Net Income = Capitalization Rate × Value). It is the rate believed to represent the proper relationship between the value of the property and the income it produces; the rate that would be a reasonable return on an investment of the type in question, or the yield necessary to attract investment of capital in property like the subject property. Often called cap rate.

Capitalize—1. To provide with cash, or capital. 2. To determine the present value of an asset using capitalization.

Capital Loss—A loss resulting from the sale of a capital asset. It may be long-term or short-term, depending on whether the asset was held for more than one year or for one year or less.

Capture, Rule of—A legal rule that grants a landowner the right to all oil and gas produced from wells on his or her land, even if it migrated from underneath land belonging to someone else.

CAR—California Association of Realtors®.

Carryback Loan—*See*: Mortgage, Purchase Money.

Carryover Clause—*See*: Safety Clause.

Cash Flow—The residual income after deducting from gross income all operating expenses and debt service.

Cash on Cash—The ratio between cash received in the first year and cash initially invested.

Caveat Emptor—A Latin phrase meaning "Let the buyer beware"; it expresses the idea that a buyer is expected to examine property carefully before buying, instead of relying on the seller to disclose problems. This was once a firm rule of law, but it has lost most of its force, especially in residential transactions.

CC&Rs—A declaration of covenants, conditions, and restrictions; usually recorded by a developer to place restrictions on all lots within a new subdivision.

CCARA—*See*: Condominium and Cooperative Abuse Relief Act.

CEQA—*See*: California Environmental Quality Act.

CERCLA—*See*: Comprehensive Environmental Response, Compensation, and Liability Act.

Certificate of Discharge—A written statement acknowledging that the debt secured by a mortgage has been paid in full. Also called a satisfaction of mortgage or mortgage release.

Certificate of Eligibility—A document issued by the Department of Veterans Affairs as evidence of a veteran's eligibility for a VA-guaranteed loan.

Certificate of Occupancy—A document issued by a local government agency (such as the building department) verifying that a newly constructed building is in compliance with all codes and may be occupied.

Certificate of Reasonable Value—A document issued by the Department of Veterans Affairs, setting forth the current market value of a property, based on a VA-approved appraisal.

Certificate of Sale—The document given to the purchaser at a mortgage foreclosure sale, instead of a deed; replaced with a sheriff's deed only after the redemption period expires.

Certiorari, Writ of—A writ in which a higher court requests a transcript of proceedings that took place in a lower court, for appellate review.

Cesspool—Underground pit used to catch and temporarily hold sewage while it decomposes and leaches into the surrounding soil.

Chain of Title—*See*: Title, Chain of.

Change, Principle of—An appraisal principle which holds that it is the future, not the past, that is of primary importance in estimating a property's value, because economic and social forces are constantly changing it.

Charter—A written instrument granting a power or a right of franchise.

Chattel—An article of personal property.

Chattel Mortgage—*See*: Mortgage, Chattel.

Chattel Real—Personal property that is closely associated with real property. The primary example is a lease.

Civil Law—The body of law concerned with the rights and liabilities of one individual in relation to another; includes contract law, tort law, and property law. *Compare*: Criminal Law.

Civil Rights—Fundamental rights guaranteed to individuals by the law. The term is primarily used in reference to constitutional and statutory protections against discrimination or government interference.

Civil Rights Act of 1866—A federal law guaranteeing all citizens the right to purchase, lease, sell, convey and inherit property, regardless of race or ancestry.

Civil Rights Act of 1964—A federal law prohibiting discrimination on the basis of race, color, national origin, or religion in many programs for which the government provides financial assistance.

Civil Suit—A lawsuit in which one private party sues another private party (as opposed to a criminal suit, in which an individual is sued—prosecuted—by the government).

Civil Wrong—*See*: Tort.

Clean Air Act—A federal law intended to maintain and enhance air quality.

Clean Water Act—A federal law intended to maintain and enhance the quality of the nation's water resources.

Client—One who employs a broker, lawyer, or appraiser. A real estate broker's client can be the seller, the buyer, or both, but is usually the seller.

Closing—The final stage in a real estate transaction, when the seller receives the purchase money, the buyer receives the deed, and title is transferred. Also called settlement.

Closing Costs—Expenses incurred in the transfer of real estate in addition to the purchase price; for example, the appraisal fee, title insurance premium, broker's commission, and documentary transfer tax.

Closing Date—The date on which all the terms of a purchase and sale agreement must be met, or the contract is terminated.

Closing Statement—*See*: Settlement Statement.

Cloud on Title—A claim, encumbrance, or apparent defect that makes the title to a property unmarketable. *See*: Title, Marketable.

Code of Ethics—A body of rules setting forth accepted standards of conduct, reflecting principles of fairness and morality; especially one that the members of an organization are expected to follow.

Codicil—An addition to, or revision of, a will.

Collateral—Anything of value used as security for a debt or obligation.

Collusion—An agreement between two or more persons to defraud another.

Color of Title—*See*: Title, Color of.

Commercial Acre—The remainder of an acre of newly subdivided land after deducting the amount of land dedicated for streets and sidewalks.

Commercial Bank—A type of financial institution that has traditionally emphasized commercial lending (loans to businesses), but which also makes many residential mortgage loans.

Commercial Paper—Negotiable instruments, such as promissory notes, sold to meet the short-term capital needs of a business.

Commercial Property—Property zoned and used for business purposes, such as a restaurant or an office building; as distinguished from residential, industrial, or agricultural property.

Commingled Funds—Funds from different sources that are deposited in the same account and thereby lose their separate character; for example, if a spouse deposits cash that is his or her separate property in an account with funds that are community property, the entire amount may be treated as community property.

Commingling—Illegally mixing trust funds held on behalf of a client with personal funds.

Commission—1. The compensation paid to a broker for services in connection with a real estate transaction (usually a percentage of the sales price). 2. A group of people organized for a particular purpose or function; usually a governmental body, such as a planning commission.

Commitment—In real estate finance, a lender's promise to make a loan. A loan commitment may be "firm" or "conditional"; a conditional commitment is contingent on something, such as a satisfactory credit report on the borrower.

Common Areas—1. The land and improvements in a condominium, planned unit development, or other housing development that are owned and used collectively by all of the residents, such as parking lots, hallways, and recreational facilities available for common use. 2. In a building with leased units or spaces, the areas that are available for use by all of the tenants.

Common Law—1. Early English law. 2. Long-established rules of law based on early English law. 3. Rules of law developed in court decisions, as opposed to statutory law.

Community Property—Property owned jointly by a married couple in California and other community property states, as distinguished from each spouse's separate property; generally, any property acquired through the labor or skill of either spouse during marriage.

Co-mortgagor—Someone (usually a family member) who accepts responsibility for the repayment of a mortgage loan, along with the primary borrower, to help the borrower qualify for the loan.

Comparable—In appraisal, a property that is similar to the subject property and that has recently been sold. The sales prices of comparables provide data for estimating the value of the subject property using the sales comparison approach. Also called a comp or a comparable sale.

Competent—1. Of sound mind, for the purposes of entering into a contract or executing an instrument. 2. Both of sound mind and having reached the age of majority.

Competition, Principle of—An appraisal principle which holds that profits tend to encourage competition, and excess profits tend to result in ruinous competition.

Completion Bond—*See*: Bond, Completion.

Compliance Inspection—A building inspection to determine, for the benefit of a lender, whether building codes, specifications, or conditions established after a prior inspection have been met before a loan is made.

Comprehensive Environmental Response, Compensation, and Liability Act—A federal law that governs liability for environmental cleanup costs.

Comprehensive Plan—*See*: General Plan.

Concurrent Ownership—*See*: Ownership, Concurrent.

Condemnation—1. Taking private property for public use through the government's power of eminent domain. 2. A declaration that a structure is unfit for occupancy and must be closed or demolished.

Condemnation Appraisal—An estimate of the value of condemned property to determine the just compensation to be paid to the owner.

Condition—1. A provision in a contract that makes the parties' rights and obligations depend on the occurrence (or nonoccurrence) of a particular event. Also called a contingency clause. 2. A provision in a deed that makes title depend on compliance with a particular restriction.

Conditional Commitment—*See*: Commitment.

Conditional Fee—*See*: Fee, Defeasible.

Conditional Use Permit—A permit that allows a special use, such as a school or hospital, to operate in a neighborhood where it would otherwise be prohibited by the zoning. Also called a special exception permit.

Condominium—Property developed for concurrent ownership, where each co-owner has a separate interest in an individual unit, combined with an undivided interest in the common areas of the property.

Condominium and Cooperative Abuse Relief Act—A federal law enacted to minimize the adverse impact of condominium and cooperative conversions.

Confirmation of Sale—Court approval of a sale of property by an executor, administrator, or guardian.

Conflict of Interest—When an agent (or other person occupying a position of trust) is in a situation where the action that would promote his or her own interests conflicts with the action that would promote the interests of the principal. The agent should inform the principal of this situation and offer to withdraw.

Conforming Loan—*See*: Loan, Conforming.

Conformity, Principle of—An appraisal principle which holds that the maximum value of property is realized when there is a reasonable degree of social and economic homogeneity in the neighborhood.

Conservation—1. Preservation of structures or neighborhoods in a sound condition. 2. Preservation or controlled use of natural resources for long-term benefits.

Conservator—A person appointed by a court to take care of the property of another who is incapable of taking care of it on his or her own.

Consideration—Anything of value given to induce another to enter into a contract, such as money, goods, services, or a promise. Sometimes called valuable consideration.

Conspiracy—An agreement or plan between two or more persons to perform an unlawful act.

Construction Lien—*See*: Lien, Construction.

Constructive—Held to be so in the eyes of the law, even if not so in fact. *See*: Annexation, Constructive; Eviction, Constructive; Notice, Constructive; Severance, Constructive.

Consumer Price Index—An index that tracks changes in the cost of goods and services for a typical consumer. Formerly called the cost of living index.

Consummate—To complete.

Contiguous—Adjacent, abutting, or in close proximity.

Contingency Clause—*See*: Condition.

Contour—The shape or configuration of a surface. A contour map depicts the topography of a piece of land by means of lines (contour lines) that connect points of equal elevation.

Contract—An agreement between two or more persons to do or not do a certain thing, for consideration.

Contract, Bilateral—A contract in which each party has made a binding promise to perform (as distinguished from a unilateral contract).

Contract, Broker and Salesperson—An employment contract between a broker and an affiliated salesperson, outlining their mutual obligations.

Contract, Conditional Sales—*See*: Contract, Land.

Contract, Executed—A contract in which both parties have completely performed their contractual obligations.

Contract, Executory—A contract in which one or both parties have not yet completed performance of their obligations.

Contract, Express—A contract that has been put into words, either spoken or written.

Contract, Implied—A contract that has not been put into words, but is implied by the actions of the parties.

Contract, Installment Sales—*See*: Contract, Land.

Contract, Land—A contract for the sale of real property in which the buyer (the vendee) pays in installments. The buyer takes possession of the property immediately, but the seller (the vendor) retains legal title until the full price has been paid. Also called a conditional sales contract, installment sales contract, real estate contract, or contract for deed.

Contract, Oral—A spoken agreement that has not been written down. Also called a parol contract.

Contract, Parol—*See*: Contract, Oral.

Contract, Real Estate—1. Any contract pertaining to real estate. 2. A land contract.

Contract, Sales—*See*: Purchase and Sale Agreement.

Contract, Unenforceable—An agreement that a court would refuse to enforce. For example, a contract is unenforceable if its contents can't be proved or the statute of limitations has run out.

Contract, Unilateral—A contract that is accepted by performance; the offeror has promised to perform his or her side of the bargain if the other party performs, but the other party has not promised to do so. *Compare*: Contract, Bilateral.

Contract, Valid—A binding, legally enforceable contract.

Contract, Void—An agreement that is not an enforceable contract, because it lacks a required element (such as consideration) or is defective in some other respect.

Contract, Voidable—A contract that one of the parties can disaffirm without liability, because of lack of capacity or a negative factor such as fraud or duress.

Contract for Deed—*See*: Contract, Land.

Contract Modification—*See*: Amendment.

Contract of Adhesion—A contract that is one-sided and unfair to one of the parties; a take-it-or-leave-it contract, in which the offeror had much greater bargaining power than the offeree.

Contract of Sale—*See*: Purchase and Sale Agreement.

Contractor—One who contracts to perform labor or supply materials for a construction project, or to do other work for a specified price.

Contractor, Independent—*See*: Independent Contractor.

Contract Rent—*See*: Rent, Contract.

Contribution, Principle of—An appraisal principle which holds that the value of real property is greatest when the improvements produce the highest return commensurate with their cost (the investment).

Conventional Financing—*See*: Loan, Conventional.

Conversion—1. Misappropriating property or funds belonging to another; for example, converting trust funds to one's own use. 2. The process of changing an apartment complex into a condominium or cooperative.

Conversion Option—A provision in many adjustable-rate mortgages that gives the borrower the option of converting to a fixed interest rate at certain times during the first years of the loan term; if the borrower chooses to do this, the loan will remain at that fixed rate for the remainder of the term.

Conveyance—The transfer of title to real property from one person to another by means of a written document, especially a deed.

Cooperating Agent—A member of a multiple listing service who attempts to find a buyer for a listing.

Cooperative—A building owned by a corporation, where the residents are shareholders in the corporation; each shareholder receives a proprietary lease on an individual unit and the right to use the common areas.

Co-ownership—*See*: Ownership, Concurrent.

Corner Influence—The increase in a commercial property's value that results from its location on or near a corner, with access and exposure on two streets.

Corporation—An association organized according to certain laws, in which individuals may purchase ownership shares; treated by the law as an artificial person, separate from the individual shareholders.

Corporation, Domestic—A corporation doing business in the state where it was created (incorporated).

Corporation, Foreign—A corporation doing business in one state, but created (incorporated) in another state, or in another country.

Correction Lines—In the government survey system, adjustment lines used to compensate for the curvature of the earth; they occur at 24-mile intervals (every fourth township line), where the distance between range lines is corrected to six miles.

Correlation—*See*: Reconciliation.

Cosign—To add one's signature to a promissory note in connection with a loan made to another person, agreeing to share responsibility for repaying the loan.

Cost—The amount paid for anything in money, goods, or services.

Cost, Replacement—In appraisal, the current cost of constructing a building with the same utility as the subject property with modern materials and construction methods.

Cost, Reproduction—In appraisal, the cost of constructing a replica (an exact duplicate) of the subject property, using the same materials and construction methods that were originally used, but at current prices.

Cost Approach to Value—One of the three main methods of appraisal, in which an estimate of the subject property's value is arrived at by estimating the cost of replacing (or reproducing) the improvements, then deducting the estimated accrued depreciation and adding the estimated market value of the land.

Cost Basis—*See*: Basis.

Cost of Living Index—*See*: Consumer Price Index.

Cost Recovery Deductions—*See*: Depreciation Deductions.

Co-tenancy—*See*: Ownership, Concurrent.

Counteroffer—A response to a contract offer, changing some of the terms of the original offer. It operates as a rejection of the original offer (not as an acceptance). Also called qualified acceptance.

County—An administrative subdivision of the state, created by the state and deriving all of its powers from the state.

Course—In a metes and bounds description, a direction, stated in terms of a compass bearing.

Covenant—1. A contract. 2. A promise. 3. A guarantee (express or implied) in a document such as a deed or lease. 4. A restrictive covenant.

Covenant, Restrictive—A promise to do or not do an act relating to real property, especially a promise that runs with the land; usually an owner's promise not to use property in a specified manner.

Covenant Against Encumbrances—In a deed, a promise that the property is not burdened by any encumbrances other than those that are disclosed in the deed.

Covenant of Quiet Enjoyment—A promise that a buyer or tenant's possession will not be disturbed by the previous owner, the lessor, or anyone else making a lawful claim against the property.

Covenant of Right to Convey—In a deed, a promise that the grantor has the legal ability to make a valid conveyance.

Covenant of Seisin—In a deed, a promise that the grantor actually owns the interest he or she is conveying to the grantee.

Covenant of Warranty—In a deed, a promise that the grantor will defend the grantee's title against claims superior to the grantor's that exist when the conveyance is made.

CPM—Certified Property Manager; a property manager who has satisfied the requirements set by the Institute of Real Estate Management of the National Association of Realtors®.

CRE—Counselor of Real Estate; a member of the American Society of Real Estate Counselors.

Credit—A payment receivable (owed to you), as opposed to a debit, which is a payment due (owed by you).

Credit Arranger—An intermediary between prospective borrowers and lenders, who negotiates loans; for example, a mortgage broker. Credit arrangers (as well as lenders) are required to comply with the Truth in Lending Act.

Credit History—An individual's record of bill payment and debt repayment, as revealed in a credit report compiled by a credit rating bureau.

Creditor—One who is owed a debt.

Creditor, Secured—A creditor with a security interest in or a lien against specific property. If the debt is not repaid, the secured creditor can repossess the property or (in the case of real estate) foreclose on the property and collect the debt from the sale proceeds.

Creditor, Unsecured—A creditor who does not have a lien against or other security interest in any of the debtor's property (and who therefore is less likely to be able to collect the debt if the debtor fails to pay it as agreed).

Credit Union—A type of financial institution that serves only the members of a particular group (such as a labor union or a professional association), and which has traditionally emphasized consumer loans.

Creditworthiness—The extent to which an individual is a good credit risk; how likely he or she is to repay a loan on the schedule set by the lender, or how likely to default.

Criminal Law—The body of law under which the government can prosecute an individual for crimes, wrongs against society. *Compare*: Civil Law.

Cubage—The cubic volume of an object; in the case of a building, determined by multiplying the width by the depth by the height (measuring from the basement floor to the outside surfaces of roof and walls).

Cul-de-Sac—A dead-end street, especially one with a semicircular turnaround at the end.

Curable—In reference to depreciation, capable of being corrected at a cost that could be recovered in the sales price if the property were subsequently sold. (Depreciation is incurable if it cannot be corrected and/or if it would cost more to correct than the correction would add to the property's value.)

Cure—To remedy a default, by paying money that is overdue or fulfilling other obligations that have not been met.

Customer—From the point of view of a real estate agent, a prospective property buyer.

Damage Deposit—*See*: Security Deposit.

Damages—In a civil lawsuit, an amount of money the defendant is ordered to pay the plaintiff.

Damages, Actual—Damages awarded to a plaintiff as compensation for injuries (personal injuries, property damage, or financial losses) caused by the defendant's act or failure to act. Also called compensatory damages.

Damages, Liquidated—A sum that the parties to a contract agree in advance (at the time the contract is made) will serve as full compensation in the event of a breach.

Damages, Punitive—In a civil lawsuit, an award added to actual damages, to punish the defendant for outrageous or malicious conduct and discourage others from similar conduct.

Datum—An artificial horizontal plane of elevation, established in reference to sea level, used by surveyors as a reference point in determining elevation.

Dealer—One who regularly buys and sells real estate in the ordinary course of business.

Dealer Property—Property held for sale to customers rather than for long-term investment; a developer's inventory of subdivision lots, for example.

Debit—A charge or debt owed to another.

Debtor—One who owes money to another.

Debt Service—The amount of money required to make the periodic payments of principal and interest on an amortized debt, such as a mortgage.

Decedent—A person who has died.

Declaration of Abandonment—A document recorded by an owner that voluntarily releases a property from homestead protection.

Declaration of Homestead—A recorded document that establishes homestead protection for a property that would not otherwise receive it.

Declaration of Restrictions—*See*: CC&Rs.

Decrement—A decrease in value; the opposite of increment.

Dedication—A voluntary or involuntary gift of private property for public use; may transfer ownership or simply create an easement.

Dedication, Common Law—Involuntary dedication, resulting from a property owner's acquiescence to public use of his or her property over a long period. Also called implied dedication.

Dedication, Statutory—A dedication required by law; for example, dedication of property for streets and sidewalks as a prerequisite to subdivision approval.

Deduction—An amount a taxpayer is allowed to subtract from his or her income before the tax on the income is calculated (as distinguished from a tax credit, which is deducted from the tax owed).

Deed—An instrument which, when properly executed and delivered, conveys title to real property from the grantor to the grantee.

Deed, Administrator's—A deed used by the administrator of an estate to convey property owned by a deceased person to the heirs.

Deed, Bargain and Sale—*See*: Deed, Special Warranty.

Deed, General Warranty—A deed in which the grantor warrants the title against defects that may have arisen before or during his or her period of ownership.

Deed, Gift—A deed that is not supported by valuable consideration; often lists "love and affection" as the consideration.

Deed, Grant—A deed that uses the word "grant" in its words of conveyance and carries certain implied warranties. The most commonly used type of deed in California.

Deed, Quitclaim—A deed that conveys any interest in a property that the grantor has at the time the deed is executed, without warranties.

Deed, Sheriff's—A deed delivered, on court order, to the holder of a certificate of sale when the redemption period after a mortgage foreclosure has expired.

Deed, Special Warranty—A deed in which the grantor warrants title only against defects that may have arisen during his or her period of ownership.

Deed, Tax—A deed given to a purchaser of property at a tax foreclosure sale.

Deed, Trust—*See*: Deed of Trust.

Deed, Trustee's—A deed given to a purchaser of property at a trustee's sale.

Deed, Warranty—1. A general warranty deed. 2. Any type of deed that carries warranties.

Deed, Wild—A deed that won't be discovered in a standard title search, because of a break in the chain of title.

Deed Executed under Court Order—A deed that is the result of a court action, such as judicial foreclosure or partition.

Deed in Lieu of Foreclosure—A deed given by a borrower to the lender to satisfy the debt and avoid foreclosure.

Deed of Partition—Deed used by co-owners (such as tenants in common or joint tenants) to divide up the co-owned property so that each can own a portion in severalty.

Deed of Reconveyance—The instrument used to release the security property from the lien created by a deed of trust when the debt has been repaid.

Deed of Trust—An instrument that creates a voluntary lien on real property to secure the repayment of a debt, and which includes a power of sale clause permitting nonjudicial foreclosure; the parties are the grantor or trustor (borrower), the beneficiary (the lender), and the trustee (a neutral third party).

Deed Release Provision—*See*: Release Clause.

Deed Restrictions—Provisions in a deed that restrict use of the property, and which may be either covenants or conditions.

Default—Failure to fulfill an obligation, duty, or promise, as when a borrower fails to make payments, or a tenant fails to pay rent.

Default Judgment—*See*: Judgment, Default.

Defeasance Clause—A clause in a mortgage, deed of trust, or lease that cancels or defeats a certain right upon the occurrence of a particular event.

Defeasible Fee—*See*: Fee, Defeasible.

Defendant—1. The person being sued in a civil lawsuit. 2. The accused person in a criminal lawsuit.

Deferred Maintenance—Depreciation resulting from maintenance or repairs that were postponed, causing physical deterioration of the building.

Deficiency Judgment—*See*: Judgment, Deficiency.

Degree—In surveying, a unit of circular measurement equal to $\frac{1}{360}$ of one complete rotation around a point in a plane.

Delivery—The legal transfer of a deed from the grantor to the grantee, which results in the transfer of title.

Demand—Desire to own coupled with ability to afford. This is one of the four elements of value, along with scarcity, utility, and transferability.

Demise—The transfer of an estate or interest in property to another for years, for life, or at will.

Density—In land use law, the number of buildings or occupants per unit of land.

Department of Housing and Urban Development (HUD)—The federal cabinet department responsible for public housing programs, FHA-insured loan programs, and enforcement of the Federal Fair Housing Act. The FHA and Ginnie Mae are both part of HUD.

Department of Real Estate—The agency of the state government that administers California's Real Estate Law.

Deposit—Money offered as an indication of commitment or as a protection, and which may be refunded under certain circumstances; for example, a good faith deposit or a tenant's security deposit.

Deposition—The formal, out-of-court testimony of a witness in a lawsuit, taken before trial for possible use later, during the trial; either as part of the discovery process, to determine the facts of the case, or when the witness will not be available during the trial.

Deposit Receipt—*See*: Purchase and Sale Agreement.

Depreciable Property—In the federal income tax code, property that is eligible for cost recovery deductions because it will wear out and have to be replaced.

Depreciation—1. A loss in value (caused by deferred maintenance, functional obsolescence, or external obsolescence). 2. For the purposes of income tax deductions, apportioning the cost of an asset over a period of time.

Depreciation, Accrued—Depreciation that has built up or accumulated over a period of time.

Depreciation, Age-Life—A method of estimating depreciation for appraisal purposes, based on the life expectancy of the property, assuming normal maintenance.

Depreciation, Curable—Deferred maintenance and functional obsolescence that would ordinarily be corrected by a prudent owner, because the correction cost could be recovered in the sales price.

Depreciation, Incurable—Deferred maintenance, functional obsolescence, or external obsolescence that is either impossible to correct, or not economically feasible to correct, because the cost could not be recovered in the sales price.

Depreciation, Straight-Line—A method of calculating depreciation for income tax or appraisal purposes, in which an equal portion of a structure's value is deducted each year over the anticipated useful life; when the full value of the improvement has been depreciated, its economic life is exhausted.

Depreciation Deductions—Under the federal income tax code, deductions from a taxpayer's income to permit the cost of an asset to be recovered; allowed only for depreciable property that is held for the production of income or used in a trade or business. Also called cost recovery deductions.

Depth Table—Mathematical table used in appraisal to estimate the differences in value between lots with different depths. Frontage has the greatest value, and land at the rear of a lot has the least value.

Dereliction—*See*: Reliction.

Descent—Property that is transferred by intestate succession instead of by will. A person who receives property by intestate succession is said to receive it by descent, rather than by devise or bequest.

Detached Residence—A home physically separated from the neighboring home(s), not connected by a common wall.

Developed Land—Land with man-made improvements, such as buildings or roads.

Developer—One who subdivides or improves land to achieve its most profitable use.

Development—1. Any development project, such as a new office park. 2. A housing subdivision. 3. In reference to a property's life cycle, the earliest stage, also called integration.

Devise—1. (noun) A gift of real property through a will. 2. (verb) To transfer real property by will. *Compare*: Bequest; Bequeath; Legacy.

Devisee—Someone who receives title to real property through a will. *Compare*: Beneficiary; Legatee.

Devisor—A testator who devises real property in his or her will.

Directional Growth—The direction in which a city's residential neighborhoods are expanding or expected to expand.

Disability—A physical or mental impairment that substantially limits a person in one or more major life activities, according to the Americans with Disabilities Act and Fair Housing Act.

Disaffirm—To ask a court to terminate a voidable contract.

Disbursements—Money paid out or expended.

Disclaimer—A denial of legal responsibility.

Discount—1. (verb) To sell a promissory note at less than its face value. 2. (noun) An amount withheld from the loan amount by the lender when the loan is originated; discount points.

Discount Points—A percentage of the principal amount of a loan, collected by the lender at the time a loan is originated, to give the lender an additional yield.

Discount Rate—The interest rate charged when a member bank borrows money from the Federal Reserve Bank.

Discrimination—Treating people unequally because of their race, religion, sex, national origin, age, or some other characteristic.

Disintegration—In a property's life cycle, the period of decline when the property's present economic usefulness is near an end and constant upkeep is necessary.

Dispossess—To force someone out of possession of real property through legal procedures, as in an eviction.

Documentary Transfer Tax—*See*: Tax, Documentary Transfer.

Domicile—The state where a person has his or her permanent home.

Donative Intent—The intent to transfer title immediately and unconditionally; required for proper delivery of a deed.

Double-Entry Bookkeeping—An accounting technique in which an item is entered in the ledger twice, once as a credit and once as a debit; used for some settlement statements.

Downpayment—The part of the purchase price of property that the buyer is paying in cash; the difference between the purchase price and the financing.

Downzoning—Rezoning land for a more limited use.

Drainage—A system to draw water off land, either artificially (e.g., with pipes) or naturally (e.g., with a slope).

Dual Agency—*See*: Agency, Dual.

Due-on-Sale Clause—*See*: Alienation Clause.

Duplex—A structure that contains two separate housing units, with separate entrances, living areas, baths, and kitchens.

Duress—Unlawful force or constraint used to compel someone to do something (such as sign a contract) against his or her will.

Dwelling—A building or a part of a building used or intended to be used as living quarters.

Earnest Money—*See*: Good Faith Deposit.

Easement—An irrevocable right to use some part of another person's real property for a particular purpose.

Easement, Access—An easement that enables the easement holder to reach and/or leave his or her property (the dominant tenement) by crossing the servient tenement. Also called an easement for ingress and egress.

Easement, Aviation—An easement by which a property owner allows aircraft to fly through the airspace over his or her property (above a specified height).

Easement, Implied—*See*: Easement by Implication.

Easement, Negative—An easement that prevents the servient tenant from using his or her own land in a certain way (instead of allowing the dominant tenant to use it); essentially the same thing as a restrictive covenant that runs with the land.

Easement, Positive—An easement that allows the dominant tenant to use the servient tenement in a particular way. This is the standard type of easement (see the first definition of Easement, above); the term "positive easement" is generally only used when contrasting a standard easement with a negative easement.

Easement, Prescriptive—An easement acquired by prescription; that is, by using the property openly and without the owner's permission for the period prescribed by statute.

Easement Appurtenant—An easement that benefits a piece of property, the dominant tenement. *Compare*: Easement in Gross.

Easement by Express Grant—An easement granted to another in a deed or other document.

Easement by Express Reservation—An easement created in a deed when a landowner is dividing the property, transferring the servient tenement but retaining the dominant tenement; an easement that the grantor reserves for his or her own use.

Easement by Implication—An easement created by law when a parcel of land is divided, if there has been long-standing, apparent prior use, and it is reasonably necessary for the enjoyment of the dominant tenement. Sometimes called an easement by necessity.

Easement by Necessity—1. A special type of easement by implication, created by law even when there has been no prior use, if the dominant tenement would be entirely useless without an easement. 2. Any easement by implication.

Easement in Gross—An easement that benefits a person instead of a piece of land. There is a dominant tenant, but no dominant tenement. *Compare*: Easement Appurtenant.

ECOA—*See*: Equal Credit Opportunity Act.

Economic Life—The period during which improved property will yield a return over and above the rent due to the land itself; also called the useful life.

Economic Obsolescence—*See*: Obsolescence, External.

Economic Rent—*See*: Rent, Economic.

Effective Age—*See*: Age, Effective.

Egress—A means of exiting; a way to leave a property; the opposite of ingress. The terms ingress and egress are most commonly used in reference to an access easement.

EIS—Environmental Impact Statement.

Ejectment—A legal action to recover possession of real property from someone who is not legally entitled to possession of it; an eviction.

Elements of Comparison—In the sales comparison approach to appraisal, considerations taken into account in selecting comparables and comparing comparables to the subject property. They include date of sale, location, physical characteristics, and terms of sale.

Emblements—Crops that are produced annually through the labor of the cultivator, such as wheat.

Emblements, Doctrine of—The legal rule that gives an agricultural tenant the right to enter the land to harvest crops after the lease ends.

Eminent Domain—The government's constitutional power to take (condemn) private property for public use, as long as the owner is paid just compensation.

Employee—Someone who works under the direction and control of another. *Compare*: Independent Contractor.

Encroachment—A physical intrusion onto neighboring property, usually due to a mistake regarding the location of the boundary.

Encumber—To place a lien or other encumbrance against the title to a property.

Encumbrance—A non-possessory interest in real property; a right or interest held by someone other than the property owner, which may be a lien, an easement, or a restrictive covenant.

Encumbrance, Financial—A lien.

Endorsement—Assignment of a negotiable instrument (such as a check or a promissory note) by the payee to another party, by signing the back of the instrument.

Endorsement, Special—An endorsement to a specific person (as opposed to an endorsement in blank).

Endorsement in Blank—An endorsement that does not specify a particular holder, so that the bearer—whoever has possession of the instrument—is entitled to payment.

Enjoin—To prohibit an act, or command performance of an act, by court order; to issue an injunction.

Entitlement—The amount of the borrower's guaranty in a VA loan.

EPA—Environmental Protection Agency.

Equal Credit Opportunity Act (ECOA)—A federal law that prohibits lenders from discriminating against consumer loan applicants on the basis of race, color, religion, national origin, sex, marital status, or age, or because the applicant's income is derived from public assistance.

Equilibrium—In the life cycle of a property, a period of stability, during which the property undergoes little, if any, change.

Equitable Interest or Title—*See*: Title, Equitable.

Equitable Remedy—In a civil lawsuit, a judgment granted to the plaintiff that is something other than an award of money (damages). An injunction, rescission, and specific performance are examples.

Equity—1. An owner's unencumbered interest in his or her property; the difference between the value of the property and the liens against it. 2. A judge's power to soften or set aside strict legal rules, to bring about a fair and just result in a particular case.

Equity of Redemption—The right of a property owner to redeem a property after a judicial foreclosure sale.

Erosion—Gradual loss of soil due to the action of water or wind.

Escalation Clause—A clause in a contract or mortgage that provides for payment or interest adjustments (usually increases) if specified events occur, such as a change in the property taxes or in the prime interest rate. Also called an escalator clause.

Escheat—Reversion of property to the state after a person dies intestate and no heirs can be located.

Escrow—An arrangement in which something of value (such as money or a deed) is held on behalf of the parties to a transaction by a disinterested third party (an escrow agent) until specified conditions have been fulfilled.

Escrow Agent—A company that is licensed to engage in the escrow business.

Escrow Instructions—A contract between an escrow agent and the parties to a transaction that sets forth the parties' obligations and the conditions for closing.

Estate—1. An interest in real property that is or may become possessory; either a freehold or a leasehold. 2. The property left by someone who has died.

Estate, Fee Simple—*See*: Fee Simple.

Estate, Periodic—*See*: Tenancy, Periodic.

Estate at Sufferance—*See*: Tenancy at Sufferance.

Estate at Will—*See*: Tenancy at Will.

Estate for Life—A freehold estate that lasts only as long as a specified person lives. That person is referred to as the measuring life. Commonly called a life estate.

Estate for Years—*See*: Tenancy, Term.

Estate of Inheritance—An estate that can pass to the holder's heirs, such as a fee simple.

Estoppel—A legal doctrine that prevents a person from asserting rights or facts that are inconsistent with his or her earlier actions or statements.

Estoppel Certificate—A document that prevents a person who signs it from later asserting facts different from those stated in the document. Also called an estoppel letter.

Et Al.—Abbreviation for the Latin phrase "et alius" or "et alii," meaning "and another" or "and others."

Ethics—A system of accepted principles or standards of moral conduct. *See*: Code of Ethics.

Et Ux.—Abbreviation for the Latin phrase "et uxor," meaning "and wife."

Eviction—Dispossession or expulsion of someone from real property.

Eviction, Actual—Physically forcing someone off of real property (or preventing them from re-entering), or using the legal process to make them leave. *Compare*: Eviction, Constructive.

Eviction, Constructive—When a landlord's act (or failure to act) interferes with the tenant's quiet enjoyment of the property, or makes the property unfit for its intended use, to such an extent that the tenant is forced to move out.

Eviction, Self-Help—The use of physical force, a lock-out, or a utility shut-off to evict a tenant, instead of the legal process. This is generally illegal.

Excess Land—Land that is part of a parcel that does not add to the value of that property. For instance, where the value of a property lies primarily in its frontage, additional depth would not increase the property's value.

Exchange—*See*: Tax-Free Exchange.

Exclusive Listing—*See*: Listing, Exclusive.

Exculpatory Clause—A clause in a contract that relieves one party of liability for certain defaults or problems. Such provisions are not always enforceable.

Execute—1. To sign an instrument and take any other steps (such as acknowledgment) that may be necessary to its validity. 2. To perform or complete. *See*: Contract, Executed.

Execution—The legal process in which a court orders an official (such as the sheriff) to seize and sell the property of a judgment debtor to satisfy a lien.

Executor—A person named in a will to carry out its provisions. If it is a woman, she may be referred to as the executrix, but that term is passing out of use.

Exemption—A provision holding that a law or rule does not apply to a particular person or group. For example, a person entitled to a tax exemption is not required to pay the tax.

Expenses, Fixed—Recurring property expenses, such as general real estate taxes and hazard insurance.

Expenses, Maintenance—Cleaning, supplies, utilities, tenant services, and administrative costs for income-producing property.

Expenses, Operating—For income-producing property, the fixed expenses, maintenance expenses, and reserves for replacement; does not include debt service.

Expenses, Variable—Expenses incurred in connection with property that do not occur on a set schedule, such as the cost of repairing a roof damaged in a storm.

Express—Stated in words, whether spoken or written. *Compare*: Implied.

Extender Clause—*See:* Safety Clause.

External Obsolescence—*See*: Obsolescence, External.

Failure of Purpose—When the intended purpose of an agreement or arrangement can no longer be achieved. In most cases, this releases the parties from their obligations.

Fair Employment and Housing Act—A California civil rights law that prohibits all housing discrimination based on race, color, religion, sex, marital status, national origin, disability, or ancestry.

Fair Housing Act—*See*: Federal Fair Housing Act.

Fannie Mae—Popular name for the Federal National Mortgage Association (FNMA).

FDIC—*See*: Federal Deposit Insurance Corporation.

Feasibility Study—A cost-benefit analysis of a proposed project, often required by lenders before giving a loan commitment.

Fed—The Federal Reserve.

Federal Deposit Insurance Corporation (FDIC)—A federal agency that insures deposits in financial institutions.

Federal Fair Housing Act—A law enacted in 1968 which makes it illegal to discriminate on the basis of race, color, religion, sex, national origin, handicap, or familial status in the sale or rental of residential property (or vacant land that will be used for residential construction).

Federal Home Loan Bank System—A federal organization that provides reserve funds for savings and loan associations, performing many of the same functions that the Federal Reserve System does for commercial banks.

Federal Home Loan Mortgage Corporation (FHLMC)—One of the government-sponsored secondary market agencies; commonly called Freddie Mac.

Federal Housing Administration (FHA)—An agency within the Department of Housing and Urban Development (HUD). Its main activity is insuring home mortgage loans, to encourage lenders to make more affordable loans.

Federal National Mortgage Association (FNMA)—One of the government-sponsored secondary market agencies; commonly called Fannie Mae.

Federal Reserve—The government body that regulates commercial banks and implements monetary policy in an attempt to keep the national economy running well. Often referred to as the Fed.

Federal Reserve System—The twelve Federal Reserve Banks, which implement federal monetary policy through setting the federal lending rates and reserve requirements.

Federal Trade Commission (FTC)—A federal agency responsible for investigating and eliminating unfair and deceptive business practices. It is also the agency charged with enforcing the Truth in Lending Act.

Fee—*See*: Fee Simple.

Fee, Defeasible—A fee simple estate that is subject to termination if a certain condition is not met or if a specified event occurs. Also called a conditional fee or qualified fee.

Fee, Qualified—*See*: Fee, Defeasible.

Fee Broker—*See*: Broker, Fee.

Fee Simple—The highest and most complete form of ownership, which is of potentially infinite duration. Also called a fee or a fee simple absolute.

Fee Simple Subject to a Condition Subsequent—*See*: Fee, Defeasible.

FHA—*See*: Federal Housing Administration. *See also*: Loan, FHA.

FHLMC—*See*: Federal Home Loan Mortgage Corporation.

Fidelity Bond—A bond to cover losses resulting from the dishonesty of an employee.

Fiduciary Relationship—A relationship of trust and confidence, where one party owes the other (or both parties owe each other) loyalty and a higher standard of good faith than is owed to third parties. For example, an agent is a fiduciary in relation to the principal; husband and wife are fiduciaries in relation to one another.

Finance Charge—Any charge a borrower is assessed, directly or indirectly, in connection with a loan. *See also*: Total Finance Charge.

Financial Statement—A summary of facts showing the financial condition of an individual or a business, including a detailed list of assets and liabilities. Also called a balance sheet.

Financing Statement—A brief instrument that is recorded to perfect and give constructive notice of a creditor's security interest in an article of personal property.

Finder's Fee—A referral fee paid to someone for directing a buyer or a seller to a real estate agent.

Firm Commitment—*See*: Commitment.

FIRPTA—*See*: Foreign Investment in Real Property Tax Act.

First Lien Position—The position held by a mortgage or deed of trust that has higher lien priority than any other mortgage or deed of trust against the property.

First Refusal, Right of—*See*: Right of First Refusal.

Fiscal Policy—The federal government's financial regime of spending, collecting revenue, and borrowing; managed by the United States Treasury.

Fiscal Year—Any twelve-month period used as a business year for accounting, tax, and other financial purposes, as opposed to a calendar year.

Fixed Disbursement Plan—A construction financing arrangement that calls for the loan proceeds to be disbursed in a series of predetermined installments at various stages of the construction.

Fixed-Rate Loan—*See*: Loan, Fixed-Rate.

Fixed Term—A period of time that has a definite beginning and ending.

Fixture—An item that used to be personal property but has been attached to or closely associated with real property in such a way that it has legally become part of the real property. *See*: Annexation, Actual; Annexation, Constructive.

Floor Area Ratio—A zoning requirement that controls the ratio between a building's floor space and the percentage of the lot it occupies.

Flowage Rights—The right to submerge or flood a piece of land. Also called a flowage easement.

FNMA—*See*: Federal National Mortgage Association.

Footloose Industry—An industry that is not tied to a particular location.

Foreclosure—Sale of property initiated by a lienholder, against the owner's wishes, so that the unpaid lien can be satisfied from the sale proceeds.

Foreclosure, Judicial—1. The sale of property pursuant to court order to satisfy a lien. 2. A lawsuit filed by a mortgagee or deed of trust beneficiary to foreclose on the security property when the borrower has defaulted.

Foreclosure, Nonjudicial—Foreclosure by a trustee under the power of sale clause in a deed of trust.

Foreign Investment in Real Property Tax Act—The Foreign Investment in Real Property Tax Act, which requires that an escrow agent must withhold funds from the sale of real property by a seller who is not a U.S. citizen, in order to prevent tax evasion.

Foreshore—Land between the mean high and mean low water marks. Also called foreshore land.

Forfeiture—Loss of a right or something else of value as a result of failure to perform an obligation or condition.

Franchise—A right or privilege granted by a government to conduct a certain business, or a right granted by a private business to use its trade name in conducting business.

Fraud—An intentional or negligent misrepresentation or concealment of a material fact, which is relied upon by another, who is induced to enter a transaction and harmed as a result.

Fraud, Actual—Intentional deceit or misrepresentation to cheat or defraud another.

Fraud, Constructive—A breach of duty that misleads the person the duty was owed to, without an intention to deceive. For example, if a seller gives a buyer inaccurate information about the property without realizing that it is false, that may be constructive fraud.

Freddie Mac—Popular name for the Federal Home Loan Mortgage Corporation (FHLMC).

Free and Clear—Ownership of real property completely free of any liens.

Freehold—A possessory interest in real property that has an indeterminable duration. It can be either a fee simple or an estate for life. Someone who has a freehold estate has title to the property (as opposed to someone who has a leasehold estate, who is only a tenant).

Frontage—The distance a property extends along a street or a body of water; the distance between the two side boundaries at the front of the lot.

Front Foot—A measurement of property for sale or valuation, with each foot of frontage presumed to extend the entire depth of the lot.

Front Money—The cash required to get a project or venture underway; includes initial expenses such as attorney's fees, feasibility studies, loan charges, and a downpayment.

Fructus Industriales—Plants planted and cultivated by people, such as crops. This is a Latin phrase meaning "fruits of industry."

Fructus Naturales—Naturally occurring plants ("fruits of nature").

Functional Obsolescence—*See*: Obsolescence, Functional.

Gain—Under the federal income tax code, that portion of the proceeds from the sale of a capital asset, such as real estate, that is recognized as taxable profit.

Garnishment—A legal process by which a creditor gains access to the funds or personal property of a debtor that are in the hands of a third party. For example, if the debtor's wages are garnished, the employer is required to turn over part of each paycheck to the creditor.

General Agent—*See*: Agent, General.

General Lien—*See*: Lien, General.

General Plan—A comprehensive, long-term plan of development for a community, which is implemented by zoning and other laws. Also called a comprehensive plan or a master plan.

Gift Funds—Money that a relative (or other third party) gives to a buyer who otherwise would not have enough cash to close the transaction.

Ginnie Mae—The Government National Mortgage Association (GNMA).

GNMA—*See*: Government National Mortgage Association.

Good Faith Deposit—A deposit that a prospective buyer gives the seller as evidence of his or her good faith intent to complete the transaction. Also called an earnest money deposit.

Good Faith Improver—*See*: Innocent Improver.

Good Will—An intangible asset of a business resulting from a good reputation with the public, serving as an indication of future return business.

Government Lot—In the government survey system, a parcel of land that is not a regular section (one mile square), because of the convergence of range lines, or because of a body of water or some other obstacle; assigned a government lot number.

Government National Mortgage Association (GNMA)—One of the three major secondary market agencies, commonly called Ginnie Mae; a federal agency that is part of the Department of Housing and Urban Development.

Government Survey System—A system of grids made up of range and township lines that divide the land into townships, which are further subdivided into sections. A particular property is identified by its location within a particular section, township, and range. Also called the rectangular survey system.

Grant—To transfer or convey an interest in real property by means of a written instrument.

Grant Deed—*See*: Deed, Grant.

Grantee—One who receives a grant of real property.

Granting Clause—Words in a deed that indicate the grantor's intent to transfer an interest in property.

Grantor—One who grants an interest in real property to another.

Gross Income Multiplier—A figure which is multiplied by a rental property's gross income to arrive at an estimate of the property's value. Also called a gross rent multiplier.

Gross Income Multiplier Method—A method of appraising residential property by reference to its rental value. Also called the gross rent multiplier method.

Group Boycott—In the real estate profession, an agreement between two or more real estate brokers to exclude other brokers from equal participation in real estate activities.

Guardian—A person appointed by a court to administer the affairs of a minor or an incompetent person.

Guide Meridians—In the government survey system, lines running north-south (parallel to the principal meridian) at 24-mile intervals.

Habendum Clause—A clause included after the granting clause in many deeds. It begins "to have and to hold" and describes the type of estate the grantee will hold.

Habitability, Implied Warranty of—A warranty implied by law in every residential lease, stating that the property is fit for habitation.

Heir—Someone entitled to inherit another's property under the laws of intestate succession.

Heirs and Assigns—A phrase used in legal documents to cover all successors to a person's interest in property. Assigns are successors who acquire title in some manner other than inheritance, such as by deed.

Hereditament—Property (real or personal) that can be inherited.

Hereditament, Corporeal—Tangible property, real or personal, that can be inherited; property with physical substance, such as a car or a house.

Hereditament, Incorporeal—Intangible property, real or personal, that can be inherited, such as an easement appurtenant or accounts receivable.

Highest and Best Use—The use which, at the time of appraisal, is most likely to produce the greatest net return from the property over a given period of time.

Historical Rent—*See*: Rent, Contract.

HMDA—*See*: Home Mortgage Disclosure Act.

Holden Act—*See*: Housing Financial Discrimination Act.

Holder in Due Course—A person who obtains a negotiable instrument for value, in good faith, without notice that it is overdue or notice of any defenses against it.

Holdover Tenant—*See*: Tenant, Holdover.

Home Mortgage Disclosure Act (HMDA)—A federal law that requires large institutional lenders to make annual reports on residential mortgage loans. The reports disclose areas where few or no home loans have been made and alert regulators to potential redlining.

Homeowners' Association—A nonprofit association made up of homeowners in a subdivision, responsible for enforcing the CC&Rs and managing other community affairs.

Homestead—An owner-occupied dwelling, together with any appurtenant outbuildings and land.

Homestead Law—A state law that provides limited protection against judgment creditors' claims for homestead property.

Housing Financial Discrimination Act—A California civil rights law that requires lenders to make lending decisions based on the merits of the borrower and the security property, rather than the neighborhood where the property is located. Also called the Holden Act.

HUD—The Department of Housing and Urban Development.

Hundred Percent Location—For a retail business, a location (normally in a city's downtown business area) that is considered the best for attracting business.

Hypothecate—To make property security for an obligation without giving up possession of it (as opposed to pledging, which involves surrender of possession).

ILSFDA—*See*: Interstate Land Sales Full Disclosure Act.

Implied—Not expressed in words, but understood from actions or circumstances. *Compare*: Express.

Impound Account—A bank account maintained by a lender for payment of property taxes and insurance premiums on the security property. The lender requires the borrower to make regular deposits, and pays the expenses out of the account. Also called a reserve account.

Improvements—Man-made additions to real property.

Improvements, Misplaced—Improvements that do not fit the most profitable use of the site. They can be overimprovements or underimprovements.

Imputed Knowledge—A legal doctrine stating that a principal is considered to have notice of information that the agent has, even if the agent never told the principal.

Inchoate—Partial, incomplete, unfinished; begun but not completed, as in the case of a contract that has not been executed by all the parties.

Inchoate Instruments—Documents that are not fully executed, or that are required to be recorded and have not been.

Inchoate Interest—A future interest in real estate, such as an interest a minor will receive when he or she comes of age.

Income, Disposable—Income remaining after income taxes have been paid.

Income, Effective Gross—A measure of a rental property's capacity to generate income; calculated by subtracting a bad debt/vacancy factor from the economic rent (potential gross income).

Income, Gross—A property's total income before making any deductions (for bad debts, vacancies, operating expenses, etc.).

Income, Net—The income that is capitalized to estimate the property's value; calculated by subtracting the property's operating expenses (fixed expenses, maintenance expenses, and reserves for replacement) from the effective gross income.

Income, Potential Gross—A property's economic rent; the income it could earn if it were available for lease in the current market.

Income, Residual—The amount of income that an applicant for a VA loan has left over after taxes, recurring obligations, and the proposed housing expense have been deducted from his or her gross monthly income.

Income, Spendable—The income that remains after deducting operating expenses, debt service, and income taxes from a property's gross income. Also called net spendable income or cash flow.

Income Approach to Value—One of the three main methods of appraisal, in which an estimate of the subject property's value is based on the net income it produces; also called the capitalization method or investor's method of appraisal.

Income Property—Property that generates rent or other income for the owner, such as an apartment building. In the federal income tax code, it is referred to as property held for the production of income.

Income Ratio—A standard used in qualifying a buyer for a loan, to determine whether he or she has sufficient income. The buyer's debts and proposed housing expense should not exceed a specified percentage of his or her income.

Incompetent—Not legally competent; not of sound mind.

Incorporeal Rights—Rights in real property that do not involve physical possession of anything, such as a dominant tenant's right to use the servient tenant's land—an easement. An easement appurtenant is an incorporeal hereditament, because it is inheritable, but an easement in gross is merely an incorporeal right, because it is not inheritable.

Increment—An increase in value; the opposite of decrement.

Independent Contractor—A person who contracts to do a job for another, but retains control over how he or she will carry out the task, rather than following detailed instructions. *Compare*: Employee.

Index—A published statistical report that indicates changes in the cost of money; used as the basis for interest rate adjustments in an ARM.

Index, Tract—An index of recorded documents in which all documents that carry a particular legal description are grouped together.

Indexes, Grantor/Grantee—Indexes of recorded documents maintained by the recorder, with each document listed in alphabetical order according to the last name of the grantor (in the grantor index) and grantee (in the grantee index). The indexes list the recording number of all documents, so that they can be located in the public record.

Ingress—A means of entering a property; the opposite of egress. The terms ingress and egress are most commonly used in reference to an access easement.

Injunction—A court order prohibiting someone from performing an act, or commanding performance of an act.

Innocent Improver—Someone who makes an improvement on land in the mistaken belief that he or she owns the land. Also called a good faith improver.

Installment Note—*See*: Note, Installment.

Installment Sale—Under the federal income tax code, a sale in which less than 100% of the sales price is received in the year the sale takes place.

Instrument—A legal document, usually one that transfers title (such as a deed), creates a lien (such as a mortgage), or establishes a right to payment (such as a promissory note or contract).

Insurance, Hazard—Insurance against damage to real property caused by fire, flood, theft, or other mishap. Also called casualty insurance.

Insurance, Homeowner's—Insurance against damage to the real property and the homeowner's personal property.

Insurance, Mortgage—Insurance that protects a lender against losses resulting from the borrower's default.

Insurance, Mutual Mortgage—The mortgage insurance provided by the FHA to lenders who make loans through FHA programs.

Insurance, Private Mortgage (PMI)—Insurance provided by private companies to conventional lenders for loans with loan-to-value ratios over 80%.

Insurance, Title—Insurance that protects against losses resulting from undiscovered title defects. An owner's policy protects the buyer, while a mortgagee's policy protects the lien position of the buyer's lender.

Insurance, Title, Extended Coverage—Title insurance that covers problems that should be discovered by an inspection of the property (such as encroachments and adverse possession), in addition to the problems covered by standard coverage policies. An extended coverage policy is sometimes referred to as an ALTA (American Land Title Association) policy.

Insurance, Title, Standard Coverage—Title insurance that protects against latent title defects (such as forged deeds) and undiscovered recorded encumbrances, but does not protect against problems that would only be discovered by an inspection of the property.

Integration—In a property's life cycle, the earliest stage, when the property is being developed. Also called development.

Interest—1. A right or share in something (such as a piece of real estate). 2. A charge a borrower pays to a lender for the use of the lender's money.

Interest, Compound—Interest computed on both the principal and its accrued interest. *Compare*: Interest, Simple.

Interest, Future—An interest in property that will or may become possessory at some point in the future, such as a remainder or reversion.

Interest, Interim—*See*: Interest, Prepaid.

Interest, Prepaid—Interest on a new loan that must be paid at the time of closing; covers the interest due for the first month of the loan term. Also called interim interest.

Interest, Simple—Interest that is computed on the principal amount of the loan only, which is the type of interest charged in connection with real estate loans. *Compare*: Interest, Compound.

Interest, Undivided—A co-owner's interest, giving him or her the right to possession of the whole property, rather than to a particular section of it.

Interpleader—A court action filed by someone who is holding funds that two or more people are claiming. The holder turns the funds over to the court; the court resolves the dispute and delivers the money to the party who is entitled to it.

Interstate Land Sales Full Disclosure Act (ILSFDA)—Federal legislation designed to provide buyers with full and accurate information in regard to subdivided property that is sold or advertised across state lines.

Intestate—Without a valid will.

Intestate Succession—Distribution of the property of a person who died intestate to his or her heirs.

Invalid—Not legally binding or legally effective; not valid.

Inventory—A detailed list of the stock-in-trade of a business.

Inverse Condemnation Action—A court action by a private landowner against the government, seeking compensation for damage to property as a result of government action.

Inverted Pyramid—A way of visualizing ownership of real property. In theory, a property owner owns all the earth, water, and air enclosed by a pyramid that has its tip at the center of the earth and extends up through the property boundaries out into the sky.

Investment Property—Unimproved property held as an investment in the expectation that it will appreciate in value.

Involuntary Conversion—For income tax purposes, when an asset is converted into cash without the voluntary action of the owner, such as through a condemnation award or insurance proceeds.

Involuntary Lien—*See*: Lien, Involuntary.

Joint Venture—Two or more individuals or companies joining together for one project or a related series of projects, but not as an ongoing business. *Compare*: Partnership.

Judgment—1. A court's binding determination of the rights and duties of the parties in a lawsuit. 2. A court order requiring one party to pay the other damages.

Judgment, Default—A court judgment in favor of the plaintiff due to the defendant's failure to answer the complaint or appear at a hearing.

Judgment, Deficiency—A personal judgment entered against a borrower in favor of the lender if the proceeds from a foreclosure sale of the security property are not enough to pay off the debt.

Judgment Creditor—A person who is owed money as a result of a judgment in a lawsuit.

Judgment Debtor—A person who owes money as a result of a judgment in a lawsuit.

Judgment Lien—*See*: Lien, Judgment.

Judicial Foreclosure—*See*: Foreclosure, Judicial.

Just Compensation—The compensation that the Constitution requires the government to pay a property owner when the property is taken under the power of eminent domain.

Laches, Doctrine of—A legal principle holding that the law will refuse to protect those who fail to assert their legal rights within the time period prescribed by the statute of limitations, or (if there is no applicable statute of limitations) within a reasonable time.

Land—In the legal sense, the solid part of the surface of the earth, everything affixed to it by nature or by man, and anything on it or in it, such as minerals and water; real property.

Land Contract—*See*: Contract, Land.

Landlocked Property—A parcel of land without access to a road or highway.

Landlord—A landowner who has leased his or her property to another. Also called a lessor.

Landmark—A monument, natural or artificial, set up on the boundary between two adjacent properties, to show where the boundary is.

Land Project—A subdivision of 50 or more unimproved parcels intended for residential use, located in a remote and thinly-populated area.

Land Residual Process—A method of appraising vacant land.

Latent Defects—Defects that are not visible or apparent (as opposed to patent defects).

Lateral Support—*See*: Support, Lateral.

Latitude Lines—*See*: Parallels.

Lawful Object—An objective or purpose of a contract that does not violate the law or a judicial determination of public policy.

Lease—A conveyance of a leasehold estate from the fee owner to a tenant; a contract in which one party pays the other rent in exchange for the possession of real estate. Also called a rental agreement.

Lease, Fixed—A lease in which the rent is set at a fixed amount, and the landlord pays most or all of the operating expenses (such as utilities, taxes, insurance, and maintenance costs). Also called a flat lease, gross lease, or straight lease.

Lease, Graduated—A lease in which it is agreed that the rental payments will increase at intervals by a specified amount or according to a speci-fied formula.

Lease, Gross—*See*: Lease, Fixed.

Lease, Ground—A lease of the land only, usually for a long term, to a tenant who intends to construct a building on the property.

Lease, Net—A lease requiring the tenant to pay all the costs of maintaining the property (such as taxes, insurance, and repairs), in addition to the rent paid to the landlord.

Lease, Percentage—A lease in which the rent is based on a percentage of the tenant's monthly or annual gross sales.

Lease, Sandwich—A leasehold interest lying between the property owner's interest and the interest of the tenant in possession. For example, when the tenant in a ground lease constructs a building and rents out space in the building, he or she is sandwiched between the landowner's interest and the interest of his or her building's tenant.

Lease, Straight—*See*: Lease, Fixed.

Leaseback—*See*: Sale-Leaseback.

Leasehold—A possessory interest in real property that has a limited duration. Also called a less-than-freehold estate.

Legacy—A gift of personal property by will. Also called a bequest.

Legal Description—A precise description of a parcel of real property; may be a lot and block description, a metes and bounds description, or a government survey description.

Legal Person—*See*: Artificial Person.

Legatee—Someone who receives personal property (a legacy) under a will.

Lender, Institutional—A bank, savings and loan, or similar organization that invests other people's funds in loans; as opposed to an individual or private lender, which invests its own funds.

Lessee—One who leases property from another; a tenant.

Lessor—One who leases property to another; a landlord.

Less-Than-Freehold—*See*: Leasehold.

Leverage—The effective use of borrowed money to finance an investment such as real estate.

Levy—To impose a tax.

Liability—1. A debt or obligation. 2. Legal responsibility.

Liability, Joint and Several—A form of liability in which two or more persons are responsible for a debt both individually and as a group.

Liability, Limited—A situation in which a business investor is not personally liable for all of the debts of the business, as in the case of a limited partner or a corporate shareholder.

Liability, Vicarious—A legal doctrine stating that a principal can be held liable for harms to third parties resulting from an agent's actions.

Liable—Legally responsible.

License—1. Official permission to do a particular thing that the law does not allow everyone to do. 2. Revocable, non-assignable permission to use another person's land for a particular purpose. *Compare*: Easement.

LID—Local Improvement District.

Lien—A non-possessory interest in real property, giving the lienholder the right to foreclose if the owner doesn't pay a debt owed to the lienholder; a financial encumbrance on the owner's title.

Lien, Attachment—A lien intended to prevent transfer of the property pending the outcome of litigation.

Lien, Construction—*See*: Lien, Mechanic's.

Lien, Equitable—A lien arising as a matter of fairness, rather than by agreement or by operation of law.

Lien, General—A lien against all the property of a debtor, rather than a particular piece of his or her property. *Compare*: Lien, Specific.

Lien, Involuntary—A lien that arises by operation of law, without the consent of the property owner. Also called a statutory lien.

Lien, Judgment—A general lien against a judgment debtor's property, which the judgment creditor creates by recording an abstract of judgment in the county where the property is located.

Lien, Materialman's—A construction lien in favor of someone who supplied materials for a project (as opposed to labor).

Lien, Mechanic's—A lien on property in favor of someone who provided labor or materials to improve it. Also called a construction lien or materialman's lien.

Lien, Property Tax—A specific lien on property to secure payment of property taxes.

Lien, Specific—A lien that attaches only to a particular piece of property (as opposed to a general lien, which attaches to all of the debtor's property).

Lien, Statutory—*See*: Lien, Involuntary.

Lien, Tax—A lien on property to secure the payment of taxes.

Lien, Voluntary—A lien placed against property with the consent of the owner; a deed of trust or a mortgage.

Lienholder, Junior—A secured creditor whose lien is lower in priority than another's lien.

Lien Priority—The order in which liens are paid off out of the proceeds of a foreclosure sale.

Lien Theory—The theory holding that a mortgage or deed of trust does not involve a transfer of title to the lender, but merely creates a lien against the property in the lender's favor. *Compare*: Title Theory.

Life Estate—A freehold estate that lasts only as long as a specified person lives. That person is referred to as the measuring life.

Life Tenant—Someone who owns a life estate; the person entitled to possession of the property during the measuring life.

Like-Kind Exchange—*See*: Tax-Free Exchange.

Limited Liability—*See*: Liability, Limited.

Limited Liability Company —A form of business entity that offers both limited liability for its owners and certain tax benefits.

Limited Partnership—*See*: Partnership, Limited.

Lineal—Relating to a line; having only length, without depth. A lineal mile is 5,280 feet in distance.

Liquidated Damages—*See*: Damages, Liquidated.

Lis Pendens—A recorded notice stating that there is a lawsuit pending that may affect title to the defendant's real estate.

Listing—A written agency contract between a seller and a real estate broker, stipulating that the broker will be paid a commission for finding (or attempting to find) a buyer for the seller's property. Also called a listing agreement.

Listing, Exclusive—Either an exclusive agency listing or an exclusive right to sell listing.

Listing, Exclusive Agency—A listing agreement that entitles the broker to a commission if anyone other than the seller finds a buyer for the property during the listing term.

Listing, Exclusive Right to Sell—A listing agreement that entitles the broker to a commission if anyone—including the seller—finds a buyer for the property during the listing term.

Listing, Net—A listing agreement in which the seller sets a net amount he or she is willing to accept for the property. If the actual selling price exceeds that amount, the broker is entitled to keep the excess as his or her commission.

Listing, Open—A nonexclusive listing, given by a seller to as many brokers as he or she chooses. If the property is sold, a broker is only entitled to a commission if he or she was the procuring cause of the sale.

Listing Agreement—*See*: Listing.

Littoral Land—Land that borders on a stationary body of water (such as a lake, as opposed to a river or stream). *Compare*: Riparian Land.

Littoral Rights—The water rights of an owner of littoral land, in regard to use of the water in the lake.

LLC—*See*: Limited Liability Company.

Loan, Amortized—A loan that requires regular installment payments of both principal and interest (as opposed to an interest-only loan). It is fully amortized if the installment payments will pay off the full amount of the principal and all of the interest by the end of the repayment period. It is partially amortized if the installment payments will cover only part of the principal, so that a balloon payment of the remaining principal balance is required at the end of the repayment period.

Loan, Called—A loan that has been accelerated by the lender. *See*: Acceleration Clause.

Loan, Carryback—*See*: Mortgage, Purchase Money.

Loan, Conforming—A loan made in accordance with the standardized underwriting criteria of the major secondary market agencies, Fannie Mae and Freddie Mac, and which therefore can be sold to those agencies.

Loan, Construction—A loan to finance the cost of constructing a building, usually providing that the loan funds will be advanced in installments as the work progresses. Also called an interim loan.

Loan, Conventional—An institutional loan that is not insured or guaranteed by a government agency.

Loan, FHA—A loan made by an institutional lender and insured by the Federal Housing Administration, so that the FHA will reimburse the lender for losses that result if the borrower defaults.

Loan, Fixed-Rate—A loan on which the interest rate will remain the same throughout the entire loan term. *Compare*: Mortgage, Adjustable-Rate.

Loan, G.I.—*See*: Loan, VA-Guaranteed.

Loan, Guaranteed—A loan in which a third party has agreed to reimburse the lender for losses that result if the borrower defaults.

Loan, Interest-Only—A loan that requires the borrower to pay only the interest during the loan term, so that the entire amount borrowed (the principal) is due at the end of the term.

Loan, Interim—*See*: Loan, Construction.

Loan, Participation—A loan in which the lender receives some yield on the loan in addition to the interest, such as a percentage of the income generated by the property, or a share in the borrower's equity in the property.

Loan, Permanent—*See*: Loan, Take-Out.

Loan, Rollover—A loan in which the interest rate is periodically renegotiated, typically every three years or every five years.

Loan, Seasoned—A loan with an established record of timely payment by the borrower.

Loan, Take-Out—Long-term financing used to replace a construction loan (an interim loan) when construction has been completed. Also called a permanent loan.

Loan, VA-Guaranteed—A home loan made by an institutional lender to an eligible veteran, where the Department of Veterans Affairs will reimburse the lender for losses if the veteran borrower defaults.

Loan Correspondent—An intermediary who arranges loans of an investor's money to borrowers, and then services the loans.

Loan Fee—A loan origination fee or assumption fee.

Loan Term—The length of time over which a mortgage will be repaid.

Loan-to-Value Ratio (LTV)—The relationship between the loan amount and either the sales price or the appraised value of the property (whichever is less), expressed as a percentage.

Local Market—*See*: Primary Mortgage Market.

Lock-In Clause—A clause in a promissory note or land contract that prohibits prepayment before a specified date, or prohibits it altogether.

Lot—A parcel of land; especially, a parcel in a subdivision.

Lot and Block Description—The type of legal description used for platted property. It states the property's lot number and block number and the name of the subdivision, referring to the plat map recorded in the county where the property is located. Sometimes called a maps and plats description.

Love and Affection—The consideration often listed on a deed when real estate is conveyed between family members with no money exchanged. The law recognizes love and affection as good consideration (as distinguished from valuable consideration, which is money, goods, or services).

LTV—*See*: Loan-to-Value Ratio.

MAI—Member of the Appraiser's Institute. The initials identify a member of the American Institute of Real Estate Appraisers of the National Association of Realtors®.

Majority, Age of—The age at which a person becomes legally competent; generally, 18 years old. *Compare*: Minor.

Maker—The person who signs a promissory note, promising to repay a debt. *Compare*: Payee.

Maps and Plats—*See*: Lot and Block Description.

Margin—In an adjustable-rate mortgage, the difference between the index rate and the interest rate charged to the borrower.

Marginal Land—Land that is of little economic value and barely repays the cost of working it.

Marketable Title—*See*: Title, Marketable.

Market Data Approach—*See*: Sales Comparison Approach.

Market-Oriented Industry—An industry that requires appropriate transportation facilities for delivery of raw materials and distribution of the finished product.

Market Price—1. The current price generally being charged for something in the marketplace. 2. The price actually paid for a property. *Compare*: Value, Market.

Market Value—See: Value, Market.

Master Plan—*See*: General Plan.

Master/Servant Relationship—A legal term for a standard employer/employee relationship.

Material Fact—An important fact; one that is likely to influence a decision.

Maturity Date—The date by which a loan is supposed to be paid off in full.

Measuring Life—*See*: Life Estate.

Meeting of Minds—*See*: Mutual Consent.

Megalopolis—An extensive, heavily populated, continuously urban area, including any number of cities.

Merger—1. Uniting two or more separate properties by transferring ownership of all of them to one person. 2. When the owner of a parcel acquires title to one or more adjacent parcels.

Meridian—An imaginary line running north and south, passing through the earth's poles. Also called a longitude line.

Meridian, Principal—In the government survey system, the main north-south line in a particular grid, used as the starting point in numbering the ranges.

Meridians, Guide—In the government survey system, lines running north-south (parallel to the principal meridian) at 24-mile intervals.

Metes—Measurements.

Metes and Bounds Description—A legal description that starts at an identifiable point of beginning, then describes the property's boundaries in terms of courses (compass directions) and distances, ultimately returning to the point of beginning.

Mill—One-tenth of one cent; a measure used to state property tax rates in some cases. For example, a tax rate of one mill on the dollar is the same as a rate of one-tenth of one percent of the assessed value of the property.

Mineral Rights—Rights to the minerals located beneath the surface of a piece of property.

Minimum Property Requirements (MPR)—A lender's requirements concerning the physical condition of a building, which must be met before a loan can be approved.

Minor—A person who has not yet reached the age of majority; generally, a person under 18.

MIP—Mortgage insurance premium; especially a premium charged in connection with an FHA-insured loan.

Misrepresentation—A false or misleading statement. *See*: Fraud.

MLS—Multiple Listing Service.

Monetary Policy—The federal government's management of the availability and cost of borrowed money; overseen by the Federal Reserve System.

Monopoly—Exclusive control over the production or sale of a product or service by a single entity or group.

Monument—A visible marker (natural or artificial) used in a survey or a metes and bounds description to establish the boundaries of a piece of property.

Mortgage—1. An instrument that creates a voluntary lien on real property to secure repayment of a debt, and which (unlike a deed of trust) does not include a power of sale, so it can only be foreclosed judicially. The parties are the mortgagor (borrower) and mortgagee (lender). 2. The term is often used more generally, to refer to either a mortgage or a deed of trust. *Note: If you do not find the specific term you are looking for here under "Mortgage," check the entries under "Loan."*

Mortgage, Adjustable-Rate (ARM)—A loan in which the interest rate is periodically increased or decreased to reflect changes in the cost of money. *Compare*: Loan, Fixed-Rate.

Mortgage, Balloon—A partially amortized mortgage loan that requires a large balloon payment at the end of the loan term.

Mortgage, Blanket—A mortgage that covers more than one parcel of property.

Mortgage, Budget—A loan in which the monthly payments include a share of the property taxes and insurance, in addition to principal and interest. The lender places the money for taxes and insurance in an impound account.

Mortgage, Chattel—An instrument that makes personal property (chattels) security for a loan. In states that have adopted the Uniform Commercial Code (including California), the chattel mortgage has been replaced by the security agreement.

Mortgage, Closed—A loan that cannot be paid off early.

Mortgage, Closed-End—A loan that does not allow the borrower to increase the balance owed; the opposite of an open-end mortgage.

Mortgage, Direct Reduction—A loan that requires a fixed amount of principal to be paid in each payment. The total payment becomes steadily smaller, because the interest portion becomes smaller with each payment as the principal balance decreases.

Mortgage, First—The mortgage on a property that has first lien position; the one with higher lien priority than any other mortgage against the property.

Mortgage, Graduated Payment—A mortgage which allows a borrower to make smaller payments at first, and larger payments as the borrower's earnings increase.

Mortgage, Growing Equity—A fixed-rate mortgage where the payment amount varies according to a schedule in order to facilitate a quicker payoff.

Mortgage, Hard Money—A mortgage given to a lender in exchange for cash, as opposed to one given in exchange for credit.

Mortgage, Junior—A mortgage that has lower lien priority than another mortgage against the same property. Sometimes called a secondary mortgage.

Mortgage, Level Payment—An amortized loan with payments that are the same amount each month, although the portion of the payment that is applied to principal steadily increases and the portion of the payment applied to interest steadily decreases. *See*: Loan, Amortized.

Mortgage, Open—A mortgage without a prepayment penalty.

Mortgage, Open-End—A loan that permits the borrower to reborrow the money he or she has repaid on the principal, usually up to the original loan amount, without executing a new loan agreement.

Mortgage, Package—A mortgage used in home financing that is secured by certain items of personal property (such as appliances or carpeting) in addition to the real property.

Mortgage, Participation—A mortgage in which the lender receives a percentage of the earnings generated by the property, as well as collecting interest on the loan. Typically used only for commercial projects.

Mortgage, Purchase Money—1. When a seller extends credit to a buyer to finance the purchase of the property, accepting a deed of trust or mortgage instead of cash. Sometimes called a takeback or carryback loan. 2. In a more general sense, any loan the borrower uses to buy the security property (as opposed to a loan secured by property the borrower already owns).

Mortgage, Reverse Equity—A mortgage that provides a steady income source for older homeowners by allowing them to receive monthly payments by borrowing against their home's equity.

Mortgage, Satisfaction of—The document a mortgagee gives the mortgagor when the mortgage debt has been paid in full, acknowledging that the debt has been paid and the mortgage is no longer a lien against the property. Also called a certificate of discharge or mortgage release.

Mortgage, Secondary—*See*: Mortgage, Junior.

Mortgage, Senior—A mortgage that has higher lien priority than another mortgage against the same property; the opposite of a junior mortgage.

Mortgage, Shared Appreciation—A mortgage in which a lender is entitled to a share of the increasing value of the property as it appreciates.

Mortgage, Wraparound—A purchase money loan arrangement in which the seller uses part of the buyer's payments to make the payments on an existing loan (called the underlying loan). The buyer takes title subject to the underlying loan, but does not assume it. When the security instrument used for wraparound financing is a deed of trust instead of a mortgage, it may be referred to as an all-inclusive trust deed.

Mortgage Banker—An intermediary who originates and services real estate loans on behalf of investors.

Mortgage Broker—An intermediary who brings real estate lenders and borrowers together and negotiates loan agreements between them.

Mortgage Company—A type of real estate lender that originates and services loans on behalf of large investors (acting as a mortgage banker) or for resale on the secondary mortgage market.

Mortgagee—A lender who accepts a mortgage as security for repayment of the loan.

Mortgage Loan—Any loan secured by real property, whether the actual security instrument used is a mortgage or a deed of trust.

Mortgage Loan Broker Law—A California law that limits the size of the fees and commissions that can be charged by a loan broker, and that requires a loan broker to give a disclosure statement to his or her customers. Also called the Necessitous Borrower Act or the Real Property Loan Law.

Mortgaging Clause—A clause in a mortgage that describes the security interest given to the mortgagee.

Mortgagor—A property owner (usually a borrower) who gives a mortgage to another (usually a lender) as security for payment of an obligation.

Multiple Listing Service (MLS)—An organization of brokers who share their exclusive listings.

Mutual Consent—When all parties freely agree to the terms of a contract, without fraud, undue influence, duress, menace, or mistake. Mutual consent is achieved through offer and acceptance; it is sometimes referred to as a "meeting of the minds."

Mutual Water Company—A company formed by property owners in a community for the purpose of obtaining a supply of water at reasonable rates. Stock in the company is issued to the members.

NAR—National Association of Realtors®.

Narrative Report—A thorough appraisal report in which the appraiser summarizes the data and the appraisal methods used, to convince the reader of the soundness of the estimate; a more comprehensive presentation than a form report or an opinion letter.

National Environmental Policy Act (NEPA)—Federal legislation that regulates development by federal agencies and private development that requires federal approval or involves federal funding.

National Market—*See*: Secondary Mortgage Market.

Natural Person—A human being, an individual (as opposed to an artificial person, such as a corporation).

Natural Servitude, Doctrine of—A legal principle which holds that a property owner is liable for any damage caused by diverting or channeling flood waters from his or her property onto someone else's.

Navigable Waters—A body of water large enough so that watercraft can travel on it in the course of commerce.

Necessitous Borrower Act—*See*: Mortgage Loan Broker Law.

Negligence—Conduct that falls below the standard of care that a reasonable person would exercise under the circumstances; carelessness or recklessness.

Negotiable Instrument—An instrument containing an unconditional promise to pay a certain sum of money to order or to bearer, on demand or at a particular time. It can be a check, promissory note, bond, draft, or stock. *See*: Note, Promissory.

Neighborhood Analysis—The gathering of data on home sizes and styles, topography, features, and amenities in a neighborhood, as part of the appraisal or property management process.

NEPA—*See*: National Environmental Policy Act.

Net Income—*See*: Income, Net.

Net Listing—*See*: Listing, Net.

Net Spendable—*See*: Income, Spendable.

Net Worth—An individual's personal financial assets, minus his or her personal liabilities.

Nominal Interest Rate—The interest rate stated in a promissory note. Also called the note rate or coupon rate. *Compare*: Annual Percentage Rate.

Nonconforming Loan—A loan that does not meet the underwriting criteria of the major secondary market agencies. *See*: Loan, Conforming.

Nonconforming Use—A property use that does not conform to current zoning requirements, but is allowed because the property was being used in that way before the present zoning ordinance was enacted.

Non-possessory Interest—An interest in property that does not include the right to possess and occupy the property; an encumbrance, such as a lien or an easement.

Nonrecognition Transaction—A transaction for which a taxpayer is not required to pay taxes in the year the gain is realized.

Notarize—To have a document certified by a notary public.

Notary Public—Someone who is officially authorized to witness and certify the acknowledgment made by someone signing a legal document.

Note—*See*: Note, Promissory.

Note, Demand—A promissory note that is due whenever the holder of the note demands payment.

Note, Installment—A promissory note that calls for regular payments of principal and interest until the debt is fully paid.

Note, Joint—A promissory note signed by two or more persons with equal liability for payment.

Note, Promissory—A written promise to repay a debt. It may or may not be a negotiable instrument.

Note, Straight—A promissory note that calls for regular payments of interest only, so that the entire principal amount is due in one lump sum at the end of the loan term.

Notice, Actual—Actual knowledge of a fact, as opposed to knowledge imputed by law (constructive notice).

Notice, Constructive—Knowledge of a fact imputed to a person by law. A person is held to have constructive notice of something when he or she should have known it (because he or she could have learned it through reasonable diligence or an inspection of the public record), even if he or she did not actually know it.

Notice of Cessation—A notice recorded when work on a construction project has ceased (although the project is unfinished), to limit the time allowed for recording construction liens.

Notice of Completion—A notice recorded when a construction project has been completed, to limit the time allowed for recording construction liens.

Notice of Default—A notice sent by a secured creditor to the debtor, informing the debtor that he or she has breached the loan agreement.

Notice of Non-responsibility—A notice that a property owner may record and post on the property to protect his or her title against construction liens, when someone other than the owner (such as a tenant) has ordered work on the property.

Notice of Sale—A notice stating that foreclosure proceedings have been commenced against a property.

Notice to Quit—A notice to a tenant, demanding that he or she vacate the leased property.

Notice to the World—Constructive notice of the contents of a document provided to the general public by recording the document.

Novation—1. The withdrawal of one party to a contract and the substitution of a new party, relieving the withdrawing party of liability. 2. The substitution of a new obligation for an old one.

Nuisance—A use of property that is offensive or annoying to neighboring landowners or to the community.

Obligatory Advances—Disbursements of construction loan funds that the lender is obligated to make (by prior agreement with the borrower) when the borrower has completed certain phases of construction.

Obsolescence—Any loss in value (depreciation) due to reduced desirability and usefulness.

Obsolescence, External—Loss in value resulting from factors outside the property itself, such as proximity to an airport. Also called economic obsolescence or external inadequacy.

Obsolescence, Functional—Loss in value due to inadequate or outmoded equipment, or as a result of a poor or outmoded design.

Offer—The action of one person (the offeror) in proposing a contract to another (the offeree). If the offeree accepts the offer, a binding contract is formed.

Offer, Illusory—An offer that is not a valid contract offer, because it requires something more than simple acceptance in order to create a contract.

Offer, Tender—*See*: Tender.

Offeree—One to whom a contract offer is made.

Offeror—One who makes a contract offer.

Officer—In a corporation, an executive authorized by the board of directors to manage the business of the corporation.

Off-Site Improvements—Improvements that add to the usefulness of a site but are not located directly on it, such as curbs, street lights, and sidewalks.

Open Listing—*See*: Listing, Open.

Open Market Operations—The Federal Reserve's manipulation of the money supply through the purchase and sale of government securities.

Option—A contract giving one party the right to do something, without obligating him or her to do it.

Optionee—The person to whom an option is given.

Optionor—The person who gives an option.

Option to Purchase—An option giving the optionee the right to buy property owned by the optionor at an agreed price during a specified period.

Ordinance—A law passed by a local legislative body, such as a city council.

Orientation—The placement of a house on its lot, with regard to its exposure to the sun and wind, privacy from the street, and protection from outside noise.

Origination Fee—A fee a lender charges a borrower upon making a new loan, intended to cover the administrative costs of making the loan. Also called a loan fee.

"Or More"—A provision in a promissory note that allows the borrower to prepay the debt.

Ostensible Agency—*See*: Agency, Apparent.

Outlawed—Barred by the statute of limitations.

Overimprovement—An improvement that is more expensive than is justified by the value of the land.

Overlying Right—A landowner's right to use percolating or diffused ground water.

Ownership—Title to property, dominion over property; the rights of possession and control.

Ownership, Concurrent—Shared ownership of one piece of property by two or more individuals, each owning an undivided interest in the property (as in a tenancy in common or joint tenancy, or with community property). Also called co-ownership or co-tenancy.

Ownership in Severalty—Ownership by one individual.

Panic Selling—*See*: Blockbusting.

Par—1. The accepted standard of comparison; the average or typical rate or amount. 2. Face value. For example, a mortgage sold at the secondary market level for 97% of par has been sold for 3% less than its face value.

Parallels—Imaginary lines running east and west, parallel to the equator. Also called latitude lines.

Parcel—A lot or piece of real estate, especially a specified part of a larger tract.

Partial Reconveyance—The instrument given to the borrower when part of the security property is released from a blanket mortgage under a partial release clause.

Partial Release Clause—*See*: Release Clause.

Partial Satisfaction—The instrument given to the borrower when part of the security property is released from a blanket mortgage under a partial release clause.

Partition—The division of a property among its co-owners, so that each owns part of it in severalty. This may occur by agreement of all of the co-owners (voluntary partition), or by court order (judicial partition).

Partner, General—A partner who has the authority to manage and contract for a general or limited partnership, and who is personally liable for the partnership's debts.

Partner, Limited—A partner in a limited partnership who is primarily an investor and does not participate in the management of the business, and who is not personally liable for the partnership's debts.

Partnership—An association of two or more persons to carry on a business for profit. The law regards a partnership as a group of individuals, not as an entity separate from its owners. *Compare*: Corporation.

Partnership, General—A partnership in which each member has an equal right to manage the business and share in the profits, as well as an equal responsibility for the partnership's debts. All of the partners are general partners.

Partnership, Limited—A partnership made up of one or more general partners and one or more limited partners.

Partnership Property—All property that partners bring into their business at the outset or later acquire for their business; property owned as tenants in partnership. *See*: Tenancy in Partnership.

Party Wall—A wall located on the boundary line between two adjoining parcels of land that is used or intended to be used by the owners of both properties.

Patent—The instrument used to convey government land to a private individual.

Payee—In a promissory note, the party who is entitled to be paid; the creditor or lender. *Compare*: Maker.

Percolation Test—A test to determine the ability of the ground to absorb or drain water; used to determine whether a site is suitable for construction, particularly for installation of a septic tank system.

Per Diem—Daily.

Periodic Tenancy—*See*: Tenancy, Periodic.

Personal Property—Any property that is not real property; movable property not affixed to land. Also called chattels or personalty.

Personalty—Personal property.

Personal Use Property—Property that a taxpayer owns for his or her own use (or family use), as opposed to income property, investment property, dealer property, or property used in a trade or business.

Petitioner—*See*: Appellant.

Physical Deterioration—Loss in value (depreciation) resulting from wear and tear or deferred maintenance.

Physical Life—An estimate of the time a building will remain structurally sound and capable of being used. *Compare*: Economic Life.

Plaintiff—The party who brings or starts a civil lawsuit; the one who sues.

Planned Unit Development (PUD)—A development (usually residential) with small, clustered lots designed to leave more open space than traditional subdivisions have.

Planning Commission—A local government agency responsible for preparing the community's general plan for development.

Plat—A detailed survey map of a subdivision, recorded in the county where the land is located. Subdivided property is often called platted property.

Plat Book—A large book containing subdivision plats, kept at the county recorder's office.

Pledge—The transfer of possession of property by a debtor to the creditor as security for repayment of the debt. *Compare*: Hypothecate.

Plot Plan—A plan showing lot dimensions and the layout of improvements (such as buildings and landscaping) on a property site.

Plottage—The increment of value that results when two or more lots are combined to produce greater value. Also called the plottage increment.

PMI—*See*: Insurance, Private Mortgage.

Point—One percent of the principal amount of a loan. *See*: Discount Points.

Point of Beginning (POB)—The starting point in a metes and bounds description; a monument or a point described by reference to a monument.

Points—*See*: Discount Points.

Police Power—The constitutional power of state and local governments to enact and enforce laws for the protection of the public's health, safety, morals, and general welfare.

Possession—1. The holding and enjoyment of property. 2. Actual physical occupation of real property.

Possessory Interest—An interest in property that includes the right to possess and occupy the property. The term includes all estates (leasehold as well as freehold), but does not include encumbrances.

Potable Water—Water that is safe to drink.

Power of Attorney—An instrument authorizing one person (the attorney in fact) to act as another's agent, to the extent stated in the instrument.

Power of Sale Clause—A clause in a deed of trust giving the trustee the right to foreclose non-judicially (sell the debtor's property without a court action) if the borrower defaults.

Preapproval—A process that allows a prospective borrower to submit a loan application to a lender and get approved for a loan before beginning the home-buying process.

Prepayment—Paying off part or all of a loan before payment is due.

Prepayment Penalty—A penalty charged to a borrower who prepays.

Prepayment Privilege—A provision in a promissory note allowing the borrower to prepay.

Prescription—Acquiring an interest in real property (usually an easement) by using it openly and without the owner's permission for the period prescribed by statute.

Price Fixing—The cooperative setting of prices by competing firms. Price-fixing is an automatic violation of antitrust laws.

Prima Facie—At first sight; on the face of it.

Primary Mortgage Market—The market in which mortgage loans are originated, where lenders make loans to borrowers. Also called the local market. *Compare*: Secondary Mortgage Market.

Prime Rate—The interest rate a bank charges its largest and most desirable customers.

Principal—1. One who grants another person (an agent) authority to represent him or her in dealings with third parties. 2. One of the parties to a transaction (such as a buyer or seller), as opposed to those who are involved as agents or employees (such as a broker or escrow agent). 3. In regard to a loan, the amount originally borrowed, as opposed to the interest.

Principal Meridian—*See*: Meridian, Principal.

Principal Residence Property—Real property that is the owner's home, his or her main dwelling. Under the federal income tax laws, a person can only have one principal residence at a time.

Prior Appropriation—*See*: Appropriation, Prior.

Private Mortgage Insurance—*See*: Insurance, Private Mortgage.

Probate—A judicial proceeding in which the validity of a will is established and the executor is authorized to distribute the estate property; or, when there is no valid will, in which an administrator is appointed to distribute the estate to the heirs.

Probate Court—A court that oversees the distribution of property under a will or intestate succession.

Procuring Cause—The real estate agent who is primarily responsible for bringing about a sale; for example, by negotiating the agreement between the buyer and seller.

Profit—A non-possessory interest; the right to enter another person's land and take something (such as timber or minerals) away from it.

Progression, Principle of—An appraisal principle which holds that a property of lesser value tends to be worth more when it is located in an area with properties of greater value than it would be if located elsewhere. The opposite is the principle of regression.

Promisee—Someone who has been promised something; someone who is supposed to receive the benefit of a contractual promise.

Promisor—Someone who has made a contractual promise to another.

Promissory Note—*See*: Note, Promissory.

Property—1. The rights of ownership in a thing, such as the right to use, possess, transfer, or encumber it. 2. Something that is owned.

Property Held for Production of Income—*See*: Income Property.

Property Manager—A person hired by a property owner to administer, merchandise, and maintain property, especially rental property.

Property Tax—*See*: Tax, Property.

Property Used in a Trade or Business—Property such as business sites and factories used in a taxpayer's trade or business.

Proprietorship, Individual or Sole—A business owned and operated by one person.

Proration—The process of dividing or allocating something (especially a sum of money or an expense) proportionately, according to time, interest, or benefit.

Public Record—The official collection of legal documents that individuals have filed with the county recorder in order to make the information contained in them public.

Public Use—A use that benefits the public. For a condemnation action to be constitutional, it must be for a public use.

Puffing—Superlative statements about the quality of a property that should not be considered assertions of fact.

Purchase and Sale Agreement—A contract in which a seller promises to convey title to real property to a buyer in exchange for the purchase price. Also called a deposit receipt, sales contract, or contract of sale.

Purchaser's Assignment of Contract and Deed—The instrument used to assign the vendee's equitable interest in a contract to another.

Pure Competitive Market—A market in which prices rise and fall in response to supply and demand without outside restrictions.

Qualified Acceptance—*See*: Counteroffer.

Qualifying Standards—The standards a lender requires a loan applicant to meet before a loan will be approved. Also called underwriting standards.

Quantity Survey Method—In appraisal, a method of estimating the replacement cost of a structure. It involves a detailed estimate of the quantities and cost of materials and labor, and overhead expenses such as insurance and contractor's profit.

Quiet Enjoyment—Use and possession of real property without interference from the previous owner, the lessor, or anyone else claiming an interest. *See*: Covenant of Quiet Enjoyment.

Quiet Title Action—A lawsuit to determine who has title to a piece of property, or to remove a cloud from the title.

Quitclaim Deed—*See*: Deed, Quitclaim.

Range—In the government survey system, a strip of land six miles wide, running north and south.

Range Lines—In the government survey system, the north-south lines (meridians) located six miles apart.

Ratify—To confirm or approve after the fact an act that was not authorized when it was performed.

Raw Materials-Oriented Industry—An industry that must locate close to the source of raw materials, and must have a cost-effective means of transporting its product to market.

Ready, Willing, and Able—A buyer is ready, willing, and able if he makes an offer that meets the seller's stated terms, and has the contractual capacity and financial resources to complete the transaction.

Real Estate—*See*: Real Property.

Real Estate Commissioner—The head of the Department of Real Estate, who is responsible for implementing and enforcing the Real Estate Law.

Real Estate Contract—1. A purchase and sale agreement. 2. A land contract. 3. Any contract having to do with real property.

Real Estate Fund—A special account into which all license fees are credited.

Real Estate Investment Trust (REIT)—A real estate investment business with at least 100 investors, organized as a trust.

Real Estate Law—A California statute that governs the licensing and business practices of real estate agents.

Real Estate Settlement Procedures Act (RESPA)—A federal law that governs residential real estate closings, requiring institutional lenders to make disclosures concerning closing costs to loan applicants, and requiring closing agents to prepare a Uniform Settlement Statement.

Realization—When a gain is separated from an asset, and therefore becomes taxable.

Real Property—Land and everything attached to or appurtenant to it. Also called realty or real estate. *Compare*: Personal Property.

Real Property Loan Law—*See*: Mortgage Loan Broker Law.

Real Property Securities Dealer—A real estate broker whose license has been endorsed to also sell real property securities.

Realtor®—A real estate agent who is an active member of a state or local real estate board that is affiliated with the National Association of Realtors®.

Realty—*See*: Real Property.

Reasonable Use Doctrine—A limitation of water rights, holding that there is no right to waste water.

Recapture—Recovery by the investor of money invested in real estate.

Recapture Clause—1. A provision in a percentage lease that allows the landlord to terminate the lease and regain the premises if a certain minimum volume of business is not maintained. 2. A provision in a ground lease that allows the tenant to purchase the property after a specified period of time.

Receiver—A person appointed by a court to manage and look after property or funds involved in litigation.

Reconciliation—The final step in an appraisal, when the appraiser assembles and interprets the data in order to arrive at a final value estimate. Also called correlation.

Reconveyance—Releasing the security property from the lien created by a deed of trust, by recording a deed of reconveyance.

Recording—Filing a document at the county recorder's office, so that it will be placed in the public record.

Recording Numbers—The numbers stamped on documents when they're recorded, used to identify and locate the documents in the public record.

Recovery Account—A special account that is funded by license fees. It is used to reimburse those injured by the unlawful acts of real estate licensees.

Rectangular Survey System—*See*: Government Survey System.

Redemption—When a defaulting borrower pays the full amount of the debt, plus costs, to avoid the loss of his or her property due to foreclosure.

Redemption, Equitable Right of—The right of a borrower to redeem property prior to the foreclosure sale.

Redemption, Statutory Right of—The right of a mortgagor to get his or her property back after a foreclosure sale.

Redlining—Refusal by a lender to make loans secured by property in a certain neighborhood because of the racial or ethnic composition of the neighborhood.

Reduction Certificate—A signed statement from a lender certifying the present balance on the loan, the rate of interest, and the maturity date. A form of estoppel certificate.

Reformation—A legal action to correct a mistake, such as a typographical error, in a deed or other document. The court will order the execution of a correction deed.

Regression, Principle of—An appraisal principle which holds that a valuable property surrounded by properties of lesser value will tend to be worth less than it would be in a different location; the opposite of the principle of progression.

Regulation Z—The Federal Reserve Board's regulation that implements the Truth in Lending Act.

Reinstate—To prevent foreclosure by curing the default.

Release—1. To give up a legal right. 2. A document in which a legal right is given up.

Release Clause—1. A clause in a blanket mortgage or deed of trust which allows the borrower to get part of the security property released from the lien when a certain portion of the debt has been paid or other conditions are fulfilled. Often called a partial release clause. 2. A clause in a land contract providing for a deed to a portion of the land to be delivered when a certain portion of the contract price has been paid. Also known as a deed release provision.

Release, Lien—A document removing a lien, given to the borrower once a mortgage or deed of trust has been paid off in full.

Reliction—The gradual receding of a body of water, exposing land that was previously under water. Also called dereliction.

Remainder—A future interest that becomes possessory when a life estate terminates, and that is held by someone other than the grantor of the life estate; as opposed to a reversion, which is a future interest held by the grantor.

Remainderman—The person who has an estate in remainder.

Remaining Economic Life—*See*: Economic Life.

Remise—To give up; a term used in quitclaim deeds.

Rent—Compensation paid by a tenant to the landlord in exchange for the possession and use of the property.

Rent, Contract—The rent that is actually being paid on property that is currently leased.

Rent, Economic—The rent that a property would be earning if it were available for lease in the current market.

Rent, Ground—The earnings of improved property that are attributed to the land itself, after allowance is made for the earnings attributable to the improvement.

Replacement Cost—*See*: Cost, Replacement.

Replevin—Legal proceedings undertaken by a tenant to recover possession of personal belongings that have been unlawfully confiscated by a landlord (usually for nonpayment of rent).

Reproduction Cost—*See*: Cost, Reproduction.

Rescission—Termination of a contract in which each party gives anything acquired under the contract back to the other party. (The verb form is rescind.) *Compare*: Cancellation.

Reservation—A right retained by a grantor when conveying property. For example, mineral rights, an easement, or a life estate can be reserved in the deed.

Reserve Account—*See*: Impound Account.

Reserve Requirements—The percentage of deposits commercial banks must keep on reserve with the Federal Reserve Bank.

Reserves for Replacement—For income-producing property, regular allowances set aside to pay for the replacement of structures and equipment that are expected to wear out.

Resident Manager—A salaried manager of a single apartment building or complex who resides on the property. Unlike a property manager, a resident manager is not required to have a real estate license.

Residual—1. The property value remaining after the economic life of the improvements has been exhausted. 2. Commissions in the form of delayed payments (when a part of the commission is paid with each installment on an installment sales contract, for example) are referred to as residuals.

Residual Income—*See*: Income, Residual.

RESPA—*See*: Real Estate Settlement Procedures Act.

Respondent—*See*: Appellee.

Respondeat Superior, Doctrine of—A legal rule holding that an employer is liable for the torts (civil wrongs) committed by an employee within the scope of his or her employment.

Restitution—Restoring something to a person that he or she was unjustly deprived of.

Restriction—A limitation on the use of real property.

Restriction, Deed—A restrictive covenant in a deed.

Restriction, Private—A restriction imposed on property by a previous owner, a neighbor, or the subdivision developer; a restrictive covenant or a condition in a deed.

Restriction, Public—A law or regulation limiting or regulating the use of real property.

Restrictive Covenant—*See*: Covenant, Restrictive.

Retainer—A fee paid up front to a professional before entering into an agency relationship.

Return—A profit from an investment.

Reversion—A future interest that becomes possessory when a temporary estate (such as a life estate) terminates, and that is held by the grantor (or his or her successors in interest). *Compare*: Remainder.

Rezone—An amendment to a zoning ordinance, usually changing the uses allowed in a particular zone. Also called a zoning amendment.

Right of First Refusal—The first opportunity to purchase or lease real property. Unlike an option agreement, the right of first refusal does not apply until the property is made available for sale.

Right of Way—An easement that gives the holder the right to cross another person's land.

Riparian Land—Land that is adjacent to or crossed by a body of water, especially flowing water such as a stream or a river. *Compare*: Littoral Land.

Riparian Rights—The water rights of a landowner whose property is adjacent to or crossed by a body of water. *Compare*: Appropriation, Prior.

Risk Analysis—*See*: Underwriting.

Rule of Capture—*See*: Capture, Rule of.

Running with the Land—Binding or benefiting the successive owners of a piece of property, rather than terminating when a particular owner transfers his or her interest. Usually said in reference to an easement or a restrictive covenant.

Safety Clause—A clause in a listing agreement providing that for a specified period after the listing expires, the broker will still be entitled to a commission if the property is sold to someone the broker dealt with during the listing term. Also called an extender clause or carryover clause.

Sale-Leaseback—A form of real estate financing in which the owner of industrial or commercial property sells the property and leases it back from the buyer. In addition to certain tax advantages, the seller/lessee obtains more cash through the sale than would normally be possible by borrowing and mortgaging the property, since lenders will not often lend 100% of the value.

Sales Comparison Approach—One of the three main methods of appraisal, in which the sales prices of comparable properties are used to estimate the value of the subject property. Also called the market data approach.

Sales Contract—*See*: Purchase and Sale Agreement.

Salesperson—A licensee who is authorized to represent a broker in a real estate transaction.

Satisfaction of Mortgage—*See*: Mortgage, Satisfaction of.

Savings and Loan Association—A type of financial institution that traditionally specialized in home mortgage loans.

Savings Bank—A type of financial institution that traditionally emphasized consumer loans and accounts for small depositors.

Scarcity—A limited or inadequate supply of something. This is one of the four elements of value (along with utility, demand, and transferability).

Secondary Financing—Money borrowed to pay part of the required downpayment or closing costs for a first loan, when the second loan is secured by the same property that secures the first loan.

Secondary Mortgage Market—The market in which investors (including Fannie Mae, Freddie Mac, and Ginnie Mae) purchase real estate loans from lenders; also called the national market.

Secret Profit—A financial benefit that an agent takes from a transaction without informing the principal.

Section—In the government survey system, a section is one mile square and contains 640 acres. There are 36 sections in a township.

Security Agreement—Under the Uniform Commercial Code, a document that creates a lien on personal property being used to secure a loan.

Securities—Shares in a corporation that represent an ownership interest but not managerial control.

Security Deposit—Money a tenant gives a landlord at the beginning of the tenancy to protect the landlord in case the tenant fails to comply with the terms of the lease. The landlord may retain all or part of the deposit to cover unpaid rent or repair costs at the end of the tenancy.

Security Instrument—A document that creates a voluntary lien to secure repayment of a loan. For debts secured by real property, it is either a mortgage or a deed of trust.

Security Interest—The interest a creditor may acquire in the debtor's property to ensure that the debt will be paid.

Security Property—The property that a borrower gives a lender a voluntary lien against, so that the lender can foreclose if the borrower defaults.

Seisin—Actual possession of a freehold estate; ownership.

Separate Property—Property owned by a married person that is not community property; includes property acquired before marriage or by gift or inheritance after marriage.

Servant—*See*: Master/Servant Relationship.

Setback Requirements—Provisions in a zoning ordinance that do not allow structures to be built within a certain distance of the property line.

Settlement—1. An agreement between the parties to a civil lawsuit in which the plaintiff agrees to drop the suit in exchange for money or the defendant's promise to do or refrain from doing something. 2. Closing.

Settlement Statement—A document that presents a final, detailed accounting for a real estate transaction, listing each party's debits and credits and the amount each will receive or be required to pay at closing. Also called a closing statement.

Severalty—*See*: Ownership in Severalty.

Severance—1. Termination of a joint tenancy. 2. The permanent removal of a natural attachment, fixture, or appurtenance from real property, which transforms the item into personal property.

Severance, Constructive—When a landowner enters into a contract to sell an appurtenance or natural attachment, the contract constructively severs the item from the land—making it the personal property of the buyer—even before the buyer has actually removed it from the land. For example, when a landowner sells a stand of timber, the trees are constructively severed from the land even before the buyer comes to chop them down.

Shareholder—An individual who holds an ownership share in a corporation (and has limited liability).

Sheriff's Deed—The document conveying title to the purchaser of a foreclosed property at a sheriff's sale, given at the end of the statutory redemption period.

Sheriff's Sale—A foreclosure sale held after a judicial foreclosure. Sometimes called an execution sale.

Sherman Act—A federal antitrust law prohibiting any agreement that has the effect of a restraint on trade, such as price fixing and tie-in arrangements.

Short Plat—The subdivision of a parcel of land into four or fewer lots.

Sinking Fund—Money set aside to accumulate (including accrued interest) so that some obligation can be satisfied or some asset can be replaced at the end of a predetermined period.

Site Analysis—The gathering of data about the physical characteristics of a property and other factors affecting its use or title, as part of the appraisal process.

Special Agent—*See*: Agent, Special.

Special Assessment—A tax levied only against the properties that have benefited from a public improvement (such as a sewer or a street light), to cover the cost of the improvement; creates a special assessment lien.

Special Exception Permit—*See*: Conditional Use Permit.

Specific Lien—*See*: Lien, Specific.

Specific Performance—A legal remedy in which a court orders someone who has breached a contract to actually perform as agreed, rather than simply paying money damages to the other party.

Square Foot Method—In appraisal, a method of estimating replacement cost by calculating the square foot cost of replacing the subject home.

SRA—A member of the Society of Real Estate Appraisers.

Stable Monthly Income—A loan applicant's gross monthly income that meets the lender's tests of quality and durability.

Statute—A law enacted by a state legislature or the U.S. Congress.

Statute of Frauds—A law that requires certain types of contracts to be in writing and signed in order to be enforceable.

Statute of Limitations—A law requiring a particular type of lawsuit to be filed within a specified time after the event giving rise to the suit occurred.

Steering—Channeling prospective buyers or tenants to or away from particular neighborhoods based on their race, religion, national origin, or ancestry.

Straight Note—*See*: Note, Straight.

Subagent—A person to whom an agent has delegated authority, so that the subagent can assist in carrying out the principal's orders; the agent of an agent.

Subcontractor—A contractor who, at the request of the general contractor, provides a specific service, such as plumbing or drywalling, in connection with the overall construction project.

Subdivided Lands Act—A California law that requires a subdivider to disclose certain information to all lot buyers.

Subdivision—1. A piece of land divided into two or more parcels. 2. A residential development.

Subdivision Map Act—A California law that gives cities and counties the power to regulate subdivisions in order to ensure that the subdivisions comply with the local general plan.

Subdivision Plat—*See*: Plat.

Subdivision Regulations—State and local laws that must be complied with before land can be subdivided.

Subjacent Support—*See*: Support, Subjacent.

Subject to—When a purchaser takes property subject to a trust deed or mortgage, he or she is not personally liable for paying off the loan. In case of default, however, the property can still be foreclosed on.

Sublease—An arrangement in which a tenant grants someone else the right to possession of the leased property for part of the remainder of the lease term; as opposed to an assignment, in which the tenant gives up possession for the entire remainder of the lease term.

Subordination Clause—A provision in a mortgage or deed of trust that permits a later mortgage or deed of trust to have higher lien priority than the one containing the clause.

Subrogation—The substitution of one person in the place of another with reference to a lawful claim or right. For instance, a title company that pays a claim on behalf of its insured, the property owner, is subrogated to any claim the owner successfully undertakes against the former owner.

Substitution, Principle of—A principle of appraisal holding that the maximum value of a property is set by how much it would cost to obtain another property that is equally desirable, assuming that there would not be a long delay or significant incidental expenses involved in obtaining the substitute.

Substitution of Liability—A buyer wishing to assume an existing loan may apply for the lender's approval; once approved, the buyer assumes liability for repayment of the loan, and the original borrower (the seller) is released from liability.

Succession—Acquiring property by will or inheritance.

Sufferance—Acquiescence, implied permission, or passive consent through a failure to act, as opposed to express permission.

Supply and Demand, Principle of—A principle holding that value varies directly with demand and inversely with supply. That is, the greater the demand the greater the value, and the greater the supply the lower the value.

Support, Lateral—The support that a piece of land receives from the land adjacent to it.

Support, Subjacent—The support the surface of a piece of land receives from the land beneath it.

Support Rights—The right to have one's land supported by the land adjacent to it and beneath it.

Surplus Productivity, Principle of—A principle of appraisal which holds that the net income that remains after paying the proper costs of labor, organization, and capital is credited to the land and tends to set its value.

Surrender—Giving up an estate (such as a life estate or leasehold) before it has expired.

Survey—The process of precisely measuring the boundaries and determining the area of a parcel of land.

Survivorship, Right of—A characteristic of joint tenancy; surviving joint tenants automatically acquire a deceased joint tenant's interest in the property.

Syndicate—An association formed to operate an investment business. A syndicate is not a recognized legal entity; it can be organized as a corporation, partnership, limited liability company, or trust.

Tacking—Adding together successive periods of use or possession by more than one person to make up the five years required for prescription or adverse possession.

Taking—When the government acquires private property for public use by condemnation, it's called "a taking." The term is also used in inverse condemnation lawsuits, when a government action has made private property virtually useless.

Tax, Ad Valorem—A tax assessed on the value of property.

Tax, Documentary Transfer—A state tax levied on every sale of real estate. Also called the real estate excise tax.

Tax, Excise—*See*: Tax, Documentary Transfer.

Tax, General Real Estate—An annual ad valorem tax levied on real property.

Tax, Improvement—*See*: Special Assessment.

Tax, Progressive—A tax, such as the federal income tax, that imposes a higher tax rate on a taxpayer who earns a higher income.

Tax, Property—1. The general real estate tax. 2. Any ad valorem tax levied on real or personal property.

Tax Credit—A credit that is subtracted directly from the amount of tax owed. *Compare*: Deduction.

Tax Deed—*See*: Deed, Tax.

Tax-Free Exchange—A transaction in which one piece of property is traded for a piece of like-kind property. If the property involved is held for investment or the production of income, or used in a trade or business, tax on the gain may be deferred.

Tax Sale—Sale of property after foreclosure of a tax lien.

Tenancy—Lawful possession of real property; an estate.

Tenancy, Joint—A form of concurrent ownership in which the co-owners have equal undivided interests and the right of survivorship.

Tenancy, Periodic—A leasehold estate that continues for successive periods of equal length (such as from week to week or month to month), until terminated by proper notice from either party. Also called a month-to-month (or week-to-week, etc.) tenancy. *Compare*: Tenancy, Term.

Tenancy, Term—A leasehold estate that lasts for a definite period (one week, three years, etc.), after which it terminates automatically. Also called an estate for years or a tenancy for years.

Tenancy at Sufferance—A situation in which a tenant (who entered into possession of the property lawfully) stays on after the lease ends without the landlord's consent.

Tenancy at Will—A leasehold estate that results when a tenant is in possession with the owner's permission, but there's no definite lease term; as when a landlord allows a holdover tenant to remain on the premises until another tenant is found.

Tenancy by the Entirety—A form of joint ownership of property by husband and wife (in some states that don't use a community property system).

Tenancy for Years—*See*: Tenancy, Term.

Tenancy in Common—A form of concurrent ownership in which two or more persons each have an undivided interest in the entire property, but no right of survivorship. *Compare*: Tenancy, Joint.

Tenancy in Partnership—The form of concurrent ownership in which general partners own partnership property, whether or not title to the property is in the partnership's name. Each partner has an equal undivided interest, but no right to transfer the interest to someone outside the partnership.

Tenant—Someone in lawful possession of real property; especially, someone who has leased property from the owner.

Tenant, Dominant—A person who has easement rights on another's property; either the owner of a dominant tenement, or someone who has an easement in gross.

Tenant, Holdover—A lessee who remains in possession of the property after the lease term has expired.

Tenant, Life—Someone who owns a life estate.

Tenant, Servient—The owner of a servient tenement; that is, someone whose property is burdened by an easement.

Tender—An unconditional offer by one of the parties to a contract to perform his or her part of the agreement. If made when the offeror believes the other party is breaching, it establishes the offeror's right to sue if the other party doesn't accept it. Also called a tender offer.

Tenement, Dominant—Property that receives the benefit of an easement appurtenant.

Tenement, Servient—Property burdened by an easement. In other words, the owner of the servient tenement (the servient tenant) must allow someone who has an easement (the dominant tenant) to use the property.

Tenements—Everything of a permanent nature associated with a piece of land that is ordinarily transferred with the land. Tenements are both tangible (buildings, for example) and intangible (air rights, for example).

Tenure—The period of time during which a person holds certain rights with respect to a piece of real property.

Tenure, Allodial—A system of real property ownership in which an individual's ownership may be complete or absolute (except for those rights held by the government, such as eminent domain and escheat).

Tenure, Feudal—A system of land ownership in which the sovereign owns all the land and grants lesser interests to others in return for services; the dominant system in Europe during the Middle Ages. *Compare*: Tenure, Allodial.

Term—A prescribed period of time; especially, the length of time a borrower has to pay off a loan, or the duration of a lease.

Term Tenancy—A leasehold estate that lasts for a definite period (one week, three years, etc.), after which it terminates automatically. Also called an estate for years.

Testament—*See*: Will.

Testate—Refers to someone who has died and left a will. *Compare*: Intestate.

Testator—A person who makes a will. (If it is a woman, she may be referred to as a testatrix.)

Third Party—1. A person seeking to deal with a principal through an agent. 2. In a transaction, someone who is not one of the principals.

Tie-in Arrangement—An agreement to sell one product, only on the condition that the buyer also purchases a different product.

Tight Money Market—A situation in which loan funds are scarce, resulting in high interest rates and discount points.

TILA—*See*: Truth in Lending Act.

Time is of the Essence—A clause in a contract that means performance on the exact dates specified is an essential element of the contract. Failure to perform on time is a material breach.

Title—Lawful ownership of real property. Also refers to the deed or other document that is evidence of that ownership.

Title, Abstract of—A brief, chronological summary of the recorded documents affecting title to a particular piece of real property.

Title, After-Acquired—Title acquired by a grantor after he or she attempted to convey property he or she didn't own.

Title, Chain of—The chain of deeds (and other documents) transferring title to a piece of property from one owner to the next, as disclosed in the public record; more complete than an abstract.

Title, Clear—A good title to property, free from encumbrances or defects; marketable title.

Title, Color of—Title that appears to be good title, but which in fact is not; commonly based on a defective instrument, such as an invalid deed.

Title, Equitable—The vendee's interest in property under a real estate contract. Also called an equitable interest.

Title, Legal—The vendor's interest in property under a real estate contract. Also called naked title.

Title, Marketable—Title free and clear of objectionable liens, encumbrances, or defects, so that a reasonably prudent person with full knowledge of the facts would not hesitate to purchase the property.

Title, Slander of—Disparaging or inaccurate statements, written or oral, concerning a person's title to property.

Title Company—A title insurance company.

Title Insurance—*See*: Insurance, Title

Title Plant—A duplicate (usually microfilmed) of a county's public record, maintained by a title company at its offices for use in title searches.

Title Report, Preliminary—A report issued by a title company, disclosing the condition of the title to a specific piece of property, before the actual title insurance policy is issued.

Title Search—An inspection of the public record to determine all rights and encumbrances affecting title to a piece of property.

Title Theory—The theory holding that a mortgage or deed of trust gives the lender legal title to the security property while the debt is being repaid. *Compare*: Lien Theory.

Topography—The contours of the surface of the land (level, hilly, steep, etc.).

Torrens System—A system of land registration used in some states, which allows title to be verified without the necessity of a title search. Title to registered land is free of all encumbrances or claims not registered with the title registrar. (Almost never used in California.)

Tort—A breach of a duty imposed by law (as opposed to a duty voluntarily taken on in a contract) that causes harm to another person, giving the injured person the right to sue the one who breached the duty. Also called a civil wrong (in contrast to a criminal wrong, a crime).

Total Finance Charge—Under the Truth in Lending Act, the total finance charge on a loan includes interest, any discount points paid by the borrower, the loan origination fee, and mortgage insurance costs.

Township—In the government survey system, a parcel of land six miles square, containing 36 sections; the intersection of a range and a township tier.

Township Lines—Lines running east-west, spaced six miles apart, in the government survey system.

Township Tier—In the government survey system, a strip of land running east-west, six miles wide and bounded on the north and south by township lines.

Tract—1. A piece of land of undefined size. 2. In the government survey system, an area made up of 16 townships; 24 miles on each side.

Trade Fixtures—Articles of personal property annexed to real property by a tenant for use in his or her trade or business, which the tenant is allowed to remove at the end of the lease.

Transferability—If an item is transferable, then ownership and possession of that item can be conveyed from one person to another. Transferability is one of the four elements of value, along with utility, scarcity, and demand.

Transfer Disclosure Statement—A form providing certain information about a piece of real property. The seller must present it to the buyer in any transaction involving one- to four-unit residential property.

Trespass—An unlawful physical invasion of property owned by another.

Trust—A legal arrangement in which title to property (or funds) is vested in one or more trustees, who manage the property on behalf of the trust's beneficiaries, in accordance with instructions set forth in the document establishing the trust.

Trust Account—A bank account, separate from a real estate broker's personal and business accounts, used to segregate trust funds from the broker's own funds.

Trust Deed—*See*: Deed of Trust.

Trustee—1. A person appointed to manage a trust on behalf of the beneficiaries. 2. A neutral third party appointed in a deed of trust to handle the nonjudicial foreclosure process in case of default.

Trustee in Bankruptcy—An individual appointed by the court to handle the assets of a person in bankruptcy.

Trustee's Sale—A nonjudicial foreclosure sale under a deed of trust.

Trust Funds—Money or things of value received by an agent, not belonging to the agent but being held for the benefit of others.

Trustor—The borrower on a deed of trust. Also called the grantor.

Truth in Lending Act (TILA)—A federal law that requires lenders and credit arrangers to make disclosures concerning loan costs (including the total finance charge and the annual percentage rate) to applicants for consumer loans (including any mortgage loan that will be used for personal, family, or household purposes), and that also requires certain disclosures in advertisements concerning consumer credit.

Underimprovement—An improvement which, because of deficiency in cost or size, is not the most profitable use of the land; not the highest and best use.

Underwriting—In real estate lending, the process of evaluating a loan application to determine the probability that the applicant would repay the loan, and matching the risk to an appropriate rate of return. Sometimes called risk analysis.

Undivided Interest—*See*: Interest, Undivided.

Undue Influence—Exerting excessive pressure on someone so as to overpower the person's free will and prevent him or her from making a rational or prudent decision; often involves abusing a relationship of trust.

Unearned Increment—An increase in the value of a property that comes about through no effort on the part of the owner, such as one resulting from a population shift or favorable zoning changes.

Unenforceable—*See*: Contract, Unenforceable.

Uniform Commercial Code—A body of law adopted in slightly varying versions in most states (including California), which attempts to standardize commercial law dealing with such matters as negotiable instruments and sales of personal property. Its main applications to real estate law concern security interests in fixtures and bulk transfers.

Uniform Settlement Statement—A settlement statement required for any transaction involving a loan that is subject to the Real Estate Settlement Procedures Act (RESPA).

Unilateral Contract—*See*: Contract, Unilateral.

Unit-in-Place Method—In appraisal, a method of estimating replacement cost by estimating the cost of each component (foundation, roof, etc.), then adding the costs of all components together.

Unjust Enrichment—An undeserved benefit; a court generally will not allow a remedy (such as forfeiture of a land contract) if it would result in the unjust enrichment of one of the parties.

Unlawful Detainer—A summary legal action to regain possession of real property; especially, a suit filed by a landlord to evict a defaulting tenant.

Unruh Civil Rights Act—A California civil rights law that guarantees the right of all persons to use the services provided by any business establishment.

Useful Life—*See*: Economic Life.

Use Value—*See*: Value, Utility.

Usury—Charging an interest rate that exceeds legal limits.

Utility—The ability of an item to satisfy some need and/or arouse a desire for possession; one of the four elements of value, along with scarcity, demand, and transferability.

VA—Department of Veterans Affairs.

Vacancy Factor—*See*: Bad Debt/Vacancy Factor.

Valid—The legal classification of a contract that is binding and enforceable in a court of law.

Valuable Consideration—*See*: Consideration.

Valuation—*See*: Appraisal.

Value—The present worth of future benefits.

Value, Assessed—The value placed on property by the taxing authority (the county assessor, for example) for the purposes of taxation.

Value, Market—The most probable price which a property should bring in a competitive and open market under all conditions requisite to a fair sale, the buyer and seller each acting prudently and knowledgeably, and assuming the price is not affected by undue stimulus. (This is the definition from the Uniform Standards of Appraisal Practice.) Sometimes called value in exchange. *Compare*: Market Price.

Value, Utility—The value of a property to its owner or to a user. Also called use value or value in use.

Value in Exchange—*See*: Value, Market.

Value in Use—*See*: Value, Utility.

Variable Interest Rate—A loan interest rate that can be adjusted periodically during the loan term, as in the case of an adjustable-rate mortgage.

Variance—Permission (from the local zoning authority) to build a structure in a way that violates the strict terms of the zoning ordinance.

Vendee—A buyer or purchaser; particularly, someone buying property under a land contract.

Vendor—A seller; particularly, someone selling property by means of a land contract.

Vicarious Liability—*See*: Liability, Vicarious.

Void—Having no legal force or effect.

Voidable—*See*: Contract, Voidable.

Voluntary Lien—*See*: Lien, Voluntary.

Voucher System—In construction lending, a system in which the general contractor gives subcontractors vouchers (instead of cash) for services rendered. The vouchers, which are statements attesting to the sum owed, are then presented to the construction lender for payment.

Waiver—The voluntary relinquishment or surrender of a right.

Warehousing—The practice, by a primary lender, of holding loans until an optimal time to sell to a secondary lender.

Warrant System—In construction lending, a system in which bills are presented to the lender for direct payment to the supplier or laborer.

Warranty, Implied—In a sale or lease of property, a guarantee created by operation of law, whether or not the seller or landlord intended to offer it.

Warranty of Habitability—*See*: Habitability, Implied Warranty of.

Waste—Destruction, damage, or material alteration of property by someone in possession who holds less than a fee estate (such as a life tenant or a lessee), or by a co-owner.

Water Rights—The right to use water from a body of water. *See*: Appropriation, Prior; Littoral Rights; Riparian Rights.

Water Table—The level at which water may be found, either at the surface or underground.

Wild Deed—*See*: Deed, Wild.

Will—A person's stipulation regarding how his or her estate should be disposed of after he or she dies. Also called a testament.

Will, Formal—A will that meets the statutory requirements for validity. As a general rule, it must be in writing and signed in the presence of at least two competent witnesses.

Will, Holographic—A will written entirely in the testator's handwriting, which may be valid even if it was not witnessed.

Will, Nuncupative—An oral will made on the testator's deathbed; valid in some states (although not in California) as to bequests of personal property worth under $1,000.

Without Recourse—A qualified or conditional endorsement on a negotiable instrument, which relieves the endorser of liability under the instrument.

Wraparound Financing—*See*: Mortgage, Wraparound.

Writ of Attachment—*See*: Attachment.

Writ of Execution—A court order directing a public officer (such as the sheriff) to seize and sell property to satisfy a debt.

Writ of Possession—A court order issued after an unlawful detainer action, informing the tenant that he or she must vacate the landlord's property within a specified period or be forcibly removed by the sheriff.

Yield—The return of profit to an investor on an investment, stated as a percentage of the amount invested.

Zone—An area of land set off for a particular use or uses, subject to certain restrictions.

Zoning—Government regulation of the uses of property within specified areas.

Zoning Amendment—*See*: Rezone.

(continued)